Access® 2019

Bible

Access® 2019

BIBLE

Michael Alexander

Dick Kusleika

WILEY

Access® 2019 Bible

Published by
John Wiley & Sons, Inc.
10475 Crosspoint Boulevard
Indianapolis, IN 46256
www.wiley.com

ISBN: 978-1-119-51475-6
ISBN: 978-1-119-51473-2 (ebk)
ISBN: 978-1-119-51474-9 (ebk)

Manufactured in the United States of America

SKY10023756_010521

For general information on our other products and services please contact our Customer Care Department within the United States at (877) 762-2974, outside the United States at (317) 572-3993 or fax (317) 572-4002.

Wiley publishes in a variety of print and electronic formats and by print-on-demand. Some material included with standard print versions of this book may not be included in e-books or in print-on-demand. If this book refers to media such as a CD or DVD that is not included in the version you purchased, you may download this material at http://booksupport.wiley.com. For more information about Wiley products, visit www.wiley.com.

Library of Congress Control Number: 2018954521

To my family. —Mike
To Matt, Jared, and Ben. —Dick

About the Authors

Michael Alexander is a Microsoft Certified Application Developer (MCAD) and author of several books on advanced business analysis with Microsoft Access and Microsoft Excel. He has more than 20 years of experience consulting and developing Microsoft Office solutions. Mike has been named a Microsoft MVP for his ongoing contributions to the Excel community. You can find Mike at www.datapigtechnologies.com.

Dick Kusleika is a 12-time Microsoft Excel MVP and has been working with Microsoft Office for more than 20 years. Dick develops Access- and Excel-based solutions for his clients and has conducted training seminars on Office products in the United States and Australia. Dick also writes a popular Excel-related blog at www.dailydoseofexcel.com.

About the Technical Editor

Joyce J. Nielsen has worked in the publishing industry for more than 25 years as an author, development editor, technical editor, and project manager, specializing in Microsoft Office, Windows, Internet, and general technology titles for leading educational and retail publishers. Joyce holds a Bachelor of Science degree in Quantitative Business Analysis from Indiana University's Kelley School of Business in Bloomington. She currently resides in Arizona.

Credits

Project Editor
David Clark

Technical Editor
Joyce J. Nielsen

Production Editor
Barath Kumar Rajasekaran

Copy Editor
Kim Cofer

Production Manager
Kathleen Wisor

Manager of Content Enablement and Operations
Pete Gaughan

Marketing Manager
Christie Hilbrich

Associate Publisher
Jim Minatel

Senior Editorial Assistant
Devon Lewis

Project Coordinator, Cover
Brent Savage

Proofreader
Kim Wimpsett

Indexer
Johnna VanHoose Dinse

Cover Designer
Wiley

Cover Image
iStockphoto.com/Aleksandar

Acknowledgments

Our deepest thanks to the professionals at John Wiley & Sons for all the hours of work put into bringing this book to life. A special thank-you goes out to our families for putting up with all the time spent locked away on this project.

Contents at a Glance

Introduction xxxix

Part I: Access Building Blocks. 1
Chapter 1: An Introduction to Database Development 3
Chapter 2: Getting Started with Access 17

Part II: Understanding Access Tables. 29
Chapter 3: Creating Access Tables... 31
Chapter 4: Understanding Table Relationships 87
Chapter 5: Working with Access Tables 129
Chapter 6: Importing and Exporting Data 169
Chapter 7: Linking to External Data 209

Part III: Working with Access Queries 237
Chapter 8: Selecting Data with Queries...239
Chapter 9: Using Operators and Expressions in Access.....................................269
Chapter 10: Going Beyond Select Queries 311

Part IV: Analyzing Data in Microsoft Access. 353
Chapter 11: Transforming Data in Access 355
Chapter 12: Working with Calculations and Dates 379
Chapter 13: Performing Conditional Analyses...405
Chapter 14: The Fundamentals of Using SQL..425
Chapter 15: Subqueries and Domain Aggregate Functions 445
Chapter 16: Running Descriptive Statistics in Access...469

Part V: Working with Access Forms and Reports 487
Chapter 17: Creating Basic Access Forms..489
Chapter 18: Working with Data on Access Forms..531
Chapter 19: Working with Form Controls..563
Chapter 20: Presenting Data with Access Reports 599
Chapter 21: Advanced Access Report Techniques 657

Part VI: Microsoft Access Programming Fundamentals 703

Chapter 22: Using Access Macros 705
Chapter 23: Using Access Data Macros 741
Chapter 24: Getting Started with Access VBA...759
Chapter 25: Mastering VBA Data Types and Procedures 801
Chapter 26: Understanding the Access Event Model 843
Chapter 27: Debugging Your Access Applications 865

Part VII: Advanced Access Programming Techniques 899

Chapter 28: Accessing Data with VBA 901
Chapter 29: Advanced Data Access with VBA...937
Chapter 30: Customizing the Ribbon 955
Chapter 31: Preparing Your Access Application for Distribution.......................993
Chapter 32: Integrating Access with SharePoint.. 1039

Index 1055

Contents

Introduction. xxxix

Part I: Access Building Blocks   1

Chapter 1: An Introduction to Database Development 3

The Database Terminology of Access 3
    Databases 3
    Tables. 5
    Records and fields 5
    Values. 6
Relational Databases 6
Access Database Objects 7
    Tables. 7
    Queries 8
    Data-entry and display forms 8
    Reports. 8
    Macros and VBA. 9
    Planning for database objects. 9
A Five-Step Design Method 9
    Step 1: The overall design—from concept to reality 10
    Step 2: Report design. 11
    Step 3: Data design. 11
    Step 4: Table design. 13
    Step 5: Form design 16

Chapter 2: Getting Started with Access 17

The Access Welcome Screen. 17
How to Create a Blank Database 18
The Access 2019 Interface. 20
    The Navigation pane 20
        Custom. 21
        Object Type 22
        Tables and Related Views. 23
        Created Date 23
        Modified Date 23
    The Ribbon 24
    The Quick Access toolbar. 25

Part II: Understanding Access Tables 29

Chapter 3: Creating Access Tables **31**

Table Types 31
    Object tables 31
    Transaction tables 32
    Join tables 32
Creating a New Table 32
    Designing tables 34
    Using the Design tab 39
        Primary Key 39
        Insert Rows 40
        Delete Rows 40
        Property Sheet 40
        Indexes 41
    Working with fields 41
        Naming a field 41
        Specifying a data type 42
        Entering a field description 49
        Specifying data validation rules 49
Creating tblCustomers 49
    Using AutoNumber fields 50
    Completing tblCustomers 50
Changing a Table Design 50
    Inserting a new field 51
    Deleting a field 51
    Changing a field location 51
    Changing a field name 51
    Changing a field size 52
    Handling data conversion issues 52
    Assigning field properties 53
        Common properties 54
        Format 55
        Input Mask 60
        Caption 63
        Validation Rule and Validation Text 63
        Required 65
        AllowZeroLength 65
        Indexed 66
Understanding tblCustomers Field Properties 68
Setting the Primary Key 71
    Choosing a primary key 71
    Creating the primary key 72
    Creating composite primary keys 72

Indexing Access Tables.. 73
 The importance of indexes 74
 Multiple-field indexes 76
 When to index tables... 78
Printing a Table Design 79
Saving the Completed Table 81
Manipulating Tables 81
 Renaming tables.. 81
 Deleting tables... 82
 Copying tables in a database 82
 Copying a table to another database 83
Adding Records to a Database Table........................... 84
Understanding Attachment Fields 84

Chapter 4: Understanding Table Relationships 87
Building Bulletproof Databases 88
Data Normalization and Denormalization.................. 90
 First normal form 90
 Second normal form... 94
  Identifying entities 94
  Less obvious entities..................................... 96
  Breaking the rules 98
 Third normal form 99
 Denormalization..101
Table Relationships 102
 Connecting the data 103
 One-to-one..105
 One-to-many...107
 Many-to-many...108
Integrity Rules 110
 No primary key can contain a null value 112
 All foreign key values must be matched by corresponding primary keys 113
Keys 113
 Deciding on a primary key 114
 Looking at the benefits of a primary key................116
 Designating a primary key 117
  Single-field versus composite primary keys.........117
  Natural versus surrogate primary keys.................118
  Creating primary keys 119
 Creating relationships and enforcing referential integrity 119
  Specifying the join type between tables 121
  Enforcing referential integrity 123
 Viewing all relationships..125
 Deleting relationships..126
 Following application-specific integrity rules 126

Contents

Chapter 5: Working with Access Tables **129**

Understanding Datasheets...130

Looking at the Datasheet Window 131

    Moving within a datasheet..132

    Using the Navigation buttons 133

    Examining the Datasheet Ribbon....................................133

        Views..134

        Clipboard 134

        Sort & Filter 134

        Records 134

        Find..134

        Window...134

        Text Formatting 135

Opening a Datasheet 135

Entering New Data 135

    Saving the record 138

    Understanding automatic data-type validation 138

    Knowing how properties affect data entry............................140

        Standard text data entry.......................................140

        Date/Time data entry...140

        Number/Currency data entry with data validation.............. 141

        OLE object data entry...141

        Long Text field data entry 141

Navigating Records in a Datasheet..142

    Moving between records...143

    Finding a specific value 143

Changing Values in a Datasheet..146

    Manually replacing an existing value 146

    Changing an existing value..146

Using the Undo Feature 148

Copying and Pasting Values 148

Replacing Values...149

Adding New Records..150

Deleting Records...150

Displaying Records...152

    Changing the field order 152

    Changing the field display width 153

    Changing the record display height 154

    Changing display fonts 155

    Displaying cell gridlines and alternate row colors 156

    Aligning data in columns..158

    Hiding and unhiding columns 159

    Freezing columns 159

Saving the changed layout...160
Saving a record 160
Sorting and Filtering Records in a Datasheet.......................................160
Sorting records..161
Filtering a selection...161
Filtering by form 164
Aggregating Data...165
Printing Records...166
Previewing Records...167

Chapter 6: Importing and Exporting Data. 169
How Access Works with External Data...169
Types of external data 169
Ways of working with external data...170
When to link to external data..171
When to import external data..172
When to export data..173
Options for Importing and Exporting...173
Importing External Data..175
Importing from another Access database.......................................175
Importing from an Excel spreadsheet..178
Importing a SharePoint list..185
Importing data from text files..185
Delimited text files...185
Fixed-width text files...188
Importing and exporting XML documents.....................................192
Importing and exporting HTML documents....................................197
Importing Access objects other than tables...................................198
Importing an Outlook folder...200
Exporting to External Formats..202
Exporting objects to other Access databases.................................202
Exporting through ODBC drivers 203
Exporting to Word 205
Merging data into Word 205
Publishing to PDF or XPS..206

Chapter 7: Linking to External Data 209
Linking External Data 210
Identifying linked tables...211
Limitations of linked data...213
Linking to other Access database tables..214
Linking to ODBC data sources 216
Linking to non-database data..217
Linking to Excel 218

Contents

Linking to HTML files..220

Linking to text files...222

Working with Linked Tables...225

Setting view properties..225

Setting relationships..226

Optimizing linked tables...226

Deleting a linked table reference..227

Viewing or changing information for linked tables..227

Refreshing linked tables...228

Splitting a Database..229

The benefits of splitting a database...229

Knowing where to put which objects...232

Using the Database Splitter add-in...232

Part III: Working with Access Queries   237

Chapter 8: Selecting Data with Queries 239

Introducing Queries...240

What queries can do..240

What queries return..241

Creating a Query..241

Adding fields to your queries..244

Adding a single field..244

Adding multiple fields...245

Running your query...247

Working with Query Fields...247

Selecting a field in the QBD grid..247

Changing field order...248

Resizing columns in the QBD grid...249

Removing a field...249

Inserting a field..249

Hiding a field...250

Changing the sort order of a field...250

Adding Criteria to Your Queries...252

Understanding selection criteria...252

Entering simple string criteria..252

Entering other simple criteria...254

Printing a Query's Recordset..255

Saving a Query..256

Creating Multi-table Queries..256

Viewing table names..258

Adding multiple fields...258

Recognizing the limitations of multi-table queries..259

Overcoming query limitations...260

Updating a unique index (primary key) 260
Replacing existing data in a query with a one-to-many
    relationship 260
Updating fields in queries 260
Working with the Table Pane 261
Looking at the join line 261
Moving a table 261
Removing a table..262
Adding more tables..262
Creating and Working with Query Joins 262
Understanding joins 262
Leveraging ad hoc table joins 265
Specifying the type of join 266
Deleting joins 267

Chapter 9: Using Operators and Expressions in Access **269**
Introducing Operators 269
Types of operators 270
    Mathematical operators 270
    Comparison operators..273
    String operators..275
    Boolean (logical) operators 278
    Miscellaneous operators 280
Operator precedence 282
    The mathematical precedence 282
    The comparison precedence 283
    The Boolean precedence 283
Using Operators and Expressions in Queries............................283
Using query comparison operators 284
Understanding complex criteria....................................285
Using functions in select queries..................................288
Referencing fields in select queries..............................289
Entering Single-Value Field Criteria 289
Entering character (Text or Memo) criteria......................289
The Like operator and wildcards 291
Specifying non-matching values....................................294
Entering numeric criteria..295
Entering true or false criteria....................................296
Entering OLE object criteria 297
Using Multiple Criteria in a Query 297
Understanding an Or operation......................................297
Specifying multiple values with the Or operator 298
Using the Or cell of the QBD pane 299
Using a list of values with the In operator......................299
Using And to specify a range..300

Contents

Using the Between...And operator 302
Searching for null data 302
Entering Criteria in Multiple Fields..304
Using And and Or across fields in a query 304
Specifying Or criteria across fields of a query 305
Using And and Or together in different fields 307
A complex query on different lines...308

Chapter 10: Going Beyond Select Queries **311**
Aggregate Queries...311
Creating an aggregate query...311
About aggregate functions 315
Group By 315
Sum, Avg, Count, StDev, Var...316
Min, Max, First, Last 317
Expression, Where...318
Action Queries..320
Make-table queries 321
Delete queries 323
Append queries 327
Update queries..332
Crosstab Queries 336
Creating a crosstab query using the Crosstab Query Wizard..................336
Creating a crosstab query manually 342
Using the query design grid to create your crosstab query 343
Customizing your crosstab queries 346
Optimizing Query Performance 348
Normalizing your database design 349
Using indexes on appropriate fields..349
Optimizing by improving query design..350
Compacting and repairing your database regularly...........................351

Part IV: Analyzing Data in Microsoft Access   **353**

Chapter 11: Transforming Data in Access. **355**
Finding and Removing Duplicate Records..355
Defining duplicate records..356
Finding duplicate records...357
Removing duplicate records..359
Common Transformation Tasks...363
Filling in blank fields 363
Concatenating...364
Concatenating fields..364
Augmenting field values with your own text....................................366

Changing case 367
Removing leading and trailing spaces from a string 368
Finding and replacing specific text 370
Adding your own text in key positions within a string...................370
Parsing strings using character markers.......................................374
Query 1 376
Query 2 376

**Chapter 12: Working with Calculations
and Dates** 379

Using Calculations in Your Analyses 379
Common calculation scenarios..380
Using constants in calculations..380
Using fields in calculations..381
Using the results of aggregation in calculations 381
Using the results of one calculation as an expression in another 381
Using a calculation as an argument in a function....................382
Constructing calculations with the Expression Builder 384
Common calculation errors 388
Understanding the order of operator precedence 388
Watching out for null values 389
Watching the syntax in your expressions................................391
Using Dates in Your Analyses 392
Simple date calculations 392
Advanced analysis using functions 392
The Date function 393
The Year, Month, Day, and Weekday functions.......................397
The DateAdd function 399
Grouping dates into quarters 400
The DateSerial function...401

Chapter 13: Performing Conditional Analyses 405

Using Parameter Queries...405
How parameter queries work 407
Ground rules of parameter queries 407
Working with parameter queries...408
Working with multiple parameter conditions...........................408
Combining parameters with operators....................................408
Combining parameters with wildcards 410
Using parameters as calculation variables..............................411
Using parameters as function arguments 411
Using Conditional Functions 414
The IIf function 414
Using IIf to avoid mathematical errors...................................415
Saving time with IIf..416

Contents

Nesting IIf functions for multiple conditions 418

Using IIf functions to create crosstab analyses.............................. 419

The Switch function 420

Comparing the IIf and Switch functions.................................... 421

Chapter 14: The Fundamentals of Using SQL **425**

Understanding Basic SQL.. 425

The SELECT statement.. 426

Selecting specific columns... 427

Selecting all columns 427

The WHERE clause 428

Making sense of joins 428

Inner joins 428

Outer joins 429

Getting Fancy with Advanced SQL Statements................................... 430

Expanding your search with the Like operator........................ 430

Selecting unique values and rows without grouping................ 432

Grouping and aggregating with the GROUP BY clause 432

Setting the sort order with the ORDER BY clause.................... 433

Creating aliases with the AS clause.. 433

Creating a column alias 433

Creating a table alias 433

Showing only the SELECT TOP or SELECT TOP PERCENT 433

Top values queries explained 434

The SELECT TOP statement 435

The SELECT TOP PERCENT statement 436

Performing action queries via SQL statements 436

Make-table queries translated.. 436

Append queries translated.. 437

Update queries translated... 437

Delete queries translated.. 437

Creating crosstabs with the TRANSFORM statement............. 437

Using SQL-Specific Queries.. 438

Merging data sets with the UNION operator 438

Creating a table with the CREATE TABLE statement............... 440

Manipulating columns with the ALTER TABLE statement 440

Adding a column with the ADD clause 441

Altering a column with the ALTER COLUMN clause............... 441

Deleting a column with the DROP COLUMN clause 441

Dynamically adding primary keys with the ADD CONSTRAINT clause.....442

Creating pass-through queries 442

Chapter 15: Subqueries and Domain Aggregate Functions **445**

Enhancing Your Analyses with Subqueries 446

Why use subqueries?..447

Subquery ground rules 447

Creating subqueries without typing SQL statements 447

Using IN and NOT IN with subqueries 451

Using subqueries with comparison operators 451

Using subqueries as expressions 452

Using correlated subqueries 453

Uncorrelated subqueries 453

Correlated subqueries 454

Using a correlated subquery as an expression 455

Using subqueries within action queries 456

A subquery in a make-table query 456

A subquery in an append query 456

A subquery in an update query 456

A subquery in a delete query 456

Domain Aggregate Functions 459

Understanding the different domain aggregate functions 460

DSum 460

DAvg 460

DCount 460

DLookup 461

DMin and DMax 461

DFirst and DLast 461

DStDev, DStDevP, DVar, and DvarP 461

Examining the syntax of domain aggregate functions 461

Using no criteria 461

Using text criteria 462

Using number criteria 462

Using date criteria 463

Using domain aggregate functions 463

Calculating the percent of total 463

Creating a running count 465

Using a value from the previous record 466

Chapter 16: Running Descriptive Statistics in Access. .469

Basic Descriptive Statistics 470

Running descriptive statistics with aggregate queries 470

Determining rank, mode, and median 471

Ranking the records in your data set 471

Getting the mode of a data set 472

Getting the median of a data set 475

Pulling a random sampling from your data set 477

Advanced Descriptive Statistics 479

Calculating percentile ranking 479

Determining the quartile standing of a record 481

Creating a frequency distribution 483

Contents

Part V: Working with Access Forms and Reports 487

Chapter 17: Creating Basic Access Forms 489

Working with Form Views 489
Understanding Different Types of Forms 490
   Creating a new form 491
      Using the Form command 492
      Using the Form Wizard 492
   Looking at special types of forms 496
      Navigation forms 496
      Multiple-items forms 498
      Split forms 500
      Datasheet forms 501
   Resizing the form area 502
   Saving your form 502
Working with Controls 503
   Categorizing controls 504
   Adding a control 506
      Using the Controls group 507
      Using the field list 508
   Selecting and deselecting controls 511
      Selecting a single control 512
      Selecting multiple controls 513
      Deselecting controls 513
   Manipulating controls 513
      Resizing a control 513
      Sizing controls automatically 515
      Moving a control 515
      Aligning controls 517
      Modifying the appearance of a control 519
      Grouping controls 519
      Changing a control's type 520
      Copying a control 522
      Deleting a control 522
      Reattaching a label to a control 522
Introducing Properties 524
   Displaying the Property Sheet 524
   Getting acquainted with the Property Sheet 525
   Changing a control's property setting 526
   Naming control labels and their captions 527

Chapter 18: Working with Data on Access Forms 531

Using Form View 532
   Looking at the Home tab of the Ribbon 532
      The Views group 534

The Clipboard group 534
The Sort & Filter group 535
The Records group..535
The Find group 535
The Window group 535
The Text Formatting group 536
Navigating among fields...536
Moving among records in a form 537
Changing Values in a Form...537
Knowing which controls you can't edit...538
Working with pictures and OLE objects...538
Entering data in the Long Text field...540
Entering data in the Date field 540
Using option groups...542
Using combo boxes and list boxes 542
Switching to Datasheet view 543
Saving a record 544
Printing a Form 544
Working with Form Properties..545
Changing the title bar text with the Caption property...................................546
Creating a bound form 547
Specifying how to view the form 548
Removing the Record Selector 549
Looking at other form properties 549
Adding a Form Header or Footer 556
Working with Section Properties 556
The Visible property 557
The Height property 557
The Back Color property..557
The Special Effect property 557
The Display When property 558
The printing properties...558
Changing the Layout..558
Changing a control's properties...558
Setting the tab order 559
Modifying the format of text in a control...560
Using the Field List to add controls...561
Converting a Form to a Report 562

Chapter 19: Working with Form Controls **563**

Setting Control Properties 563
Customizing default properties..565
Looking at common controls and properties 566
The Text Box control 566
The Command Button control...568

Contents

The Combo Box and List Box controls 568
The Check Box and Toggle Button controls 570
The Option Group control 570
The Web Browser control 570
Creating a Calculated Control 571
Working with Subforms 572
Form Design Tips..573
Using the Tab Stop property 573
Tallying check boxes...573
Setting up combo boxes and list boxes 574
Tackling Advanced Forms Techniques 576
Using the Page Number and Date/Time controls...................................576
Using the Image control 577
Morphing a control..578
Using the Format Painter 579
Offering more end-user help 580
Adding background pictures..580
Limiting the records shown on a form 582
Using the Tab Control...583
Using Dialog Boxes to Collect Information..586
Designing the query 587
Setting up the command buttons..587
Adding a default button 588
Setting a Cancel button 589
Removing the control menu 589
Designing a Form from Scratch...589
Creating the basic form..589
Creating a subform 590
Adding the subform..591
Changing the form's behavior 593
Setting the form properties 593
Looking up values during data entry...594
Saving the record..595
Changing the form's appearance 596

Chapter 20: Presenting Data with Access Reports **599**
Introducing Reports...599
Identifying the different types of reports 600
Tabular reports 600
Columnar reports 601
Mailing label reports..602
Distinguishing between reports and forms 603
Creating a Report, from Beginning to End..604
Defining the report layout 604
Assembling the data...604

Creating a report with the Report Wizard 605
    Creating a new report..605
    Selecting the grouping levels..606
    Defining the group data 607
    Selecting the sort order...608
    Selecting summary options..608
    Selecting the layout..609
    Opening the report design 610
    Adjusting the report's layout 611
    Choosing a theme 612
    Creating new theme color schemes 614
    Using the Print Preview window 617
    Publishing in alternate formats 618
    Viewing the report in Design view..619
  Printing or viewing the report 620
    Printing the report 620
    Viewing the report 621
  Saving the report 622
Banded Report Design Concepts 622
  The Report Header section 625
  The Page Header section 625
  The Group Header section..626
  The Detail section 626
  The Group Footer section..627
  The Page Footer section 627
  The Report Footer section 627
Creating a Report from Scratch 628
  Creating a new report and binding it to a table...629
  Defining the report page size and layout...631
  Placing controls on the report 633
  Resizing a section 634
    Modifying the appearance of text in a control....................................635
  Working with Text Box controls...636
    Adding and using Text Box controls 636
    Entering an expression in a Text Box control 636
    Sizing a Text Box control or Label control 637
    Deleting and cutting attached labels from Text Box controls.................638
    Pasting labels into a report section 640
    Moving Label and Text Box controls 640
    Modifying the appearance of multiple controls....................................642
  Changing Label and Text Box control properties 643
  Growing and shrinking Text Box controls..644
  Sorting and grouping data 645
    Creating a group header or footer 645

Sorting data within groups 647
Removing a group 648
Hiding a section 648
Sizing a section 648
Moving controls between sections 649
Adding page breaks 650
Improving the Report's Appearance 651
Adjusting the page header 652
Creating an expression in the group header 653
Creating a report header 654

Chapter 21: Advanced Access Report Techniques **657**

Grouping and Sorting Data...658
Grouping alphabetically 658
Grouping on date intervals..662
Hiding repeating information...665
Hiding a page header 668
Starting a new page number for each group....................................670
Formatting Data...670
Creating numbered lists 671
Creating bulleted lists..674
Adding emphasis at run time 677
Avoiding empty reports 679
Inserting vertical lines between columns..680
Adding a blank line every *n* records...682
Even-odd page printing..684
Using different formats in the same text box 686
Centering the title...687
Aligning control labels 687
Micro-adjusting controls 687
Adding Data 688
Adding more information to a report 688
Adding the user's name to a bound report 688
Adding Even More Flexibility...690
Displaying all reports in a combo box...690
Fast printing from queried data..692
Using snaking columns in a report..692
Exploiting two-pass report processing...699
Assigning unique names to controls 701

Part VI: Microsoft Access Programming Fundamentals   703

Chapter 22: Using Access Macros **705**

An Introduction to Macros...705

Creating a macro 706
Assigning a macro to an event..708
Understanding Macro Security 709
Enabling sandbox mode 710
The Trust Center..712
Multi-action Macros...713
Submacros...716
Conditions...720
Opening reports using conditions 720
Multiple actions in conditions 723
Temporary Variables...723
Enhancing a macro you've already created.............................723
Using temporary variables to simplify macros.......................725
Using temporary variables in VBA...727
Error Handling and Macro Debugging...728
The OnError action 730
The MacroError object 732
Debugging macros 733
Embedded Macros...734
Macros versus VBA Statements..736
Choosing between macros and VBA 737
Converting existing macros to VBA..737

Chapter 23: Using Access Data Macros 741
Introducing Data Macros...742
Understanding Table Events..742
"Before" events 743
"After" events...744
Using the Macro Builder for Data Macros 745
Understanding the Action Catalog...747
Program flow...748
Data blocks 748
Data actions..749
Creating Your First Data Macro 751
Managing Macro Objects 755
Collapsing and expanding macro items....................................755
Moving macro items...756
Saving a macro as XML...756
Recognizing the Limitations of Data Macros...............................757

Chapter 24: Getting Started with Access VBA 759
Introducing Visual Basic for Applications....................................760
Understanding VBA Terminology..761
Starting with VBA Code Basics 762
Creating VBA Programs..763

Contents

Modules and procedures 763

    Modules 764

    Procedures and functions 767

Working in the code window 770

    White space 770

    Line continuation 771

    Multi-statement lines 772

    IntelliSense 773

    Compiling procedures 776

    Saving a module 777

Understanding VBA Branching Constructs 777

    Branching 777

        The If keyword 778

        The Select Case...End Select statement 781

    Looping 783

        The Do...Loop statement 783

        The For...Next statement 784

Working with Objects and Collections 786

    An object primer 786

    Properties and methods 788

        Properties 788

        Methods 788

    The With statement 789

    The For Each statement 790

Exploring the Visual Basic Editor 792

    The Immediate window 792

    The Project Explorer 793

    The Object Browser 794

    VBE options 794

        The Editor tab of the Options dialog box 795

        The Project Properties dialog box 797

Chapter 25: Mastering VBA Data Types and Procedures **801**

Using Variables 802

    Naming variables 803

    Declaring variables 804

        The Dim keyword 807

        The Public keyword 807

        The Private keyword 808

Working with Data Types 809

    Comparing implicit and explicit variables 811

    Forcing explicit declaration 813

    Using a naming convention with variables 813

    Understanding variable scope and lifetime 816

        Examining scope 816

Determining a variable's lifetime 817
Deciding on a variable's scope.. 819
Using constants 819
Declaring constants 820
Using a naming convention with constants.. 821
Eliminating hard-coded values.. 821
Working with arrays 822
Fixed arrays 822
Dynamic arrays... 825
Array functions 826
Understanding Subs and Functions.. 829
Understanding where to create a procedure 830
Calling VBA procedures 830
Creating subs 831
Creating Functions.. 835
Handling parameters 836
Calling a function and passing parameters 836
Creating a function to calculate sales tax.. 838
Simplifying Code with Named Arguments 840

Chapter 26: Understanding the Access Event Model **843**
Programming Events 844
Understanding how events trigger VBA code.. 844
Creating event procedures... 845
Identifying Common Events.. 847
Form event procedures.. 848
Essential form events 848
Form mouse and keyboard events... 849
Form data events 850
Control event procedures... 851
Report event procedures 853
Report section event procedures... 854
Paying Attention to Event Sequence.. 856
Looking at common event sequences.. 857
Writing simple form and control event procedures 858
Opening a form with an event procedure 859
Running an event procedure when closing a form............................ 862
Using an event procedure to confirm record deletion 862

Chapter 27: Debugging Your Access Applications. **865**
Organizing VBA Code.. 866
Testing Your Applications 867
Testing functions 868
Compiling VBA code... 871
Traditional Debugging Techniques... 873

Contents

Using MsgBox..874

Using Debug.Print 878

Using the Access Debugging Tools 879

Running code with the Immediate window...880

Suspending execution with breakpoints..881

Looking at variables with the Locals window...887

Setting watches with the Watches window 889

Using conditional watches..891

Using the Call Stack window 892

Trapping Errors in Your Code...893

Understanding error trapping...893

On Error Resume Next...893

On Error Goto 0..895

On Error GoTo Label..895

The Resume keyword...895

The Err object 896

Including error handling in your procedures..897

Part VII: Advanced Access Programming Techniques   899

Chapter 28: Accessing Data with VBA 901

Working with Data 901

Understanding DAO Objects 904

The DAO DBEngine object 906

The DAO Workspace object...906

The DAO Database object..907

The DAO TableDef object 908

The DAO QueryDef object..909

The DAO Recordset object...911

Navigating recordsets..912

Detecting the recordset end or beginning 914

Counting records...915

The DAO Field objects (recordsets) 916

Understanding ADO Objects 917

The ADO Connection object 918

The ADO Command object...920

The ADO Recordset object...922

Writing VBA Code to Update a Table 923

Updating fields in a record using ADO 924

Updating a calculated control..926

Recalculating a control when updating or adding a record......................................927

Checking the status of a record deletion..929

Eliminating repetitive code 931

Adding a new record..932

Bulletproofing an Application 1022
   Using error trapping on all Visual Basic procedures 1023
      Maintaining usage logs 1023
   Separating tables from the rest of the application...................... 1027
   Building bulletproof forms 1027
   Validating user input.. 1028
   Using the /runtime option 1028
   Encrypting or encoding a database 1029
      Removing a database password 1031
   Protecting Visual Basic code.. 1032
Securing the Environment 1034
   Setting startup options in code 1035
   Disabling startup bypass... 1036
   Setting property values 1037
   Getting property values 1038

Chapter 32: Integrating Access with SharePoint. 1039
Introducing SharePoint 1039
Understanding SharePoint Sites 1040
   SharePoint documents 1040
   SharePoint lists... 1041
Sharing Data between Access and SharePoint................................. 1043
   Linking to SharePoint lists 1043
   Importing SharePoint lists 1046
   Exporting Access tables to SharePoint.................................... 1047
   Moving Access tables to SharePoint 1049
Using SharePoint Templates 1052

Index. 1055

Introduction

Welcome to *Access 2019 Bible*, your personal guide to the most powerful desktop database management system available today.

If you've picked up this book, you've probably already recognized that Microsoft Access can help you manage your data in ways that no other application can. Even the king of applications, Microsoft Excel, can't do what Access can. Now, it may seem silly to compare Access (a database management application) with Excel (a spreadsheet application), but there is no doubt that Excel is being used every day to manage and analyze large amounts of data in all kinds of organizations. Indeed, you may be opening this book because you need to get past the limitations of Excel.

Access is an excellent (many would say logical) next step for the analyst who faces an ever-increasing data pool. Access takes very few performance hits with larger data sets. It has no predetermined row limitations. And it can effectively manage the relationships between disparate data tables. In addition, Access comes with tools that help you build your own distributable applications.

Today, when we have more data than ever and more demands for complex data analysis, power analysts need to add some tools to their repertoire in order to get away from being simply "spreadsheet mechanics." That's why this book is such an important step in the evolution of your skillset. Throughout this book, not only will you get an introduction to Access, but you'll also learn various ways in which you can use Access to improve your daily data management and analysis.

Is This Book for You?

This book contains everything you need in order to learn Access 2019 to a mid-advanced level. The book starts off with database basics and builds, chapter by chapter.

This book is designed to enhance the skillset of users at all levels (beginning, intermediate, and even advanced users of Access). Start at the beginning if you're new to Access. If you're already familiar with Access and comfortable building Access applications, you may want to start with the later parts of this book.

If you're new to the world of database management, this book has everything you need to get started with Access 2019. It also offers advanced topics for reference and learning. Beginning developers should pay particular attention to Part I, where we cover the essential skills necessary for building successful and efficient databases. Your ability as a database designer is constantly judged by how well the applications you build perform and how well they handle data entrusted to them by their users.

If you want to learn the basics of Visual Basic for Applications (VBA) programming, you'll find what you need in this book. Although the topic of VBA is a rich one that deserves its own book, this book offers a robust set of chapters that will get you started leveraging VBA to enhance your Access databases. Part VI of this book explains the nuts and bolts—with a lot of gritty technical details—of writing VBA procedures and building Access applications around the code you add to your databases.

Conventions Used in This Book

We use the following conventions in this book:

- When you're instructed to press a key combination (press and hold down one key while pressing another key), the key combination is separated by a plus sign. For example, Ctrl+Esc indicates that you must hold down the Ctrl key and press the Esc key; then release both keys.
- *Point the mouse* refers to moving the mouse so that the mouse pointer is on a specific item. *Click* refers to pressing the left mouse button once and releasing it. *Double-click* refers to pressing the left mouse button twice in rapid succession and then releasing it. *Right-click* refers to pressing the right mouse button once and releasing it. *Drag* refers to pressing and holding down the left mouse button while moving the mouse.
- We use *italics* for new terms and for emphasis.
- We use **bold** for material that you need to type directly into a field in Access.

How This Book Is Organized

This book is divided into nine parts:

- **Part I: Access Building Blocks:** Part I provides a solid understanding of the basic elements of databases, introduces you to the keywords of database management, and teaches you how to plan tables and work with Access data types. In this part, you'll also get your first look into Access and the Access interface.
- **Part II: Understanding Access Tables:** In Part II, you get the skills you need to build Access tables, manage relationships between tables, and link to disparate data sources like Excel files, text files, SQL Server, and other Access databases.
- **Part III: Working with Access Queries:** Part III introduces you to some of the basic analytical tools available in Access. Here, you'll explore the Query Builder, as well as techniques to create both simple and advanced analytical outputs from your Access tables. We cover query basics, aggregate queries, action queries, and cross-tab queries.
- **Part IV: Analyzing Data in Microsoft Access:** Part IV demonstrates many of the advanced techniques that truly bring data analysis to the next level. Here, you'll explore how to transform your data via queries, create custom calculations, perform

conditional analysis, build powerful subqueries, and apply statistical analysis to your queries.

- **Part V: Working with Access Forms and Reports:** Part V focuses on building forms and reports using Access. Here, we cover the basics of turning data into slick-looking user interfaces and PDF-style Access reports. You'll also explore how to enhance the look and feel of your Access applications via advanced form controls.

- **Part VI: Microsoft Access Programming Fundamentals:** In Part VI, you'll take the next step and dive into programming. The chapters in this part start you with Access macros, take you into VBA fundamentals, and eventually work up to leveraging VBA to improve your Access database. This part helps you understand the complex object and event models that drive Access applications and how to construct the VBA code necessary to take advantage of this rich programming environment.

- **Part VII: Advanced Access Programming Techniques:** Part VII turns your attention to automation and integration, showing you how your reporting mechanisms can be enhanced by leveraging other programs and platforms. In these chapters, you'll not only learn the fundamental skills required to become more proficient in VBA, but you'll also discover many insider tricks to apply to your Access application development projects. You'll also discover the extended Microsoft SharePoint integration capabilities in Access that allow you to publish Access tables, forms, and reports on SharePoint sites.

How to Use This Book

Although each chapter is an integral part of the book as a whole, each chapter can also stand on its own and has its own example files, available on the book's website. This book is not necessarily meant to be read cover to cover. Instead, it's a reference book that you can consult when

- You're stuck while trying to do something.
- You need to do something that you've never done before.
- You have some time on your hands, and you're interested in learning something new about Access.

In short, you can read the book in any order you want, skipping from chapter to chapter and from topic to topic. This book's index is particularly thorough; you can refer to the index to find the location of a particular topic you're interested in.

What's on the Website

The examples demonstrated throughout this book can be found on this book's website. The URL is www.wiley.com/go/access2019bible.

Getting Additional Help with Access

As you experiment with the new functions and tools you learn here in this book, you may sometimes need an extra push in the right direction. The first place you should look is Access's Help system. The Help system in Access isn't perfect. To a new user, the Help system may seem like a clunky add-in that returns a perplexing list of topics that has nothing to do with the original topic being searched. The truth is, however, once you learn how to use the Access Help system effectively, it's often the fastest and easiest way to get extra help on a topic.

Following are some tips that will help you get the most out of Access's Help system:

- **Location matters when asking for help.** You may remember the Help system in older versions of Access being a lot more user-friendly and more effective than newer versions of Access. Well, rest assured that you aren't just imagining it. The fact is, Microsoft fundamentally changed the mechanics of the Access Help system.

  In Access 2019, there are actually two Help systems: one providing help on Access features and another providing help on VBA programming topics. Instead of doing a global search with your criteria, Access throws your search criteria only against the Help system that is relevant to your current location. This essentially means that the help you get is determined by the area of Access in which you're working. So, if you need help on a topic that involves VBA programming, you'll need to be in the VBA Editor while performing your search. On the other hand, if you need help on building a query, it's best to be in the Query Design view. This will ensure that your keyword search is performed on the correct Help system.

- **Online help is better than offline help.** When you search for help on a topic, Access checks to see if you're connected to the Internet. If you are, Access returns help results based on online content from Microsoft's website. If you aren't, Access uses the Help files that are locally stored with Microsoft Office. One way to maximize the help you get in Access is to use the online help. Online help is generally better than offline help because the content you find with online help is often more detailed and includes updated information, as well as links to other resources not available offline.

- **Diversify your knowledge base with online resources.** Familiarize yourself with a handful of websites and forums dedicated to Access. These resources can serve as supplemental help, not only for basic Access topics, but also to give you situation-specific tips and tricks. The following list of sites should get you started:

  - www.allenbrowne.com
  - https://developer.microsoft.com/en-us/access
  - www.mvps.org/access
  - www.utteraccess.com

These sites are free to use and are particularly helpful when you need an extra push in the right direction.

Part I

Access Building Blocks

E ach part of this book builds on previous parts, and the chapters in each part contain examples that draw on techniques explained in previous parts and chapters. As a developer, your applications will benefit from the skills you acquire by reading the chapters and practicing the examples contained in this book.

But everyone has to start somewhere when approaching a new discipline, and Part I of this book presents the essential skills necessary for anyone to succeed at database development with Access. The topics covered in this part explain the concepts and techniques that are necessary to successfully use database environments and give you the skills necessary to normalize data and plan and implement effective tables.

If you're already familiar with the concepts involved in database design, you may want to skim these chapters. If you're new to the world of databases, spend some time here gaining a thorough understanding of these important topics.

IN THIS PART

Chapter 1
An Introduction to Database Development

Chapter 2
Getting Started with Access

An Introduction to Database Development

IN THIS CHAPTER

Examining the differences between databases, tables, records, fields, and values

Discovering why multiple tables are used in a database

Exploring Access database objects

Designing a database system

Database development is unlike most other ways you work with computers. Unlike Microsoft Word or Excel, where the approach to working with the application is relatively intuitive, good database development requires prior knowledge. You have to learn a handful of fundamentals, including database terminology, basic database concepts, and database best practices.

Throughout this chapter, we cover the fundamentals of database development.

 If your goal is to get right into Access, you might want to skip to Chapter 2.

The Database Terminology of Access

Access follows most, but not all, traditional database terminology. The terms *database*, *table*, *record*, *field*, and *value* indicate a hierarchy from largest to smallest. These same terms are used with virtually all database systems.

Databases

Generally, the word *database* is a computer term for a collection of information concerning a certain topic or business application. Databases help you organize this related information in a logical fashion for easy access and retrieval.

> **NOTE**
> Some older database systems used the term *database* to describe individual tables; the current use of *database* applies to all elements of a database system.

Databases aren't only for computers. There are also manual databases; we sometimes refer to these as *manual filing systems* or *manual database systems*. These filing systems usually consist of people, papers, folders, and filing cabinets—paper is the key to a manual database system. In manual database systems, you typically have in and out baskets and some type of formal filing method. You access information manually by opening a file cabinet, taking out a file folder, and finding the correct piece of paper. Users fill out paper forms for input, perhaps by using a keyboard to input information that's printed on forms. You find information by manually sorting the papers or by copying information from many papers to another piece of paper (or even into an Excel spreadsheet). You may use a spreadsheet or calculator to analyze the data or display it in new and interesting ways.

An Access database is nothing more than an automated version of the filing and retrieval functions of a paper filing system. Access databases store information in a carefully defined structure. Access tables store a variety of different kinds of data, from simple lines of text (such as name and address) to complex data (such as pictures, sounds, or video images). Storing data in a precise format enables a database management system (DBMS) like Access to turn data into useful information.

Tables serve as the primary data repository in an Access database. Queries, forms, and reports provide access to the data, enabling a user to add or extract data and presenting the data in useful ways. Most developers add macros or Visual Basic for Applications (VBA) code to forms and reports to make their Access applications easier to use.

A relational database management system (RDBMS), such as Access, stores data in *related* tables. For example, a table containing employee data (names and addresses) may be related to a table containing payroll information (pay date, pay amount, and check number).

Queries allow the user to ask complex questions (such as "What is the sum of all paychecks issued to Jane Doe in 2012?") from these related tables, with the answers displayed as onscreen forms and printed reports.

One of the fundamental differences between a relational database and a manual filing system is that, in a relational database system, data for a single person or item may be stored in separate tables. For example, in a patient management system, the patient's name, address, and other contact information is likely to be stored in a different table from the table holding patient treatments. In fact, the treatment table holds all treatment information for all patients, and a patient identifier (usually a number) is used to look up an individual patient's treatments in the treatment table.

In Access, a *database* is the overall container for the data and associated objects. It's more than the collection of tables, however—a database includes many types of objects, including queries, forms, reports, macros, and code modules.

As you open an Access database, the objects (tables, queries, and so on) in the database are presented for you to work with. You may open several copies of Access at the same time and simultaneously work with more than one database, if needed.

Many Access databases contain hundreds or even thousands of tables, forms, queries, reports, macros, and modules. With a few exceptions, all the objects in an Access 2016 database reside within a single file with an extension of ACCDB or ACCDE. Access databases can also have an extension of MDB or MDE. Databases with these extensions are backward-compatible with Access 2003 and prior versions.

Tables

A table is just a container for raw information (called *data*), similar to a folder in a manual filing system. Each table in an Access database contains information about a single topic, such as employees or products, and the data in the table is organized into rows and columns.

 In Chapters 3 and 4, you learn the very important rules governing relational table design and how to incorporate those rules into your Access databases. These rules and guidelines ensure that your applications perform well while protecting the integrity of the data contained within your tables.

In Access, a table is an entity. As you design and build Access databases, or even when working with an existing Access application, you must think of how the tables and other database objects represent the physical entities managed by your database and how the entities relate to one another.

After you create a table, you can view the table in a spreadsheet-like form, called a *datasheet*, comprising rows and columns (known as *records* and *fields*, respectively—see the following section, "Records and fields"). Although a datasheet and a spreadsheet are superficially similar, a datasheet is a very different type of object.

 Chapter 5 discusses Access datasheets and the differences between datasheets and spreadsheets. You can find much more about fields and field properties in Chapter 3.

Records and fields

A datasheet is divided into rows (called *records*) and columns (called *fields*), with the first row (the heading on top of each column) containing the names of the fields in the database.

Each row is a single record containing fields that are related to that record. In a manual system, the rows are individual forms (sheets of paper), and the fields are equivalent to the blank areas on a printed form that you fill in.

Each column is a field that includes many properties that specify the type of data contained within the field and how Access should handle the field's data. These properties include the name of the field (Company) and the type of data in the field (Text). A field may include other properties as well. For example, the Address field's Size property tells Access the maximum number of characters allowed for the address.

NOTE

When working with Access, the term *field* is used to refer to an attribute stored in a record. In many other database systems, including Microsoft SQL Server, *column* is the expression you'll hear most often in place of *field*. *Field* and *column* mean the same thing. The terminology used relies somewhat on the context of the database system underlying the table containing the record.

Values

At the intersection of a record and a field is a *value*—the actual data element. For example, if you have a field called Company, a company name entered into that field would represent one data value. Certain rules govern how data is contained in an Access table.

 See Chapters 3 and 4 for more on these rules.

Relational Databases

Access is a relational database management system. Access data is stored in related tables, where data in one table (such as Customers) is related to data in another table (such as Orders). Access maintains the relationships between related tables, making it easy to extract a customer and all the customer's orders, without losing any data or pulling order records not owned by the customer.

Multiple tables simplify data entry and reporting by decreasing the input of redundant data. By defining two tables for an application that uses customer information, for example, you don't need to store the customer's name and address every time the customer purchases an item.

After you've created the tables, they need to be related to each other. For example, if you have a Customers table and a Sales table, you can relate the two tables using a common field between them. In this case, Customer Number would be a good field to have in both tables. This will allow you to see sales in the Sales table where the Customer Number matches the Customers table.

The benefit of this model is that you don't have to repeat key attributes about a customer (like customer name, address, city, state, zip) each time you add a new record to the Sales table. All you need is the customer number. When a customer changes address, for example, the address changes only in one record in the Customers table.

Separating data into multiple tables within a database makes a system easier to maintain because all records of a given type are within the same table. By taking the time to properly segment data into multiple tables, you experience a significant reduction in design and work time. This process is known as *normalization*.

 You can read about normalization in Chapter 4.

Why Create Multiple Tables?

The prospect of creating multiple tables almost always intimidates beginning database users. Most often, beginners want to create one huge table that contains all the information they need—for example, a Customers table with all the sales placed by the customer and the customer's name, address, and other information. After all, if you've been using Excel to store data so far, it may seem quite reasonable to take the same approach when building tables in Access.

A single large table for all customer information quickly becomes difficult to maintain. You have to input the customer information for every sale a customer makes (repeating the name and address information over and over in every row). The same is true for the items purchased for each sale when the customer has purchased multiple items as part of a single purchase. This makes the system more inefficient and prone to data-entry mistakes. The information in the table is inefficiently stored—certain fields may not be needed for each sales record, and the table ends up with a lot of empty fields.

You want to create tables that hold a minimum of information while still making the system easy to use and flexible enough to grow. To accomplish this, you need to consider making more than one table, with each table containing fields that are related only to the focus of that table. Then, after you create the tables, you can use other Access database objects to link them and create meaningful views and reports. We'll dive into those topics in the next section.

Access Database Objects

If you're new to databases (or even if you're an experienced database user), you need to understand a few key concepts before starting to build Access databases. The Access database contains six types of top-level objects, which consist of the data and tools that you need to use Access:

- **Table:** Holds the actual data
- **Query:** Searches for, sorts, and retrieves specific data
- **Form:** Lets you enter and display data in a customized format
- **Report:** Displays and prints formatted data
- **Macro:** Automates tasks without programming
- **Module:** Contains programming statements written in the VBA (Visual Basic for Applications) programming language

Tables

As you've discovered earlier in this chapter, tables serve as the primary data repository in an Access database. You interact with tables through a special kind of object called a datasheet. Although not a permanent database object, a datasheet displays a table's content in a row-and-column format, similar to an Excel worksheet. A datasheet displays a table's information in a raw form, without transformations or filtering. The Datasheet view is the default mode for displaying all fields for all records.

You can scroll through the datasheet using the directional keys on your keyboard. You can also display related records in other tables while in a datasheet. In addition, you can make changes to the displayed data.

Queries

Queries extract information from a database. A query selects and defines a group of records that fulfill a certain condition. Most forms and reports are based on queries that combine, filter, or sort data before it's displayed. Queries are often called from macros or VBA procedures to change, add, or delete database records.

An example of a query is when a person at the sales office tells the database, "Show me all customers, in alphabetical order by name, who are located in Massachusetts and bought something over the past six months" or "Show me all customers who bought Chevrolet car models within the past six months and display them sorted by customer name and then by sale date."

Instead of asking the question in plain English, a person uses the query by example (QBE) method. When you enter instructions into the Query Designer window and run the query, the query translates the instructions into Structured Query Language (SQL) and retrieves the desired data.

 Chapter 8 discusses the Query Designer window and building queries.

Data-entry and display forms

Data-entry forms help users get information into a database table quickly, easily, and accurately. Data-entry and display forms provide a more structured view of the data than what a datasheet provides. From this structured view, database records can be viewed, added, changed, or deleted. Entering data through the data-entry forms is the most common way to get the data into the database table.

Data-entry forms can be used to restrict access to certain fields within the table. Forms can also be enhanced with data validation rules or VBA code to check the validity of your data before it's added to the database table.

Most users prefer to enter information into data-entry forms rather than into Datasheet views of tables. Forms often resemble familiar paper documents and can aid the user with data-entry tasks. Forms make data entry easy to understand by guiding the user through the fields of the table being updated.

Read-only forms are often used for inquiry purposes. These forms display certain fields within a table. Displaying some fields and not others means that you can limit a user's access to sensitive data while allowing access to other fields within the same table.

Reports

Reports present your data in PDF-style formatting. Access allows for an extraordinary amount of flexibility when creating reports. For instance, you can configure a report to list all records in a given table (such as a Customers table), or you can have the report contain only the records meeting certain criteria (such as all customers living in Arizona). You do this by basing the report on a query that selects only the records needed by the report.

Reports often combine multiple tables to present complex relationships among different sets of data. An example is printing an invoice. The Customers table provides the customer's name and address (and other relevant data) and related records in the sales table to print the individual line-item information for each product ordered. The report also calculates the sales totals and prints them in a specific format. Additionally, you can have Access output records into an *invoice report*, a printed document that summarizes the invoice.

Macros and VBA

Just as Excel has macros and VBA programming functionality, Microsoft Access has its equivalents. This is where the true power and flexibility of Microsoft Access data analysis resides. Whether you are using them in custom functions, batch analysis, or automation, macros and VBA modules can add a customized flexibility that is hard to match using any other means. For example, you can use macros and VBA to automatically perform redundant analyses and recurring analytical processes, leaving you free to work on other tasks. Macros and VBA also allow you to reduce the chance of human error and to ensure that analyses are preformed the same way every time. Starting in Chapter 22, you will explore the benefits of macros and VBA, and learn how you can use them to schedule and run batch analysis.

> **TIP**
> When you design your database tables, keep in mind all the types of information that you want to print. Doing so ensures that the information you require in your various reports is available from within your database tables.

Planning for database objects

To create database objects, such as tables, forms, and reports, you first complete a series of design tasks. The better your design is, the better your application will be. The more you think through your design, the faster and more successfully you can complete any system. The design process is not some necessary evil, nor is its intent to produce voluminous amounts of documentation. The sole intent of designing an object is to produce a clear-cut path to follow as you implement it.

A Five-Step Design Method

The five design steps described in this section provide a solid foundation for creating database applications—including tables, queries, forms, reports, macros, and simple VBA modules.

The time you spend on each step depends entirely on the circumstances of the database you're building. For example, sometimes users give you an example of a report they want printed from their Access database, and the sources of data on the report are so obvious that designing the report takes a few minutes. Other times, particularly when the users' requirements are complex or the business processes supported by the application require a great deal of research, you may spend many days on Step 1.

As you read through each step of the design process, *always* look at the design in terms of outputs and inputs.

Step 1: The overall design—from concept to reality

All software developers face similar problems, the first of which is determining how to meet the needs of the end user. It's important to understand the overall user requirements before zeroing in on the details.

For example, your users may ask for a database that supports the following tasks:

- Entering and maintaining customer information (name, address, and financial history)
- Entering and maintaining sales information (sales date, payment method, total amount, customer identity, and other fields)
- Entering and maintaining sales line-item information (details of items purchased)
- Viewing information from all the tables (sales, customers, sales line items, and payments)
- Asking all types of questions about the information in the database
- Producing a monthly invoice report
- Producing a customer sales history
- Producing mailing labels and mail-merge reports

When reviewing these eight tasks, you may need to consider other peripheral tasks that weren't mentioned by the user. Before you jump into designing, sit down and learn how the existing process works. To accomplish this, you must do a thorough needs analysis of the existing system and how you might automate it.

Prepare a series of questions that give insight to the client's business and how the client uses his data. For example, when considering automating any type of business, you might ask these questions:

- What reports and forms are currently used?
- How are sales, customers, and other records currently stored?
- How are billings processed?

As you ask these questions and others, the client will probably remember other things about the business that you should know.

A walkthrough of the existing process is also helpful to get a feel for the business. You may have to go back several times to observe the existing process and how the employees work.

As you prepare to complete the remaining steps, keep the client involved—let the users know what you're doing and ask for input on what to accomplish, making sure it's within the scope of the user's needs.

Step 2: Report design

Although it may seem odd to start with reports, in many cases, users are more interested in the printed output from a database than they are in any other aspect of the application. Reports often include every bit of data managed by an application. Because reports tend to be comprehensive, they're often the best way to gather important information about a database's requirements.

When you see the reports that you'll create in this section, you may wonder, "Which comes first, the chicken or the egg?" Does the report layout come first, or do you first determine the data items and text that make up the report? Actually, these items are considered at the same time.

It isn't important how you lay out the data in a report. The more time you take now, however, the easier it will be to construct the report. Some people go so far as to place gridlines on the report to identify exactly where they want each bit of data to be.

Step 3: Data design

The next step in the design phase is to take an inventory of all the information needed by the reports. One of the best methods is to list the data items in each report. As you do so, take careful note of items that are included in more than one report. Make sure that you keep the same name for a data item that is in more than one report because the data item is really the same item.

For example, you can start with all the customer data you'll need for each report, as shown in Table 1.1.

TABLE 1.1 Customer-Related Data Items Found in the Reports

Customers Report	Invoice Report
Customer Name	Customer Name
Street	Street
City	City
State	State
zip code	zip code
Phone Numbers	Phone Numbers
E-Mail Address	
Web Address	
Discount Rate	
Customer Since	
Last Sales Date	
Sales Tax Rate	
Credit Information (four fields)	

As you can see by comparing the type of customer information needed for each report, there are many common fields. Most of the customer data fields are found in both reports. Table 1.1 shows only some of the fields that are used in each report—those related to customer information. Because the related row and field names are the same, you can easily make sure that you have all the data items. Although locating items easily isn't critical for this small database, it becomes very important when you have to deal with large tables containing many fields.

After extracting the customer data, you can move on to the sales data. In this case, you need to analyze only the Invoice report for data items that are specific to the sales. Table 1.2 lists the fields in the report that contain information about sales.

TABLE 1.2 Sales Data Items Found in the Reports

Invoice Report	Line Item Data
Invoice Number	Product Purchased
Sales Date	Quantity Purchased
Invoice Date	Description of Item Purchased
Payment Method	Price of Item
Salesperson	Discount for Each Item
Discount (overall for sale)	
Tax Location	
Tax Rate	
Product Purchased (multiple lines)	
Quantity Purchased (multiple lines)	
Description of Item Purchased (multiple lines)	
Price of Item (multiple lines)	
Discount for each item (multiple lines)	
Payment Type (multiple lines)	
Payment Date (multiple lines)	
Payment Amount (multiple lines)	
Credit Card Number (multiple lines)	
Expiration Date (multiple lines)	

As you can see when you examine the type of sales information needed for the report, a few items (fields) are repeating (for example, the Product Purchased, Quantity Purchased, and Price of Item fields). Each invoice can have multiple items, and each of these items needs the same type of information—number ordered and price per item. Many sales have more than one purchased item. Also, each invoice may include partial payments, and it's possible that this payment information will have multiple lines of payment information, so these repeating items can be put into their own grouping.

You can take all the individual items that you found in the sales information group in the preceding section and extract them to their own group for the invoice report. Table 1.2 shows the information related to each line item.

Step 4: Table design

Now for the difficult part: you must determine which fields are needed for the tables that make up the reports. When you examine the multitude of fields and calculations that make up the many documents you have, you begin to see which fields belong to the various tables in the database. (You already did much of the preliminary work by arranging the fields into logical groups.) For now, include every field you extracted. You'll need to add others later (for various reasons), although certain fields won't appear in any table.

It's important to understand that you don't need to add every little bit of data into the database's tables. For example, users may want to add vacation and other out-of-office days to the database to make it easy to know which employees are available on a particular day. However, it's very easy to burden an application's initial design by incorporating too many ideas during the initial development phases. Because Access tables are so easy to modify later, it's probably best to put aside noncritical items until the initial design is complete. Generally speaking, it's not difficult to accommodate user requests after the database development project is underway.

After you've used each report to display all the data, it's time to consolidate the data by purpose (for example, grouped into logical groups) and then compare the data across those functions. To do this step, first look at the customer information and combine all its different fields to create a single set of data items. Then do the same thing for the sales information and the line-item information. Table 1.3 compares data items from these groups of information.

TABLE 1.3 **Comparing the Data Items**

Customer Data	Invoice Data	Line Items	Payment Information
Customer Company Name	Invoice Number	Product Purchased	Payment Type
Street	Sales Date	Quantity Purchased	Payment Date
City	Invoice Date	Description of Item Purchased	Payment Amount
State	Discount (overall for this sale)	Price of Item	Credit Card Number

Continues

TABLE 1.3   *(continued)*

Customer Data	Invoice Data	Line Items	Payment Information
zip code	Tax Rate	Discount for Each Item	Expiration Date
Phone Numbers (two fields)		Taxable?	
E-Mail Address			
Web Address			
Discount Rate			
Customer Since			
Last Sales Date			
Sales Tax Rate			
Credit Information (four fields)			

Consolidating and comparing data is a good way to start creating the individual table, but you have much more to do.

As you learn more about how to perform a data design, you also learn that the customer data must be split into two groups. Some of these items are used only once for each customer, while other items may have multiple entries. An example is the Sales column—the payment information can have multiple lines of information.

You need to further break these types of information into their own columns, thus separating all related types of items into their own columns—an example of the *normalization* part of the design process. For example, one customer can have multiple contacts with the company or make multiple payments toward a single sale. Of course, we've already broken the data into three categories: customer data, invoice data, and line-item details.

Keep in mind that one customer may have multiple invoices, and each invoice may have multiple line items on it. The invoice-data category contains information about individual sales and the line-items category contains information about each invoice. Notice that these three columns are all related; for example, one customer can have multiple invoices, and each invoice may require multiple line items.

The relationships between tables can be different. For example, each sales invoice has one and only one customer, while each customer may have multiple sales. A similar relationship exists between the sales invoice and the line items of the invoice.

Database table relationships require a unique field in both tables involved in a relationship. A unique identifier in each table helps the database engine to properly join and extract related data.

Only the Sales table has a unique identifier (Invoice Number), which means that you need to add at least one field to each of the other tables to serve as the link to other tables—for example, adding a Customer ID field to the Customers table, adding the same field to the Invoice table, and establishing a relationship between the tables through Customer ID in each table. The database engine uses the relationship between customers and invoices to connect customers with their invoices. Relationships between tables are facilitated through the use of key fields.

 We cover creating and understanding relationships and the normalization process in Chapter 4.

With an understanding of the need for linking one group of fields to another group, you can add the required key fields to each group. Table 1.4 shows two new groups and link fields created for each group of fields. These linking fields, known as *primary keys* and *foreign keys*, are used to link these tables together.

The field that uniquely identifies each row in a table is the *primary key*. The corresponding field in a related table is the *foreign key*. In our example, Customer ID in the Customers table is a primary key, while Customer ID in the Invoices table is a foreign key.

Let's assume a certain record in the Customers table has 12 in its Customer ID field. Any record in the Invoices table with 12 as its Customer ID is "owned" by customer 12.

TABLE 1.4 Tables with Keys

Customers Data	Invoice Data	Line Items Data	Sales Payment Data
Customer ID	Invoice ID	Invoice ID	Invoice ID
Customer Name	Customer ID	Line Number	Payment Type
Street	Invoice Number	Product Purchased	Payment Date
City	Sales Date	Quantity Purchased	Payment Amount
State	Invoice Date	Description of Item Purchased	Credit Card Number
zip code	Payment Method	Price of Item	Expiration Date
Phone Numbers (two fields)	Salesperson	Discount for Each Item	
E-Mail Address	Tax Rate		
Web Address			
Discount Rate			
Customer Since			
Last Sales Date			
Sales Tax Rate			

With the key fields added to each table, you can now find a field in each table that links it to other tables in the database. For example, Table 1.4 shows Customer ID in both the Customers table (where it's the primary key) and the Invoice table (where it's a foreign key).

You've identified the three core tables for your system, as reflected by the first three columns in Table 1.4. This is the general, or first, cut toward the final table designs. You've also created an additional fact table to hold the sales payment data. Normally, payment details (such as the credit card number) are not part of a sales invoice.

Taking time to properly design your database and the tables contained within it is arguably the most important step in developing a database-oriented application. By designing your database efficiently, you maintain control of the data, eliminating costly data-entry mistakes and limiting your data entry to essential fields.

Although this book is not geared toward teaching database theory and all its nuances, this is a good place to briefly describe the art of database normalization. You'll read the details of normalization in Chapter 4, but in the meantime you should know that *normalization* is the process of breaking data down into constituent tables. Earlier in this chapter you read about how many Access developers add dissimilar information, such as customers, invoice data, and invoice line items, into one large table. A large table containing dissimilar data quickly becomes unwieldy and hard to keep updated. Because a customer's phone number appears in every row containing that customer's data, multiple updates must be made when the phone number changes.

Step 5: Form design

After you've created the data and established table relationships, it's time to design your forms. *Forms* are made up of the fields that can be entered or viewed in Edit mode. Generally speaking, your Access screens should look a lot like the forms used in a manual system.

When you're designing forms, you need to place three types of objects onscreen:

- **Labels and text-box data-entry fields:** The fields on Access forms and reports are called *controls*.
- **Special controls (command buttons, multiple-line text boxes, option buttons, list boxes, check boxes, business graphs, and pictures).**
- **Graphical objects to enhance the forms (colors, lines, rectangles, and three-dimensional effects).**

Ideally, if the form is being developed from an existing printed form, the Access data-entry form should resemble the printed form. The fields should be in the same relative place on the screen as they are in the printed counterpart.

Labels display messages, titles, or captions. Text boxes provide an area where you can type or display text or numbers that are contained in your database. Check boxes indicate a condition and are either unchecked or checked. Other types of controls available with Access include command buttons, list boxes, combo boxes, option buttons, toggle buttons, and option groups.

 Starting with Part V, we cover in detail the topic of creating forms.

Getting Started with Access

IN THIS CHAPTER

Looking at the Access welcome screen

Creating a database from scratch

Opening a new database

Getting acquainted with the Access interface

n this chapter, you'll gain an understanding of the major components of the Microsoft Access user interface.

The Access Welcome Screen

If you open Access 2019 via Windows (Start ⇨ Access), you'll see the default welcome screen shown in Figure 2.1. The welcome screen gives you several options for opening an existing Access database or creating a new database.

> **NOTE**
> If you open an Access database directly from File Explorer (by double-clicking it), you won't see the welcome screen. Instead, you'll go directly to the database interface covered later in this chapter.

In the upper-left corner of the welcome screen, you'll notice the Recent section. The files listed here are databases that you've previously opened through Access 2019. You can click any of the database files listed there to open them.

> **NOTE**
> Access does not distinguish existing databases from deleted databases when populating the Recent section. This means you could see a database in the Recent list that you know for a fact you've deleted. Clicking an already deleted database in the Recent list will simply activate an error message stating that Access could not find the database.

Below the Recent section, you'll see the Open Other Files hyperlink. Click this link to browse for and open databases on your computer or network.

FIGURE 2.1

The Access welcome screen provides a number of ways to start working with Access.

At the top of the welcome screen, you can search for Access database templates online. These templates are typically starter databases that have various purposes. Microsoft makes them available free of charge.

In the center of the welcome screen, you'll see various predefined templates that you can click to download and use. Microsoft established the online templates repository as a way to provide people with the opportunity to download partially or completely built Access applications. The template databases cover many common business requirements, such as inventory control and sales management. You may want to take a moment to explore the online templates, but they aren't covered in this book.

In the center of the welcome screen, you'll also see an option for Blank Database. This option allows you to create a database from scratch.

> **NOTE**
>
> Access 2013 and Access 2016 offered an option to create a Web database. These were databases that could be published as a custom web application on SharePoint. Microsoft has deprecated Access web applications and no longer makes Web databases available as an option in Access 2019.

How to Create a Blank Database

To create a new blank database, you can click the Blank Database option on the welcome screen (refer to Figure 2.1). When you do, the dialog box shown in Figure 2.2 appears, allowing you to specify the name and location of your database.

> **NOTE**
>
> The default location of the new database will be your `Documents` folder. If you want to use a different folder, click the Browse button (it looks like a File Explorer folder) to the right of the File Name box to browse to the location you want to use.
>
> You can also permanently tell Access to start with your own custom default location by clicking the File tab, choosing Options, and then changing the Default database folder setting (found on the General tab).

FIGURE 2.2

Enter the name of the new database in the File Name box.

When the new database is created by clicking the Create button, Access automatically opens the database for you. In Figure 2.3, notice that Access opens the new database with a blank table already added to the database, ready to be filled in with fields and other design details.

FIGURE 2.3

Your new database is created.

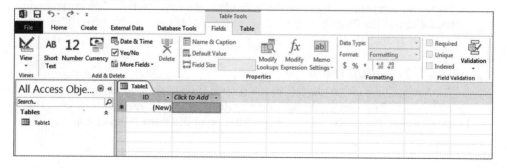

Access File Formats

Since Access 2007, the default file format for Access database files has been ACCDB instead of MDB. It's worth a moment of your time to understand why this changed and how it affects how Access 2019 works with older Access database files.

Since its inception, Access has used a database engine named Jet (an acronym for Joint Engine Technology). With Access 2007, the Access development team wanted to add significant new features to Access, such as multivariable and attachment fields. Because the new features were so significant, they couldn't retrofit Jet with the code necessary to support the new features. As a result, Microsoft developed an entirely new database engine, the Access Connectivity Engine (ACE).

Access 2019 supports several file formats, including the following:

- Access 2007–2019 ACCDB
- Access 2002–2003 MDB
- Access 2000 MDB

If you are unfortunate enough to work in an environment where Access 2003 is still being used, you will need to stick with the Access 2002–2003 MDB format for compatibility purposes. In that same light, if you are using older databases that use database replication or user-level security, you will need to stick with the MDB formats. Access ACCDB files do not support replication or user-level security.

In Access 2019, you can open older Access 2002–2003 and Access 2000 MDB files and make any desired changes to them, but you'll only be able to use features specific to those versions. Some of the new Access features won't be available, particularly those features that rely on the ACE database engine.

You can convert a database saved in a previous format by opening the database in Access 2019, choosing File ⇨ Save As, and then, in the Save As dialog box, choosing any one of the different Access formats.

The Access 2019 Interface

After you create or open a new database, the Access screen will look similar to Figure 2.4. Across the top of the screen is the Access Ribbon. On the left, you see the Navigation pane. These two components make up the bulk of the Access interface. In addition, you have at your disposal the Quick Access toolbar, which you can customize with the commands you use most frequently.

The Navigation pane

The Navigation pane, at the left of the screen, is your primary navigation aid when working with Access. The Navigation pane shows tables, queries, forms, reports, and other Access object types. It can also display a combination of different types of objects.

Click the drop-down list in the Navigation pane's title bar to reveal the navigation options (see Figure 2.5).

FIGURE 2.4

The Access interface starts with the Ribbon at the top and the Navigation pane at the left.

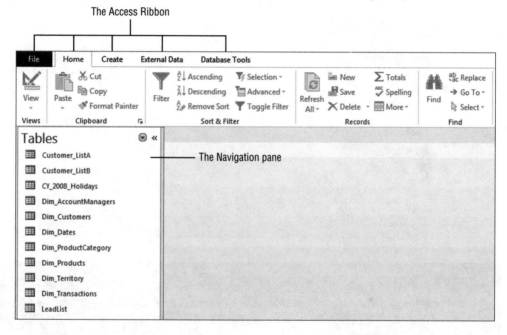

The navigation options are divided into two categories: Navigate To Category and Filter By Group. First, you choose an option under Navigate To Category, and then you choose an option under Filter By Group. The Filter By Group options you're presented with depend on the Navigate To Category option you select. We cover each of the Navigate To Category options in the following sections, along with the corresponding Filter By Group options.

Custom

The Custom option creates a new grouping in the Navigation pane. This new tab is titled Custom Group 1 by default and contains objects that you drag and drop into the tab's area. Items added to a custom group still appear in their respective object type views described in the next section.

When you select Custom, the Filter By Group category is populated with all the custom groups you've previously created. You can use the Filter By Group category to filter to any of the created custom groups.

FIGURE 2.5

Choosing an alternate display for the Navigation pane.

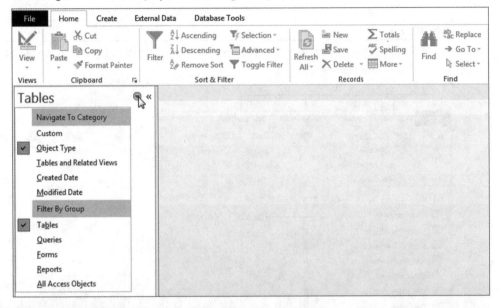

> **TIP**
>
> Custom groups are a great way to group dissimilar objects (like tables, queries, and forms) that are functionally related. For example, you could create a Customers custom group and add all the database objects related to customer activities. Items contained in a custom group can appear in other groups as well.

Object Type

The Object Type option is most similar to previous versions of Access.

When you select Object Type, you have the following options under Filter By Group:

- Tables
- Queries
- Forms
- Reports
- All Access Objects

By default, the Navigation pane shows all objects in the current database. Select All Access Objects when you've been working with one of the filtered views and want to see every object in the database.

Tables and Related Views

The Tables and Related Views option requires a bit of explanation. Access tries very hard to keep the developer informed of the hidden connections between objects in the database. For example, a particular table may be used in a number of queries or referenced from a form or report. Selecting Tables and Related Views allows you to understand which objects are affected by each table.

When you select Tables and Related Views, the Filter By Group category is populated with the Tables in your database. Clicking each object in the Filter By Group category will filter the list to that object and all the other dependent and precedent objects related to it.

Created Date

This option groups the database objects by the created date. This setting is useful when you need to know when an object was created.

When you select Created Date, some or all of the following options are available under Filter By Group:

- Today
- Yesterday
- Last Week
- Two Weeks Ago
- Older

Modified Date

This option groups the database objects by the modified date. This setting is useful when you need to know when an object was last modified.

When you select Modified Date, some or all of the following options are available under Filter By Group:

- Today
- Yesterday
- Last Week
- Two Weeks Ago
- Older

Tabbed Windows

A common complaint among some developers with earlier versions of Access was the fact that when multiple objects were simultaneously opened in the Access environment, the objects would often overlap and obscure each other, making it more difficult to navigate between the objects.

Microsoft has added a tabbed document interface to Access, preventing objects from obscuring other objects that are open at the same time. You can simply select a tab associated with an object, and the object is brought to the top.

TIP

Don't like the new tabbed windows configuration? You can go back to the old overlapping windows by choosing File ⌴ Options. In the Access Options dialog box, select the Current Database tab, and change the Document Window Options setting from Tabbed Documents to Overlapping Windows. You'll have to close and reopen your database to have the change take effect.

The Ribbon

The Ribbon occupies the top portion of the main Access screen. Starting with Access 2007, the Ribbon replaced the menus and toolbars seen in previous versions of Access.

The Ribbon is divided into six tabs, each containing any number of controls and commands (refer to Figure 2.4):

- **File:** When you click the File tab, the Office Backstage view opens. Backstage view contains a number of options for creating databases, opening databases, saving databases, and configuring databases. We delve deeper into the Office Backstage view in the nearby sidebar.

- **Home:** The theme of the Home tab is "frequently used." Here, you find generally unrelated commands that are repeatedly called upon during the course of working with Access. For example, there are commands for formatting, copying and pasting, sorting, and filtering.

- **Create:** The Create tab contains commands that create the various objects in Access. This tab is where you'll spend most of your time. Here, you can initiate the creation of tables, queries, forms, reports, and macros. As you read this book, you'll be using the Create tab all the time.

- **External Data:** The External Data tab is dedicated to integrating Access with other sources of data. On this tab, you find commands that allow you to import and export data, establish connections to outside databases, and work with SharePoint or other platforms.

- **Database Tools:** The Database Tools tab contains the commands that deal with the inner workings of your database. Here, you find tools to create relationships between tables, analyze the performance of your database, document your database, and compact and repair your database.

- **Help:** Access 2019 also contains a Help tab which doesn't have database functionality, but does provide links to support and training.

In addition to the standard six tabs on the Access Ribbon, you'll also see contextual tabs. *Contextual tabs* are special types of tabs that appear only when a particular object is selected. For example, when you're working with the Query Builder, you'll see the Query Tools Design tab, as shown in Figure 2.6.

FIGURE 2.6

Contextual tabs contain commands that are specific to whichever object is active.

Office Backstage View

Office Backstage view is the gateway to a number of options for creating, opening, or configuring Access databases. You get to Backstage view by clicking the File tab on the Ribbon (see the preceding section).

The Backstage options include activities that are used infrequently when you're working within the main Access window, but that are necessary for saving, printing, or maintaining Access databases. Putting these options into the Backstage area means they don't have to appear anywhere on the Ribbon as you're working with Access.

We cover the Backstage commands in the chapters that follow.

The Quick Access toolbar

The Quick Access toolbar (shown in Figure 2.7) is a customizable toolbar that allows you to add commands that are most important to your daily operations. By default, the Quick Access toolbar contains three commands: Save, Undo, and Redo.

FIGURE 2.7

The Quick Access toolbar is located above the Ribbon.

If you click the drop-down arrow next to the Quick Access toolbar, you'll see that many more commands are available (see Figure 2.8). Place a check mark next to any of these options to add it to the Quick Access toolbar.

FIGURE 2.8

Commands you can add to the Quick Access toolbar.

You're not limited to the commands shown in this drop-down list. You can add all kinds of commands. To add a command to the Quick Access toolbar, follow these steps:

1. **Click the drop-down arrow next to the Quick Access toolbar, and select the More Commands option.** The Quick Access Toolbar tab of the Access Options dialog box (shown in Figure 2.9) appears.

2. **In the Choose Commands From drop-down list on the left, select All Commands.**

3. **From the alphabetical list of commands, select the one you're interested in and click the Add button.**

4. **When you're done, click OK.**

FIGURE 2.9

Adding more commands to the Quick Access toolbar.

> **TIP**
>
> To change the order of the icons on the Quick Access toolbar, select the Quick Access Toolbar tab of the Access Options dialog box (refer to Figure 2.9). The list on the right shows all the commands that are currently in the Quick Access toolbar. You can click a command and then click the up and down arrow buttons on the right to move the command up or down in the list. This will change the order of the commands.

Part II

Understanding Access Tables

The topics covered in this part explain the techniques for creating and managing Access database tables, the core of any application you build in Access.

These chapters go well beyond simply describing how to build tables. Here, you learn fundamental concepts that are key to using the capabilities documented in the remaining parts of this book.

Chapter 3 lays the foundation by defining tables and their component parts. In Chapter 4, you learn the importance of table relationships and how to effectively build and manage the relationships between the tables in your database. Chapter 5 demonstrates the techniques to effectively sort, filter, and work with your raw tables and datasheets. Finally, Chapters 6 and 7 explain how you can reach outside your database and create tables from imported or linked external data sources.

IN THIS PART

Chapter 3
Creating Access Tables

Chapter 4
Understanding Table Relationships

Chapter 5
Working with Access Tables

Chapter 6
Importing and Exporting Data

Chapter 7
Linking to External Data

Creating Access Tables

IN THIS CHAPTER

Creating a new table

Modifying the design of a table

Working with field properties

Specifying the primary key

Adding indexes

Documenting a table's design

Saving a new table

Working with tables

Adding data to a table

Using attachment fields

I n this chapter, you learn how to create a new Access database and its tables. You establish the database container to hold your tables, forms, queries, reports, and code that you build as you learn Access. Finally, you create the actual tables used by the Collectible Mini Cars database.

ON THE WEB

This chapter uses the examples in the database named `Chapter03.accdb`. If you haven't yet downloaded this file from the book's website, please do so now.

Table Types

To Access, a table is always just a table. But to your Access application, different tables serve different purposes. A database table fits into one of three types: an object table, a transaction table, or a join table. Knowing what type of table you're creating helps to determine how you create it.

Object tables

Object tables are the most common. Each record of this type of table holds information that relates to a real-world object. A customer is a real-world object, and a record in a table named tblCustomers holds information about that customer. The fields in an object table reflect the characteristics of the object they represent. A City field describes one characteristic of the customer—namely, the actual city where the customer is. When creating an object table, think about the characteristics of that object that make it unique or that are important.

Transaction tables

The next most common type of table is a transaction table. Each record of a transaction table holds information about an event. Placing an order for a book is an example of an event. To hold the details of all the orders, you might have a table named tblBookOrders. Transaction tables almost always have a Date/Time field because when the event happened is usually an important piece of information to record. Another common type of field is a field that refers to an object table, such as a reference to the customer in tblCustomers that placed the order. When creating a transaction table, think about the information created by the event and who was involved.

Join tables

Join tables are the easiest to design and are vitally important to a well-designed database. Usually relating two tables is a simple process: A customer orders a book, for instance, and you can easily relate that order to that customer. But sometimes the relationship isn't so clear. A book may have many authors, and an author may have many books. When this relationship exists, called a *many-to-many relationship*, a join table sits in the middle of the two tables. A join table usually has a name that reflects the association, such as tblAuthorBook. A join table generally has only three fields: a unique field to identify each record, a reference to one side of the association, and a reference to the other side of an association.

Creating a New Table

Creating database tables is as much art as it is science. Acquiring a good working knowledge of the user's requirements is a fundamental step for any new database project.

 Chapter 4 covers the details of applying database design rules to the creation of Access tables.

In this chapter, we show you the steps required to create basic Access tables. In the following sections, you'll study the process of adding tables to an Access database, including the relatively complex subject of choosing the proper data type to assign to each field in a table.

It's always a good idea to plan tables first, before you use the Access tools to add tables to the database. Many tables, especially small ones, really don't require a lot of forethought before adding them to the database. After all, not much planning is required to design a table holding lookup information, such as the names of cities and states. However, more complex entities, such as customers and products, usually require considerable thought and effort to implement properly.

Although you can design the table without any forethought as you create it in Access, carefully planning a database system is a good idea. You can make changes later, but doing so wastes time; generally, the result is a system that's harder to maintain than one that you've planned well from the beginning.

In the following sections, we explore the new, blank table added to the Chapter03.accdb database. It's important to understand the steps required to add new tables to an Access database.

The Importance of Naming Conventions

Most Access developers eventually adopt a naming convention to help identify database objects. Most naming conventions are relatively simple and involve nothing more than adding a prefix indicating an object's type to the object's name. For example, an employees form might be named frmEmployees.

As your databases grow in size and complexity, establishing a naming convention for the objects in your databases becomes more valuable. Even with the Perform Name AutoCorrect option turned on (click the File tab and choose Options ⇨ Current Database ⇨ Name AutoCorrect Options), Access only corrects the most obvious name changes. Changing the name of a table breaks virtually every query, form, and report that uses the information from that table. Your best defense is to adopt reasonable object names, use a naming convention early on as you begin building Access databases, and stick with the naming convention throughout the project.

Access imposes very few restrictions on the names assigned to database objects. Therefore, it's entirely possible to have two distinctly different objects (for example, a form and a report, or a table and a macro) with the same name. (You can't, however, have a table and a query with the same name, because tables and queries occupy the same namespace in the database.)

Although simple names like Contacts and Orders are adequate, as a database grows in size and complexity, you might be confused about which object a particular name refers to. For example, later in this book, you'll read about manipulating database objects through code and macros. When working with Visual Basic for Applications (VBA), the programming language built into Access, there must be no ambiguity or confusion between referenced objects. Having both a form and a report named Contacts might be confusing to you *and* your code.

The simplest naming convention is to prefix object names with a three- or four-character string indicating the type of object carrying the name. Using this convention, tables are prefixed with tbl and queries with qry. The generally accepted prefixes for forms, reports, macros, and modules are frm, rpt, mcr, and bas or mod, respectively.

In this book, most compound object names appear in *camel case*: tblBookOrders, tblCustomers, and so on. Most people find camel-case names easier to read and remember than names that appear in all-uppercase or all-lowercase characters (such as TBLBOOKORDERS or tblbookorders).

Also, at times, we use informal references for database objects. For example, the formal name of the table containing contact information in the previous examples is tblContacts. An informal reference to this table might be "the Contacts table."

3

In most cases, your users never see the formal names of database objects. One of your challenges as an application developer is to provide a seamless user interface that hides all data-management and data-storage entities that support the user interface. You can easily control the text that appears in the title bars and surfaces of the forms, reports, and other user-interface components to hide the actual names of the data structures and interface constituents.

Access allows table names up to 64 characters. Take advantage of this to give your tables, queries, forms, and reports descriptive, informative names. There is no reason why you should confine a table name to BkOrd when tblBookOrders is handled just as easily and is much easier to understand.

Descriptive names can be carried to an extreme, of course. There's no point in naming a form frmUpdateContactInformation if frmUpdateInfo does just as well. Long names are more easily misspelled or misread than shorter names, so use your best judgment when assigning names.

Although Access lets you use spaces in database object names, you should avoid doing so. Spaces don't add to readability over camel case and can cause major headaches, particularly when upsizing to client/server environments or using OLE automation with other applications. Even if you don't anticipate extending your Access applications to client/server or incorporating OLE or DDE automation into your applications, get into the habit of not using spaces in object names.

Finally, you can use some special characters, like an underscore, in your table names. Some developers use an underscore to separate words in a table name as part of a larger naming convention. Unless you use a specific convention that includes special characters, you should avoid them.

Designing tables

Designing a table is a multistep process. By following the steps in order, your table design can be created readily and with minimal effort:

1. **Create the new table.**
2. **Enter field names, data types, properties, and (optionally) descriptions.**
3. **Set the table's primary key.**
4. **Create indexes for appropriate fields.**
5. **Save the table's design.**

Generally speaking, some tables are never really finished. As users' needs change or the business rules governing the application change, you might find it necessary to open an existing table in Design view. This book, like most books on Access, describes the process of creating tables as if every table you ever work on is brand new. The truth is, however, that most of the work that you do on an Access application is performed on existing objects in the database. Some of those objects you've added yourself, while other objects may have been added by another developer at some time in the past. However, the process of maintaining an existing database component is very much the same as creating the same object from scratch.

TIP

A quick note about modifying tables once they're built: adding a new field to a table almost never causes problems. Existing queries, forms, reports, and even VBA code will continue using the table as before. These objects won't reference the new field because the field was added after their creation. The new field will not be automatically added to existing objects, but you can add the new field where needed in your application, and everything works as expected.

The trouble comes when you remove or rename a field in a table. Even with AutoCorrect turned on, Access won't update field name references in VBA code, in control properties, and in expressions throughout the database. Changing an existing field (or any other database object, for that matter) is always a bad idea. You should always strive to provide your tables, fields, and other database objects with good, strong, descriptive names when you add them to the database, instead of planning to go back later and fix them.

TIP

Many Access developers routinely turn off AutoCorrect. (Use the File tab to access the Backstage, select Options, and then select Current Database. In the Name AutoCorrect Options, make sure Track name AutoCorrect info is unchecked.) The AutoCorrect feature negatively affects performance because it constantly watches for name changes in an application and takes corrective action when needed. Furthermore, because AutoCorrect never quite corrects all the names in an application, there is always more work to perform when you change the name of a database object.

Begin by selecting the Create tab on the Ribbon at the top of the Access screen. The Create tab (shown in Figure 3.1) contains all the tools necessary to create not only tables, but also forms, reports, and other database objects.

ON THE WEB

The following examples use the `Chapter03.accdb` database found on this book's website.

FIGURE 3.1

The Create tab contains tools necessary for adding new objects to your Access database.

There are two main ways to add new tables to an Access database, both of which are invoked from the Tables group on the Create tab:

- **Clicking the Table button:** Adds a table in Datasheet view to the database with one AutoNumber field named ID
- **Clicking the Table Design button:** Adds a table in Design view to the database

For this example, we'll be using the Table Design button, but first, let's take a look at the Table button.

Clicking the Table button adds a new table to the Access environment. The new table appears in Datasheet view in the area to the right of the Navigation pane. The new table is shown in Figure 3.2. Notice that the new table appears in Datasheet view, with an ID column already inserted and a Click to Add column to the right of the ID field.

FIGURE 3.2

The new table in Datasheet view.

The Click to Add column is intended to permit users to quickly add fields to a table. All you have to do is begin entering data in the new column. You assign the field a name by right-clicking the field's heading, selecting Rename Field, and entering a name for the field. In other words, building an Access table can be very much like creating a spreadsheet in Excel.

NOTE

In previous versions of Access, this approach was usually referred to as "creating a table in Datasheet view."

Once you've added the new column, the tools on the Fields tab of the Ribbon (shown in Figure 3.3) allow you to set the specific data type for the field, along with its formatting, validation rules, and other properties.

FIGURE 3.3

Field design tools are located on the Fields tab of the Ribbon.

The second method of adding new tables is to click the Table Design button in the Tables group on the Create tab. Access opens a new table in Design view, allowing you to add fields to the table's design. Figure 3.4 shows a new table's design after a few fields have been added. Table Design view provides a somewhat more deliberate approach to building Access tables.

FIGURE 3.4

A new table added in Design view.

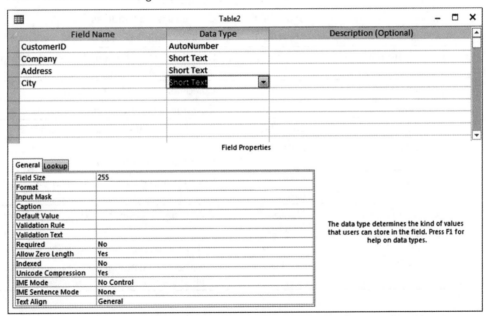

The Table Designer is easy to understand, and each column is clearly labeled. At the far left is the Field Name column, where you input the names of fields you add to the table. You assign a data type to each field in the table and (optionally) provide a description for the field. Data types are discussed in detail later in this chapter.

For this exercise, you create the Customers table for the Collectible Mini Cars application. The basic design of this table is outlined in Table 3.1. We cover the details of this table's design in the "Creating tblCustomers" section, later in this chapter.

TABLE 3.1   The Collectible Mini Cars Customers Table

Field Name	Data Type	Description
CustomerID	AutoNumber	Primary key
Company	Short Text	Contact's employer or other affiliation
Address	Short Text	Contact's address
City	Short Text	Contact's city
State	Short Text	Contact's state
zipcode	Short Text	Contact's zip code
Phone	Short Text	Contact's phone
Fax	Short Text	Contact's fax
Email	Short Text	Contact's e-mail address
WebSite	Short Text	Contact's web address
OrigCustomerDate	DateTime	Date the contact first purchased something from Collectible Mini Cars
CreditLimit	Currency	Customer's credit limit in dollars
CurrentBalance	Currency	Customer's current balance in dollars
CreditStatus	Short Text	Description of the customer's credit status
LastSalesDate	DateTime	Most recent date the customer purchased something from Collectible Mini Cars
TaxRate	Number (Double)	Sales tax applicable to the customer
DiscountPercent	Number (Double)	Customary discount provided to the customer
Notes	Long Text	Notes and observations regarding this customer
Active	Yes/No	Whether the customer is still buying or selling to Collectible Mini Cars

The Short Text fields in the preceding table use the default 255 character Field Size. While it's unlikely that anyone's name will occupy 255 characters, there's no harm in providing for very long names. Access only stores as many characters as are actually entered into a text field. So, allocating 255 characters doesn't actually *use* 255 characters for every name in the database.

Looking once again at Figure 3.4, you see that the Table Design window consists of two areas:

- **The field entry area:** Use the field entry area, at the top of the window, to enter each field's name and data type. You can also enter an optional description.
- **The field properties area:** The area at the bottom of the window is where the field's properties are specified. These properties include field size, format, input mask, and default value, among others. The actual properties displayed in the properties area depend upon the data type of the field. You learn much more about these properties in the "Assigning field properties" section, later in this chapter.

> **TIP**
>
> You can switch between the upper and lower areas of the Table Designer by clicking the mouse when the pointer is in the desired pane or by pressing F6. The F6 key cycles through all open panes, such as the Navigation pane and the Property search, so you may have to press it multiple times to get where you're going.

Using the Design tab

The Design tab of the Access Ribbon (shown in Figure 3.5) contains many controls that assist in creating a new table definition.

FIGURE 3.5

The Design tab of the Ribbon.

The controls on the Design tab affect the important table design considerations. Only a few of the controls shown in Figure 3.5 are described in the following sections. You'll learn much more about the other buttons in the "Creating tblCustomers" section, later in this chapter, and in subsequent chapters of this book.

Primary Key

Click this button to designate which of the fields in the table you want to use as the table's primary key. Traditionally, the primary key appears at the top of the list of fields in the table, but it could appear anywhere within the table's design. Primary keys are discussed in detail in the "Setting the Primary Key" section later in this chapter.

> **TIP**
>
> To move a field, simply left-click the selector to the left of the field's name to highlight the field in the Table Designer and drag the field to its new position.

Insert Rows

Although it makes little difference to the database engine, many developers are fussy about the sequence of fields in a table. Many of the wizards in Access display the fields in the same order as the table. Keeping an address field above a city field, for example, can make development easier.

 Composite keys, consisting of multiple fields combined as a single key, are discussed in detail in Chapter 4.

Clicking the Insert Rows button inserts a blank row just *above* the position occupied by the mouse cursor. For example, if the cursor is currently in the second row of the Table Designer, clicking the Insert Rows button inserts an empty row in the second position, moving the existing second row to the third position.

Delete Rows

Clicking the Delete Rows button removes a row from the table's design.

CAUTION

Access doesn't ask you to confirm the deletion before actually removing the row.

Property Sheet

Clicking the Property Sheet button opens the Property Sheet for the entire table (shown in Figure 3.6). These properties enable you to specify important table characteristics, such as a validation rule to apply to the entire table, or an alternate sort order for the table's data.

FIGURE 3.6

The Property Sheet.

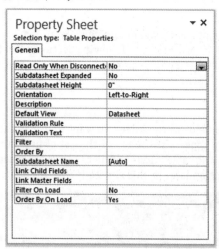

Indexes

Indexes are discussed in much more detail in the "Indexing Access Tables" section, later in this chapter. Clicking the Indexes button opens the Indexes dialog box, which enables you to specify the details of indexes on the fields in your table.

Working with fields

You create fields by entering a field name and a field data type in the upper field entry area of the Table Design window. The (optional) Description property can be used to indicate the field's purpose. The description appears in the status bar at the bottom of the screen during data entry and may be useful to people working with the application. After entering each field's name and data type, you can further specify how each field is used by entering properties in the field properties area.

Naming a field

A field name should be descriptive enough to identify the field to you as the developer, to the user of the system, and to Access. Field names should be long enough to quickly identify the purpose of the field, but not overly long. (Later, as you enter validation rules or use the field name in a calculation, you'll want to save yourself from typing long field names.)

To enter a field name, position the pointer in the first row of the Table Design window under the Field Name column. Then type a valid field name, observing these rules:

- Field names can be from 1 to 64 characters in length.
- Field names can include letters, numbers, and special characters, except period (.), exclamation point (!), accent grave (`), and brackets ([]).
- Field names can include spaces. Spaces should be avoided in field names for some of the same reasons you avoid them in table names.
- You can't use low-order ASCII characters—for example Ctrl+J or Ctrl+L (ASCII values 0 through 31).
- You can't start with a blank space.

You can enter field names in uppercase, lowercase, or mixed case. If you make a mistake while typing the field name, position the cursor where you want to make a correction and type the change. You can change a field name at any time, even if the table contains data.

> **NOTE**
> Access is not case sensitive, so the database itself doesn't care whether you name a table tblCustomers or TblCustomers. Choosing uppercase, lowercase, or mixed case characters is entirely your decision and should be aimed at making your table names descriptive and easy to read.

> **CAUTION**
>
> After your table is saved, if you change a field name that is also used in queries, forms, or reports, you have to change it in those objects as well. One of the leading causes of errors in Access applications stems from changing the names of fundamental database objects, such as tables and fields, but neglecting to make all the changes required throughout the database. Overlooking a field name reference in the control source of a control on the form or report, or deeply embedded in VBA code somewhere in the application, is far too easy.

Specifying a data type

When you enter a field, you must also decide what type of data each of your fields will hold. In Access, you can choose any of several data types. The available data types are shown in Table 3.2.

TABLE 3.2 Data Types Available in Microsoft Access

Data Type	Type of Data Stored	Storage Size
Short Text	Alphanumeric characters	255 characters or fewer
Long Text	Alphanumeric characters	1GB of characters or less
Number	Numeric values	1, 2, 4, or 8 bytes; 16 bytes for Replication ID (GUID)
Large Number	Numeric values	8 bytes
Date/Time	Date and time data	8 bytes
Currency	Monetary data	8 bytes
AutoNumber	Automatic number increments	4 bytes; 16 bytes for Replication ID (GUID)
Yes/No	Logical values: Yes/No, True/False	1 bit (0 or –1)
OLE Object	Pictures, graphs, sound, video	Up to 1GB (disk space limitation)
Hyperlink	Link to an Internet resource	1GB of characters or less
Attachment	A special field that enables you to attach external files to an Access database	Varies by attachment
Calculated	A field that stores a calculation based on other fields in the table	Determined by setting the Result Type property
Lookup Wizard	Displays data from another table	Generally 4 bytes

Figure 3.7 shows the Data Type drop-down list used to select the data type for the field you just created.

FIGURE 3.7

The Data Type drop-down list.

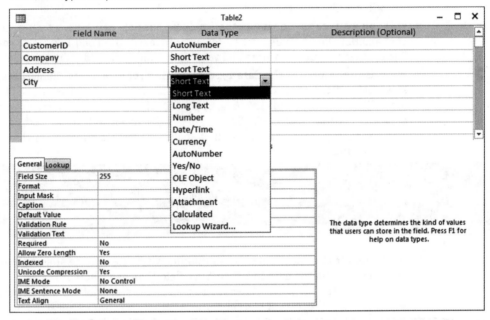

One of these data types must be assigned to each of your fields. Some of the data types have additional options, such as Field Size for Short Text fields and Number fields.

Here are the basic questions to consider when choosing the data type for new fields in your tables:

- **What is the data type?** The data type should reflect the data stored in the field. For example, you should select one of the numeric data types to store numbers like quantities and prices. Don't store data like phone numbers or Social Security numbers in numeric fields, however; your application won't be performing numeric operations like addition or multiplication on phone numbers. Instead, use text fields for common data, such as Social Security numbers and phone numbers.

NOTE

Numeric fields never store leading zeros. Putting a zip code such as 02173 into a numeric field means only the last four digits (2173) are actually stored.

- **What are the storage requirements of the data type you've selected?** Although you can use the Numeric data type with a field size of Long Integer in place of Integer or Byte, the storage requirements of a Long Integer (4 bytes) are twice that of Integer. This means that twice as much memory is required to use and manipulate the number and twice as much disk space is required to store its value. Use the smallest data type/field size you can that will still hold the largest value you will ever have in that field.

- **Will you want to sort or index the field?** Because of their binary nature, Long Text and OLE Object fields can't be sorted or indexed. Use Long Text fields sparingly. The overhead required to store and work with Long Text fields is considerable.

- **What is the impact of the data type on sorting requirements?** Numeric data sorts differently from text data. Using the numeric data type, a sequence of numbers will sort as expected: 1, 2, 3, 4, 5, 10, 100. The same sequence stored as text data will sort like this: 1, 10, 100, 2, 3, 4, 5. If it's important to sort text data in a numeric sequence, you'll have to first apply a conversion function to the data before sorting.

TIP

If it's important to have text data representing numbers to sort in the proper order, you might want to prefix the numerals with zeros (001, 002, and so on). Then the text values will sort in the expected order: 001, 002, 003, 004, 005, 010, 100.

- **Is the data text or date data?** When working with dates, you're almost always better off storing the data in a Date/Time field than as a Short Text field. Text values sort differently from dates (dates are stored internally as numeric values), which can upset reports and other output that rely on chronological order.

NEW FEATURE

The Large Number data type was added to Access 2019. Its main purpose is to support compatibility with other databases that use this data type, such as SQL Server. If you use Large Number, your database will not be compatible with older versions of Access. Only use Large Number if you have a specific reason to do so.

Don't be tempted to store dates in one Date/Time field and time in another Date/Time field. The Date/Time field is specifically designed to handle both dates and times, and, as you'll see throughout this book, it's quite easy to display only the date or time portion of a Date/Time value.

A Date/Time field is also meant to store a discrete date and time, and not a time interval. If keeping track of durations is important, you could use two Date/Time fields—one to record the start and the other at the end of a duration—or one Long Integer field to store the number of elapsed seconds, minutes, hours, and so forth.

- **What reports will be needed?** You won't be able to sort or group Long Text or OLE data on a report. If it's important to prepare a report based on Long Text or OLE data, add a Tag field like a date or sequence number, which can be used to provide a sorting key, to the table.

Short Text

The Short Text data type holds information that is simply characters (letters, numbers, punctuation). Names, addresses, and descriptions are all text data, as are numeric data that are not used in a calculation (such as telephone numbers, Social Security numbers, and zip codes).

Although you specify the size of each Short Text field in the property area, you can enter no more than 255 characters of data in any Short Text field. Access uses variable length fields to store text data. If you designate a field to be 25 characters wide and you use only 5 characters for each record, then only enough room to store 5 characters is used in your database.

You'll find that the ACCDB database file might quickly grow quite large, but text fields are usually not the cause. However, it's good practice to limit Short Text field widths to the maximum you believe is likely for the field. Names can be tricky because fairly long names are common in some cultures. However, it's a safe bet that a postal code will be fewer than 12 characters, while a U.S. state abbreviation is always 2 characters. By limiting a Short Text field's width, you also limit the number of characters users can enter when the field is used in a form.

Long Text

The Long Text data type holds a variable amount of data up to 1GB. Long Text fields use only as much memory as necessary for the data stored. So, if one record uses 100 characters, another requires only 10, and yet another needs 3,000, you use only as much space as each record requires.

You don't specify a field size for the Long Text data type. Access allocates as much space as necessary for the data.

In versions prior to Access 2013, the Short Text data type was called simply Text, and the Long Text data type was called Memo. If you're working in previous versions, you'll need to refer to the old data type names. The properties and limitations of those data types did not change; only the name has.

Number

The Number data type enables you to enter *numeric* data—that is, numbers that will be used in mathematical calculations or represent scalar quantities such as inventory counts. (If you have data that will be used in monetary calculations, use the Currency data type, which performs calculations without rounding errors.)

The exact type of numeric data stored in a number field is determined by the Field Size property. Table 3.3 lists the various numeric data types, their maximum and minimum ranges, the decimal points supported by each numeric data type, and the storage (bytes) required by each numeric data type.

TABLE 3.3 Numeric Field Settings

Field Size Setting	Range	Decimal Places	Storage Size
Byte	0 to 255	None	1 byte
Integer	–32,768 to 32,767	None	2 bytes
Long Integer	–2,147,483,648 to 2,147,483,647	None	4 bytes
Single	-3.4×10^{38} to 3.4×10^{38}	7	4 bytes
Double	-1.797×10^{308} to 1.797×10^{308}	15	8 bytes
Replication ID	N/A	N/A	16 bytes
Decimal	-9.999×10^{27} to 9.999×10^{27}	15	12 bytes

CAUTION

Many errors are caused by choosing the wrong numeric type for number fields. For example, notice that the maximum value for the Integer data type is 32,767. We once saw a database that ran perfectly for several years and then started crashing with overflow errors. It turned out that the overflow was caused by a particular field being set to the Integer data type, and when the company occasionally processed very large orders, the 32,767 maximum was exceeded.

Be aware that overflow may occur simply by adding two numbers together or by performing any mathematical operation that results in a value too large to be stored in a field. Some of the most difficult bugs occur only when circumstances (such as adding or multiplying two numbers) cause an overflow condition at run time.

Design your tables very conservatively and allow for larger values than you ever expect to see in your database. This is not to say that using the Double data type for all numeric fields is a good idea. The Double data type is very large (8 bytes) and might be somewhat slow when used in calculations or other numeric operations. Instead, the Single data type is probably best for most floating-point calculations, and Long Integer is a good choice where decimal points are irrelevant.

Large Number

The Large Number data type holds values from -2^{63} to $2^{63}-1$. Those are bigger numbers than most people need. It was added to Access mainly for compatibility with other databases that have this data type, specifically SQL Server.

If you use Large Number, be aware that not all versions of Access prior to 2019 support this data type. If you're linking to or importing from a database that uses this data type, check the Support Large Number (BigInt) Data Type for Linked/Imported Tables check box in the Current Database tab of Access Options.

Date/Time

The Date/Time data type is a specialized number field for holding dates or times (or dates *and* times). When dates are stored in a Date/Time field, it's easy to calculate days between dates and other calendar operations. Date data stored in Date/Time fields sort and filter properly as well. The Date/Time data type holds dates from January 1, 100, to December 31, 9999.

Currency

The Currency data type is another specialized number field. Currency numbers are not rounded during calculations and preserve 15 digits of precision to the left of the decimal point and 4 digits to the right. Because Currency fields use a fixed decimal point position, they're faster in numeric calculations than doubles.

AutoNumber

The AutoNumber field is another specialized Number data type. When an AutoNumber field is added to a table, Access automatically assigns a long integer (32-bit) value to the field (beginning at 1) and increments the value each time a record is added to the table. Alternatively (determined by the New Values property), the value of the AutoNumber field is a random integer that is automatically inserted into new records.

Only one AutoNumber field can appear in a table. Once assigned to a record, the value of an AutoNumber field can't be changed programmatically or by the user. AutoNumber fields are stored as a Long Integer data type and occupy 4 bytes. AutoNumber fields can accommodate up to 4,294,967,296 unique numbers—more than adequate as the primary key for most tables.

> **NOTE**
>
> An AutoNumber field is not guaranteed to generate a continuous, unbroken set of sequential numbers. For example, if the process of adding a new record is interrupted (such as the user pressing the Esc key while entering the new record's data) an AutoNumber field will "skip" a number. AutoNumber fields should not be used to provide a stream of sequential numbers. Instead, sequential numbers can be easily added to a table through a data macro (data macros are explained in Chapter 22) or VBA code.

> **TIP**
>
> When you create a relationship between two tables and one of the fields in that relationship is an AutoNumber field, the other field should be made a Long Integer data type to prevent overflow errors. Creating relationships between tables is explained in Chapter 4.

Yes/No

Yes/No fields accept only one of two possible values. Internally stored as –1 (Yes) or 0 (No), the Yes/No field is used to indicate yes/no, on/off, or true/false. A Yes/No field occupies a single bit of storage.

OLE Object

The OLE Object field stores OLE data, highly specialized binary objects such as Word documents, Excel spreadsheets, sound or video clips, and images. The OLE object is created by an application that Windows recognizes as an OLE server and can be linked to the parent application or embedded in the Access table. OLE objects can be displayed only in bound object frames in Access forms and reports. OLE fields can't be indexed.

Hyperlink

The Hyperlink data type field holds combinations of text and numbers stored as text and used as a hyperlink address. It can have up to four parts:

- The text that appears in a control (usually formatted to look like a clickable link).
- The address—the path to a file or web page.
- Any sub-address within the file or page. An example of a sub-address is a picture on a web page. Each part of the hyperlink's address is separated by the pound sign (#).
- The text that appears in the screen tip when the user hovers over the link.

Access hyperlinks can even point to forms and reports in other Access databases. This means that you can use a hyperlink to open a form or report in an external Access database and display the form or report on the user's computer.

Attachment

The Attachment data type was introduced in Access 2007. In fact, the Attachment data type is one of the reasons Microsoft changed the format of the Access data file. The older MDB format is unable to accommodate attachments.

The Attachment data type is relatively complex, compared to the other types of Access fields, and it requires a special type of control when displayed on Access forms. For details on this interesting type of field, turn to "Understanding Attachment Fields," later in this chapter.

Calculated

A Calculated field holds an expression that can include numbers, text, fields from within the same table, and Access functions. It cannot reference fields from other tables. "Calculated" isn't a data type although Access includes it in the data type list. It has a ResultType property that determines what kind of data the field holds.

You might use a Calculated field if you find you're performing the same calculations in queries over and over. For example, if you had a TaxableAmount field and a SalesTaxRate field, you could create a SalesTaxAmount field that multiplies them together.

Using this field comes dangerously close to violating the third normal form (see Chapter 4 for information on data normalization). The field actually stores the formula and not the calculated value. But this is what queries are for and you may find that keeping the data in your tables and the calculations in your queries is a good way to organize your application.

Lookup Wizard

The Lookup Wizard data type inserts a field that enables the end user to choose a value from another table or from the results of a SQL statement. The values may also be presented as a combo box or list box. At design time, the Lookup Wizard leads the developer through the process of defining the lookup characteristics when this data is assigned to a field.

As you drag an item from the Lookup Wizard field list, a combo box or list box is automatically created on the form. The list box or combo box also appears on a query datasheet that contains the field.

Entering a field description

The field description is completely optional; you use it only to help you remember, or to let another developer understand, the field's purpose. Often, you don't use the Description column at all, or you use it only for fields whose purpose is not obvious. If you enter a field description, it appears in the status bar whenever you use that field in Access—in the datasheet or in a form. The field description can help clarify a field whose purpose is ambiguous or give the user a more complete explanation of the appropriate values for the field during data entry.

Specifying data validation rules

The last major design decision concerns data validation, which becomes important as users enter data. You want to make sure that only good data (data that passes certain defined tests) gets into your system. You have to deal with several types of data validation. You can test for known individual items, stipulating that the Gender field can accept only the values Male, Female, or Unknown, for example. Or you can test for ranges, specifying that the value of Weight must be between 0 and 1,500 pounds. You'll read more about validation rules in the "Validation Rule and Validation Text" section, later in this chapter.

Creating tblCustomers

Working with the different data types, you should be ready to create the final working copy of tblCustomers.

ON THE WEB

This chapter uses a variety of data from the database named `Chapter03.accdb`. If you haven't already downloaded it, you'll need to do so now. The tables in this database have the same names as the tables described in this chapter except for the "Complete" suffix. If you'd like to see what the table should look like if you follow the steps, inspect one of these tables.

Using AutoNumber fields

Access gives special considerations to AutoNumber fields. You can't change a previously defined field from another type to AutoNumber if any data has been added to the table. If you try to change an existing field to an AutoNumber, you'll see an error that says:

```
Once you enter data in a table, you can't change the data type of any
field to AutoNumber, even if you haven't yet added data to that
field.
```

You'll have to add a new AutoNumber field and begin working with it instead of changing an existing field to AutoNumber.

> **NOTE**
>
> Only one AutoNumber field can be added to an Access table. Generally speaking, it's better to use AutoNumber fields where their special characteristics are needed by an application.

Completing tblCustomers

With tblCustomers in Design view, you're ready to finalize its design. Table 3.1, shown earlier in this chapter, lists the field definitions for tblCustomers. Enter the field names and data types as shown in Table 3.1. The next few pages explain how to change existing fields (which includes rearranging the field order, changing a field name, and deleting a field).

Here are the steps for adding fields to a table structure:

1. **Place the cursor in the Field Name column in the row where you want the field to appear.**
2. **Enter the field name and press Enter or Tab to move to the Data Type column.**
3. **Select the field's data type from the drop-down list in the Data Type column.**
4. **If desired, add a description for the field in the Description column.**

Repeat each of these steps to create each of the data entry fields for tblCustomers. You can press the down arrow (↓) key to move between rows, or use the mouse and click on any row. Pressing F6 switches the focus from the top to the bottom of the Table Design window, and vice versa.

Changing a Table Design

Even the best planned table may require changes from time to time. You might find that you want to add another field, remove a field, change a field name or data type, or simply rearrange the order of the field names.

Although a table's design can be changed at any time, special considerations must be given to tables containing data. Be careful of making changes that damage data in the table, such as making text fields smaller or changing the Field Size property of Number fields. You can always add new fields to a table without problems, but changing existing fields might be an issue. And, with very few exceptions, it's almost always a bad idea to change a field's name after a table has been put into use in an application.

Inserting a new field

To insert a new field, in the Table Design window, place your cursor on an existing field, right-click on a field in the table's design surface, and select Insert Rows, or just click the Insert Rows button on the Design tab of the Ribbon. A new row is added to the table, and existing fields are pushed down. You can then enter a new field definition. Inserting a field doesn't disturb other fields or existing data. If you have queries, forms, or reports that use the table, you might need to add the field to those objects as well.

Deleting a field

There are three ways to delete a field. While the table is in Design view:

- Select the field by clicking the row selector and then press Delete.
- Right-click the selected field and choose Delete Rows from the shortcut menu.
- Select the field and click the Delete Rows button from the Tools group on the Design tab of the Ribbon.

When you delete a field containing data, you'll see a warning that you'll lose data in the table for the selected field. If the table contains data, make sure that you want to eliminate the data for that field (column). You'll also have to delete the same field from queries, forms, reports, macros, and VBA code that use the field name.

> **TIP**
>
> If you try to delete a field that's part of a relationship (a primary or secondary key field), Access informs you that you can't delete the field until you remove the relationship in the Relationships window.
>
> Table relationships and the Relationships window are discussed in Chapter 4.

If you delete a field, you must also fix all references to that field throughout Access. Because you can use a field name in forms, queries, reports, and even table data validation, you must examine your system carefully to find any instances in which you might have used the specific field name.

Changing a field location

The order of your fields, as entered in the table's Design view, determines the left-to-right column sequence in the table's Datasheet view. If you decide that your fields should be rearranged, click on a field selector and use the mouse to drag the field to its new location.

Changing a field name

You change a field's name by selecting the field's name in the Table Design window and entering a new name. Access updates the table design automatically. As long as you're creating a new table, this process is easy. For existing tables that are referenced elsewhere in your application, changing the field name can cause problems, as discussed in the "Designing tables" section earlier in this chapter.

Changing a field size

Making a field size larger is simple in a table design. You simply increase the Field Size property for text fields or specify a different field size for number fields. You must pay attention to the Decimal Places property in number fields to make sure you don't select a new size that supports fewer decimal places than you currently have.

> **CAUTION**
>
> When you want to make a field size smaller, make sure that none of the data in the table is larger than the new field width. Choosing a smaller field size may result in data loss.

> **TIP**
>
> Remember that each text field uses only the number of characters actually entered in the field. You should still try to make your fields only as large as the largest value so that Access can stop someone from entering a value that might not fit on a form or report.

Handling data conversion issues

If, in spite of your best efforts, it becomes necessary to change the data type of a field containing data, you might suffer data loss as the data-type conversion occurs. You should be aware of the effects of a data-type conversion on existing data:

- **Any data type to AutoNumber:** Can't be done. The AutoNumber field type must be created fresh in a new field.
- **Short Text to Number, Currency, Date/Time, or Yes/No:** In most cases, the conversion will be made without damaging the data. Inappropriate values are automatically deleted. For instance, a Short Text field containing "January 28, 2018" will be faithfully converted to a Date/Time field. If, however, you change a field containing "January 28, 2018" to a Yes/No data type, its value will be deleted.
- **Long Text to Short Text:** A straightforward conversion with no corruption of data. Any text longer than the field size specified for the Short Text field is truncated and lost.
- **Number or Large Number to Short Text:** No loss of information. The number value is converted to text using the General Number format.
- **Number or Large Number to Currency:** Because the Currency data type uses a fixed decimal point, some precision may be lost as the number is truncated.
- **Date/Time to Short Text:** No loss of information. Date and time data are converted to text with the General Date format.

- **Currency to Short Text:** No loss of information. The currency value is converted to text without the currency symbol.
- **Currency to Number:** Simple, straightforward conversion. Some data may be lost as the currency value is converted to fit the new number field. For example, when converting Currency to Long Integer, the decimal portion is truncated (cut off).
- **AutoNumber to Short Text:** Conversion occurs without loss of data, except in a case where the width of the text field is inadequate to hold the entire AutoNumber value. In this case, the number is truncated.
- **AutoNumber to Number:** Simple, straightforward conversion. Some data may be lost as the AutoNumber value is converted to fit the new number field. For example, an AutoNumber larger than 32,767 will be truncated if it is converted to an Integer field.
- **Yes/No to Short Text:** Simple conversion of Yes/No value to text. No loss of information.

> **NOTE**
> The OLE Object data type cannot be converted to any other type of data.

Assigning field properties

The field properties built into Access tables are powerful allies that can help you manage the data in your tables. In most cases, the field property is enforced by the database engine, which means the property is consistently applied wherever the field's value is used. For example, if you've set the Default Value property in the table design, the default value is available in the table's Datasheet view, on forms, and in queries.

In fact, field properties are among the many differences between Access tables and Excel worksheets. Understanding field properties is just one of several skills necessary to begin using Access tables to store data, rather than Excel worksheets.

Each field data type has its own set of properties. For example, Number fields have a Decimal Places property, and Short Text fields have a Text Align property. Although many data types share a number of properties (such as Caption) in common, there are enough different field properties to make it easy to become confused or to incorrectly use the properties. The following sections discuss some of the more important and frequently used field properties.

> **NOTE**
> The following sections include many references to properties, and property settings in the Access Table Designer. The formal name for a property (such as DefaultValue) never contains a space, while the property's expression in the Table Designer usually contains a space for readability (Default Value). These relatively minor differences become important when referencing properties in expressions, VBA code, and macros. When making a formal reference to a property in code or a macro, always use the *spaceless* version of the property's name, not the property reference you see in the Access user interface.

Common properties

Here's a list of all the general properties (note that they may not all be displayed, depending on which data type you chose):

- **Field Size:** When applied to Short Text fields, limits the size of the field to the specified number of characters (1–255). The default is 255.
- **New Values:** Applies to AutoNumber fields. Allows specification of Increment or Random type.
- **Format:** Changes the way data appears after you enter it (uppercase, dates, and so on). There are many different types of formats that may be applied to Access data. Many of these differences are explained in the "Format" section, later in this chapter.
- **Input Mask:** Used for data entry into a predefined format (phone numbers, zip codes, Social Security numbers, dates, customer IDs). Applicable to both numeric and text data types.
- **Decimal Places:** Specifies the number of decimal places for the Currency, Number, and Large Number data types.
- **Caption:** Optional label that's used in place of the field's name. Access uses the Caption property when displaying a control in a datasheet or on a form or report.
- **Default Value:** The value automatically provided for new data entry into the field. This value can be any value appropriate for the field's data type. A default is no more than an initial value; you can change it during data entry. To specify a default value, simply enter the desired value into the Default Value property setting. A default value can be an expression, as well as a number or a text string.

> **NOTE**
>
> Because the Default Value for Number and Currency data types is set to 0 by default, these fields are set automatically to 0 when you add a new record. In many situations, such as medical test results and many financial applications, 0 is not an appropriate default value for numeric fields. Be sure to verify that 0 is an appropriate default value in your Access applications.

- **Validation Rule:** Ensures that data entered into the field conforms to some business rule, such as "greater than zero," "date must occur after January 1, 2000," and so on.
- **Validation Text:** The message displayed when data fails validation.
- **Required:** Specifies whether you must enter a value into a field.
- **Allow Zero Length:** Determines whether you may enter an empty string ("") into a Short Text or Long Text field to distinguish it from a null value.
- **Indexed:** Speeds up data access and (if desired) limits data to unique values. Indexing is explained in greater detail later in this chapter.
- **Unicode Compression:** Used for multilanguage applications. Requires about twice the data storage but enables Office documents, including Access reports, to be

displayed correctly no matter what language or symbols are used. Generally speaking, Unicode is of no value unless the application is likely to be used in Asian environments.

- **IME Mode:** Also known as the Kanji conversion mode property, this is used to show whether the Kanji mode is maintained when the control is lost. The setting has no relevance in English or European-language applications.
- **IME Sentence Mode:** Used to determine the Sequence mode of fields of a table or controls of a form that switch when the focus moves in or out of the field. The setting has no relevance in English or European-language applications.

Format

The Format property specifies how the data contained in table fields appears whenever the data is displayed or printed. When set at the table level, the format is in effect throughout the application. There are different format options for each data type.

Access provides built-in format options for most field data types. The exact format used to display field values is influenced by the Region and Language settings in Windows Settings.

The Format property affects only the way a value is displayed and not the value itself or how the value is stored in the database.

If you elect to build a custom format, construct a string in the field's Format property box. There are a number of different symbols you use for each **data type**. Access provides global format specifications to use in any custom format:

- **(space):** Displays spaces as characters.
- **"SomeText":** Displays the text between the quotes as literal text.
- **! (exclamation point):** Left-aligns the display.
- *** (asterisk):** Fills empty space with the next character.
- **\ (backslash):** Displays the next character as literal text. Use the backslash to display characters that otherwise have special meaning to Access.
- **[color]:** Displays the output in the color (black, blue, green, cyan, red, magenta, yellow, or white) indicated between the brackets.

The Format property takes precedence when both a format and an input mask have been defined.

Number and Currency field formats

There is a wide variety of valid formats for Number and Currency fields. You can use one of the built-in formats or construct a custom format of your own:

- **General Number:** The number is displayed in the format in which it was entered. (This is the default format for numeric data fields.)
- **Currency:** Add a thousands separator (usually a comma), add a decimal point with two digits to the right of the decimal, and enclose negative numbers in

parentheses. A Currency field value is shown with the currency symbol (such as a dollar sign or euro sign) specified by the Region and Language settings in Windows Settings.

- **Fixed:** Always display at least one digit to the left and two digits to the right of the decimal point.
- **Standard:** Use the thousands separator with two digits to the right of the decimal point.
- **Percent:** The number value is multiplied by 100 and a percent sign is added to the right. Percent values are displayed with two decimal places to the right of the decimal point.
- **Scientific:** Scientific notation is used to display the number.
- **Euro:** Prefixes the euro currency symbol to the number.

The built-in numeric formats are summarized in Table 3.4.

TABLE 3.4 Numeric Format Examples

Format Type	Number as Entered	Number as Displayed	Format Defined
General	987654.321	987654.321	#.###
Currency	987654.321	$987,654.32	$#,##0.00;($#,##0.00)
Euro	987654.321	€987,654.32	€#,##0.00; (€#,##0.00)
Fixed	987654.321	987654.32	#.##
Standard	987654.321	987,654.32	#,##0.00
Percent	.987	98.70%	#.##%
Scientific	987654.321	9.88E+05	0.00E+00

All the previous formats are the default formats based on setting the Decimal Places property to Auto. The exact format applied also depends on the Field Size and Region and Language settings in Windows Settings.

Custom numeric formats

Custom formats are created by combining a number of symbols to create a format. The symbols used with Number and Currency fields are listed here:

- **. (period):** Specifies where the decimal point should appear.
- **, (comma):** The thousands separator.
- **0 (zero):** A placeholder for 0 or a digit.
- **# (pound sign):** A placeholder for nothing or a digit.
- **$ (dollar sign):** Displays the dollar sign character.
- **% (percent sign):** Multiplies the value by 100 and adds a percent sign.

- **E– or e–:** Uses scientific notation to display the number. Uses a minus sign to indicate a negative exponent and no sign for positive exponents.
- **E+ or e+:** Uses scientific notation to display the number. Uses a plus sign to indicate a positive exponent.

You create custom formats by composing a string made up of one to four sections separated by semicolons. Each section has a different meaning to Access:

- **First section:** The format for positive values
- **Second section:** The format for negative values
- **Third section:** The format for zero values
- **Fourth section:** The format for null values

Each section is a combination of a numeric formatting string and an optional color specification. Here's an example of a custom format:

```
0,000.00[Green];(0,000.00)[Red];"Zero";"—"
```

This format specifies showing the number with zeros in all unused positions, using the comma thousands separator, enclosing negative numbers in parentheses, using "Zero" to indicate zero values, and using a dash for null values.

Built-in Date/Time formats

The following are the built-in Date/Time formats. Note that these examples are based on the "English (United States)" Region and Language settings in Windows Settings.

- **General Date:** If the value contains a date only, don't display a time value, and vice versa. Dates are displayed in the built-in Short Date format (m/d/yyyy), while time data is displayed in the Long Time format.
- **Long Date:** Thursday, November 12, 2015
- **Medium Date:** 12-Nov-15
- **Short Date:** 11/12/2015
- **Long Time:** 5:34:23 PM
- **Medium Time:** 5:34 PM
- **Short Time:** 17:34

Date and time formats are influenced by the Region and Language settings in Windows Settings.

Custom Date/Time formats

Custom formats are created by constructing a specification string containing the following symbols:

- **: (colon):** Separates time elements (hours, minutes, seconds)
- **/ (forward slash):** Separates date elements (days, months, years)
- **c:** Instructs Access to use the built-in General Date format

3

- **d:** Displays the day of the month as one or two digits (1–31)
- **dd:** Displays the day of the month using two digits (01–31)
- **ddd:** Displays the day of the week as a three-character abbreviation (Sun, Mon, Tue, Wed, Thu, Fri, Sat)
- **dddd:** Uses the full name of the day of the week (Sunday, Monday, Tuesday, Wednesday, Thursday, Friday, Saturday)
- **ddddd:** Uses the built-in Short Date format
- **dddddd:** Uses the built-in Long Date format
- **w:** Uses a number to indicate the day of the week
- **ww:** Shows the week of the year
- **m:** Displays the month of the year using one or two digits
- **mm:** Displays the month of the year using two digits (with a leading zero if necessary)
- **mmm:** Displays the month as a three-character abbreviation (Jan, Feb, Mar, Apr, May, Jun, Jul, Aug, Sep, Oct, Nov, Dec)
- **mmmm:** Displays the full name of the month (for example, January)
- **q:** Displays the date as the quarter of the year
- **y:** Displays the day of the year (1 through 366)
- **yy:** Displays the year as two digits (for example, 15)
- **yyyy:** Displays the year as four digits (2015)
- **h:** Displays the hour using one or two digits (0–23)
- **hh:** Displays the hour using two digits (00–23)
- **n:** Displays the minutes using one or two digits (0–59)
- **nn:** Displays the minutes using two digits (00–59)
- **s:** Displays the seconds using one or two digits (0–59)
- **ss:** Displays the seconds using two digits (00–59)
- **ttttt:** Uses the built-in Long Time format
- **AM/PM:** Uses a 12-hour format with uppercase AM or PM
- **am/pm:** Uses a 12-hour format with lowercase am or pm
- **A/P:** Uses a 12-hour format with uppercase A or P
- **a/p:** Uses a 12-hour format with lowercase a or p

Short Text and Long Text field formats

When applied to Short Text fields, formats help clarify the data contained within the fields. tblCustomers uses several formats. The State text field has a > in the Format property to display the data entry in uppercase. The Active field has a Yes/No format with lookup Display Control property set to Text Box.

Short Text and Long Text fields are displayed as plain text by default. If a particular format is to be applied to Short Text or Long Text field data, use the following symbols to construct the format:

- **@:** A character or space is required.
- **&:** A character is optional (not required).
- **<:** Force all characters to their lowercase equivalents.
- **>:** Force all characters to their uppercase equivalents.

The custom format may contain as many as three different sections, separated by semicolons:

- **First section:** Format for fields containing text
- **Second section:** Format for fields containing zero-length strings
- **Third section:** Format for fields containing null values

If only two sections are given, the second section applies to both zero-length strings and null values. For example, the following format displays None when no string data is contained in the field and Unknown when a null value exists in the field. Otherwise, the simple text contained in the field is displayed:

```
@;"None";"Unknown"
```

Several examples of custom text formats using the "English (United States)" Regional & Language Settings in Windows Settings are presented in Table 3.5.

TABLE 3.5 Format Examples

Format Specified	Data as Entered	Formatted Data as Displayed
>	Adam Smith	ADAM SMITH
<	Adam Smith	adam smith
@@-@@	Adam	Ad-am
&-@@	Ad	-Ad
@;"Empty"	""	Empty
@;"Empty"	Null	Empty

Yes/No field formats

A Yes/No field displays Yes, No, True, False, On, or Off, depending on the value stored in the field and the setting of the Format property for the field. Access predefines these rather obvious format specifications for the Yes/No field type:

- **Yes/No:** Displays Yes or No
- **True/False:** Displays True or False
- **On/Off:** Displays On or Off

Yes, True, and On all indicate the same "positive" value, while No, False, and Off indicate the opposite ("negative") value.

Access stores Yes/No data in a manner different from what you might expect. The Yes data is stored as −1, whereas No data is stored as 0. You'd expect it to be stored as 0 for No and 1 for Yes, but this isn't the case. Without a format setting, Access will display −1 or 0, and it will be stored and displayed that way.

Regardless of the format set, you can enter data into a Yes/No field using any of the words in the built-in formats or as numbers. To enter No, you can enter **False**, **No**, **Off**, or 0. To enter Yes, you can enter **True**, **Yes**, **On**, or any number other than zero. If you enter a number other than 0 or −1, Access converts it to −1.

You're also able to specify a custom format for Yes/No fields. For example, assume you've got a table with a field that indicates whether the employee has attended an orientation meeting. Although a yes or no answer is appropriate, you might want to get a little fancy with the field's display. By default, a check box is used to indicate the value of the Yes/No field (checked means Yes). To customize the appearance of the Yes/No field, set its Format property according to the following pattern:

```
;"Text for Yes values";"Text for No values"
```

Notice the placeholder semicolon at the front of this string. Also, notice that each text element must be surrounded by quotes. In the case of the employee table, you might use the following Format property specifier:

```
;"Attendance OK";"Must attend orientation"
```

You must also set the Yes/No field's Display Control property to Text Box in order to change the default check box display to text.

Hyperlink field format

Access also displays and stores hyperlink data in a manner different from what you would expect. The format of this type is comprised of up to four parts, separated by pound signs (#):

- **Display Text:** The text that is displayed as a hyperlink in the field or control
- **Address:** The path to a file (UNC) or page (URL) on the Internet
- **Sub-Address:** A specific location within a file or page
- **ScreenTip:** The text that is displayed when a user hovers over the link

The Display Text property is the text that is visible in the field or control, while the address and sub-address are hidden. In the following example, "Microsoft MSN Home Page" is the displayed text, while http://www.msn.com is the hyperlink's address.

```
Microsoft MSN Home Page#http://www.msn.com
```

Input Mask

The Input Mask property makes it easier for users to enter the data in the correct format. An input mask limits the way the user inputs data into the application. For example, you can restrict entry to only digits for phone numbers, Social Security numbers, and employee

IDs. An input mask for a Social Security number might look like "000-00-0000." This mask requires input into every space, restricts entry to digits only, and does not permit characters or spaces.

A field's input mask is applied anywhere the field appears (query, form, report).

The Input Mask property value is a string containing as many as three semicolon-separated sections:

- **First section:** Contains the mask itself, comprised of the symbols shown later.
- **Second section:** Tells Access whether to store the literal characters included in the mask along with the rest of the data. For example, the mask might include dashes to separate the parts of the Social Security number, while a phone number might include parentheses and dashes. Using a zero tells Access to store the literal characters as part of the data while 1 tells Access to store only the data itself.
- **Third section:** Defines the "placeholder" character that tells the user how many characters are expected in the input area. Many input masks use pound signs (#) or asterisks (*) as placeholders.

The following characters are used to compose the input mask string:

- **0:** A digit is required, and plus (+) and minus (–) signs are not permitted.
- **9:** A digit is optional, and plus (+) and minus (–) signs are not permitted.
- **#:** Optional digit or space. Spaces are removed when the data is saved in the table. Plus and minus signs are allowed.
- **L:** A letter from A to Z is required.
- **?:** A letter from A to Z is optional.
- **A:** A character or digit is required.
- **a:** A character or digit is optional.
- **&:** Permits any character or space (required).
- **C:** Permits any character or space (optional).
- **. (period):** Decimal placeholder.
- **, (comma):** Thousands separator.
- **: (colon):** Date and time separator.
- **; (semicolon):** Separator character.
- **– (dash):** Separator character.
- **/ (forward slash):** Separator character.
- **< (less-than sign):** Converts all characters to lowercase.
- **> (greater-than sign):** Converts all characters to uppercase.
- **! (exclamation point):** Displays the input mask from right to left. Characters fill the mask from right to left.
- **\ (backslash):** Displays the next character as a literal.

The same masking characters are used on a field's Property Sheet in a query or form.

3

An input mask is ignored when importing data or adding data to a table with an action query.

An input mask is overridden by the Format property assigned to a field. In this case, the input mask is in effect only as data is entered and reformatted according to the Format when the entry is complete.

The Input Mask Wizard

Although you can manually enter an input mask, you can easily create an input mask for Short Text or Date/Time type fields with the Input Mask Wizard. When you click the Input Mask property, a Builder button (three periods) appears in the property's input box. Click the Builder button to start the wizard. Figure 3.8 shows the first screen of the Input Mask Wizard.

FIGURE 3.8

The Input Mask Wizard for creating input masks for Text field types.

The Input Mask Wizard shows not only the name of each predefined input mask, but also an example for each name. You can choose from the list of predefined masks. Click in the Try It text box and enter a test value to see how data entry will look. After you choose an input mask, the next wizard screen enables you to refine the mask and specify the placeholder symbol (perhaps a # or @). Another wizard screen enables you to decide whether to store special characters (such as the dashes in a Social Security number) with the data. When you complete the wizard, Access adds the input mask characters in the field's Property Sheet.

> **TIP**
>
> You can create your own Input Mask properties for Short Text and Date/Time fields by simply clicking the Edit List button in the Input Mask Wizard and entering a descriptive name, input mask, placeholder character, and sample data content. Once created, the new mask will be available the next time you use the Input Mask Wizard.

Enter as many custom masks as you need. You can also determine the international settings so that you can work with multiple country masks. A custom input mask you create in one database is available in other databases.

Caption

The Caption property determines what appears in the default label attached to a control created by dragging the field from the field list onto a form or report. The caption also appears as the column heading in Datasheet view for tables or queries that include the field.

> **CAUTION**
>
> Be careful using the Caption property. Because the caption text appears as the column heading in Datasheet view, you might be misled by a column heading in a query's Datasheet view. When the field appears in a query, you don't have immediate access to the field's properties, so you must be aware that the column heading is actually determined by the Caption property and may not reflect the field's name. To be even more confusing, the caption assigned in the table's Design view and the caption assigned in a field's Property Sheet in the Query Design view are different properties and can contain different text.

Captions can be as long as 2,048 characters, more than adequate for all but the most verbose descriptions.

Validation Rule and Validation Text

The Validation Rule property establishes requirements for input into the field. Enforced by the ACE database engine, the Validation Rule ensures that data entered into the table conforms to the requirements of the application.

Validation properties are a great way to enforce business rules, such as ensuring that a product is not sold for zero dollars, or requiring that an employee review date come after her hire date. And, like other field properties, validation rules are enforced wherever the field is used in the application.

The value of the Validation Rule property is a string containing an expression that is used to test the user's input. The expression used as a field's Validation Rule property can't contain user-defined functions or any of the Access domain or aggregate functions (DCount, DSum, and so on). A field's Validation Rule property can't reference forms, queries, or other tables in the application. (These restrictions don't apply to validation rules applied

3

63

to controls on a form, however.) Field validation rules can't reference other fields in the table, although a rule applied to a record in a table can reference fields in the same table (a record-level validation rule is set in the table's Property Sheet, rather than in an individual field).

The Validation Text property contains a string that is displayed in a message box when the user's input doesn't satisfy the requirements of the Validation Rule property. The maximum length of the Validation Text property value is 255 characters.

When using the Validation Rule property, you should always specify a Validation Text value to avoid triggering the generic message box Access displays when the rule is violated. Use the Validation Text property to provide users with a helpful message that explains acceptable values for the field. Figure 3.9 shows the message box displayed when the value specified by the Validation Rule attached to the CreditLimit field is exceeded.

FIGURE 3.9

A data-validation warning box appears when the user enters a value in the field that does not match the rule specified in the design of the table.

The Validation Rule property doesn't apply to check boxes, option buttons, or toggle buttons within an option group on a form. The option group itself has a Validation Rule property that applies to all the controls within the group.

Validation properties are often used to ensure that certain dates fall after other dates (for example, an employee's retirement date must fall after his starting date), that nonnegative numbers are entered for values such as inventory quantities, and that entries are restricted to different ranges of numbers or text.

Dates used in Access expressions, such as a Validation Rule property, are surrounded, or *delimited*, by pound signs (#). If you want to limit the LastSalesDate data entry to dates between January 1, 2018, and December 31, 2019, enter **Between #1/1/2018# And #12/31/2019#**.

> **TIP**
>
> If you want to limit the upper end to the current date, you can enter a different set of dates, such as Between #1/1/2018# And Date(). `Date()` is a built-in VBA function that returns the current date; it's completely acceptable as part of a validation rule or other expression.

When a field is dragged onto a form, the Validation Rule property of the new control is not set to the field's Validation Rule. Unless you enter a new Validation Rule value in the control's Property Sheet, Access enforces the rule set at the table level.

Field and control Validation Rule properties are enforced when the focus leaves the table field or form control. Validation Rule properties applied to both a field and a control bound to the field are enforced for both entities. The table-level rule is applied as data is edited on the bound control and as focus leaves the control.

You can't create table-level Validation Rule properties for linked "foreign" tables, such as from Excel, text files, other databases. Instead, you must apply Validation Rule properties to the controls bound to fields in linked foreign tables.

Required

The Required property instructs Access to require input into the field. When set to Yes, input is required in the field within a table or in a control on a form bound to the field. The value of a required field can't be Null.

The Required property is invalid for AutoNumber fields. By default, all AutoNumber fields are assigned a value as new records are created.

The Access database engine enforces the Required property. An error message is generated if the user tries to leave a Text Box control bound to a field with its Required property set to Yes.

The Required property can be used in conjunction with the AllowZeroLength property to determine when the value of a field is unknown or doesn't exist.

AllowZeroLength

The AllowZeroLength property specifies whether you want a zero-length string ("") to be a valid entry for a Short Text or Long Text field. AllowZeroLength accepts the following values:

- **Yes:** A zero-length string is a valid entry.
- **No:** The table will not accept zero-length strings, and instead inserts a Null value into the field when no valid text data is supplied.

Combining the AllowZeroLength and Required properties enables you to differentiate between data that doesn't exist (which you'll probably want to represent as a zero-length string) and data that is unknown (which you'll want to store as a null value). In some cases, you'll want to store the proper value in the Short Text or Long Text field.

An example of data that doesn't exist is the case of a customer who doesn't have an e-mail address. The e-mail address field should be set to an empty (zero-length) string, indicating that you know the user doesn't have an e-mail address. Another customer who is entirely new to the company should have a null value in the e-mail address field, indicating that you don't know whether the customer has an e-mail address.

An input mask can help your application's users distinguish when a field contains a null value. For example, the input mask could be set to display No email when the field contains a zero-length string and Unknown when the value is null.

The Required property determines whether a null value is accepted by the field, while the AllowZeroLength property permits zero-length strings in the field. Together, these independent properties provide the means to determine whether a value is unknown or absent for the field.

The interaction between Required and AllowZeroLength can be quite complicated. Table 3.6 summarizes how these two properties combine to force the user to input a value, or to insert either a null or zero-length string into a field.

TABLE 3.6   Required and AllowZeroLength Property Combinations

AllowZeroLength	Required	Data Entered by User	Value Stored in Table
No	No	Null	Null
No	No	Space	Null
No	No	Zero-length string	Disallowed
Yes	No	Null	Null
Yes	No	Space	Null
Yes	No	Zero-length string	Zero-length string
No	Yes	Null	Disallowed
No	Yes	Space	Disallowed
No	Yes	Zero-length string	Disallowed
Yes	Yes	Null	Disallowed
Yes	Yes	Space	Zero-length string
Yes	Yes	Zero-length string	Zero-length string

Indexed

The Indexed property tells Access that you want to use a field as an index in the table. Indexed fields are internally organized to speed up queries, sorting, and grouping operations. If you intend to frequently include a certain field in queries (for example, the employee ID or Social Security number) or if the field is frequently sorted or grouped on reports, you should set its Indexed property to Yes.

The valid settings for the Indexed property are as follows:

- **No:** The field is not indexed (default).

- **Yes (Duplicates OK):** The field is indexed and Access permits duplicate values in the column. This is the appropriate setting for values such as names, where it's likely that names like Smith will appear more than once in the table.
- **Yes (No Duplicates):** The field is indexed and no duplicates are permitted in the column. Use this setting for data that should be unique within the table, such as Social Security numbers, employee IDs, and customer numbers.

Indexes are discussed in more detail later in this chapter.

In addition to the primary key, you can index up to 31 other fields to provide optimum performance. Keep in mind that each index extracts a small performance hit as new records are added to the table. Access dynamically updates the indexing information each time a new record is added. If a table includes an excessive number of indexes, a noticeable delay might occur as each new record is added.

The Indexed property is set in the field's Property Sheet or on the table's Property Sheet. You must use the table's Property Sheet to set multifield indexes. Multifield indexes are discussed later in this chapter.

The AutoIndex option

The Access Options dialog box (File ⇨ Options ⇨ Object Designers) contains an entry (AutoIndex on Import/Create) that directs Access to automatically index certain fields as they're added to a table's design. By default, fields that begin or end with ID, key, code, or num (for example, EmployeeID or TaskCode) are automatically indexed as the field is created. Every time a new record is added to the table, the field's value is added to the field's index. If there are other field name patterns you'd like Access to automatically index, add new values to the AutoIndex on Import/Create check box on the Object Designers tab in the Access Options dialog box (see Figure 3.10).

FIGURE 3.10

The Table Design View area on the Options dialog box contains a box for setting the AutoIndex on Import/Create options.

When to index

Generally speaking, you should index fields that are frequently searched or sorted. Remember that indexes slow down certain operations, such as inserting records and some action queries.

Long Text and OLE Object fields can't be indexed. It would be impossible for Access to maintain an index on these complex data types.

An index should not be used if a field contains very few unique values. For example, you won't see a significant benefit from indexing a field containing a person's gender or a Yes/No field. Because there is a limited range of values in such fields, Access easily sorts the data in these fields.

Use a multiple-field index in situations where sorts are often simultaneously performed on multiple fields (for example, first and last names). Access will have a much easier time sorting such a table.

Understanding tblCustomers Field Properties

After you enter the field names, data types, and field descriptions, you may want to go back and further refine each field. Every field has properties, and these are different for each data type. In tblCustomers, you must enter properties for several data types. Figure 3.11 shows the property area for the field named CreditLimit. Notice that there are two tabs on the property box: General and Lookup.

FIGURE 3.11

The property area for the Currency field named CreditLimit.

General	Lookup
Format	Currency
Decimal Places	2
Input Mask	
Caption	
Default Value	0
Validation Rule	<=2500
Validation Text	The value entered exceeds the maximum credit limit.
Required	No
Indexed	No
Text Align	General

TIP

Figure 3.11 shows ten properties available for the CreditLimit Currency field. Other types, such as Number, Date/Time, Short Text, or Yes/No, show more or fewer options.

Pressing F6 switches between the field entry grid and the Field Properties pane. (You may have to press F6 several times before you reach the desired pane.) You can also move between panes by clicking the desired pane. Some properties display a list of possible values, along with a downward-pointing arrow when you move the pointer into the field. When you click the arrow, the values appear in a drop-down list.

The Field Properties pane of the Table Design window has a second tab: the Lookup tab. After clicking this tab, you may see a single property, the Display Control property. This property is used for Short Text, Number, and Yes/No fields.

Figure 3.12 shows the Lookup Property window for the Active Yes/No field where Display Control is the only property. This property has three choices: Check Box, Text Box, and Combo Box. Choosing one of these determines which control type is used when a particular field is added to a form. Generally, all controls are created as text boxes except Yes/No fields, which are created as check boxes by default. For Yes/No data types, however, you may want to use the Text Box setting to display Yes/No, True/False, or another choice that you specifically put in the format property box.

FIGURE 3.12

The Lookup tab for a Yes/No field.

3

 You learn about combo boxes in Chapter 19.

If you're working with Short Text fields instead of a Yes/No field and know a certain Short Text field can only be one of a few combinations, select the combo box choice for the display control. Figure 3.13 shows the Lookup tab when combo box has been selected as the display control for the Credit Status field. There are only two acceptable values for Credit Status: OK and Not OK. These two values (separated by a semicolon) are specified as the combo box's Row Source, and the Row Source Type is set to Value List.

FIGURE 3.13

Setting up a combo box as the display control for Credit Status.

Combo box is selected

General	Lookup
Display Control	Combo Box
Row Source Type	Value List
Row Source	OK;Not OK
Bound Column	1
Column Count	1
Column Heads	No
Column Widths	
List Rows	16
List Width	Auto
Limit To List	No
Allow Multiple Values	No
Allow Value List Edits	No
List Items Edit Form	
Show Only Row Source V	No

Values displayed for this field

Although Figure 3.13 shows a combo box using a value list for its items, you could also specify a query or SQL statement as the combo box's Row Source.

Figure 3.14 shows how the Credit Status field appears when tblCustomers is displayed as a datasheet. The user can select only OK or Not OK as the credit status, and the same combo box appears when the field is added to an Access form.

FIGURE 3.14

Using a combo box as a lookup control to restrict user input on a field.

OrigCustom ▾	CreditLimit ▾	CurrentBalai ▾	CreditStatus ▾	LastSalesDat ▾	TaxRate ▾
$41,044.00	$2,000.00	$0.00	OK	3/28/2012	0.06
$40,766.00	$2,500.00	$57.00	OK	3/28/2012	0.05
$40,976.00	$750.00	$0.00	OK	2/26/2007	0.05
$41,613.00	$900.00	$958.00	OK	3/28/2012	0.07
$41,060.00	$1,400.00	$168.00	OK	3/28/2012	0.06
$41,167.00	$1,500.00	$1,599.00	OK		0.05
	$0.00	$0.00	OK		0.05
	$0.00	$0.00	OK		0.06
	$0.00	$0.00	Not OK		0.07
	$0.00	$0.00			0.06
	$0.00	$0.00			0.07
$0.00	$0.00	$0.00			
$0.00	$0.00	$0.00			

Record: I◄ ◄ 28 of 33 ► ►I ►☆ No Filter Search

The properties for a Lookup field are different for each data type. The Yes/No data type fields differ from Short Text and Long Text fields or Number fields. Because a Lookup field is really a combo box, the standard properties for a combo box are displayed when you select a Lookup field data type.

Setting the Primary Key

Every table should have a *primary key*—one field or a combination of fields with a unique value for each record. (This principle is called *entity integrity* in the world of database management.) In tblCustomers, the CustomerID field is the primary key. Each customer has a unique CustomerID value so that the database engine can distinguish one record from another. CustomerID 17 refers to one and only one record in the Contacts table. If you don't specify a primary key (unique value field), Access can create one for you.

Choosing a primary key

Without the CustomerID field, you'd have to rely on another field or combination of fields for uniqueness. You couldn't use the Company field because two customers could easily have the same company name. In fact, you couldn't even use the Company and City fields together (in a multifield key), for the same reason—it's entirely possible that two customers with the same company name exist in the same city. You need to come up with a field or combination of fields that makes every record unique.

The easiest way to solve this problem is to add an AutoNumber field to serve as the table's primary key. The primary key in tblCustomers is CustomerID, an AutoNumber field.

If you don't designate a field as a primary key, Access can add an AutoNumber field and designate it as the table's primary key. AutoNumber fields make very good primary keys because Access creates the value for you, the number is never reused within a table, and you can't change the value of an AutoNumber field.

Good primary keys:

- Uniquely identify each record.
- Cannot be null.
- Must exist when the record is created.
- Must remain stable. (Never change a primary key value once it's established.)
- Should be simple and contain as few attributes as possible.

In addition to uniquely identifying rows in a table, primary keys provide other benefits:

- A primary key is always an index.
- An index maintains a presorted order of one or more fields that can greatly speed up queries, searches, and sort requests.

- When you add new records to your table, Access checks for duplicate data and doesn't allow any duplicates for the primary key field.
- By default, Access displays a table's data in the order of its primary key.

By designating a field such as CustomerID as the primary key, data is displayed in a meaningful order. In our example, because the CustomerID field is an AutoNumber, its value is assigned automatically by Access in the order that a record is put into the system.

The ideal primary key is, then, a single field that is immutable and guaranteed to be unique within the table. For these reasons, the Collectible Mini Cars database uses the AutoNumber field exclusively as the primary key for all tables.

Creating the primary key

The primary key can be created in any of three ways. With a table open in Design view:

- Select the field to be used as the primary key and click the Primary Key button (the key icon) in the Tools group on the Design tab of the Ribbon.
- Right-click the field and select Primary Key from the shortcut menu.
- Save the table without creating a primary key, and allow Access to automatically create an AutoNumber field.

After you designate the primary key, a key icon appears in the gray selector area to the left of the field's name to indicate that the primary key has been created.

Creating composite primary keys

You can designate a combination of fields to be used as a table's primary key. Such keys are often referred to as *composite primary keys*. As indicated in Figure 3.15, select the fields that you want to include in the composite primary key; then click the Primary Key button on the Tools tab of the Ribbon. To create a primary key from fields that are not next to each other, hold down Ctrl while selecting the fields.

Composite primary keys are primarily used when the developer strongly feels that a primary key should be comprised of data that occurs naturally in the database. There was a time when all developers were taught that every table should have a *natural primary key* (data that occurs naturally in the table).

Composite primary keys are seldom used these days because developers have come to realize that data is highly unpredictable. Even if your users promise that a combination of certain fields will never be duplicated in the table, things have a way of turning out differently than planned. Using a *surrogate primary key* (a key field that does not naturally occur in the table's data, such as an Employee ID with an AutoNumber data type) separates the table's design from the table's data. The problem with natural primary keys is that, eventually, given a large enough data set, the values of fields chosen as the table's primary key are likely to be duplicated.

FIGURE 3.15

Creating a composite primary key.

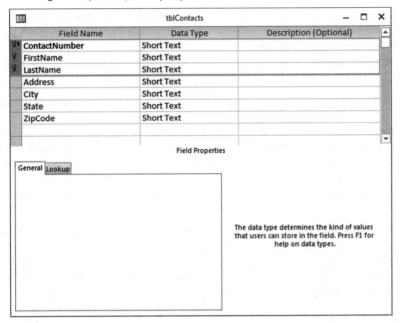

Furthermore, when using composite keys, maintaining relationships between tables becomes more complicated because the fields comprising the primary key must be duplicated in all the tables containing related data. Using composite keys simply adds to the complexity of the database without adding stability, integrity, or other desirable features.

Indexing Access Tables

Data is rarely, if ever, entered into tables in a meaningful order. Usually, records are added to tables in random order (with the exception of time-ordered data). For example, a busy order-entry system will gather information on a number of different customer orders in a single day. Most often, this data will be used to report orders for a single customer for billing purposes or for extracting order quantities for inventory management. The records in the Orders table, however, are in chronological order, which is not necessarily helpful when preparing reports detailing customer orders. In that case, you'd rather have data entered in customer ID order.

To further illustrate this concept, consider the Rolodex card file many people used to use to store names, addresses, and phone numbers. Assume for a moment that the cards in the file were fixed in place. You could add new cards, but only to the end of the card file. This limitation would mean that "Jones" might follow "Smith," which would in turn be followed by "Baker." In other words, there is no particular order to the data stored in this file.

An unsorted Rolodex like this would be very difficult to use. You'd have to search each and every card looking for a particular person, a painful and time-consuming process. Of course, this isn't how you use address card files. When you add a card to the file, you insert it into the Rolodex at the location where it *logically* belongs. Most often, this means inserting the card in alphabetical order, by last name, into the Rolodex.

Records are added to Access tables as described in the fixed card file example earlier. New records are always added to the end of the table, rather than in the middle of the table where they may logically belong. However, in an order-entry system, you'd probably want new records inserted next to other records on the same customer. Unfortunately, this isn't how Access tables work. The *natural order* of a table is the order in which records were added to the table. This order is sometimes referred to as *entry order* or *physical order* to emphasize that the records in the table appear in the order in which they were added to the table.

Using tables in natural order is not necessarily a bad thing. Natural order makes perfect sense if the data is rarely searched or if the table is very small. Also, there are situations where the data being added to the table is highly ordered to start with. If the table is used to gather sequential data (like readings from an electric meter) and the data will be used in the same sequential order, there is no need to impose an index on the data.

But for situations where natural order doesn't suffice, Access provides *indexing* to help you find and sort records faster. You specify a *logical* order for the records in a table by creating an *index* on that table. Access uses the index to maintain one or more internal sort orders for the data in the table. For example, you may choose to index the LastName field that will frequently be included in queries and sorting routines.

Access uses indexes in a table as you use an index in a book: to find data, Access looks up the data's location in the index. Most often, your tables will include one or more *simple indexes*. A simple index is one that involves a single field in the table. Simple indexes may arrange the table's records in ascending or descending order. Simple indexes are created by setting the field's Indexed property to one of the following values:

- Yes (Duplicates OK)
- Yes (No Duplicates)

By default, Access fields are not indexed, but it's hard to imagine a table that doesn't require some kind of index. The next section discusses why indexing is important to use in Access tables.

The importance of indexes

Microsoft's data indicates that more than half of all tables in Access databases contain *no* indexes. This number doesn't include the tables that are improperly indexed—it includes only those tables that have no indexes at all. It appears that a lot of people don't appreciate the importance of indexing the tables in an Access database.

ON THE WEB

As a demonstration of the power and value of indexes, this book's website includes a database named `IndexTest.accdb`. This database includes two identical tables containing approximately 355,000 random words. One table is indexed on the Word field, and the other is not. A small form (shown in Figure 3.16) lets you query either the indexed or unindexed table and shows the number of milliseconds the search takes.

FIGURE 3.16

frmIndexTest provides a quick and easy way to verify the importance of indexes.

The buttons run each test 10 times and display the results in the list box below the button. The indexed table consistently finds a word in 10 to 30 milliseconds, while the unindexed search takes between 300 and 350 milliseconds. Displaying the results you see in Figure 3.16 takes almost no time at all and doesn't contribute to the overall time required to run the query. It goes without saying that the actual time required to run a query depends very much on the computer's hardware, but performance enhancements of 500 percent and more are not at all uncommon when adding an index to a field.

Because an index means that Access maintains an internal sort order on the data contained in the indexed field, you can see why query performance is enhanced by an index. You should index virtually every field that is frequently involved in queries or is frequently sorted on forms or reports.

Without an index, Access must search each and every record in the database looking for matches. This process is called a *table scan* and is analogous to searching through each and every card in a Rolodex file to find all the people who work for a certain company. Until you reach the end of the deck, you can't be sure you've found every relevant card in the file.

As mentioned earlier in this chapter, a table's primary key field is always indexed. This is because the primary key is used to locate records in the table. Indexing the primary key makes it much easier for Access to find the required tables in either the current table or a foreign table related to the current table. Without an index, Access has to search all records in the related table to make sure it has located all the related records.

> **TIP**
>
> The performance losses due to unindexed tables can have a devastating effect on the overall performance of an Access application. Anytime you hear a complaint about the performance of an application, consider indexing as a possible solution.

Multiple-field indexes

Multiple-field indexes (also called *composite indexes*) are easy to create. In Design view, click the Indexes button on the Design tab of the Ribbon. The Indexes dialog box (shown in Figure 3.17) appears, allowing you to specify the fields to include in the index.

FIGURE 3.17

Multiple-field (composite) indexes can enhance performance.

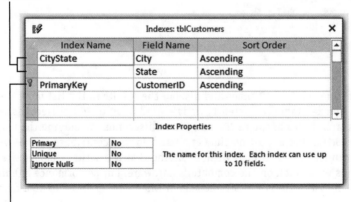

Composite index

Primary Key index

Enter a name for the index (CityState in Figure 3.17) and tab to the Field Name column. Use the drop-down list to select the fields to include in the index. In this example, City and State are combined as a single index. Any row appearing immediately below this row that does not contain an index name is part of the composite index. Access considers both these fields when creating the sort order on this table, speeding queries and sorting operations that include both the City and State fields.

> **NOTE**
>
> The order of the fields in a composite index is important. The CityState index described in this chapter will be used by Access when only the City is provided in a query, but it will provide no benefit when only the State is provided.

As many as ten fields can be included in a composite index. As long as the composite index is not used as the table's primary key, any of the fields in the composite index can be empty.

Figure 3.18 shows how to set the properties of an index. The cursor is placed in the row in the Indexes dialog box containing the name of the index. Notice the three properties appearing in the bottom half of the Indexes dialog box.

FIGURE 3.18

It's easy to set the properties of an index.

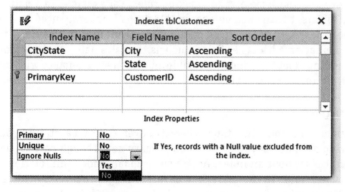

The index properties are quite easy to understand (these properties apply to single-field and composite indexes equally):

- **Primary:** When set to Yes, Access uses this index as the table's primary key. More than one field can be designated as the primary key, but keep the rules governing primary keys in mind, particularly those requiring each primary key value to be unique and that no field in a composite primary key can be empty. The default for the Primary property is No.

■ **Unique:** When set to Yes, the index must be unique within a table. A Social Security number field is a good candidate for a unique index because the application's business rules may require one and only one instance of a Social Security number in the table. In contrast, a last name field should not be uniquely indexed, because many last names, like Smith and Jones, are very common, and having a unique index on the last name field will only cause problems.

When applied to composite keys, the *combination* of field values must be unique— each field within the composite key can duplicate fields found within the table.

■ **Ignore Nulls:** If a record's index field contains a null value (which happens in a composite index only if all fields in the composite index are null) the record's index won't contribute anything to the overall indexing. In other words, unless a record's index contains some kind of value, Access doesn't know where to insert the record in the table's internal index sort lists. Therefore, you might want to instruct Access to ignore a record if the index value is null. By default, the Ignore Nulls property is set to No, which means Access inserts records with a Null index value into the indexing scheme along with any other records containing Null index values.

You should test the impact of the index properties on your Access tables and use the properties that best suit the data handled by your databases.

A field can be both the primary key for a table and part of a composite index. You should index your tables as necessary to yield the highest possible performance without worrying about over-indexing or violating some arcane indexing rules. For example, in a database such as Collectible Mini Cars, the invoice number in tblSales is frequently used in forms and reports and should be indexed. In addition, there are many situations in which the invoice number is used in combination with other fields, such as the sales date or salesperson ID. You should consider adding composite indexes combining the invoice number with sales date, and salesperson ID, to the sales table.

When to index tables

Depending on the number of records in a table, the extra overhead of maintaining an index may not justify creating an index beyond the table's primary key. Though data retrieval is somewhat faster than it is without an index, Access must update index information whenever you enter or change records in the table. In contrast, changes to nonindexed fields do not require extra file activity. You can retrieve data from nonindexed fields as easily (although not as *quickly*) as from indexed fields.

Generally, it's best to add secondary indexes when tables are quite large and when indexing fields other than the primary key speeds up searches. Even with large tables, however, indexing can slow performance if the records in tables will be changed often or new records will be added frequently. Each time a record is changed or added, Access must update all indexes in the table.

Given all the advantages of indexes, why not index everything in the table? What are the drawbacks of indexing too many fields? Is it possible to over-index tables?

First, indexes increase the size of the Access database somewhat. Unnecessarily indexing a table that doesn't really require an index eats up a bit of disk space for each record in the table. More important, indexes extract a performance hit for each index on the table every time a record is added to the table. Because Access automatically updates indexes each time a record is added (or removed), the internal indexing must be adjusted for each new record. If you have ten indexes on a table, Access makes ten adjustments to the indexes each time a new record is added or an existing record is deleted, causing a noticeable delay on large tables (particularly on slow computers).

Sometimes changes to the data in records cause adjustments to the indexing scheme. This is true if the change causes the record to change its position in sorting or query activities. Therefore, if you're working with large, constantly changing data sets that are rarely searched, you may choose *not* to index the fields in the table, or to minimally index by indexing only those few fields that are likely to be searched.

As you begin working with Access tables, you'll probably start with the simplest one-field indexes and migrate to more complex ones as your familiarity with the process grows. Keep in mind, however, the trade-offs between greater search efficiency and the overhead incurred by maintaining a large number of indexes on your tables.

It's also important to keep in mind that indexing does not modify the physical arrangement of records in the table. The natural order of the records (the order in which the records were added to the table) is maintained after the index is established.

3

NOTE

A compact and repair cycle on an Access database forces Access to rebuild the indexes in all the tables, and physically rearranges tables in primary key order in the ACCDB file. The maintenance operations ensure that your Access databases operate at maximum efficiency. See Chapter 31 for more on the Compact and Repair utility.

Printing a Table Design

You can print a table design by clicking the Database Documenter button in the Analyze group on the Database Tools tab of the Ribbon. The Analyze group contains a number of tools that make it easy to document your database objects. When you click the Database Documenter button, the Documenter dialog box appears, letting you select objects to print. In Figure 3.19, tblCustomers is selected on the Tables tab of the Documenter dialog box.

You can also set various options for printing. When you click the Options button, the Print Table Definition dialog box (shown in Figure 3.20) appears, enabling you to select which information from the Table Design to print. You can print the various field names, all their properties, the indexes, and even network permissions.

FIGURE 3.19

The Documenter dialog box.

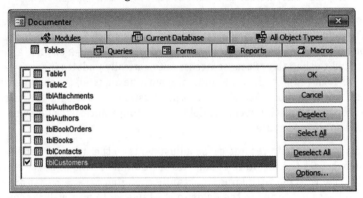

FIGURE 3.20

Printing options in the Print Table Definition dialog box.

CAUTION

Don't select too many options in the Print Table Definition dialog box. Printing every detail of a table's design can take many pages to output. It's probably best to print just a few items for a table, and add to the options when necessary.

After you select the options you want, Access generates a report. You can view the report in a Print Preview window or send it to a printer. You may want to save the report within the database as part of the application's documentation.

> **TIP**
> The Database Documenter creates a table of all the objects and object properties you specify. You can use this utility to document such database objects as forms, queries, reports, macros, and modules.

Saving the Completed Table

You can save the completed table design by choosing File ➪ Save or by clicking the Save button on the Quick Access toolbar in the upper-left corner of the Access environment. If you're saving the table for the first time, Access asks for its name. Table names can be up to 64 characters long and follow standard Access object naming conventions: They may include letters and numbers, can't begin with a number, and can't include punctuation. If you try to close an unsaved table, Access will prompt you to save it.

If you've saved this table before and want to save it with a different name, choose File ➪ Save As ➪ Save Object As, click the Save As button, and enter a different table name. This action creates a new table design and leaves the original table with its original name untouched. If you want to delete the old table, select it in the Navigation pane and press the Delete key.

Manipulating Tables

As you add many tables to your database, you may want to use them in other databases or make copies of them as backups. In many cases, you may want to copy only the table's design and not include all the data in the table. You can perform many table operations in the Navigation pane, including:

- Renaming tables
- Deleting tables
- Copying tables in a database
- Copying a table to another database

You perform these tasks by direct manipulation or by using menu items.

Renaming tables

Rename a table by right-clicking its name in the Navigation pane and selecting Rename from the shortcut menu or by selecting the table in the Navigation pane and pressing the F2 key. After you change the table name, it appears in the Tables list, which re-sorts the tables in alphabetical order.

> **CAUTION**
>
> If you rename a table, you must change the table name in any objects in which it was previously referenced, including queries, forms, and reports.

Deleting tables

Delete a table by right-clicking its name in the Navigation pane and selecting Delete from the shortcut menu or by selecting the table in the Navigation pane and pressing the Delete key. Like most delete operations, you have to confirm the delete by clicking Yes in a confirmation box.

> **CAUTION**
>
> Be aware that holding down the Shift key while pressing the Delete key deletes the table (or any other database object, for that matter) *without* confirmation. You'll find the Shift+Delete key combination useful for removing items but also dangerous if not carefully applied.

Copying tables in a database

The copy and paste options in the Clipboard group on the Home tab allow you to copy any table in the database. When you paste the table back into the database, the Paste Table As dialog box appears, asking you to choose from three options:

- **Structure Only:** Clicking the Structure Only option creates a new, empty table with the same design as the copied table. This option is typically used to create a temporary table or an archive table to which you can copy old records.
- **Structure and Data:** When you click Structure and Data, a complete copy of the table design and all its data is created.
- **Append Data to Existing Table:** Clicking the Append Data to Existing Table option adds the data of the selected table to the bottom of another table. This option is useful for combining tables, such as when you want to add data from a monthly transaction table to a yearly history table.

Follow these steps to copy a table:

1. **Right-click the table name in the Navigation pane and choose Copy from the shortcut menu, or click the Copy button in the Clipboard group on the Home tab.**

2. **Right-click anywhere in the Navigation pane and choose Paste from the shortcut menu, or click the Paste button in the Clipboard group on the Home tab.**
   The Paste Table As dialog box appears (see Figure 3.21).

3. **Enter the name of the new table.** When you're appending data to an existing table (see the next step), you must type the name of an existing table.

4. **Choose one of the Paste options**—Structure Only, Structure and Data, or Append Data to Existing Table—from the Paste Table As dialog box.

5. **Click OK to complete the operation.**

FIGURE 3.21

Pasting a table opens the Paste Table As dialog box.

Copying a table to another database

Just as you can copy a table within a database, you can copy a table to another database. There are many reasons why you may want to do this. Maybe you share a common table among multiple systems, or maybe you need to create a backup copy of your important tables within the system.

When you copy tables to another database, the relationships between tables are not copied. Access copies only the table design and the data to the other database. The method for copying a table to another database is essentially the same as for copying a table within a database:

1. **Right-click the table name in the Navigation pane and choose Copy from the shortcut menu, or click the Copy button in the Clipboard group on the Home tab.**

2. **Open the other Access database and right-click anywhere in the Navigation page. Choose Paste from the shortcut menu, or click the Paste button in the Clipboard group on the Home tab.** The Paste Table As dialog box appears.

3. **Enter the name of the new table.**

4. **Choose one of the Paste options:** Structure Only, Structure and Data, or Append Data to Existing Table.

5. **Click OK to complete the operation.**

Adding Records to a Database Table

Adding records to a table is as simple as double-clicking the table name in the Navigation pane to open the table in Datasheet view. Once the table is opened, enter values for each field. Figure 3.22 shows the process of adding records in Datasheet view to the table.

You can enter information into all fields except CustomerID. AutoNumber fields automatically provide a number for you.

FIGURE 3.22

Using Datasheet view to add records to a table.

▦	tblCustomers							− ☐ ✕
Custon ▾	Company ▾	Address ▾	City ▾	Stat ▾	ZipCo ▾			
21	All Star Toys	971 E Main St	Detroit	MI	12345-67	(		
22	Carl's Collectibles	105 Main Street	Columbia	MA	12237	(		
23	Your Favorite Thing	75 Main Street	Bedford	NY	10506	(		
24	Gleason's	196 East Street	Derby	CT	06418	(		
25	Tommy's Toys	46 School Street	Oneco	CT	06373	(		
26	Too Many Toys	54 E Center Street	Granby	CT	06035	(		
27	Grandma's Closet	986 Buckingham St	Brewster	NY	10509	(		
29	Tommy's Trains	4962 Holly St	Stillwell	NY	04113	(		
30	Toy Warehouse	3738 Stonecoal Road	Toledo	OH	43609	(		
31	Toy Box	1337 Victoria Court	Portland	ME	04101	(		
32	Gothic Goodies	4408 Main Street	Seattle	WA	98101	(		
33	Comstock Collectil	916 Cambridge Drive	Phoenix	AZ	85027	(		
35	Wee Ones Toys	123 Main Street						
*	(New)							

Record: I◄ ◄ 33 of 33 ► ►I ►⁕ | ▼⨯ No Filter | Search | ◄ | ► |

Although you can add records directly into the table through the Datasheet view, it isn't the recommended way. Adding records using forms is better because code behind a form can dynamically provide default values (perhaps based on data already added to the form) and communicate with the user during the data entry process.

 Part V of this book discusses building forms to enter data.

Understanding Attachment Fields

Microsoft recognizes that database developers must deal with many different types of data. Although the traditional Access data types (Short Text, Currency, OLE Object, and so on) are able to handle many different types of data, until recently there was no way to accommodate *complete files* as Access data without performing some transformation on the file (such as conversion to OLE data).

Since Access 2010, Access has included the Attachment data type, enabling you to bring entire files into your Access database as "attachments" to a table. When you click an attachment field, a small Attachments dialog box (shown in Figure 3.23) appears, enabling you to locate files to attach to the table.

The Add button in Figure 3.23 opens the familiar Choose File dialog box, enabling you to search for one or more files to attach to the field. The selected files are added to the list you see in Figure 3.23. Notice also that the Attachments dialog box includes buttons for removing attachments from the field, and for saving attachments back to the computer's disk.

FIGURE 3.23

Managing attachments in an Attachment field.

The significant thing to keep in mind about the Attachment data type is that a single attachment field in a table can contain multiple files of different types. It's entirely possible to store a Word document, several audio or video clips, and a number of photographs, within a single attachment field.

CAUTION

Obviously, because the attached data is incorporated into the database, the ACCDB file will quickly grow if many attachments are added. You should use the Attachment data type only when its benefits outweigh the burden it places on an Access application.

Understanding Table Relationships

IN THIS CHAPTER

Understanding bulletproof database design

Normalizing database data

Looking at common table relationships

Understanding integrity rules

Adding key fields to tables

W e've already covered one of the most basic assumptions about relational database systems—that data is spread across a number of tables that are related through primary and foreign keys. Although this basic principle is easy to understand, it can be much more difficult to understand why and when data should be broken into separate tables.

Because the data managed by a relational database such as Access exists in a number of different tables, there must be some way to connect the data. The more efficiently the database performs these connections, the better and more flexible the database application as a whole will function.

Although databases are meant to model real-world situations, or at least manage the data involved in real-world situations, even the most complex situation is reduced to a number of relationships between pairs of tables. As the data managed by the database becomes more complex, you may need to add more tables to the design. For example, a database to manage employee affairs for a company will include tables for employee information (name, Social Security number, address, hire date, and so on), payroll information, benefits programs the employee belongs to, and so on.

This chapter uses a variety of data from different business situations, including Northwind Traders (the traditional Access example database), a small bookstore, and the Collectible Mini Cars application used in other chapters of this book. Each data set has somewhat different objectives from the others and is used to emphasize different aspects of relational theory. All the tables described in this chapter are contained in the Chapter04.accdb database.

When working with the actual data, however, you concentrate on the relationship between two tables at a time. You might create the Employees and Payroll tables first, connecting these tables with a relationship to make it easy to find all the payroll information for an employee.

Building Bulletproof Databases

In Chapters 1, 2, and 3, you saw examples of common relationships found in many Access databases. By far the most common type of table relationship is the one-to-many. The Collectible Mini Cars application has many such relationships: each record in the Customers table is related to one or more records in the Sales table. (Each contact may have purchased more than one item through Collectible Mini Cars.)

 We cover one-to-many relationships in detail in the "Table Relationships" section later in this chapter.

You can easily imagine an arrangement that would permit the data contained in the Customers and Sales tables to be combined within a single table. All that would be needed is a separate row for each order placed by each of the contacts. As new orders come in, new rows containing the customer and order information would be added to the table.

The Access table shown in Figure 4.1, tblCustomersAndOrders, is an example of such an arrangement. In this figure, the OrderID column contains the order number placed by the contact (the data in this table has been sorted by CustomerID to show how many orders have been placed by each contact). The table in Figure 4.1 was created by combining data from the Customers and Orders tables in the Northwind Traders sample database and is included in the `Chapter04.accdb` database file on this book's website.

Notice the OrderID column to the right of the CompanyName column. Each contact (like Alfreds Futterkiste) has placed a number of orders. Columns to the far right in this table (beyond the right edge of the figure) contain more information about each contact, including address and phone numbers, while columns beyond the company information contain the specific order information. In all, this table contains 24 different fields.

The design shown in Figure 4.1 is what happens when a spreadsheet application such as Excel is used for database purposes. Because Excel is entirely spreadsheet oriented, there is no provision for breaking up data into separate tables, encouraging users to keep everything in one massive spreadsheet.

FIGURE 4.1

An Access table containing customer, contact, *and* orders data.

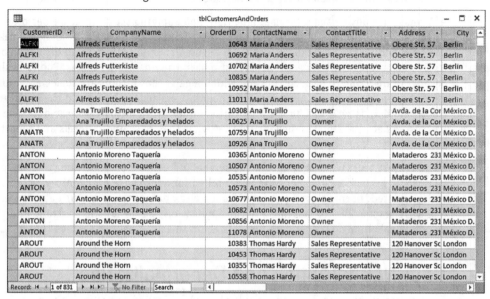

CustomerID	CompanyName	OrderID	ContactName	ContactTitle	Address	City
ALFKI	Alfreds Futterkiste	10643	Maria Anders	Sales Representative	Obere Str. 57	Berlin
ALFKI	Alfreds Futterkiste	10692	Maria Anders	Sales Representative	Obere Str. 57	Berlin
ALFKI	Alfreds Futterkiste	10702	Maria Anders	Sales Representative	Obere Str. 57	Berlin
ALFKI	Alfreds Futterkiste	10835	Maria Anders	Sales Representative	Obere Str. 57	Berlin
ALFKI	Alfreds Futterkiste	10952	Maria Anders	Sales Representative	Obere Str. 57	Berlin
ALFKI	Alfreds Futterkiste	11011	Maria Anders	Sales Representative	Obere Str. 57	Berlin
ANATR	Ana Trujillo Emparedados y helados	10308	Ana Trujillo	Owner	Avda. de la Cor	México D.
ANATR	Ana Trujillo Emparedados y helados	10625	Ana Trujillo	Owner	Avda. de la Cor	México D.
ANATR	Ana Trujillo Emparedados y helados	10759	Ana Trujillo	Owner	Avda. de la Cor	México D.
ANATR	Ana Trujillo Emparedados y helados	10926	Ana Trujillo	Owner	Avda. de la Cor	México D.
ANTON	Antonio Moreno Taquería	10365	Antonio Moreno	Owner	Mataderos 231	México D.
ANTON	Antonio Moreno Taquería	10507	Antonio Moreno	Owner	Mataderos 231	México D.
ANTON	Antonio Moreno Taquería	10535	Antonio Moreno	Owner	Mataderos 231	México D.
ANTON	Antonio Moreno Taquería	10573	Antonio Moreno	Owner	Mataderos 231	México D.
ANTON	Antonio Moreno Taquería	10677	Antonio Moreno	Owner	Mataderos 231	México D.
ANTON	Antonio Moreno Taquería	10682	Antonio Moreno	Owner	Mataderos 231	México D.
ANTON	Antonio Moreno Taquería	10856	Antonio Moreno	Owner	Mataderos 231	México D.
ANTON	Antonio Moreno Taquería	11078	Antonio Moreno	Owner	Mataderos 231	México D.
AROUT	Around the Horn	10383	Thomas Hardy	Sales Representative	120 Hanover Sc	London
AROUT	Around the Horn	10453	Thomas Hardy	Sales Representative	120 Hanover Sc	London
AROUT	Around the Horn	10355	Thomas Hardy	Sales Representative	120 Hanover Sc	London
AROUT	Around the Horn	10558	Thomas Hardy	Sales Representative	120 Hanover Sc	London

Record: 1 of 831   No Filter   Search

Such an arrangement has several problems:

- **The table quickly becomes unmanageably large.** The Northwind Traders Customers table contains 11 different fields, while the Orders table contains 14 more. One field, OrderID, overlaps both tables. Each time an order is placed, all 24 data fields in the combined table would be added for each record added to the table, including a lot of data (such as the Contact Name and Contact Title) not directly relevant to an order.

- **Data is difficult to maintain and update.** Making simple changes to the data in the large table—for example, changing a contact's phone or fax number—involves searching through all records in the table and changing every occurrence of the phone number. It's easy to make an erroneous entry or miss one or more instances. The fewer records needing changes, the better off the user will be.

- **A monolithic table design is wasteful of disk space and other resources.** Because the combined table contains a huge amount of redundant data (for example, a contact's address is repeated for every sale), a large amount of hard disk space is consumed by the redundant information. In addition to wasted disk space, network traffic, computer memory, and other resources would be poorly utilized.

A much better design—the relational design—moves the repeated data into a separate table, leaving a field in the first table to serve as a reference to the data in the second

4

table. The additional field required by the relational model is a small price to pay for the efficiencies gained by moving redundant data out of the table.

A second huge advantage of normalizing data and applying strict database design rules to Access applications is that the data becomes virtually bulletproof. In an appropriately designed and managed database, users are ensured that the information displayed on forms and reports truly reflects the data stored in the underlying tables. Poorly designed databases are prone to data corruption, which means that records are sometimes "lost" and never appear on forms and reports, even though users added the data to the application, or the wrong data is returned by the application's queries. In either case, the database can't be trusted because users are never sure that what they're seeing in forms and reports is correct.

Users tend to trust what they see on the screen and printed on paper. Imagine the problems that would occur if a customer were never billed for a purchase or inventory were incorrectly updated. Nothing good can come from a weak database design. As database developers, we're responsible for making sure the applications we design are as strong and resilient as possible. Following proper data normalization rules can help us achieve that goal.

Data Normalization and Denormalization

The process of splitting data across multiple tables is called *normalizing* the data. There are several stages of normalization; the first through the third stages are the easiest to understand and implement and are generally sufficient for the majority of applications. Although higher levels of normalization are possible, they're usually ignored by all but the most experienced and fastidious developers.

To illustrate the normalization process, we'll use a little database that a book wholesaler might use to track book orders placed by small bookstores in the local area. This database must handle the following information:

- The dates on which the books were ordered
- The customers who placed the orders
- The quantity of each book ordered
- The title of each book ordered

Although this dataset is very simple, it's typical of the type of data you might manage with an Access database application, and it provides a valid demonstration of normalizing a set of data.

First normal form

The initial stage of normalization, called *first normal form* (1NF), requires that the table conform to the following rule:

Each field of a table must contain only a single value, and the table must not contain repeating groups of data.

A table is meant to be a two-dimensional storage object, and storing multiple values within a field or permitting repeating groups within the table implies a third dimension to the data. Figure 4.2 shows the first attempt at building a table to manage bookstore orders (tblBookOrders1). Notice that some bookstores have ordered more than one book. A value like 7 Cookie Magic in the BookTitle field means that the contact has ordered seven copies of the cookbook titled *Cookie Magic*. Storing both a quantity and the item's name in the same cell is just one of several ways that this table violates first normal form.

FIGURE 4.2

An unnormalized tblBookOrders table.

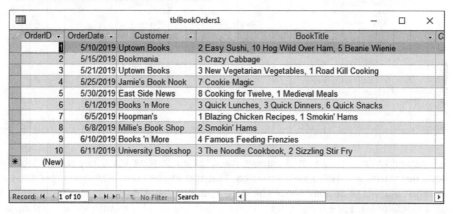

The table in Figure 4.2 is typical of a *flat-file approach* to building a database. Data in a flat-file database is stored in two dimensions (rows and columns) and neglects the third dimension (related tables) possible in a relational database system such as Access.

Notice how the table in Figure 4.2 violates the first rule of normalization. Many of the records in this table contain multiple values in the BookTitle field. For example, the book titled *Smokin' Hams* appears in records 7 and 8. There is no way for the database to handle this data easily—if you want to cross-reference the books ordered by the bookstores, you'd have to parse the data contained in the BookTitle field to determine which books have been ordered by which contacts.

A slightly better design is shown in Figure 4.3 (tblBookOrders2). The books' quantities and titles have been separated into individual columns. Each row still contains all the data for a single order. This arrangement makes it somewhat easier to retrieve quantity and title information, but the repeating groups for quantity and title (the columns Quant1, Title1, Quant2, Title2, and so on) continue to violate the first rule of normalization. (The row height in Figure 4.3 has been adjusted to make it easier to see the table's arrangement.)

4

FIGURE 4.3

Only a slight improvement over the previous design.

OrderID	OrderDate	Customer	Quant1	Title1	Quant2	Title2	Quant3	Title3	Quant4
1	5/10/2019	Uptown Books	2	Easy Sushi	10	Hog Wild Over Ham	5	Beanie Wienie	
2	5/15/2019	Bookmania	3	Crazy Cabbage					
3	5/21/2019	Uptown Books	3	New Vegetarian Vegetables	1	Road Kill Cooking			
4	5/25/2019	Jamie's Book Nook	7	Cookie Magic					
5	5/30/2019	East Side News	8	Cooking for Twelve	1	Medieval Meals			
6	6/1/2019	Books 'n More	3	Quick Lunches	3	Quick Dinners	6	Quick Snacks	
7	6/5/2019	Hoopman's	1	Blazing Chicken Recipes	1	Smokin' Hams			
8	6/8/2019	Millie's Book Shop	2	Smokin' Hams					
9	6/10/2019	Books 'n More	4	Famous Feeding Frenzies					
10	6/11/2019	University Bookshop	3	The Noodle Cookbook	2	Sizzling Stir Fry			
* (New)			0		0		0		0

Record: 1 of 10   No Filter   Search

The design in Figure 4.3 is still clumsy and difficult to work with. The columns to hold the book quantities and titles are permanent features of the table. The developer must add enough columns to accommodate the maximum number of books that could be purchased on a single order. For example, let's assume that the developer anticipates that no bookstore will ever order more than 50 books at a time. This means that 100 columns are added to the table (two columns—Quantity and Title—are required for each book title ordered). If a bookstore orders a single book, 98 columns would sit empty in the table, a very wasteful and inefficient situation.

Based on the design shown in Figure 4.3, it would be exceedingly difficult to query tblBookOrders2 to get the sales figure for a particular book. The quantity sold for any book is scattered all over the table, in different rows and different columns, making it very difficult to know where to look for a book's sales data.

Also, if any book order exceeds 50 books, the table has to be redesigned to accommodate the additional columns needed by the order. Of course, the user might add a second row for the order, making the data in the table more difficult to work with than intended.

Figure 4.4 shows tblBookOrders3, a new table created from the data in Figure 4.3 in first normal form. Instead of stacking multiple book orders within a single record, in tblBookOrders3 each record contains a single book ordered by a customer. More records are required, but the data is handled much more easily. First normal form is much more efficient because the table contains no unused fields. Every field is meaningful to the table's purpose.

FIGURE 4.4

First normal form at last!

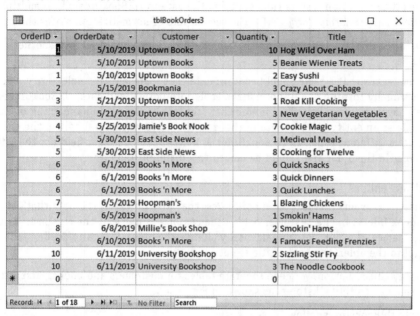

OrderID ▾	OrderDate ▾	Customer ▾	Quantity ▾	Title ▾
1	5/10/2019	Uptown Books	10	Hog Wild Over Ham
1	5/10/2019	Uptown Books	5	Beanie Wienie Treats
1	5/10/2019	Uptown Books	2	Easy Sushi
2	5/15/2019	Bookmania	3	Crazy About Cabbage
3	5/21/2019	Uptown Books	1	Road Kill Cooking
3	5/21/2019	Uptown Books	3	New Vegetarian Vegetables
4	5/25/2019	Jamie's Book Nook	7	Cookie Magic
5	5/30/2019	East Side News	1	Medieval Meals
5	5/30/2019	East Side News	8	Cooking for Twelve
6	6/1/2019	Books 'n More	6	Quick Snacks
6	6/1/2019	Books 'n More	3	Quick Dinners
6	6/1/2019	Books 'n More	3	Quick Lunches
7	6/5/2019	Hoopman's	1	Blazing Chickens
7	6/5/2019	Hoopman's	1	Smokin' Hams
8	6/8/2019	Millie's Book Shop	2	Smokin' Hams
9	6/10/2019	Books 'n More	4	Famous Feeding Frenzies
10	6/11/2019	University Bookshop	2	Sizzling Stir Fry
10	6/11/2019	University Bookshop	3	The Noodle Cookbook
* 0			0	

Record: ◄ ◄ 1 of 18 ► ►I ►❙ ⲧ No Filter   Search

The table in Figure 4.4 contains the same data as shown in Figure 4.2 and Figure 4.3. The new arrangement, however, makes it much easier to work with the data. For example, queries are easily constructed to return the total number of a particular book ordered by customers or to determine which titles have been ordered by a particular bookstore.

TIP

Your tables should *always* be in first normal form. Make sure each cell of the table contains a single value, don't mix values within a cell, and don't have repeating groups (as you saw in Figure 4.3).

The table design optimization is not complete at this point, however. Much remains to be done with the BookOrders data and the other tables in this application. In particular, the table shown in Figure 4.4 contains redundant information. The book titles are repeated each time customers order the same book, and the order number and order date are repeated for all the rows for an order.

A subtler issue is the fact that the OrderID can no longer be used as the table's primary key. Because the OrderID is duplicated for each book title in an order, it can't be used to identify individual records in the table. Instead, the OrderID field is now a key field for the table and can be used to locate all the records relevant to a particular order. The next step of optimization corrects this situation.

4

Second normal form

A more efficient design results from splitting the data in tblBookOrders into multiple tables to achieve *second normal form* (2NF). The second rule of normalization states the following:

> Data not directly dependent on the table's primary key is moved into another table.

This rule means that a table should contain data that represents a single entity. Because we're gradually turning one unnormalized table into normalized data, tblBookOrders3 doesn't have a primary key. We'll ignore that fact for the time being and think of each row in a table as an entity. All the data in that row that isn't an integral part of the entity is moved to a different table. In tblBookOrders3, neither the Customer field nor the Title field is integral to the order and should be moved to a different table.

Identifying entities

But aren't customers integral to an order? Yes, they are. However, the data that's stored in tblBookOrders3 in the Customer field is the customer's name. If the customer were to change names, it would not fundamentally change the order. Similarly, while the book is integral to the order, the book's title is not.

To remedy this situation, we need separate tables for customers and books. First, create a new table named tblBookstores, as shown in Figure 4.5.

To create tblBookstores follow these steps:

1. **Click Table Design on the Create tab of the Ribbon.**
2. **Add an AutoNumber field named BookstoreID.**
3. **Click Primary Key on the Table Tools Design tab of the Ribbon.**
4. **Add a Short Text field named StoreName.**
5. **Set the Field Size of StoreName to 50.**
6. **Save the table as tblBookstores.**

You can imagine that we want to store some more information about customers, such as their mailing addresses and phone numbers. For now, we're getting our data into 2NF by moving data that isn't integral to an order to its own table.

Next create a table for books by following these steps:

1. **Click Table Design on the Create tab of the Ribbon.**
2. **Add an AutoNumber field named BookID.**
3. **Click Primary Key on the Table Tools Design tab of the Ribbon.**
4. **Add a Short Text field named BookTitle.**
5. **Save the table as tblBooks.**

FIGURE 4.5

Moving customer data to its own table.

The customer and the book are still integral to the order (just not the name and title), and we need a way to relate the tables to each other. While the customer may change names, the customer can't change the BookstoreID because we created it and we control it. Similarly, the publisher may change the book's title but not the BookID. The primary keys of tblBookstores and tblBooks are reliable pointers to the objects they identify, regardless of what other information may change.

Figure 4.6 shows our three tables, but instead of a customer name and a book title, tblBookOrders4 now contains the primary key of its related record in both tblBookstores and tblBooks. When the primary key of one table is used as a field in another table, it's called a *foreign key*.

Before we split out the customer data to its own table, if Uptown Books changed its name to Uptown Books and Periodicals, we would have to identify all the rows in tblBookOrders3 that had a customer of Uptown Books and change the field's value for each row identified.

Overlooking an instance of the customer's name during this process is called an *update anomaly* and results in records that are inconsistent with the other records in the database. From the database's perspective, Uptown Books and Uptown Books and Periodicals are two completely different organizations, even if we know that they're the same store. A query to retrieve all the orders placed by Uptown Books and Periodicals will miss any records that still have Uptown Books in the Customer field because of the update anomaly.

FIGURE 4.6

The first step in making our table 2NF.

Another advantage of removing the customer name from the orders table is that the name now exists in only one location in the database. If Uptown Books changes its name to Uptown Books and Periodicals, we now only have to change its entry in the tblBookstores table. This single change is reflected throughout the database, including all forms and reports that use the customer name information.

Identifying separate entities and putting their data into separate tables is a great first step to achieving second normal form. But we're not quite done. Our orders table still doesn't have a unique field that we can use as the primary key. The OrderID field has repeating values that provide a clue that there is more work to be done to achieve 2NF.

Less obvious entities

Customers and books are physical objects that are easy to identify as separate entities. The next step is a little more abstract. Our orders table, now called tblBookOrders4, still contains information about two separate, but related, entities. The order is one entity, and the order details (the individual lines on the order) are entities all their own.

The first three records of tblBookOrders4, shown in Figure 4.6, contain the same OrderID, OrderDate, and BookStoreID. These three fields are characteristics of the order as a whole, not of each individual line on the order. The Quantity and BookID fields contain different values in those three first records. Quantity and BookID are characteristics of a particular line on the order.

TIP

Values that repeat in multiple records, like OrderID in tblBookOrders4 shown in Figure 4.6, are an indication that your data is not yet in second normal form. Some data, like foreign keys, is meant to repeat. Other data, like dates and quantities, repeats naturally and is not indicative of a problem.

The last step to get our order data into second normal form is to put the information integral to the order as a whole into a separate table from the information for each line on the order. Create a new table named tblBookOrderDetails with the fields BookOrderDetailID, Quantity, and BookID. BookOrderDetailID is an AutoNumber field that will serve as the primary key, and BookID is a foreign key field that we use to relate the two tables. Figure 4.7 shows our new orders table, tblBookOrders5, and our new details table, tblBookOrderDetails.

The OrderID field in tblBookOrders5 was deleted and a new AutoNumber field named OrderID was created. Now that we have a unique field in the orders table, we can set OrderID as the primary key. All the data in each record of tblBookOrders5 directly relates to an order entity. Or, in 2NF language, all the data is directly dependent on the primary key.

The OrderID field in tblBookOrderDetails is a foreign key that is used to relate the two tables together. Figure 4.7 shows that the first three records in tblBookOrderDetails show an OrderID of 1 that maps to the first record of tblBookOrders5.

All the fields in tblBookOrderDetails are directly dependent on the primary key BookOrderDetailID. The quantity from the first record, 10, relates directly to that line item on the order. It only relates to the order as a whole indirectly, just as the quantities from the next two records, 5 and 7, do. That indirect relationship is created by including the OrderID foreign key in the record.

The original table, tblBookOrders1, contained data about several different entities in each record. Through a series of steps, we split the data into four tables—tblBookOrders5, tblBookOrderDetails, tblBookstores, and tblBooks—each of which contains data about one entity. Our data is finally in the second normal form.

Breaking a table into individual tables, each of which describes some aspect of the data, is called *decomposition*. Decomposition is a very important part of the normalization process. Even though the tables appear smaller than the original table (refer to Figure 4.2), the data contained within the tables is the same as before.

4

FIGURE 4.7

We have achieved second normal form.

A developer working with the bookstore tables is able to use queries to recombine the data in the four tables in new and interesting ways. It'd be quite easy to determine how many books of each type have been ordered by the different customers, or how many times a particular book has been ordered. When coupled with a table containing information such as book unit cost, book selling price, and so on, the important financial status of the book wholesaler becomes clear.

Notice also that the number of records in tblBookOrders5 has been reduced. This is one of several advantages to using a relational database. Each table contains only as much data as is necessary to represent the entity (in this case, a book order) described by the table. This is far more efficient than adding duplicate field values (refer to Figure 4.2) for each new record added to a table.

Breaking the rules

From time to time, you might find it necessary to break the rules. For example, let's assume that the bookstores are entitled to discounts based on the volume of purchases over the last year. Strictly following the rules of normalization, the discount percentage should be included in the tblBookstores table. After all, the discount is dependent on the customer, not on the order.

But maybe the discount applied to each order is somewhat arbitrary. Maybe the book wholesaler permits the salespeople to cut special deals for valued customers. In this case, you might want to include a Discount column in the table containing book orders information, even if it means duplicating information in many records. You could store the traditional discount as part of the customer's record in tblBookstores, and use it as the default value for the Discount column but permit the salesperson to override the discount value when a special arrangement has been made with the customer.

In fact, it only appears that this breaks the second normal form. The default discount is directly dependent on the customer. The actual discount given is directly dependent on the order. A similar situation might exist with shipping addresses. A customer may have most of their orders shipped to them, but occasionally they may want to have an order shipped directly to their customer. The customer's shipping address directly relates to the customer, and the address where the order was actually shipped relates directly to the order. Values in object tables that serve as default values in transaction tables are common in large databases.

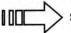 See Chapter 3 for a discussion of object tables and transaction tables.

Third normal form

The last step of normalization, called *third normal form* (3NF), requires removing all fields that can be derived from data contained in other fields in the table or other tables in the database. For example, let's say the sales manager insists that you add a field to contain the total number of books in an order in the Orders table. This information, of course, would be calculated from the Quantity field in tblBookOrderDetails.

It's not really necessary to add the new OrderTotal field to the Orders table. Access easily calculates this value from data that is available in the database. The only advantage of storing order totals as part of the database is to save the few milliseconds required for Access to retrieve and calculate the information when the calculated data is needed by a form or report.

Removing calculated data maintains the integrity of the data in your database. Figure 4.7 shows three records in tblBookOrderDetails that relate to the order with OrderID of 1. Summing the Quantity field, you can see that 22 books were ordered. If there were an OrderTotal field and the total were incorrectly entered as 33 instead of 22, the data would be inconsistent. A report showing total books ordered using the OrderTotal field would show a different number than a report based on the Details table.

Depending on the applications you build, you might find good reasons to store calculated data in tables, particularly if performing the calculations is a lengthy process, or if the stored value is necessary as an audit check on the calculated value printed on reports. It might be more efficient to perform the calculations during data entry (when data is being handled one record at a time) instead of when printing reports (when many thousands of records are manipulated to produce a single report).

4

As you'll read in the "Denormalization" section later in this chapter, there are some good reasons why you might choose to include calculated fields in a database table. As you'll read in this section, most often the decision to denormalize is based on a need to make sure the same calculated value is stored in the database as is printed on a report.

> **TIP**
>
> Although higher levels of normalization are possible, you'll find that, for most database applications, third normal form is more than adequate. At the very least, you should always strive for first normal form in your tables by moving redundant or repeating data to another table.

More on Anomalies

This business about update anomalies is important to keep in mind. The whole purpose of normalizing the tables in your databases is to achieve maximum performance with minimum maintenance effort.

Three types of errors can occur from an unnormalized database design. Following the rules outlined in this chapter will help you avoid the following pitfalls:

- **Insertion anomaly:** An error occurs in a related table when a new record is added to another table. For example, let's say you've added the OrderTotal field described in the previous section. After the order has been processed, the customer calls and changes the number of books ordered or adds a new book title to the same order. Unless you've carefully designed the database to automatically update the calculated OrderTotal field, the data in that field will be in error as the new data is inserted into the table.

  If insertion anomalies are a problem in your applications, you may be able to use macros (see Chapter 22) to help synchronize the data in your tables when changes are made.

- **Deletion anomaly:** A deletion anomaly causes the accidental loss of data when a record is deleted from a table. Let's assume that the tblBookOrders3 table contains the name, address, and other contact information for each bookstore. Deleting the last remaining record containing a particular customer's order causes the customer's contact information to be unintentionally lost. Keeping the customer contact information in a separate table preserves and protects that data from accidental loss. Avoiding deletion anomalies is one good reason not to use cascading deletes in your tables. (See the "Table Relationships" section later in this chapter for more on cascading deletes.)

- **Update anomaly:** Storing data that is not dependent on the table's primary key causes you to have to update multiple rows anytime the independent information changes. Keeping the independent data (such as the bookstore information) in its own table means that only a single instance of the information needs to be updated.

Denormalization

After hammering you with all the reasons why normalizing your databases is a good idea, let's consider when you might deliberately choose to denormalize tables or use unnormalized tables.

Generally speaking, you normalize data in an attempt to improve the performance of your database. For example, in spite of all your efforts, some lookups will be time consuming. Even when using carefully indexed and normalized tables, some lookups require quite a bit of time, especially when the data being looked up is complicated or there's a large amount of it.

Similarly, some calculated values may take a long time to calculate. You may find it faster to simply store a calculated value than to calculate it on the fly. This is particularly true when the user base is working on older, memory-constrained, or slow computers.

Another common reason for denormalizing data is to provide the ability to exactly reproduce a document as it was originally produced. For example, if you need to reprint an invoice from a year ago but the customer's name has changed in the last year, reprinting the invoice will show the new name in a perfectly normalized database. If there are business reasons that dictate the invoice be reproducible precisely, the customer's name may need to be stored in the invoice record at the time the invoice is created.

Be aware that most steps to denormalize a database schema result in additional programming time required to protect the data and user from the problems caused by an unnormalized design. For example, in the case of the calculated OrderTotal field, you must insert code that calculates and updates this field whenever the data in the fields underlying this value changes. This extra programming, of course, takes time to implement and time to process at run time.

> **CAUTION**
>
> Make sure that denormalizing the design does not cause other problems. If you know you've deliberately denormalized a database design and you're having trouble making everything work (particularly if you begin to encounter any of the anomalies discussed in the previous section), look for workarounds that permit you to work with a fully normalized design.

4

Finally, always document whatever you've done to denormalize the design. It's entirely possible that you or someone else will be called in to provide maintenance or to add new features to the application. If you've left design elements that seem to violate the rules of normalization, your carefully considered work may be undone by another developer in an effort to "optimize" the design. The developer doing the maintenance, of course, has the best of intentions, but he may inadvertently re-establish a performance problem that was resolved through subtle denormalization.

One thing to keep in mind is that denormalization is almost always done for reporting or performance purposes, rather than simply to maintain data in tables. Consider a situation in which a customer has been given a special discount that doesn't correspond to his traditional discount. It may be very useful to store the actual amount invoiced to the customer, instead of relying on the database to calculate the discount each time the report is printed. Storing the actual amount ensures that the report always reflects the amount invoiced to the customer, instead of reporting a value that depends on other fields in the database that may change over time.

Table Relationships

Many people start out using a spreadsheet application like Excel to build a database. Unfortunately, a spreadsheet stores data as a two-dimensional worksheet (rows and columns) with no easy way to connect individual worksheets together. You must manually connect each cell of the worksheet to the corresponding cells in other worksheets—a tedious process at best.

Two-dimensional storage objects like worksheets are called *flat-file databases* because they lack the three-dimensional quality of relational databases. Figure 4.8 shows an Excel worksheet used as a flat-file database.

FIGURE 4.8

An Excel worksheet used as a flat-file database.

	A	B	C	D	E	F	G	H
1	EmployeeID	LastName	FirstName	Title	PayrollDate	CheckNumber	CheckAmount	
2	1	Davolio	Nancy	Marketing Manager	8/23/2016	10344	1417.38	
3	2	Fuller	Andrew	Vice President, Sales	8/23/2016	10345	3327.56	
4	3	Leverling	Janet	Sales Representative	8/23/2016	10346	1952.19	
5	4	Peacock	Margaret	Sales Representative	8/23/2016	10347	1417.38	
6	5	Buchanan	Steven	Sales Manager	8/23/2016	10348	2113.76	
7	6	Suyama	Michael	Sales Representative	8/23/2016	10349	2113.76	
8	7	King	Robert	Sales Representative	8/23/2016	10350	978.55	
9	8	Callahan	Laura	Inside Sales Coordinator	8/23/2016	10351	1952.19	
10	9	Dodsworth	Anne	Sales Representative	8/23/2016	10352	1952.19	
11	1	Davolio	Nancy	Marketing Manager	8/30/2016	10353	1417.38	
12	2	Fuller	Andrew	Vice President, Sales	8/30/2016	10354	3327.56	
13	3	Leverling	Janet	Sales Representative	8/30/2016	10355	1952.19	
14	4	Peacock	Margaret	Sales Representative	8/30/2016	10356	1417.38	
15	5	Buchanan	Steven	Sales Manager	8/30/2016	10357	1215.92	
16								
17								

Sheet1 ⊕

The problems with flat-file databases should be immediately apparent from viewing Figure 4.8. Notice that the employee information is duplicated in multiple rows of the worksheet. Each time a payroll check is issued to an employee, a new row is added to the worksheet. Obviously, this worksheet would rapidly become unmanageably large and unwieldy.

Consider the amount of work required to make relatively simple changes to the data in Figure 4.8. For example, changing an employee's title requires searching through numerous records and editing the data contained within individual cells, creating many opportunities for errors.

Through clever programming in the Excel VBA language, it would be possible to link the data in the worksheet shown in Figure 4.8 with another worksheet containing paycheck detail information. It would also be possible to programmatically change data in individual rows. But such Herculean efforts are not necessary when you harness the power of a relational database such as Access.

Connecting the data

A table's primary key uniquely identifies the records in a table. In a table of employee data, the employee's Social Security number, a combination of first and last names, or an employee ID might be used as the primary key. Let's assume the employee ID is selected as the primary key for the Employees table. When the relationship to the Payroll table is formed, the EmployeeID field is used to connect the tables together. Figure 4.9 shows this sort of arrangement (see the "One-to-many" section later in this chapter).

Some of the issues related to using natural keys (such as Social Security number) are discussed in the "Natural versus surrogate primary keys" section later in this chapter.

Although you can't see the relationship in Figure 4.9, Access knows it's there because a formal relationship has been established between tblEmployees and tblPayroll. (This process is described in the "Creating relationships and enforcing referential integrity" section later in this chapter.) Because of the relationship between these tables, Access is able to instantly retrieve all the records from tblPayroll for any employee in tblEmployees.

The relationship example shown in Figure 4.9, in which each record of tblEmployees is related to several records in tblPayroll, is the most common type found in relational database systems, but it's by no means the only way that data in tables is related. This book, and most books on relational databases such as Access, discusses the three basic types of relationships between tables:

- One-to-one
- One-to-many
- Many-to-many

Figure 4.10 shows most of the relationships in the Collectible Mini Cars database.

4

FIGURE 4.9

The relationship between the Employees and Payroll tables is an example of a typical one-to-many relationship.

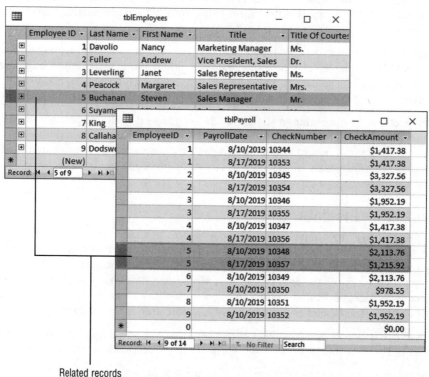

Related records

Notice that there are several one-to-many relationships between the tables (for example, tblSales-to-tblSalesLineItems, tblProducts-to-tblSalesLineItems, and tblCustomers-to-tblSales). The relationship that you specify between tables is important. It tells Access how to find and display information from fields in two or more tables. The program needs to know whether to look for only one record in a table or look for several records on the basis of the relationship. tblSales, for example, is related to tblCustomers as a many-to-one relationship. This is because the focus of the Collectible Mini Cars system is on sales. This means that there will *always* be only one customer related to every sales record. That is, many sales can be associated with a single customer. In this case, the Collectible Mini Cars system is actually using tblCustomers as a lookup table.

FIGURE 4.10

Most of the Collectible Mini Cars table relationships.

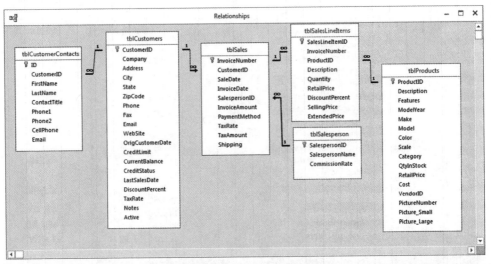

> **NOTE**
>
> Relationships can be very confusing—they depend upon the focus of the system. For example, when working with tblCustomers and tblSales, you can always create a query that has a one-to-many relationship to tblSales from tblCustomers. Although the system is concerned with sales (invoices), sometimes you'll want to produce reports or views that are customer related instead of invoice related. Because one customer can have more than one sale, there will always be one record in tblCustomers and at least one record in tblSales. In fact, there could be many related records in tblSales. So, Access knows to find only one record in the Customers table and to look for any records in the Sales table (one or more) that have the same customer number.

One-to-one

A one-to-one relationship between tables means that for every record in the first table, one and only one record exists in the second table. Figure 4.11 illustrates this concept.

Pure one-to-one relationships are not common in relational databases. In most cases, the data contained in the second table is included in the first table. As a matter of fact, one-to-one relationships are generally avoided because they violate the rules of normalization. Following the rules of normalization, data should not be split into multiple tables if the data describes a single entity. Because a person has one and only one birth date, the birth date should be included in the table containing a person's other data.

FIGURE 4.11

A one-to-one relationship.

There are times, however, when storing certain data along with other data in the table isn't a good idea. For example, consider the situation illustrated in Figure 4.11. The data contained in tblSecurityIDs is confidential. Normally, you wouldn't want anyone with access to the public customer information (name, address, and so on) to have access to the confidential security code that the customer uses for purchasing or billing purposes. If necessary, tblSecurityIDs could be located on a different disk somewhere on the network, or even maintained on removable media to protect it from unauthorized access.

Another instance of a one-to-one relationship is a situation known as *subtyping*. For example, your database may contain a Customers table and a Vendors table. If both your customers and vendors are businesses, a lot of the information for both entities may be similar. In that case, you may prefer to have a Companies table that contains all the data that is similar, such as CompanyName, Address, and TaxIdentificationNumber. Then your Customers and Vendors table would contain a reference to the Companies table and include additional fields that are particular to customers and vendors, respectively. The customer and vendor entities are subtypes of the companies and related one-to-one.

A common situation for one-to-one relationships is when data is being transferred or shared among databases. Perhaps the shipping clerk in an organization doesn't need to see all of a customer's data. Instead of including irrelevant information—such as job titles, birth dates, alternate phone numbers, and e-mail addresses—the shipping clerk's database contains only the customer's name, address, and other shipping information. A record in the Customers table in the shipping clerk's database has a one-to-one relationship with the corresponding record in the master Customers table located on the central computer somewhere within the organization. Although the data is contained within separate ACCDB files, the links between the tables can be *live* (meaning that changes to the master record are immediately reflected in the shipping clerk's ACCDB file).

One-to-many

A far more common relationship between tables in a relational database is the one-to-many. In one-to-many relationships, each record in the first table (the *parent*) is related to one or more records in the second table (the *child*). Each record in the second table is related to one and only one record in the first table.

Without a doubt, one-to-many relationships are the most common type encountered in relational database systems. Examples of one-to-many situations abound:

- **Customers and orders:** Each customer (the "one" side) has placed several orders (the "many" side), but each order is sent to a single customer.
- **Teacher and student:** Each teacher has many students, but each student has a single teacher (within a particular class, of course).
- **Employees and paychecks:** Each employee has received several paychecks, but each paycheck is given to one and only one employee.
- **Patients and appointments:** Each patient has zero or more doctor appointments, but each appointment is for one patient.

As we discuss in the "Creating relationships and enforcing referential integrity" section later in this chapter, Access makes it very easy to establish one-to-many relationships between tables. A one-to-many relationship is illustrated in Figure 4.12. This figure, using tables from the Northwind Traders database, clearly demonstrates how each record in the Customers table is related to several different records in the Orders table. An order can be sent to only a single customer, so all requirements of one-to-many relationships are fulfilled by this arrangement.

Although the records on the "many" side of the relationship illustrated in Figure 4.12 are sorted by the Customer field in alphabetical order, there is no requirement that the records in the "many" table be arranged in any particular order.

4

> **NOTE**
>
> Although *parent-child* is the most common expression used to explain the relationship between tables related in a one-to-many relationship, you may hear other expressions used, such as *master-detail*, applied to this design. The important thing to keep in mind is that the intent of referential integrity is to prevent lost records on the "many" side of the relationship. Referential integrity guarantees that there will never be an *orphan* (a child record without a matching parent record). As you work with related tables, it's important to keep in mind which table is on the "one" side and which is on the "many" side.

FIGURE 4.12

The Northwind Traders database contains many examples of one-to-many relationships.

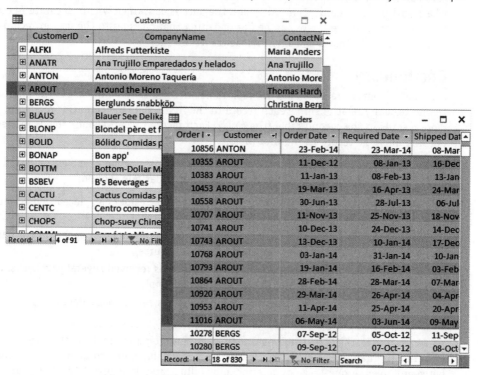

Notice how difficult it would be to record all the orders for a customer if a separate table were not used to store the order's information. The flat-file alternative discussed earlier in this section requires much more updating than the one-to-many arrangement shown in Figure 4.12. Each time a customer places an order with Northwind Traders, a new record is added to the Orders table. In a one-to-many arrangement, only the CustomerID (for example, AROUT) is added to the Orders table. The CustomerID is a foreign key that relates the order back to the Customers table. Keeping the customer information is relatively trivial because each customer record appears only once in the Customers table.

Many-to-many

You'll come across many-to-many situations from time to time. In a many-to-many arrangement, each record in both tables can be related to zero, one, or many records in the other table. An example is shown in Figure 4.13. Each student in tblStudents can belong to more than one club, while each club in tblClubs has more than one member.

As indicated in Figure 4.13, many-to-many relationships are somewhat more difficult to understand because they can't be directly modeled in relational database systems like Access. Instead, the many-to-many relationship is broken into two separate one-to-many relationships, joined through a linking table (called a *join table*). The join table has one-to-many relationships with both of the tables involved in the many-to-many relationship. This principle can be a bit confusing at first, but close examination of Figure 4.13 soon reveals the beauty of this arrangement.

In Figure 4.13, you can see that Jeffrey Walker (StudentID 12) belongs to both the Horticulture and Photography clubs (ClubID = 2 and ClubID = 3), an example of one student belonging to many clubs. You can also see that the French club (ClubID = 4) has Barry Williams and David Berry (StudentIDs 7 and 9), an example of one club having many students. Each student belongs to multiple clubs, and each club contains multiple members.

FIGURE 4.13

A database of students and the clubs they belong to is an example of a many-to-many relationship.

Because of the additional complication of the join table, many-to-many relationships are often considered more difficult to establish and maintain. Fortunately, Access makes such relationships easy to establish, if a few rules are followed. These rules are explained in various places in this book. For example, in order to update either side of a many-to-many relationship (for example, to change club membership for a student), the join table must contain the primary keys of both tables joined by the relationship.

Many-to-many relationships are common in business environments:

- **Lawyers to clients (or doctors to patients):** Each lawyer may be involved in several cases, while each client may be represented by more than one lawyer on each case.
- **Patients and insurance coverage:** Many people are covered by more than one insurance policy. For example, if you and your spouse are both provided medical insurance by your employers, you have multiple coverage.
- **Video rentals and customers:** Over a year's time, each video is rented by several people, while each customer rents more than one video during the year.
- **Magazine subscriptions:** Most magazines have circulations measured in the thousands or millions. Most people who subscribe to a magazine, subscribe to more than one at a time.

The Collectible Mini Cars database has a many-to-many relationship between tblCustomers and tblSalesPayments, linked through tblSales. Each customer might have purchased more than one item, and each item might be paid for through multiple payments. In addition to joining contacts and sales payments, tblSales contains other information, such as the sale date and invoice number. The join table in a many-to-many relationship often contains information regarding the joined data.

As shown in Figure 4.13 join tables can contain information other than the primary keys of the tables they join. The tblStudentToClubJoin table includes a field to record the date that the related student joined the related club.

Integrity Rules

Access permits you to apply referential integrity rules that protect data from loss or corruption. *Referential integrity* means that the relationships between tables are preserved during updates, deletions, and other record operations. The relational model defines several rules meant to enforce the referential integrity requirements of relational databases. In addition, Access contains its own set of referential integrity rules that are enforced by the ACE database engine.

Imagine a payroll application that contained no rules regulating how data in the database is used. It would be possible to issue payroll checks that aren't linked to an employee, for instance. From a business perspective, issuing paychecks to "phantom" employees is a very serious situation. Eventually, the issue will be noticed when the auditors step in and notify management of the discrepancy.

Referential integrity operates strictly on the basis of the tables' key fields. Referential integrity means that the database engine checks each time a key field (whether primary or foreign) is added, changed, or deleted. If a change to a value in a key field invalidates a relationship, it is said to violate referential integrity. Tables can be set up so that referential integrity is automatically enforced.

Figure 4.14 illustrates a relationship between a Customers table and a Sales table. tblCustomers is related to tblSales through the CustomerID field. The CustomerID field in tblCustomers is the primary key, while the CustomerID field in tblSales is a foreign key. The relationship connects each customer with a sales invoice. In this relationship, tblCustomers is the parent table, while tblSales is the child table.

Orphaned records are very bad in database applications. Because sales information is almost always reported as which products were sold to which customers, a sales invoice that is not linked to a valid customer will not be discovered under most circumstances. It's easy to know which products were sold to Fun Zone, but given an arbitrary sales record, it may not be easy to know that there is no valid customer making the purchase. In Figure 4.14, the invoice records related to Fun Zone are indicated by boxes drawn around the data in tblSales.

FIGURE 4.14

A typical database relationship.

Because the referential integrity rules are enforced by the Access database engine, data integrity is ensured wherever the data appears in the database: in tables, queries, or forms.

Once you've established the integrity requirements of your applications, you don't have to be afraid that data in related tables will become lost or disorganized.

We can't overemphasize the need for referential integrity in database applications. Many developers feel that they can use VBA code or user interface design to prevent orphaned records. The truth is that, in most databases, the data stored in a particular table may be used in many different places within the application, or even in other applications that use the data. Also, given the fact that many database projects extend over many years, and among any number of developers, it's not always possible to recall how data should be protected. By far, the best approach to ensuring the integrity of data stored in any database system is to use the power of the database engine to enforce referential integrity.

The general relational model referential integrity rules ensure that records contained in relational tables are not lost or confused. For obvious reasons, it's important that the primary keys connecting tables be protected and preserved. Also, changes in a table that affect other tables (for example, deleting a record on the "one" side of a one-to-many relationship) should be rippled to the other tables connected to the first table. Otherwise, the data in the two tables will quickly become unsynchronized.

No primary key can contain a null value

The first referential integrity rule states that no primary key can contain a null value. A *null value* is one that simply does not exist. The value of a field that has never been assigned a value (even a default value) is null. No row in a database table can have null in its primary key because the main purpose of the primary key is to guarantee uniqueness of the row. Obviously, null values cannot be unique, and the relational model would not work if primary keys could be null. Access will not allow you to set a field that already contains null values as the primary key.

Furthermore, Access can't evaluate a null value. Because a null value doesn't exist, it can't be compared with any other value. It isn't larger or smaller than any other value; it simply doesn't exist. Therefore, a null value can't be used to look up a record in a table or to form a relationship between two tables.

Access automatically enforces the first referential integrity rule. As you add data to tables, you can't leave the primary key field empty without generating a warning (one reason the AutoNumber field works so well as a primary key). Once you've designated a field in an Access table as the primary key, Access won't let you delete the data in the field, nor will it allow you to change the value in the field so that it duplicates a value in another record.

When using a composite primary key made up of several fields, all the fields in the composite key must contain values. None of the fields is allowed to be empty. The combination of values in the composite primary key must be unique.

All foreign key values must be matched by corresponding primary keys

The second referential integrity rule says that all foreign key values must be matched by corresponding primary keys. This means that every record in a table on the "many" (or child) side of a one-to-many relationship must have a corresponding record in the table on the "one" (or parent) side of the relationship. A record on the "many" side of a relationship without a corresponding record on the "one" side is said to be *orphaned* and is effectively removed from the database schema. Identifying orphaned records in a database can be very difficult, so you're better off avoiding the situation in the first place.

The second rule means the following:

- **Rows cannot be added to a "many" side table (the child) if a corresponding record does not exist on the "one" side (the parent).** If a child record contains a ParentID field, the ParentID value *must* match an existing record in the parent table.
- **The primary key value in a "one" side table cannot be changed if the change would create orphaned child records.**
- **Deleting a row on the "one" side must not orphan corresponding records on the "many" side.**

For example, in the sales example, the foreign key in each record in tblSales (the "many" side) must match a primary key in tblCustomers. You can't delete a record in tblCustomers (the "one" side) without deleting the corresponding records in tblSales.

One of the curious results of the rules of referential integrity is that it's entirely possible to have a parent record that isn't matched by any child records. Intuitively, this makes sense. A company may certainly have employees who haven't yet been issued paychecks. Or the Collectible Mini Cars company may hire a new employee who hasn't made any sales yet. Eventually, of course, most parent records are matched by one or more child records, but this condition is not a requirement of relational databases.

As you'll see in the next section, Access makes it easy to specify the integrity rules you want to employ in your applications. You should be aware, however, that not using the referential integrity rules means that you might end up with orphaned records and other data integrity problems.

Keys

When you create database tables, like those created in Chapter 3, you should assign each table a primary key. This key is a way to make sure that the table records contain only one unique value; for example, you may have several contacts named Michael Heinrich, and you may even have more than one Michael Heinrich (for example, father and son) living at the same address. So, in a case like this, you have to decide how you can create a record in the Customers database that will let you identify each Michael Heinrich separately.

Uniquely identifying each record in a table is precisely what a primary key field does. For example, using Collectible Mini Cars as an example, the CustomerID field (a unique number that you assign to each customer placing an order) is the primary key in tblCustomers—each record in the table has a different CustomerID number. (No two records have the same number.) This is important for several reasons:

- You don't want to have two records in tblCustomers for the same customer, because this can make updating the customer's record virtually impossible.
- You want assurance that each record in the table is accurate so that the information extracted from the table is accurate.
- You don't want to make the table (and its records) any larger than necessary. Adding redundant or duplicate fields and records just complicates the database without adding value.

The ability to assign a single, unique value to each record makes the table clean and reliable. This is known as *entity integrity*. By having a different primary key value in each record (such as the CustomerID in tblCustomers), you can tell two records (in this case, customers) apart, even if all other fields in the records are the same. This is important because you can easily have two individual customers with a common name, such as Fred Smith, in your table.

Theoretically, you could use the customer's name and address, but two people named Fred D. Smith could live in the same town and state, or a father and son (Fred David Smith and Fred Daniel Smith) could live at the same address. The goal of setting primary keys is to create individual records in a table that *guarantees* uniqueness.

If you don't specify a primary key when creating Access tables, Access asks whether you want one. If you say yes, Access uses the AutoNumber data type to create a primary key for the table. An AutoNumber field is automatically inserted each time a record is added to the table, and it can't be changed once its value has been established. Furthermore, once an AutoNumber value has appeared in a table, the value will never be reused, even if the record containing the value is deleted and the value no longer appears in the table. In fact, because an AutoNumber field is added to a new record before any of the other data, if the new row is not saved for some reason, the new AutoNumber is never used in the table at all.

Deciding on a primary key

As you learned earlier, a table normally has a field (or combination of fields)—the primary key for that table—which makes each record unique. The primary key is an identifier that is often a text, numeric, or AutoNumber data type. To determine the contents of this ID field, you specify a method for creating a unique value for the field. Your method can be as simple as letting Access automatically assign an AutoNumber value or using the first letter of the real value you're tracking along with a sequence number (such as A001, A002, A003, B001, B002, and so on). The method may rely on a random set of letters and numbers for the field content (as long as each field has a unique value) or a complicated calculation based on information from several fields in the table.

However, there is no reason why the primary key value has to be *meaningful* to the application. A primary key exists in a table solely to ensure uniqueness for each row and to provide an anchor for table relationships. Many Access developers routinely use AutoNumber fields as primary keys simply because they meet all the requirements of a primary key without contributing to an application's complexity.

In fact, meaningful primary keys can cause confusion as the data in the table changes. For example, if the primary key for a table of employee information is the first letter of the employee's last name plus a sequential number, then Jane Doe might have an EmployeeID of D001. If Jane were to get married and change her last name, her EmployeeID would no longer be consistent with the data in her record. Her EmployeeID may still be unique, but it may also cause confusion if someone were to rely on that data.

Table 4.1 lists the Collectible Mini Cars tables and describes one *possible* plan for deriving the primary key values in each table. As this table shows, it doesn't take a great deal of work (or even much imagination) to derive a plan for key values. Any rudimentary scheme with a good sequence number always works. Access automatically tells you when you try to enter a duplicate key value. To avoid duplication, you can simply add the value of 1 to the sequence number.

TABLE 4.1   Deriving the Primary Key

Table	Possible Derivation of Primary Key Value
tblCustomers	Companies: AutoNumber field assigned by Access
tblSales	Invoice Number: AutoNumber field
tblSalesLineItems	Invoice Number (from Sales) and an AutoNumber field
tblProducts	Product Number, entered by the person putting in a new product
tblSalesPayments	Invoice Number (from Sales) and an AutoNumber field
tblSalesperson	Sales Person ID: AutoNumber field
tblCategories	Category of Items: Entered by the person putting in a new record

Even though it isn't difficult to use logic (implemented, perhaps, though VBA code) to generate unique values for a primary key field, by far the simplest and easiest approach is to use AutoNumber fields for the primary keys in your tables. The special characteristics of the AutoNumber field (automatic generation, uniqueness, the fact that it can't be changed, and so on) make it the ideal candidate for primary keys. Furthermore, an AutoNumber value is nothing more than a 4-byte integer value, making it very fast and easy for the database engine to manage. For all these reasons, the Collectible Mini Cars exclusively uses AutoNumber fields as primary keys in its tables.

NOTE

AutoNumber fields are guaranteed to be unique, but they are not guaranteed to be sequential. There are a number of reasons why gaps in AutoNumbers can be introduced, such as deleting records, and you should never rely on AutoNumbers being sequential.

You may be thinking that all these sequence numbers make it hard to look up information in your tables. Just remember that, in most cases, you never look up information by an ID field. Generally, you look up information according to the *purpose* of the table. In tblCustomers, for example, you would look up information by customer name—last name, first name, or both. Even when the same name appears in multiple records, you can look at other fields in the table (zip code, phone number) to find the correct customer. Unless you just happen to know the customer ID number, you'll probably never use it in a search for information.

Looking at the benefits of a primary key

Have you ever placed an order with a company for the first time and then decided the next day to increase your order? When you call the people at the order desk, they may ask you for your customer number. You tell them that you don't know your customer number. Next, they ask you for some other information—generally, your zip code and last name. Then, as they narrow down the list of customers, they ask your address. Once they've located you in their database, they can tell you your customer number. Some businesses use phone numbers or e-mail addresses as starting points when searching for customer records.

Primary and foreign keys are discussed in Chapter 1, but because these concepts are so important in database applications, they're covered again in this chapter.

Database systems usually have more than one table, and the tables are related in some manner. For example, in the Collectible Mini Cars database, tblCustomers and tblSales are related to each other through the CustomerID field. Because each customer is *one* person or organization, you only need one record in tblCustomers.

Each customer can make many purchases, however, which means you need to set up a second table to hold information about each sale—tblSales. Again, each invoice is *one* sale (on a specific day at a specific time). CustomerID is used to relate the customer to the sales.

A *foreign key* in the child table (the CustomerID field in the tblSales table) is related to the *primary key* in the parent table (CustomerID in tblCustomers).

Besides being a common link field between tables, the primary key field in an Access database table has the following advantages:

- Primary key fields are always indexed, greatly speeding up queries, searches, and sorts that involve the primary key field.
- Access forces you to enter a value (or automatically provides a value, in the case of AutoNumber fields) every time you add a record to the table. You're guaranteed that your database tables conform to the rules of referential integrity.
- As you add new records to a table, Access checks for duplicate primary key values and prevents duplicate entries, thus maintaining data integrity.
- By default, Access displays your data in primary key order.

TIP

An *index* is a special internal file that is created to put the records in a table in some specific order. For example, the primary key field in tblCustomers is an index that puts the records in order by CustomerID field. Using an indexed table, Access uses the index to quickly find records within the table.

Designating a primary key

From the preceding sections, you're aware that choosing a table's primary key is an important step toward bulletproofing a database's design. When properly implemented, primary keys help stabilize and protect the data stored in your Access databases. As you read the following sections, keep in mind that the cardinal rule governing primary keys is that the values assigned to the primary key field within a table must be unique. Furthermore, the ideal primary key is stable.

Single-field versus composite primary keys

Sometimes, when an ideal primary key doesn't exist within a table as a single value, you may be able to combine fields to create a *composite* primary key. For example, it's unlikely that a first name or last name alone is enough to serve as a primary key, but by combining first and last names with birth dates, you may be able to come up with a unique combination of values to serve as the primary key. As you'll see in the "Creating relationships and enforcing referential integrity" section later in this chapter, Access makes it very easy to combine fields as composite primary keys.

There are several practical considerations when using composite keys:

- **None of the fields in a composite key can be null.**
- **Sometimes building a composite key from data naturally occurring within the table can be difficult.** Sometimes records within a table differ by one or two fields, even when many other fields may be duplicated within the table.
- **Each of the fields can be duplicated within the table, but the combination of composite key fields cannot be duplicated.**

4

However composite keys have a number of issues:

- **Composite keys tend to complicate a database's design.** If you use three fields in a parent table to define the table's primary key, the same three fields must appear in every child table.
- **Ensuring that a value exists for all the fields within a composite key (so that none of the fields is null) can be quite challenging.**

TIP

Most developers avoid composite keys unless absolutely necessary. In many cases, the problems associated with composite keys greatly outweigh the minimal advantage of using composite keys generated from data within the record.

Natural versus surrogate primary keys

Many developers maintain that you should use only natural primary keys. A *natural primary key* is derived from data already in the table, such as a Social Security number or employee number. If no single field is enough to uniquely identify records in the table, these developers suggest combining fields to form a *composite primary key*.

However, there are many situations where no "perfect" natural key exists in database tables. Although a field like SocialSecurityNumber may seem to be the ideal primary key, there are a number of problems with this type of data:

- **The value is not universal.** Not everyone has a Social Security number.
- **The value may not be known at the time the record is added to the database.** Because primary keys can never be null, provisions must be made to supply some kind of "temporary" primary key when the Social Security number is unknown, and then other provisions must be made to fix up the data in the parent and child tables once the value becomes known.
- **Values such as Social Security number tend to be rather large.** A Social Security number is at least nine characters, even omitting the dashes between groups of numbers. Large primary keys unnecessarily complicate things and run more slowly than smaller primary keys.
- **Legal and privacy issues inhibit its use.** A Social Security number is considered "personally identifiable information" and (in the United States) its use is limited under the Social Security Protection Act of 2005.

CAUTION

By far the largest issue is that adding a record to a table is impossible unless the primary key value is known at the time the record is committed to the database. Even if temporary values are inserted until the permanent value is known, the amount of fix-up required in related tables can be considerable. After all, unless Cascade Update is enabled on the relationship, you can't change the value of a primary key if related child records exist in other tables.

Although an AutoNumber value does not naturally occur in the table's data, because of the considerable advantages of using a simple numeric value that is automatically generated and cannot be deleted or changed, in most cases an AutoNumber is the ideal primary key candidate for most tables.

Creating primary keys

A primary key is created by opening a table in Design view, selecting the field(s) that you want to use as a primary key, and clicking the Primary Key button on the Table Tools Design tab of the Ribbon. If you're specifying more than one field to create a composite key, hold down the Ctrl key while using the mouse to select the fields before clicking the Primary Key button.

 Setting a table's primary key is covered in detail in Chapter 3.

Creating relationships and enforcing referential integrity

The Relationships window lets you establish the relationships and referential integrity rules that you want to apply to the tables involved in a relationship. Creating a permanent, managed relationship that ensures referential integrity between Access tables is easy:

1. **Select Database Tools ⇨ Relationships.** The Relationships window appears.

2. **Click the Show Table button on the Ribbon, or right-click the Relationships window and select Show Table from the shortcut menu.** The Show Table dialog box (shown in Figure 4.15) appears.

FIGURE 4.15

Double-click a table name to add it to the Relationships window.

3. **Add tblBookOrders5 and tblBookOrderDetails to the Relationships window (double-click each table in the Show Table dialog box, or select each table and click the Add button).**

4. **Create a relationship by dragging the primary key field in the "one" table and dropping it on the foreign key in the "many" table.** Alternatively, drag the foreign key field and drop it on the primary key field.

   For this example, drag OrderID from tblBookOrders5 and drop it on OrderID in tblBookOrderDetails. Access immediately opens the Edit Relationships dialog box (shown in Figure 4.16) to enable you to specify the details about the relationship you intend to form between the tables. Notice that Access recognizes the relationship between tblBookOrders5 and tblBookOrderDetails as a one-to-many.

5. **Check the Enforce Referential Integrity checkbox.** In Figure 4.16, notice the Cascade Delete Related Records check box. If this check box is left unchecked, Access won't permit you to delete records in tblBookOrders5 (the "one" table) until all the corresponding records in tblBookOrderDetails (the "many" table) are first deleted. With this box checked, deletions across the relationship "cascade" automatically. Cascading deletes can be a dangerous operation because the deletions in the "many" table occur without confirmation.

FIGURE 4.16

You enforce referential integrity in the Edit Relationships dialog box.

6. **Click the Create button.** Access draws a line between the tables displayed in the Relationships window, indicating the type of relationship. In Figure 4.17, the 1 symbol indicates that tblBookOrders5 is the "one" side of the relationship while the infinity symbol (∞) designates tblBookOrderDetails as the "many" side.

FIGURE 4.17

A one-to-many relationship between tblBookOrders5 and tblBookOrderDetails.

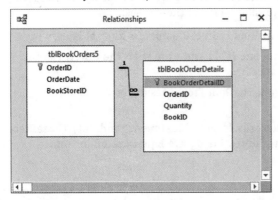

Specifying the join type between tables

The right side of the Edit Relationships dialog box has four buttons:

- **Create:** The Create button returns you to the Relationships window with the changes specified.
- **Cancel:** The Cancel button cancels the current changes and returns you to the Relationships window.
- **Join Type:** The Join Type button opens the Join Properties dialog box.
- **Create New:** The Create New button lets you specify an entirely new relationship between the two tables and fields.

By default, when you process a query on related tables, Access returns only records that appear in both tables. Considering the payroll example from the "Integrity Rules" section earlier in this chapter, this means that you would see only employees who have valid paycheck records in the paycheck table. You wouldn't see any employees who haven't yet received a paycheck. Such a relationship is sometimes called an *inner join* because the only records that appear are those that exist on *both* sides of the relationship.

However, the inner join is not the only type of join supported by Access. Click the Join Type button to open the Join Properties dialog box. The alternative settings in the Join Properties dialog box allow you to specify that you prefer to see all the records from either the parent table or child table, regardless of whether they're matched on the other side. (It's possible to have an unmatched child record as long as the foreign key in the child table is null.) Such a join (called an *outer join*) can be very useful because it accurately reflects the state of the data in the application.

4

In the case of the Collectible Mini Cars example, seeing all the customers, regardless of whether they have records in the Sales table, is what you're shooting for. To specify an outer join connecting customers to sales, perform these steps:

1. **From the Relationships window, add tblCustomers and tblSales.**

2. **Drag the CustomerID from one table and drop it on the other.** The Edit Relationships dialog box appears.

3. **Click the Join Type button.** The Join Properties dialog box (shown in Figure 4.18) appears.

4. **Select the Include ALL Records from 'tblCustomers' and Only Those Records from 'tblSales' Where the Joined Fields Are Equal option button.**

FIGURE 4.18

The Join Properties dialog box, used to set up the join properties between tblCustomers and tblSales. Notice that it specifies all records from the Customers table.

5. **Click OK.** You're returned to the Edit Relationships dialog box.

6. **Click Create.** You're returned to the Relationships window. The Relationships window should now show an arrow going from the Customers table to the Sales table. At this point, you're ready to set referential integrity between the two tables on an outer join relationship.

> **TIP**
>
> To change an existing relationship, double-click the line in the Relationships window for the relationship you'd like to change. The Edit Relationships dialog box appears, and you can change referential integrity and join type settings.

Given the join properties shown in Figure 4.18, any time the Customers and Sales tables are involved in a query, all the customer records are returned by default, even if a customer hasn't yet placed any orders. This setting should give a more complete impression of the company's customer base instead of restricting the returned records to customers who've placed orders.

Establishing a join type for every relationship in your database isn't absolutely necessary. In the following chapters, you'll see that you can specify outer joins for each query in your application. Many developers choose to use the default inner join for all the relationships in their databases and to adjust the join properties on each query to yield the desired results.

Enforcing referential integrity

After using the Edit Relationships dialog box to specify the relationship, to verify the table and related fields, and to specify the type of join between the tables, you should set referential integrity between the tables. Select the Enforce Referential Integrity check box in the lower portion of the Edit Relationships dialog box to indicate that you want Access to enforce the referential integrity rules on the relationship between the tables.

CAUTION

If you choose not to enforce referential integrity, you can add new records, change key fields, or delete related records without warnings about referential integrity violations—thus, making it possible to change critical fields and damaging the application's data. With no integrity active, you can create tables that have orphans (Sales without a Customer). With normal operations (such as data entry or changing information), referential integrity rules should be enforced.

Enforcing referential integrity also enables two other options that you may find useful— cascading updates and cascading deletes. These options are near the bottom of the Edit Relationships dialog box (refer to Figure 4.16).

NOTE

You might find, when you select Enforce Referential Integrity and click the Create button (or the OK button if you've reopened the Edit Relationships dialog box to edit a relationship), that Access won't allow you to create a relationship and enforce referential integrity. The most likely reason for this behavior is that you're asking Access to create a relationship that violates referential integrity rules, such as a child table with orphans in it. In such a case, Access warns you by displaying a dialog box similar to the one shown in Figure 4.19. The warning happens in this example because there are some records in the Sales table with no matching value in the Salesperson table. This means that Access can't enforce referential integrity between these tables because the data within the tables already violates the rules.

TIP

To solve any conflicts between existing tables, you can create a Find Unmatched query by using the Query Wizard to find the records in the "many" table that violate referential integrity. Then you can convert the Unmatched query to a Delete query to delete the offending records or add the appropriate value to the SalespersonID field.

You could remove the offending records, return to the Relationships window, and set referential integrity between the two tables. Whether it's appropriate to clean up data by deleting records depends entirely on the business rules governing the application. Deleting orders just because referential integrity can't be enforced would be considered a bad idea in most environments.

FIGURE 4.19

A dialog box warning that referential integrity can't be enforced because of integrity violations.

Choosing the Cascade Update Related Fields option

If you specify Enforce Referential Integrity in the Edit Relationships dialog box, Access enables the Cascade Update Related Fields check box. This option tells Access that, as a user changes the contents of a related field (the primary key field in the primary table—CustomerID, for example), the new CustomerID is rippled through all related tables.

> **NOTE**
> If the primary key field in the primary table is a related field between several tables, the Cascade Update Related Fields option must be selected for all related tables or it won't work.

Generally speaking, however, there are very few reasons why the value of a primary key may change. The example we give in the "Connecting the data" section earlier in this chapter, of a missing Social Security number, is one case where you may need to replace a temporary Social Security number with the permanent Social Security number after employee data has been added to the database. However, when using an AutoNumber or another surrogate key value, there is seldom any reason to have to change the primary key value once a record has been added to the database. In fact, an AutoNumber primary key cannot be changed.

Choosing the Cascade Delete Related Records option

The Cascade Delete Related Records option instructs Access to delete all related child records when a parent record is deleted. Although there are instances in which this option can be quite useful, the cascading deletes option comes with a number of warnings.

For example, if you've chosen Cascade Delete Related Records and try to delete a particular customer (who moved away from the area), Access first deletes all the related records from the child tables—Sales and SalesLineItems—and then deletes the customer record. In other words, Access deletes all the records in the sales line items for each sale for each customer—the detail items of the sales, the associated sales records, and the customer record—with one step.

Perhaps you can already see the main problem with cascading deletes. If all of a customer's sales records are deleted when the customer record is deleted, you have no way of properly reporting sales for the period. You couldn't, for instance, reliably report on the previous year's sales figures because all the sales records for "retired" customers have been deleted from the database. Also, in this particular example, you would lose the opportunity to report on sales trends, product category sales, and a wide variety of other uses of the application's data.

It would make much more sense to use an Active field (Yes/No data type) in the Customers table to indicate which customers are still active. It would be quite easy to include the Active field in queries where only current customers are needed (Active = Yes) and ignore the Active field in queries where all sales (regardless of the customer's active status) are required.

> **TIP**
>
> To use the Cascade Delete Related Records option, you must specify Cascade Delete Related Records for all the table's relationships in the database. If you don't specify this option for all the tables in the chain of related tables, Access won't cascade deletions.

In general, it's probably not a good idea to enable cascading deletes in a database. It's far too easy to accidentally delete important data. Consider a situation where a user accidentally deletes a customer, wiping out the customer's entire sales history, including payments, shipping, backorders, promotions, and other activities. There are very few situations where users should be permitted to delete many different types of data as a single action.

Viewing all relationships

With the Relationships window open, click All Relationships on the Relationship Tools Design tab of the Ribbon to see all the relationships in the database. If you want to simplify the view you see in the Relationships window, you can "hide" a relationship by deleting the tables you see in the Relationships window. Click a table, press the Delete key, and Access removes the table from the Relationships window. Removing a table from the Relationships window doesn't delete any relationships between the table and other tables in the database.

When building database tables, make sure that the Required property of the foreign key field in the related table (in the case of tblBookOrders5 and tblBookOrderDetails, the foreign key is OrderID in tblBookOrderDetails) is set to Yes. This action forces the user to enter a value in the foreign key field, providing the relationship path between the tables.

The relationships formed in the Relationships window are permanent and are managed by Access. When you form permanent relationships, they appear in the Query Design window by default as you add the tables. (Queries are discussed in detail in Part III.) Even without permanent relationships between tables, you form temporary relationships any time you include multiple tables in the Query Design window.

4

Deleting relationships

During the design phase, even in meticulously planned designs, table structures change, which may necessitate deleting and re-establishing some of the relationships. The Relationships window is simply a picture of the relationships between tables. If you open the Relationships window, click each of the tables in the relationship, and press the Delete key, you delete the picture of the tables in the relationship, but not the relationship itself. You must first click the line connecting the tables and press Delete to delete the relationship, and then delete each of the table pictures to completely remove the relationship.

Following application-specific integrity rules

In addition to the referential integrity rules enforced by the ACE Database Engine, you can establish a number of business rules that are enforced by the applications you build in Access. In many cases, your clients or users will tell you the business rules that must be enforced by the application. It's up to you as the developer to compose the Visual Basic code, table design, field properties, and so on that implement the business rules expected by your users.

Typical business rules include items such as the following:

- The order-entry clerk must enter his ID number on the entry form.
- Quantities can never be less than zero.
- The unit selling price can never be less than the unit cost.
- The order ship date must come after the order date.

Often these rules are added to a table at design time. Enforcing such rules goes a long way toward preserving the value of the data managed by the database. For example, in Figure 4.20, the ValidationRule property of the Quantity field (>=0) ensures that the quantity can't be a negative number. If the inventory clerk tries to put a negative number into the Quantity field, an error message box pops up containing the validation text: Must not be a negative number.

You can also establish a table-wide validation rule using the Validation Rule property on the table's Property Sheet that provides some protection for the data in the table. Unfortunately, only one rule can be created for the entire table, making it difficult to provide specific validation text for all possible violations.

The Validation Rule property has some limitations. For instance, you can't use user-defined functions in a rule. Also, you can't reference other fields, data in other records, or other tables in your rules. Validation rules prevent user entry rather than provide warnings that the user can bypass. If you need to provide a warning but still allow the user to continue, you shouldn't use a validation rule.

FIGURE 4.20

A simple validation rule goes a long way toward preserving the database's integrity.

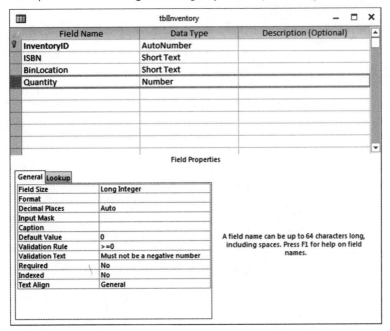

You can read examples of using VBA to enforce business rules throughout this book.

Working with Access Tables

IN THIS CHAPTER

Understanding datasheets

Looking at the Datasheet window

Opening a datasheet

Entering new data

Navigating records

Changing values in a datasheet

Using the Undo feature

Copying and pasting values in a datasheet

Replacing values in a datasheet

Adding records to a datasheet

Deleting records from a datasheet

Displaying records in a datasheet

Sorting and filtering records

Aggregating data

Printing records

I n this chapter, you'll use a datasheet to enter data into an Access table and display the data many different ways. Using Datasheet view allows you to see many records at once, in the familiar spreadsheet-style format. In this chapter, you'll work with tblContacts and tblProducts to add, change, and delete data, as well as learn about different features available in Datasheet view.

ON THE WEB

This chapter uses the database named `Chapter05.accdb`. If you haven't already downloaded it from this book's website, you'll need to do so now.

Understanding Datasheets

Using a datasheet is just one of the ways to view data in Access. A datasheet is visually similar to a spreadsheet in that it displays data as a series of rows and columns. Figure 5.1 shows a typical Datasheet view of a table. Each row represents a single record, and each column represents a single field in the table. Scroll up or down in the datasheet to see the rows (records) that don't fit on the screen; scroll left or right to see the columns (fields) that don't fit.

FIGURE 5.1

A typical Datasheet view. Each row represents a single record in the table; each column represents a single field (like Description or ModelYear) in the table.

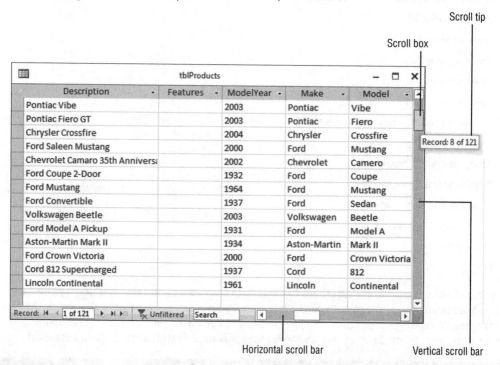

> **NOTE**
>
> Many of the behaviors described in this chapter apply equally to Access forms. Most Access forms display data from a single record at a time, and interacting with the data on such a form is much like working with data in a single row of a datasheet.

You can customize datasheets, which allows you to view data in many ways. For example, you can change the font size, column widths, and row heights to make more or less of the data fit on the screen. Or you can rearrange the order of the rows and/or columns to organize the records and fields logically. You can also lock columns, making them stay in position as you scroll to other parts of the datasheet, or hide them to make them disappear. To hide records, you can filter data that doesn't match specific criteria.

> **NOTE**
>
> You can view both tables and queries in Datasheet view. Even forms can be displayed as datasheets. Depending on the source of your data, some of the datasheet behaviors described in this chapter may not work exactly as described. This is particularly true when the underlying data source is a query or form. With these data sources, you might find the datasheet is read only.

A Quick Review of Records and Fields

A *table* is a container for storing related information—customer records, a holiday card list, birthday reminders, payroll information, and so on. Each table has a formal structure comprised of fields, each with a unique name to identify and describe the stored information and a specific data type—Short Text, Number, Date/Time, and so on—to limit what users enter in these fields. When displayed in a *datasheet* (a two-dimensional sheet of information), Access displays these fields in columns.

The table is comprised of records that hold information about a single entity (like a single customer or a single product). One record is made up of information stored in the fields of the table structure. For example, if a table has three fields—name, address, and phone number—then the first record only has one name, one address, and one phone number in it. The second record also has one name, one address, and one phone number in it.

A datasheet is an ideal way of looking at many of the table's records at once. A single record appears as a row in the datasheet; each row contains information for that specific record. The fields appear as columns in the datasheet; each column contains an individual field's contents. This row-and-column format lets you see lots of data at once.

Looking at the Datasheet Window

The datasheet arranges the records initially by primary key and arranges the fields by the order in the table design. At the top of the Access window, you see the title bar (displaying the database filename), the Quick Access toolbar, and the Ribbon. At the bottom of the Access window, you see the status bar, which displays information about the datasheet. For example, it might contain field description information, error messages, warnings, or a progress bar.

5

Generally, error messages and warnings appear in dialog boxes in the center of the screen rather than in the status bar. If you hover the mouse over items in the status bar, a ScreenTip appears with a short message about what it is or what it does.

The right side of the Datasheet window contains a scroll bar for displaying a different subset of records (assuming all of the records don't fit on one screen). As you scroll, a scroll tip (shown in Figure 5.1) tells you which record will be the first visible record. The size of the scroll box (the part of the scroll bar that moves) gives you a proportional look at how many of the total number of records are being displayed. The bottom of the Datasheet window also contains a scroll bar for displaying different fields (left to right). The Navigation buttons for moving among records also appear in the bottom-left corner of the Datasheet window.

Moving within a datasheet

You easily move within the Datasheet window using the mouse to indicate where you want to change or add to your data—just click a field within a record. In addition, the Ribbon tabs, scroll bars, and Navigation buttons make it easy to move among fields and records. Think of a datasheet as a spreadsheet without the row numbers and column letters. Instead, columns have field names, and rows are unique records that have identifiable values in each cell.

Table 5.1 lists the navigational keys you use for moving within a datasheet.

TABLE 5.1 Navigating in a Datasheet

Navigational Direction	Keystrokes
Next field	Tab
Previous field	Shift+Tab
First field of current record	Home
Last field of current record	End
Next record	Down arrow ($\downarrow$)
Previous record	Up arrow ($\uparrow$)
First field of first record	Ctrl+Home
Last field of last record	Ctrl+End
Scroll down one page	PgDn
Scroll up one page	PgUp
Scroll right one page	Ctrl+PgDn
Scroll left one page	Ctrl+PgUp

Using the Navigation buttons

The *Navigation buttons* (shown in Figure 5.2) are the six controls located at the bottom of the Datasheet window, which you use to move to a different record. The two leftmost controls move you to the first record or the previous record in the datasheet, respectively. The three rightmost controls position you on the next record, last record, or new record in the datasheet, respectively. If you know the record number (the row number of a specific record), you can click the record-number box, enter a record number, and press Enter.

FIGURE 5.2

The Navigation buttons of a datasheet.

NOTE

If you enter a record number greater than the number of records in the table, an error message appears stating that you can't go to the specified record.

Examining the Datasheet Ribbon

The Datasheet Ribbon (shown in Figure 5.3) provides a way to work with the datasheet. The Home tab has some familiar objects on it, as well as some new ones. This section provides an overview of the groups on the Home tab; the individual commands are described in more detail later in this chapter.

FIGURE 5.3

The Datasheet Ribbon's Home tab.

We explain how to customize the Ribbon in Chapter 30.

Views

The Views group allows you to switch between Datasheet view and Design view. You can see both choices by clicking the View command's downward-pointing arrow. Clicking Design View permits you to make changes to the object's design (table, query, and so on). Clicking Datasheet View returns you to the datasheet.

Clipboard

The Clipboard group contains the Cut, Copy, and Paste commands. These commands work like the commands in other applications (such as Word and Excel). The Paste command's down arrow gives you three choices: Paste, Paste Special, and Paste Append. Paste Special gives you the option of pasting the contents of the Clipboard in different formats (text, CSV, records, and so on). Paste Append pastes the contents of the Clipboard as a new record—as long as a row with a similar structure was copied to the Clipboard.

Sort & Filter

The Sort & Filter group lets you change the order of the rows, as well as limit the rows being displayed, based on the criteria you want.

Records

The Records group lets you save, delete, or add a new record to the datasheet. It also contains commands to show totals, check spelling, freeze and hide columns, and change the row height and field width.

Find

The Find group lets you find and replace data and go to specific records in the datasheet. Use the Select command to select a record or all records.

Window

The Window group includes two buttons that help you control the items (forms, reports, tables, and so on) that are open in the main Access window:

- **Size to Fit Form:** The Size to Fit Form button resizes the form in the window to fit the size set when the form was created. By default, Access forms have a sizeable border, which means the user might drag the form to a new size. The Size to Fit Form button restores a form to the size specified at design time.
- **Switch Windows:** The Switch Windows button lets you choose a different open window to work with. A form or report needed by the user might be under another form or report, and the Switch Windows button provides a quick way to select which object is on top of the other objects in the Access main window.

> **NOTE**
>
> The Window group does not show on the Home tab if you're using tabbed documents (the default setting in Access 2019). To change between overlapping windows and tabbed documents, set the Document Window Options in the Current Database section of Access Options.

Text Formatting

The Text Formatting group lets you change the look of text fields in the datasheet. Use these commands to change the font, size, bold, italic, color, and so on. Selecting a font attribute (such as bold) applies the attribute to all fields in the datasheet. (See the following Note for the only exception to this rule.) Use the Align Left, Align Right, and Center commands to align the data in the selected column. Click the Gridlines command to toggle gridlines on and off. Use the Alternate Row Color or Background Color command to change the colors of alternating rows or to make them all the same.

> **NOTE**
>
> The controls in the Text Formatting group behave differently when the currently selected field in the datasheet happens to be the Long Text data type. When a Long Text field is selected, you can change the font attributes (bold, underline, italics, and so on) of individual characters and words in the field, but only if the Text Format property is set to Rich Text. The Text Format property (which applies only to the Long Text data type) is set to Plain Text by default.

Opening a Datasheet

Follow these steps to open a datasheet from the Database window:

1. **Using the `Chapter05.accdb` database from this book's website, click Tables in the Navigation pane.**
2. **Double-click the table name you want to open (in this example, tblProducts).**

An alternative method for opening the datasheet is to right-click tblProducts and select Open from the shortcut menu.

> **TIP**
>
> If you're in any of the design windows, click the Datasheet View command in the View group of the Ribbon to view your data in a datasheet.

Entering New Data

All the records in your table are visible when you first open it in Datasheet view. If you just created your table, the new datasheet doesn't contain any data. Figure 5.4 shows an empty

5

datasheet and a portion of the Fields tab of the Ribbon. When the datasheet is empty, the first row contains an asterisk (*) in the record selector, indicating it's a new record.

FIGURE 5.4

An empty datasheet. Notice that the first record is blank and has an asterisk in the record selector.

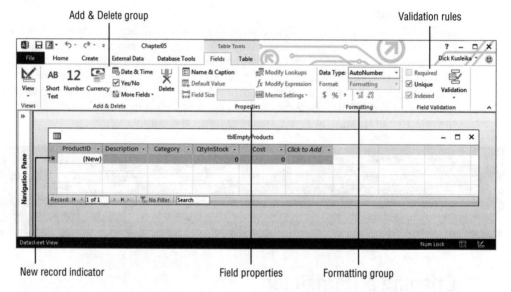

The Table Tools tab group of the Ribbon includes virtually all the tools needed to build a complete table. You can specify the data type, default formatting, indexing, field and table validation, and other table construction tasks from the controls in the Table Tools tab group.

The New row appears at the bottom of the datasheet when the datasheet already contains records. Click the New command in the Records group of the Ribbon, or click the New Record button in the group of Navigation buttons at the bottom of the datasheet to move the cursor to the New row—or simply click the last row, which contains the asterisk. The asterisk turns into a pencil when you begin entering data, indicating that the record is being edited. A new row—containing an asterisk—appears below the one you're entering data into. The new record pointer always appears in the last row of the datasheet. Figure 5.5 shows adding a new record to tblProducts.

FIGURE 5.5

Entering a new record into the Datasheet view of tblProducts.

Description	Features	ModelYear	Make
Reo Touring		1917	Reo
Buick Roadmaster		1949	Buick
Ducati 996		2001	Ducati
Chrysler LeBaron		1932	Chrysler
Cleveland 40 Roadster		1920	Cleveland
Chrysler Imperial		1955	Chrysler
Cadillac Fleetwood		1938	Cadillac
Studebaker Avanti		1963	Studebaker
Ford Coupe		1940	Ford
Chrysler Town and Country		1948	Chrysler
Reo Touring		1917	Reo
Packard LeBaron		1930	Packard
Harley Davidson FLHRC Road King		2001	Harley Davidso
Hummer Hard Top		2002	Hummer
Ducati Monster		2001	Ducati
1990 BMW M3		1990	BMW

Record: I◄ ◄ 121 of 121 ► ►I ►⊞ 🏷Unfiltered Search

Edit indicator   New row   Edited cell

To add a new record to the open Datasheet view of tblProducts, follow these steps:

1. Click the New button in the Records group of the Home tab of the Ribbon.

2. Type in values for all fields of the table, moving between fields by pressing the Enter key or the Tab key.

When adding or editing records, you might see three different record pointers:

- **Record being edited:** A pencil icon
- **Record is locked (multiuser systems):** A padlock icon
- **New record:** An asterisk icon

CAUTION

If the record contains an AutoNumber field, Access shows the name (New) in the field. You can't enter a value in this type of field; instead, simply press the Tab or Enter key to skip the field. Access automatically puts the number in when you begin entering data.

5

Saving the record

Moving to a different record saves the record you're editing. Tabbing through all the fields, clicking the Navigation buttons, clicking Save in the Records group of the Ribbon, and closing the table all write the edited record to the database. You'll know the record is saved when the pencil disappears from the record selector.

To save a record, you must enter valid values into each field. The fields are validated for data type, uniqueness (if indexed for unique values), and any validation rules that you've entered into the Validation Rule property. If your table has a primary key that's not an AutoNumber field, you'll have to make sure you enter a unique value in the primary key field to avoid the error message shown in Figure 5.6. One way to avoid this error message while entering data is to use an AutoNumber field as the table's primary key.

FIGURE 5.6

The error message Access displays when attempting to save a record with a duplicate primary key value entered into the new record. Use an AutoNumber field as your primary key to avoid this error.

> **TIP**
>
> The Undo button in the Quick Access toolbar reverses changes to the current record and to the last saved record. After you change a second record, you can't undo a previously saved record.

> **TIP**
>
> You can save the record to disk without leaving the record by pressing Shift+Enter.

Now you know how to enter, edit, and save data in a new or existing record. In the next section, you learn how Access validates your data as you make entries into the fields.

Understanding automatic data-type validation

Access validates certain types of data automatically. Therefore, you don't have to enter any data validation rules for these data types when you specify table properties. The data types that Access automatically validates include:

- Number/Currency
- Date/Time
- Yes/No

Access validates the data type when you move off the field. When you enter a letter into a Number or Currency field, you don't initially see a warning that the characters are invalid. When you tab out of the field or click a different field, you get a warning like the one shown in Figure 5.7. This particular warning lets you choose to enter a new value or change the column's data type to Text. You'll see this message if you enter other invalid characters (symbols, letters, and so on), enter more than one decimal point, or enter a number too large for the specified numeric data type.

FIGURE 5.7

The warning Access displays when entering data that doesn't match the field's data type. Access gives you a few choices to correct the problem.

Access validates Date/Time fields for valid date or time values. You'll see a warning similar to the one shown in Figure 5.7 if you try to enter a date such as 14/45/05, a time such as 37:39:12, or an invalid character in a Date/Time field.

Yes/No fields require that you enter one of these defined values:

- **Yes:** Yes, True, On, −1, or a number other than 0 (which displays as −1)
- **No:** No, False, Off, or 0

5

Of course, you can define your own acceptable values in the Format property for the field, but generally these values are the only acceptable ones. If you enter an invalid value, the warning appears with the message to indicate an inappropriate value.

> **TIP**
>
> The default value of a Yes/No field's Display Control is Check Box. Displaying a check box in Yes/No fields prevents users from entering invalid data.

Knowing how properties affect data entry

Because field types vary, you use different data-entry techniques for each type. In the "Saving the record" section earlier in this chapter, you learned that some data-type validation is automatic. Designing tblContacts, however, means entering certain user-defined format and data validation rules. The following sections examine the types of data entry.

Standard text data entry

The first field—ContactID—in tblContacts is an AutoNumber field, while other fields in the table are Short Text fields. After skipping ContactID, you simply enter a value in each field and move on. The zipcode field uses an input mask (00000\-9999;0;_) for data entry. The Phone and Fax fields also use an input mask (!\(999") "000\-0000;0;_). A 0 in an input mask represents a required numeric entry. A 9 in an input mask represents an optional numeric entry. The zipcode input mask requires the first five digits, but the plus 4 portion is optional. Short Text fields accept any characters, unless you restrict them with an input mask.

> **TIP**
>
> To enter multiple lines in a Short Text or Long Text field, press Ctrl+Enter to add a new line. This is useful, for example, in large text strings for formatting a multiple-line address field.

Date/Time data entry

The OrigCustDate and LastSalesDate fields in tblContacts are Date/Time data types, which both use a Short Date format (3/16/2019). However, you could have defined the format as Medium Date (16-Mar-19) or Long Date (Saturday, March 16, 2019). Using either of these formats simply means that no matter how you type in the date—using month and year; day, month, and year; or month, day, and year—the date always displays in the specified format (short date [3/16/2019], medium date [16-Mar-19], or long date [Saturday, March 16, 2019]). Therefore, if you type 3/16/19 or 16 Mar 19, Access displays the value in the specified format as you leave the field. Dates are actually stored in the database without any formatting, so the format you select for a field doesn't affect how the data is stored.

NOTE

Formats affect only the display of the data. They don't change storage of data in the table.

CAUTION

In general, it isn't a good idea to apply an input mask on Date/Time data. Microsoft Access does a more than adequate job of validating date and time values. You're far more likely to encounter data entry problems with an input mask on a date-containing control than you are to avoid trouble by using an input mask.

Number/Currency data entry with data validation

The CreditLimit field in tblContacts has a validation rule assigned to it. It has a Validation Rule property to limit the amount of credit to less than $250,000. If the rule is violated, a dialog box appears with the validation text entered for the field. If you want to allow a contact to have $250,000 or more of credit, change the validation rule in the table design.

The exact currency character used by Access (in this case, the dollar sign) is determined by the regional options set in the Region and Language Settings in Windows Settings.

OLE object data entry

You can enter Object Linking and Embedding (OLE) object data into a datasheet, even though you don't see the object. An OLE Object field holds many different item types, including:

- Bitmap pictures
- Sound files
- Business graphs
- Word or Excel files

Any object that an OLE server supports can be stored in an Access OLE Object field. OLE objects are generally entered into a form so you can see, hear, or use the value. When OLE objects appear in datasheets, you see text that tells what the object is (for example, you may see Bitmap Image in the OLE Object field). You can enter OLE objects into a field in two ways:

- By pasting from the Clipboard
- By right-clicking the OLE Object field and selecting Insert Object from the shortcut menu

Long Text field data entry

The Features field in tblProducts is a Long Text data type. This type of field allows up to 1GB of text for each field. As you enter text into a Long Text field, you see only a few

5

characters at a time—the rest of the string scrolls out of sight. Pressing Shift+F2 displays a Zoom window with a scroll bar (see Figure 5.8) that lets you see more characters at a time. Click the Font button at the bottom of the window to view all the text in a different font or size. (The font in Figure 5.8 has been enlarged considerably over the 8-point default font size for the Zoom window.)

FIGURE 5.8

The Zoom window. Notice that you can see all of the field's data event at a larger font size.

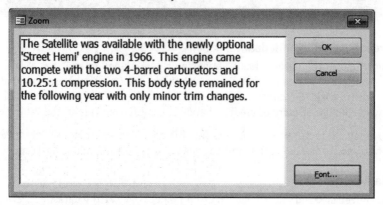

When you first display text in the Zoom window, all the text is selected. You can deselect the text by clicking anywhere in the window. If you accidentally delete all the text or change something you didn't want to change, click Cancel to exit back to the datasheet with the field's original data.

> **TIP**
> Use the Zoom window (Shift+F2) when designing Access objects (tables, forms, reports, and queries) to see text that normally scrolls out of view.

Navigating Records in a Datasheet

Wanting to make changes to records after you've entered them is not unusual. You might need to change records because you receive new information that changes existing values or because you discover errors in existing values.

When you decide to edit data in a table, the first step is to open the table, if it isn't already open. From the list of tables in the Navigation pane, double-click tblProducts to open it in

Datasheet view. If you're already in Design view for this table, click the Datasheet View button to switch views.

When you open a datasheet in Access that has related tables, a column with a plus sign (+) is added to indicate the related records, or subdatasheets. Click a row's plus sign to open the subdatasheet for the row.

Moving between records

You can move to any record by scrolling through the records and positioning your cursor on the desired record. With a large table, scrolling through all the records might take a while, so you'll want to use other methods to get to specific records quickly.

Use the vertical scroll bar to view more records. The scroll bar arrows move one record at a time. To move through many records at a time, drag the scroll box or click the areas between the scroll box and the scroll bar arrows.

> **TIP**
> Watch the scroll tip when you use a scroll bar to move to another area of the datasheet. Access doesn't update the record number box until you click a field.

Use the five Navigation buttons (refer to Figure 5.2) to move between records. You simply click these buttons to move to the desired record. If you know the record number (the row number of a specific record), click the record number box, enter a record number, and press Enter.

Also, use the Go To command in the Find group of the Ribbon to navigate to the First, Previous, Next, Last, and New records.

Finding a specific value

Although you can move to a specific record (if you know the record number) or to a specific field in the current record, usually you'll want to find a certain value in a record. You can use one of these methods for locating a value in a field:

- Select the Find command (a magnifying glass) from the Find group of the Ribbon.
- Press Ctrl+F.
- Use the Search box at the bottom of the Datasheet window.

The first two methods display the Find and Replace dialog box (shown in Figure 5.9). To limit the search to a specific field, place your cursor in the field you want to search before you open the dialog box. Change the Look In drop-down list to Current Document to search the entire table for the value.

5

FIGURE 5.9

The Find and Replace dialog box. The fastest way to activate it is to simply press Ctrl+F.

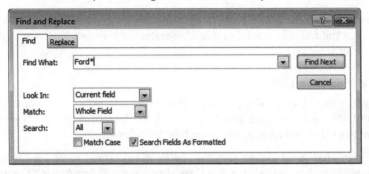

The Find and Replace dialog box lets you control many aspects of the search. Enter the value you want to search for in the Find What combo box, which contains a list of recently used searches. You can enter a specific value or choose to use wildcard characters. Table 5.2 lists the wildcard characters available in the Find dialog box.

TABLE 5.2   Wildcard Characters

Character	Description	Example
* (asterisk)	Matches any number of characters	Ford* finds Ford Mustang
? (question mark)	Matches any single character	F?rd finds Ford
[ ] (brackets)	Matches one of a list of characters	19[67]1 finds 1961 and 1971
! (exclamation point)	With brackets, excludes a list of characters	19[!67]1 finds 1951 but not 1961
- (hyphen)	With brackets, matches a range of characters	196[2–8] finds 1962 to 1968
# (hash)	Matches one number	1:## finds 1:18 but not 1:9

You can combine wildcard characters for more robust searches. For example, 196[!2–8] will find 1961 and 1969, but nothing in between.

The Match drop-down list contains three choices:

- **Any Part of Field:** If you select Any Part of Field, Access searches to see whether the value is contained anywhere in the field. This search finds Ford anywhere in the field, including values like Ford Mustang, 2008 Ford F-150, and Ford Galaxy 500.
- **Whole Field:** The default is Whole Field, which finds fields containing exactly what you've entered. For example, the Whole Field option finds Ford only if the value in the field being searched is exactly Ford, and nothing else.
- **Start of Field:** A search for Ford using the Start of Field option searches from the beginning of the field and returns all the rows containing Ford as the first four characters of the description.

In addition to these drop-down lists, you can use two check boxes at the bottom of the Find and Replace dialog box:

- **Match Case:** Match Case determines whether the search is case sensitive. The default is not case sensitive (not checked). A search for SMITH finds smith, SMITH, or Smith. If you check the Match Case check box, you must then enter the search string in the exact case of the field value. (The data types Number, Currency, and Date/Time don't have any case attributes.)

  If you've checked Match Case, Access doesn't use the value Search Fields As Formatted (the second check box), which limits the search to the actual values displayed in the table. (If you format a field for display in the datasheet, you should check the box.)

- **Search Fields As Formatted:** The Search Fields As Formatted check box, the selected default, finds only text that has the same pattern of characters as the text specified in the Find What box. Clear this box to find text regardless of the formatting. For example, if you're searching the Cost field for a value of $16,500, you must enter the comma if Search Fields As Formatted is checked. Uncheck this box to search for an unformatted value (16500).

CAUTION

Checking Search Fields As Formatted may slow the search process.

The search begins when you click the Find Next button. If Access finds the value, the cursor highlights it in the datasheet. To find the next occurrence of the value, click the Find Next button again. The dialog box remains open so that you can find multiple occurrences. Choose one of three search direction choices (Up, Down, or All) in the Search drop-down list to change the search direction. When you find the value that you want, click Close to close the dialog box.

5

Use the search box at the bottom of the Datasheet window (refer to Figure 5.1) to quickly search for the first instance of a value. When using the search box, Access searches the entire datasheet for the value in any part of the field. If you enter **FORD** in the search box, the datasheet moves to the closest match as you type each letter. First, it finds a field with *F* as the first character, then it finds *FO*, and so on. Once it finds the complete value, it stops searching. To find the next instance, press the Enter key.

Changing Values in a Datasheet

If the field that you're in has no value, you can type a new value into the field. When you enter new values into a field, follow the same rules as for a new record entry.

Manually replacing an existing value

Generally, you enter a field with either no characters selected or the entire value selected. If you use the keyboard (Tab or arrow keys) to enter a field, you select the entire value. (You know that the entire value is selected when it's displayed in reverse video.) When you begin to type, the new content replaces the selected value automatically.

When you click in a field, the value is not selected. To select the entire value with the mouse, use any of these methods:

- Click just to the left of the value when the cursor is shown as a large plus sign.
- Click to the left of the value, hold down the left mouse button, and drag the mouse to select the whole value.
- Click in the field and press F2.

> **TIP**
>
> You may want to replace an existing value with the value from the field's Default Value property. To do so, select the value and press Ctrl+Alt+Spacebar. To replace an existing value with that of the same field from the preceding record, press Ctrl+' (apostrophe). Press Ctrl+; (semicolon) to place the current date in a field.

> **CAUTION**
>
> Pressing Ctrl+- (minus sign) deletes the current record. Access will ask you to confirm a deletion before any data is lost.

Changing an existing value

If you want to change an existing value instead of replacing the entire value, use the mouse and click in front of any character in the field to activate Insert mode; the existing value moves to the right as you type the new value. If you press the Insert key, your entry changes to Overtype mode; you replace one character at a time as you type. Use the arrow keys to move between characters without disturbing them. Erase characters to the left by pressing Backspace, or to the right of the cursor by pressing Delete.

Table 5.3 lists editing techniques.

TABLE 5.3 **Editing Techniques**

Editing Operation	Keystrokes
Move the insertion point within a field.	Press the right-arrow (→) and left-arrow (←) keys.
Insert a value within a field.	Select the insertion point and type new data.
Toggle entire field and insertion point.	Press F2.
Move insertion point to the beginning of the field.	Press the Home key.
Move insertion point to the end of the field.	Press the End key.
Select the previous character.	Press Shift+left-arrow (←) key.
Select the next character.	Press Shift+right-arrow (→) key.
Select from the insertion point to the beginning of the word.	Press Ctrl+Shift+left-arrow (←) key.
Select from the insertion point to the end of the word.	Press Ctrl+Shift+right-arrow (→) key.
Select from the insertion point to the beginning of the field.	Press Ctrl+Shift+Home.
Select from the insertion point to the end of the field.	Press Ctrl+Shift+End.
Replace an existing value with a new value.	Select the entire field and type a new value.
Replace a value with the value of the previous field.	Press Ctrl+' (apostrophe).
Replace the current value with the default value.	Press Ctrl+Alt+Spacebar.
Insert a line break in a Short Text or Long Text field.	Press Ctrl+Enter.
Save the current record.	Press Shift+Enter or move to another record.
Insert the current date.	Press Ctrl+; (semicolon).
Insert the current time.	Press Ctrl+: (colon).
Add a new record.	Press Ctrl++ (plus sign).
Delete the current record.	Press Ctrl+− (minus sign).
Toggle values in a check box or option button.	Press Spacebar.
Undo a change to the current field.	Press Esc or click the Undo button.
Undo a change to the current record.	Press Esc or click the Undo button a second time after you undo the current field.

5

Fields That You Can't Edit

Some fields cannot be edited, such as:

- **AutoNumber fields:** Access maintains AutoNumber fields automatically, calculating the values as you create each new record. AutoNumber fields can be used as the primary key.

- **Calculated fields:** Forms or queries may contain fields that are the result of expressions. These values are not actually stored in your table and are not editable.

- **Fields in multiuser locked records:** If another user is editing a record, it can be locked and you can't edit any fields in that record.

Using the Undo Feature

The Undo button on the Quick Access toolbar is often dimmed because there's nothing to undo. As soon as you begin editing a record, however, you can use this button to undo the typing in the current field. You can also undo a change with the Esc key; pressing Esc cancels any changes to a field that you're actively editing or cancels the changes to the last field you edited if you're not currently editing a field. Pressing Esc twice undoes changes to the entire current record.

After you type a value into a field, click the Undo button to undo changes to that value. After you move to another field, you can undo the change to the preceding field's value by clicking the Undo button. You can also undo all the changes to an unsaved current record by clicking the Undo button after you undo a field. After you save a record, you can still undo the changes by clicking the Undo button. However, after the next record is edited, changes to the previous record are permanent.

> **CAUTION**
>
> Don't rely on the Undo command to save you after you edit multiple records. When working in a datasheet, changes are saved when you move from record to record, and you can undo changes only to the current record.

Copying and Pasting Values

Copying or cutting data to the Clipboard is performed by Microsoft Office or Microsoft Windows, depending on the type of data; it isn't a specific function of Access. After you cut or copy a value, you can paste into another field or record by using the Paste command in the Clipboard group of the Ribbon. You can cut, copy, or paste data from any Windows application or from one task to another in Access. Using this technique, you can copy entire records between tables or databases, and you can copy datasheet values to and from Word and Excel.

The Paste command's down arrow gives you three choices:

- **Paste:** Inserts the contents of the Clipboard into one field
- **Paste Special:** Gives you the option of pasting the contents of the Clipboard in different formats (text, CSV, records, and so on)
- **Paste Append:** Pastes the contents of the Clipboard as a new record—provided a row with a similar structure was copied

> **TIP**
>
> Select a record or group of records using the record selector to cut or copy one or more records to the Clipboard. Then use Paste Append to add them to a table with a similar structure.

Replacing Values

To replace an existing value in a field, you can manually find the record to update, or you can use the Find and Replace dialog box. Display the Find and Replace dialog box using these methods:

- Select the Replace command from the Find group of the Ribbon.
- Press Ctrl+H.

The Find and Replace dialog box allows you to replace a value in the current field or in the entire table. Use it to find a certain value and replace it with a new value everywhere it appears in the field or table.

After the Find and Replace dialog box is active, select the Replace tab and type in the value that you want to find in the Find What box. After you've selected all the remaining search options (turn off Search Fields As Formatted, for example), click the Find Next button to find the first occurrence of the value. To change the value of the current found item (under the cursor), enter a value in the Replace With box and click the Replace button. For example, Figure 5.10 shows that you want to find the value Mini Vans in the current field and change it to Minivans.

You can select your search options on the Find tab and then select the Replace tab to continue the process. However, it's far easier to simply do the entire process using the Replace tab. Enter the value you want to find and the value that you want to replace it with. After you've completed the dialog box with all the correct information, select one of the command buttons on the side:

- **Find Next:** Finds the next field that has the value in the Find What field.
- **Cancel:** Closes the form and performs no find and replace.
- **Replace:** Replaces the value in the current field only. (Note: You must click the Find Next button first.)

5

■ **Replace All:** Finds all the fields with the Find What value and replaces them with the Replace With value. Use this if you're sure that you want to replace all the values; double-check the Look In drop-down list to make sure you don't replace the values in the entire datasheet if you don't want to.

FIGURE 5.10

The Find and Replace dialog box with the Replace tab showing. In this case, you want to replace Mini Vans with Minivans.

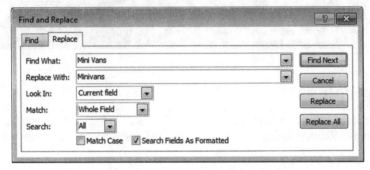

Adding New Records

There are a number of ways to add a record to a datasheet:

■ Click the datasheet's last line, where the record pointer is an asterisk.
■ Click the New (blank) record navigation button (the furthest button on the right).
■ Click the New command from the Records group of the Ribbon.
■ Choose Go To ⇨ New from the Find group of the Ribbon.
■ Move to the last record and press the down-arrow (↓) key.
■ Press Ctrl++ (plus sign).
■ Right-click any record selector and choose New Record from the shortcut menu. The new record is still appended to the bottom regardless of which record's selector you click.

Once you move to a new record, enter data into the desired fields and save the record.

Deleting Records

To delete records, select one or more records using the record selectors, and then press the Delete key, click the Delete command in the Records group of the Ribbon, or right-click a record's selector. The Delete command's drop-down list contains the Delete Record command, which deletes the current record, even if it isn't selected. When you delete a record, a dialog box asks you to confirm the deletion (see Figure 5.11). If you select Yes, the records are deleted; if you select No or press the Esc key, no changes are made.

CAUTION

The Default value for this dialog box is Yes. Pressing the Enter key automatically deletes the records. If you accidentally erase records using this method, the action can't be reversed.

FIGURE 5.11

The Delete Record dialog box warns you that you're about to delete a specific number of records. The default response is Yes (okay to delete), so be careful when deleting records.

CAUTION

If you have relationships set between tables and checked Enforce Referential Integrity—for example, the tblContacts (Customer) table is related to tblSales—then you can't delete a parent record (tblContacts) that has related child records (in tblSales) unless you also check the Cascade Delete Related Records check box. Otherwise, you receive an error message dialog box that reports: `The record can't be deleted or changed because the table '<tablename>' includes related records.`

To select multiple contiguous records, click the record selector of the first record that you want to select and drag the mouse to the last record that you want to select. Or click to select the first record, and then hold the Shift key and click the last record that you want in the selection.

TIP

To select multiple contiguous records with the keyboard, press Shift+Spacebar to select the current record and Shift+down-arrow (↓) key or Shift+up-arrow (↑) key to extend the selection to neighboring records.

5

Displaying Records

A number of techniques can increase your productivity when you add or change records. Change the field order, hide and freeze columns, change row height or column width, change display fonts, and change the display or remove gridlines to make data entry easier.

Changing the field order

By default, Access displays the fields in a datasheet in the same order in which they appear in the table design. Sometimes, you want to see certain fields next to each other in order to better analyze your data. To rearrange your fields, select a column by clicking the column heading, and then drag the column to its new location (as shown in Figure 5.12).

FIGURE 5.12

Select and drag a column to change the field order.

Description	Features	ModelYear	Make	Model	Ca
Alfa-Romeo GT Coupe		2004	Alfa-Romeo	GT	Spe
Ford GT40 Concept Car		2002	Ford	GT40	
Dodge Viper RT/10		2003	Dodge	Viper	
Chrysler ME Four-Twelve		2004	Chrysler		
Ford F-100 Tow Truck		1956	Ford	F-100	Tru
ALF 700 Pumper Truck		1954	ALF	Fire Truck	Tru
Mack CF Pumper		1968	Mack	Fire Truck	Tru
E-One Rescue Truck		1999	E-One	Fire Truck	Tru
White Delivery Van		1920	White	Truck	Tru
Chrysler Airflow		1936	Chrysler	Coupe	
Hudson 3 Window		1930	Hudson	Coupe	
Ford Model T Pickup		1932	Ford	Model T	Tru
Volvo XC90		2004	Volvo	XC90	
Pontiac GTO		1969	Pontiac	GTO	
Hummer Soft Top		2002	Hummer		
Jaguar E-Type		1971	Jaguar		
Lincoln Model K		1937	Lincoln		

Record: 1 of 121   Unfiltered   Search

You can select and drag columns one at a time, or select multiple columns to move at the same time. Suppose you want ModelYear to appear before Features in the tblProducts datasheet. Follow these steps to make this change:

1. **Position the mouse pointer over the ModelYear column heading.** The cursor changes to a down arrow.

2. **Click to select the column.** The entire ModelYear column is now highlighted.

3. **Release the mouse button.**

4. **Click the mouse button on the column heading again.** The pointer changes to an arrow with a box under it.

5. **Drag the column to the left, between the Description and Features fields.** A thin black column appears between them (refer to Figure 5.12).

6. **Release the mouse button.** The column moves in front of the Features field of the datasheet.

With this method, you can move any individual field or contiguous field selection. To select multiple fields, click and drag the mouse across multiple column headings. Then you can move the fields left or right or past the right or left boundary of the window.

> **NOTE**
>
> Moving fields in a datasheet does not affect the field order in the table design.

Changing the field display width

You can change the *field display width* (column width) either by specifying the width in a dialog box (in number of characters) or by dragging the column border. When you hover the mouse over a column border, the cursor changes to the double-arrow symbol.

To widen a column or to make it narrower, follow these steps:

1. **Place the mouse pointer between two column names on the field separator line.** The mouse pointer turns into a small line with arrows pointing to the left and right—if you have it in the correct location.

2. **Drag the column border to the left to make the column smaller or to the right to make it larger.**

> **TIP**
>
> You can instantly resize a column to the best fit (based on the longest visible data value) by double-clicking the right column border after the cursor changes to the double arrow.

> **NOTE**
>
> Resizing the column doesn't change the number of characters allowed in the table's field size. You're simply changing the amount of viewing space for the data contained in the column.

Alternatively, you can resize a column by right-clicking the column header and selecting Field Width from the shortcut menu to display the Column Width dialog box, as shown in Figure 5.13. Set the Column Width box to the number of characters you want to fit in the column or click the Standard Width check box to set the column to its default size. Click Best Fit to size the column to the widest visible value.

5

FIGURE 5.13

The Column Width dialog box.

Changing the record display height

You might need to increase the row height to accommodate larger fonts or text that uses multiple lines. Change the record (row) height of all rows by dragging a row's border to make the row height larger or smaller.

When you drag a record's border, the cursor changes to the vertical two-headed arrow you see at the left edge of Figure 5.14.

To increase or decrease a row's height, follow these steps:

1. **Place the mouse pointer between record selectors of two rows.** The cursor changes to the double-pointing arrow (up and down).

2. **Drag the row border up to shrink all row heights or down to increase all row heights.**

You can also resize rows by choosing More ⇨ Row Height in the Records group of the Ribbon. The Row Height dialog box appears; there you enter the row height in point size. Check the Standard Height check box to return the rows to their default size.

FIGURE 5.14

Changing a row's height. Position the mouse as shown and drag to the desired height.

Description	⌄	Features	⌄	ModelYear	⌄	Make	⌄	Model	⌄	Category	⌄
Alfa-Romeo GT Coupe				2004		Alfa-Romeo		GT		Special Intere	
Ford GT40 Concept Car				2002		Ford		GT40			
Dodge Viper RT/10				2003		Dodge		Viper			
Chrysler ME Four-Twelve				2004		Chrysler					
Ford F-100 Tow Truck				1956		Ford		F-100		Trucks	
ALF 700 Pumper Truck				1954		ALF		Fire Truck		Trucks	
Mack CF Pumper				1968		Mack		Fire Truck		Trucks	
E-One Rescue Truck				1999		E-One		Fire Truck		Trucks	
White Delivery Van				1920		White		Truck		Trucks	
Chrysler Airflow				1936		Chrysler		Coupe			
Hudson 3 Window				1930		Hudson		Coupe			
Ford Model T Pickup				1932		Ford		Model T		Trucks	
Volvo XC90				2004		Volvo		XC90			
Pontiac GTO				1969		Pontiac		GTO			
Hummer Soft Top				2002		Hummer					
Jaguar E-Type				1971		Jaguar					
Lincoln Model K				1937		Lincoln					

Record: ◄ ◄ 81 of 121 ► ►► ►▣ ▼x Unfiltered Search

> **CAUTION**
>
> If you drag a record's gridline up to meet the gridline immediately above it in the previous record, all rows are hidden. This also occurs if you set the row height close to 0 (for example, a height of 0.1) in the Row Height dialog box. In that case, you must use the Row Height dialog box to set the row height to a larger number to redisplay the rows.

Changing display fonts

By default, Access displays all data in the datasheet in the Calibri 11-point Regular font. Use the commands and drop-down lists in the Text Formatting group of the Ribbon (shown in Figure 5.15) to change the datasheet's text appearance.

5

FIGURE 5.15

Changing the datasheet's font directly from the Ribbon. Choose font type style, size, and other font attributes for the entire datasheet.

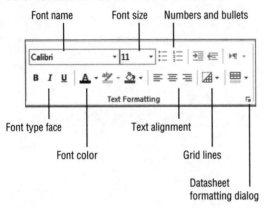

Setting the font display affects the entire datasheet. If you want to see more data on the screen, you can use a very small font. You can also switch to a higher-resolution display size if you have the necessary hardware. If you want to see larger characters, you can increase the font size or click the Bold button.

Displaying cell gridlines and alternate row colors

Normally gridlines appear between fields (columns) and between records (rows). You can set how you want the gridlines to appear using the Gridlines command in the Text Formatting group of the Ribbon (shown in Figure 5.15). Choose from the following options in the Gridlines drop-down list:

- Gridlines: Both
- Gridlines: Horizontal
- Gridlines: Vertical
- Gridlines: None

Use the Background Color and Alternate Row Color drop-down lists, also in the Text Formatting group, to change the background colors of the datasheet. The Background Color palette changes the color of all the rows in the datasheet. The Alternate Row Color palette changes the color of the even-numbered rows. When Alternate Row Color is set, the Background Color palette only affects the odd-numbered rows. To remove coloring from alternate rows, set Alternate Row Color to No Color.

After changing the gridline settings or alternate row colors, Access will ask whether to save the changes to the datasheet's layout. Be sure to click Yes if you want to make the changes permanent.

The Datasheet Formatting dialog box (shown in Figure 5.16) gives you complete control over the datasheet's look. Open this dialog box by clicking the Datasheet Formatting launcher in the bottom-right corner of the Text Formatting group of the Ribbon. Use the Flat, Sunken, and Raised option buttons under Cell Effect to change the grid to a 3-D look. Click the Horizontal and Vertical check boxes under Gridlines Shown to toggle which gridlines you want to see. Change the Background Color, Alternate Background Color, and Gridline Color using the available color palettes. The sample in the middle of the dialog box shows you a preview of changes.

FIGURE 5.16

Use the Datasheet Formatting dialog box to customize the look of the datasheet.

Use the Border and Line Styles drop-down lists to change the look of the gridlines. You can change the styles for the Datasheet Border and the Column Header Underline. Choose a different line style for each of the selections in the first drop-down list. The different line styles you can select from include:

- Transparent Border
- Solid
- Dashes
- Short Dashes
- Dots
- Sparse Dots
- Dash-Dot
- Dash-Dot-Dot
- Double Solid

5

Figure 5.17 shows a datasheet with dashes instead of solid lines and a higher contrast between alternating rows. You can use the various colors and styles to customize the datasheet's look to your liking.

FIGURE 5.17

Different line styles and row colors for the datasheet.

	ContactID	ContactType	FirstName	LastName	Company	A
⊞	1	Buyer	John	Jones	Nopa Auto Par	112
+	2	Seller	Hank	Masters	Jiffy Auto Sale:	62:
⊞	3	Both	Larry	Minkler	All Start Autos	971
+	11	Both	Joe	Hammerman	Columbia Chev	10!
⊞	12	Buyer	Cary	James	James Auto Par	59 !
+	13	Buyer	Mark	Uno	Fillion Sales Ar	89(
⊞	14	Buyer	Brandon	Aley	Tip Top Chevy	191
+	15	Both	Michael	Dennis	Newbury Auto	75
⊞	16	Both	Mark	Martin	Peekskill Sales	51
+	17	Both	Karl	Johnson	KJ Auto Repair	35(
⊞	18	Both	William	Gleason	R & G Monda Ir	19€
+	19	Both	Alex	Tomaso	Tires National	46
⊞	20	Both	Karla	Hayes	Hayes Auction:	54
+	21	Seller	Teresa	Aikins	Middletown A(	10(
⊞	22	Both	John	Marino	Bill Thomas Sal	98€
+	23	Both	Donald	Peterson	Yantic Auto Par	8 O
⊞	24	Seller	Dennie	Parkson	ACC Car Sales	96:
+	25	Buyer	Ann	Bond	A-1 Auto Sales	54

Record: I◄ ◄ 14 of 58 ► ►I ►▣ No Filter Search

Aligning data in columns

Align the data to the left or right, or center it within a column using the alignment buttons. Choose alignments different from the default alignments Access chooses based on a field's data type (text aligns left, numbers/dates align right). Follow these steps to change the alignment of the data in a column:

1. **Position the cursor anywhere within the column that you want to change the alignment.**

2. **Click the Align Left, Center, or Align Right commands in the Text Formatting group of the Ribbon (refer to Figure 5.15) to change the alignment of the column's data.**

Hiding and unhiding columns

Hide columns by dragging the column gridline to the preceding field or by setting the column width to 0:

1. **Position the cursor anywhere within the column that you want to hide.**

2. **Choose More ⇨ Hide Fields in the Records group of the Ribbon.** The column disappears because the column width is simply set to 0. You can hide multiple columns by first selecting them and then choosing More ⇨ Hide Fields.

After you've hidden a column, you can redisplay it by choosing More ⇨ Unhide Fields in the Records group of the Ribbon. A dialog box appears, letting you selectively unhide columns by checking next to each field (see Figure 5.18). Click Close to return to the datasheet showing the desired columns. You can also use this dialog box to hide one or more columns by unchecking the check box next to each field you want to hide.

FIGURE 5.18

Hide and unhide columns using the Unhide Columns dialog box.

Freezing columns

When you want to scroll left and right among many columns but want to keep certain columns from scrolling out of view, choose More ⇨ Freeze Fields in the Records group of the Ribbon. With this command, for example, you can keep the ProductID and Description fields visible while you scroll through the datasheet to find the product's features. The frozen columns are visible on the far-left side of the datasheet while other fields scroll horizontally out of sight. The fields must be contiguous if you want to freeze more than one at a time.

5

(Of course, you can first move your fields to place them next to each other.) When you're ready to unfreeze the datasheet columns, simply choose More ⇨ Unfreeze All Fields.

> **TIP**
>
> When you unfreeze columns, the column doesn't move back to its original position. You must move it back manually.

Saving the changed layout

When you close the datasheet, you save all your data changes, but you might lose all your layout changes. As you make all these display changes to your datasheet, you probably won't want to make them again the next time you open the same datasheet. If you make any layout changes, Access prompts you to save the changes to the layout when you close the datasheet. Choose Yes to save the changes. You can also save the layout changes manually by clicking Save on the Quick Access toolbar.

> **CAUTION**
>
> If you're following the example, don't save the changes to tblProducts if you want your screen to match the figures in the rest of this chapter.

Saving a record

Access saves each record when you move off it. Pressing Shift+Enter or selecting Save from the Records group of the Ribbon saves a record without moving off it. Closing the datasheet also saves a record.

Sorting and Filtering Records in a Datasheet

The Sort & Filter group of the Ribbon (shown in Figure 5.19) lets you rearrange the order of the rows and reduce the number of rows. Using the commands in this group, you'll display the records you want in the order you want to see them. The following sections demonstrate how to use these commands.

FIGURE 5.19

The Sort & Filter group lets you change the record order and reduce the number of visible rows.

Sorting records

You can sort selected columns into either ascending or descending order using the Ascending and Descending commands in the Sort & Filter group. To use these commands, click in a field you want to sort by, and then click Ascending or Descending. The data redisplays instantly in the sorted order. Right-clicking a column and selecting either of the Sort buttons also sorts the data. The captions on the right-click menu change depending on the data type of the field. Short Text fields display Sort A to Z and Sort Z to A, while numeric fields display Sort Smallest to Largest and Sort Largest to Smallest. Some fields, such as OLE and Long Text fields, can't be sorted.

To sort your data on the basis of values in multiple fields, highlight more than one column: Highlight a column (see the "Changing the field order" section earlier in this chapter) and before you release the mouse button, drag the cursor to the right or left. When you select one of the sort commands, Access sorts the records into major order (by the first highlighted field) and then into orders within orders (based on subsequent fields). If you need to select multiple columns that aren't contiguous (next to each other), you can move them next to each other (see the "Changing the field order" section earlier in this chapter).

> **TIP**
> To display the records in their original order, use the Remove Sort command in the Sort & Filter group of the Ribbon.

> **TIP**
> Another way you can select multiple columns is to click a column header and release the mouse button. Then, while holding down the Shift key, click and release another column header. All of the columns between the columns will be selected.

Filtering a selection

Filter by Selection lets you select records on the basis of the current field value. For example, using tblProducts, place your cursor in a row containing Trucks in the Category column, click the Selection command in the Sort & Filter group of the Ribbon, and choose Equals "Trucks." Access filters the datasheet to show only those records where the Category is trucks.

Access gives you four choices when you click the Selection command:

- Equals "Trucks"
- Does Not Equal "Trucks"
- Contains "Trucks"
- Does Not Contain "Trucks"

The area to the right of the Navigation buttons—at the bottom of the Datasheet window—tells you whether the datasheet is currently filtered; in addition, the Toggle Filter command on the Ribbon is highlighted, indicating that a filter is in use. When you click this command, it removes the filter. The filter specification doesn't go away; it's simply turned off. Click the Toggle Filter command again to apply the same filter.

Filtering by selection is additive. You can continue to select values, each time clicking the Selection command.

TIP

Right-click the field content that you want to filter by and then select from the available menu choices.

If you want to further specify a selection and then see everything that *doesn't* match that selection (for example, where the Make field isn't Chevrolet), move the cursor to the field (the Make field where the value is Chevrolet), right-click the datasheet, and then select Does Not Equal "Chevrolet" from the filter options that appear in the shortcut menu.

When using the Selection command on numeric or date fields, select Between from the available commands to enter a range of values. Enter the smallest and largest numbers or oldest and newest dates to limit the records to values that fall in the desired range.

Imagine using this technique to review sales by salespeople for specific time periods or products. Filtering by selection provides incredible opportunities to drill down into successive layers of data. Even when you click the Toggle Filter command to redisplay all the records, Access still stores the query specification in memory. Figure 5.20 shows the filtered datasheet, with the Filter by Selection list still open on the Category field.

When a datasheet is filtered, each column has an indicator in the column heading letting you know if a filter is applied to that column. Hover the mouse over the indicator to see a ScreenTip displaying the filter. Click the indicator to specify additional criteria for the column using the shortcut menu shown in Figure 5.21. Click the column heading's down-arrow for an unfiltered column to display a similar menu.

The menu contains commands to sort the column in ascending or descending order, clear the filter from the field, select a specific filter, and check values you want to see in the datasheet. The available commands change based on the data type of the column. In this case, Text Filter lets you enter a criterion that filters the data based on data you type in.

The check boxes in this menu contain data that appear in the column. In this case, the choices are: (Select All), (Blanks), and one entry for each Make in the table. The Mack entry is unchecked in this example. Click (Select All) to see all the records regardless of this field's value. Click (Blanks) to see the records that don't contain data. Select any of the data values to limit the records where the field contains the selected values. Place a check next to each Make you'd like to see and remove the check for each Make you want to exclude.

FIGURE 5.20

Using Filter by Selection. In this case, you see all trucks that are not Mack models.

FIGURE 5.21

Filtering the Make field. Use the column filter menu to select criteria for a field.

If you want to filter data but you can't find the value that you want to use and you know the value, click the Text Filters (or Number Filters, Date Filters, and so on) command and choose one of the available commands (Equals, Does Not Equal, Begins With, and so on) to display a dialog box where you type in the desired value.

Filtering by form

Filter by Form lets you enter criteria into a single row on the datasheet. Clicking the Filter By Form button transforms the datasheet into a single row containing a drop-down list in every column. The drop-down list contains all the unique values for the column. An Or tab at the bottom of the window lets you specify *OR* conditions for each group. Choose Advanced ➪ Filter By Form in the Sort & Filter group of the Ribbon to enter Filter by Form mode, shown in Figure 5.22.

FIGURE 5.22

Using Filter by Form lets you set multiple conditions for filtering at one time. Notice the Or tab at the bottom of the window.

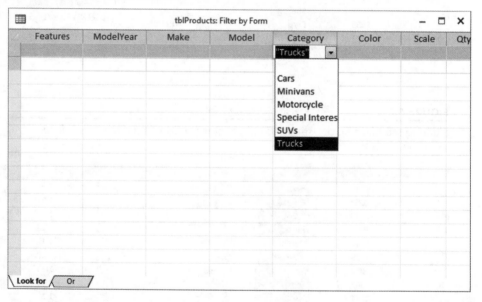

Select values from the combo boxes or type values you want to search for in the field. If you want to see records where the Category is Trucks or SUVs, select Trucks from the Category drop-down list, select the Or tab at the bottom of the window, and then select SUVs from the Category drop-down list. To see records where Category is SUV and QtyInStock is 1, select SUV from the Category drop-down and type 1 in QtyInStock. Once you enter the desired criteria, click the Toggle Filter command to apply the filter. (The Toggle Filter button is shown in Figure 5.19.)

Enter as many conditions as you need using the Or tab. If you need even more advanced manipulation of your selections, you can choose Advanced ⇨ Advanced Filter/Sort from the Sort & Filter group of the Ribbon to get an actual Query by Example (QBE) screen that you can use to enter more-complex criteria.

 Chapter 8 discusses queries, and Chapter 9 discusses operators and expressions.

Aggregating Data

Access datasheets support a Total row at the bottom of datasheets. The Total row is opened by clicking the Totals button in the Records group on the Home tab of the Ribbon (the Totals button is marked with a Greek sigma character, much like the AutoSum button in Excel). Each column in the Total row can be set to a different aggregate calculation (Sum, Average, Minimum, Maximum, Count, Standard Deviation, or Variance).

To use the Total row, open a table or form in Datasheet view and click the Totals button in the Records group (see Figure 5.23) on the Home tab of the Ribbon. Access adds a Total row at the bottom of the datasheet, just below the New row.

FIGURE 5.23

The datasheet Total row.

Model	Category	Color	Scale	QtyInStock	RetailPrice	Cost	V
Coupe	Cars		1:18	0	$29.99	$17.99	
Station Wagon			1:18	0	$19.99	$11.99	
			1:18	0	$29.99	$17.99	
			1:18	0	$39.99	$23.99	
	Motorcycle		1:18	0	$19.99	$11.99	
			1:18	0	$21.99	$13.19	
	Motorcycle		1:9	0	$49.99	$29.99	
				0	$0.00	$0.00	
*				0	$0.00	$0.00	
					$35.89		

tblProducts

None
Sum
Average
Count
Maximum
Minimum
Standard Deviation
Variance

Record: I◄ ◄ Totals ► ►I ►▣ 🝟 Unfiltered Search

5

Clicking a column in the Total row transforms the datasheet cell to a drop-down list. The items in the drop-down list are specific to the column's data type. For example, in text columns, the drop-down list shows only None and Count, while a numeric column contains a full complement of totals calculations (Sum, Average, Count, and so on). Date/Time columns include None, Average, Count, Minimum, and Maximum.

The Totals calculation you choose is dynamic. As you change data in the datasheet or underlying table, the calculation results displayed in the Total row are automatically updated after a very short delay. Recalculating a lot of totals extracts a small performance penalty, so you might want to hide the Total row when you aren't using it.

The Totals options you choose for the columns in a datasheet persist. If you close the datasheet and re-open it, the Total row is still there.

To remove the Total row, open the datasheet and click the Totals button in the Records group on the Ribbon. Here's one interesting behavior of the Total row: if you choose to remove it, you can restore it later (by clicking the Totals button again). The row is restored to its original setting.

Printing Records

You can print all the records in your datasheet in a simple row-and-column layout. In Chapter 20, you learn to produce formatted reports. For now, the simplest way to print is to click File ⇨ Print and choose one of the Print options as shown in Figure 5.24.

If you choose Print, and not Quick Print or Print Preview, Access shows the Print dialog box. From the Print dialog box, customize your printout by selecting from several options:

- **Print Range:** Prints the entire datasheet or only selected pages or records
- **Copies:** Determines the number of copies to be printed
- **Collate:** Determines whether multiple copies are collated

You can also change the printer, click the Properties button, and set options for the selected printer. The Setup button allows you to set margins and print headings.

The printout reflects all layout options that are in effect when the datasheet is printed. Hidden columns don't print. Gridlines print only if the cell gridline properties are on. The printout also reflects the specified row height and column width.

Only so many columns and rows can fit on a page; the printout takes up as many pages as required to print all the data. Access breaks up the printout as necessary to fit on each page. For example, the tblProducts printout might be nine pages—three pages across are needed to print all the fields in tblProducts, and all the records require three pages in length. The records of tblContacts might need four pages in length. The number of pages depends on your layout and your printer.

FIGURE 5.24

The Microsoft Access Print menu.

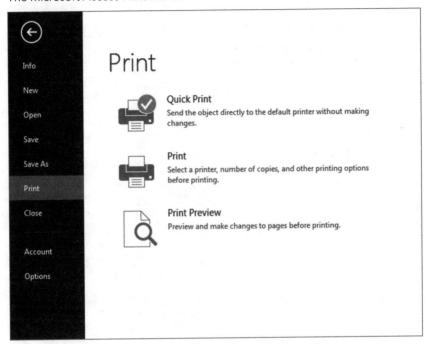

Previewing Records

Although you may have all the information in the datasheet ready to print, you may be unsure of whether to change the width or height of the columns or rows or whether to adjust the fonts to improve your printed output. To preview your print job, click the Print Preview command under the Print menu to display the Print Preview window. The default view is the first page in single-page preview. Use the Ribbon commands to select different views and zoom in and out. Click Print to print the datasheet to the printer. Click the Close Print Preview command on the right side of the Ribbon to return to Datasheet view.

Importing and Exporting Data

IN THIS CHAPTER

Understanding external data

Selecting the import and export options that are right for you

Creating import specifications

Exporting to external tables and files

I n this chapter, we show you how to bring data into your Access database from an outside source by importing. We also show you how to create external files from the data by exporting. An import process adds data to an Access database from some external source, such as an XML file. An export from Access means you create something outside the Access database, like an XML or Excel file containing data stored in Access.

On the Web

This chapter uses various files for importing, plus two Access databases: `Chapter06_1.accdb` and `Chapter06_2.accdb`. Both databases are used for importing and exporting examples. The tables from the completed imports have been renamed in the files. If you haven't already downloaded these files onto your machine from this book's website, you'll need to do so now. The website contains the two databases and a number of auxiliary files in different formats (XLS, XML, TXT, and so on). Be sure to copy these files to your computer.

How Access Works with External Data

Exchanging information between Access and another program is an essential capability in today's database world. Information is usually stored in a wide variety of application programs and data formats. Access, like many other products, has its own native file format, designed to support referential integrity and provide support for rich data types, such as OLE objects. Most of the time, Access alone is sufficient for the job. Occasionally, however, you need to move data from one Access database file to another or use data from another program with a different format.

Types of external data

Access can use and exchange data among a wide range of applications. For example, you may need to get data from a Microsoft Excel file, a SQL Server, Oracle, or even a text file. Access can move data among several categories of applications, including other Windows applications, Macintosh applications, database management systems, text files, and even mainframe files.

Ways of working with external data

Often, you need to move data from another application or file into your Access database, or vice versa. You might need to get information you already have in an external spreadsheet file. You can reenter all that information by hand or have it automatically imported into your database.

Access has tools that enable you to exchange data with another database or spreadsheet file. In fact, Access can exchange data with many different file types, including the following:

- Access database objects (all types)
- Text files
- Excel files
- ODBC databases (SQL Server, Sybase Server, Oracle Server, and other ODBC-compliant databases)
- HTML tables, lists, and documents
- XML documents
- Outlook tables
- Microsoft Exchange documents
- SharePoint lists
- Azure databases
- Word documents
- Rich Text Format (RTF) documents

Access works with these external data sources in several ways:

- **Linking:** Linking to data creates a connection to a table in another Access database or links to the data from a different format. Linking uses the data in the source file format (such as Excel or XML). The linked data remains in its original file. The file containing the linked data should not be moved, deleted, or renamed; otherwise, Access won't be able to locate the data the next time it's needed. If moving or renaming the linked data source is unavoidable, Access provides tools for relinking to the source.
- **Importing:** Importing copies data from a data source, another Access database, or another application's database file into an Access table. The imported data is converted to the appropriate Access data type, stored in a table, and managed by Access from that point on.

- **Exporting:** Exporting copies data from an Access table into a text file, another Access database, or another application's file. Like importing, changing the source data does not affect the exported data.

Each method has clear advantages and disadvantages, as covered in the following sections.

 Linking between Access and external data is discussed in Chapter 7.

When to link to external data

Linking in Access enables you to work with the data in another application's format—thus, sharing the file with the existing application. If you leave data in another database format, Access can read the data while the original application is still using it. This capability is useful when you want to work with data in Access that other programs also need to work with. However, there are limitations as to what you can do with linked data. For example, you can't update data in a linked Excel spreadsheet or a linked text file. The ability to work with external data is also useful when you use Access as a front end for a SQL Server database—you can link to a SQL Server table and directly update the data, without having to batch-upload it to the SQL Server.

Access databases are often linked to external data so that people can use Access forms to add and update the external data or to use the external data in Access reports.

You can link to the following types of data in Access:

- Other Access tables (ACCDB, ACCDE, ACCDR, MDB, MDA, MDE)
- Excel spreadsheets
- Outlook folders
- Text files
- XML files
- HTML documents
- SharePoint lists
- ODBC databases

> **CAUTION**
>
> Access is capable of linking to certain formats (like HTML tables, text files, Excel files, and XML documents) for read-only access. You can use and look at tables in HTML or text format; however, the tables can't be updated and records can't be added to them using Access.

A big disadvantage of working with linked tables is that you lose the capability to enforce referential integrity between tables (unless all the linked tables are in the same external Access database or all are in some other database management system that supports referential integrity). Linked tables may exhibit somewhat poorer performance than local tables. Depending on the source and the location of the source data, users might experience a noticeable delay when they open a form or report that is based on linked data.

Performance issues become more pronounced when joining linked and local data in a query. Because Access is unable to apply optimization techniques to foreign data, many joins are inefficient and require more memory and CPU time to complete than joining local tables. However, Access can work with many different types of external data, which makes it the ideal platform for applications requiring these features.

When to import external data

Importing data enables you to bring an external table or data source into a new or existing Access table. By importing data, Access automatically converts data from the external format and copies it into Access. You can even import data objects into a different Access database or Access project from the one that is currently open. If you know that you'll use your data in Access only, you should import it. Generally, Access works faster with its own local tables.

> **NOTE**
>
> Because importing makes another copy of the data, you might want to delete the old file after you import the copy into Access. Sometimes, however, you'll want to preserve the old data file. For example, the data might be an Excel spreadsheet still in use. In cases such as this, simply maintain the duplicate data and accept that storing it will require more disk space (and that the two files are going to get out of sync).

One of the principal reasons to import data is to customize it to meet your needs. After a table has been imported into an Access database, you can work with the new table as if you'd built it in the current database. With linked tables, on the other hand, you're greatly limited in the changes you can make. For example, you can't specify a primary key or assign a data entry rule, which means that you can't enforce integrity against the linked table. Also, because linked tables point to external files, which Access expects to find in a specific location, it can make distributing your application more difficult.

Data is frequently imported into an Access database from an obsolete system being replaced by a new Access application. When the import process is complete, the obsolete application can be removed from the user's computer.

> **TIP**
>
> If you'll be importing data from the same source frequently, you can automate the process with a macro or a VBA procedure. This can be helpful for those times when you have to import data from an external source on a regular schedule or when you have complex transformations that must be applied to the imported data.

When to export data

Exporting data enables you to pass data to other applications. When you export data, you direct Access to convert data to an external format and copy it to a file that can be read by an external application. As we've already mentioned, sometimes you have to import data into Access as opposed to just linking to the external data source if you want to be able to modify the data. If you still need to be able to work with the modified data in the external application, you have little choice but to create a new file by exporting the modified data.

A common reason to export data is because you want to share the data with other users who don't have Access installed.

Working with Data in Unsupported Programs

Although unsupported formats are rare, you might occasionally need to work with data from a program that isn't stored in a supported external database or file format. In such cases, the programs usually can export or convert their data into one of the formats recognized by Access. To use the data in these programs, export it into a format recognized by Access and then import it into Access.

For example, many applications can export to the XML file format. If the XML format is not available, most programs, even those on different operating systems, can export data to delimited or fixed-width text files, which you can then import into Access.

Options for Importing and Exporting

Before examining the processes of importing and exporting, let's take a brief look at the various options for importing and exporting data with Access.

Access is often described as a "landing pad" for many types of data. This means that Access can use and exchange data among a wide range of applications. For example, you might need to get data from SQL Server or Oracle, a text file, or even an XML document. Access can move data among several categories of applications, database engines, and even platforms (mainframes and Macintosh computers).

Open the Chapter06_1.accdb database in Access, and click the External Data tab of the Ribbon (see Figure 6.1). You'll see the following groups: Import & Link, Export, and Web Linked Lists.

FIGURE 6.1

The External Data tab of the Ribbon hints at the variety of external data sources available to Access.

The Import & Link group includes the following options:

- New Data Source
- Saved Imports
- Linked Table Manager

The New Data Source drop-down includes four categories containing several data formats each:

- From File
    - Excel
    - HTML Document
    - XML File
    - Text File
- From Database
    - Access
    - From SQL Server
    - From Azure Database
    - dBASE File
- From Online Services
    - SharePoint List
    - From Dynamics 365 (online)
    - From Salesforce
    - Data Services
- From Other Sources
    - ODBC Database
    - Outlook Folder

The Export group includes the following options:

- Saved Exports
- Excel

- Text File
- XML File
- PDF or XPS
- Email
- Access
- Word Merge
- More: Click this button to open the More drop-down list, which has the following options:
  - Word
  - SharePoint List
  - ODBC Database
  - HTML Document
  - dBASE File

Obviously, Microsoft has prepared Access well for its role as a "landing pad" for data.

Importing External Data

An import copies external data into an Access database. The external data remains in its original state, but, after the import, a copy exists within Access. When you import a file (unlike when you link tables), Access converts a copy of the data from an external source into records in an Access table. The external data source is not changed during the import. No connection to the external data source is maintained once the import process is complete.

You can import information to new or existing tables. Every type of data can be imported to a new table. However, some types of imports—such as spreadsheets and text files—don't necessarily have a table structure compatible with Access. In those cases, Access will create a table structure for you. If you want to control the structure of the table, you should create the table before importing.

Importing from another Access database

You can import items from a source database into the current database. The objects you import can be tables, queries, forms, reports, macros, or modules. Import an item into the current Access database by following these steps:

1. **Open the destination database you want to import into.** In this case, open the Chapter06_1.accdb database.

2. **Select the External Data tab.**

3. **Click Import & Link ⇨ New Data Source ⇨ From Database ⇨ Access, and then click the Browse button to select the filename of the source database (Chapter06_2.accdb).**

4. **Select the Import Tables, Queries, Forms, Reports, Macros, and Modules into the Current Database option button and click OK.** The Import Objects dialog box (shown in Figure 6.2) appears. It gives you options for importing a database object.

NOTE

When working with an external Access database, you can import any type of object, including tables, queries, forms, reports, macros, and VBA code modules.

FIGURE 6.2

Many types of Access database objects can be imported from one Access database into another.

5. **Select a table and click OK.** If an object already exists in the destination database, then a sequential number is added to the name of the imported object, distinguishing it from the original item. For example, if tblDepartments already exists, the new imported table is named tblDepartments1.

The Get External Data – Save Import Steps dialog box appears, with a very useful feature that allows you to store the import process as a saved import, as shown in Figure 6.3.

FIGURE 6.3

The Save Import Steps feature lets you save frequently executed import processes for future use.

6. **Check the Save import steps check box.** Access will display the Save as and Description fields.

7. **Provide a name for the import process to make it easy to recall the saved import's purpose and then click Save Import.** You can execute the saved import again at a later date by clicking the Saved Imports button in the Import & Link group of the External Data tab of the Ribbon. From the Manage Data Tasks dialog box (see Figure 6.4), you can change the name of the saved import, the location of the source file, and the description of the saved import. All other information about the saved import (such as the destination table name) can't be changed. If you need to change other information, create a new saved import with the proper parameters.

> ### TIP
> The Manage Data Tasks dialog box includes the Create Outlook Task button to set up the import procedure as a scheduled Outlook Task. This is a convenient way to automatically execute the import process on a regular schedule.

> ### NOTE
> Each time you run a Saved Import, a new table is created with the imported data. If, for example, you import tblDepartments, a table named tblDepartments is created. Running the saved import again creates a table named tblDepartments1. Running the saved import a second time creates a table name tblDepartments2, and so on. Saved Imports do not replace the originally imported table.

FIGURE 6.4

The Saved Imports feature lets you rerun previous saved import processes.

Importing from an Excel spreadsheet

You can import data from Excel spreadsheets to a new or existing table. The primary rule when importing Excel data is that each cell in a column must contain the same type of data. When you're importing Excel data into a new table, Access guesses at the data type to assign to each field in the new table based on the first few rows of Excel data (other than column headings). An import error may occur if any Excel row past the first few rows contains incompatible data. In Figure 6.5, the Age column should contain all numeric data, but it contains an age written out as words. This is likely to cause an error during the import process. The data in Row 5 should be changed so that the entire column contains numeric data (as shown in Figure 6.6).

You can import all the data from an Excel spreadsheet, or just the data from a named range of cells. Naming a range of cells in your spreadsheet can make importing into Access easier. Often a spreadsheet is formatted into groups of cells (or *ranges*). One range may contain a listing of sales by customer, for example, while another may include total sales for all customers, totals by product type, or totals by month purchased. By providing a range name for each group of cells, you can limit the import to just one section of the spreadsheet data.

FIGURE 6.5

Access can import data from an Excel spreadsheet, but there are some restrictions.

This data will cause import problems.

FIGURE 6.6

Excel worksheet columns should contain consistent data.

All data is now numeric

To import EMPLIST.xls, follow these steps:

1. **Open the Chapter06_1.accdb database.**
2. **Click Import & Link ⇨ New Data Source ⇨ From File ⇨ Excel on the External Data tab.**
3. **Browse to the Excel file.**

4. **Select Import the Source Data into a New Table in the Current Database and click OK.** The first Import Spreadsheet Wizard screen (see Figure 6.7) shows lists of worksheets or named ranges, and a preview of the data, in the Excel spreadsheet.

FIGURE 6.7

The Import Spreadsheet Wizard.

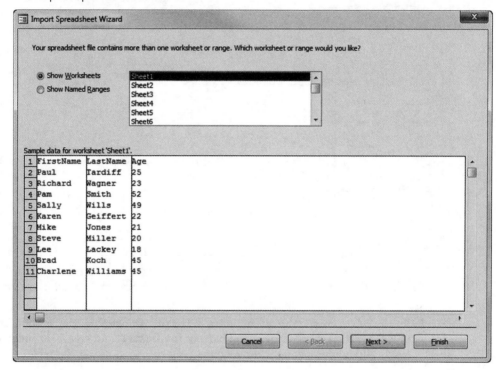

5. **Select a worksheet or named range and click Next.**

6. **On the next screen (shown in Figure 6.8), select the First Row Contains Column Headings check box and click Next.** Normally you don't want the Excel column headings stored as field data. Access uses the column headings as the field names in the new table.

FIGURE 6.8

Does the first row contain column headings?

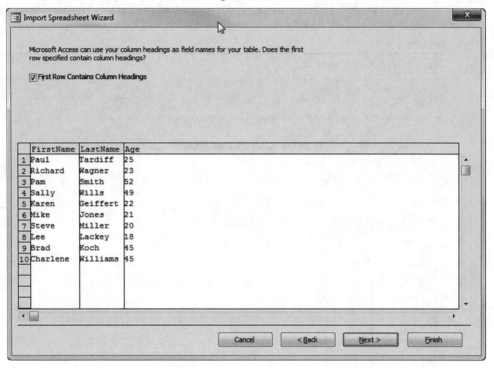

7. **On the next screen (shown in Figure 6.9), you can override the default field name and data type, remove fields from the import, and create an index on a field. When you're done, click Next.**

FIGURE 6.9

You can override any of the default settings Access has chosen.

8. **On the next screen, set a primary key for the new table (see Figure 6.10) and click Next.** A primary key uniquely identifies each row in a table.

FIGURE 6.10

Specify a primary key for the new table.

> **CAUTION**
>
> Be somewhat wary when choosing a primary key for the imported file. The field you choose must conform to the rules of primary keys: no value can be null, and no duplicates are allowed. The purpose of a table's primary key is to uniquely identify the rows in the table, so if no column in the Excel spreadsheet is appropriate for this purpose, it's probably best to let Access add a default primary key field. The primary key added by Access is always an AutoNumber and always conforms to data normalization rules.
>
> Primary keys are discussed in Chapters 3 and 4.

9. **Specify the new table's name and click Finish.**

> **CAUTION**
>
> If you import an Excel file with the same name as an Excel file you've already linked, Access will ask if you want to overwrite the existing file. Unless you actually intend to replace the linked table, you must give the newly imported table a new name.

10. **If you want to, save the import process for later execution.** The new table now appears in the Navigation pane.

Importing a SharePoint list

SharePoint lists are candidate data sources for Access databases. Because SharePoint lists reside on web servers, SharePoint data is accessible across a network to qualified users. This gives Access the ability to share data virtually anywhere in the world.

 Part VIII is dedicated to understanding and working with SharePoint Services.

Because SharePoint is deployed on a large number of corporate intranets, Access is likely to continue as a component in enterprise environments.

Importing data from text files

There are many reasons for text file output, such as business-to-business (B2B) data transfers. Also, mainframe data is often output as text files to be consumed in desktop applications. Access can import from two different types of text files: delimited and fixed width. The Access Import Text Wizard assists you in importing or exporting both delimited and fixed-width text files.

Delimited text files

In *delimited text files* (sometimes known as *comma-delimited text files, comma-separated-values text files,* or *tab-delimited text files*), each record is on a separate line in the text file. The fields on the line contain no trailing spaces, normally use commas or tab characters as field separators, and might have certain fields that are enclosed in *qualifying characters* (such as single or double quotation marks). Here's an example of a comma-delimited text file:

```
1,Davolio,Nancy,5/1/14 0:00:00,4000
2,Fuller,Andrew,8/14/14 0:00:00,6520
3,Leverling,Janet,4/1/14 0:00:00,1056
4,Peacock,Margaret,5/3/15 0:00:00,4000
5,Buchanan,Steven,10/17/15 0:00:00,5000
6,Suyama,Michael,10/17/15 0:00:00,1000
7,King,Robert,1/2/14 0:00:00,1056
8,Callahan,Laura,3/5/14 0:00:00,1056
9,Dodsworth,Joseph,11/15/14 0:00:00,1056
```

Notice that the file has nine records (rows of text) and five fields. A comma separates each field. In this example, text fields are not qualified with double quotation marks. Notice also that the rows are different lengths because of the variable data within each row.

To import a delimited text file named `ImportDelim.txt`, follow these steps:

1. **Open the `Chapter06_1.accdb` database.**

2. **Select the External Data tab.**

3. **Click Import & Link ⇨ New Data Source ⇨ From File ⇨ Text File.**

4. **Browse to the `ImportDelim.txt` file, select the Import option button, and click OK.** The first screen of the Import Text Wizard (shown in Figure 6.11) appears. The Import Text Wizard displays the data in the text file and lets you choose between delimited or fixed width.

FIGURE 6.11

The first screen of the Import Text Wizard.

5. **Select Delimited and click Next.** The next screen of the Import Text Wizard (shown in Figure 6.12) appears. As you can see in Figure 6.12, this screen enables you to specify the separator used in the delimited file. A *separator* is the character placed between fields in a delimited text file. The separator is often a comma or semicolon, although it can be another character.

FIGURE 6.12

The second Import Text Wizard screen.

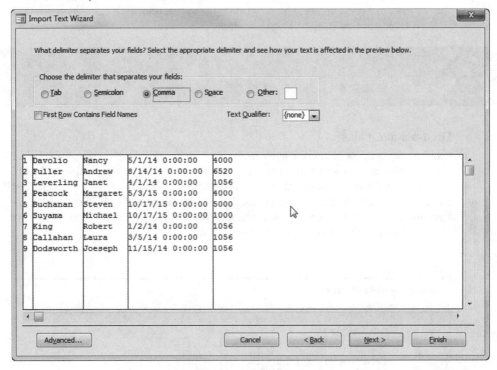

6. **Select the delimiter that separates your fields; if an uncommon delimiter is used, select Other and enter the delimiter in the Other box.**

> **CAUTION**
>
> There can be a problem with the separator used if any of the fields in the text file contains the separator character as data. For example, if you use a comma to delimit fields and one of the fields is Acme Widgets, Inc., Access will have a problem importing the file. The solution is to wrap text fields in double quotes ("Acme Widgets, Inc.") so that the comma is not misinterpreted as a field separator. This use of double quotes is referred to as the *text qualifier*. Most often single- or double-quote marks are used for this purpose and usually resolve issues with special characters contained within data fields.

7. **If the first row contains field names for the imported table, select the First Row Contains Field Names check box. When you're done with this screen, click Next.** The next few screens are very similar to the steps involved when importing

Excel worksheets. You can change field names, specify a primary key, and save the import for future use. Save the imported text file with a descriptive Access table name. Access creates the new table, using the text file's name by default. The new table appears in the Navigation pane.

Fixed-width text files

Fixed-width text files also place each record on a separate line. However, each field has the same number of characters for every record (the character counts are fixed, thus the name). If a field has fewer characters than its fixed width, spaces are added to the end until it has the proper number of characters. Figure 6.13 shows an example of a fixed-width file. Even though the first column only contains one character, spaces are added so that the second column starts in the same place for every record.

FIGURE 6.13

A typical fixed-width text file.

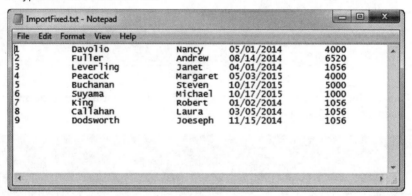

Notice that the fields in a fixed-width text file are not separated by delimiters. Instead, they start at exactly the same position in each record, and each record has exactly the same length.

Text values, such as first and last names, are not surrounded by quotation marks. Because there are no column delimiters, there's no chance that an illegal character can occur in a field, which would require the field to be text qualified. Anything within a field's position in a row is considered that field's data.

NOTE

If the Access table being imported has a primary key field, the text file cannot have any duplicate primary key values. If duplicate primary keys are found, the import will report an error and fail to import rows with duplicate primary keys.

To import a fixed-width text file, follow these steps:

1. **Open the `Chapter06_1.accdb` database.**

2. **Select the External Data tab.**

3. **Click Import & Link ⇨ New Data Source ⇨ From File ⇨ Text File.**

4. **Browse to `ImportFixed.txt`, select the Import option button, and click OK.** The first screen of the Import Text Wizard (refer to Figure 6.11) appears. The Import Text Wizard displays the data in the text file and lets you choose between delimited or fixed width.

5. **Select Fixed Width and click Next.** The next screen of the Import Text Wizard (shown in Figure 6.14) appears.

FIGURE 6.14

The Import Text Wizard screen for fixed-width text files.

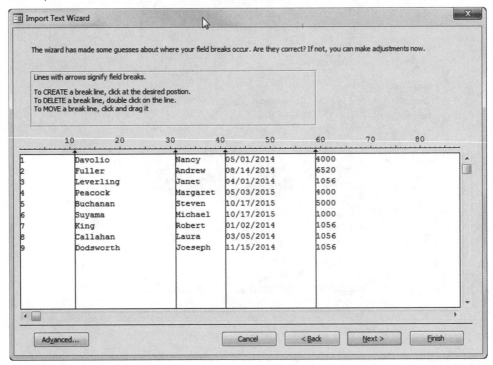

6. **Adjust field widths as needed.** Access guesses at the best breaks to use for fields, based on the most consistent spacing across rows. In this case, the field breaks are very consistent. If necessary, however, use the mouse to grab a dividing line and move it left or right to change the width of fields in the file.

> **TIP**
>
> To add a new dividing line, single click the mouse within the data area and then move the line to the desired position. To delete an existing line, double-click the line.

7. **Click the Advanced button at the bottom of the wizard.** The Import Specification dialog box (shown in Figure 6.15) appears. The Import Specification dialog box lets you change the default formats for dates, times, field names, indexing, and data types. It also provides an option for skipping fields you don't want to import. (For detailed information on this dialog box, see the following sidebar.)

FIGURE 6.15

The Import Specification dialog box for importing a fixed-width text file.

8. **Ensure that the Date Order is set to MDY and the Four Digit Years check box is selected.**

9. **Select the Leading Zeros in Dates check box.**

10. **Click OK to dismiss the Import Specification dialog box.**

11. **Continue through the remaining Import Text Wizard screens.**

Using the Import Specification Dialog Box

One advantage of using the Import Specification dialog box is the fact that you can specify the type of file to be imported from or exported to. The Language and Code Page drop-down lists determine the fundamental type of format. The Code Page drop-down list displays the code pages that are available for the selected language.

You can also specify the Field Delimiter option for delimited text files. Four built-in field-separator choices (semicolon, tab, space, and comma) are available in this combo box, or you can specify another character by typing into the combo box, if needed.

You can also specify the text qualifier used to surround text fields. Normally, text fields in a delimited file are enclosed by characters such as quotation marks that set the text data apart from other fields. This is useful for specifying numeric data like Social Security and phone numbers as text data rather than numeric.

The Text Qualifier drop-down list is actually a combo box, so you can enter a different qualifier by typing it in the text area.

When Access imports or exports data, it converts dates to a specific format (such as MMDDYY). You can specify how date fields are to be converted, using one of the six choices in the Date Order combo box:

- DMY
- DYM
- MDY
- MYD
- YDM
- YMD

These choices specify the order for each portion of a date. The *D* is the day of the month (1–31), *M* is the calendar month (1–12), and *Y* is the year. The default date order is set to the U.S. format (month, day, year). When you work with European dates, the order is often changed to day, month, and year.

You use the Date Delimiter field to specify the date delimiter character. The default is a forward slash (/), but you can change this to any other delimiter, such as a period. European dates are often separated by periods, as in 22.10.2019.

> **NOTE**
>
> When you import text files with Date-type data, you must have a separator between the month, day, and year. Access reports an error if the field is specified as a Date/Time type and no delimiter is used. When you're exporting date fields, the separator is not needed.
>
> With the Time Delimiter option, you can specify a separator (usually a colon) between the parts of time values in a text file. To change the separator, simply enter another in the Time Delimiter box.
>
> Select the Four Digit Years check box to specify that the year portion of a date field is formatted with four digits. By checking this box, you can import dates that include the century (such as in 1981 or 2001). The default setting is to use four-digit years.
>
> The Leading Zeros in Dates option specifies that date values include leading zeros. This means that date formats include leading zeros (as in 02/04/03), if needed.

Importing and exporting XML documents

Importing XML documents is easy with Microsoft Access. XML is often used to transfer information between disparate platforms, databases, operating systems, applications, or companies. XML is used for raw data, *metadata* (data that describes other data), and even processing data. It's safe to say that most Access developers eventually import or export data in XML format.

Presenting XML in Access needs to be done in an odd way. You could easily import a simple XML document in your Access database, but the best way to find out how well Access uses XML is to begin by exporting something into XML.

Follow these steps to export data from Access to an XML file:

1. **Open the `Chapter06_1.accdb` database.**
2. **Open tblDepartments in Datasheet view.**
3. **Select the External Data tab, and click XML File in the Export section.**
4. **Name the XML file `tblDepartments.xml`, and click OK.** The Export XML dialog box (shown in Figure 6.16) appears.

FIGURE 6.16

The Export XML dialog box.

5. **Click OK to complete the export process.**

The Export XML dialog box includes options for specifying advanced options for the XML export process. Clicking the More Options button opens a dialog box (see Figure 6.17) with several important XML settings.

FIGURE 6.17

Advanced XML export options.

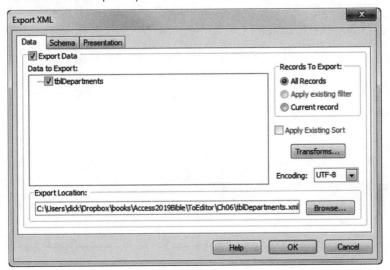

The data contained in an XML file may be relational or hierarchical. For example, a single XML file might contain information on both product categories and the products themselves. A *schema file* is needed for complex XML to be understood by other applications. Access automatically produces a schema file (XSD extension) for data exported in XML format. Figure 6.18 shows the Schema tab of the Export XML dialog box.

The XML schema file includes information such as the data type of each field and the source table's primary key and indexes.

A further refinement of the XML export process is to specify how the XML data should be presented in an application using the exported data. (The presentation is specified using HTML conventions.) In most cases, the XML presentation file (XSL extension) is not needed, because the application that is designed to use the XML file displays the data as required by its users. Figure 6.19 shows the Presentation tab of the Export XML dialog box. Notice that none of the options on this tab is selected by default.

FIGURE 6.18

Exporting XML schema information.

FIGURE 6.19

XML presentation options.

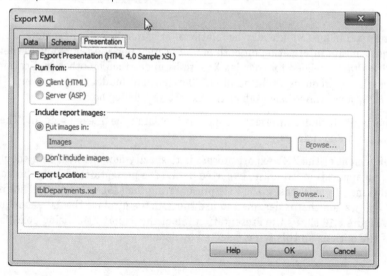

6

In a text editor, such as Notepad, open `tblDepartments.xml`. You'll see the contents of the XML file, as shown in Figure 6.20.

The first two lines of the text file define the version of XML that was used and the schema. The exported data and structure start on the third line. XML is a hierarchy of tags that define the structure of the data, and each piece of data is within an opening and closing tag. Each record begins with a tag for the name of the table. In this example `<tblDepartments>` is the tag that defines the table. A few lines down, there is a closing tag, `</tblDepartments>`, signifying the end of the record.

> **NOTE**
>
> XML uses tags to give context to the data. Opening tags define the start of a structure and consist of text between a less-than symbol (<) and a greater-than symbol (>). Closing tags define the end of the structure. Closing tags are formatted similarly to opening tags except that a forward slash is included after the less-than symbol (<).

FIGURE 6.20

An exported XML file in plain text.

In between these two tags are the fields and data for that record. The first field of the first record is recorded as `<DeptNumber>1000</DeptNumber>`. An application that understands XML will interpret that line to mean there is a field named DeptNumber, and this record has 1000 in that field. This hierarchy of tags and data continues for each field in the record and for each record in the table.

Just as Access can export to XML, it can also import it. To import the tblDepartments .xml file that you just exported, follow these steps:

1. **Click Import & Link ➪ New Data Source ➪ From File ➪ XML File on the External Data tab.**

2. **Browse to tblDepartments.xml, click Open, and then click OK.** The Import XML dialog box, shown in Figure 6.21, displays how Access interprets the XML data.

3. **Click OK.**

4. **Click Close.** You can save the import steps before closing as described earlier in this chapter.

FIGURE 6.21

Access understands XML data.

196

Access converted the well-formed XML into a table. The `<tblDepartments>` tag determines what the imported table will be named, the tags within the `<tblDepartments>` tag and its closing tag define the fields, and the data in between the field tags will become data in the new table.

Importing and exporting HTML documents

Access enables you to import HTML tables as easily as any other database, Excel spreadsheet, or text file. You simply select an HTML file to import and use the HTML Import Wizard. The HTML Import Wizard works exactly like the other import wizards described earlier in this chapter.

And just like we demonstrated XML in the previous section, we'll do an HTML import in reverse. First, you export a table to generate an HTML file, and then you import the file back into Access to create a new table:

1. **Open the `Chapter06_1.accdb` database and select tblEmployees from the Navigation pane.**

2. **Select the External Data tab, click the More drop-down button in the Export group, and select HTML Document.**

3. **Specify an HTML file as the export destination in the Export – HTML Document dialog box (see Figure 6.22).**

4. **Select your HTML output options and click OK.** The HTML export is completed as soon as you click the OK button. Unless you check Export Data with Formatting and Layout, no options other than what you see in Figure 6.22 are available when exporting HTML data.

Exporting Data with Formatting and Layout, an option in the Export – HTML Document dialog box, presents additional exporting options. The most important option is that it allows you to specify an HTML template for your export. An HTML template is a normal HTML file, except that it includes special tags that Access recognizes. These tags instruct Access where to place certain data when exporting, allowing you to define the other aspects of the HTML document, such as styling and logos.

FIGURE 6.22

The Export – HTML Document dialog box.

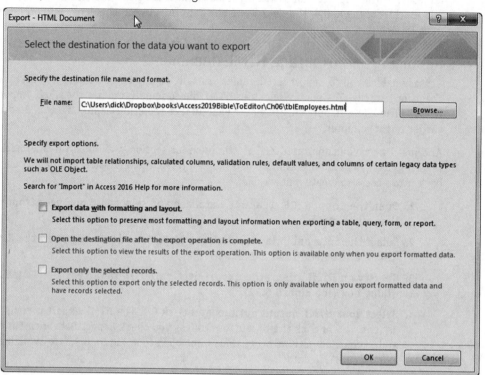

Importing the HTML is much like importing a text file shown previously in this chapter. In fact, the Import HMTL Wizard has most of the same screens and options as the Import Text Wizard, such as defining data types for fields and identifying the primary key.

Importing Access objects other than tables

You can import other Access database tables or any other object in another database, which means you can import an existing table, query, form, report, macro, or module from another Access database. You can also import custom toolbars and menus.

As a simple demonstration, follow these steps:

1. **Open the Chapter06_1.accdb database.**

2. **Click Import & Link ⇨ New Data Source ⇨ From Database ⇨ Access, and select the option to import from another Access database.** The screen in Figure 6.23 appears. Notice that this dialog box enables you to specify whether to import database objects or link to tables in an external Access database.

3. **Browse to the Chapter06_2.accdb database, click Open, and then click OK.** Figure 6.24 shows that you can import every type of Access object.

FIGURE 6.23

The same wizard imports objects and links to external Access tables.

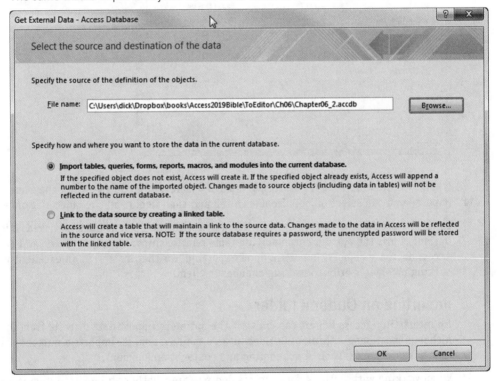

FIGURE 6.24

Importing Access objects.

When including tables, queries, forms, reports, macros, or modules—all in the same import—you can select objects from each tab and then import all the objects at once.

Figure 6.24 shows the Import Objects dialog box with the Options button clicked. Clicking Options shows the options for importing table relationships, menus, toolbars, and other Access database objects. Importing (and exporting, for that matter) is an excellent way of backing up objects prior to making changes to them.

Importing an Outlook folder

An interesting Access import capability is the option to import data directly from Outlook. Although most people think of Outlook as an e-mail system, it supports a number of important business needs, such as scheduling and contact management.

When working with Outlook data, Access doesn't care whether an imported item is an e-mail or contact. Access handles all types of Outlook objects with equal ease.

Select New Data Source ➪ From Other Sources ➪ Outlook Folder from the Import & Link group to open the initial Outlook Folder import dialog box (shown in Figure 6.25). Access provides options for importing Outlook data, adding it to an existing Access table, or linking to it from the current Access database.

FIGURE 6.25

The initial Outlook import options.

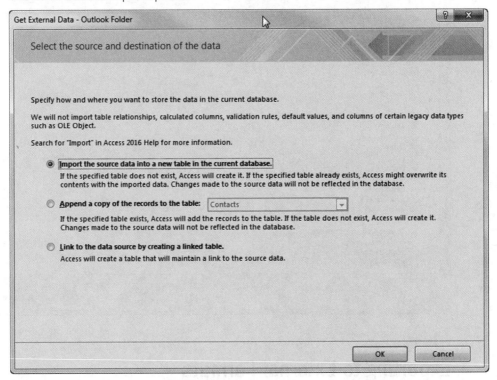

Selecting the import option opens the Import Exchange/Outlook Wizard (shown in Figure 6.26). As shown in this dialog box, Access can import Outlook e-mail, contacts, calendars, journals, and other folders.

Depending on which item you select in the Import Exchange/Outlook Wizard, the remaining wizard screens walk you through the process of bringing Outlook data into Access. You can import Outlook data into a new or existing table, add a primary key, specify data types, and save the import process for later execution.

FIGURE 6.26

Importing Outlook objects into Access.

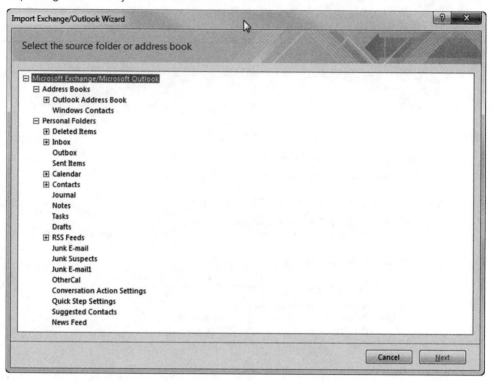

Exporting to External Formats

An export copies data from an Access table to some other application or data source, such as an XML document. The exported result uses the format of the destination data source and not the format of an Access database. You can copy data from an Access table or query into a new external file. You can export tables to several different sources.

> **NOTE**
>
> In general, anything imported can also be exported, unless otherwise stated in this chapter.

Exporting objects to other Access databases

When the destination of an export process is an Access database, you can export every type of Access object (tables, queries, forms, reports, and so on). Unlike importing, which allows you to import many objects at once, exporting only allows you to export one object at a time. To export an object to another Access database, follow these generic steps:

1. **Open the source database and select an object to export.**
2. **Click the Access button in the Export group of the External Data tab.** The Export – Access Database dialog box appears.
3. **Use the Browse button to locate the destination Access database.**

4. **Click Save and then click OK.** The Export dialog box is shown.

If an object already exists in the target database, you'll be asked whether you want to replace the object in the target database. If you don't, you can create a new object in the target database.

5. **Choose Definition and Data and click OK.**
6. **The last step of the wizard enables you to save the export configuration for future use.** This option is handy if you'll be frequently performing the same export process.

Exporting through ODBC drivers

Access can export to any Open Database Connectivity (ODBC)–compliant database. ODBC-compliant databases come with an ODBC driver that serves as the connection between Access and the database. Many of the most popular databases, including Access, are ODBC-compliant.

To export through an ODBC driver, follow these steps:

1. **Open Chapter06_1.accdb and select an object to export, such as tblEmployees.**
2. **Click More ⇨ ODCB Database in the Export group of the External Data tab.** The Export dialog box appears as shown in Figure 6.27.

FIGURE 6.27

Naming the table in an ODBC destination.

3. **Type a name for the table or simply click OK to use the default name.**

4. **Select the appropriate driver for your database from the Select Data Source dialog box (see Figure 6.28).** This example uses SQLite3, a free, open-source, ODBC-compliant database. Consult your database's documentation for the name of its driver.

FIGURE 6.28

Selecting the ODBC driver.

5. **Save export steps, if desired.**

Some ODBC drivers will prompt for additional information, such as the database name or table name. Others, such as SQLite3, store the filename in the driver file and name the table the same as the exported table. When the export is complete, you can use the new table in the other database. Figure 6.29 shows that tblEmployees was successfully exported to a SQLite3 database.

FIGURE 6.29

The Employees table has successfully exported to a SQLite3 database.

Exporting to Word

Access provides two ways to transfer data to Word: Export to Rich Text Format and Word Merge. Rich Text Format (RTF) is a plain text file with special characters that define the formatting. Exporting to RTF creates a document with an RTF extension, not a native Word document (though Word can read RTF, as can WordPad and many other text editors).

Merging data into Word

The real power of exporting to Word is to use the data in Word Merge. With Word Merge, you can control where your data ends up in the Word document. This is useful for such tasks as sending letters, addressing envelopes, producing reports, and creating file folder labels.

To create file folder labels for each department in tblDepartments, follow these steps:

1. **Open tblDepartments in Datasheet view.**

2. **Click the Word Merge button in the Export group on the External Data tab.**

3. **On the first screen of the Microsoft Word Mail Merge Wizard, shown in Figure 6.30, select Create a New Document and Then Link the Data to It, and click OK.** Word opens to a new document and the Mail Merge task pane appears on the right.

FIGURE 6.30

The Microsoft Word Mail Merge Wizard allows you to export data to existing or new documents.

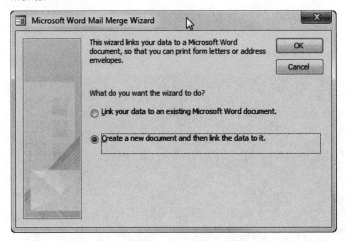

4. **Follow the steps in Word's Mail Merge Wizard.** Select Labels as the document type and choose the style of label you have.

5. **Arrange the DeptNumber and DeptDescription on the label and template and complete the merge.** Use the Insert Merge Field button on the Mailings tab of the Ribbon to place the fields on the label. You can add other text and punctuation and even put fields on their own lines. Figure 6.31 shows the results of a merge where the department number and description are separated by a colon.

> **NOTE**
>
> You can import from Word into Access by converting the Word document into a text file first. You could even use Word in combination with Excel to produce a delimited text file.

Publishing to PDF or XPS

The PDF and XPS file formats were developed to display data as it would appear on a printed page. Data displayed in these formats is generally not editable. Publishing to PDF or XPS outputs a relatively small file and is useful when you want to share data but don't want the other person to be able to change it.

FIGURE 6.31

A completed Word Merge.

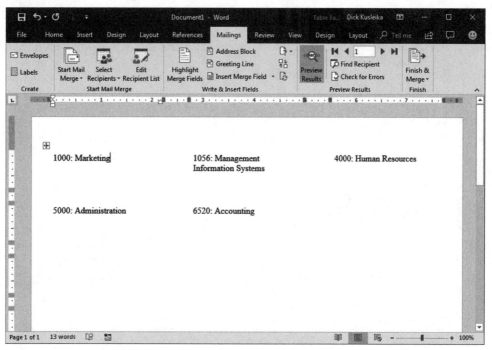

To export tblEmployees to a PDF file, follow these steps:

1. **Select tblEmployees in the Navigation pane.**
2. **Select PDF or XPS from the Export group on the External Data tab of the Ribbon.** The Publish as PDF or XPS dialog box appears.
3. **Select PDF from the Save As Type drop-down list (see Figure 6.32).**
4. **Click the Publish button.**

The result, as shown in Figure 6.33, is a PDF file that can be opened by many different PDF reader programs. Most computers have some PDF reader software installed, which makes it a great format for sharing data you don't want changed.

FIGURE 6.32

Select PDF or XPS as a file format.

FIGURE 6.33

A table published in the PDF file format.

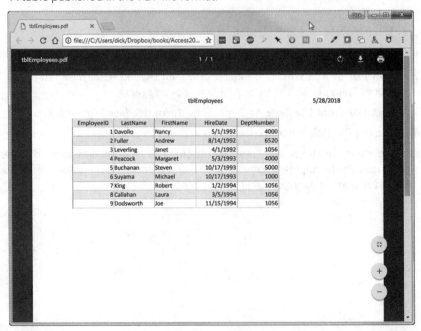

Linking to External Data

IN THIS CHAPTER

Examining the types of external data and methods for working with them

Linking an Access database to external data

Using linked tables

Splitting an Access database

I n Chapter 6, you learned about the types of external data that you can import to and export from Access. You also learned when to import and export and when to link. This chapter describes the methods for using external data in Access through a live, updating link to the data.

ON THE WEB

This chapter uses the `Chapter07.accdb` database, as well as several other files that you'll use for linking. If you haven't already downloaded these files onto your machine from this book's website, you'll need to do so now.

Note that, because the point of this chapter is to show how Access works with external data, there are examples of external data that you need to copy to your machine. Unfortunately, when working with external data, Access requires an exact path to each file—it can't work with relative paths. That means that when you copy `Chapter07.accdb` to your machine, it won't work until you relink the various external files. We show you how to do that in this chapter. For now, be aware that the following tables are linked to the files indicated:

Table	External File Type	Filename
ContactsFixed	Text File	`ContactsFixed.txt`
Customers	Excel 8.0	`CollectibleMiniCars.xls`
CustomerTypes	HTML	`CustomerTypes.html`
Products	Excel 8.0	`CollectibleMiniCars.xls`
tblSales	Access	`Chapter07_Link.accdb`
tblSalesLineItems	Excel 8.0	`tblSalesLineItems.xls`
tblSalesPayments	Access	`Chapter07_Link.accdb`

The data linked to Access applications comes in a variety of formats. There is no practical way to document every possible type of linking operation in a single chapter. So, this chapter discusses the essential steps required to link to external data and gives a few examples demonstrating how these processes are performed in Access, instead of filling page after page with examples that may or may not be relevant to your work.

As you'll soon see, knowledge of the external data format is critical to a successful linking operation. You must have some notion of the external data format before you can successfully import data into your Access application or incorporate the data into an Access database through linking. This chapter points out many of the issues involved if you choose to link to external data; it's intended to serve as a guide as you perform these operations in your Access applications.

Fixing Links

We'll discuss the Linked Table Manager later in this chapter in detail. For now, follow these steps to fix the linked tables in Chapter07.accdb:

1. Copy the Chapter 07 folder to your computer and make a note of the location.
2. Open Chapter07.accdb.
3. Click Linked Table Manager in the Import & Link group on the External Data tab of the Ribbon. The Linked Table Manager appears.
4. Click the Select All button, make sure Always Prompt For New Location is checked, and then click OK. You'll be prompted for the new location for each of the linked tables.
5. Using the table of filenames provided earlier in this chapter, browse to each file. The Linked Table Manager displays a message that all selected linked tables were successfully refreshed. The name of the table it's currently trying to refresh is in the title bar of the file dialog box.
6. Click Close to close the Linked Table Manager.

Now you can follow along with the examples in this chapter.

Linking External Data

As the database market continues to grow, the need to work with information from many different sources will escalate. If you have information captured in a SQL Server database or an old Excel spreadsheet, you don't want to reenter the information from these sources into Access. Also, the processes or policies at your company may require that the data live in these external files, and you don't want to risk having duplicate data that gets out of sync. Ideally, you want to open an Access table containing the data and use the information in its native format, without having to copy it or write a translation program to access it. In many cases, the capability of accessing information from one database format while working in another is often an essential starting point for many business projects.

Using code to copy or translate data from one application format to another is both time-consuming and costly. The time it takes can mean the difference between success and failure. Therefore, you want an intermediary between the different data sources in your environment.

Access can simultaneously link to multiple tables contained within other database systems. After an external file is linked, Access stores the link specification and uses the external data as if it were contained in a local table. Access easily links to other Access database tables as well as to non-Access database tables that support ODBC. A recommended practice is to split an Access database into two separate databases for easier use in a multiuser or client-server environment. Splitting your database in this manner is discussed in detail later in this chapter.

Identifying linked tables

In the "Ways of working with external data" section in Chapter 6, you saw a list of database tables and other types of files that Access links to. Access displays the names of linked tables in the object list and uses a special icon to indicate that the table is linked, not local. An arrow pointing to an icon indicates that the table name represents a linked data source. Figure 7.1 shows several linked tables in the list. (The arrow icon indicates that the file is linked. The icon also indicates which type of file is linked to the current Access database. For example, Excel files show the Excel logo and HTML tables show a globe-on-paper icon.)

FIGURE 7.1

Linked tables in an Access database. Notice that each linked table has an arrow icon indicating its status as a linked table.

After you link an external database table to your Access database, you use it as you would any other table. For example, Figure 7.2 shows a query using several linked tables: tblCustomers (a local Access table), tblSales (a linked Access table), tblSalesLineItems (from an Excel file), and Products (from another Excel file). As you can see, there's nothing that distinguishes the fact that the tables are from external sources—Access treats them no differently from any other tables.

FIGURE 7.2

A query using externally linked tables.

This query shows the potential benefit of linking to a variety of data sources and seamlessly displays data from internal and linked tables. Figure 7.3 shows the datasheet returned by this query. This datasheet combines four different data sources.

Figure 7.3 illustrates an important concept regarding using linked data in Access: users won't know, nor will they care, where the data resides. All they want is to see the data in a format they expect. Only you, the developer, understand the issues involved in bringing this data to the user interface (UI). Other than the limitations of linked data (explained in the next section), users won't be able to tell the difference between native and linked data.

> **NOTE**
>
> After you link an external table to an Access database, don't move the source table to another drive or directory. Access doesn't bring the external data file into the ACCDB file; it maintains the link via the filename and file path. If you move the external table, you have to update the link using the Linked Table Manager, explained in the "Viewing or changing information for linked tables" section, later in this chapter.

FIGURE 7.3

The Datasheet view of externally linked data.

Company	InvoiceNum	SaleDate	ProductID	Quantity	Description
Fun Zone	4	3/28/2012	59	1	GMC Pickup
Fun Zone	4	3/28/2012	45	1	Ford Woody
Fun Zone	4	3/28/2012	2	1	Cord 810
Zoomy Collectibles	5	5/10/2012	4	5	Chevrolet Corvette Convertible
Zoomy Collectibles	5	5/10/2012	34	1	Porsche 935
Zoomy Collectibles	5	5/10/2012	5	2	Chevrolet Bel Air Convertible
Zoomy Collectibles	5	5/10/2012	3	1	Chevrolet Corvette Convertible
Your Favorite Things	6	5/7/2012	6	3	Ford Fairlane
Your Favorite Things	6	5/7/2012	8	1	Pontiac Vibe
Grandma's Closet	7	7/5/2012	2	1	Cord 810
Grandma's Closet	7	7/5/2012	7	4	Buick T-Type
Grandma's Closet	7	7/5/2012	57	1	Chevy Bel Air
Too Many Toys	8	8/4/2012	51	3	Chevy Bel Air Hardtop
Too Many Toys	8	8/4/2012	38	1	Eagle #6 Bobby Unser
Too Many Toys	8	8/4/2012	1	3	Buick Skylark
Too Many Toys	8	8/4/2012	8	1	Pontiac Vibe
Paul's Best Toys	9	8/12/2012	56	1	Datsun 240Z
Paul's Best Toys	9	8/12/2012	1	1	Buick Skylark
Fun Zone	10	9/25/2012	33	3	Shelby Coupe

Record: 1 of 88 — No Filter — Search

Limitations of linked data

Although this chapter describes using linked data as if it existed as native Access tables, certain operations can't be performed on linked data. Plus, the prohibited operations depend, to a certain extent, on the type of data linked to Access.

These limitations are relatively easy to understand. Linked data is never "owned" by Access. External files that are linked to Access are managed by their respective applications. For example, an Excel worksheet is managed by Excel. It would be presumptive—and dangerous—for Access to freely modify data in an Excel worksheet. For example, because many Excel operations depend on the relative positions of rows and columns in a worksheet, inserting a row into a worksheet might break calculations and other operations performed by Excel on the data. Deleting a row might distort a named range in the Excel worksheet, causing similar problems. Because there is no practical way for Access to understand all the operations performed on an external data file by its respective owner, Microsoft has chosen to take a conservative route and not allow Access to modify data that might cause problems for the data's owner.

The following list describes the limitations of linked data:

- **Access data:** There are no limitations to what you can do with the data in linked tables. You can't delete or rename the source table. Nor can you change the fields or data types of the source table.

- **Excel data:** Existing data in an Excel worksheet can't be changed, nor can rows be deleted or new rows be added to a worksheet. Excel data is essentially treated as read-only by Access.

- **Text files:** For all practical purposes, data linked to text files is treated as read-only in Access. Although the data can be used in forms and reports, you can't simply and easily update rows in a linked text file, nor can you delete existing rows in a text file. Oddly enough, you can *add* new rows to a text file; presumably, this is because new rows won't typically break existing operations the way that deleting or changing the contents of an existing row might.

- **HTML:** HTML data is treated exactly as Excel data. You can't modify, delete, or add rows to an HTML table.

- **Outlook contacts:** Outlook contacts can be displayed in Access forms and reports, but they can't be added, deleted, or changed.

- **ODBC:** ODBC is a data access technology that uses a driver between an Access database and an external database file, such as SQL Server or Oracle. Generally speaking, because the linked data source is a database table, you can perform whatever database operations (modifying, deleting, adding) you would with a native Access table, provided you've defined a unique index in Access. (We discuss ODBC database tables in some detail in the "Linking to ODBC data sources" section later in this chapter.)

Linking to other Access database tables

Access seamlessly incorporates data located in the other Access files by linking to those tables. This process makes it easy to share data among Access applications across the network or on the local computer. The information presented in this section applies to virtually any Access data file you linked to from an Access database. Later in this chapter, you'll see short sections explaining the differences between linking to an Access table and linking to each of the other types of data files recognized by Access.

> **NOTE**
>
> A common practice among Access developers is splitting an Access database into two pieces. One piece contains the queries, forms, reports, and other UI components of an application, while the second piece contains the tables and relationships. There are many advantages to splitting Access databases, including certain performance benefits, as well as easier maintenance. You can read about splitting Access databases later in this chapter. The process of linking to external Access tables described in this section is an essential part of the split database paradigm.

After you link to another Access table, you use it just as you use any table in the open database (with the exception that it can't be used in a relationship to other tables not in the source database). Follow these steps to link to tblSalesPayments in the Chapter07_Link.accdb database from the Chapter07.accdb database file:

1. **Open Chapter07.accdb.**

2. **Select the External Data tab of the Ribbon, and then click Import & Link ➪ New Data Source ➪ From Database ➪ Access.** The Get External Data – Access Database dialog box (shown in Figure 7.4) appears.

FIGURE 7.4

Use the Get External Data dialog box to select the type of operation you want to perform on the external data sources.

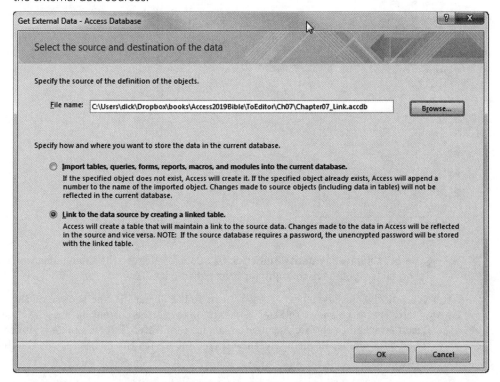

3. **Click the Browse button.** The File Open dialog box appears.

4. **Locate `Chapter07_Link.accdb` and click Open.** The File Open dialog box closes and you're taken back to the Get External Data – Access Database dialog box.

5. **Select the option button for linking and click OK in the Get External Data – Access Database dialog box.** The Link Tables dialog box enables you to select one or more tables from the selected database (in this case, Chapter07_Link). Figure 7.5 shows the Link Tables dialog box open on `Chapter07_Link.accdb`.

FIGURE 7.5

Use the Link Tables dialog box to select the Access table(s) for linking.

6. **Select tblSalesPayments and click OK.** Double-clicking the table name won't link the table—you have to highlight it and then click OK.

After you link tblSalesPayments, Access returns to the object list and shows you the newly linked table. Figure 7.6 shows tblSalesPayments linked to the current database. Notice the special icon attached to tblSalesPayments. This icon indicates that this table is linked to an external data source. Hovering over the linked table with the mouse reveals the linked table's data source.

> **TIP**
>
> You can link more than one table at a time by selecting multiple tables before you click the OK button in the Link Tables dialog box. Clicking the Select All button selects all the tables. Once you've selected all the tables, you can click individual selections to unselect them.

Linking to ODBC data sources

One significant advance with regard to data sharing is the establishment of the Open Database Connectivity (ODBC) standard by Microsoft and other vendors. ODBC is a specification that software vendors use to create drivers for database products. This specification lets your Access application work with data in a standard fashion across many different database platforms. If you write an application conforming to ODBC specifications, then your application will be able to use any other ODBC-compliant back end.

FIGURE 7.6

The Navigation pane with tblSalesPayments added. Hovering over the linked table icon reveals its source.

For example, say you create an Access application that uses a SQL Server database back end. The most common way to accomplish this requirement is to use the SQL Server ODBC driver. After developing the application, you find that one of your branch offices would like to use the application as well, but they're using Oracle as a database host. If your application has conformed closely to ODBC syntax, then you should be able to use the same application with Oracle by acquiring an Oracle ODBC driver. Not only are vendors supplying drivers for their own products, but there are now software vendors who only create and supply ODBC drivers.

Linking to non-database data

You can also link to non-database data, such as Excel, HTML, and text files. When you select one of these types of data sources, Access runs a Link Wizard that prompts you through the process.

Linking to Excel

Here are the main issues to keep in mind when linking to Excel data:

- An Excel workbook file might contain multiple worksheets. You must choose which worksheet within a workbook file to link to (unless you're using named ranges).

- You may link to named ranges within an Excel worksheet. Each range becomes a separate linked table in Access.

- Excel columns may contain virtually any type of data. Just because you've successfully linked to an Excel worksheet doesn't mean that your application will be able to use all the data contained in the worksheet. Because Excel doesn't limit the types of data contained in a worksheet, your application may encounter multiple types of data within a single column of a linked Excel worksheet. This means that you may have to add code or provide other strategies for working around the varying types of data contained in an Excel worksheet.

ON THE WEB

This book's website contains an Excel spreadsheet created by exporting the Products table from the Collectible Mini Cars application. Use this file to practice linking to Excel data, keeping in mind that, in practice, the data you're likely to encounter in Excel spreadsheets is far more complex and less orderly than the data contained in `CollectibleMiniCars.xls`.

Follow these steps to link to the Excel `CollectibleMiniCars.xls` spreadsheet:

1. **In the `Chapter07.accdb` database, click Import & Link ⇨ New Data Source ⇨ From File ⇨ Excel on the External Data tab of the Ribbon.** The Get External Data – Excel Spreadsheet dialog box (shown in Figure 7.7) appears.

2. **Select Link to the Data Source by Creating a Linked Table, and then click Browse.** The same Get External Data dialog box is used for both import and link operations, so be sure the correct operation is selected before continuing.

 We cover importing data into Access in Chapter 6.

3. **Locate and open the Excel file.** Select the CollectibleMiniCars spreadsheet file from the File Open dialog box and click Open.

4. **Click OK on the Get External Data - Excel Spreadsheet dialog box.** The Link Spreadsheet Wizard (see Figure 7.8) is shown. Notice that the Link Spreadsheet Wizard contains options for selecting either worksheets or named ranges within the workbook file. In this example, there are three different worksheets (named Products, Sales, and Customers) within the spreadsheet file.

FIGURE 7.7

The first screen of the Get External Data – Excel Spreadsheet dialog box.

5. **Select the Products worksheet.** The Link Spreadsheet Wizard walks you through a number of different screens where you specify details such as First Row Contains Column Headings and the data type you want to apply to each column in the Excel worksheet. The last screen of the Link Spreadsheet Wizard asks for the name of the newly linked table.

6. **Click Finish.** The linked table is established, and you're returned to the Access environment.

As with so many other things in database development, many decisions involved in linking to external data sources are based on how the data is to be used in the application. Also, the names you provide for fields and other details have a direct impact on your application.

FIGURE 7.8

The main Link Spreadsheet Wizard screen.

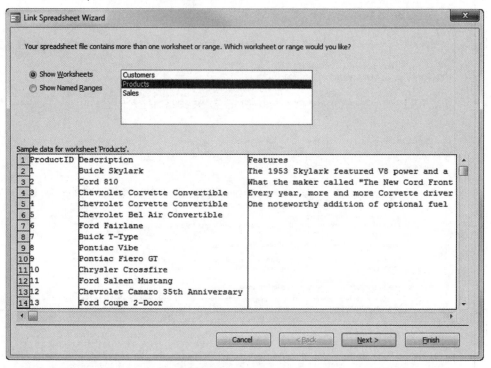

Linking to HTML files

Linking to data contained in HTML documents is not covered in detail in this book because of the rather severe limitations imposed by Access on this process. For example, Access is unable to retrieve data from an arbitrary HTML file. The data must be presented as an HTML table, in a row-and-column format, and the data has to be relatively clean (absent any unusual data or mix of data, such as text, image, and numeric data combined within a single HTML table).

You're likely to encounter problems if more than one HTML table appears on the page or if the data is presented in a hierarchical fashion (parent and child data).

TIP

Linking to arbitrary HTML documents is hit or miss at best. You're much better off linking to an HTML document specifically prepared as a data source for your Access application than trying to work with arbitrary HTML files.

If someone is going to the trouble of creating specialized HTML documents to be used as Access data sources, producing comma-separated values (CSV) or fixed-width text files is probably a better choice than HTML. CSV files, where the fields in each row are separated by commas, are commonly used for moving data from one application to another. CSV and fixed-width file types are discussed in the next section.

The process of linking HTML data is similar to linking to Excel spreadsheets:

1. **Click Import & Link ➪ New Data Source ➪ From File ➪ HTML Document on the External Data tab of the Ribbon.** The Get External Data – HTML Document dialog box appears.

2. **Select the Link to the Data Source by Creating a Linked Table option, and click Browse.** The File Open dialog box appears, enabling you to search for the HTML file you want to link.

From this point on, the process of linking to HTML data is similar to linking to other types of data files, including providing field names and other details of the linked data. Figure 7.9 shows the first screen of the Link HTML Wizard. Click the Advanced button to get to the Link Specification dialog box (shown in Figure 7.10), where you can provide the field names and other details.

FIGURE 7.9

The Link HTML Wizard dialog box showing the data in the HTML file.

FIGURE 7.10

The Link Specification dialog box that is used to name the column headings (field names) for the linked table.

Linking to text files

A far more common situation than linking to HTML files is linking to data stored in plain text files. Most applications, including Word and Excel, are able to publish data in a variety of text formats. The most common formats you're likely to encounter are:

- **Fixed-width:** In a fixed-width text file, each line represents one row of a database table. Each field within a line occupies exactly the same number of characters as the corresponding field in the lines above and below the current line. For example, a Last Name field in a fixed-width text file might occupy 20 characters, while a phone number field may only use 10 or 15 characters. Each data field is padded with spaces to the right to fill out the width allocated to the field. Figure 7.11 shows a typical fixed-width file open in Notepad.

FIGURE 7.11

A typical fixed-width text file.

- **Comma-separated values (CSV):** CSV files are somewhat more difficult to understand than fixed width. Each field is separated from the other fields by a comma character (,), and each field occupies as much space as necessary to contain the data. Generally, there is no blank space between fields in a CSV file. The advantage of CSV files is that the data can be contained in a smaller file because each field occupies only as much disk space as necessary to contain the data. The difficult part is that sometimes there are commas within a field, requiring text qualifiers, like double quotes, around the field.

  CSV files can be difficult to read when opened in Notepad. Figure 7.12 shows a typical CSV text file.

Text files often are used as intermediate data-transfer vehicles between dissimilar applications. For example, there might be an obsolete data management system in your environment that's incompatible with any of the link or import data types in Access. If you're lucky, the obsolete system is able to output either fixed-width or CSV files. Linking to or importing the fixed-width or CSV files might be the best option for sharing data with the obsolete system. At the very least, much less time is required to link or import the data than would be involved in re-keying all the information from the obsolete system into Access.

Follow these steps to link to `Contacts_FixedWidth.txt` or `Contacts_CSV.txt`:

1. **Open `Chapter07.accdb` and select the External Data tab of the Ribbon.**

2. **Click Import & Link ➪ New Data Source ➪ From File ➪ Text File on the External Data tab of the Ribbon. The Get External Data – Text File dialog box appears.**

FIGURE 7.12

CSV data is more compact than fixed-width text, but it's more difficult to read.

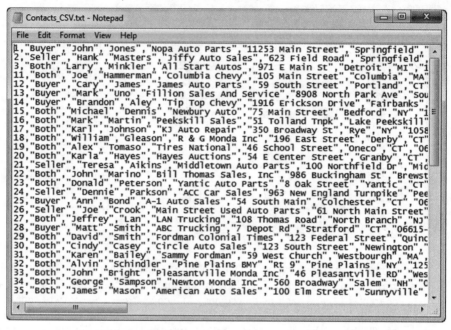

3. **Be sure the Link to the Data Source by Creating a Linked Table option is selected, and then click Browse.** The File Open dialog box appears.

4. **Locate the text file (either `Contacts_FixedWidth.txt` or `Contacts_CSV .txt`) and click Open.**

5. **Click OK on the Get External Data – Text File dialog box.** You'll be taken to the Link Text Wizard.

Access usually makes a pretty good guess at how the data in the file is delimited. Linking to text data can involve nothing more than clicking Next and verifying that Access has correctly identified the data in the file.

Working with Linked Tables

After you link to an external table from another database, you use it just as you would any other Access table. You use linked tables with forms, reports, and queries just as you would native Access tables. When working with external tables, you can modify many of their features (for example, setting view properties and relationships, setting links between tables in queries, and renaming the tables).

One note on renaming linked tables: providing a different name for the table inside Access doesn't change the name of the file that's linked to the application. The name that Access refers to in a linked table is maintained within the Access application and doesn't influence the physical table that's linked.

Setting view properties

Although an external table is used like another Access table, you can't change the structure (delete, add, or rearrange fields) of an external table. You can, however, set several properties for the fields in a linked table:

- Format
- Decimal places
- Caption
- Input mask
- Unicode compressions
- IME sequence mode
- Display control

To change these properties, open the linked table in Design view. When you open a linked table in Design view, Access warns you that the design can't be modified. Figure 7.13 shows a warning when the ContactsFixed table is opened in Design view. Despite that warning, these properties can be changed.

FIGURE 7.13

Opening linked tables in Design view comes with a warning.

Setting relationships

> **TIP**
>
> Access enables you to set permanent relationships at the table level between linked non-Access tables and native Access tables through the Relationships window. You can't, however, set referential integrity between linked tables or between linked tables and internal tables. Access enables you to create forms and reports based on relationships set up in the Relationships window, such as building a SQL statement used as the RecordSource property of a form or report.

Linking to external Access tables maintains the relationships that might exist between the external tables. Therefore, when linking to a back-end database, the relationships you've established in the back end, as well as any validation and default values, are recognized and honored by the front-end database. This is a good thing, because it means that the rules you've defined will be enforced regardless of how many front ends are created to use the tables.

 We discuss relationships in detail in Chapter 4.

Optimizing linked tables

When working with linked tables, Access has to retrieve records from an external file. This process takes time, especially when the table resides on a network or in a SQL database. When working with external data, optimize performance by observing these basic rules:

- **Avoid using functions in query criteria.** This is especially true for aggregate functions, such as DTotal or DCount, which retrieve all records from the linked table before performing the query operation.
- **Limit the number of external records to view.** Create a query using criteria that limit the number of records from an external table. This query can then be used by other queries, forms, or reports.
- **Avoid excessive movement in datasheets.** View only the data you need to in a datasheet. Avoid paging up and down and jumping to the first or last record in very large tables. (The exception is when you're adding records to the external table.)

■ **If you add records to external linked tables, create a form to add records and set the DataEntry property to True.** This makes the form an entry form that starts with a blank record every time it's executed. Data entry forms are not pre-populated with data from the bound table. Using a dedicated data entry form is much more efficient than building a normal form, populating it with data from the linked source, and then moving to the end of the linked data just to add a new record.

Deleting a linked table reference

Deleting a linked table from your database is a simple matter of performing three steps:

1. **In the Navigation pane, select the linked table you want to delete.**

2. **Press the Delete key, or right-click the linked table and select Delete from the shortcut menu.**

3. **Click OK in the Access dialog box to delete the file.**

> **NOTE**
>
> Deleting an external table deletes only its name from the database object list. The actual data is not deleted from its source location.

Viewing or changing information for linked tables

Use the Linked Table Manager to update the links when you move, rename, or modify tables, indexes, or relationships associated with linked tables. Otherwise, Access won't be able to find the data file referenced by the link.

1. **Select the External Data tab of the Ribbon and click the Linked Table Manager button.** The Linked Table Manager (shown in Figure 7.14) appears, letting you locate the data files associated with the linked tables in the database.

2. **Click the check box next to a linked table and click OK.**

3. **Find the missing file and relink to Access.** If all the files are already linked correctly, clicking OK makes Access verify all the linkages associated with all the selected tables.

4. **If you know all the linked data sources have been moved, select the Always Prompt for New Location check box, and then click OK.** Access then prompts you for the new location and links all the tables as a batch process. This is much faster than linking one or two tables at a time. If all your tables come from different sources, though, the Linked Table Manager still requires you to select each source one at a time.

FIGURE 7.14

The Linked Table Manager lets you relocate external tables that have been moved.

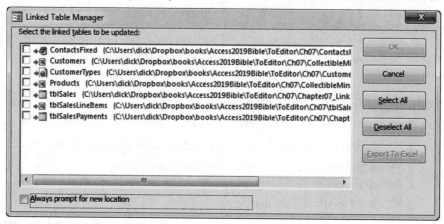

Refreshing linked tables

Access keeps the data in linked tables in sync with the source data automatically. No user intervention is required to have up-to-date data. When a linked table is open in Datasheet view or otherwise being used, Access attempts to restrict access to the source data depending on what kind of data it is. For instance, Access locks linked text files that are in use so that you can't open them in a text editor.

To demonstrate how linked data is synchronized automatically, create a linked table to a text file and edit that text file by following these steps:

1. **Click Import & Link ➪ New Data Source ➪ From File ➪ Text File on the External Data tab of the Ribbon.**

2. **Create a linked text file from the file named** ContactsFixed.txt, **a fixed-length text file.** The file is well formatted, so Access will guess correctly about where the fields begin. Don't worry about field names for this exercise.

3. **Open the linked table ContactsFixed.** Note that it contains 12 records. If you attempt to open ContactsFixed.txt in a text editor, Windows will tell you that it's being used by another process and won't allow you to open it.

4. **Close the ContactsFixed table.**

5. **Add a new row to the text file using your favorite plain text editor, such as Notepad.** Don't use Word for this process, because you'll risk saving it in a format that's not plain text. Figure 7.15 shows the new ContactsFixed.txt file.

FIGURE 7.15

A new row in the text file will sync with Access automatically.

```
ContactsFixed.txt - Notepad

File  Edit  Format  View  Help
01    Jones       John      Nopa Auto Parts      Springfield      MA 02/22/1994
02    Masters     Hank      Jiffy Auto Sales     Springfield      MO 01/01/2005
03    Minkler     Larry     All Start Autos      Detroit          MI 06/17/2011
04    Hammerman   Joe       Columbia Chevy       Columbia         MA 03/13/2003
05    James       Cary      James Auto Parts     Portland         CT 04/04/2011
06    Uno         Mark      Fillion Sales And    South Windsor    CT 07/08/2004
07    Aley        Brandon   Tip Top Chevy        Fairbanks        MA 05/25/1999
08    Dennis      Michael   Newbury Auto         Bedford          NY 06/26/2013
09    Martin      Mark      Peekskill Sales      Lake Peekskill   NY 10/20/2010
10    Johnson     Karl      KJ Auto Repair       Rye              NY 09/29/2001
11    Gleason     William   R & G Monda Inc      Derby            CT 01/10/2009
12    Tomaso      Alex      Tires National       Oneco            CT 02/01/2011
13    Smith       Jerry     Smith Service        Detroit          MI 03/01/2012
```

6. **Save the file and close the text editor.**

7. **In Access, open the ContactsFixed linked table.** The linked table now contains a 13th row.

Splitting a Database

There are many great reasons to link tables between Access databases. One of the best, and most common, reasons is to split the database. Splitting a database means creating two ACCDB files from one. One of the files, generally called the *back end*, contains only tables and relationships. The other file, the *front end*, contains queries, macros, code, and UI elements, such as forms and reports. The front end also contains links to all the tables in the back end.

The benefits of splitting a database

There is at least one extremely good reason why you should consider splitting your Access databases. Although you can place a single copy of an ACCDB file onto a shared computer on the network, the performance degradation from such a design is considerable.

Using an Access database stored on a remote computer involves much more than simply moving data from the remote computer to the local machine. All the form, menu, and Ribbon definitions must be transported to the local computer so that Windows can "construct" the UI on the local computer's monitor. The Windows installation on the local computer must intercept and transmit any keyboard and mouse events to the remote computer so that the proper code will run in response to these events. Finally, the single copy of Access on the remote computer must fulfill all data requests, no matter how trivial or demanding. The impact of all these actions is compounded by increasing the number of users working with the same remotely installed copy of the database.

Fortunately, most of these issues disappear when the database application is split into front-end and back-end components. The local Windows installation handles the UI from information stored in the front-end database. All code is run on the user's desktop computer, rather than on the remote machine. Also, the locally installed copy of Access is able to handle all local data requirements, while only those requests for remote data are passed on to the back-end database.

Before getting into the details of splitting a database, let's consider some of the problems associated with single-file databases. To begin with, unlike some other development systems, all the objects in an Access database application are stored in a single file, the familiar ACCDB file you work with every day. Many other database systems like FoxPro for Windows maintain a number of different files for each application, usually one file per object (form, table, and so on). Although having to deal with multiple files complicates database development and maintenance somewhat, updating a single form or query involves nothing more than replacing the related file with the updated form or query file.

Updating an Access database object is somewhat more complicated. As you've probably discovered, replacing a form or query in an Access database used by a large number of users can be quite a problem. Replacing a form or other database object often requires hours of work importing the object into each user's copy of the database.

A second consideration is the network traffic inherent in single-file Access databases. Figure 7.16 shows an example of the problem. This figure illustrates a common method of sharing an Access database. The computer in the upper-left corner of the figure is the file server and holds the Access database file. Assume for a moment that the entire database is contained within a single ACCDB on the file server, and the database has been enabled for shared data access. Each workstation in Figure 7.16 has a full copy of Access (or the Access RunTime) installed.

Now, what happens when the user on Workstation C opens the database? The Access installation on that machine must locate the ACCDB on the file server, open that file, and start up the application. This means that any splash forms, queries, and other startup activities must take place across the network before the user is able to work with the database. Any time a form is opened or a query is run, the information necessary to fulfill the query must travel across the network, slowing the operation. (In Figure 7.16, the network load is indicated by a wide network cable.)

The situation shown in Figure 7.16 is made even worse when more than one user is using the same database. In this case, the network traffic is increased by the queries, opening of forms, and other operations performed by each additional user's copy of Access. Imagine the line getting thicker with each operation across the network.

The split-database model is illustrated in Figure 7.17. The back-end database resides on the server while individual copies of the front-end database are placed on each workstation.

Each front-end database contains links to the tables stored in the back-end ACCDB file. The front-end databases also contain the forms, reports, queries, and other user-interface components of the application. Each database, back-end and front-end, is smaller than if they were combined.

FIGURE 7.16

A database kept on a file server can generate a large amount of traffic on the network.

The network traffic is reduced (indicated by a thinner network cable) in Figure 7.17 because only linking information and data returned by queries is moved across the network. A user working with the database application uses the forms, queries, reports, macros, and code stored in the local front-end ACCDB file. Because the front end is accessed by a single user, response time is much improved because the local copy of Access is able to instantly open the database and begin the startup operations. Only when actually running queries does the network traffic increase.

The second major benefit of the split database design is that updating the forms, reports, and other application components requires nothing more than replacing the front-end database on each user's computer and reestablishing the links to the table in the back-end database. In fact, the design in Figure 7.17 supports the notion of customized front ends, depending on the requirements of the user sitting at each workstation. For example, a manager sitting at Workstation A might need access to personnel information that is not available to the people sitting at workstations B and C. In this case, the front-end database on Workstation A includes the forms, queries, and other database objects necessary to view the personnel information.

FIGURE 7.17

A database kept on a file server can generate a large amount of traffic on the network.

Knowing where to put which objects

The local ACCDB contains all the UI objects, including forms, reports, queries, macros, and modules. Keeping the UI components on the local machine dramatically improves performance. You don't need to move forms, queries, or reports across the network—these objects are much more easily manipulated on the local machine than when accessed across the network.

All shared tables should be placed in the back-end database kept on the server, along with all relationships between those tables. The server database is opened in Shared mode, making all its objects accessible to multiple users. The tables in the server database are linked to the front-end ACCDB on each user's Desktop. (There is no problem with simultaneously linking the same table to multiple databases.)

Obviously, with more than one person using the data within a table, the same record might be edited by multiple users. The Access database engine handles this problem by locking a record as it's edited by a user. A lock contention occurs when more than one user tries to update the same record. Only one user will have "live" access to the record—all other users will either be locked or have their changes held up until the record holder is done making changes.

Using the Database Splitter add-in

The Database Splitter helps you split an application into front-end and back-end databases. This wizard enables you to build and test your database to your heart's content, and then lightens the burden of preparing the application for multiuser access.

As an experiment, let's take a look at splitting the Northwind Traders database into front-end and back-end ACCDB files. You start the Database Splitter by selecting the Database Tools tab of the Ribbon and then clicking the Access Database button in the Move Data group. The opening wizard screen (shown in Figure 7.18) explains the actions of the Database Splitter and suggests that you make a backup of the database before proceeding.

FIGURE 7.18

The Database Splitter is a simple wizard.

The only other information that the Database Splitter requires is where you want to put the back-end database. Figure 7.19 shows the familiar Explorer-style Create Back-end Database dialog box that lets you specify the location of the back-end ACCDB file. By default, the back-end database has the same name as the original database with a _be suffix added to the name (for example, MyDB_be.accdb).

CAUTION

You can access a network location through a Universal Naming Convention (UNC) path or through a mapped drive. A UNC path starts with two back slashes, the server name, and the path to the network location. An example of a UNC path is \\MyServer\MyDatashare\MyFolder\. A mapped drive assigns a letter to a particular UNC path (such as S:). Mapped drives are unique to each computer, and there is no guarantee that a mapped drive on one computer will be the same on another. When creating a back-end database, always use a UNC path to link the tables because UNC paths are the same for all computers on the same network. To use UNC paths, navigate to the network location through the Network shortcut.

FIGURE 7.19

Specify the permanent location of the back-end database in the Create Back-end Database dialog box.

When you click the Split button (refer to Figure 7.19), the Database Splitter creates the back-end database, exports all tables to it, deletes the tables in the local database, and creates links to the back-end tables. In other words, the Database Splitter performs precisely the same steps you'd have to perform manually if the Database Splitter weren't available.

> **NOTE**
>
> Be prepared for this process to take a little while, especially on large databases. Because Access has to create the new database, transfer tables to it, and create the links back to the original database, the splitting process can easily require more than a few minutes. If the process appears to be taking longer than you expect, it means that splitting your database was a good idea and you'll see some great performance improvements.
>
> Also, keep in mind that the Database Splitter is rather simplistic and tends to ignore system considerations such as available disk space. Make sure adequate disk space exists on the target machine to accommodate the back-end database.

Figure 7.20 shows the Access Navigation pane after splitting the Northwind Traders database. The back-end database contains only the tables exported from `Northwind.accdb`. Notice that the icons associated with all the tables in `Northwind.accdb` have been changed, indicating that they're now pointing to copies in the back-end database. You'll have to import any local tables from the back-end database before distributing the front end to the users.

FIGURE 7.20

The Database Splitter creates links for all tables in the database.

Part III

Working with Access Queries

The chapters in Part III introduce you to some of the basic analytical tools and techniques available in Access. Specifically, you get a solid foundation in building Access queries.

Queries draw various data sources together and present the combined information in useful views. They enable you to synthesize the raw data in your Access tables into meaningful analysis.

Chapter 8 starts by exploring the Query Designer along with techniques to create simple analytical outputs from your Access tables. Chapter 9 outlines the various operators and expressions that can be used to add complexity to your Access data analysis. Finally, in Chapter 10, you dive deeply into more advanced query concepts. Here, you learn how to go beyond simply selecting data from your tables and explore how to aggregate query outputs, how to perform action queries, and how to create versatile crosstab queries.

IN THIS PART

Chapter 8
Selecting Data with Queries

Chapter 9
Using Operators and Expressions in Access

Chapter 10
Going Beyond Select Queries

Selecting Data with Queries

IN THIS CHAPTER

Understanding what queries are and what they can do for you

Creating queries

Specifying the fields in a query

Displaying a query's results

Adding and removing fields from a query's design

Sorting a query's results

Filtering records with query criteria

Printing records returned by a query

Saving a query

Including more than one table in a query

Adding, deleting, and moving tables in a query

Joining tables in a query's design

Understanding the options for joining tables in a query

Queries are an essential part of any database application. Queries are the tools that enable you and your users to extract data from multiple tables, combine it in useful ways, and present it to the user as a datasheet, on a form, or as a printed report.

You may have heard the old cliché, "Queries convert data to information." To a certain extent, this statement is true—that's why it's a cliché. The data contained within tables is not particularly useful because, for the most part, the data in tables appears in no particular order. Also, in a properly normalized database, important information is spread out among a number of different tables. Queries are what draw these various data sources together and present the combined information in such a way that users can actually work with the data.

ON THE WEB

The starting database for this walkthrough, `Chapter08.accdb`, can be downloaded from this book's website.

Introducing Queries

The word *query* comes from the Latin word *quaerere*, which means "to ask or inquire." Over the years, the word *query* has become synonymous with *quiz, challenge, inquire,* or *question.*

An Access query is a question that you ask about the information stored in Access tables. You build queries with the Access query tools. Your query can be a simple question about data in a single table, or it can be a more complex question about information stored in several tables. For example, you might ask your database to show you only trucks that were sold in the year 2012. After you submit the question in the form of a query, Access returns only the information you requested.

What queries can do

Queries are flexible. They allow you to look at your data in virtually any way you can imagine. Most database systems are continually evolving and changing over time. Quite often, the original purpose of a database is very different from its current use.

Here's just a sampling of what you can do with Access queries:

- **Choose tables.** You can obtain information from a single table or from many tables that are related by some common data. Suppose you're interested in seeing the customer name along with the items purchased by each type of customer. When using several tables, Access combines the data as a single recordset (a set of records that meet given criterion).
- **Choose fields.** Specify which fields from each table you want to see in the recordset. For example, you can select the customer name, zip code, sales date, and invoice number from tblCustomers and tblSales.
- **Provide criteria.** Record selection is based on selection criteria. For example, you might want to see records for only a certain category of products.
- **Sort records.** You might want to sort records in a specific order. For example, you might need to see customer contacts sorted by last name and first name.
- **Perform calculations.** Use queries to perform calculations such as averages, totals, or counts of data in records.
- **Create tables.** Create a brand-new table based on data returned by a query.
- **Display query data on forms and reports.** The recordset you create from a query might have just the right fields and data needed for a report or form. Basing a report or form on a query means that, every time you print the report or open the form, you see the most current information contained in the tables.
- **Use a query as a source of data for other queries (subquery).** You can create queries that are based on records returned by another query. This is very useful for performing ad hoc queries, where you might repeatedly make small changes to the criteria. In this case, the second query filters the first query's results.
- **Make changes to data in tables.** Action queries can modify multiple rows in the underlying tables as a single operation. Action queries are frequently used to maintain data, such as updating values in specific fields, appending new data, or deleting obsolete information.

What queries return

Access combines a query's records and, when executed, displays them in Datasheet view by default. The set of records returned by a query is commonly called (oddly enough) a *recordset*. A recordset is a dynamic set of records. The recordset returned by a query is not stored within the database, unless you've directed Access to build a table from those records.

 You can read much more about Datasheet view in Chapter 5.

When you save a query, only the structure of the query is saved, not the returned records. That is to say, only the SQL syntax used to build the query is stored.

 We cover the SQL syntax behind queries in Chapter 14.

Consider these benefits of *not* saving the recordset to a physical table:

- A smaller amount of space on a storage device (usually a hard disk) is needed.
- The query uses updated versions of records.

Every time the query is executed, it reads the underlying tables and re-creates the recordset. Because recordsets themselves are not stored, a query automatically reflects any changes to the underlying tables made since the last time the query was executed—even in a real-time, multiuser environment. Depending on your needs, a query's recordset can be viewed as a datasheet or in a form or report. When a form or report is based on a query, the query's recordset is re-created and bound to the form or report each time it's opened.

A query's recordset can also be used in macros and VBA procedures to help drive any number of automated tasks.

Creating a Query

After you create your tables and place data in them, you're ready to work with queries. To begin a query, select the Create tab on the Ribbon, and click the Query Design button in the Queries group. This opens the Query Designer shown in Figure 8.1.

Figure 8.1 shows two windows. The underlying window is the Query Designer. Floating on top of the Query Designer is the Show Table dialog box. The Show Table dialog box is *modal*, which means that you must do something in the dialog box before continuing with the query. Before you continue, you add the tables required for the query. In this case, tblProducts is highlighted and ready to be added.

The Show Table dialog box (refer to Figure 8.1) displays the tables and queries in your database. Double-click tblProducts to add it to the query design, or highlight tblProducts in the list and click the Add button. Close the Show Table dialog box after adding tblProducts. Figure 8.2 shows tblProducts added to the query.

FIGURE 8.1

The Show Table dialog box and the query design window.

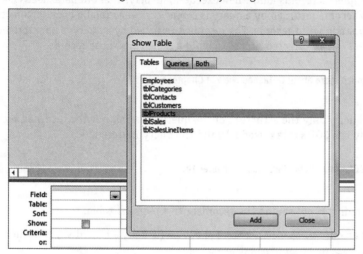

To add additional tables to the query, right-click anywhere in the upper portion of the Query Designer and select Show Table from the shortcut menu that appears. Once the Show Table dialog box is open, you would typically select all the table and query objects needed to build your query.

Alternatively, you can drag tables or queries from the Navigation pane to the upper portion of the Query Designer. This is a handy trick if you've already dismissed the Show Table dialog box and you need a quick addition to your query. There is also a Show Table button on the Design tab of the Ribbon.

Removing a table from the Query Designer is easy. Simply right-click the table in the Query Designer and select Remove Table from the shortcut menu.

The query design window has three primary views:

- **Design view:** Where you create the query
- **Datasheet view:** Displays the records returned by the query
- **SQL view:** Displays the SQL statement behind a query

The Query Designer consists of two sections:

- **The table/query pane (top):** This is where tables or queries and their respective field lists are added to the query's design. You'll see a separate field list for each object to add. Each field list contains the names of all the fields in the respective table or query. You can resize a field list by clicking the edges and dragging it to a different size. You may want to resize a field list so that all of a table's fields are visible.

FIGURE 8.2

The query design window with tblProducts added.

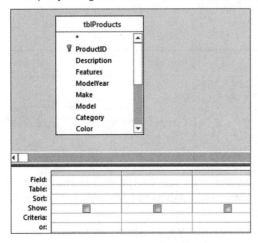

- **The Query by Design (QBD) grid (bottom):** The QBD grid holds the field names involved in the query and any criteria used to select records. Each column in the QBD grid contains information about a single field from a table or query contained within the upper pane.

The two window panes are separated horizontally by a pane-resizing scroll bar (refer to Figure 8.2). You can use the scroll to shift the design grid left or right or use the mouse to click and drag the bar up or down to change the relative sizes of the upper and lower panes.

Switch between the upper and lower panes by clicking the desired pane or by pressing F6. Each pane has horizontal and vertical scroll bars to help you move around.

You actually build the query by dragging fields from the upper pane to the QBD grid.

Figure 8.2 displays an empty QBD grid at the bottom of the Query Designer. The QBD grid has six labeled rows:

- **Field:** This is where field names are entered or added.
- **Table:** This row shows the table the field is from. This is useful in queries with multiple tables.
- **Sort:** This row enables sorting instructions for the query.
- **Show:** This row determines whether to display the field in the returned recordset.
- **Criteria:** This row consists of the criteria that filter the returned records.
- **Or:** This row is the first of a number of rows to which you can add multiple query criteria.

You learn more about these rows as you create queries in this chapter.

The Query Tools Design Ribbon (shown in Figure 8.3) contains many buttons specific to building and working with queries. Although each button is explained as it's used in the chapters of this book, here are the main buttons:

FIGURE 8.3

The Query Tools Design Ribbon.

- **View:** Switches between the Datasheet view and Design view in the query design window. The View drop-down control also enables you to display the underlying SQL statement behind the query.
- **Run:** Runs the query. Displays a select query's datasheet, serving the same function as selecting Datasheet View from the View button. However, when working with action queries, the Run button performs the operations (append, make-table, and so on) specified by the query.
- **Select:** Clicking the Select button transforms the opened query into a Select query.
- **Make Table, Append, Update, Crosstab, and Delete:** Each of these buttons specifies the type of query you're building. In most cases, you transform a select query into an action query by clicking one of these buttons.
- **Show Table:** Opens the Show Table dialog box.

The remaining buttons are used for creating more-advanced queries and displaying a query's Property Sheet.

Adding fields to your queries

There are several ways to add fields to a query. You can add fields one at a time, select and add multiple fields, or select all the fields in a field list.

Adding a single field

You add a single field in several ways. One method is to double-click the field name in the table in the top pane of the Query Designer. The field name immediately appears in the first available column in the QBD pane. Alternatively, drag a field from a table in the top pane of the Query Designer, and drop it on a column in the QBD grid. Dropping a field between two fields in the QBD grid pushes other fields to the right.

In Figure 8.4 you can see that the Cost field was brought into the QBD grid. Once a field is added, you can simply add the next field you need to see in the query.

FIGURE 8.4

To add fields from your table to the QBD grid, simply double-click or drag the field.

Each cell in the Table row of the QBD grid contains a drop-down list of the tables contained in the upper pane of the Query Designer.

Adding multiple fields

You can add multiple fields in a single action by selecting the fields from the field list window and dragging them to the QBD grid. The selected fields don't have to be contiguous (one after the other). Hold down the Ctrl key while selecting multiple fields. Figure 8.5 illustrates the process of adding multiple fields.

FIGURE 8.5

Selecting multiple fields to add to the QBD grid.

8

245

The fields are added to the QBD grid in the order in which they occur in the table.

You can also add all the fields in the table by double-clicking the field list's header (where it says tblProducts in Figure 8.6) to highlight all the fields in the table. Then drag the highlighted fields to the QBD grid.

Alternatively, you can click and drag the asterisk (*) from the field list to the QBD grid (or double-click the asterisk to add it to the QBD grid). Although this action doesn't add all the fields to the QBD grid, the asterisk directs Access to include all fields in the table in the query.

FIGURE 8.6

Adding the asterisk to the QBD grid selects all fields in the table.

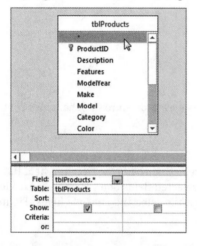

> **TIP**
>
> Unlike selecting all the fields, the asterisk places a reference to all the fields in a single column. When you drag multiple columns, as in the preceding example, you drag names to the QBD grid. If you later change the design of the table, you will also have to change the design of the query if you need to use the changed fields. The advantage of using the asterisk for selecting all fields is that changes to the underlying tables don't require changes to the query. The asterisk means to select all fields in the table, regardless of the field names or changes in the number of fields in the table.

> **CAUTION**
>
> The downside of using the asterisk to specify all fields in a table is that the query, as instructed, returns all the fields in a table, regardless of whether every field is used on a form or report. Retrieving unused data can be an inefficient process. Very often, performance problems can be traced to the asterisk returning many more fields than necessary to a form or report. You also have no control over the order in which the fields appear in the datasheet.

Running your query

After selecting the fields, run the query by clicking the Run button on the Query Tools Design Ribbon (see Figure 8.7).

FIGURE 8.7

Click the Run button to display the results of your query.

To return to the QBD grid, you can go up to the Home tab and choose View ⇨ Design View. Alternatively, you can right-click the tab header for the query (as shown in Figure 8.8) and select Design View.

FIGURE 8.8

Right-click the query's tab header and select Design View to return to the QBD grid.

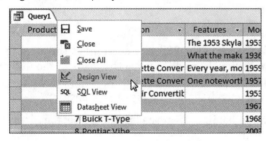

Working with Query Fields

Sometimes you'll want to work with the fields you've already selected—rearranging their order, inserting a new field, or deleting an existing field. You may even want to add a field to the QBD grid without showing it in the datasheet. Adding a field without showing it enables you to sort on the hidden field or to use the hidden field as criteria.

Selecting a field in the QBD grid

Before you can move a field's position, you must first select it. To select it, you will work with the field selector row.

The *field selector* is the thin gray area at the top of each column in the QBD grid at the bottom of the Query Designer. Each column represents a field. To select the Category field, move the mouse pointer until a small selection arrow (in this case, a dark downward arrow) is visible in the field selector and then click and drag the column. Figure 8.9 shows the selection arrow above the Category column just before it's selected.

FIGURE 8.9

Selecting a column in the QBD grid. The pointer changes to a downward-pointing arrow when you move over the field selector.

Field:	ProductID	Description	Category	QtyInStock	Cost
Table:	tblProducts	tblProducts	tblProducts	tblProducts	tblProducts
Sort:					
Show:	✓	✓	✓	✓	✓
Criteria:					
or:					

> **TIP**
>
> Select multiple contiguous fields by clicking the first field you want to select and then dragging across the field selector bars of the other fields.

Changing field order

The left-to-right order in which fields appear in the QBD grid determines the order in which they appear in Datasheet view. You might want to move the fields in the QBD grid to achieve a new sequence of fields in the query's results. With the fields selected, you can move the fields on the QBD design by simply dragging them to a new position.

Left-click a field's selector bar and, while holding down the left mouse button, drag the field into a new position in the QBD grid.

Figure 8.10 shows the Category field highlighted. As you move the selector field to the left, the column separator between the fields ProductID and Description changes (gets wider) to show you where Category will go.

FIGURE 8.10

Moving the Category field to between ProductID and Description. Notice the QBD field icon below the arrow near the Description column.

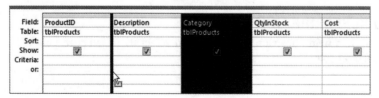

Field:	ProductID	Description	Category	QtyInStock	Cost
Table:	tblProducts	tblProducts	tblProducts	tblProducts	tblProducts
Sort:					
Show:	✓	✓	✓	✓	✓
Criteria:					
or:					

Resizing columns in the QBD grid

The QBD grid generally shows eight to ten fields (depending on how wide your screen is) in the viewable area. The remaining fields are viewed by moving the horizontal scroll bar at the bottom of the window.

You might want to shrink some fields to be able to see more columns in the QBD grid. You adjust the column width to make them smaller (or larger) by moving the mouse pointer to the margin between two fields and dragging the column resizer left or right (see Figure 8.11).

FIGURE 8.11

Resizing columns in the QBD grid.

The width of a column in the QBD grid has no effect on how the field's data is displayed in a datasheet, form, or report. The column width in the QBD grid is just a convenience to you, the developer. Also, QBD column width is not preserved when you save and close the query.

Removing a field

Remove a field from the QBD grid by selecting the field and pressing the Delete key. You can also right-click a field's selector bar and choose Cut from the shortcut menu.

Inserting a field

Insert new fields in the QBD grid by dragging a field from a field list window in the tables pane above the QBD grid and dropping it onto a column in the QBD grid. The new column is inserted to the left of the column on which you dropped the field. Double-clicking a field in a field list adds the new column at the far-right position in the QBD grid.

Hiding a field

While you're performing queries, you might want to show only some of the fields in the QBD grid. For example, suppose you've chosen FirstName, LastName, Address, City, and State. Then you decide that you want to temporarily look at the same data, without the State field. Instead of completely removing the State field, you can simply hide it by unchecking the Show check box in the State column (see Figure 8.12).

FIGURE 8.12

The Show check box is unchecked for the State field so that field will not show in the results.

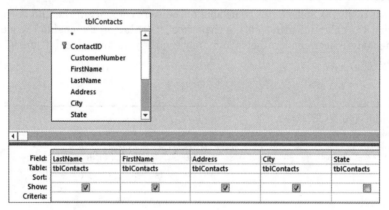

A common reason to hide a field in the query is because the field is used for sorting or as criteria, but its value is not needed in the query results. For example, consider a query involving invoices. For a number of reasons, the users might want to see the invoices sorted by the order date, even though the actual order date is irrelevant for this particular purpose. You could simply include the OrderDate field in the QBD grid, set the sort order for the OrderDate field, and uncheck its Show box. Access sorts the data by the OrderDate field even though the field is not shown in the query's results.

> **NOTE**
>
> If you save a query that has an unused field (its Show box is unchecked and no criteria or sort order is applied to the field), Access eliminates the field from the query as part of the query optimization process. The next time you open the query, the field won't be included in the query's design.

Changing the sort order of a field

When viewing a recordset, you often want to display the data in a sorted order to make it easier to analyze the data. For example, you may want to review the results from the tblProducts table sorted by category.

Sorting places the records in alphabetical or numeric order. The sort order can be ascending or descending. You can sort on a single field or multiple fields.

You input sorting directions in the Sort row in the QBD grid. To specify a sort order on a particular field (such as LastName), perform these steps:

1. **Position the cursor in the Sort cell in the LastName column.**

2. **Click the drop-down list that appears in the cell and select the sort order (Ascending or Descending) you want to apply.** Figure 8.13 shows the QBD grid with ascending sorts specified for the LastName and FirstName fields. Notice the word *Ascending* is being shown in the fields' Sort cells.

FIGURE 8.13

An ascending sort has been specified for the LastName and FirstName fields.

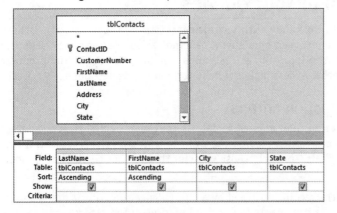

8

The left-to-right order in which fields appear in the QBD grid is important when sorting on more than one field. Not only do the fields appear in the datasheet in left-to-right order, but they're sorted in the same order; this is known as *sort order precedence*. The leftmost field containing sort criteria is sorted first, the first field to the right containing sort criteria is sorted next, and so on. In the example shown in Figure 8.13, the LastName field is sorted first, followed by the FirstName field.

Figure 8.14 shows the results of the query shown in Figure 8.13. Notice that the data is sorted by LastName and then by FirstName. This is why Ann Bond appears before John Bond, and John Jones appears before Kevin Jones in the query's data.

FIGURE 8.14

The order of the fields in the QBD grid is critical when sorting on multiple fields.

LastName	FirstName	City	State
Aikins	Teresa	Middletown	CT
Aley	Brandon	Fairbanks	MA
Bailey	Karen	Westbourgh	MA
Baker	Harry	Mohegan Lake	NY
Bond	Ann	Colchester	CT
Bond	John	Colchester	CT
Calson	Larry	Chicota	TX
Jackson	Harry	Tuskahoma	OK
Jones	John	Springfield	MA
Jones	Kevin	Eastville	MA

Adding Criteria to Your Queries

Most often users want to work only with records conforming to some criteria. Otherwise, too many records may be returned by a query, causing serious performance issues. For example, you might want to look only at customers who haven't bought any products within the last six months. Access makes it easy for you to specify a query's criteria.

Understanding selection criteria

Selection criteria are filtering rules applied to data as they're extracted from the database. Selection criteria tell Access which records you want to look at in the recordset. A typical criterion might be "all sellers," or "only those vehicles that are not trucks," or "products with retail prices greater than $75."

Selection criteria limit the records returned by a query. Selection criteria aid the user by selecting only the records a user wants to see and ignoring all the others.

You specify criteria in the Criteria row of the QBD grid. You designate criteria as an expression. The expression can be simple (like "trucks" or "not trucks"), or it can take the form of complex expressions using built-in Access functions.

Proper use of query criteria is critical to an Access database's success. In most cases, the users have no idea what data is stored in a database's tables and accept whatever they see on a form or report as truthfully representing the database's status. Poorly chosen criteria might hide important information from the application's users, leading to bad business decisions or serious business issues later on.

Entering simple string criteria

Character-type criteria are applied to Text-type fields. Most often, you'll enter an example of the text you want to retrieve. Here is a small example that returns only product records where the product type is "Cars":

1. **Add tblProducts and choose the Description, Cost, QtyInStock, and Category fields.**

2. **Type** CARS **into the Criteria cell under the Category column (see Figure 8.15).**
   Notice that Access adds double quotes around the value. Unlike many other
   database systems, Access automatically makes assumptions about what you
   want.

3. **Run the query.** Note that only cars are displayed in the query's results.

FIGURE 8.15

Specifying Cars as the query's criteria.

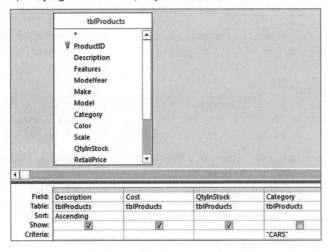

When looking at the results of the query, you may argue that there is no point in displaying Cars in every row. In fact, because this query only returns information about
cars, the user can assume that every record references a car, and there's no need to
display a product category in the query. Unchecking the Category field's Show box in
the query's design removes Category from the datasheet, making the data easier to
understand.

You could enter the criteria expression in any of these other ways:

    CARS
    = CARS
    "CARS"
    = "Cars"

By default, Access is *not* case sensitive, so any form of the word *cars* works just as well as
this query's criteria.

Figure 8.15 is an excellent example for demonstrating the options for various types of simple character criteria. You could just as well enter **Not Cars** in the criteria for the column to return all products that are not cars (trucks, vans, and so on).

Generally, when dealing with character data, you enter equalities, inequalities, or a list of acceptable values.

This capability is a powerful tool. Consider that you only have to supply an example, and Access not only interprets it but also uses it to create the query recordset. This is exactly what *Query by Example* means: you enter an example and let the database build a query based on the example.

To erase the criteria in the cell, select the contents and press Delete, or select the contents and right-click Cut from the shortcut menu that appears.

Entering other simple criteria

You can also specify criteria for Numeric, Date, and Yes/No fields. Simply enter the example data in the criteria field just as you did for text fields. In almost every case, Access understands the criteria you enter and adjusts to correctly apply the criteria to the query's fields.

It's also possible to add more than one criteria to a query. For example, suppose that you want to look only at contacts who live in Connecticut and have been customers since January 1, 2010 (where OrigCustDate is greater than or equal to January 1, 2010). This query requires criteria in both the State and OrigCustDate fields. To do this, it's critical that you place both examples on the same criteria row. Follow these steps to create this query:

1. **Create a new query starting with tblContacts.**
2. **Add OrigCustDate, LastName, FirstName, and State to the QBD grid.**
3. **Enter** CT **in the Criteria cell in the State column.**
4. **Enter** >= 01/01/2010 **in the Criteria cell in the OrigCustDate column.** Access adds pound sign characters (#) around the date in the criteria box. Figure 8.16 shows how the query should look.
5. **Run the query.**

Access displays records of customers who live in Connecticut and who became customers after January 1, 2010.

Access uses comparison operators to compare Date fields to a value. These operators include less than (<), greater than (>), equal to (=), or a combination of these operators.

Notice that Access automatically adds pound sign (#) delimiters around the date value. Access uses these delimiters to distinguish between date and text data. The pound signs are just like the quote marks Access added to the "Cars" criteria. Because OrigCustDate is a DateTime field, Access understands what you want and inserts the proper delimiters for you.

FIGURE 8.16

Specifying text and date criteria in the same query.

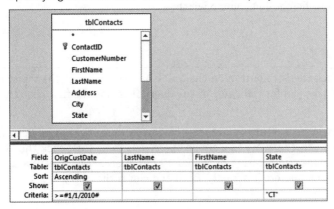

Field:	OrigCustDate	LastName	FirstName	State
Table:	tblContacts	tblContacts	tblContacts	tblContacts
Sort:	Ascending			
Show:	☑	☑	☑	☑
Criteria:	>=#1/1/2010#			"CT"

Be aware that Access interprets dates according to the region and language settings in the Windows Control Panel. For example, in most of Europe and Asia, #5/6/2010# is interpreted as June 5, 2010, while in the United States this date is May 6, 2010. It's very easy to construct a query that works perfectly but returns the wrong data because of subtle differences in regional settings.

 We cover operators and precedence in more detail in Chapter 9.

Printing a Query's Recordset

After you create your query, you can easily print all the records in the recordset. Although you can't specify a type of report, you can print a simple matrix-type report (rows and columns) of the recordset created by your query.

You do have some flexibility when printing a recordset. If you know that the datasheet is set up just as you want, you can specify some options as you follow these steps:

1. **Run the query you just created for Connecticut customers who've been active since January 1, 2010.**

2. **Choose File ⇨ Print. This will present you with three options: you can Quick Print without specifying any print settings, you can Print using specific print settings, or you can Print Preview to preview the output before printing. In this case, let's select the Print command.**

3. **Specify the print options that you want in the Print dialog box and click OK.**

The printout reflects all layout options in effect when you print the recordset. Hidden columns don't print, and gridlines print only if the Gridlines option is on. The printout reflects the specified row height and column width.

Saving a Query

To save your query, click the Save button on the Quick Access toolbar at the top of the Access screen. Access asks you for the name of the query if this is the first time the query has been saved.

After saving the query, Access returns you to the mode you were working in. Occasionally, you'll want to save and exit the query in a single operation. To do this, click the Close Window button in the upper-right corner of the Query Designer. Access always asks you to confirm saving the changes before it actually saves and closes the query.

Creating Multi-table Queries

Using a query to get information from a single table is common; often, however, you need information from several related tables. For example, you might want to obtain a buyer's name and product purchased by the customer. This query requires four tables: tblCustomers, tblSales, tblSalesLineItems, and tblProducts.

 In Chapter 4, you learned the importance of primary and foreign keys and how they link tables together. You learned how to use the Relationships window to create relationships between tables. Finally, you learned how referential integrity affects data in tables.

After you create the tables for your database and decide how the tables are related to one another, you're ready to build multi-table queries to obtain information from several related tables. A multi-table query presents data as if it existed in one large table.

The first step in creating a multi-table query is to add the tables to the query design window:

1. **Create a new query by clicking the Query Design button on the Create tab of the Ribbon.**

2. **Add tblCustomers, tblSales, tblSalesLineItems, and tblProducts by double-clicking each table's name in the Show Table dialog box.**

3. **Click the Close button.**

NOTE
You can also add each table by highlighting the table in the list separately and clicking Add.

Figure 8.17 shows the top pane of the query design window (the section in gray) with the four tables you just added. Because the relationships were set at table level, the join lines are automatically added to the query.

FIGURE 8.17

The query design window with four tables added. Notice that the join lines are already present.

NOTE

You can add more tables at any time by choosing Show Table from the Query Tools Design Ribbon. Alternatively, you can right-click the design window and select the Show Table option from the shortcut menu.

8

You add fields from more than one table to the query in exactly the same way as you do when you're working with a single table. You can add fields one at a time, multiple fields as a group, or all the fields from a table.

When you select a field that has a common name in multiple tables, Access adds the table's name, followed by a period and the field name. For example, if ProductID is a field found in more than one table used in the query design window (let's say tblProducts and tblSales-LineItems), adding the ProductID field from tblSalesLineItems will display that field in the design grid as tblSalesLineItems.ProductID. This helps you select the correct field name. Using this method, you can select a common field name from a specific table.

TIP

The easiest way to select fields is still to double-click the field names in the top pane of the Query Designer. To do so, you might have to resize the field list windows to see the fields that you want to select.

Viewing table names

When you're working with multiple tables in a query, the field names in the QBD grid can become confusing. You might find yourself asking, for example, just which table the Description field is from.

Access automatically maintains the table name that is associated with each field displayed in the QBD grid. Figure 8.18 shows the Query Designer with the name of each table displayed under the field name in the QBD grid.

FIGURE 8.18

The QBD grid with table names displayed. Notice that it shows all four table names.

Source Table Names

Adding multiple fields

The process of adding multiple fields in a multi-table query is identical to adding multiple fields in a single-table query. When you're adding fields from several tables, you must add them from one table at a time. The easiest way to do this is to select multiple fields and drag them together down to the QBD grid.

Select multiple contiguous fields by clicking the first field of the list and then clicking the last field while holding down the Shift key. You can also select noncontiguous fields in the list by holding down the Ctrl key while clicking individual fields.

CAUTION

Selecting the asterisk (*) does have some drawbacks: You can't specify criteria on the asterisk column itself. You have to add an individual field from the table and enter the criterion. You also can't sort on individual fields when selecting the asterisk. Again, you have to add the individual field from the table in order to apply the needed sorting.

Recognizing the limitations of multi-table queries

When you create a query with multiple tables, there are limits to which fields can be edited. Generally, you can change data in a query's recordset, and your changes are saved in the underlying tables. The main exception is a table's primary key—a primary key value can't be edited if referential integrity is in effect and the field is part of a relationship.

There may be instances when you will want to make manual edits to the resulting recordset of a query. In Access, the records in your tables might not always be updateable. Table 8.1 shows when a field in a table is updateable. As Table 8.1 shows, queries based on one-to-many relationships are updateable in both tables (depending on how the query was designed).

TABLE 8.1 **Rules for Updating Queries**

Type of Query or Field	Updateable	Comments
One table	Yes	
One-to-one relationship	Yes	
Results contain Long Text field	Yes	Long Text field updateable if the underlying query is not based on a many-to-many relationship
Results contain a hyperlink	Yes	Hyperlink updateable if the underlying query is not based on a many-to-many relationship
Results contain an OLE object	Yes	OLE object updateable if the underlying query is not based on a many-to-many relationship
One-to-many relationship	Usually	Restrictions based on design methodology (see text)
Many-to-many relationship	No	Can update data in a form or data access page if Record Type = Recordset
Two or more tables with no join line	No	Must have a join to determine updateability
Crosstab	No	Creates a snapshot of the data
Totals query (Sum, Avg, and so on)	No	Works with grouped data creating a snapshot
Unique Value property is Yes	No	Shows unique records only in a snapshot
SQL-specific queries	No	Union and pass-through work with ODBC data
Calculated fields	No	Will recalculate automatically
Read-only fields	No	If opened read-only or on read-only drive (CD-ROM)

8

Continues

TABLE 8.1 *(continued)*

Type of Query or Field	Updateable	Comments
Permissions denied	No	Insert, replace, or delete not granted in older MDB databases that use user-level security
ODBC tables with no unique identifier	No	Unique identifier must exist
Paradox table with no primary key	No	Primary key file must exist
Locked by another user	No	Can't be updated while a field is locked by another

Overcoming query limitations

Table 8.1 shows that there are times when queries and fields in tables are not updateable. As a general rule, any query that performs aggregate operations or uses an ODBC data source is not updateable; most other queries can be updated. When your query has more than one table and some of the tables have a one-to-many relationship, some fields might not be updateable (depending on the design of the query).

Updating a unique index (primary key)

If a query uses two tables involved in a one-to-many relationship, the query must include the primary key from the "one" table. Access must have the primary key value so that they can find the related records in the two tables.

Replacing existing data in a query with a one-to-many relationship

Normally, all the fields in the "many" table (such as the tblSales table) are updateable in a one-to-many query. All the fields (*except* the primary key) in the "one" table (tblCustomers) can be updated. This is sufficient for most database application purposes. Also, the primary key field is rarely changed in the "one" table because it's the link to the records in the joined tables.

Updating fields in queries

If you want to add records to both tables of a one-to-many relationship, include the foreign key from the "many" table and show the field in the datasheet. After doing this, records can be added starting with either the "one" or "many" table. The "one" table's primary key field is automatically copied to the "many" table's join field.

If you want to add records to multiple tables in a form (covered in Chapters 17 and 18), remember to include all (or most) of the fields from both tables; otherwise, you won't have a complete set of the record's data on your form.

Working with the Table Pane

The upper (table) pane of the Query Designer contains information that's important to your query. Understanding the table pane and how to work with field lists is critically important to building complex queries.

Looking at the join line

A *join line* connects tables in the Query Designer (refer to Figure 8.17). The join line connects the primary key in one table to the foreign key in another table. The *join line* represents the relationship between two tables in the Access database. In this example, a join line goes from tblSales to tblCustomers, connecting CustomerID in tblCustomers to the CustomerID field in tblSales. The join line is added by Access because relationships were set in the Relationships window.

 These lines were predrawn because you already set the relationships between the tables as described in Chapter 4.

If referential integrity is set on the relationship, Access uses a somewhat thicker line for the join connecting to the table in the Query Designer. A one-to-many relationship is indicated by an infinity symbol (∞) on the "many" table end of the join line.

Access auto-joins two tables if the following conditions are met:

- Both tables have fields with the same name.
- The same-named fields are the same data type (text, numeric, and so on). Note that the AutoNumber data type is the same as Numeric (Long Integer).
- One of the fields is a primary key in its table.

NOTE

After a relationship is created between tables, the join line remains between the two fields. As you move through a table selecting fields, the line moves relative to the linked fields. For example, if you scroll downward, toward the bottom of the window in tblCustomers, the join line moves upward with the customer number, eventually stopping at the top of the table window.

When you're working with many tables, these join lines can become confusing as they cross or overlap. As you scroll through the table, the line eventually becomes visible, and the field it's linked to becomes obvious.

Moving a table

You can move the field lists around the Query Designer by grabbing the title bar of a field list window (where the name of the table is) with the mouse and dragging the field list. You can also resize a field list by clicking its borders and adjusting the height and width.

Access makes some attempts to save the arrangement when you save and close the query. Generally speaking, the field lists will appear in the same configuration the next time you open the query.

Removing a table

You might need to remove tables from a query. Use the mouse to select the table you want to remove in the top pane of the query design window and press the Delete key. Or right-click the field list window and choose Remove Table from the shortcut menu.

Removing a table from a query's design does not remove the table from the database, of course.

> **CAUTION**
>
> When you remove a table from a query design, join lines to that table are deleted as well. There is no warning or confirmation before removal. The table is simply removed from the screen, along with any of the table's fields added to the QBD grid. Be aware, however, that deleted tables referenced in calculated fields will not be removed. The "phantom" table references may cause errors when you try to run the query.

 Calculated fields are discussed in detail in Chapter 12.

Adding more tables

You might decide to add more tables to a query or you might accidentally delete a table and need to add it back. You accomplish this task by clicking the Show Table button on the Query Setup group in the Design Ribbon. The Show Table dialog box appears in response to this action.

Creating and Working with Query Joins

You'll often need to build queries that require two or more related tables to be joined to achieve the desired results. For example, you may want to join an employee table to a transaction table in order create a report that contains both transaction details and information on the employees who logged those transactions. The type of join used will determine the records that will be output.

Understanding joins

There are three basic types of joins: inner joins, left outer joins, and right outer joins.

- **Inner joins:** An *inner join* operation tells Access to select only those records from both tables that have matching values. Records with values in the joined field that do not appear in both tables are omitted from the query results. Figure 8.19 represents the inner join operation visually.

FIGURE 8.19

An inner join operation will select only the records that have matching values in both tables. The arrows point to the records that will be included in the results.

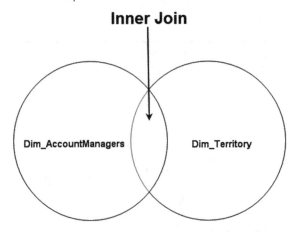

- **Left outer joins:** A *left outer join* operation (sometimes called a "left join") tells Access to select all the records from the first table regardless of matching *and* only those records from the second table that have matching values in the joined field. Figure 8.20 represents the left join operation visually.

FIGURE 8.20

A left outer join operation will select all records from the first table and only those records from the second table that have matching values in both tables. The arrows point to the records that will be included in the results.

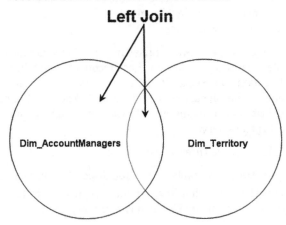

- **Right outer joins:** A *right outer join* operation (sometimes called a "right join") tells Access to select all the records from the second table regardless of matching *and* only those records from the first table that have matching values in the joined field (see Figure 8.21).

FIGURE 8.21

A right outer join operation will select all records from the second table and only those records from the first table that have matching values in both tables. The arrows point to the records that will be included in the results.

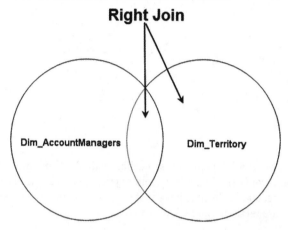

By default, an Access query returns only records where data exists on both sides of a relationship (inner join). For example, a query that extracts data from the Contacts table and the Sales table only returns records where contacts have actually placed sales and will not show contacts who haven't yet placed a sale. If a contact record isn't matched by at least one sales record, the contact data isn't returned by the query. This means that, sometimes, the query might not return all the records you expect.

Although this is the most common join type between tables in a query, users sometimes want to see all the data in a table regardless of whether those records are matched in another table. In fact, users often want to specifically see records that are *not* matched on the other side of the join. Consider a sales department that wants to know all the contacts that have *not* made a sale in the last year. You must modify the default query join characteristics in order to process this type of query.

You can create joins between tables in these three ways:

- By creating relationships between the tables when you design the database.
- By selecting two tables for the query that have a field in common that has the same name and data type in both tables. The field is a primary key field in one of the tables.
- By modifying the default join behavior.

The first two methods occur automatically in the query design window. Relationships between tables are displayed in the Query Designer when you add the related tables to a query. It also creates an automatic join between two tables that have a common field, as long as that field is a primary key in one of the tables and the Enable AutoJoin choice is selected (by default) in the Options dialog box.

If relationships are set in the Relationships window, you might not see the auto-join line if:

- The two tables have a common field, but it isn't the same name.
- A table isn't related and can't be logically related to the other table (for example, tblCustomers can't directly join the tblSalesLineItems table).

If you have two tables that aren't related and you need to join them in a query, use the query design window. Joining tables in the query design window does *not* create a permanent relationship between the tables; instead, the join (relationship) applies only to the tables while the query operates.

Leveraging ad hoc table joins

Figure 8.22 shows a simple query containing tblSales, tblSalesLineItems, tblProducts, and tblCategories. This is an ad hoc join, formed when the Categories table was added to the query.

FIGURE 8.22

An ad hoc join between tblProducts and tblCategories.

No direct relationship yet exists between tblProducts and tblCategories. However, Access found the Category field in both the tables, determined that the Category data type is the same in both tables, and determined that the Category field in tblCategories is the primary key. Therefore, Access added an ad hoc join between the tables.

NOTE

Tables are not joined automatically in a query if they aren't already joined at the table level, if they don't have a common named field for a primary key, or if the Enable AutoJoin option is off.

If Access hasn't auto-joined tblProducts and tblCategories (perhaps because the Category field was named differently in the tables), you can easily add an ad hoc join by dragging the Category field from one table and dropping it on the corresponding field in the other table.

Specifying the type of join

The problem with most joins is that, by default, they exhibit inner join behavior as the query executes. In the case of the query in Figure 8.22, if a product record exists that doesn't have an assigned category (for example, a car that was never assigned to a category), the query doesn't return any records where a product record isn't matched by a category.

The problem is that you can't even tell records are missing. The only way you'd ever determine that there should be more records returned by this query is by carefully examining the sales records, by composing another query that counts all sales, or by performing some other audit operation.

You must modify the join characteristics between tblProducts and tblCategories to get an accurate picture of sales. Carefully right-click the thin join line between tblProducts and tblCategories, and select the Join Properties command from the shortcut menu. This action opens the Join Properties dialog box (see Figure 8.23), enabling you to specify an alternate join between the tables.

FIGURE 8.23

Selecting an outer join for the query.

In Figure 8.23, the third option (Include ALL Records from 'tblProducts'...) has been selected (the first option is the default). Options 2 and 3 are left outer join and right outer join, respectively. These options direct Access to retrieve all records from the left (or right) table involved in the join, regardless of whether those records are matched on the other side of the join.

Figure 8.24 shows the result of the new join. In the lower-right corner of this figure you see how an outer join appears in the Access Query Designer.

FIGURE 8.24

A right outer join corrects the "missing products" problem in Figure 8.22.

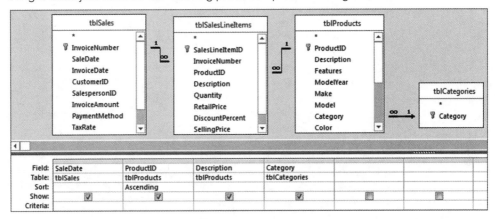

Of course, you can easily create joins that make no sense, but when you view the data, it'll be pretty obvious that you got the join wrong. If two joined fields have no values in common, you'll have a datasheet in which no records are selected.

You would never want to create a meaningless join. For example, you wouldn't want to join the City field from tblCustomers to the SalesDate field of tblSales. Although Access enables you to create this join, the resulting recordset will have no records in it.

> **NOTE**
>
> Access enables you to create multi-field joins between tables (more than one line can be drawn). The two fields must have data in common; if not, the query won't find any records to display.

Deleting joins

To delete a join line between two tables, select the join line and press the Delete key. Select the join line by placing the mouse pointer on any part of the line and clicking once.

> **CAUTION**
>
> If you delete a join between two tables and the tables remain in the query design window unjoined to any other tables, the solution will have unexpected results. Without the joins, Access will essentially create a view that contains every possible combination of records from both tables. This is typically referred to as a Cartesian product.
>
> Note that deleting the join in the query design window will only affect the query currently being worked on. The underlying relationship built in the Relationships window remains intact.

Using Operators and Expressions in Access

IN THIS CHAPTER

Understanding operators in expressions

Creating complex queries

Building queries with simple criteria

Using multiple criteria in a query

Composing complex query criteria

In the preceding chapter, you created queries using selected fields from one or more tables. You also sorted the data and set criteria to limit the results of a query. This chapter focuses on using operators and expressions to calculate information, compare values, and display data in a different format—using queries to build examples.

This chapter uses queries to demonstrate the use of operators and functions, but the principles in this chapter's exercises apply anywhere operators and expressions appear in Access.

ON THE WEB
The starting database for this walkthrough, `Chapter09.accdb`, can be downloaded from this book's website.

Introducing Operators

Operators let you compare values, put text strings together, format data, and perform a wide variety of tasks. You use operators to instruct Access to perform a specific action against one or more *operands*. The combination of operators and operands is known as an *expression*.

> **NOTE**
>
> You'll see the term *evaluate* a lot in this chapter. When you present Access with a field, expression, variable, and so on, Access *evaluates* the item and (internally) represents the item as a value. It's very important to compose expressions in such a way that Access evaluates them as we expect. If Access incorrectly evaluates an expression, the application won't perform as expected. Understanding how Access evaluates a query's criteria or an expression used in VBA code is critically important to success as an Access developer.

You'll use operators every time you create an equation in Access. For example, operators specify data validation rules in table properties, create calculated fields in forms and reports, and specify criteria in queries.

Types of operators

Operators can be grouped into the following types:

- Mathematical
- Comparison
- String
- Boolean (logical)
- Miscellaneous

Mathematical operators

Mathematical operators are also known as arithmetic operators, because they're used for performing numeric calculations. By definition, you use mathematical operators to work with numbers as operands. When you work with mathematical operators, numbers can be any numeric data type. The number can be a constant value, the value of a variable, or a field's contents. You use these numbers individually or combine them to create complex expressions.

There are seven basic mathematical operators:

+ Addition
– Subtraction
* Multiplication
/ Division
\ Integer division
^ Exponentiation
Mod Modulo

 The mathematical operators discussed in this section are typically used in calculated fields. Calculated fields are covered in detail in Chapter 12.

The addition operator: +

If you want to create a calculated field in a query for adding the value of tax to the price, use an expression similar to the following:

    [TaxAmt] + [Price]

The subtraction operator: –

The subtraction operator (–) performs simple subtraction, such as calculating a final invoice amount by subtracting a discount from the price:

    [Price] - ([Price] * [DiscountPercent])

NOTE

Although parentheses are not mathematical operators, they play an important role in many expressions, as discussed in the "Operator precedence" section later in this chapter.

The multiplication operator: *

A simple example of when to use the multiplication operator (*) is to calculate the total price of several items. You could design a query to display the number of items purchased and the price for each item. Then you could add a calculated field containing the value of the number of items purchased times the price per item. In this case, the expression would be:

    [Quantity] * [Price]

The division operator: /

Use the division operator (/) to divide two numbers. Suppose, for example, that a pool of 212 people win a $1,000,000 lottery. The expression to determine each individual's payoff of $4,716.98 is:

    1000000 / 212

NOTE

Notice that the 1000000 value does not contain commas. Access is not able to perform a mathematical operation on numeric values containing punctuation.

*The integer division operator: *

The integer division operator (\\) takes any two numbers (*number1* and *number2*), rounds them up or down to integers, divides the first by the second (*number1 / number2*), and then

9

drops the decimal portion, leaving only the integer value. Here are some examples of how integer division differs from normal division:

Normal Division	Integer Conversion Division
100 / 6 = 16.667	100 \ 6 = 16
100.9 / 6.6 = 15.288	100.9 \ 6.6 = 14
102 / 7 = 14.571	102 \ 7 = 14

> **NOTE**
>
> Access rounds whole numbers based on a principle known as *banker's rounding* or *round half to even*. Rounding is always done to the nearest even number: 6.5 becomes 6, and 7.5 becomes 8. This can produce unexpected results only when the rounded value is exactly midway between two whole numbers. As you'd expect, 6.51 rounds to 7, and 6.49 rounds to 6. Access does this to minimize round-off errors.

The exponentiation operator: ^

The exponentiation operator (^) raises a number to the power of an exponent. Raising a number simply means multiplying a number by itself. For example, multiplying the value 4 x 4 x 4 (that is, 4^3) is the same as entering the formula 4^3.

The exponent does not have to be a whole number; it can even be negative. For example, 2^2.1 returns 4.28709385014517, and 4^-2 is 0.0625.

The modulo division operator: Mod

The modulo operator (Mod) takes any two numbers (*number1* and *number2*), rounds them up or down to integers, divides the first by the second (*number1* / *number2*), and then returns the remainder. Here are some examples of how modulo division compares to normal division:

Normal Division	Modulo Division	Explanation
10 / 5 = 2	10 Mod 5 = 0	10 is evenly divided by 5
10 / 4 = 2.5	10 Mod 4 = 2	10 / 4 = 2 with a remainder of 2
22.24 / 4 = 5.56	22.24 Mod 4 = 2	22 / 4 = 5 with a remainder of 2
22.52 / 4 = 5.63	22.52 Mod 4 = 3	23 / 4 = 5 with a remainder of 3

The tricky thing about modulo division is that the returned value is the remainder after integer division is performed on the operands. The Mod operator is often used to determine whether a number is even or odd by performing modulo division with 2 as the divisor:

```
5 Mod 2 = 1
4 Mod 2 = 0
```

If Mod returns 1, the dividend is odd. Mod returns 0 when the dividend is even.

Comparison operators

Comparison operators compare two values or expressions in an equation. There are six basic comparison operators:

= Equal
<> Not equal
< Less than
<= Less than or equal to
> Greater than
>= Greater than or equal to

The expressions built from comparison operators always return True, False, or Null. Null is returned when the expression can't be evaluated.

As you read the following descriptions, please keep in mind that Access is case insensitive in most situations. When comparing strings, for example, "CAR," "Car," and "car" are the same to Access.

> **NOTE**
>
> Access actually returns a numeric value for comparison operator expressions. Access uses −1 to represent True and 0 to represent False.

If either side of an equation is a null value, the result is always Null.

The equal operator: =

The equal operator (=) returns True if the two expressions are the same. For example:

[Category] = "Car" returns True if Category is Car; returns False for any
other category.

[SaleDate] = Date() returns True if the date in SaleDate is today; returns
False for any other date.

The not-equal operator: <>

The not-equal operator (<>) is the opposite of the equal operator. For example:

[Category] <> "Car" returns True if Category is anything but Car and False
only when Category is Car.

The less-than operator: <

The less-than operator (<) returns a logical True if the left side of the equation is less than the right side, as in this example:

[Price] < 1000 returns True if the Price field contains a value of less than 1,000;
returns False whenever Price is greater than or equal to 1,000.

Interestingly, the less-than operator is easily applied to string values (the same is true for most comparison operators). For example, the following expression is `False`:

    "Man" > "Woman"

Without getting philosophical about the expression, what actually happens is that Access does a character-by-character comparison of the strings. Because *M* appears before *W* in the alphabet, the word *Man* is not greater than *Woman*. The ability to compare strings can be of significant value when sorting string data or arranging names in a particular order.

Again, because Access string comparisons are not case sensitive, *XYZ* is not greater than *xyz*.

> **NOTE**
>
> You may not get the results you were expecting when doing string-based comparisons on numbers. For instance, 10 will come before 9 because textually, 1 comes before 9.

The less-than-or-equal-to operator: <=

The less-than-or-equal-to operator (`<=`) returns `True` if the operand on the left side of the equation is either less than or equal to the right-side operand, as in this example:

    [Price] <= 2500 returns True if Price equals 2500 or is less than 2500; returns
    False for any Price that is more than 2500.

> **CAUTION**
>
> Comparison operators must be composed properly. Access reports an error if you enter `=<`. The order of the characters in this operator is important. It must be less than or equal to: `<=`.

The greater-than operator: >

The greater-than operator (`>`) is the opposite of less than. This operator returns `True` when the left-side operand is greater than the operand on the right side. For example:

    [TaxRate] > 3.5 returns True if TaxRate is greater than 3.5; returns False
    whenever TaxRate is less than or equal to 3.5.

The greater-than-or-equal-to operator: >=

The greater-than-or-equal-to operator (`>=`) returns `True` if the left side is greater than or equal to the right side. For example:

    [TaxRate] >= 5 returns True if TaxRate is 5 or greater; returns False when
    TaxRate is less than 5.

String operators

Access has three string operators for working with strings. Unlike the mathematical and logical operators, the string operators are specifically designed to work with the string data type:

    `&`   Concatenates operands.

    `Like`   Operands are similar.

    `Not Like`   Operands are dissimilar.

The concatenation operator: &

The concatenation operator joins two strings into a single string. In some ways, concatenation is similar to addition. Unlike addition, however, concatenation always returns a string:

```
[FirstName] & [LastName]
```

However, there is no space between the names in the returned string. If `[FirstName]` is "Fred" and `[LastName]` is "Smith," the returned string is `FredSmith`. If you want a space between the names, you must explicitly add a space between the strings, as follows:

```
[FirstName] & " " & [LastName]
```

The concatenation operator easily joins a string with a numeric- or date-type value. Using the `&` operator eliminates the need for special functions to convert numbers or dates to strings.

Suppose, for example, that you have a number field (HouseNumber) and a text field (StreetName), and you want to combine both fields:

```
[HouseNumber] & " " & [StreetName]
```

If `HouseNumber` is "1600" and `StreetName` is "Pennsylvania Avenue N.W.," the returned string is:

```
"1600 Pennsylvania Avenue N.W."
```

> **NOTE**
> Quotes are added around the returned string to clarify the result.

Maybe you want to print the OperatorName and current date at the bottom of a report page. This can be accomplished with the following:

```
"This report was printed " & Now() & " by " & [OperatorName]
```

Notice the spaces after the word *printed* and before and after the word *by*. If the date is March 21, 2012, and the time is 4:45 p.m., this expression looks like:

```
This report was printed 3/21/12 4:45:40 PM by Jim Rosengren
```

9

The addition operator (+) also concatenates two character strings. For example, to combine FirstName and LastName from tblContacts to display them as a single string, the expression is:

```
[FirstName] + " " + [LastName]
```

> **TIP**
>
> Knowing how the concatenation operator works makes maintaining your database expressions easier. If you always use the concatenation operator (&)—instead of the addition operator (+)—when working with strings, you won't have to be concerned with the data types of the concatenation operands. Any expression that uses the concatenation operator converts all operands to strings for you. Using the addition operator to concatenate strings can sometimes lead to unpredictable results because Access must decide whether the operands are numbers or strings and act accordingly. The concatenation operator forces Access to treat the operands as strings and always returns a string as a result.

Although & and + both serve as concatenation operators, using + might exhibit unexpected results in some situations. The & operator *always* returns a string when concatenating two values. The operands passed to & may be strings, numeric or date/time values, field references, and so on, and a string is always returned.

Because it always returns a string, & is often used to prevent Invalid use of null errors when working with data that might be null. For example, let's assume a particular text box on an Access form may or may not contain a value because we can't be sure the user has entered anything in the text box. When assigning the contents of the text box to a variable (discussed in Chapter 24), some developers concatenate an empty string to the text box's contents as part of the assignment:

```
MyVariable = txtLastName & ""
```

& ensures that, even if the text box contains a null value, the variable is assigned a string and no error is raised.

+, on the other hand, returns a null value when one of the operands is null:

```
MyVariable = txtLastName + ""
```

In this case, if txtLastName is truly null, the user may encounter an Invalid use of null error because the result of the concatenation is null (assuming, once again, that txtLastName contains a null value).

Most experienced Access developers reserve + for arithmetical operations and always use & for string concatenation.

The Like and Not Like operators

The Like operator and its opposite, the Not Like operator, compare two string expressions. These operators determine whether one string matches, or doesn't match, the pattern of another string. The returned value is True, False, or Null. The Like and Not Like operators are case insensitive.

The Like operator uses the following syntax:

expression Like *pattern*

Like looks for the expression in the pattern; if it's present, the operation returns True. For example:

[FirstName] Like "John" returns True if the first name is John.

[LastName] Like "SMITH*" returns True if the last name is Smith, Smithson, or any other name beginning with "Smith," regardless of capitalization.

[State] Not Like "NY" returns True for any state other than New York.

> **NOTE**
>
> If either operand in a Like operation is null, the result is null.

The Like and Not Like operators provides powerful and flexible tools for string comparisons. Wildcard characters extend the flexibility of the Like operator.

Using Wildcards

The following table shows the five wildcards you can use with the Like operator:

Wildcard	Purpose
?	A single character (0–9, Aa–Zz)
*	Any number of characters (0–*n*)
#	Any single digit (0–9)
[list]	Any single character in the list
[!list]	Any single character *not* in the list

Both [list] and [!list] can use the hyphen between two characters to signify a range.

Here are some wildcard examples:

[tblContacts].[LastName] Like "Mc*" returns True for any last name that begins with "Mc" or "MC," such as "McDonald," "McJamison," and "MCWilliams." Anything that doesn't start with "Mc" or "MC" returns False.

[Answer] Like "[A-D]" returns True if the Answer is A, B, C, D, a, b, c, or d. Any other character returns False.

Continues

9

continued

`"AB1989" Like "AB####"` Returns `True` because the string begins with "AB" and is followed by four digits.

`"AB198" Like "AB####"` Returns `False` because the string begins with "AB" and is not followed by four digits.

`"AB19893" Like "AB####"` Returns `False` because the string begins with "AB" and is followed by more than four digits.

`[LastName] Not Like "[A,E,I,O,U]*"` Returns `True` for any last name that does *not* begin with a vowel. "Smith" and "Jones" return `True` while "Adams" and "O'Malley" return `False`.

`[City] Like "?????"` Returns `True` for any city that is exactly five characters long.

TIP

If the pattern you're trying to match contains a wildcard character, you must enclose the wildcard character in brackets. In the following example, the [*] in the pattern treats asterisks in the third position as data:

```
"AB*Co" Like "AB[*]C*"
```

Since the asterisk character is enclosed in brackets, it won't be mistaken for an asterisk wildcard character..

Boolean (logical) operators

Boolean operators (also referred to as *logical operators*) are used to create multiple conditions in expressions. Like comparison operators, these operators always return `True`, `False`, or `Null`. Boolean operators include the following:

And returns `True` when both `Expression1` and `Expression2` are true.

Or returns `True` when either `Expression1` or `Expression2` is true.

Not returns `True` when the `Expression` is not true.

Xor returns `True` when either `Expression1` or `Expression2` is true, but not both.

Eqv returns `True` when both `Expression1` and `Expression2` are true or both are false.

Imp performs bitwise comparisons of identically positioned bits in two numerical expressions.

The And operator

Use the `And` operator to perform a logical *conjunction* of two expressions. The operator returns `True` if both expressions are true. The general syntax of `And` is as follows:

```
Expression1 And Expression2
```

For example:

```
[tblContacts].[State] = "MA" And
  [tblContacts].[ZipCode] = "02379"
```

Returns True only if both expressions are true.

The logical And operator depends on how the two operands are evaluated by Access. Table 9.1 describes all the possible results when the operands are True or False. Notice that And returns True only when *both* operands are true.

TABLE 9.1 And Operator Results

Expression1	Expression2	Expression1 And Expression2
True	True	True
True	False	False
True	Null	Null
False	True	False
False	False	False
False	Null	False
Null	True	Null
Null	False	False
Null	Null	Null

The Or operator

The Or operator performs a logical *disjunction* of two expressions. Or returns True if *either* condition is true. The general syntax of Or is as follows:

```
Expression1 Or Expression2
```

The following examples show how the Or operator works:

[LastName] = "Casey" Or [LastName] = "Gleason" returns True if LastName is either Casey or Gleason.

[TaxLocation] = "TX" Or [TaxLocation] = "CT" returns True if TaxLocation is either TX or CT.

The Or operator (like And) returns True or False depending on how Access evaluates its operands. Table 9.2 shows all possible combinations with two operands. Notice that Or returns False only when *both* operands are false.

9

TABLE 9.2 Or Expression Results

Expression1	Expression2	Expression1 Or Expression2
True	True	True
True	False	True
True	Null	True
False	True	True
False	False	False
False	Null	Null
Null	True	True
Null	False	Null
Null	Null	Null

The Not operator

The Not operator negates a numeric or Boolean expression. The Not operator returns True if the expression is false, and False if the expression is true. The general syntax of Not is:

    Not [numeric|boolean] expression

The following examples show how to use the Not operator:

    Not [Price] <= 100000 returns True if Price is greater than 100,000.

    If Not (City = "Seattle") Then returns True for any city that is not Seattle.

If the operand is null, the Not operator returns Null. Table 9.3 shows all the possible values.

TABLE 9.3 Not Operator Results

Expression	Not Expression
True	False
False	True
Null	Null

Miscellaneous operators

Access has three very useful miscellaneous operators:

    Between...And Range
    In   List comparison
    Is   Reserved word

The Between...And operator

Between...And determines whether an expression's value falls within a range of values:

```
expression Between value1 And value2
```

If the value of the expression falls within *value 1* and *value 2*, or is the same as *value 1* or *value 2*, the result is True; otherwise, it's False. Note that the Between ... And operator is inclusive, the equivalent of >= and <=.

The following examples show how to use the Between...And operator:

[TotalCost] Between 10000 And 19999 returns True if the TotalCost is
between 10,000 and 19,999, or equal to 10,000 or 19,999

[SaleDate] Between #1/1/2012# And #12/31/2012# returns True when the
SaleDate occurs within the year 2012.

The Between...And operator can also be used with the Not operator to negate the logic:

Not [SaleDate] Between #1/1/2012# And #3/31/2012# returns True only
when SaleDate is *not* within the first quarter of 2012.

The In operator

The In operator determines whether an expression's value is the same as any value within a list. The general syntax of In is:

```
Expression In (value1, value2, value3, ...)
```

If the expression's value is found within the list, the result is True; otherwise, the result is False.

The following example uses the In operator as a query's criteria in the Category column:

In ('SUV','Trucks')

This query displays only those models that are SUVs or trucks.

The In operator is also used in VBA code:

If [tblCustomers].[City] In("Seattle", "Tacoma") Then

In this case the body of the If...Then...Else statement executes only if the City field is either Seattle or Tacoma.

The return value of the In operator can be negated with Not:

If strCity Not In ("Pittsburgh", "Philadelphia") Then

In this case, the body of the If...Then...Else statement executes only if strCity is not set to either Pittsburgh or Philadelphia.

9

The Is operator

The Is operator is generally used with the keyword Null to determine whether the value of an object is null:

> *expression* Is Null

In the VBA environment, the Is operator can be used to compare various objects to determine if they represent the same entity.

The following example uses the Is operator:

> [LastName] Is Null returns True if the LastName field is null; returns False if the LastName field contains any value.

It is important to note that the Is operator applies only to objects and object variables, such as fields in tables. The Is operator can't be used with simple variables such as strings or numbers.

Operator precedence

When you work with complex expressions that have many operators, Access must determine which operator to evaluate first and then which is next, and so forth. Access has a built-in predetermined order for mathematical, logical, and Boolean operators, known as *operator precedence*. Access always follows this order unless you use parentheses to override its default behavior.

Operations within parentheses are performed before operations outside parentheses. Within parentheses, Access follows the default operator precedence.

Precedence is determined first according to category of the operator. The operator rank by order of precedence is:

1. Mathematical
2. Comparison
3. Boolean

Each category contains its own order of precedence, which we explain in the following sections.

The mathematical precedence

Mathematical operators follow this order of precedence:

1. Exponentiation
2. Negation
3. Multiplication and/or division (left to right)
4. Integer division
5. Modulus division

6. Addition and/or subtraction (left to right)

7. String concatenation

The comparison precedence

Comparison operators observe this order of precedence:

1. Equal

2. Not equal

3. Less than

4. Greater than

5. Less than or equal to

6. Greater than or equal to

7. Like

The Boolean precedence

The Boolean operators follow this order of precedence:

1. Not

2. And

3. Or

4. Xor

5. Eqv

6. Imp

Using Operators and Expressions in Queries

One of the most common uses of operators and expressions is when building complex query criteria. A thorough understanding of how these constructs work can ease the process of building sophisticated, useful queries. This section deals specifically with building query criteria using operators and expressions. Some of the information in the remainder of this chapter parallels earlier discussions, but the context is specifically query design.

Knowing how to specify criteria is critical to designing and writing effective queries. Although queries can be used against a single table for a single criterion, many queries extract information from several tables using more complex criteria.

Because of this complexity, your queries are able to retrieve only the data you need, in the order that you need it. You might, for example, want to select and display data from the database to get the following information:

- All buyers of Chevy car or Ford truck models
- All buyers who have purchased something during the past 60 days

9

- All sales for items greater than $90
- The number of customers in each state
- Customers who have made comments or complaints

As your database system evolves, you'll want to retrieve subsets of information like these examples. Using operators and expressions, you create complex select queries to limit the number of records returned by the query. This section discusses select queries that use operators and expressions. Later, you'll apply this knowledge when working with forms, reports, and VBA code.

 Feel free to visit Chapter 8 for a refresher on designing queries in Access.

Using query comparison operators

When working with select queries, you may need to specify one or more criteria to limit the scope of information shown. You specify criteria by using comparison operators in equations and calculations. The categories of operators are mathematical, relational, logical, and string. In select queries, operators are used in either the Field cell or the Criteria cell of the Query by Design (QBD) grid.

Table 9.4 shows the most common operators used with select queries.

TABLE 9.4 Common Operators Used in Select Queries

Mathematical	Relational	Logical	String	Miscellaneous
* (multiply)	= (equal)	And	& (concatenate)	Between...And
/ (divide)	<> (not equal)	Or	Like	In
+ (add)	> (greater than)	Not	Not Like	Is Null
– (subtract)	< (less than)			Is Not Null

Using these operators, you can ferret out groups of records like these:

- Product records that include a picture
- A range of records, such as all sales between November and January
- Records that meet both And *and* Or criteria, such as all records that are cars and are not either a truck or an SUV
- All records that do *not* match a value, such as any category that is not a car

When you add criteria to a query, use the appropriate operator with an example of what you want. In Figure 9.1, the example is Cars. The operator is equal (=). Notice that the equal sign is *not* shown in the figure because it's the default operator for select queries.

FIGURE 9.1

The QBD pane shows a simple criterion asking for all models where the category is Cars.

Understanding complex criteria

You build complex query criteria using any combination of the operators shown in Table 9.4. For many queries, complex criteria consist of a series of Ands and Ors, as in these examples:

- State must be Connecticut *or* Texas.
- City must be Sunnyville *and* state must be Georgia.
- State must be MA *or* MO *and* city must be Springfield.

These examples demonstrate the use of both logical operators: And/Or. Many times, you can create complex criteria by entering example data in different cells of the QBD pane, as shown in Figure 9.2. In Figure 9.2, criteria is specified in both the State and Category columns. Within the State column, the criteria specifies "either California or Arizona," while the additional criteria in the Category column adds "not Cars." When combined, the criteria in the two columns limit the returned records to those where the customer state is either California or Arizona, and the product category is not cars.

9

FIGURE 9.2

Using And and Or criteria in a query

Field:	Company	State	Category	SaleDate	Description	Cost	
Table:	tblCustomers	tblCustomers	tblProducts	tblSales	tblProducts	tblProducts	
Sort:							
Show:	☑	☑	☑	☑	☑	☑	☐
Criteria:		"CA" Or "AZ"	<> "Cars"				

However, using explicit Boolean operators is not the only way to select records based on multiple criteria. Figure 9.3 demonstrates a common Access technique using complex criteria without entering the operator keywords And/Or at all. In this example, the criteria "stacked" within a single column specifies Or. For example, in the State column, the criteria is interpreted as "CA" Or "AZ". The presence of criteria in another column in the QBD grid implies And. Therefore, the criteria in the Category column is combined with the state criteria and is interpreted as:

```
(State = "CA" And Category <> "Cars") Or
(State = "AZ" And Category <> "Cars")
```

In any case, the queries in Figures 9.2 and 9.3 are equivalent and return the same data.

One confusing aspect about the query in Figure 9.3 is that the criteria in the Category column must appear twice, once for each value in the State column. If the Category criteria appeared only once, perhaps in the same row as "AZ" in the State column, the combined criteria would be interpreted as:

```
(State = "AZ" and Category <> "Cars") Or (State = "CA")
```

You learn how to create this type of complex query in the "Entering Criteria in Multiple Fields" section, later in this chapter.

TIP

In the QBD pane, enter And criteria in the same row and Or criteria in different rows.

FIGURE 9.3

Creating complex criteria without using the And/Or operators.

Access takes your graphical query and creates a single SQL SELECT statement to actually extract the information from your tables. Click the drop-down in the Ribbon's View group and select SQL View to change the window's contents to display the SQL SELECT statement (shown in Figure 9.4), which Access creates from the fields and criteria placed in the QBD pane in Figure 9.3.

The SQL statement in Figure 9.4 has been slightly rearranged by the author for clarification purposes. When you switch to SQL view in your database, you'll see one long multi-line statement with no breaks between sections.

An expression for this query's criteria is:

```
(tblCustomers.State = "CA" AND tblProducts.Category <> "Cars") OR
(tblCustomers.State = "AZ" AND tblProducts.Category <> "Cars")
```

You must enter the category criteria (<> "Cars") for each state in the QBD pane, as shown in Figure 9.3. In the "Entering Criteria in Multiple Fields" section later in this chapter, you learn to use the And/Or operators in a Criteria cell of the query, which eliminates the redundant entry of these fields.

> **TIP**
>
> In this example, you looked for all models that didn't contain cars in the Category field. To find records that *do* match a value, drop the <> operator with the value. For example, enter Cars to find all records with Cars as the category. You don't have to use the equal sign in the QBD pane when working with select queries.

9

The And/Or operators are the most common operators when working with complex criteria. The operators consider two different expressions (one on each side of the And/Or operators) and then determine whether the expressions are true or false. Then the operators compare the results of the two expressions against each other for a logical true/false answer. For example, take the first And statement in the expression given in the preceding paragraph:

```
(tblCustomers.State = "CA" AND tblProducts.Category <> "Cars")
```

The right side of the criteria (tblProducts.Category <> "Cars") evaluates to True if the Category is anything other than Cars. The And operator compares the logical true/false from the left and right expressions to return a true/false answer.

> **NOTE**
>
> A field has a null value when it has no value at all. Null indicates the lack of entry of information in a field. Null is neither true nor false, nor is it the same as a space character or 0. Null simply has no value. If you never enter a name in the City field and just skip it, Access leaves the field empty (unless a default value is provided in the table's design). This state of emptiness is known as *null*.

When the result of an And/Or operation is True, the overall condition is true, and the query displays the records meeting the true condition.

Notice that the result of an And operation is true only when *both* sides of the expression are true, whereas the result of an Or operation is true when *either* side of the expression is true. In fact, one side can be a null value, and the result of the Or operation will still be true if the other side is true. This is the fundamental difference between And/Or operators.

Using functions in select queries

When you work with queries, you might want to use built-in Access functions to display information. For example, you might want to display items such as:

- The day of the week for sales dates
- All customer names in uppercase
- The difference between two date fields

You can display all this information by creating calculated fields for the query.

 We discuss calculated fields in depth in Chapter 12 (and throughout this book).

Referencing fields in select queries

When you reference table names and field names in queries, it is a best practice to enclose names in square brackets ([]). Access actually requires brackets around any field names that contains spaces or punctuation characters. An example of a field name in brackets is:

```
[tblSales].[SaleDate] + 30
```

In this example, 30 days is added to the SaleDate field in tblSales.

> **CAUTION**
>
> If you omit the brackets ([]) around a field name in the QBD grid, Access might place quotes around the field name and treat it as literal text instead of a field name.

Entering Single-Value Field Criteria

You'll encounter situations in which you want to limit the query records returned on the basis of a single field criterion, such as in these queries:

- Customer (buyer) information for customers living in New York
- Sales of truck models
- Customers who bought anything in the month of January

Each of these queries requires a single-value criterion. Simply put, a *single-value criterion* is the entry of only one expression in the QBD grid. The expression can be example data, such as "CA", or a function, such as `DatePart("m", [SaleDate]) = 1`. Criteria expressions can be specified for virtually any data type: Text, Numeric, Date/Time, and so forth. Even OLE Object and Calculated field types can have criteria specified.

Entering character (Text or Memo) criteria

You use character criteria for Text or Memo data-type fields. These are either examples or patterns of the contents of the field. To create a query that returns customers who live in New York, for example, follow these steps:

1. **Open a new query in Design view based on tblCustomers and add the Company, Phone, and State fields to the QBD pane.**

2. **Click the Criteria cell for State field.**

3. **Type NY in the cell.** Your query should look like Figure 9.5. Notice that only one table is open and only three fields are selected. Click the Datasheet View button in the Home Ribbon's Views group to see this query's results.

9

FIGURE 9.4

The SQL view for the query in Figure 9.3. Notice that it contains a single OR and two AND operators (in the WHERE clause).

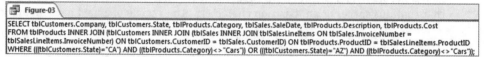

```
Figure-03
SELECT tblCustomers.Company, tblCustomers.State, tblProducts.Category, tblSales.SaleDate, tblProducts.Description, tblProducts.Cost
FROM tblProducts INNER JOIN (tblCustomers INNER JOIN (tblSales INNER JOIN tblSalesLineItems ON tblSales.InvoiceNumber =
tblSalesLineItems.InvoiceNumber) ON tblCustomers.CustomerID = tblSales.CustomerID) ON tblProducts.ProductID = tblSalesLineItems.ProductID
WHERE (((tblCustomers.State)="CA") AND ((tblProducts.Category)<>"Cars")) OR (((tblCustomers.State)="AZ") AND ((tblProducts.Category)<>"Cars"));
```

FIGURE 9.5

The query design window showing tblCustomers open.

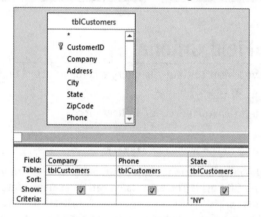

You don't have to enter an equal sign before the literal word NY, because this is a select query. To see all states except New York, you must enter either the <> (not equal) or the Not operator before NY.

You also don't have to type quotes around NY. Access assumes that you're using a literal string NY and adds the quotes for you automatically.

Special considerations apply when data in the field contains quotation marks. For example, consider a query to find a person whose name is given as Robert "Bobby" Jones. Ideally, the contacts table would include a nickname field to capture "Bobby," but, in the absence of a nickname field, the data entry clerk may enter the first name as Robert "Bobby," using the quotation marks around "Bobby."

In this case, Access sees the double-quotation characters as data, and you may want to include the quotes in the criteria. The simplest solution is to use a criteria expression such as the following:

```
'Robert "Bobby"'
```

Notice the single quotes surrounding the criteria string. Access correctly interprets the single quotes as delimiting characters and understands that the double quotes within the single quotes are just data. You shouldn't use an expression such as the following:

```
"Robert 'Bobby'"
```

This is, of course, the opposite use of quotation marks as the previous example. In this case, Access expects to find single quotes around "Bobby" in the first name field, and no records will be returned.

The Like operator and wildcards

In previous sections, you worked with *literal* criteria. You specified the exact field contents for Access to find, which was NY in the previous example. Access used the literal to retrieve the records. Sometimes, however, you know only a part of the field contents, or you might want to see a wider range of records on the basis of a pattern.

For example, you might want to see all product information for items with "convertible" in the description. Many different makes and models may be convertibles, and there's no field where "convertible" will work by itself as the query's criteria. You'll need to use wildcards to make sure you successfully select all records containing "convertible" in the description.

Here's another example: Suppose you have a buyer who has purchased a couple of red models in the last year. You remember making a note of it in the Notes field about the color, but you don't remember which customer it was. To find these records, you're required to use a wildcard search against the Notes field in tblCustomers to find records that contain the word *red*.

Use the Like operator in the Criteria cell of a field to perform wildcard searches against the field's contents. Access searches for a pattern in the field; you use the question mark (?) to represent a single character or the asterisk (*) for several characters. In addition to ? and *, Access uses three other characters for wildcard searches. The table in the "Using Wildcards" sidebar earlier in this chapter lists the wildcards that the Like operator can use.

The question mark (?) stands for any single character located in the same position as the question mark in the example expression. An asterisk (*) stands for any number of characters in the same position in which the asterisk is placed. The pound sign (#) stands for a single digit (0–9) found in the position occupied by the pound sign. The brackets ([ ]) and the list they enclose stand for any single character that matches any one character in the list located within the brackets. Finally, the exclamation point (!) inside the brackets represents the Not operator for the list—that is, any single character that does *not* match any character in the list.

These wildcards can be used alone or in conjunction with each other. They can even be used multiple times within the same expression.

9

To create an example using the `Like` operator, let's suppose you want to find the customer who likes red model cars. You know that *red* is used in one of the Notes field in tblCustomers. To create the query, follow these steps:

1. **Add tblCustomers, tblSales, tblSalesLineItems, and tblProducts to the query.**

2. **Add Company and Notes from tblCustomers, SalesDate from tblSales, and Description from tblProducts to the QBD pane.**

3. **Click the Criteria cell of the Notes field and enter * red * as the criteria.** Be sure to put a space between the first asterisk and the *r* and the last asterisk and the *d*— in other words, put spaces before and after the word *red*.

> **TIP**
>
> In the preceding steps, you put a space before and after the word *red*. If you didn't, Access would find all words that have the word *red* in them—like *aired, bored, credo, fired, geared, restored,* and on and on. By placing a space before and after the word *red*, Access is being told to look for the word *red* only.
>
> You may point out that if the Notes field starts with the word *Red* (as in "Red cars are the customer's preference"), Access would not include this record because the word *Red* is not preceded by a space. You're right!
>
> You should expect to have to experiment a bit when you build the criteria for your queries. Because the data in your tables (especially text fields) can be unpredictable, you may have to create several queries to capture every scenario. In this case, you could create a supplemental query with the criteria `"red *"` to try to capture this record.

There is, however, one issue with this example. Notice that the criteria (`"* red *"`) requires a space after the word *red*. This means that a record containing the following note will not be returned by this query:

```
Customer wants any model of car, as long as it's red!
```

Because there is no space immediately after *red,* this record will be missed. The proper criteria to use is:

```
Like "* red[ ,.!]*"
```

The brackets around " ,.!" instruct Access to select records when the Notes field ends with the word *red,* followed by a space or punctuation character. Obviously, there may be other characters to consider within the brackets, and you must have a good idea of the variety of data in the queried field.

When you click outside the Criteria cell, Access automatically adds the `Like` operator and the quotation marks around the expression. Your query QBD pane should look like Figure 9.6.

After creating this query, click the Datasheet View command to view the query's results. It should look like Figure 9.7.

FIGURE 9.6

Using the Like operator in a select query.

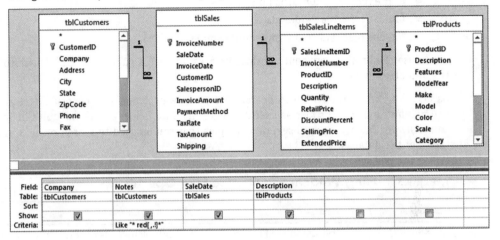

FIGURE 9.7

The results of using the Like operator with a select query in a Memo field. The query looks for the word *red* in the Notes field.

Company	Notes	SaleDate	Description
Terriffic Toys	I'd prefer cars that were red, blue or yellow.	11/6/2012	Ford Fairlane
Carmen's Collectibles	Customer wants any model of car, as long as it's red!	11/17/2012	Chevrolet Bel Air
Carmen's Collectibles	Customer wants any model of car, as long as it's red!	11/17/2012	Chevrolet 150
Carmen's Collectibles	Customer wants any model of car, as long as it's red!	11/17/2012	Volkswagen Beetle
Rockin And Rollin	Seems to like red models.	12/26/2012	Ford Galaxy 500
Rockin And Rollin	Seems to like red models.	12/26/2012	Ford Convertible
Rockin And Rollin	Seems to like red models.	12/26/2012	Ford Galaxy 500
Rockin And Rollin	Seems to like red models.	1/13/2013	Buick T-Type
Carmen's Collectibles	Customer wants any model of car, as long as it's red!	3/29/2013	Ford Convertible
Carmen's Collectibles	Customer wants any model of car, as long as it's red!	5/9/2013	Honda F1 RA272
Terriffic Toys	I'd prefer cars that were red, blue or yellow.	6/30/2013	Chevrolet Bel Air
Terriffic Toys	I'd prefer cars that were red, blue or yellow.	6/30/2013	Lincoln Continental Limo
Terriffic Toys	I'd prefer cars that were red, blue or yellow.	6/30/2013	Honda F1 RA272

If you click the Datasheet View command on the Ribbon, you see that a number of records match your query's criteria. The recordset returned by this query includes redundant information in the Company and Notes columns, but the redundancy is the result of asking for this information along with the sales and product data.

Access automatically adds the Like operator and quotation marks if you meet these conditions:

- Your expression contains no spaces.
- You use only the wildcards ?, *, or #.
- You use brackets ([]) inside quotation marks (" ").

If you use the brackets without quotation marks, you must supply the Like operator and the quotation marks.

Using the Like operator with wildcards is the best way to perform pattern searches through memo fields. It's just as useful in text and date fields, as the examples in Table 9.5 demonstrate. Table 9.5 shows several examples that can be used to search records in the tables of the database.

TABLE 9.5 Using Wildcards with the Like Operator

Expression	Field Used In	Results of Criteria
Like "Ca*"	tblCustomers.LastName	Finds all records of contacts whose last name begins with Ca (for example, Carson and Casey).
Like "* red *"	tblProducts.Features	Finds all records where the Features field starts and ends with any character and has *red* somewhere in the text.
Like "C*"	tblSales.PaymentMethod	Finds all sales where the payment method starts with a C.
Like "## South Main"	tblCustomers.Address	Finds all records of contacts with houses containing house numbers between 10 and 99 inclusively (for example, 10, 22, 33, 51) on South Main.
Like "[CDF]*"	tblCustomers.City	Finds all records of contacts for customers who live in any city with a name beginning with C, D, or F.
Like "[!EFG]*"	tblCustomers.City	Finds all records of contacts who live in any city with a name beginning with any letter except E, F, or G.

Specifying non-matching values

To specify a non-matching value, you simply use either the Not or the <> operator in front of the expression that you don't want to match. For example, you might want to see all contacts that have purchased a vehicle, but you want to exclude buyers from New York. Follow these steps to see how to specify this non-matching value:

1. **Open a new query in Design view and add tblCustomers.**

2. **Add Company and State from tblCustomers.**

3. **Click in the Criteria cell of State.**

4. **Type <> NY in the cell.** Access automatically places quotation marks around NY if you don't do so before you leave the field. The query should look like Figure 9.8. The query selects all records *except* those for customers who live in the state of New York.

FIGURE 9.8

Using the Not operator in criteria.

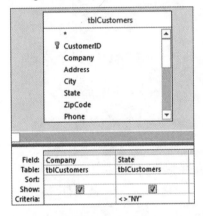

NOTE

You can use the Not operator instead of <> in Step 4 of the previous instructions to exclude New York (NY). The result is the same with either operator. These two operators are interchangeable except with the use of the keyword Is. You can't say Is <> Null. Instead, you must say Not Is Null or, more accurately, Is Not Null.

Entering numeric criteria

You use numeric criteria with numeric or currency data-type fields. You simply enter the numbers and the decimal symbol—if required—following the mathematical or comparison operator (but do *not* use commas). For example, you might want to see all sales where the product's inventory count is less than ten:

1. **Open a new query in Design view and add tblProducts.**

2. **Add ProductID, Description, Make, Model, and QtyInStock from tblProducts to the QBD grid.**

3. **Click in the Sort cell for Make and select Ascending from the drop-down list.**

4. **Click in the Criteria cell for QtyInStock and enter** <10 **in the cell.** Your query should look like Figure 9.9. When working with numeric data, Access doesn't enclose the expression with quotes, as it does with string criteria.

FIGURE 9.9

Criteria set for products with low inventory.

The criteria applied to numeric fields usually include comparison operators, such as less than (<), greater than (>), or equal to (=). If you want to specify a comparison other than equal, you must enter the operator as well as the value. Remember that Access defaults to equal when running a select query. That's why you needed to specify <10 in the QtyInStock column in the example shown in Figure 9.9.

Access does not surround the criteria with quotes because QtyInStock is numeric and requires no delimiter.

Entering true or false criteria

True and false criteria are used with Yes/No type fields. The example data that you supply as criteria must evaluate to true or false. You can also use the Not and the <> operators to signify the opposite, but the Yes/No data also has a null state that you might want to consider. Access recognizes several forms of true and false.

Thus, instead of typing **Yes**, you can type any of these in the Criteria: cell: **On**, **True**, **Not No**, **<> No**, **<No**, or **–1**.

> **NOTE**
>
> A Yes/No field can have three states: Yes, No, and Null. Null occurs only when no default value was set in a table and the value has not yet been entered. Checking for `Is Null` displays only records containing `Null` in the field, and checking for `Is Not Null` always displays all records with `Yes` or `No` in the field. After a Yes/No field check box is checked (or checked and then deselected), it can never be `Null`. It must be either `Yes` or `No` (–1 or 0).

Entering OLE object criteria

You can specify criteria for OLE objects: `Is Null` or `Is Not Null`. For example, suppose you don't have pictures for all the products and you want to view only those records that have a picture—that is, those in which the picture is not null. You specify the `Is Not Null` criterion for the Picture field of tblProducts.

> **TIP**
>
> Although `Is Not Null` is the correct syntax, you can also use `Not Null` in the QBD grid, and Access supplies the `Is` operator for you.

Using Multiple Criteria in a Query

In previous sections of this chapter, you worked with single-condition criteria on a single field. As you learned in those sections, you can specify single-condition criteria for any field type. In this section, you work with multiple criteria based on a single field. For example, you might be interested in seeing all records in which the buyer comes from New York, California, or Arizona. Or maybe you want to view the records of all the products sold during the first quarter of the year 2012.

The QBD pane has the flexibility to solve these types of problems. You can specify criteria for several fields in a select query. Using multiple criteria, for example, you can determine which products were sold for the past 90 days. Either of the following expressions could be used as criteria in the SaleDate field's criteria:

```
Between Date() And Date() - 90
Between Date() And DateAdd("d",-90,Date())
```

Of these, the expression using the `DateAdd` function is less ambiguous and more specific to the task.

 We delve deeper into the topic of creating calculations with dates in Chapter 12.

Understanding an Or operation

You use an `Or` operator in queries when you want a field to meet either of two conditions. For example, you might want to see all the records where the customer has an address in

9

either New York or California. In other words, you want to see all records where a customer has addresses in NY, in CA, or both. The general expression for this operation is:

```
[State] = "NY" Or [State] = "CA"
```

If either side of this expression is true, the resulting answer is also true. To clarify this point, consider these conditions:

- Customer 1 has an address in NY: The expression is true.
- Customer 2 has an address in CA: The expression is true.
- Customer 3 has an address in NY and CA: The expression is true.
- Customer 4 has an address in CT: The expression is false.

Specifying multiple values with the Or operator

The Or operator is used to specify multiple values for a field. For example, you use the Or operator if you want to see all records of buyers who live in AZ or CA or NY. To do this, follow these steps:

1. **Open a new query in Design view and add tblCustomers and tblSales.**

2. **Add Company and State from tblCustomers and SalesDate from tblSales.**

3. **Click in the Criteria cell of State.**

4. **Type** AZ Or CA Or NY **in the cell.** Your QBD pane should resemble the one shown in Figure 9.10. Access automatically places quotation marks around your example data—AZ, CA, and NY.

FIGURE 9.10

Using the Or operator. Notice the two Or operators under the State field—AZ Or CA Or NY.

Using the Or cell of the QBD pane

Besides using the literal Or operator as a single expression on the Criteria row under the State field, you can supply individual criteria for the field vertically on separate rows of the QBD pane, as shown in Figure 9.11.

> **TIP**
>
> Access allows up to nine Or cells for each field. If you need to specify more Or conditions, use the Or operator between conditions (for example, AZ Or CA Or NY Or PA).

Access rearranges the design shown in Figure 9.11 when the query is saved to match the query in Figure 9.10. In fact, when you open the Figure-11 query in the Chapter09 .accdb example database, you'll see that it is exactly the same as the Figure-10 query because of the way Access rearranged the criteria when the Figure-11 query was originally saved. When you build a query using "vertical" Or criteria, Access optimizes the SQL statement behind the query by placing all the Or criteria into a single expression.

FIGURE 9.11

Using the Or cell of the QBD pane. You can place criteria vertically in the QBD grid.

Using a list of values with the In operator

Another method for specifying multiple values of a single field is using the In operator. The In operator finds a value from a list of values. For example, use the expression IN(AZ, CA, NY) under the State field in the query used in Figure 9.11. The list of values in the parentheses becomes an example criterion. Your query should resemble the query shown in Figure 9.12.

Access automatically adds quotation marks around AZ, CA, and NY.

FIGURE 9.12

Using the In operator to find all records for buyer state being either AZ, CA, or NY.

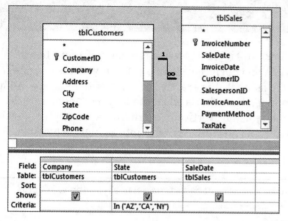

Using And to specify a range

The And operator is frequently used in fields that have numeric or date/time data types. It's seldom used with text data types, although it can be this way in some situations. For example, you might be interested in viewing all buyers whose names start with the letters *d, e,* or *f.* The And operator can be used here (>="D" And <="G"), although the Like operator is better (Like " [DEF]*") because it's much easier to understand.

You use the And operator in queries when you want a field to meet two or more conditions that you specify. For example, you might want to see records of buyers who have purchased products between October 1, 2012, and March 31, 2013. In other words, the sale had to have occurred during the last quarter of the year 2012 and the first quarter of 2013. The general expression for this example is:

    (SaleDate >= #10/1/2012#) And (SaleDate <= #3/31/2013#)

Unlike the Or operation (which has several conditions under which it is true), the And operation is true only when *both* sides of the expression are true. To clarify the use of the And operator, consider these conditions:

- SaleDate (9/22/2012) is not greater than 10/01/2012 but is less than 3/31/2013: The result is false.
- SaleDate (4/11/2013) is greater than 10/01/2012 but is not less than 3/31/2013: The result is false.
- SaleDate (11/22/2012) is greater than 10/01/2012 and less than 3/31/2013: The result is true.

Using an And operator with a single field sets a range of acceptable values in the field. Therefore, the key purpose of an And operator in a single field is to define a range of records to be viewed. For example, you can use the And operator to create a range criterion to display all buyers who have purchased products between October 1, 2012 and March 31, 2013, inclusively. To create this query, follow these steps:

1. **Create a new query using tblCustomers and tblSales.**
2. **Add Company from tblCustomers and SaleDate from tblSales.**
3. **Click in the Criteria cell of SaleDate.**
4. **Type** >= #10/1/2012# And <= #3/31/2013# **in the cell.** The query should resemble Figure 9.13.

FIGURE 9.13

Using an And operator to specify complex query criteria.

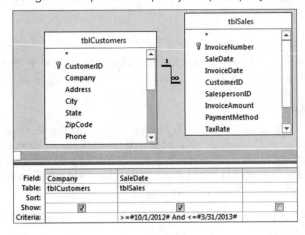

Notice the pound signs (#) used to delimit the dates in the expressions on both sides of the And operator. Access recognizes pound signs as delimiters for date and time values.

Without the pound signs, Access evaluates the date values as numeric expressions (10 divided by 1 divided by 2012, for example).

Using the Between...And operator

You can request a range of records using another method—the Between...And operator. With Between...And, you can find records that meet a range of values—for example, all sales where the list price of the product was between $50 and $100. Using the previous example with dates, create the query shown in Figure 9.14.

FIGURE 9.14

Using the Between...And operator. The results are the same as the query in Figure 9.13.

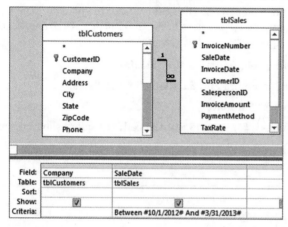

The operands for the Between...And operator are inclusive. This means that sales on 10/1/2012 and 3/31/2013 are included in the query results.

Searching for null data

A field might have no contents for several reasons. For example, perhaps the value wasn't known at the time of data entry, or the person who did the data entry simply forgot to enter the information, or the field's information was removed. Access does nothing with this field. Unless a default value is specified in the table design, the field simply remains empty. (A field is said to be *null* when it's truly empty.)

Logically, null is neither true nor false. A null field is not equivalent to all spaces or to zero. A null field simply has no value.

What Is a Null Value?

Databases must work with all kinds of information. We're all familiar with text, numeric, date, and other types of data, and in most cases, the value is known. For example, we almost certainly know a new employee's first and last names, but we may not yet know his middle name. How does a database represent a value that is unknown and that may, in fact, not exist? That's where null comes in. By default, most fields in a database table are null until a value is provided. The value may come from a user entering a value on a form, or it may be provided through the field's default value property. If we learn that the employee doesn't have a middle name, we may enter an empty string ("") in the field holding the middle name. In this case, an empty string means that there is no middle name. But as long as the value is unknown, the field is null.

Access lets you work with null value fields by means of two special operators:

- `Is Null`
- `Is Not Null`

You use these operators to limit criteria based on the null state of a field. Earlier in this chapter, you learned that a null value can be used to query for products having a picture on file. In the next example, you look for buyers that don't have the Notes field filled in:

1. **Create a new query using tblCustomers and tblSales.**
2. **Add Notes and Company from tblCustomers, and SaleDate from tblSales.**
3. **Enter** Is Null **as the criteria in the Notes field.**
4. **Uncheck the Show box in the Notes field.**

Your query should look like Figure 9.15. Select the Datasheet View command to see the records that don't have a value in the Notes field.

You unchecked the Show box because there is no need to display the Notes field in the query results. The criteria selects only those rows where the Notes field is null, so there is, quite literally, nothing to see in the Notes field and no reason to display it in the results.

9

TIP

When using the `Is Null` and `Is Not Null` operators, you can enter Null or Not Null, and Access automatically adds the `Is` to the Criteria field.

FIGURE 9.15

Use `Is Null` to select rows containing fields that contain no data.

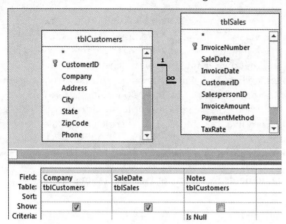

Entering Criteria in Multiple Fields

Earlier in this chapter, you worked with single and multiple criteria specified in single fields. In this section, you work with criteria across several fields. When you want to limit the records based on several field conditions, you do so by setting criteria in each of the fields that will be used for the scope. Suppose you want to search for all sales of models to resellers in Kansas. Or suppose you want to search for motorcycle model buyers in Massachusetts or Connecticut. Or suppose you want to search for all motorcycle buyers in Massachusetts or trucks in Connecticut. Each of these queries requires placing criteria in multiple fields and on multiple lines.

Using And and Or across fields in a query

To use the `And` operator and the `Or` operator across fields, place your example or pattern data in the Criteria cells (for the `And` operator) and the Or cells of one field relative to the placement in another field. When you want to use `And` between two or more fields, you place the example or pattern data across the same row in the QBD pane. When you want to use `Or` between two fields, you place the criteria on different rows in the QBD pane. Figure 9.16 shows the QBD pane and a rather extreme example of this placement.

The query in Figure 9.16 displays a record if a value matches any of the following criteria:

- ModelYear = 1932 And Make = Ford And Model = Coupe (all must be true).
- Color = Green (this can be true even if either or both of the other two lines are false).
- Category = Cars (this can be true even if either or both of the other two lines are false).

As long as one of these three criteria is true, the record appears in the query's results.

FIGURE 9.16

The QBD pane with And/Or criteria between fields using the Criteria and Or rows.

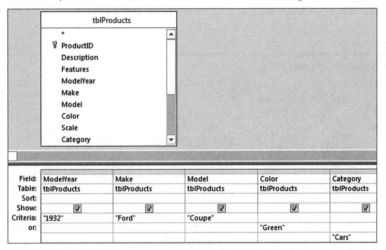

Here's the core SQL statement behind the query in Figure 9.16:

```
SELECT ModelYear, Make, Model, Color, Category
FROM tblProducts
WHERE ((ModelYear="1932") AND (Make="Ford") AND (Model="Coupe"))
OR (Color="Green")
OR (Category="Cars")
```

The locations of the parentheses in this SQL statement are significant. One set of parentheses surrounds the criteria for Field1, Field2, and Field3, while parentheses surround each of the criteria applied to Field4 and Field5. This means, of course, that ModelYear, Make, and Model are applied as a group, while Color and Category are included individually.

Specifying Or criteria across fields of a query

Although the Or operator isn't used across fields as commonly as the And operator, occasionally Or is very useful. For example, you might want to see records of any models bought by contacts in Connecticut or you might want to see records on truck models, regardless of the state the customers live in. To create this query, follow these steps:

1. **Add tblCustomers, tblSales, tblSalesLineItems, and tblProducts to a new query.**

2. **Add Company and State from tblCustomers, and Description and Category from tblProducts.**

3. **Enter CT as the criteria for State.**

4. **Enter** Trucks **in the** Or **cell under Category.** Your query should resemble Figure 9.17. Notice that the criteria entered are not in the same row of the QBD

pane for State and Category. When you place criteria on different rows in the QBD grid, Access interprets this as an Or between the fields. This query returns customers who either live in Connecticut or have bought truck models.

FIGURE 9.17

Using the Or operator between fields.

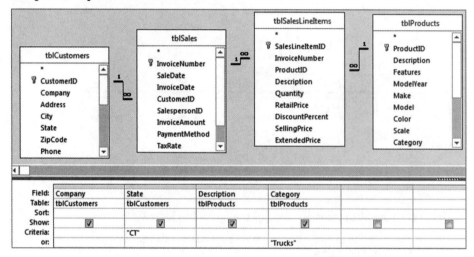

Here's the SQL statement behind the query in Figure 9.17:

```
SELECT tblCustomers.Company, tblCustomers.State,
tblProducts.Description, tblProducts.Category
FROM tblProducts
INNER JOIN (tblCustomers
INNER JOIN (tblSales INNER JOIN tblSalesLineItems
ON tblSales.InvoiceNumber = tblSalesLineItems.InvoiceNumber)
ON tblCustomers.CustomerID = tblSales.CustomerID)
ON tblProducts.ProductID = tblSalesLineItems.ProductID
WHERE (tblCustomers.State="CT") OR (tblProducts.Category="Trucks")
```

Notice the placement of parentheses in the WHERE clause. Either condition (State = "CT" or Category="Trucks") can be true, and the record is returned by the query.

Moving "Trucks" to the same row as "CT" in the QBD grid changes the query's logic to return customers who live in Connecticut *and* have bought truck models. The rearranged query is shown in Figure 9.18.

Here's the SQL statement for this minor rearrangement:

```
SELECT tblCustomers.Company, tblCustomers.State,
tblProducts.Description, tblProducts.Category
FROM tblProducts
INNER JOIN (tblCustomers
INNER JOIN (tblSales INNER JOIN tblSalesLineItems
ON tblSales.InvoiceNumber = tblSalesLineItems.InvoiceNumber)
ON tblCustomers.CustomerID = tblSales.CustomerID)
ON tblProducts.ProductID = tblSalesLineItems.ProductID
WHERE (tblCustomers.State="CT") AND (tblProducts.Category="Trucks")
```

FIGURE 9.18

A simple rearrangement in the QBD grid results in a very different query.

The difference is significant because the rearrangement is considerably more restrictive when returning records. Only one record is returned by the Figure-18 query, while the Figure-17 query returns 17 rows.

Using And and Or together in different fields

After you've worked with And and Or separately, you're ready to create a query using And and Or in different fields. In the next example, the query displays records for all buyers of car models in Connecticut and buyers of truck models in New York:

1. **Use the query from the previous example, emptying the two criteria cells first.**

2. **Enter** CT **in the Criteria row in the State column.**

3. **Enter** NY **in the** OR **row under CT in QBD grid.**

4. **Type** Cars **as criteria in the Category field.**

5. **Enter** Trucks **under Cars in the Category field.** Figure 9.19 shows how the query should look. Notice that CT and Cars are in the same row; NY and Trucks are in another row. This query represents two Ands across fields, with an Or in each field.

FIGURE 9.19

Using Ands and Ors in a select query.

The important thing to notice about this query is that Access returns, essentially, two sets of data: car model owners in Connecticut and truck model owners in New York. All other customers and model combinations are ignored.

A complex query on different lines

Suppose you want to view all records of Chevy models bought in the first six months of 2012 where the buyer lives in Massachusetts or any type of vehicle from buyers in California, regardless of when they were bought. In this example, you use three fields for setting criteria: tblCustomers.State, tblProducts.Description, and tblSales.SaleDate. Here's the expression for setting these criteria:

```
(tblSales.SaleDate Between #1/1/2012# And #6/30/2012#) AND
(tblCustomers.State="MA")) OR (tblCustomers.State="CA")
```

The query design is shown in Figure 9.20.

FIGURE 9.20

Using multiple Ands and Ors across fields. This is a rather complex select query.

Field:	Company	SaleDate	State	Description		
Table:	tblCustomers	tblSales	tblCustomers	tblProducts		
Sort:						
Show:	☑	☑	☑	☑	☐	
Criteria:		Between #1/1/2012#	"MA" Or "CA"	Like "*Chev*"		

> **CAUTION**
>
> Be aware that Access interprets dates based on the region and language settings in the Windows Control Panel. Those settings could tell Access to interpret short dates as mm/dd/yyyy or dd/mm/yyyy, depending on the region. Make sure that you account for these regional differences when working with dates.
>
> Also, keep in mind that Access, by default, interprets two-digit years from 00 to 30 as 2000 to 2030, while all two-digit years between 31 and 99 are taken to be 1931 to 1999. This is one reason why consistently using four-digit years during data entry is always a good idea.

9

Going Beyond Select Queries

IN THIS CHAPTER

Working with aggregate queries

Using action queries

Creating crosstab queries

Optimizing query performance

Retrieving and displaying specific records with a select query is indeed a fundamental task when analyzing data in Access. However, it's just a small portion of what makes up data analysis. The scope of data analysis is broad and includes grouping and comparing data, updating and deleting data, performing calculations on data, and shaping and reporting data. Access has built-in tools and functionalities designed specifically to handle each of these tasks.

In this chapter, we give you an in-depth look at the various tools available to you in Access and how they can help you go beyond select queries.

ON THE WEB

The starting database for this walkthrough, `Chapter10.accdb`, can be downloaded from this book's website.

Aggregate Queries

An *aggregate query*, sometimes referred to as a *group-by query*, is a type of query you can build to help you quickly group and summarize your data. With a select query, you can retrieve records only as they appear in your data source. But with an aggregate query, you can retrieve a summary snapshot of your data that shows you totals, averages, counts, and more.

Creating an aggregate query

To get a firm understanding of what an aggregate query does, consider the following scenario: You've just been asked to provide the sum of total revenue by period. In response to this request, start a query in Design view and bring in the Dim_Dates.Period and Dim_Transactions.LineTotal fields, as shown in Figure 10.1. If you run this query as is, you'll get every record in your data set instead of the summary you need.

FIGURE 10.1

Running this query will return all the records in your data set, not the summary you need.

TIP

Here's a quick reminder on how to start a query in Design view: Go to the Ribbon and select the Create tab. From there, select Query Design. The Show Table dialog box opens on top of a blank Query Design view. Select the table(s) you need to work with.

If you need more information, refer to Chapter 8 for a quick refresher on the basics of Access queries.

In order to get a summary of revenue by period, you'll need to activate Totals in your design grid. To do this, go to the Ribbon and select the Design tab, and then click the Totals button. As you can see in Figure 10.2, after you've activated Totals in your design grid, you'll see a new row in your grid called *Total*. The Total row tells Access which aggregate function to use when performing aggregation on the specified fields.

Notice that the Total row contains the words *Group By* under each field in your grid. This means that all similar records in a field will be grouped to provide you with a unique data item. We'll cover the different aggregate functions in depth later in this chapter.

The idea here is to adjust the aggregate functions in the Total row to correspond with the analysis you're trying perform. In this scenario, you need to group all the periods in your data set and then sum the revenue in each period. Therefore, you'll need to use the Group By aggregate function for the Period field, and the Sum aggregate function for the LineTotal field.

Since the default selection for Totals is the Group By function, no change is needed for the Period field. However, you'll need to change the aggregate function for the LineTotal field from Group By to Sum. This tells Access that you want to sum the revenue figures in the LineTotal field, not group them. To change the aggregate function, simply click the Total drop-down list under the LineTotal field, shown in Figure 10.3, and select Sum. At this point, you can run your query.

FIGURE 10.2

Activating Totals in your design grid adds a Total row to your query grid that defaults to Group By.

FIGURE 10.3

Change the aggregate function under the LineTotal field to Sum.

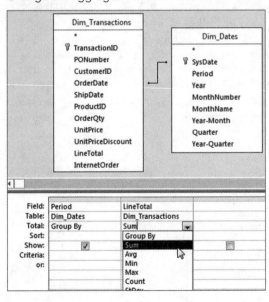

10

313

As you can see in Figure 10.4, the resulting table gives a summary of your data set, showing total revenue by period.

FIGURE 10.4

After running your query, you have a summary showing your total revenue by period.

Period	SumOfLineTotal
201107	$1,282,530.35
201108	$3,008,547.90
201109	$2,333,985.05
201110	$1,982,360.35
201111	$4,338,025.75
201112	$3,457,253.40
201201	$1,928,725.30
201202	$3,712,032.10
201203	$3,109,211.70
201204	$2,224,498.50
201205	$4,308,999.75

Creating Aliases for Your Column Names

Notice that in Figure 10.4, Access automatically changed the name of the LineTotal field to SumOfLineTotal. This is a common courtesy extended by Access to let you know that the figures you see here are a result of summing the LineTotal field. This renaming may be convenient in some cases, but if you need to distribute these results to other people, you may want to give the field a better name. This is where aliases come in handy.

An *alias* is an alternate name you can give to a field in order to make it easier to read the field's name in the query results. There are two methods for creating an alias for your field:

- Method 1: Preface the field with the text you would like to see as the field name, followed by a colon. The following figure demonstrates how you would create aliases to ensure that your query results have user-friendly column names. Running this query will result in a data set with a column called Period and column called Total Revenue.

- Method 2: Right-click the field name and select Properties. The Property Sheet for Field Properties appears. In this dialog box, enter the desired alias in the Caption input, as shown in the following figure.

Property Sheet	▾ ✕
Selection type: Field Properties	
General Lookup	
Description	
Format	
Decimal Places	
Input Mask	
Caption	TotalRevenue

About aggregate functions

In the example shown in Figure 10.3, you selected the Sum aggregate function from the Total drop-down list. Obviously, you could've selected any one of the 12 functions available. Indeed, you'll undoubtedly come across analyses where you'll have to use a few of the other functions available to you. So, it's important to know what each one of these aggregate functions means for your data analysis.

Group By

The Group By aggregate function aggregates all the records in the specified field into unique groups. Here are a few things to keep in mind when using the Group By aggregate function:

- **Access performs the** Group By **function in your aggregate query before any other aggregation.** If you're performing a Group By along with another aggregate function, the Group By function will be performed first. The example shown in Figure 10.4 illustrates this concept. Access groups the Period field before summing the LineTotal field.
- **Access sorts each group-by field in ascending order.** Unless otherwise specified, any field tagged as a group-by field will be sorted in ascending order. If your query has multiple group-by fields, each field will be sorted in ascending order starting with the leftmost field.

10

■ **Access treats multiple group-by fields as one unique item.** To illustrate this point, create a query that looks similar to the one shown in Figure 10.5. This query counts all the transactions that were logged in the 201201 period.

FIGURE 10.5

This query returns only one line showing total records for the 201201 period.

Now return to the Query Design view and add ProductID, as shown in Figure 10.6. This time, Access treats each combination of Period and ProductID as a unique item. Each combination is grouped before the records in each group are counted. The benefit here is that you've added a dimension to your analysis. Not only do you know how many transactions per ProductID were logged in 201201, but if you add up all the transactions, you'll get an accurate count of the total number of transactions logged in 201201.

Sum, Avg, Count, StDev, Var

These aggregate functions all perform mathematical calculations against the records in your selected field. It's important to note that these functions exclude any records that are set to null. In other words, these aggregate functions ignore any empty cells.

■ Sum: Calculates the total value of all the records in the designated field or grouping. This function will work only with the following data types: AutoNumber, Currency, Date/Time, and Number.

■ Avg: Calculates the average of all the records in the designated field or grouping. This function will work only with the following data types: AutoNumber, Currency, Date/Time, and Number.

FIGURE 10.6

This query results in a few more records, but if you add up the counts in each group, they'll total 503.

- Count: Counts the number of entries within the designated field or grouping. This function works with all data types.
- StDev: Calculates the standard deviation across all records within the designated field or grouping. This function will work only with the following data types: AutoNumber, Currency, Date/Time, and Number.
- Var: Calculates the amount by which all the values within the designated field or grouping vary from the average value of the group. This function will work only with the following data types: AutoNumber, Currency, Date/Time, and Number.

Min, Max, First, Last

Unlike other aggregate functions, these functions evaluate all the records in the designated field or grouping and return a single value from the group.

- Min: Returns the value of the record with the lowest value in the designated field or grouping. This function will work only with the following data types: AutoNumber, Currency, Date/Time, Number, and Text.
- Max: Returns the value of the record with the highest value in the designated field or grouping. This function will work only with the following data types: AutoNumber, Currency, Date/Time, Number, and Text.
- First: Returns the value of the first record in the designated field or grouping. This function works with all data types.
- Last: Returns the value of the last record in the designated field or grouping. This function works with all data types.

10

Expression, Where

One of the steadfast rules of aggregate queries is that every field must have an aggregation performed against it. However, in some situations you'll have to use a field as a utility—that is, use a field to simply perform a calculation or apply a filter. These fields are a means to get to the final analysis you're looking for, rather than part of the final analysis. In these situations, you'll use the Expression function or the Where clause. The Expression function and the Where clause are unique in that they don't perform any grouping action per se.

- Expression: The Expression aggregate function is generally applied when you're utilizing custom calculations or other functions in an aggregate query. Expression tells Access to perform the designated custom calculation on each individual record or group separately.
- Where: The Where clause allows you to apply a criterion to a field that is not included in your aggregate query, effectively applying a filter to your analysis.

To see the Expression aggregate function in action, create a query in Design view that looks like the one shown in Figure 10.7. Note that you're using two aliases in this query: "Revenue" for the LineTotal field and "Cost" for the custom calculation defined here. Using an alias of "Revenue" gives the sum of LineTotal a user-friendly name.

FIGURE 10.7

The Expression aggregate function allows you to perform the designated custom calculation on each Period group separately.

Now you can use [Revenue] to represent the sum of LineTotal in your custom calculation. The Expression aggregate function ties it all together by telling Access that

[Revenue]*0.33 will be performed against the resulting sum of LineTotal for each individual Period group. Running this query will return the total Revenue and Cost for each Period group.

To see the `Where` clause in action, create a query in Design view that looks like the one shown in Figure 10.8. As you can see in the Total row, you're grouping ProductID and summing LineTotal. However, Period has no aggregation selected because you only want to use it to filter out one specific period. You've entered **201201** in the criteria for Period. If you run this query as is, you'll get the following error message:

```
Your query does not include the specified expression 'Dim_
Dates.Period="201201"' as part of an aggregate function.
```

FIGURE 10.8

Running this query will cause an error message because you have no aggregation defined for Period.

To run this query successfully, click the Total drop-down list for the Period field and select `Where`. At this point, your query should look similar to the one shown here in Figure 10.9. With the `Where` clause specified, you can successfully run this query.

> **NOTE**
>
> Here is one final note about the `Where` clause. Notice in Figure 10.9 that the check box in the Show row has no check in it for the Period. This is because fields that are tagged with the `Where` clause can't be shown in an aggregate query. Therefore, this check box must remain empty. If you check the Show check box of a field with a `Where` clause, you'll get an error message stating that you can't display the field for which you entered `Where` in the Total row.

10

FIGURE 10.9

Adding a Where clause remedies the error and allows you to run the query.

Action Queries

As we mentioned earlier, in addition to querying data, the scope of data analysis includes shaping data, changing data, deleting data, and updating data. Access provides action queries as data analysis tools to help you with these tasks. Unfortunately, many people don't use these tools; instead, they export small chunks of data to Excel to perform these tasks. That may be fine if you're performing these tasks as a one-time analysis with a small data set. But what do you do when you have to carry out the same analysis on a weekly basis, or if the data set you need to manipulate exceeds Excel's limits? In these situations, it would be impractical to routinely export data into Excel, manipulate the data, and then re-import the data back into Access. Using action queries, you can increase your productivity and reduce the chance of errors by carrying out all your analytical processes within Access.

You can think of an action query the same way you think of a select query. Like a select query, an action query extracts a data set from a data source based on the definitions and criteria you pass to the query. The difference is that when an action query returns results it doesn't display a data set; instead, it performs some action on those results. The action it performs depends on its type.

> **NOTE**
>
> Unlike select queries, you can't use action queries as a data source for a form or a report, as they do not return a data set that can be read.

There are four types of action queries: make-table queries, delete queries, append queries, and update queries. Each query type performs a unique action.

Make-table queries

A *make-table query* creates a new table consisting of data from an existing table. The table that is created consists of records that have met the definitions and criteria of the make-table query.

In simple terms, if you create a query, and you want to capture the results of your query in its own table, you can use a make-table query to create a hard table with your query results. Then you can use your new table in some other analytical process.

> **CAUTION**
>
> When you build a make-table query, you have to specify the name of the table that will be made when the make-table query is run. If you give the new table the same name as an existing table, the existing table will be overwritten. If you accidentally write over another table with a make-table query, you won't be able to recover the old table. Be sure that you name the tables created by your make-table queries carefully to avoid overwriting existing information.

> **NOTE**
>
> The data in a table made by a make-table query is not, in any way, linked to its source data. This means that the data in your new table will not be updated when data in the original table is changed.

Let's say you've been asked to provide the marketing department with a list of customers, along with information on each customer's sales history. A make-table query will get you the data you need. To create a make-table query, follow these steps:

1 **Create a query in the Query Design view that looks similar to the one shown in Figure 10.10.**

FIGURE 10.10

Create this query in Design view.

2. **Select the Design tab of the Ribbon, and then click the Make Table button.** The Make Table dialog box (shown in Figure 10.11) appears.

3. **In the Table Name field, enter the name you want to give to your new table.** For this example, type **SalesHistory**. Be sure not to enter the name of a table that already exists in your database, because it'll be overwritten.

FIGURE 10.11

Enter the name of your new table.

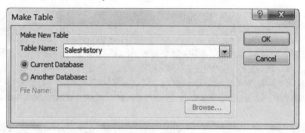

4. **Click OK to close the dialog box, and then click the Run command to run your query.** Access displays the warning message shown in Figure 10.12, letting you know that you won't be able to undo this action.

5. **Click Yes to confirm and create your new table.**

FIGURE 10.12

Click Yes to run your query.

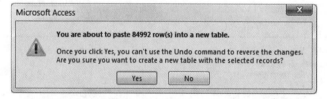

When your query has finished running, you'll find a new table called SalesHistory in your Table objects.

Turning Aggregate Query Results into Hard Data

The results of aggregate queries are inherently not updatable. This means you won't be able to edit any of the records returned from an aggregate query because there is no relationship between the aggregated data and the underlying data.

However, you can change your aggregate query into a Make Table query and create a hard table with your aggregate query's results. With your new hard table, you'll be able to edit to your heart's content.

To illustrate how this works, create the query shown in the following figure in Design view. Then change the query into a make-table query, enter a name for your new table, and run it.

Notice that in the figure you defined a column with an alias of "Customer." After the alias, you simply enter "All" (in quotes). When you run the query, you'll notice that your new table has a column named Customer in which the value for every record is All. This example illustrates that when running a make-table query, you can create your own columns on the fly simply by creating an alias for the column and defining its contents after the colon.

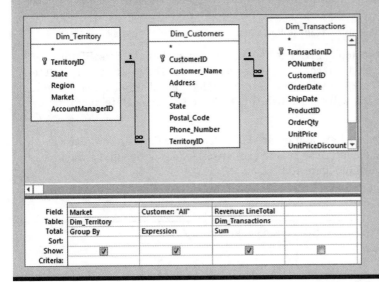

Delete queries

A *delete query* deletes records from a table based on the definitions and criteria you specify. That is, a delete query affects a group of records that meet a specified criterion that you apply.

Although you can delete records by hand, in some situations using a delete query is more efficient. For example, if you have a very large data set, a delete query deletes your records faster than a manual delete can. In addition, if you want to delete certain records based on several complex criteria, you'll want to use a delete query. Finally, if you need to delete records from one table based on a comparison to another table, a delete query is the way to go.

CAUTION

Like all other action queries, you can't undo the effects of a delete query. However, a delete query is much more dangerous than the other action queries because there is no way to remedy accidentally deleted data.

10

Given the fact that deleted data can't be recovered, get in the habit of taking one of the following actions in order to avoid a fatal error:

- Run a select query to display the records you're about to delete. Then review the records to confirm that these records are indeed the ones you want to delete, and then run the query as a delete query.

- Run a select query to display the records you're about to delete. Then change the query into a make-table query. Run the make-table query to make a backup of the data you're about to delete. Finally, run the query again as a delete query to delete the records.

- Make a backup of your database before running your delete query.

Now let's say the marketing department has informed you that the SalesHistory table you gave them includes records that they don't need. They want you to delete all history before the 201206 Period. A delete query based on the SalesHistory table you created a moment ago will accomplish this task. To create a delete query, follow these steps:

1. **Bring in the Period field and enter** <PD201206 **in the Criteria row.** Access will automatically add quotations around your criteria. Your design grid should look like the one shown in Figure 10.13.

FIGURE 10.13

This query will select all records with a Period earlier than 201206.

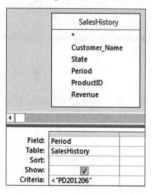

2. **Perform a test by running the query.**

3. **Review the records that are returned, and take note that 2,781 records meet your criteria.** You now know that 2,781 records will be deleted if you run a delete query based on these query definitions.

4. **Return to Design view.**

5. **Select the Design tab of the Ribbon, and then click the Delete button.**

6. **Run your query again.** Access displays the message shown in Figure 10.14, telling you that you're about to delete 2,781 rows of data and warning you that you won't be able to undo this action. This is the number you were expecting to see, because the test you ran earlier returned 2,781 records.

7. **Because everything checks out, click Yes to confirm and delete the records.**

FIGURE 10.14

Click Yes to continue with your delete action.

> **NOTE**
>
> If you're working with a very large data set, Access may display a message telling you that the Undo command won't be available because the operation is too large or there isn't enough free memory. Many people mistakenly interpret this message as meaning that the operation can't be done because there isn't enough memory. But this message is simply telling you that Access won't be able to give the option of undoing this change if you choose to continue with the action. This is applicable to delete queries, append queries, and update queries.

Deleting Records from One Table Based on the Records from Another Table

You'll encounter many analyses in which you have to delete records from one table based on the records from another table. This task is relatively easy. However, many users get stuck on it because of one simple mistake.

The query in the following figure looks simple enough. It's telling Access to delete all records from the Customer_ListA table if the customer is found in the Customer_ListB table.

Continues

10

continued

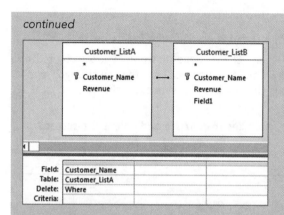

If you run this query, Access will display the message shown in the following figure. This message is asking you to specify which table contains the records you want to delete.

This message stumps many Access users. Unfortunately, this message doesn't clearly state what you need in order to remedy the mistake. Nevertheless, the remedy is a simple one: First, clear the query grid by deleting the CustomerName field. Next, double-click the asterisk (*) in the Customer_ListA table. This explicitly tells Access that the Customer_ListA table contains the records you want to delete. The following figure demonstrates the correct way to build this query.

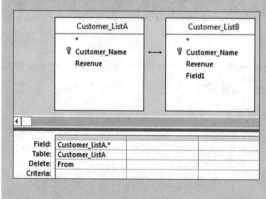

Append queries

An *append query* appends records to a table based on the definitions and criteria you specify in your query. In other words, with an append query, you can add the results of your query to the end of a table, effectively adding rows to the table.

With an append query, you're essentially copying records from one table or query and adding them to the end of another table. Append queries come in handy when you need to transfer large data sets from one existing table to another. For example, if you have a table called Old Transactions in which you archive your transaction records, you can add the latest batch of transactions from the New Transactions table simply by using an append query.

> **CAUTION**
>
> It's possible that not all the records you think you're appending to a table actually make it to the table (for the reasons we outline in the following list). Also, you'll want to be wary of running the same append query more than once, so that data is duplicated.

There are generally two reasons why records can get lost during an append process:

- **Type conversion failure:** This failure occurs when the character type of the source data doesn't match that of the destination table column. For example, imagine that you have a table with a field called *Cost*. Your Cost field is set as a Text character type because you have some entries that are tagged as TBD (to be determined), because you don't know the cost yet. If you try to append that field to another table whose Cost field is set as a Number character type, all the entries that have TBD will be changed to null, effectively deleting your TBD tag.
- **Key violation:** This violation occurs when you're trying to append duplicate records to a field in the destination table that is set as a primary key or is indexed as No Duplicates. In other words, when you have a field that prohibits duplicates, Access won't let you append any record that is a duplicate of an existing record in that field.

Another hazard of an append query is that the query will simply fail to run. There are two reasons why an append query will fail:

- **Lock violation:** This violation occurs when the destination table is open in Design view or is opened by another user on the network.
- **Validation rule violation:** This violation occurs when a field in the destination table has one of the following property settings:
  - **Required field is set to Yes:** If a field in the destination table has been set to Required Yes and you don't append data to this field, your append query will fail.
  - **Allow Zero Length is set to No:** If a field in the destination table has been set to Zero Length No and you don't append data to this field, your append query will fail.

10

- **Validation rule set to anything:** If a field in the destination table has a validation rule and you break the rule with your append query, your append query will fail. For example, if you have a validation rule for the Cost field in your destination table set to >0, you can't append records with a quantity less than or equal to zero.

Luckily, Access will clearly warn you if you're about to cause any of these errors. Figure 10.15 demonstrates this warning message, which tells you that you can't append all the records due to errors. It also tells you exactly how many records won't be appended because of each error. In this case, 5,979 records won't be appended because of key violations. You have the option of clicking Yes or No. If you click Yes, the warning is ignored and all records are appended, minus the records with the errors. If you click No, the query will be canceled, which means that no records will be appended.

FIGURE 10.15

The warning message tells you that you'll lose records during the append process.

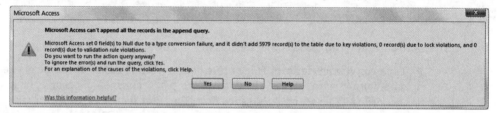

CAUTION

Keep in mind that like all other action queries, you won't be able to undo your append query once you've pulled the trigger.

TIP

If you can identify the records you recently appended in your destination table, you could technically undo your append action simply by deleting the newly appended records. This would obviously be contingent upon your providing yourself with a method of identifying appended records. For example, you could create a field that contains some code or tag that identifies the appended records. This code can be anything from a date to a simple character.

Let's say the marketing department tells you that they made a mistake—they actually need all the sales history for the 2012 fiscal year. So, they need periods 201201 through 201205 added back to the SalesHistory report. An append query is in order.

In order to get them what they need, follow these steps:

1. **Create a query in the Query Design view that looks similar to the one shown in Figure 10.16.**

2. **Select the Design tab of the Ribbon, and then click the Append button.** The Append dialog box (shown in Figure 10.17) appears.

3. **In the Table Name field, enter the name of the table to which you would like to append your query results.** In this example, enter **SalesHistory**.

4. **Once you've entered your destination table's name, click OK.** Your query grid has a new row called Append To under the Sort row (see Figure 10.18). The idea is to select the name of the field in your destination table where you want to append the information resulting from your query. For example, the Append To row under the Period field shows the word *Period*. This means that the data in the Period field of this query will be appended to the Period field in the SalesHistory table.

FIGURE 10.16

This query selects all records contained in Periods 201201 through 201205.

FIGURE 10.17

Enter the name of the table to which you want to append your query results.

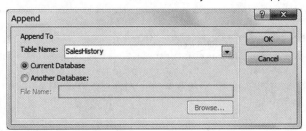

10

FIGURE 10.18

In the Append To row, select the name of the field in your destination table where you want to append the information resulting from your query.

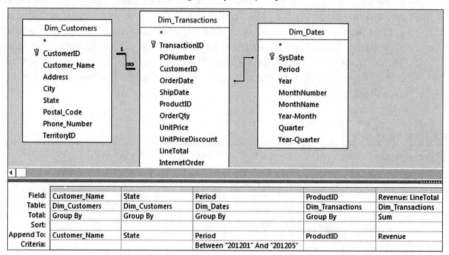

Field:	Customer_Name	State	Period	ProductID	Revenue: LineTotal
Table:	Dim_Customers	Dim_Customers	Dim_Dates	Dim_Transactions	Dim_Transactions
Total:	Group By	Group By	Group By	Group By	Sum
Sort:					
Append To:	Customer_Name	State	Period	ProductID	Revenue
Criteria:			Between "201201" And "201205"		

5. **Run your query.** Access displays a message, as shown in Figure 10.19, telling you that you're about to append 2,781 rows of data and warning you that you won't be able to undo this action.

6. **Click Yes to confirm and append the records.**

FIGURE 10.19

Click Yes to continue with your append action.

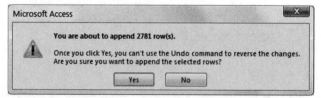

Adding a Total Row to Your Data Set

Your manager wants you to create a revenue summary report that shows the total revenue for each account manager in each market. He also wants to see the total revenue for each market. Instead of giving your manager two separate reports, you can give him one table that has account manager details and market totals. This is an easy process:

1. Create a query in the Query Design view that looks similar to the one shown in the following figure. Note that you're creating an alias for the LineTotal Field.

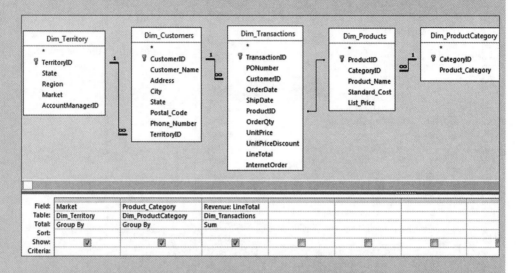

2. Change the query into a make-table query and name your table RevenueSummary.
3. Run this query.
4. Now use the RevenueSummary table you just created to summarize revenue by Market; to do this, create a query in the Query Design view that looks similar to the one shown in the following figure.

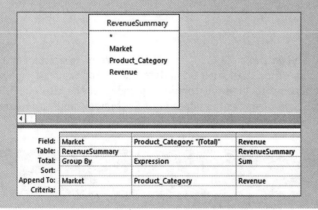

Continues

continued

Take a moment and look at the query in this figure. You'll notice that you're making a custom Product_Category field, filling it with "(Total)". This will ensure that the summary rows you append to the RevenueSummary table will be clearly identifiable, as they'll have the word "(Total)" in the Product_Category field.

5. Change the query into an append query and append these results to the RevenueSummary table.

Market	Product_Category	Revenue
Baltimore	(Total)	$19,387.00
Baltimore	Bar Equipment	$80.00
Baltimore	Fryers	$352.00
Baltimore	Ovens and Ranges	$7,470.00
Baltimore	Refrigerators and Coolers	$10,730.00
Baltimore	Warmers	$755.00
Buffalo	(Total)	$5,283,983.55
Buffalo	Bar Equipment	$37,397.90
Buffalo	Commercial Appliances	$237,297.85
Buffalo	Concession Equipment	$187,711.00
Buffalo	Fryers	$127,287.70
Buffalo	Ovens and Ranges	$1,654,376.65
Buffalo	Refrigerators and Coolers	$2,030,464.50
Buffalo	Warmers	$1,009,447.95
California	(Total)	$11,363,506.25

Now you can open the RevenueSummary table and sort by Market and Product_Category. As you can see in the preceding figure, you've successfully created a table that has a total revenue line for every product category and a total revenue line for each market, all in one table.

Update queries

The primary reason to use *update queries* is to save time. There is no easier way to edit large amounts of data at one time than with an update query. For example, imagine you have a Customers table that includes customers' zip codes. If the zip code 32750 has been changed to 32751, you can easily update your Customers table to replace 32750 with 32751.

CAUTION

As is the case with all other action queries, you must always take precautions to ensure that you aren't in a situation where you can't undo the effects of an update query. To give yourself a way back to the original data in the event of a misstep, make a backup of your database before running your update query. Alternatively, you can run a select query to display and then change the query into a make-table query; run the make-table query to make a backup of the data you're about to update; and then run the query again as an update query to overwrite the records.

Let's say you've just received word that the zip code for all customers in the 33605 zip code has been changed to 33606. In order to keep your database accurate, you'll have to update all the 33605 zip codes in your Dim_Customers table to 33606. Here's how:

1. **Create a query in the Query Design view that looks similar to the one shown in Figure 10.20.**

FIGURE 10.20

This query will select all customers that are in the 33605 zip code.

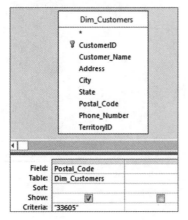

2. **Perform a test by running the query.**

3. **Review the records that are returned, and take note that six records meet your criteria.** You now know that six records will be updated if you run an update query based on these query definitions.

4. **Return to the Design view.**

5. **Select the Design tab of the Ribbon, and click the Update button.** Your query grid now has a new row called Update To. The idea is to enter the value to which you would like to update the current data. In this scenario, shown in Figure 10.21, you want to update the zip code for the records you're selecting to 33606.

6. **Run the query.** Access displays the message shown in Figure 10.22, telling you that you're about to update six rows of data and warning you that you won't be able to undo this action. This is the number you were expecting to see, because the test you ran earlier returned six records.

7. **Since everything checks out, click Yes to confirm and update the records.**

10

FIGURE 10.21

In this query, you are updating the zip code for all customers that have a code of 33605 to 33606.

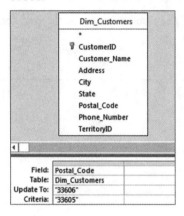

FIGURE 10.22

Click Yes to continue with your update action.

Using Expressions in Your Update Queries

You'll come across situations in which you have to execute record-specific updates. That is, you aren't updating multiple records with one specific value; instead, you're updating each record individually based on an expression.

To demonstrate this concept, start a query in Design view based on the SalesHistory table you created in the "Make-table queries" section earlier in this chapter. Build your query like the one shown in the following figure.

This query is telling Access to update the Period to the concatenated text "PD" with the value in the Period field.

After you run this query, all the values in the Period field will have a prefix of PD. For example, 201201 will be updated to PD201201.

Remember: This is just one example of an expression you can use to update your records. You can use almost any expression with an update query, ranging from mathematical functions to string operations.

A Word on Updatable Data Sets

Not all data sets are updatable. That is, you may have a data set that Access can't update for one reason or another. If your update query fails, you'll get one of these messages: `Operation must use an updatable query` or `This recordset is not updatable`.

Your update query will fail if any one of the following applies:

- Your query is using a join to another query. To work around this issue, create a temporary table that you can use instead of the joined query.

- Your query is based on a crosstab query, an aggregate query, a union query, or a subquery that contains aggregate functions. To work around this issue, create a temporary table that you can use instead of the query.

- Your query is based on three or more tables and there is a many-to-one-to-many relationship. To work around this issue, create a temporary table that you can use without the relationship.

- Your query is based on a table where the Unique Values property is set to Yes. To work around this issue, set the Unique Values property of the table to No.

Continues

10

continued

- Your query is based on a table that's locked by another user. To work around this issue, ensure the table is not in Design view or locked by another user.

- Your query is based on a table in a database that is open as read-only or is located on a read-only drive. To work around this issue, obtain write access to the database or drive.

- Your query is based on a linked ODBC table with no unique index or a paradox table without a primary key. To work around this issue, add a primary key or a unique index to the linked table.

- Your query is based on a SQL pass-through query. To work around this issue, create a temporary table that you can use instead of the query.

Crosstab Queries

A *crosstab query* is a special kind of aggregate query that summarizes values from a specified field and groups them in a matrix layout by two sets of dimensions, one set down the left side of the matrix and the other set listed across the top of the matrix. Crosstab queries are perfect for analyzing trends over time or providing a method for quickly identifying anomalies in your data set.

The anatomy of a crosstab query is simple. You need a minimum of three fields in order to create the matrix structure that will become your crosstab. The first field makes up the row headings; the second field makes up the column headings; and the third field makes up the aggregated data in the center of the matrix. The data in the center can represent a Sum, Count, Average, or any other aggregate function. Figure 10.23 demonstrates the basic structure of a crosstab query.

FIGURE 10.23

The basic structure of a crosstab query.

Region Name	QTR1	QTR2	QTR3	QTR4
Region A	data	data	data	data
Region B	data	data	data	data
Region C	data	data	data	data

There are two methods to create a crosstab query. You can use the Crosstab Query Wizard or create a crosstab query manually using the query design grid.

Creating a crosstab query using the Crosstab Query Wizard

To use the Crosstab Query Wizard to create a crosstab query, follow these steps:

1. **Select the Create tab of the Ribbon and then click the Query Wizard button.** The New Query dialog box, shown in Figure 10.24, appears.

FIGURE 10.24

Select Crosstab Query Wizard from the New Query dialog box.

2. **Select Crosstab Query Wizard from the selection list, and then click OK.**

   The first step in the Crosstab Query Wizard is to identify the data source you'll be using. As you can see in Figure 10.25, you can choose either a query or a table as your data source. In this example, you'll be using the Dim_Transactions table as your data source.

3. **Select Dim_Transactions and then click the Next button.**

   The next step is to identify the fields you want to use as the row headings.

4. **Select the ProductID field and click the button with the > symbol on it to move it to the Selected Fields list.** The dialog box should look like Figure 10.26. Notice that the ProductID field is shown in the sample diagram at the bottom of the dialog box.

   You can select up to three fields to include in your crosstab query as row headings. Remember that Access treats each combination of headings as a unique item. That is, each combination is grouped before the records in each group are aggregated.

5. **Click the Next button.**

   The next step is to identify the field you want to use as the column heading for your crosstab query. Keep in mind that there can be only one column heading in your crosstab.

6. **Select the OrderDate field from the field list.** Notice in Figure 10.27 that the sample diagram at the bottom of the dialog box updates to show the OrderDate.

NOTE

If the field that is being used as a column heading includes data that contains a period (.), an exclamation point (!), or a bracket ([or]), those characters will be changed to an underscore character (_) in the column heading. This does not happen if the same data is used as a row heading. This behavior is by design, as the naming convention for field names in Access prohibits use of these characters.

10

FIGURE 10.25

Select the data source for your crosstab query.

FIGURE 10.26

Select the ProductID field and then click the Next button.

FIGURE 10.27

Select the OrderDate field and then click the Next button.

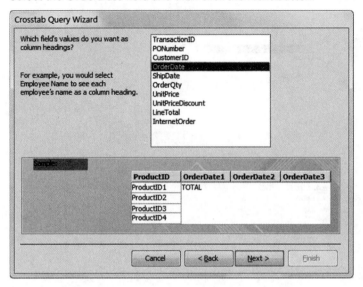

If your Column Heading is a date field, as the OrderDate is in this example, you'll see the step shown in Figure 10.28. In this step, you'll have the option of specifying an interval to group your dates by.

7. **Select Quarter and notice that the sample diagram at the bottom of the dialog box updates accordingly.**

   You're almost done. In the second-to-last step, shown in Figure 10.29, you'll identify the field you want to aggregate and the function you want to use.

8. **Select the LineTotal field from the Fields list, and then select Sum from the Functions list.** Notice the Yes, Include Row Sums check box. This box is checked by default to ensure that your crosstab query includes a Total column that contains the sum total for each row. If you don't want this column, simply remove the check from the check box.

   If you look at the sample diagram at the bottom of the dialog box, you will get a good sense of what your final crosstab query will do. In this example, your crosstab will calculate the sum of the LineTotal field for each ProductID by Quarter.

   The final step, shown in Figure 10.30, is to name your crosstab query.

9. **In this example, name your crosstab Product Summary by Quarter.** After you name your query, you have the option of viewing your query or modifying the design.

10

FIGURE 10.28

Select Quarter and then click Next.

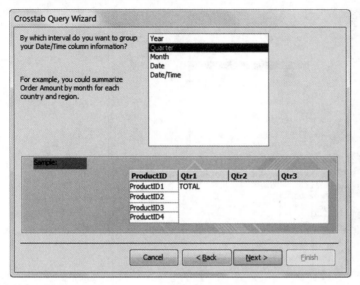

FIGURE 10.29

Select the LineTotal and Sum, and then click the Next button.

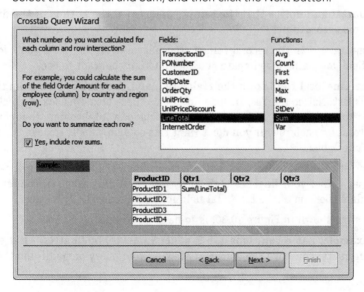

10. **In this case, you want to view your query results so simply click the Finish button.**

In just a few clicks, you've created a powerful look at the revenue performance of each product by quarter (see Figure 10.31).

FIGURE 10.30

Click Finish to see your query results.

FIGURE 10.31

A powerful analysis in just a few clicks.

ProductID	Total Of LineTotal	Qtr 1	Qtr 2	Qtr 3	Qtr 4
709	$28,663.80	$3,787.20	$8,000.40	$9,485.40	$7,390.80
710	$353,507.05	$69,334.85	$64,463.10	$62,870.60	$156,838.50
718	$732,725.50		$171,432.25	$414,166.75	$147,126.50
719	$5,853,748.80	$1,244,884.20	$1,541,942.70	$1,616,661.00	$1,450,260.90
720	$495,413.50			$495,413.50	
732	$160,733.00	$23,115.00	$49,948.50	$36,247.00	$51,422.50
733	$57,352.00		$22,411.50	$13,065.00	$21,875.50
753	$9,373,695.50	$2,286,041.00	$2,949,132.00	$1,824,659.50	$2,313,863.00
755	$582,601.20	$145,650.30	$166,482.60	$103,370.40	$167,097.90
756	$526,095.55	$133,975.65	$155,210.75	$85,507.75	$151,401.40
757	$250,742.10	$82,378.10	$83,924.30		$84,439.70
759	$517,812.55	$116,694.85	$147,762.65	$124,890.65	$128,464.40
760	$1,680,850.20	$340,321.65	$439,951.80	$489,024.00	$411,552.75
761	$1,609,727.40	$346,173.30	$433,207.60	$433,159.70	$397,186.80
762	$1,970,584.00	$412,384.00	$521,899.00	$558,061.00	$478,240.00
763	$1,381,724.40	$298,040.80	$374,013.60	$373,272.00	$336,398.00
764	$953,558.70	$211,096.10	$263,555.85	$245,037.80	$233,868.95

Turning Your Crosstab Query into Hard Data

You'll undoubtedly encounter scenarios in which you'll have to convert your crosstab query into hard data in order to use the results on other analyses. A simple trick for doing this is to use your saved crosstab query in a make-table query to create a new table with your crosstab results.

Start by creating a new select query in Design view and add your saved crosstab query. In the following figure, you'll notice that you're using the Product Summary by Quarter crosstab you just created. Bring in the fields you want to include in your new table.

At this point, simply convert your query into a make-table query and run it. After you run your make-table query, you'll have a hard table that contains the results of your crosstab.

Creating a crosstab query manually

Although the Crosstab Query Wizard makes it easy to create a crosstab in just a few clicks, it does have limitations that may inhibit your data analysis efforts:

- **You can select only one data source on which to base your crosstab.** This means that if you need to crosstab data residing across multiple tables, you'll need to take extra steps to create a temporary query to use as your data source.
- **There is no way to filter or limit your crosstab query with criteria from the Crosstab Query Wizard.**
- **You're limited to only three row headings.**
- **You can't explicitly define the order of your column headings from the Crosstab Query Wizard.**

The good news is that you can create a crosstab query manually through the query design grid. Manually creating your crosstab query allows you greater flexibility in your analysis.

Using the query design grid to create your crosstab query

Here's how to create a crosstab query using the query design grid:

1. **Create the aggregate query shown in Figure 10.32.** Notice that you're using multiple tables to get the fields you need. One of the benefits of creating a crosstab query manually is that you don't have to use just one data source—you can use as many sources as you need in order to define the fields in your query.

FIGURE 10.32

Create an aggregate query as shown here.

2. **Select the Design tab of the Ribbon and click the Crosstab button.** A row called Crosstab has been added to your query grid (see Figure 10.33). The idea is to define what role each field will play in your crosstab query.

FIGURE 10.33

Set each field's role in the Crosstab row.

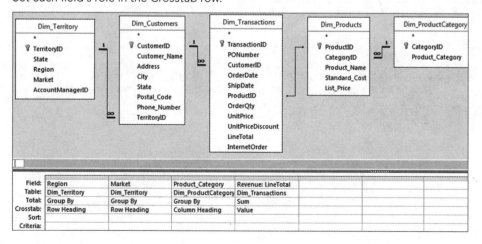

3. **Under each field in the Crosstab row, select whether the field will be a row heading, a column heading, or a value.**

4. **Run the query to see your crosstab in action.**

When building your crosstab in the query design grid, keep the following in mind:

- You must have a minimum of one row heading, one column heading, and one value field.
- You can't define more than one column heading.
- You can't define more than one value heading.
- You are not limited to only three row headings.

Creating a Crosstab View with Multiple Value Fields

One of the rules of a Crosstab query is that you cannot have more than one Value field. However, there is a trick to work around this limitation and analyze more than one metric with the same data groups.

Start by creating the Crosstab query shown in the following figure. Note that your Column heading is a custom field that will give you the region name and the word "Revenue" next to it.

Next, create another crosstab query as shown in the following figure and save it as **Crosstab-2**. Again, your column heading is a custom field that will give you the region name and the word *Transactions* next to it.

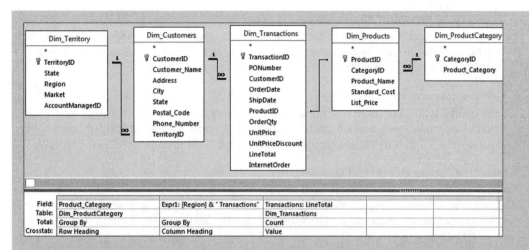

Field:	Product_Category	Expr1: [Region] & " Transactions"	Transactions: LineTotal		
Table:	Dim_ProductCategory		Dim_Transactions		
Total:	Group By	Group By	Count		
Crosstab:	Row Heading	Column Heading	Value		

Finally, create a select query that will join the two crosstab queries on the row heading. In the example shown in the following figure, the row heading is the Product_Category field. Bring in all the fields in the appropriate order. When you run this query, the result will be an analysis that incorporates both crosstab queries, effectively giving you multiple value fields.

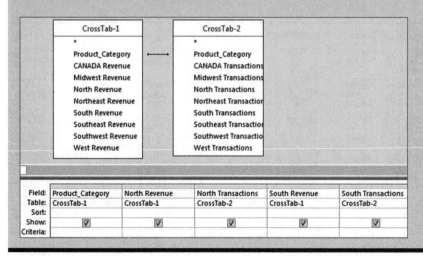

Field:	Product_Category	North Revenue	North Transactions	South Revenue	South Transactions
Table:	CrossTab-1	CrossTab-1	CrossTab-2	CrossTab-1	CrossTab-2
Sort:					
Show:	☑	☑	☑	☑	☑
Criteria:					

NOTE

Keep in mind that if you have more than one row heading, you'll have to create a join on each row heading.

Customizing your crosstab queries

As useful as crosstab queries can be, you may find that you need to apply some of your own customizations in order to get the results you need. In this section, we explain a few of the ways you can customize your crosstab queries to meet your needs.

Defining criteria in a crosstab query

The ability to filter or limit your crosstab query is another benefit of creating crosstab queries manually. To define a filter for your crosstab query, simply enter the criteria as you normally would for any other aggregate query. Figure 10.34 demonstrates this concept.

Changing the sort order of your crosstab query column headings

By default, crosstab queries sort their column headings in alphabetical order. For example, the crosstab query in Figure 10.35 will produce a data set where the column headings read this order: Canada, Midwest, North, Northeast, South, Southeast, Southwest, and West.

This may be fine in most situations, but if your company headquarters is in California, the executive management may naturally want to see the West region first. You can specify the column order of a crosstab query by changing the Column Headings attribute in the Query Properties.

FIGURE 10.34

You can define a criterion to filter your crosstab queries.

FIGURE 10.35

This crosstab query will display all regions as columns in alphabetical order.

To get to the Column Headings attribute:

1. **Open the query in Design view.**

2. **Right-click in the gray area above the white query grid and select Properties.**
   The Property Sheet for the Query Properties, shown in Figure 10.36, appears.

3. **Enter the order in which you want to see the column headings by changing the Column Headings attribute.**

FIGURE 10.36

The Column Headings attribute is set to have the columns read in this order: West, Canada, Midwest, North, Northeast, South, Southeast, and Southwest.

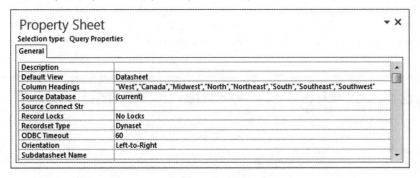

> **TIP**
>
> Adjusting the Column Headings attribute comes in handy when you're struggling with showing months in month order instead of alphabetical order. Simply enter the month columns in the order you want to see them. For example: "Jan", "Feb","Mar","Apr","May","Jun", "Jul","Aug","Sep","Oct","Nov","Dec".

When working with the Column Headings attribute, keep in mind the following:

- You must enter each column name in quotes and separate each column with commas.
- Accidentally misspelling a column name will result in that column being excluded from the crosstab results and a dummy column with the misspelled name being included with no data in it.
- The Column Headings attribute is not case sensitive. You can enter Jan or JAN and still get the same results.
- Column names you enter into the Column Headings attribute will show up in the final results even if no data exists for that column.
- You must enter every column you want to include in your crosstab report. Excluding a column from the Column Headings attribute will exclude that column from the crosstab results.
- Clearing the Column Headings attribute will ensure that all columns are displayed in alphabetical order.

Optimizing Query Performance

When you're analyzing a few thousand records, query performance is not an issue. Analytical processes run quickly and smoothly with few problems. However, when you're moving and crunching hundreds of thousands of records, performance becomes a huge issue. There is no getting around the fact that the larger the volume of data, the slower your queries will run. That said, there are steps you can take to optimize query performance and reduce the time it takes to run your large analytical processes.

Understanding the Access Query Optimizer

Most relational database programs have a built-in optimizer to ensure efficient performance, even in the face of large volumes of data. Access also has a built-in query optimizer. Have you ever noticed that when you build a query, close it, and then open it again, Access sometimes shuffles your criteria and expressions around? This is because of its built-in query optimizer.

The query optimizer is charged with the task of establishing a query execution strategy. The query execution strategy is a set of instructions given to the Access database engine (ACE) that tells it how to run the query in the quickest, most cost-effective way possible. Access's query optimizer bases its query execution strategy on the following factors:

- The size of the tables used in the query
- Whether indexes exist in the tables used in the query
- The number of tables and joins used in the query
- The presence and scope of any criteria or expressions used in the query

This execution strategy is created when the query is first run, and it's recompiled each time you save a query or compact your database. Once a query execution strategy has been established, the ACE database engine simply refers to it each time the query is run, effectively optimizing the execution of the query.

You've heard the term *garbage in, garbage out*, referring to the fact that the results you get out of a database are only as good as the data you put in. This concept also applies to Access's query optimizer. Since Access's optimization functionality largely depends on the makeup and utility of your tables and queries, poorly designed tables and queries can limit the effectiveness of Access's query optimizer.

Normalizing your database design

Many users who are new to Access build one large, flat table and call it a database. This structure seems attractive because you don't have to deal with joins and you only have to reference one table when you build your queries. However, as the volume of data grows in a structure such as this one, query performance will take a nosedive.

When you normalize your database to take on a relational structure, you break up your data into several smaller tables. This has two effects:

- You inherently remove redundant data, giving your query less data to scan.
- You can query only the tables that contain the information you need, preventing you from scanning your entire database each time you run a query.

Using indexes on appropriate fields

Imagine that you have a file cabinet that contains 1,000 records that aren't alphabetized. How long do you think it would take you to pull out all the records that start with *S?* You would definitely have an easier time pulling out records in an alphabetized filing system. Indexing fields in an Access table is analogous to alphabetizing records in a file cabinet.

When you run a query in which you're sorting and filtering on a field that hasn't been indexed, Access has to scan and read the entire data set before returning any results. As you can imagine, on large data sets this can take a very long time. By contrast, queries that sort and filter on fields that have been indexed run much more quickly because Access uses the index to check positions and restrictions.

10

You can create an index on a field in a table by going into the table's Design view and adjusting the Indexed property.

 Refer to Chapter 3 for a refresher on indexes.

Now, before you go out and start creating an index on every field in your database, there is one caveat to indexing: although indexes do speed up select queries dramatically, they significantly slow down action queries such as update, delete, and append. This is because when you run an action query on indexed fields, Access has to update each index in addition to changing the actual table. To that end, it's important that you limit the fields that you index.

A best practice is to limit your indexes to the following types of fields:

- Fields in which you'll routinely filter values using criteria
- Fields that you anticipate using as joins on other tables
- Fields in which you anticipate sorting values regularly

Optimizing by improving query design

You'd be surprised how a few simple choices in query design can improve the performance of your queries. Take a moment to review some of the actions you can take to speed up your queries and optimize your analytical processes:

- Avoid sorting or filtering fields that aren't indexed.
- Avoid building queries that select * from a table. For example, SELECT * FROM MyTable forces Access to look up the field names from the system tables every time the query is run.
- When creating a totals query, include only the fields needed to achieve the query's goal. The more fields you include in the GROUP BY clause, the longer the query will take to execute.
- Sometimes you need to include fields in your query design only to set criteria against them. Fields that aren't needed in the final results should be set to "not shown." In other words, remove the check from the check box in the Show row of the query design grid.
- Avoid using open-ended ranges such as > or <. Instead, use the Between...And statement.
- Use smaller temporary tables in your analytical processes instead of your large core tables. For example, instead of joining two large tables together, consider creating smaller temporary tables that are limited to only the relevant records and then joining those two. You'll often find that your processes will run faster even with the extra steps of creating and deleting temporary tables.

- Use fixed column headings in crosstab queries whenever possible. This way, Access doesn't have to take the extra step of establishing column headings in your crosstab queries.
- Avoid using calculated fields in subqueries or domain aggregate functions. Subqueries and domain aggregate functions already come with an inherent performance hit. Using calculated fields in them compounds your query's performance loss considerably.

 Subqueries and domain aggregate queries are discussed in detail in Chapter 15.

Compacting and repairing your database regularly

Over time, your database will change due to the rigors of daily operation. The number of tables may have increased or decreased; you may have added and removed several temporary tables and queries; you may have abnormally closed the database once or twice; and the list goes on. All this action may change your table statistics, leaving your previously compiled queries with inaccurate query execution plans.

When you compact and repair your database, you force Access to regenerate table statistics and re-optimize your queries so that they'll be recompiled the next time the query is executed. This ensures that Access will run your queries using the most accurate and efficient query execution plans. To compact and repair your database, simply select the Database Tools tab on the Ribbon and choose the Compact and Repair Database command.

You can set your database to automatically compact and repair each time you close it by doing the following:

1. **On the Ribbon, select File.**
2. **Click Options. The Access Options dialog box appears.**
3. **Select Current Database to display the configuration settings for the current database.**
4. **Place a check mark next to Compact on Close and click OK to confirm the change.**

Part IV

Analyzing Data in Microsoft Access

Now that you know how to organize the data into tables and how to use queries to interact with that data, Part IV highlights the tools and functionalities in Access 2019 that can drive more meaningful data analysis. Indeed, using Access for your data analysis needs can help you streamline your analytical processes, increase your productivity, and analyze the larger data sets.

Chapter 11 covers data transformation, providing examples of how to clean and shape raw data into staging areas. Chapter 12 provides in-depth instruction on how to create and utilize custom calculations in analysis; this chapter also shows you how to work with dates, using them in simple date calculations. Chapter 13 introduces you to some conditional analysis techniques that allow for the addition of business logic into analytical processes. Chapter 14 explores SQL syntax and some of the SQL-specific queries that can be leveraged to improve analytics. Chapter 15 introduces you to powerful subquery and domain aggregate functionality. Chapter 16 demonstrates many of the advanced statistical analyses that can be performed using subqueries and domain aggregate functions.

IN THIS PART

Chapter 11
Transforming Data in Access

Chapter 12
Working with Calculations and Dates

Chapter 13
Performing Conditional Analyses

Chapter 14
The Fundamentals of Using SQL

Chapter 15
Subqueries and Domain Aggregate Functions

Chapter 16
Running Descriptive Statistics in Access

Transforming Data in Access

IN THIS CHAPTER

Finding and removing duplicate records

Filling in blank fields

Concatenating

Changing case

Removing leading and trailing spaces

Finding and replacing specific text

Padding strings

Parsing strings

Data transformation generally entails certain actions that are meant to "clean" your data—actions such as establishing a table structure, removing duplicates, cleaning text, removing blanks, and standardizing data fields.

You'll often receive data that is unpolished or raw—that is, the data may have duplicates, there may be blank fields, there may be inconsistent text, and so on. Before you can perform any kind of meaningful analysis on data in this state, it's important to go through a process of data transformation or data cleanup.

In this chapter, we introduce you to some of the tools and techniques in Access that make it easy for you to clean and massage your data without turning to Excel.

ON THE WEB
The starting database for this walkthrough, `Chapter11.accdb`, can be downloaded from this book's website.

Finding and Removing Duplicate Records

Duplicate records are absolute analysis killers. The effect duplicate records have on your analysis can be far reaching, corrupting almost every metric, summary, and analytical assessment you produce. For this reason, finding and removing duplicate records should be your first priority when you receive a new data set.

Defining duplicate records

Before you jump into your data set to find and remove duplicate records, it's important to consider how you define a *duplicate record*. To demonstrate this point, look at the table shown in Figure 11.1, where you see 11 records. Out of the 11 records, how many are duplicates?

FIGURE 11.1

Are there duplicate records in this table? It depends on how you define one.

SicCode	PostalCode	CompanyNumber	DollarPotential	City	State	Address
1389	77032	11147805	$9,517.00	houston	tx	6000 n sem heirten pkwy e
1389	77032	11147848	$9,517.00	houston	tx	43410 e herdy rd
1389	77042	11160116	$7,653.00	houston	tx	40642 rachmend ave ste 600
1389	77051	11165400	$9,517.00	houston	tx	5646 helmis rd
1389	77057	11173241	$9,517.00	houston	tx	2514 san filape st ste 6600
1389	77060	11178227	$7,653.00	houston	tx	100 n sem heirten pkwy e ste 100
1389	77073	11190514	$9,517.00	houston	tx	4660 rankan rd # 400
1389	77049	11218412	$7,653.00	houston	tx	4541 mallir read 6
1389	77040	13398882	$18,379.00	houston	tx	3643 wandfirn rd
1389	77040	13399102	$18,379.00	houston	tx	3643 wandfirn rd
1389	77077	13535097	$7,653.00	houston	tx	44160 wisthiamir rd ste 100

If you were to define a duplicate record in Figure 11.1 as a duplication of just SicCode, you would find 11 duplicate records. Now, if you were to expand your definition of a duplicate record to a duplication of both SicCode and PostalCode, you'd find only two duplicates: the duplication of PostalCodes 77032 and 77040. Finally, if you were to define a duplicate record as a duplication of the unique value of SicCode, PostalCode, and CompanyNumber, you would find no duplicates.

This example shows that having two records with the same value in a column doesn't necessarily mean that you have a duplicate record. It's up to you to determine which field or combination of fields will best define a unique record in your data set.

Once you have a clear idea about which field(s) best make up a unique record in your table, you can easily test your table for duplicate records by attempting to set them as a primary or combination key. To demonstrate this test, open the LeadList table in Design view, and then tag the CompanyNumber field as a primary key. If you try to save this change, you'll get the error message shown in Figure 11.2. This message means there is some duplication of records in your data set that needs to be dealt with.

 Revisit Chapter 3 to get a refresher on designing tables.

FIGURE 11.2

If you get this error message when trying to set a primary key, you have duplicate records in your data set.

Finding duplicate records

If you've determined that your data set does, indeed, contain duplicates, it's generally a good idea to find and review the duplicate records before removing them. Giving your records a thorough review will ensure you don't mistake a record as a duplicate and remove it from your analysis. You may find that you're mistakenly identifying valid records as duplicates, in which case you'll need to include another field in your definition of what makes a unique record.

The easiest way to find the duplicate records in your data set is to run the Find Duplicates Query Wizard:

1. **Select the Create tab of the Ribbon and click the Query Wizard button.** The New Query dialog box appears (see Figure 11.3).

2. **Select Find Duplicates Query Wizard and then click OK.**

FIGURE 11.3

Select the Find Duplicates Query Wizard and then click OK.

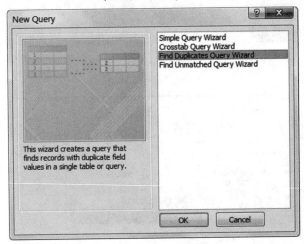

3. **Select the particular data set you will use in your Find Duplicate query (see Figure 11.4) and then click Next.**

4. **Identify which field, or combination of fields, best defines a unique record in your data set, and then click Next.** In the example shown in Figure 11.5, the CompanyNumber field alone defines a unique record.

FIGURE 11.4

Select the data set in which you want to find duplicates, and then click Next.

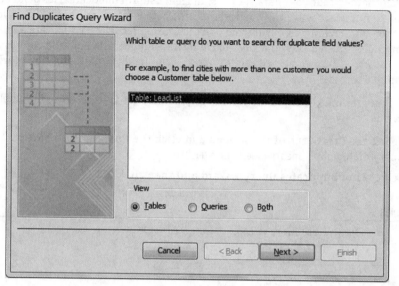

FIGURE 11.5

Select the field(s) that make up a unique record in your data set.

5. **Identify any additional fields you would like to see in your query (see Figure 11.6), and then click Next.**

FIGURE 11.6

Select the field(s) you want to see in your query.

6. **Name your query and click Finish (see Figure 11.7).** Your new Find Duplicates query will immediately open for your review. Figure 11.8 shows the resulting query. Now that Access has found the records that are repeating, you can remove duplicates simply by deleting the duplicate records.

> **NOTE**
>
> The records shown in your Find Duplicates query are not only the duplications. They include one unique record plus the duplication. For example, in Figure 11.8, notice that there are four records tagged with the CompanyNumber 11145186. Three of the four are duplicates that can be removed, while one should remain as a unique record.

Removing duplicate records

If you're working with a small data set, removing the duplicates can be as easy as manually deleting records from your Find Duplicates query. However, if you're working with a large data set, your Find Duplicates query may result in more records than you care to manually delete. Believe it when someone tells you that manually deleting records from a 5,000-row Find Duplicates query is an eyeball-burning experience. Fortunately, there is an alternative to burning out your eyeballs.

FIGURE 11.7

Name your query and click Finish.

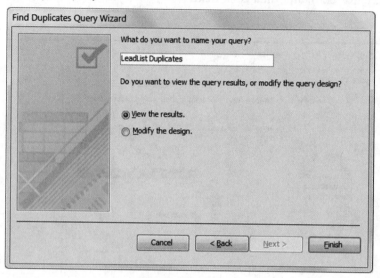

```
Find Duplicates Query Wizard

                        What do you want to name your query?

                        LeadList Duplicates

                        Do you want to view the query results, or modify the query design?

                        ◉ View the results.
                        ○ Modify the design.


                        Cancel      < Back      Next >      Finish
```

FIGURE 11.8

Your Find Duplicates query.

CompanyNumber	DollarPotential	Address	City	State	PostalCode
10625840	$47,039.00	1100 landirs rd	n little rock	ar	72117
10625840	$47,039.00	1100 landirs rd	n little rock	ar	72117
11145186	$60,770.00	5364 iost fwy	houston	tx	77029
11145186	$60,770.00	5364 iost fwy	houston	tx	77029
11145186	$60,770.00	5364 iost fwy	houston	tx	77029
11145186	$60,770.00	5364 iost fwy	houston	tx	77029
11166089	$60,770.00	6632 biffalo spiidway	houston	tx	77054
11166089	$60,770.00	6632 biffalo spiidway	houston	tx	77054
11166089	$60,770.00	6632 biffalo spiidway	houston	tx	77054
11166089	$60,770.00	6632 biffalo spiidway	houston	tx	77054
11220179	$60,770.00	40420 tilge rd	houston	tx	77095
11220179	$60,770.00	40420 tilge rd	houston	tx	77095
11220179	$60,770.00	40420 tilge rd	houston	tx	77095

The idea is to remove duplicates en masse by taking advantage of the built-in protections Access has against duplicate primary keys. To demonstrate this technique, follow these steps:

1. **Right-click the LeadList table and select Copy.**

2. **Right-click again and select Paste. The Paste Table As dialog box, shown in Figure 11.9, appears.**

3. **Name your new table** LeadList_NoDups **and select Structure Only from the Paste Options section.** A new empty table that has the same structure as your original is created.

FIGURE 11.9

Activate the Paste Table As dialog box to copy your table's structure into a new table called LeadList_NoDups.

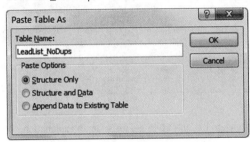

4. **Open your new LeadList_NoDups table in Design view and set the appropriate field or combination of fields as primary keys.** It's up to you to determine which field or combination of fields will best define a unique record in your data set. As you can see in Figure 11.10, the CompanyNumber field alone defines a unique record; therefore, only the CompanyNumber field will be set as a primary key.

FIGURE 11.10

Set as a primary key the field(s) that best defines a unique record.

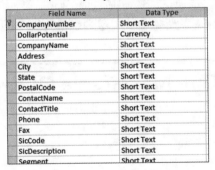

Field Name	Data Type
CompanyNumber	Short Text
DollarPotential	Currency
CompanyName	Short Text
Address	Short Text
City	Short Text
State	Short Text
PostalCode	Short Text
ContactName	Short Text
ContactTitle	Short Text
Phone	Short Text
Fax	Short Text
SicCode	Short Text
SicDescription	Short Text
Segment	Short Text

Pause here a moment and review what you have so far. At this point, you should have a table called LeadList and a table called LeadList_NoDups. The LeadList_NoDups table is empty and has the CompanyNumber field set as a primary key.

5. Create an append query that appends all records from the LeadList table to the LeadList_NoDups table. When you run the append query, you'll get a message similar to the one shown in Figure 11.11.

FIGURE 11.11

Now you can append all records excluding the duplicates.

 Not familiar with append queries? Turn back to Chapter 10 to get an in-depth explanation.

Because the CustomerNumber field in the LeadList_NoDups table is set as the primary key, Access won't allow duplicate customer numbers to be appended. In just a few clicks, you've effectively created a table free from duplicates. You can now use this duplicate-free table as the source for any subsequent analysis!

CAUTION

Be aware that Access makes no fuzzy logical determination to see if records may duplicate. It processes your request literally. For instance, a simple mistyping of an address or phone number would mean that rows that actually are duplicates would be allowed. You'll want to keep this in mind, especially when working with textual fields where data entry is manual.

Removing Duplicates with One Make-Table Query

Here's a trick that will allow you to remove duplicates by running a make-table query:

1. Select the Create tab and choose Query Design.
2. In the Show Table dialog box, select your table that contains duplicates.
3. Add all fields from your table to the query design grid.
4. On the Query Tools Design tab, select the Property Sheet command. The Property Sheet shown in the following figure appears.

All you have to do here is change the Unique Values property to Yes. Close the Property Sheet and change the query type to a Make Table Query.

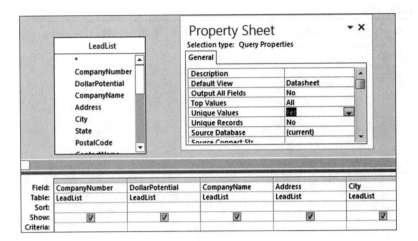

Common Transformation Tasks

Besides duplicate records, you'll find that many of the unpolished data sets that come to you will require other types of transformation actions. This section covers some of the more common transformation tasks you'll have to perform.

Filling in blank fields

Often, you'll have fields that contain empty values. These values are considered null—a value of nothing. Nulls are not necessarily a bad thing. In fact, if used properly, they can be an important part of a well-designed relational database. That said, you may find that you need to fill in blank fields with some logical code that indicates a missing value.

Filling in the null fields in your data set is as simple as running an update query. In the example shown in Figure 11.12, you're updating the null values in the DollarPotential field to zero.

It's important to note that there are actually two kinds of blank values: null and empty string (""). When filling in the blank values of a text field, include the empty string as a criterion in your update query to ensure that you don't miss any fields. In the example shown in Figure 11.13, you're updating the blank values in the Segment field to "Other."

FIGURE 11.12

This query will update the null values in the DollarPotential field to a value of 0.

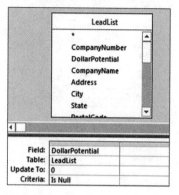

FIGURE 11.13

This query will update blank values in the Segment field to a value of "Other."

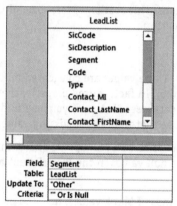

Concatenating

It's always amazing to see anyone export data out of Access and into Excel, only to concatenate (join two or more character strings end to end) and then re-import the data back into Access. You can easily concatenate any number of ways in Access with a simple update query.

Concatenating fields

Look at the update query shown in Figure 11.14. In this query, you're updating the MyTest field with the concatenated row values of the Type field and the Code field.

FIGURE 11.14

This query concatenates the row values of the Type field and the Code field.

TIP

It's a good idea to create a test field in order to test the effects of your data transformation actions before applying changes to the real data.

Take a moment to analyze the following query breakdown:

- **[Type]:** This tells Access to use the row values of the Type field.
- **&:** The ampersand is a character operator that joins strings together.
- **[Code]:** This tells Access to use the row values of the Code field.

Figure 11.15 shows the results of this query.

FIGURE 11.15

The MyTest field now contains the concatenated values of the Type field and the Code field.

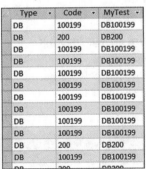

CAUTION

When running update queries that perform concatenations, make sure the field you're updating is large enough to accept the concatenated string. For example, if the length of your concatenated string is 100 characters, and the field size of the field you're updating is 50 characters, your concatenated string will be cut short without warning.

Augmenting field values with your own text

You can augment the values in your fields by adding your own text. For example, you may want to concatenate the row values of the Type field and the Code field but separate them with a colon. The query in Figure 11.16 does just that.

FIGURE 11.16

This query concatenates the row values of the Type field and the Code field and separates them with a colon.

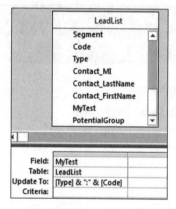

Take a moment to analyze the following query breakdown:

- **[Type]:** This tells Access to use the row values of the Type field.
- **&:** The ampersand is a character operator that joins strings together.
- **":":** This text will add a colon to the concatenated string.
- **&:** The ampersand is a character operator that joins strings together.
- **[Code]:** This tells Access to use the row values of the Code field.

Figure 11.17 shows the results of this query.

NOTE

When specifying your own text in a query, you must enclose the text in quotes. You can concatenate numeric data without the quotes.

FIGURE 11.17

The MyTest field now contains the concatenated values of the Type field and the Code field, separated by a colon.

Type	Code	MyTest
DB	100199	DB:100199
DB	200	DB:200
DB	100199	DB:100199
DB	100199	DB:100199
DB	100199	DB:100199
DB	100199	DB:100199
DB	100199	DB:100199
DB	100199	DB:100199
DB	100199	DB:100199
DB	200	DB:200
DB	100199	DB:100199

Changing case

Making sure the text in your database has the correct capitalization may sound trivial, but it's important. Imagine you receive a customer table that has an address field where all the addresses are lowercase. How is that going to look on labels, form letters, or invoices? Fortunately, for those who are working with tables containing thousands of records, Access has a few built-in functions that make changing the case of your text a snap.

The LeadList table shown in Figure 11.18 contains an Address field that is in all lowercase letters.

FIGURE 11.18

The Address field is in all lowercase letters.

Address	City	State	PostalCode
46 gin criaghten w ebrems dr	agawam	ma	01001
426 bewlis rd	agawam	ma	01001
651 sheimekir ln	agawam	ma	01001
44 almgrin dr	agawam	ma	01001
35 mall ln	brimfield	ma	01010
460 fillir rd	chicopee	ma	01020
320 mimeraal dr ste 4	chicopee	ma	01020
4010 shiradan st	chicopee	ma	01022
5046 wistevir rd	chicopee	ma	01022
40 meple st	east longmeadow	ma	01028
242 biich st	holyoke	ma	01040
42 whatang ferms rd	holyoke	ma	01040

To fix the values in the Address field, you can use the StrConv function, which is a function that converts a string to a specified case. To use the StrConv function, you must provide two required arguments: the string to be converted and the conversion type.

```
StrConv(string to be converted, conversion type,)
```

The string to be converted is simply the text you're working with. In a query environment, you can use the name of a field to specify that you're converting all the row values of that field.

The conversion type tells Access whether you want to convert the specified text to all uppercase, all lowercase, or proper case. A set of constants identifies the conversion type:

- **Conversion type 1:** Converts the specified text to uppercase characters.
- **Conversion type 2:** Converts the specified text to lowercase characters.
- **Conversion type 3:** Converts the specified text to proper case. That is, the first letter of every word is uppercase.

For example:

StrConv("My Text",1) would be converted to "MY TEXT."

StrConv("MY TEXT",2) would be converted to "my text."

StrConv("my text",3) would be converted to "My Text."

The update query shown in Figure 11.19 will convert the values of the Address field to proper case.

FIGURE 11.19

This query will convert addresses to proper case.

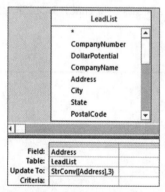

> **NOTE**
> You can also use the UCase and LCase functions to convert your text to uppercase and lowercase text, respectively. See Access Help for more details on the UCase and LCase functions.

Removing leading and trailing spaces from a string

When you receive a data set from a mainframe system, a data warehouse, or even a text file, it is not uncommon to have field values that contain leading and trailing spaces.

These spaces can cause some abnormal results, especially when you're appending values with leading and trailing spaces to other values that are clean. To demonstrate this, look at the data set in Figure 11.20.

This is intended to be an aggregate query that displays the sum of the dollar potential for California, New York, and Texas. However, the leading spaces are causing Access to group each state into two sets, preventing you from discerning the accurate totals.

FIGURE 11.20

The leading spaces are preventing an accurate aggregation.

State	SumOfDollarPotential
ca	$26,561,554.00
ny	$7,483,960.00
tx	$13,722,782.00
ca	$12,475,489.00
ny	$827,563.00
tx	$7,669,208.00

You can easily remove leading and trailing spaces by using the Trim function. Figure 11.21 demonstrates how you would update a field to remove the leading and trailing spaces by using an update query.

FIGURE 11.21

Simply pass the field name through the Trim function in an update query to remove the leading and trailing spaces.

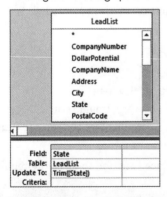

NOTE

Using the LTrim function will remove only the leading spaces, while the RTrim function will remove only the trailing spaces.

Finding and replacing specific text

Imagine that you work in a company called BLVD, Inc. One day, the president of your company informs you that the abbreviation "blvd" on all addresses is now deemed an infringement on your company's trademarked name and must be changed to "Boulevard" as soon as possible. How would you go about meeting this new requirement? Your first thought may be to use the built-in Find and Replace functionality that exists in all Office applications. However, when your data consists of hundreds of thousands of rows, the Find and Replace function will only be able to process a few thousand records at a time. This clearly would not be very efficient.

The `Replace` function is ideal in a situation like this:

```
Replace(Expression, Find, Replace[, Start[, Count[, Compare]]])
```

There are three required arguments in a `Replace` function and three optional arguments:

- **`Expression` (required):** This is the full string you're evaluating. In a query environment, you can use the name of a field to specify that you're evaluating all the row values of that field.
- **`Find` (required):** This is the substring you need to find and replace.
- **`Replace` (required):** This is the substring used as the replacement.
- **`Start` (optional):** The position within a substring to begin the search; the default is 1.
- **`Count` (optional):** The number of occurrences to replace; the default is all occurrences.
- **`Compare` (optional):** The kind of comparison to use. You can specify a binary comparison, a textual comparison, or the default comparison algorithm. See Access Help for more details.

For example:

`Replace("Pear", "P", "B")` would return "Bear."

`Replace("Now Here", " H", "h")` would return "Nowhere."

`Replace("Microsoft Access", "Microsoft ", "")` would return "Access."

`Replace("Roadsign Road", "Road", "Rd",9)` would start the replace function at the ninth character, returning "Roadsign Rd."

Figure 11.22 demonstrates how you would use the Replace function to meet the requirements in this scenario.

Adding your own text in key positions within a string

When transforming your data, you'll sometimes have to add your own text in key positions with a string. For example, in Figure 11.23, you'll see two fields. The Phone field is the raw phone number received from a mainframe report, while the MyTest field is the same phone number transformed into a standard format. As you can see, the two parentheses and the dash were added in the appropriate positions within the string to achieve the correct format.

FIGURE 11.22

This query finds all instances of "blvd" and replaces them with "Boulevard."

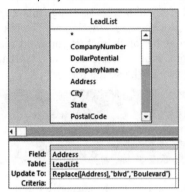

Field:	Address
Table:	LeadList
Update To:	Replace([Address],"blvd","Boulevard")
Criteria:	

FIGURE 11.23

The phone number has been transformed into a standard format by adding the appropriate characters to key positions with the string.

Phone	MyTest
6025526111	(602)552-6111
1406664640	(140)666-4640
5404362224	(540)436-2224
5302442400	(530)244-2400
1105225600	(110)522-5600
6606415600	(660)641-5600
5431426300	(543)142-6300
5434251100	(543)425-1100
5403155400	(540)315-5400
6066540220	(606)654-0220
5451534634	(545)153-4634

The edits demonstrated in Figure 11.23 were accomplished using the Right function, the Left function, and the Mid function in conjunction with each other. The Right, Left, and Mid functions allow you to extract portions of a string starting from different positions:

- The Left function returns a specified number of characters starting from the leftmost character of the string. The required arguments for the Left function are the text you're evaluating and the number of characters you want returned. For example, Left("70056-3504", 5) would return five characters starting from the leftmost character (70056).

- The Right function returns a specified number of characters starting from the rightmost character of the string. The required arguments for the Right function are the text you're evaluating and the number of characters you want returned.

For example, `Right("Microsoft", 4)` would return four characters starting from the rightmost character (`soft`).

- The `Mid` function returns a specified number of characters starting from a specified character position. The required arguments for the `Mid` function are the text you're evaluating, the starting position, and the number of characters you want returned. For example, `Mid("Lonely", 2, 3)` would return three characters, starting from the second character, or character number two in the string (`one`).

> **TIP**
>
> In a `Mid` function, if there are fewer characters in the text being used than the length argument, the entire text will be returned. For example, `Mid("go",1,10000)` will return `go`. As you'll see later in this chapter, this behavior comes in handy when you're working with nested functions.

Figure 11.24 demonstrates how the MyTest field was updated to the correctly formatted phone number.

Take a moment to analyze the query breakdown:

- `"("`: This text will add an open parenthesis to the resulting string.
- `&`: The ampersand is a character operator that joins strings together.
- `Left([Phone],3)`: This function will extract the left 3 characters of the [Phone] field.
- `&`: The ampersand is a character operator that joins strings together.
- `")"`: This text will add a close parenthesis to the resulting string.
- `&`: The ampersand is a character operator that joins strings together.
- `Mid([Phone],4,3)`: This function will extract the three characters of the [Phone] field starting from character number four.
- `&`: The ampersand is a character operator that joins strings together.
- `"-"`: This text will add a dash to the resulting string.
- `&`: The ampersand is a character operator that joins strings together.
- `Right([Phone],4)`: This function will extract the right four characters of the [Phone] field.

Padding Strings to a Specific Number of Characters

You may encounter a situation where key fields are required to be a certain number of characters in order for your data to be able to interface with peripheral platforms such as ADP payroll systems or SAP databases.

For example, imagine that the CompanyNumber field must be ten characters long. Those that are not ten characters long must be padded with enough leading zeros to create a ten-character string.

Number fields (fields with the Number data type) cannot have padded zeros, as Access will simply remove them. If you need a number string to have padded zeros, you will need to set the field to have a Short Text data type.

The secret to this trick is to add ten zeros to every company number, regardless of the current length, and then pass them through a Right function that will extract only the right ten characters. For example, company number 29875764 would first be converted to 000000000029875764; then it would go into a Right function that extracted only the right ten characters: Right("000000000029875764",10). This would leave you with 0029875764.

Although this is essentially two steps, you can accomplish the same thing with just one update query. The following figure demonstrates how this is done. This query first concatenates each company number with 0000000000, and then passes that concatenated string through a Right function that extracts only the left ten characters.

The following figure shows the results of this query. The CompanyNumber field now contains ten-character company numbers.

FIGURE 11.24

This query will update the MyTest field with a properly formatted phone number.

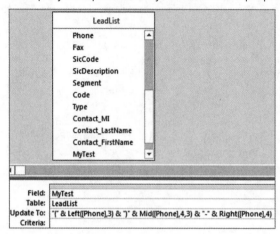

Parsing strings using character markers

Have you ever gotten a data set where two or more distinct pieces of data were jammed into one field and separated by commas? For example, in Figure 11.25, you can see that the values in the ContactName field are strings that represent "Last name, First name, Middle initial." You'll need to parse this string into three separate fields.

Although this is not a straightforward undertaking, it can be done with the help of the InStr function:

```
InStr(Start, String, Find, Compare)
```

The InStr function searches for a specified string in another string and returns its position number. There are two required arguments in an InStr function and two optional arguments:

- **Start (optional):** This is the character number with which to start the search; the default is 1.
- **String (required):** This is the string to be searched.
- **Find (required):** This is the string to search for.
- **Compare (optional):** This specifies the type of string comparison. If you specify a Compare argument, the Start argument becomes not optional.

FIGURE 11.25

You need to parse the values in the ContactName field into three separate fields.

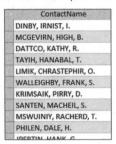

ContactName
DINBY, IRNIST, I.
MCGEVIRN, HIGH, B.
DATTCO, KATHY, R.
TAYIH, HANABAL, T.
LIMIK, CHRASTEPHIR, O.
WALLEIGHBY, FRANK, S.
KRIMSAIK, PIRRY, D.
SANTEN, MACHEIL, S.
MSWUINIY, RACHERD, T.
PHILEN, DALE, H.
IPERTIN, HANK, G.

For example:

> InStr("Alexander, Mike, H",",") would return 10 because the first comma of the string is character number 10.
> InStr(11,"Alexander, Mike, H",",") would return 16 because the first comma from character number 11 is character number 16.

If the InStr function only returns a number, how can it help you? Well, the idea is to use the InStr function with the Left, Right, or Mid functions in order to extract a string. For example, instead of using a hard-coded number in your Left function to pass it the required length argument, you can use a nested InStr function to return that number. For example, Left("Alexander, Mike",9) is the same as Left("Alexander, Mike", Instr("Alexander, Mike", ",")-1).

NOTE

When you're nesting an InStr function inside a Left, Right, or Mid function, you may have to add or subtract a character, depending on what you want to accomplish. For example, Left("Zey, Robert", InStr("Zey, Robert", ",")) would return "Zey,". Why is the comma included in the returned result? The InStr function returns 4 because the first comma in the string is the fourth character. The Left function then uses this 4 as a length argument, effectively extracting the left four characters: "Zey, "

If you want a clean extract without the comma, you'll have to modify your function to read as follows:

Left("Zey, Robert", InStr("Zey, Robert", ",")-1)

Subtracting 1 from the InStr function would leave you with 3 instead of 4. The Left function then uses this 3 as the length argument, effectively extracting the left three characters: "Zey."

The easiest way to parse the contact name field, shown in Figure 11.26, is to use two update queries.

CAUTION

This is a tricky process, so you'll want to create and work in test fields, giving yourself a way back from any mistakes you may make.

Query 1

The first query, shown in Figure 11.26, will parse out the last name in the ContactName field and update the Contact_LastName field. It will then update the Contact_FirstName field with the remaining string.

FIGURE 11.26

This query will update the Contact_LastName and Contact_FirstName fields.

If you open the LeadList table, you'll be able to see the impact of your first update query. Figure 11.27 shows your progress so far.

Query 2

The second query, shown in Figure 11.28, will update the Contact_FirstName field and the Contact_MI field.

After you run your second query, you can open your table and see the results, shown in Figure 11.29.

FIGURE 11.27

Check your progress so far.

Contact_LastName	Contact_FirstName
DINBY	IRNIST, I.
MCGEVIRN	HIGH, B.
DATTCO	KATHY, R.
TAYIH	HANABAL, T.
LIMIK	CHRASTEPHIR, O.
WALLEIGHBY	FRANK, S.
KRIMSAIK	PIRRY, D.
SANTEN	MACHEIL, S.
MSWUINIY	RACHERD, T.
PHILEN	DALE, H.
IRERTIN	HANK, C.

FIGURE 11.28

This query parses out the first name and the middle initial from the Contact_FirstName field.

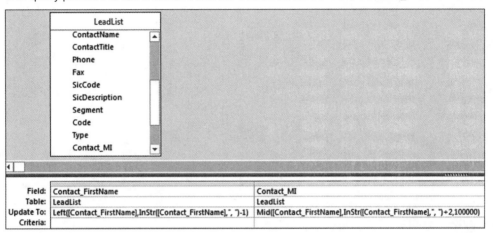

FIGURE 11.29

With two queries, you've successfully parsed the ContactName field into three separate fields.

ContactName	Contact_LastName	Contact_FirstName	Contact_MI
DINBY, IRNIST, I.	DINBY	IRNIST	I.
MCGEVIRN, HIGH, B.	MCGEVIRN	HIGH	B.
DATTCO, KATHY, R.	DATTCO	KATHY	R.
TAYIH, HANABAL, T.	TAYIH	HANABAL	T.
LIMIK, CHRASTEPHIR, O.	LIMIK	CHRASTEPHIR	O.
WALLEIGHBY, FRANK, S.	WALLEIGHBY	FRANK	S.
KRIMSAIK, PIRRY, D.	KRIMSAIK	PIRRY	D.
SANTEN, MACHEIL, S.	SANTEN	MACHEIL	S.
MSWUINIY, RACHERD, T.	MSWUINIY	RACHERD	T.
PHILEN, DALE, H.	PHILEN	DALE	H.
IDERTIN, HANK, G.	IDERTIN	HANK	G.

Working with Calculations and Dates

IN THIS CHAPTER

Using calculations in your analyses

Using dates in your analyses

The truth is that few organizations can analyze their raw data at face value. More often than not, some preliminary analysis with calculations and dates must be carried out before the big-picture analysis can be performed. As you'll learn in this chapter, Access provides a wide array of tools and built-in functions that make working with calculations and dates possible.

ON THE WEB
The database for this walkthrough, `Chapter12.accdb`, can be downloaded from this book's website. When you use the sample database, you'll be able to open the queries shown in the figures. Some of the queries look a bit different from the screenshots shown here. Don't be alarmed—Access sometimes shuffles around criteria and expressions because of its built-in query optimizer. The query optimizer is charged with the task of structuring the query in the quickest, most cost-effective way possible.

Using Calculations in Your Analyses

If you're an Excel user trying to familiarize yourself with Access, one of the questions you undoubtedly have is, "Where do the formulas go?" In Excel, you have the flexibility to enter a calculation via a formula directly into the data set you're analyzing. You can't do this in Access. So, the question is, "Where do you store calculations in Access?"

As you've already learned, things work differently in Access. A best practice when working in a database environment is to keep your data separate from your analysis. In this light, you won't be able to store a calculation (a formula) in your data set. Now, it's true that you can store the calculated results in your tables, but using tables to store calculated results is problematic for several reasons:

- Stored calculations take up valuable storage space.
- Stored calculations require constant maintenance as the data in your table changes.
- Stored calculations generally tie your data to one analytical path.

Instead of storing the calculated results as hard data, it's a better practice to perform calculations in real time, at the precise moment when they're needed. This ensures the most current and accurate results and doesn't tie your data to one particular analysis.

Common calculation scenarios

In Access, calculations are performed using expressions. An *expression* is a combination of values, operators, or functions that are evaluated to return a separate value to be used in a subsequent process. For example, 2+2 is an expression that returns the integer 4, which can be used in a subsequent analysis. Expressions can be used almost anywhere in Access to accomplish various tasks: in queries, forms, reports, data access pages, and even tables to a certain degree. In this section, you'll learn how to expand your analysis by building real-time calculations using expressions.

Using constants in calculations

Most calculations typically consist of hard-coded numbers or constants. A *constant* is a static value that doesn't change. For example, in the expression [List_Price]*1.1, 1.1 is a constant; the value of 1.1 will never change. Figure 12.1 demonstrates how a constant can be used in an expression within a query.

In this example, you're building a query that will analyze how the current price for each product compares to the same price with a 10 percent increase. The expression, entered under the alias "Increase" will multiply the List_Price field of each record with a constant value of 1.1, calculating a price that is 10 percent over the original value in the List_Price field.

FIGURE 12.1

In this query, you're using a constant to calculate a 10 percent price increase.

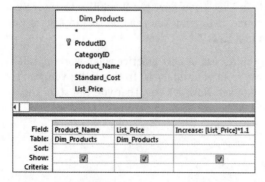

Using fields in calculations

Not all your calculations will require you to specify a constant. In fact, many of the mathematical operations you'll carry out will be performed on data that already resides in fields within your data set. You can perform calculations using any fields formatted as number or currency.

For instance, in the query shown in Figure 12.2, you aren't using any constants. Instead, your calculation will be executed using the values in each record of the data set. This is similar to referencing cell values in an Excel formula.

FIGURE 12.2

In this query, you're using two fields in a Dollar Variance calculation.

Using the results of aggregation in calculations

Using the result of an aggregation as an expression in a calculation allows you to perform multiple analytical steps in one query. In the example in Figure 12.3, you're running an aggregate query. This query will execute in the following order:

1. **The query groups your records by market.**
2. **The query calculates the count of orders and the sum of revenue for each market.**
3. **The query assigns the aliases you've defined respectively (OrderCount and Rev).**
4. **The query uses the aggregation results for each branch as expressions in your AvgDollarPerOrder calculation.**

Using the results of one calculation as an expression in another

Keep in mind that you aren't limited to one calculation per query. In fact, you can use the results of one calculation as an expression in another calculation. Figure 12.4 illustrates this concept.

FIGURE 12.3

In this query, you're using the aggregation results for each market as expressions in your calculation.

In this query, you're first calculating an adjusted forecast, and then you're using the results of that calculation in another calculation that returns the variance of actual versus adjusted forecast.

FIGURE 12.4

This query uses the results of one calculation as an expression in another.

Using a calculation as an argument in a function

Look at the query in Figure 12.5. The calculation in this query will return a number with a fractional part. That is, it will return a number that contains a decimal point followed by many trailing digits. You would like to return a round number, however, making the resulting data set easier to read.

FIGURE 12.5

The results of this calculation will be difficult to read because they'll all be fractional numbers that have many digits trailing a decimal point. Forcing the results into round numbers will make for easier reading.

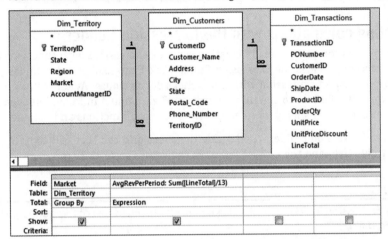

To force the results of your calculation into an integer, you can use the Int function. The Int function is a mathematical function that will remove the fractional part of a number and return the resulting integer. This function takes one argument, a number. However, instead of hard-coding a number into this function, you can use your calculation as the argument. Figure 12.6 demonstrates this concept.

FIGURE 12.6

You can use your calculation as the argument in the Int function, allowing you to remove the fractional part from the resulting data.

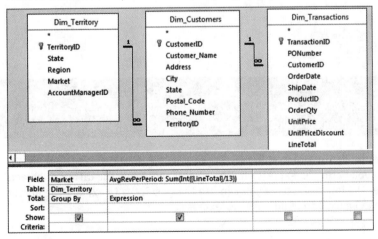

NOTE

You can use calculations that result in a numeric value in any function where a numeric value is accepted as an argument.

Constructing calculations with the Expression Builder

If you aren't yet comfortable manually creating complex expressions with functions and calculations, Access provides the Expression Builder. The Expression Builder guides you through constructing an expression with a few clicks of the mouse. Avid Excel users may relate the Expression Builder to the Insert Function Wizard found in Excel. The idea is that you build your expression simply by selecting the necessary functions and data fields.

To activate the Expression Builder, click inside the query grid cell that will contain your expression, right-click, and then select Build, as shown in Figure 12.7.

FIGURE 12.7

Activate the Expression Builder by right-clicking inside the Field row of the query grid and selecting Build.

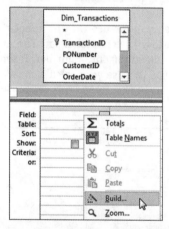

TIP

You can activate the Expression Builder by right-clicking anywhere you would write expressions, including control properties in forms, control properties in reports, and field properties in tables, as well as in the query design grid.

As you can see in Figure 12.8, the Expression Builder has four panes to work in. The upper pane is where you enter the expression. The lower panes show the different objects available to you. In the lower-left pane you can use the plus icons to expand the database objects that can be used to build out your expression.

FIGURE 12.8

The Expression Builder will display any database object you can use in your expression.

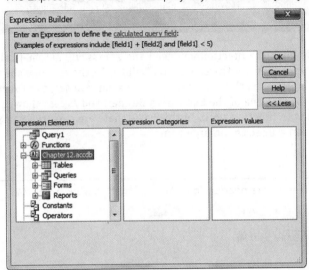

Double-click any of the database objects to drill down to the next level of objects. By double-clicking the Functions object, for example, you'll be able to drill into the Built-In Functions folder where you'll see all the functions available to you in Access. Figure 12.9 shows the Expression Builder set to display all the available math functions.

FIGURE 12.9

The Expression Builder displays all the functions available to you.

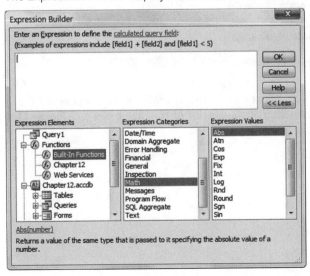

The idea is that you double-click the function you need and Access will automatically enter the function in the upper pane of the Expression Builder. In the example shown in Figure 12.10, the selected function is the Round function. As you can see, the function is immediately placed in the upper pane of the Expression Builder, and Access shows you the arguments needed to make the function work. In this case, there are two arguments identified: a Number argument and a Precision argument.

FIGURE 12.10

Access tells you which arguments are needed to make the function work.

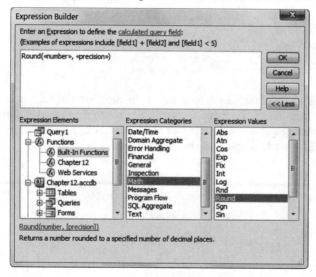

If you don't know what an argument means, simply highlight the argument in the upper pane and then click the hyperlink at the bottom of the dialog box (see Figure 12.11). A Help window provides an explanation of the function.

FIGURE 12.11

Help files are available to explain each function in detail.

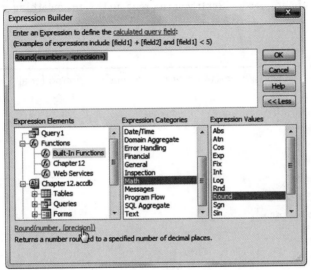

As you can see in Figure 12.12, instead of using a hard-coded number in the Round function, an expression is used to return a dynamic value. This calculation will divide the sum of [Dim_Transactions]![LineTotal] by 13. Since the Precision argument is optional, that argument is left off.

FIGURE 12.12

The function here will round the results of the calculation, ([Dim_Transactions]![Line Total])/13.

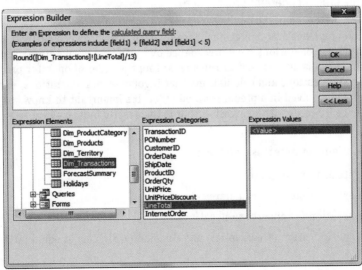

When you're satisfied with your newly created expression, click OK to insert it into the query grid. Figure 12.13 shows that the new expression has been added as a field. Note that the new field has a default alias of Expr1; you can rename this to something more meaningful.

FIGURE 12.13

Your newly created expression will give you the average revenue per period for all transactions.

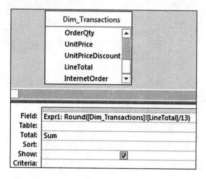

Common calculation errors

No matter which platform you're using to analyze your data, there's always the risk of errors when working with calculations. There is no magic function in Access that will help you prevent errors in your analysis. However, there are a few fundamental actions you can take to avoid some of the most common calculation errors.

Understanding the order of operator precedence

You might remember from your algebra days that when working with a complex equation, executing multiple mathematical operations, the equation does not necessarily evaluate from left to right. Some operations have precedence over others and therefore must occur first. The Access environment has similar rules regarding the order of operator precedence. When you're using expressions and calculations that involve several operations, each operation is evaluated and resolved in a predetermined order. It's important to know the order of operator precedence in Access. An expression that is incorrectly built may cause errors on your analysis.

The order of operations for Access is as follows:

1. Evaluate items in parentheses.
2. Perform exponentiation (^ calculates exponents).
3. Perform negation (- converts to negative).
4. Perform multiplication (* multiplies) and division (/ divides) at equal precedence.

5. Perform addition (+ adds) and subtraction (- subtracts) at equal precedence.

6. Evaluate string concatenation (&).

7. Evaluate comparison and pattern matching operators (>, <, =, <>, >=, <=, Like, Between, Is) at equal precedence.

8. Evaluate logical operators in the following order: Not, And, Or.

> **NOTE**
> Operations that are equal in precedence are performed from left to right.

How can understanding the order of operations ensure that you avoid analytical errors? Consider this basic example: The correct answer to the calculation, (20+30)*4, is 200. However, if you leave off the parentheses—as in 20+30*4—Access will perform the calculation like this: 30*4 = 120 + 20 = 140. The order of operator precedence mandates that Access perform multiplication before subtraction. Therefore, entering 20+30*4 will give you the wrong answer. Because the order of operator precedence in Access mandates that all operations in parentheses be evaluated first, placing 20+30 inside parentheses ensures the correct answer.

Watching out for null values

A *null value* represents the absence of any value. When you see a data item in an Access table that is empty or has no information in it, it is considered null.

If Access encounters a null value, it doesn't assume that the null value represents zero; instead, it immediately returns a null value as the answer. To illustrate this behavior, build the query shown in Figure 12.14.

FIGURE 12.14

To demonstrate how null values can cause calculation errors, build this query in Design view.

Run the query, and you'll see the results shown in Figure 12.15. Notice that the Variance calculation for the first record doesn't show the expected results; instead, it shows a null value. This is because the forecast value for that record is a null value.

FIGURE 12.15

When any variable in your calculation is null, the resulting answer is a null value.

Market	Actual	Forecast	Variance
Baltimore	$8,571.00		
Buffalo	$2,103,749.00	$2,163,175.64	($59,426.64)
California	$3,970,922.40	$3,743,168.24	$227,754.16
CANADA	$1,300,568.10	$1,198,797.92	$101,770.18
Charlotte	$8,586,372.20	$7,969,278.04	$617,094.16
Chicago	$159,293.00	$140,286.23	$19,006.77
Dakotas	$149,198.70	$140,938.93	$8,259.77
Dallas	$2,130,941.40	$2,067,835.02	$63,106.38
Denver	$1,302,986.85	$1,221,948.00	$81,038.85
Florida	$36,117,372.05	$37,622,262.55	($1,504,890.50)
Great Lakes	$614,349.10	$573,346.94	$41,002.16
Kansas City	$950,374.15	$904,571.09	$45,803.06
Knoxville	$17,361.00	$16,564.09	$796.91
New England	$772,343.10	$731,248.87	$41,094.23
Omaha	$744,337.50	$687,854.12	$56,483.38
Phoenix	$1,703,992.80	$1,635,833.09	$68,159.71
Seattle	$156,448.00	$162,705.92	($6,257.92)
Tulsa	$987,686.75	$928,425.55	$59,261.20

Looking at Figure 12.15, you can imagine how a null calculation error can wreak havoc on your analysis, especially if you have an involved analytical process. Furthermore, null calculation errors can be difficult to identify and fix.

That being said, you can avoid null calculation errors by using the Nz function, which enables you to convert any null value that is encountered to a value you specify:

```
Nz(variant, valueifnull)
```

The Nz function takes two arguments:

- *variant*: The data you're working with
- *valueifnull*: The value you want returned if the *variant* is null

Nz([MyNumberField],0) converts any null value in *MyNumberField* to zero.

Because the problem field is the Forecast field, you would pass the Forecast field through the Nz function. Figure 12.16 shows the adjusted query.

As you can see in Figure 12.17, the first record now shows a variance value even though the value in the Forecast field is null. Note that the Nz function did not physically place a zero in the null value. The Nz function merely told Access to treat the nulls as zeros when calculating the Variance field.

FIGURE 12.16

Pass the Forecast field through the Nz function to convert null values to zero.

Field:	Market	Actual	Forecast	Variance: [Actual]-Nz([Forecast],0)
Table:	ForecastSummary	ForecastSummary	ForecastSummary	
Sort:				
Show:	☑	☑	☑	☑
Criteria:				

FIGURE 12.17

The first record now shows a variance value.

Market	Actual	Forecast	Variance
Baltimore	$8,571.00		$8,571.00
Buffalo	$2,103,749.00	$2,163,175.64	($59,426.64)
California	$3,970,922.40	$3,743,168.24	$227,754.16
CANADA	$1,300,568.10	$1,198,797.92	$101,770.18
Charlotte	$8,586,372.20	$7,969,278.04	$617,094.16
Chicago	$159,293.00	$140,286.23	$19,006.77
Dakotas	$149,198.70	$140,938.93	$8,259.77
Dallas	$2,130,941.40	$2,067,835.02	$63,106.38
Denver	$1,302,986.85	$1,221,948.00	$81,038.85
Florida	$36,117,372.05	$37,622,262.55	($1,504,890.50)
Great Lakes	$614,349.10	$573,346.94	$41,002.16
Kansas City	$950,374.15	$904,571.09	$45,803.06
Knoxville	$17,361.00	$16,564.09	$796.91
New England	$772,343.10	$731,248.87	$41,094.23
Omaha	$744,337.50	$687,854.12	$56,483.38
Phoenix	$1,703,992.80	$1,635,833.09	$68,159.71
Seattle	$156,448.00	$162,705.92	($6,257.92)
Tulsa	$987,686.75	$928,425.55	$59,261.20

Watching the syntax in your expressions

Basic syntax mistakes in your calculation expressions can also lead to errors. Follow these basic guidelines to avoid slip-ups:

- If you're using fields in your calculations, enclose their names in square brackets ([ ]).
- Make sure you spell the names of the fields correctly.
- When assigning an alias to your calculated field, be sure you don't inadvertently use a field name from any of the tables being queried.
- Don't use illegal characters—period (.), exclamation point (!), square brackets ([ ]), or ampersand (&)—in your aliases.

Using Dates in Your Analyses

In Access, every possible date starting from December 31, 1899, is stored as a positive serial number. For example, December 31, 1899, is stored as 1; January 1, 1900, is stored as 2; and so on. This system of storing dates as serial numbers, commonly called the *1900 system*, is the default date system for all Office applications. You can take advantage of this system to perform calculations with dates.

Simple date calculations

Figure 12.18 shows one of the simplest calculations you can perform on a date. In this query, you're adding 30 to each ship date. This will effectively return the order date plus 30 days, giving you a new date.

FIGURE 12.18

You're adding 30 to each ship date, effectively creating a date that is equal to the ship date plus 30 days.

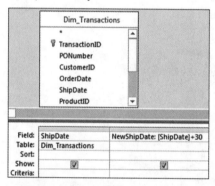

> **CAUTION**
>
> To be calculated correctly, dates must reside in a field that is formatted as a Date/Time field. If you enter a date into a Short Text field, the date will continue to look like a date, but Access will treat it like a string. The end result is that any calculation done on dates in this Text-formatted field will fail. Ensure that all dates are stored in fields that are formatted as Date/Time.

You can also calculate the number of days between two dates. The calculation in Figure 12.19, for example, essentially subtracts the serial number of one date from the serial number of another date, leaving you the number of days between the two dates.

Advanced analysis using functions

There are 25 built-in date/time functions available in Access 2019. Some of these are functions you'll very rarely encounter, whereas others you'll use routinely in your analyses.

FIGURE 12.19

In this query, you're calculating the number of days between two dates.

This section discusses a few of the basic date/time functions that will come in handy in your day-to-day analysis.

The Date function

The Date function is a built-in Access function that returns the current system date—in other words, today's date. With this versatile function, you never have to hard-code today's date in your calculations. That is, you can create dynamic calculations that use the current system date as a variable, giving you a different result every day. In this section, we look at some of the ways you can leverage the Date function to enhance your analysis.

Finding the number of days between today and a past date

Imagine that you have to calculate aged receivables. You need to know the current date to determine how overdue the receivables are. Of course, you could type in the current date by hand, but that can be cumbersome and prone to error.

To demonstrate how to use the Date function, create the query shown in Figure 12.20.

FIGURE 12.20

This query returns the number of days between today's date and each order date.

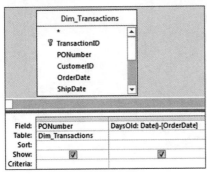

Using the Date function in a criteria expression

You can use the Date function to filter out records by including it in a criteria expression. For example, the query shown in Figure 12.21 will return all records with an order date older than 90 days.

FIGURE 12.21

No matter what day it is today, this query will return all orders older than 90 days.

Calculating an age in years using the Date function

Imagine that you've been asked to provide a list of account managers along with the number of years they have been employed by the company. To accomplish this task, you have to calculate the difference between today's date and each manager's hire date.

The first step is to build the query shown in Figure 12.22.

FIGURE 12.22

You're calculating the difference between today's date and each manager's hire date.

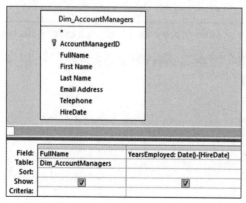

When you look at the query results, shown in Figure 12.23, you'll realize that the calculation results in the number of *days* between the two dates, not the number of *years*.

FIGURE 12.23

This data set shows the number of days, not the number of years.

FullName	YearsEmployed
Ian Harrell	3430
Kirstie Paulson	3396
Megan Winston	3360
Austen Cope	3288
Maleah Menard	3180
Annabel Locklear	3096
Norman Stackhouse	2970
Pauline Mccollum	2914
Martin Stamps	2897
Rosetta Kimbrough	2851
Truman Dubois	2816
Carma Gough	2752

To fix this problem, switch back to Design view and divide your calculation by 365.25. Why 365.25? That's the average number of days in a year when you account for leap years. Figure 12.24 demonstrates this change. Note that your original calculation is now wrapped in parentheses to avoid errors due to order of operator precedence.

FIGURE 12.24

Divide your original calculation by 365.25 to convert the answer to years.

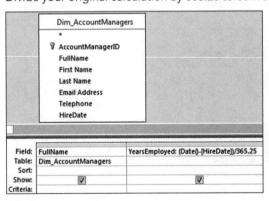

A look at the results, shown in Figure 12.25, proves that you're now returning the number of years. All that's left to do is to strip away the fractional portion of the date using the Int function. Why the Int function? The Int function doesn't round the year up or down; it merely converts the number to a readable integer.

FIGURE 12.25

Your query is now returning years, but you have to strip away the fractional portion of your answer.

FullName	YearsEmployed
Ian Harrell	9.39082819986311
Kirstie Paulson	9.29774127310062
Megan Winston	9.19917864476386
Austen Cope	9.00205338809035
Maleah Menard	8.70636550308008
Annabel Locklear	8.47638603696099
Norman Stackhouse	8.13141683778234
Pauline Mccollum	7.97809719370294
Martin Stamps	7.9315537303217
Rosetta Kimbrough	7.80561259411362
Truman Dubois	7.709787816564
Carma Gough	7.53456536618754

Wrapping your calculation in the Int function ensures that your answer will be a clean year without fractions (see Figure 12.26).

FIGURE 12.26

Running this query will return the number of years each employee has been with the company.

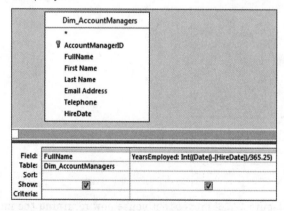

The Year, Month, Day, and Weekday functions

The Year, Month, Day, and Weekday functions are used to return an integer that represents their respective parts of a date. All these functions require a valid date as an argument. For example:

Year(#12/31/2019#) returns 2019.
Month(#12/31/2019#) returns 12.
Day(#12/31/2019#) returns 31.
Weekday(#12/31/2019#) returns 3.

> **NOTE**
>
> The dates in this chapter correspond to the U.S. English date format: month/day/year. For example, 5/1/2019 refers to May 1, 2019, not January 5, 2019. We realize this may seem illogical to those of you who are accustomed to seeing dates in the day/month/year format, but that's how your humble authors have been trained. We trust you can make the adjustment while reading this chapter.

> **NOTE**
>
> The Weekday function returns the day of the week from a date. In Access, weekdays are numbered from 1 to 7, starting with Sunday. Therefore, if the Weekday function returns 4, then the day of the week represented is Wednesday. If Sunday is not the first day of the week in your part of the world, you can use the optional FirstDayOfWeek argument. This argument specifies which day you want to count as the first day of the week. Enter 1 in this argument to make the first day Sunday, 2 for Monday, 3 for Tuesday, and so on. If this argument is omitted, the first day is a Sunday by default.

Figure 12.27 demonstrates how you would use these functions in a query environment.

FIGURE 12.27

The Year, Month, Day, and Weekday functions enable you to parse out a part of a date.

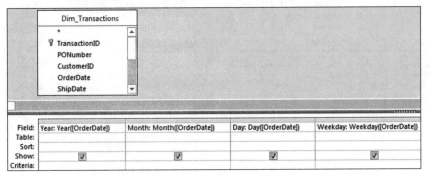

An Easy Way to Query Only Workdays

Suppose that you've been asked to provide the total amount of revenue generated by product, but only revenue generated during workdays in calendar year 2013. Workdays are defined as days that are not weekends or holidays.

The first thing you need to accomplish this task is a table that lists all the company holidays in 2013. The following figure shows that a holidays table can be nothing more than one field listing all the dates that constitute a holiday.

After you've established a table that contains all the company holidays, it's time to build the query. The following figure demonstrates how to build a query that filters out non-workdays.

Take a moment to analyze what is going on in the preceding figure:

1. You create a left join from Dim_Transactions to Holidays to tell Access that you want all the records from Dim_Transactions.
2. You then use the Is Null criteria under Holidays. This limits the Dim_Transactions table to only those dates that do not match any of the holidays listed in the Holidays table.
3. You then use the Weekday function to return the weekday of every service date in the Dim_Transactions table.
4. You filter the newly created Weekday field to filter out those weekdays that represent Saturdays and Sundays (1 and 7).
5. Finally, you filter for only those records whose order dates fall in the year 2013.

The DateAdd function

A common analysis for many organizations is to determine on which date a certain benchmark will be reached. For example, most businesses want to know on what date an order will become 30 days past due. Furthermore, what date should a warning letter be sent to the customer? An easy way to perform these types of analyses is to use the DateAdd function, which returns a date to which a specified interval has been added:

```
DateAdd(interval, number, date)
```
There are three required arguments in the DateAdd function.

- **interval (required):** The interval of time you want to use. The intervals available are as follows:
    - "yyyy": Year
    - "q": Quarter
    - "m": Month
    - "y": Day of year
    - "d": Day
    - "w": Weekday
    - "ww": Week
    - "h": Hour
    - "n": Minute
    - "s": Second
- number **(required):** The number of intervals to add. A positive number returns a date in the future, whereas a negative number returns a date in the past.
- date **(required):** The date value with which you're working. For example:

```
DateAdd("ww",1,#11/30/2019#) returns 12/7/2019.
DateAdd("m",2,#11/30/2019#) returns 1/30/2020.
DateAdd("yyyy",-1,#11/30/2019#) returns 11/30/2018.
```

The query shown in Figure 12.28 illustrates how the DateAdd function can be used in determining the exact date a specific benchmark is reached. You're creating two new fields with this query: Warning Date and Overdue Date. The DateAdd function used in the Warning Date field will return the date that is three weeks from the original order date. The DateAdd function used in the Overdue Date field will return the date that is one month from the original order date.

FIGURE 12.28

This query will give you the original order date, the date you should send a warning letter, and the date on which the order will be 30 days overdue.

Grouping dates into quarters

Why would you need to group your dates into quarters? Most databases store dates rather than quarter designations. Therefore, if you wanted to analyze data on a quarter-over-quarter basis, you would have to convert dates into quarters. Surprisingly, there is no date/time function that allows you to group dates into quarters. There is, however, the Format function.

The Format function belongs to the Text category of functions and allows you to convert a variant into a string based on formatting instructions. From the perspective of analyzing dates, there are several valid instructions you can pass to a Format function:

```
Format(#01/31/2019#, "yyyy") returns 2019.
Format(#01/31/2019#, "yy") returns 19.
Format(#01/31/2019#, "q") returns 1.
Format(#01/31/2019#, "mmm") returns Jan.
Format(#01/31/2019#, "mm") returns 01.
Format(#01/31/2019#, "d") returns 31.
Format(#01/31/2019#, "w") returns 5.
Format(#01/31/2019#, "ww") returns 5.
```

NOTE

Keep in mind that the value returned when passing a date through a `Format` function is a string that cannot be used in subsequent calculations.

The query in Figure 12.29 shows how you would group all the order dates into quarters and then group the quarters to get a sum of revenue for each quarter.

FIGURE 12.29

You can group dates into quarters by using the `Format` function.

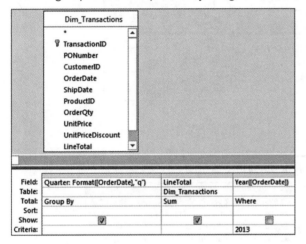

If you want to get fancy, you can insert the `Format` function in a crosstab query, using Quarter as the column (see Figure 12.30).

As you can see in Figure 12.31, the resulting data set is a clean look at revenue by product by quarter.

The DateSerial function

The `DateSerial` function allows you to construct a date value by combining given year, month, and day components. This function is perfect for converting disparate strings that, together, represent a date, into an actual date:

```
DateSerial(Year, Month, Day)
```

The `DateSerial` function has three arguments:

- **Year (required):** Any number or numeric expression from 100 to 9999
- **Month (required):** Any number or numeric expression
- **Day (required):** Any number or numeric expression

FIGURE 12.30

You can also use the `Format` function in a crosstab query.

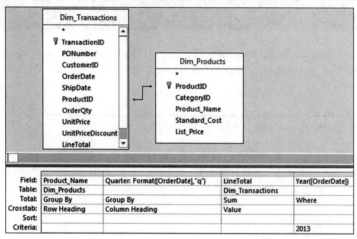

Field:	Product_Name	Quarter: Format([OrderDate],"q")	LineTotal	Year([OrderDate])
Table:	Dim_Products		Dim_Transactions	
Total:	Group By	Group By	Sum	Where
Crosstab:	Row Heading	Column Heading	Value	
Sort:				
Criteria:				2013

FIGURE 12.31

You've successfully grouped your dates into quarters.

Product_Name	1	2	3	4
Filter Sheets 13 1/2" X 24"	$11,970.00	$22,548.75	$55,258.00	$29,307.25
Filter Sheets 14" X 22"	$28,284.60	$57,696.10	$190,679.15	$129,965.20
Filter Sheets 16 1/2" X 25 1/2"	$3,018.35	$3,402.60	$58,183.40	$63,390.65
Filter Sheets 16 3/8" X 24 3/8"	$49,286.10	$101,954.70	$106,431.90	$111,335.50
Food Warmer Pickup Stations 24"W		$7,901.60	$15,529.50	$9,389.10
Food Warmer Pickup Stations 72"W	$11,804.00	$18,532.80		
Fry Basket Black Handle		$336.00	$7,469.40	$6,965.40
Fry Basket Yellow Handle			$7,360.00	$11,592.00
Fryer Brush	$3,497.00	$6,325.15	$49,318.10	$143,146.90
Funnel Cake Fryer			$347,907.20	$282,902.80
Garnish Center	$5,376.00	$15,484.50	$8,742.00	$3,450.00
Gas Char Broiler 2 Burners			$61,779.90	$78,141.70

For example, the following statement would return `April 3, 2019`:

```
DateSerial(2019, 4, 3)
```

So, how is this helpful? Well, now you can put a few twists on this by performing calculations on the expressions within the `DateSerial` function. Consider some of the possibilities:

- Get the first day of last month by subtracting 1 from the current month and using 1 as the Day argument:

```
DateSerial(Year(Date()), Month(Date()) - 1, 1)
```

- Get the first day of next month by adding 1 to the current month and using 1 as the Day argument:

  `DateSerial(Year(Date()), Month(Date()) + 1, 1)`
- Get the last day of this month by adding 1 to the current month and using 0 as the Day argument:

  `DateSerial(Year(Date()), Month(Date())+1, 0)`
- Get the last day of next month by adding 2 to the current month and using 0 as the Day argument:

  `DateSerial(Year(Date()), Month(Date()) +2, 0)`

TIP

Passing a 0 to the Day argument will automatically get you the last day of the month specified in the DateSerial function. It's worth mentioning that DateSerial is smart enough to work across years. Month(Date()) - 1 will still work correctly in January, and Month(Date()) + 1 will work correctly in December.

12

Performing Conditional Analyses

IN THIS CHAPTER

Using parameter queries

Using conditional functions

Comparing the `IIf` and `Switch` functions

U ntil now your analyses have been straightforward. You build a query, you add some criteria, you add a calculation, you save the query, and then you run the query whenever you need to. What happens, however, if the criteria that governs your analysis changes frequently or if your analytical processes depend on certain conditions being met? In these situations, you would use a *conditional analysis*: an analysis whose outcome depends on a predefined set of conditions. Barring VBA and macros, there are several tools and functions that enable you to build conditional analyses; some of these are parameter queries, the `IIf` function, and the `Switch` function.

In this chapter, you learn how these tools and functions can help you save time, organize your analytical processes, and enhance your analyses.

ON THE WEB
The database for this walkthrough, `Chapter13.accdb`, can be downloaded from this book's website.

Using Parameter Queries

You'll find that when building your analytical processes, anticipating every single combination of criteria that may be needed will often be difficult. This is where parameter queries can help.

A *parameter query* is an interactive query that prompts you for criteria before the query is run. A parameter query is useful when you need to ask a query different questions using different criteria each time it's run. To get a firm understanding of how a parameter query can help you, build the query shown in Figure 13.1. With this query, you want to see all the purchase orders logged during the 201205 period.

FIGURE 13.1

This query has a hard-coded criterion for system period.

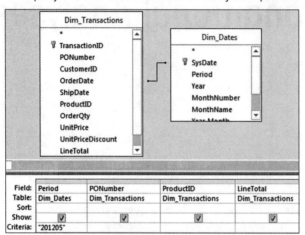

Although this query will give you what you need, the problem is that the criterion for system period is hard-coded as 201205. That means if you want to analyze revenue for a different period, you essentially have to rebuild the query. Using a parameter query will allow you to create a conditional analysis—that is, an analysis based on variables you specify each time you run the query. To create a parameter query, simply replace the hard-coded criteria with text that you've enclosed in square brackets ([ ]), as shown in Figure 13.2.

FIGURE 13.2

To create a parameter query, replace the hard-coded criteria with text enclosed in square brackets ([ ]).

Running a parameter query forces the Enter Parameter Value dialog box to open and ask for a variable. Note that the text you typed inside the brackets of your parameter appears in the dialog box. At this point, you would simply enter your parameter into a dialog box (see Figure 13.3).

FIGURE 13.3

The Parameter Value dialog box lets you specify the criteria each time you run your query.

How parameter queries work

When you run a parameter query, Access attempts to convert any text to a literal string by wrapping the text in quotes. However, if you place square brackets ([]) around the text, Access thinks that it's a variable and tries to bind some value to the variable using the following series of tests:

1. Access checks to see if the variable is a field name. If Access identifies the variable as a field name, that field is used in the expression.

2. If the variable is not a field name, Access checks to see if the variable is a calculated field. If Access determines the expression is indeed a calculated field, it simply carries out the mathematical operation.

3. If the variable is not a calculated field, Access checks to see if the variable is referencing an object such as a control on an open form or open report.

4. If all else fails, the only remaining option is to ask the user what the variable is, so Access displays the Enter Parameter Value dialog box, showing the text you entered in the Criteria row.

Ground rules of parameter queries

As with other functionality in Access, parameter queries come with their own set of ground rules that you should follow in order to use them properly:

- You must place square brackets ([]) around your parameter. If you don't, Access will automatically convert your text into a literal string.

- You can't use the name of a field as a parameter. If you do, Access will simply replace your parameter with the current value of the field.

- You can't use a period (.), an exclamation point (!), square brackets ([]), or an ampersand (&) in your parameter's prompt text.
- You must limit the number of characters in your parameter's prompt text. Entering parameter prompt text that is too long may result in your prompt being cut off in the Enter Parameter Value dialog box. Moreover, you should make your prompts as clear and concise as possible.

TIP

If you really want to use a field name in your parameter's prompt, you can follow the field name with other characters. For example, instead of using `[System_Period]`, you could use `[System_Period: ?]`. As you read this, keep in mind that there is nothing magic about the colon (:) or the question mark (?). Any set of characters will do. In fact, it may be more useful to provide your users with a sense of how the needed parameter should be formatted—for example: `[System_Period: yyyymm]`.

Working with parameter queries

The example shown in Figure 13.2 uses a parameter to define a single criterion. Although this is the most common way to use a parameter in a query, there are many ways to exploit this functionality. In fact, it's safe to say that the more innovative you get with your parameter queries, the more elegant and advanced your impromptu analysis will be. This section covers some of the different ways you can use parameters in your queries.

Working with multiple parameter conditions

You aren't in any way limited in the number of parameters you can use in your query. Figure 13.4 demonstrates how you can utilize more than one parameter in a query. When you run this query, you'll be prompted for both a system period and a product ID, allowing you to dynamically filter on two data points without ever having to rewrite your query.

Combining parameters with operators

You can combine parameter prompts with any operator you would normally use in a query. Using parameters in conjunction with standard operators allows you to dynamically expand or contract the filters in your analysis without rebuilding your query. To demonstrate how this works, build the query shown in Figure 13.5.

This query uses the BETWEEN...AND operator and the < (less than) operator to limit the results of the query based on the user-defined parameters. Since there are three parameter prompts built into this query, you'll be prompted for inputs three times: once for a starting period, once for an ending period, and once for a dollar amount. The number of records returned depends on the parameters you input. For instance, if you input 201201 as the starting period, 201203 as the ending period, and 5000 as the dollar amount, you'll get 1,700 records.

FIGURE 13.4

You can employ more than one parameter in a query.

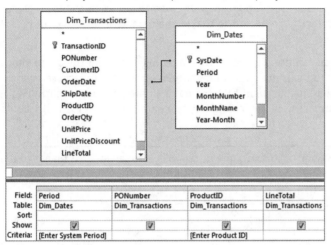

Field:	Period	PONumber	ProductID	LineTotal
Table:	Dim_Dates	Dim_Transactions	Dim_Transactions	Dim_Transactions
Sort:				
Show:	☑	☑	☑	☑
Criteria:	[Enter System Period]		[Enter Product ID]	

FIGURE 13.5

This query combines standard operators with parameters in order to limit the results.

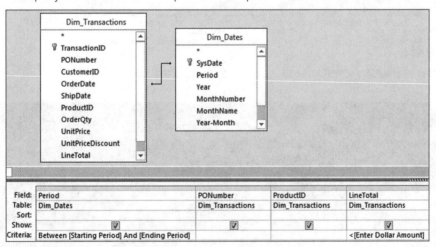

Field:	Period		PONumber	ProductID	LineTotal
Table:	Dim_Dates		Dim_Transactions	Dim_Transactions	Dim_Transactions
Sort:					
Show:	☑		☑	☑	☑
Criteria:	Between [Starting Period] And [Ending Period]				< [Enter Dollar Amount]

Combining parameters with wildcards

One of the problems with a parameter query is that if the parameter is left blank when the query is run, the query will return no records. One way to get around this problem is to combine your parameter with a wildcard so that if the parameter is blank, all records will be returned.

To demonstrate how you can use a wildcard with a parameter, build the query shown in Figure 13.6. When you run this query, it'll prompt you for a period. Because you're using the * wildcard, you have the option of filtering out a single period by entering a period designator into the parameter, or you can ignore the parameter to return all records.

FIGURE 13.6

If the parameter in this query is ignored, the query will return all records thanks to the wildcard (*).

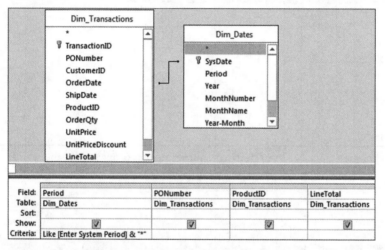

Using parameters as calculation variables

You are not limited to using parameters as criteria for a query; you can use parameters anywhere you use a variable. In fact, a particularly useful way to use parameters is in calculations. For example, the query in Figure 13.7 enables you to analyze how a price increase will affect current prices based on the percent increase you enter. When you run this query, you'll be asked to enter a percentage by which you want to increase your prices. Once you pass your percentage (you'll need to enter a decimal), the parameter query uses it as a variable in the calculation.

FIGURE 13.7

You can use parameters in calculations, enabling you to change the calculation variables each time you run the query.

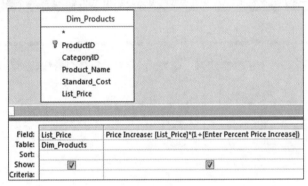

Using parameters as function arguments

You can also use parameters as arguments within functions. Figure 13.8 demonstrates the use of the `DateDiff` function using parameters instead of hard-coded dates. When this query is run, you'll be prompted for a start date and an end date. Those dates will then be used as arguments in the `DateDiff` function. Again, this allows you to specify new dates each time you run the query without ever having to rebuild the query.

FIGURE 13.8

You can use parameters as arguments in functions instead of hard-coded values.

Field:	Start: [Enter Start Date]	End: [Enter End Date]	Age in Weeks: DateDiff("ww",[Enter Start Date],[Enter End Date])
Table:			
Total:	Group By	Group By	Group By
Sort:			
Show:	☑	☑	☑
Criteria:			

13

CAUTION

Be aware that values you enter into your parameters must fit into the data type required for the function's argument. For example, if you're using a parameter in a `DateDiff` function, the variable you assign that parameter must be a date; otherwise, the function won't work.

NOTE

When you run the query in Figure 13.8, you'll only have to enter the start date and the end date one time, even though they're both used in two places in the query. This is because once you assign a variable to a parameter, the assignment persists to every future instance of that parameter.

If you are prompted more than once for a parameter used more than once in your query, odds are there's a slight variation in how the parameter names were typed. Consider copying your parameters to avoid this.

Creating a Parameter Prompt That Accepts Multiple Entries

The parameter query in the following figure enables you to filter results dynamically by a variable period that you specify within the parameter. However, this query does not allow you to see results for more than one period at a time.

You could use more than one parameter, as shown in the following figure. Unlike the query in the preceding figure, this query allows you to include more than one period in your query results. However, you would still be limited to the number of parameters built into the query (in this case, three).

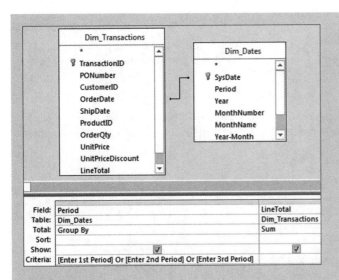

So, how do you allow for any number of parameter entries? The answer is relatively easy. You create a parameter that is passed through an `InStr` function to test for a position number.

The query shown in the following figure demonstrates how to do this:

Continues

continued

Notice that the parameter is not being used as criteria for the Period field. Instead, it is being used in an InStr function to test for the position number of the variable you enter into the parameter prompt, as follows:

```
InStr([Enter Periods Separated by Commas],[Period])
```

If the InStr function finds your variable, it returns a position number; if not, it returns zero. Therefore, you only want records that return a position number greater than zero (hence, the criteria for the parameter).

When you run this query, the Enter Parameter Value dialog box (shown in the following figure) appears. You can then type in as many variables as you want.

Using Conditional Functions

Parameter queries aren't the only tools in Access that allow for conditional analysis. Access also has built-in functions that facilitate value comparisons, data validation, and conditional evaluation. Two of these functions are the IIf function and the Switch function. These conditional functions (also called *program flow functions*) are designed to test for conditions and provide different outcomes based on the results of those tests. In this section, you'll learn how to control the flow of your analyses by utilizing the IIf and Switch functions.

The IIf function

The IIf (immediate if) function replicates the functionality of an IF statement for a single operation. The IIf function evaluates a specific condition and returns a result based on a true or false determination:

```
IIf(Expression, TrueAnswer, FalseAnswer)
```

To use the IIf function, you must provide three required arguments:

- **Expression (required):** The expression you want to evaluate
- **TrueAnswer (required):** The value to return if the expression is true
- **FalseAnswer (required):** The value to return if the expression is false

> **TIP**
>
> Think of the commas in an `IIf` function as `THEN` and `ELSE` statements. Consider the following `IIf` function, for instance:
>
> ```
> IIf(Babies = 2 , "Twins", "Not Twins")
> ```
>
> This function literally translates to: If Babies equals 2, then Twins, else Not Twins.

Using IIf to avoid mathematical errors

To demonstrate a simple problem where the `IIf` function comes in handy, build the query shown in Figure 13.9.

FIGURE 13.9

This query will perform a calculation on the Actual and the Forecast fields to calculate a percent to forecast.

When you run the query, you'll notice that not all the results are clean. As you can see in Figure 13.10, you're getting some errors due to division by zero. That is, you're dividing actual revenues by forecasts that are zero.

FIGURE 13.10

The errors shown in the results are due to the fact that some revenues are being divided by zeros.

Product	Actual	Forecast	Percent
90830	171	0	#Div/0!
90830	520	658	79.03%
90830	706	727	97.11%
90830	1,025	1,206	84.99%
90830	1,064	1,400	76.00%
90830	1,195	0	#Div/0!
90830	1,370	0	#Div/0!
90830	1,463	0	#Div/0!
90830	1,483	1,786	83.03%
90830	1,522	1,951	78.01%

Although this seems like a fairly benign issue, in a more complex, multilayered analytical process, these errors could compromise the integrity of your data analysis. To avoid these errors, you can perform a conditional analysis on your data set using the IIf function, evaluating the Forecast field for each record before performing the calculation. If the forecast is zero, you'll bypass the calculation and simply return a value of zero. If the forecast is not zero, you'll perform the calculation to get the correct value. The IIf function would look like this:

```
IIf([Forecast]=0,0,[Actual]/[Forecast])
```

Figure 13.11 demonstrates how this IIf function is put into action.

FIGURE 13.11

This IIf function enables you to test for forecasts with a value of zero and bypass them when performing your calculation.

As you can see in Figure 13.12, the errors have been avoided.

FIGURE 13.12

The IIf function helped you avoid the division by zero errors.

Saving time with IIf

You can also use the IIf function to save steps in your analytical processes and, ultimately, save time. For example, imagine that you need to tag customers in a lead list as either large customers or small customers, based on their dollar potential. You decide that you'll update the MyTest field in your data set with "LARGE" or "SMALL" based on the revenue potential of the customer.

Without the IIf function, you would have to run the two update queries shown in Figures 13.13 and 13.14 to accomplish this task.

FIGURE 13.13

This query will update the MyTest field to tag all customers that have a revenue potential at or above $10,000 with the word "LARGE."

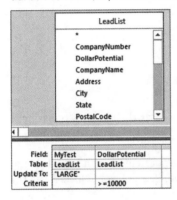

FIGURE 13.14

This query will update the MyTest field to tag all customers that have a revenue potential less than $10,000 with the word "SMALL."

Will the queries in Figures 13.13 and 13.14 do the job? Yes. However, you could accomplish the same task with one query using the IIf function.

The update query shown in Figure 13.15 illustrates how you can use an IIf function as the update expression.

FIGURE 13.15

You can accomplish the same task in one query using the `IIf` function.

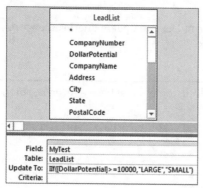

Take a moment and look at the `IIf` function being used as the update expression:

```
IIf([DollarPotential]>=10000,"LARGE","SMALL")
```

This function tells Access to evaluate the DollarPotential field of each record. If the DollarPotential field is greater than or equal to 10,000, use the word "LARGE" as the update value; if not, use the word "SMALL."

> **TIP**
>
> You can use conditional operators (AND, OR, BETWEEN) within your `IIf` functions to add a layer to your condition expression. For example, the following function tests for a dollar potential and segment to get a true or false value:
>
> ```
> IIf([DollarPotential]>10000 And [Segment]="Metal Fabrication","True","False")
> ```

Nesting IIf functions for multiple conditions

Sometimes the condition you need to test for is too complex to be handled by a basic `IF...THEN...ELSE` structure. In such cases, you can use nested `IIf` functions—that is, `IIf` functions that are embedded in other `IIf` functions. Consider the following example:

```
IIf([VALUE]>100,"A",IIf([VALUE]<100,"C","B"))
```

This function will check to see if VALUE is greater than 100. If it is, then `"A"` is returned; if not (else), a second `IIf` function is triggered. The second `IIf` function will check to see if VALUE is less than 100. If yes, then `"C"` is returned; if not (else), `"B"` is returned.

The idea here is that because an `IIf` function results in a true or false answer, you can expand your condition by setting the false expression to another `IIf` function instead of to a hard-coded value. This triggers another evaluation. There is no limit to the number of nested `IIf` functions you can use.

Using IIf functions to create crosstab analyses

Many seasoned analysts use the `IIf` function to create custom crosstab analyses in lieu of using a crosstab query. Among the many advantages of creating crosstab analyses without a crosstab query is the ability to categorize and group otherwise unrelated data items.

In the example shown in Figure 13.16, you're returning the number of account managers hired before and after 2014. Categorizations this specific would not be possible with a crosstab query.

FIGURE 13.16

This query demonstrates how to create a crosstab analysis without using a crosstab query.

The result, shown in Figure 13.17, is every bit as clean and user-friendly as the results would be from a crosstab query.

FIGURE 13.17

The resulting data set gives you a clean crosstab-style view of your data.

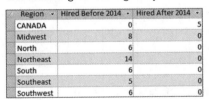

Region	Hired Before 2014	Hired After 2014
CANADA	0	5
Midwest	8	0
North	6	0
Northeast	14	0
South	6	0
Southeast	5	0
Southwest	6	0

Another advantage of creating crosstab analyses without a crosstab query is the ability to include more than one calculation in your crosstab report. For example, Figure 13.18 illustrates a query where the sum of units and revenue will be returned in crosstab format.

FIGURE 13.18

Creating crosstab-style reports using the `IIf` function allows you to calculate more than one value.

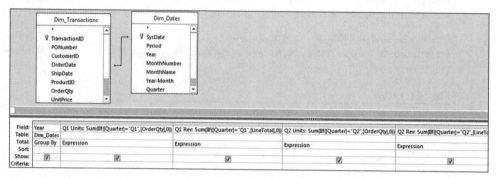

As you can see in Figure 13.19, the resulting data set provides a great deal of information in an easy-to-read format. Because a standard crosstab query does not allow more than one value calculation (in this case, units and revenue are values), this particular view would not be possible with a standard crosstab query.

FIGURE 13.19

This analysis would be impossible to create in a standard crosstab query, where multiple calculations are not allowed.

Year	Q1 Units	Q1 Rev	Q2 Units	Q2 Rev
2011	0	$0.00	0	$0.00
2012	4517	$8,749,969.10	5865	$9,761,310.90
2013	12352	$9,262,135.00	18603	$12,554,344.60
2014	31540	$18,071,842.70	43700	$22,996,203.25

The Switch function

The `Switch` function enables you to evaluate a list of expressions and return the value associated with the expression determined to be true. To use the `Switch` function, you must provide a minimum of one expression and one value:

```
Switch(Expression, Value)
```

- **Expression (required):** The expression you want to evaluate
- **Value (required):** The value to return if the expression is true

The power of the `Switch` function comes in evaluating multiple expressions at one time and determining which one is true. To evaluate multiple expressions, simply add another `Expression` and `Value` to the function, as follows:

```
Switch(Expression1, Value1, Expression2, Value2, Expression3, Value3)
```

When executed, this Switch function evaluates each expression in turn. If an expression evaluates to true, the value that follows that expression is returned. If more than one expression is true, the value for the first true expression is returned (and the others are ignored). Keep in mind that there is no limit to the number of expressions you can evaluate with a Switch function.

CAUTION

If none of the expressions in your Switch function evaluate as true, the function will return a null value. For example, the following function evaluates Count and returns a value based on it:

```
Switch([Count] < 10, "Low", [Count] > 15, "High")
```

The problem with this function is that if Count comes in between 10 and 15, you will get a null value because none of the expressions include those numbers. This may indirectly cause errors in other parts of your analysis.

To avoid this scenario, you can add a "catch-all" expression and provide a value to return if none of your expressions is determined to be true:

```
Switch([Count] < 10, "Low", [Count] > 15, "High", True, "Middle")
```

Adding True as the last expression will force the value "Middle" to be returned instead of a null value if none of the other expressions evaluate as true.

Comparing the IIf and Switch functions

Although the IIf function is a versatile tool that can handle most conditional analyses, the fact is that the IIf function has a fixed number of arguments that limits it to a basic IF...THEN...ELSE structure. This limitation makes it difficult to evaluate complex conditions without using nested IIf functions. Although there is nothing wrong with nesting IIf functions, there are analyses in which the numbers of conditions that need to be evaluated make building a nested IIf impractical at best.

To illustrate this point, consider this scenario. It's common practice to classify customers into groups based on annual revenue or how much they spend with your company. Imagine that your organization has a policy of classifying customers into four groups: A, B, C, and D (see Table 13.1).

TABLE 13.1 Customer Classifications

Annual Revenue	Customer Classification
>= $10,000	A
>=5,000 but < $10,000	B
>=$1,000 but < $5,000	C
<$1,000	D

You've been asked to classify the customers in the Dim_Transactions table, based on each customer's sales transactions. You can actually do this using either the IIf function or the Switch function.

The problem with using the IIf function is that this situation calls for some hefty nesting. That is, you'll have to use IIf expressions within other IIf expressions to handle the easy layer of possible conditions. Here's how the expression would look if you opted to use the IIf function (note that [REV] is the alias used for the [LineTotal] field):

```
IIf([REV]>=10000,"A",IIf([REV]>=5000 And [REV]<10000,"B",
IIf([REV]>1000 And [REV]<5000,"C","D")))
```

As you can see, not only is it difficult to determine what's going on here, but this is so convoluted that the chances of making a syntax or logic error are high.

In contrast to the preceding nested IIf function, the following Switch function is rather straightforward:

```
Switch([REV]<1000,"D",[REV]<5000,"C",[REV]<10000,"B",True,"A")
```

This function tells Access to return a value of "D" if REV is less than 1000. If REV is less than 5000, a value of "C" is returned. If REV is less than 10000, "B" is returned. If all else fails, use "A". Figure 13.20 demonstrates how you would use this function in a query.

FIGURE 13.20

Using the Switch function is sometimes more practical than using nested IIf functions. This query will classify customers by how much they spend.

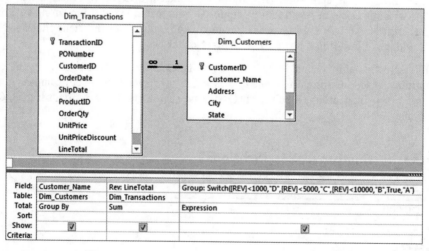

NOTE

You may shrewdly notice that those records that are less than 1,000 will also be less than 10,000. So, why don't all the records get tagged with a value of B? Remember that the `Switch` function evaluates your expressions from left to right and only returns the value of the first expression that evaluates to true.

In this light, you'll want to sort the expressions in your `Switch` function accordingly, using an order that is conducive to the logic of your analysis.

When you run the query, you'll see the resulting data set shown in Figure 13.21.

FIGURE 13.21

Each customer is conditionally tagged with a group designation based on annual revenue.

Customer_Name	Rev	Group
ACASCO Corp.	$253.00	D
ACECUL Corp.	$14,771.00	A
ACEHUA Corp.	$9,095.00	B
ACOPUL Corp.	$10,190.00	A
ACORAR Corp.	$4,750.00	C
ACSBUR Corp.	$33.00	D
ADACEC Corp.	$395.00	D
ADADUL Corp.	$5,637.00	B
ADANAS Corp.	$8,573.00	B
ADCOMP Corp.	$4,206.00	C
ADDATI Corp.	$1,020.00	C
ADDOUS Corp.	$921.00	D

13

The Fundamentals of Using SQL

IN THIS CHAPTER

Understanding basic SQL

Getting fancy with advanced SQL

Using SQL-specific queries

S tructured Query Language (SQL) is the language that relational database management systems (such as Access) use to perform their various tasks. In order to tell Access to perform any kind of query, you have to convey your instructions in SQL. Don't panic—the truth is, you've already been building and using SQL statements, even if you didn't realize it.

In this chapter, you'll discover the role that SQL plays in your dealings with Access and learn how to understand the SQL statements generated when building queries. You'll also explore some of the advanced actions you can take with SQL statements, allowing you to accomplish actions that go beyond the Access user interface. The basics you learn here will lay the foundation for your ability to perform the advanced techniques you'll encounter throughout the rest of this book.

ON THE WEB
The starting database for this walkthrough, `Chapter14.accdb`, can be downloaded from this book's website.

Understanding Basic SQL

A major reason your exposure to SQL is limited is that Access is more user friendly than most people give it credit for being. The fact is, Access performs a majority of its actions in user-friendly environments that hide the real grunt work that goes on behind the scenes.

For a demonstration of this, build in Design view the query you see in Figure 14.1. In this relatively simple query, you're asking for the sum of revenue by period.

FIGURE 14.1

Build this relatively simple query in Design view.

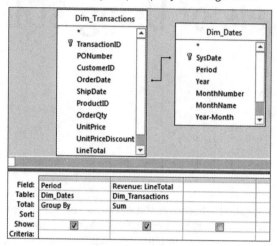

Next, select the Design tab on the Ribbon and choose View ⇨ SQL View. Access switches from Design view to the view you see in Figure 14.2.

FIGURE 14.2

You can get to SQL view by selecting View ⇨ SQL View.

```
SELECT Dim_Dates.Period, Sum(Dim_Transactions.LineTotal) AS Revenue
FROM Dim_Dates INNER JOIN Dim_Transactions ON Dim_Dates.SysDate = Dim_Transactions.OrderDate
GROUP BY Dim_Dates.Period;
```

As you can see in Figure 14.2, while you were busy designing your query in Design view, Access was diligently creating the SQL statement that allows the query to run. This example shows that with the user-friendly interface provided by Access, you don't necessarily need to know the SQL behind each query. The question now becomes: If you can run queries just fine without knowing SQL, why bother to learn it?

Admittedly, the convenient query interface provided by Access does make it a bit tempting to go through life not really understanding SQL. However, if you want to harness the real power of data analysis with Access, you need to understand the fundamentals of SQL.

The SELECT statement

The SELECT statement, the cornerstone of SQL, enables you to retrieve records from a data set. The basic syntax of a SELECT statement is as follows:

```
SELECT column_name(s)
FROM table_name
```

The SELECT statement is always used with a FROM clause. The FROM clause identifies the table(s) that make up the source for the data.

Try this: Start a new query in Design view. Close the Show Table dialog box (if it's open), select the Design tab on the Ribbon, and choose View ➪ SQL View. In SQL view, type in the SELECT statement shown in Figure 14.3, and then run the query by selecting Run on the Design tab of the Ribbon.

FIGURE 14.3

A basic SELECT statement in SQL view.

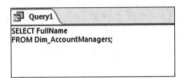

Congratulations! You've just written your first query manually.

> **NOTE**
>
> You may notice that the SQL statement automatically created by Access in Figure 14.2 has a semicolon at the end of it. The semicolon is a standard way to end a SQL statement and is required by some database programs. However, it isn't necessary to end your SQL statements with a semicolon in Access, because Access will automatically add it when the query compiles.

Selecting specific columns

You can retrieve specific columns from your data set by explicitly defining the columns in your SELECT statement, as follows:

```
SELECT AccountManagerID, FullName, [Email Address]
FROM Dim_AccountManagers
```

> **CAUTION**
>
> Any column in your database with a name that includes spaces or a non-alphanumeric character must be enclosed within brackets ([]) in your SQL statement. For example, the SQL statement selecting data from a column called Email Address would be referred to as [Email Address].

Selecting all columns

Using the wildcard (*) allows you to select all columns from a data set without having to define every column explicitly:

```
SELECT * FROM Dim_AccountManagers
```

14

The WHERE clause

You can use the WHERE clause in a SELECT statement to filter your data set and conditionally select specific records. The WHERE clause is always used in combination with an operator such as: = (equal), <> (not equal), > (greater than), < (less than), >= (greater than or equal to), <= (less than or equal to), or BETWEEN (within general range).

The following SQL statement retrieves only those employees whose last name is Winston:

```
SELECT AccountManagerID, [Last Name], [First Name]
FROM Dim_AccountManagers
WHERE [Last Name] = "Winston"
```

And this SQL statement retrieves only those employees whose hire date is later than May 16, 2012:

```
SELECT AccountManagerID, [Last Name], [First Name]
FROM Dim_AccountManagers
WHERE HireDate > #5/16/2012#
```

> **NOTE**
>
> Notice in the preceding two examples that the word Winston is wrapped in quotes ("Winston") and the date 5/16/2012 is wrapped in pound signs (#5/16/2012#). When referring to a text value in a SQL statement, you must place quotes around the value; when referring to a date, pound signs must be used.

Making sense of joins

You'll often need to build queries that require that two or more related tables be joined to achieve the desired results. For example, you may want to join an employee table to a transaction table in order to create a report that contains both transaction details and information on the employees who logged those transactions. The type of join used will determine the records that will be output.

 For a detailed review of joins, check out Chapter 8.

Inner joins

An *inner join* operation tells Access to select only those records from both tables that have matching values. Records with values in the joined field that do not appear in both tables are omitted from the query results.

The following SQL statement selects only those records in which the employee numbers in the AccountManagerID field are in both the Dim_AccountManagers table and the Dim_Territory table:

```
SELECT Region, Market,
Dim_AccountManagers.AccountManagerID, FullName
```

```
FROM Dim_AccountManagers INNER JOIN Dim_Territory ON
Dim_AccountManagers.AccountManagerID =
Dim_Territory.AccountManagerID
```

Outer joins

An *outer join* operation tells Access to select all the records from one table and only the records from a second table with matching values in the joined field. There are two types of outer joins: left joins and right joins.

A *left join* operation (sometimes called an *outer left join*) tells Access to select all the records from the first table regardless of matching *and* only those records from the second table that have matching values in the joined field.

This SQL statement selects all records from the Dim_AccountManagers table and only those records in the Dim_Territory table where values for the AccountManagerID field exist in the Dim_AccountManagers table:

```
SELECT Region, Market,
Dim_AccountManagers.AccountManagerID, FullName
FROM Dim_AccountManagers LEFT JOIN Dim_Territory ON
Dim_AccountManagers.AccountManagerID =
Dim_Territory.AccountManagerID
```

A *right join* operation (sometimes called an *outer right join*) tells Access to select all the records from the second table, regardless of matching, *and* only those records from the first table that have matching values in the joined field.

This SQL statement selects all records from the Dim_Territory table and only those records in the Dim_AccountManagers table where values for the AccountManagerID field exist in the Dim_Territory table:

```
SELECT Region, Market,
Dim_AccountManagers.AccountManagerID, FullName
FROM Dim_AccountManagers RIGHT JOIN Dim_Territory ON
Dim_AccountManagers.AccountManagerID =
Dim_Territory.AccountManagerID
```

14

TIP

Notice that in the preceding join statements, table names are listed before each column name separated by a dot (for example, Dim_AccountManager.AccountManagerID). When you're building a SQL statement for a query that utilizes multiple tables, it's generally a good practice to refer to the table names as well as field names in order to avoid confusion and errors. Access does this for all queries automatically. You'll also need to use the square brackets if the table or field being referenced contains special characters such as spaces.

Getting Fancy with Advanced SQL Statements

You'll soon realize that the SQL language is quite versatile, allowing you to go far beyond basic SELECT, FROM, and WHERE statements. In this section, you'll explore some of the advanced actions you can accomplish with SQL.

Expanding your search with the Like operator

By itself, the Like operator is no different from the equal (=) operator. For instance, these two SQL statements will return the same number of records:

```
SELECT AccountManagerID, [Last Name], [First Name]
FROM Dim_AccountManagers
WHERE [Last Name] = "Winston"
```

```
SELECT AccountManagerID, [Last Name], [First Name]
FROM Dim_AccountManagers
WHERE [Last Name] Like "Winston"
```

The Like operator is typically used with wildcard characters to expand the scope of your search to include any record that matches a pattern. The wildcard characters that are valid in Access are as follows:

- *: The asterisk represents any number and type characters.
- ?: The question mark represents any single character.
- #: The pound sign represents any single digit.
- []: The brackets allow you to pass a single character or an array of characters to the Like operator. Any values matching the character values within the brackets will be included in the results.
- [!]: The brackets with an embedded exclamation point allow you to pass a single character or an array of characters to the Like operator. Any values matching the character values following the exclamation point will be excluded from the results.

Listed in Table 14.1 are some example SQL statements that use the Like operator to select different records from the same table column.

TABLE 14.1 **Selection Methods Using the Like Operator**

Wildcard Character(s) Used	SQL Statement Example	Result
*	SELECT Field1 FROM Table1 WHERE Field1 Like "A*"	Selects all records where Field1 starts with the letter A

Wildcard Character(s) Used	SQL Statement Example	Result
*	SELECT Field1 FROM Table1 WHERE Field1 Like "*A*"	Selects all records where Field1 includes the letter *A*
?	SELECT Field1 FROM Table1 WHERE Field1 Like "???"	Selects all records where the length of Field1 is three characters long
?	SELECT Field1 FROM Table1 WHERE Field1 Like "B??"	Selects all records where Field1 is a three-letter string that starts with *B*
#	SELECT Field1 FROM Table1 WHERE Field1 Like "###"	Selects all records where Field1 is a number that is exactly three digits long
#	SELECT Field1 FROM Table1 WHERE Field1 Like "A#A"	Selects all records where the value in Field1 is a three-character value that starts with *A*, contains one digit, and ends with *A*
#, *	SELECT Field1 FROM Table1 WHERE Field1 Like "A#*"	Selects all records where Field1 begins with *A* and any digit
[], *	SELECT Field1 FROM Table1 WHERE Field1 Like "*[$%!*/]*"	Selects all records where Field1 includes any one of the special characters shown in the SQL statement
[!], *	SELECT Field1 FROM Table1 WHERE Field1 Like "*[!a-z]*"	Selects all records where the value of Field1 is not a text value, but a number value or special character such as the @ symbol
[!], *	SELECT Field1 FROM Table1 WHERE Field1 Like "*[!0-9]*"	Selects all records where the value of Field1 is not a number value, but a text value or special character such as the @ symbol

14

Selecting unique values and rows without grouping

The DISTINCT predicate enables you to retrieve only unique values from the selected fields in your data set. For example, the following SQL statement will select only market names from the PvTblFeed table, resulting in 14 records:

```
SELECT DISTINCT Market
FROM PvTblFeed
```

If your SQL statement selects more than one field, the combination of values from all fields must be unique for a given record to be included in the results.

If you require that the entire row be unique, you could use the DISTINCTROW predicate. The DISTINCTROW predicate enables you to retrieve only those records for which the entire row is unique. That is to say, the combination of all values in the selected fields does not match any other record in the returned data set. You would use the DISTINCTROW predicate just as you would in a SELECT DISTINCT clause:

```
SELECT DISTINCTROW AccountManagerID
FROM Dim_AccountManagers
```

Grouping and aggregating with the GROUP BY clause

The GROUP BY clause makes it possible to aggregate records in your data set by column values. When you create an aggregate query in Design view, you're essentially using the GROUP BY clause. The following SQL statement will group the Market field and give you the count of states in each market:

```
SELECT Market, Count(State)
FROM Dim_Territory
GROUP BY Market
```

When you're using the GROUP BY clause, any WHERE clause included in the query is evaluated before aggregation occurs. However, you may have scenarios when you need to apply a WHERE condition after the grouping is applied. In these cases, you can use the HAVING clause.

For instance, this SQL statement will group the records where the value in the Market field is Dallas, and then only return those customer records where the sum of Revenue is less than 100. Again, the grouping is done before checking if the sum of Revenue is less than 100:

```
SELECT Customer_Name, Sum(Revenue) AS Sales
FROM PvTblFeed
Where Market = "Dallas"
GROUP BY Customer_Name
HAVING (Sum(Revenue)<100)
```

Setting the sort order with the ORDER BY clause

The ORDER BY clause enables you to sort data by a specified field. The default sort order is ascending; therefore, sorting your fields in ascending order requires no explicit instruction. The following SQL statement will sort the resulting records by Last Name ascending and then First Name ascending:

```
SELECT AccountManagerID, [Last Name], [First Name]
FROM Dim_AccountManagers
ORDER BY [Last Name], [First Name]
```

To sort in descending order, you must use the DESC reserved word after each column you want sorted in descending order. The following SQL statement will sort the resulting records by Last Name descending and then First Name ascending:

```
SELECT AccountManagerID, [Last Name], [First Name]
FROM Dim_AccountManagers
ORDER BY [Last Name] DESC, [First Name]
```

Creating aliases with the AS clause

The AS clause enables you to assign aliases to your columns and tables. There are generally two reasons you would want to use aliases: either you want to make column or table names shorter and easier to read, or you're working with multiple instances of the same table and you need a way to refer to one instance or the other.

Creating a column alias

The following SQL statement will group the Market field and give you the count of states in each market. In addition, the alias State Count has been given to the column containing the count of states by including the AS clause:

```
SELECT Market, Count(State) AS [State Count]
FROM Dim_Territory
GROUP BY Market
HAVING Market = "Dallas"
```

Creating a table alias

This SQL statement gives the Dim_AccountManagers the alias "MyTable":

```
SELECT AccountManagerID, [Last Name], [First Name]
FROM Dim_AccountManagers AS MyTable
```

Showing only the SELECT TOP or SELECT TOP PERCENT

When you run a SELECT query, you're retrieving all records that meet your definitions and criteria. When you run the SELECT TOP statement, or a top values query, you're telling Access to filter your returned data set to show only a specific number of records.

14

Top values queries explained

To get a clear understanding of what the SELECT TOP statement does, build the aggregate query shown in Figure 14.4.

FIGURE 14.4

Build this aggregate query in Design view. Take note that the query is sorted descending on the Sum of LineTotal.

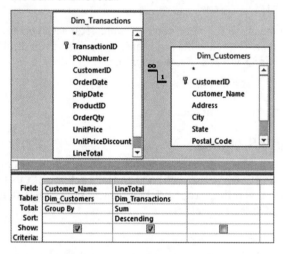

On the Query Tools Design tab, click the Property Sheet command. This will activate the Property Sheet shown in Figure 14.5. Alternatively, you can use the F4 key on your keyboard to activate the Property Sheet.

In the Property Sheet, change the Top Values property to 25.

FIGURE 14.5

Change the Top Values property to 25.

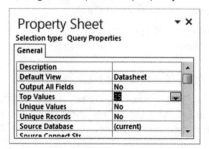

As you can see in Figure 14.6, after you run this query, only the customers who fall into the top 25 by sum of revenue are returned. If you want the bottom 25 customers, simply change the sort order of the LineTotal field to Ascending.

FIGURE 14.6

Running the query will give you the top 25 customers by revenue.

Customer_Name	SumOfLineTotal
SUASHU Corp.	$2,738,933.20
GUPDYU Corp.	$2,062,418.05
CATYOF Corp.	$2,007,139.00
SCULOS Corp.	$1,374,781.70
WHATLU Corp.	$1,357,050.30
MADOSM Corp.	$1,282,750.00
USANGE Corp.	$1,226,356.55
CORULA Corp.	$1,201,995.95
RADASS Corp.	$1,198,185.00
SMEAS Corp.	$1,191,758.00
GRECUW Corp.	$1,187,312.80
AVAATA Corp.	$1,174,196.45
ZUQHYR Corp.	$1,173,088.50
ANATUD Corp.	$1,093,389.95
THEMOG Corp.	$1,087,385.00
BASHUQ Corp.	$1,081,070.55
ATLANT Corp.	$1,077,585.85
CUGGAN Corp.	$1,071,389.30
WORUTC Corp.	$1,068,895.55
EBANAU Corp.	$1,025,716.70
USLAND Corp.	$1,005,005.95
QAAKUY Corp.	$996,152.20
MUUZEO Corp.	$946,096.70
CUANTY Corp.	$937,880.00
SUASHF Corp.	$912,274.15

NOTE

Access does not break ties. If the 24th, 25th, and 26th customers all have the same total, you'll actually get 26 rows back.

14

The SELECT TOP statement

The SELECT TOP statement is easy to spot. This is the same query used to run the results in Figure 14.6:

```
SELECT TOP 25 Customer_Name, Sum(LineTotal) AS SumOfLineTotal
FROM Dim_Customers INNER JOIN Dim_Transactions ON
Dim_Customers.CustomerID = Dim_Transactions.CustomerID
GROUP BY Customer_Name
ORDER BY Sum(LineTotal) DESC
```

Bear in mind that you don't have to be working with totals or currency to use a top values query. In the following SQL statement, you're returning the ten account managers who have the earliest hire date in the company, effectively producing a seniority report:

```
SELECT Top 10 AccountManagerID, [Last Name], [First Name]
FROM Dim_AccountManagers
ORDER BY HireDate ASC
```

CAUTION

Note the use of the DESC and ASC clauses in the previous SQL statements. When you're using the SELECT TOP, it's important to specify the sort direction accurately because it can make the difference between selecting the biggest ten results or the smallest ten results. Keep in mind that you can sort on a field without displaying that field—for instance, the HireDate field in the previous example.

The SELECT TOP PERCENT statement

The SELECT TOP PERCENT statement works in exactly the same way as SELECT TOP except the records returned in a SELECT TOP PERCENT statement represent the *n*th percent of total records rather than the *n*th number of records. For example, the following SQL statement will return the top 25 percent of records by revenue:

```
SELECT TOP 25 PERCENT Customer_Name, Sum(LineTotal) AS SumOfLineTotal
FROM Dim_Customers INNER JOIN Dim_Transactions ON
Dim_Customers.CustomerID = Dim_Transactions.CustomerID
GROUP BY Customer_Name
ORDER BY Sum(LineTotal) DESC
```

NOTE

Keep in mind that SELECT TOP PERCENT statements give you only the top or bottom percent of the total number of records in the returned data set, not the percent of the total value in your records. For example, the preceding SQL statement won't give you only those records that make up 25 percent of the total value in the LineTotal field. It will give you the top 25 percent of total records in the queried data set. In other words, if you'd get 5,961 records using just SELECT, then SELECT TOP 25 PERCENT will return 1,491 rows.

Performing action queries via SQL statements

You may not have thought about it before, but when you build an action query, you're building a SQL statement that is specific to that action. These SQL statements make it possible for you to go beyond just selecting records.

Make-table queries translated

Make-table queries use the SELECT...INTO statement to make a hard-coded table that contains the results of your query. The following example first selects account manager number, last name, and first name; and then it creates a new table called Employees:

```
SELECT AccountManagerID, [Last Name], [First Name] INTO Employees
FROM Dim_AccountManagers
```

Append queries translated

Append queries use the `INSERT INTO` statement to insert new rows into a specified table. The following example inserts new rows into the Employees table from the Dim_AccountManagers table:

```
INSERT INTO Employees (AccountManagerID, [Last Name], [First Name])
SELECT AccountManagerID, [Last Name], [First Name]
FROM Dim_AccountManagers
```

Update queries translated

Update queries use the `UPDATE` statement in conjunction with `SET` in order to modify the data in a data set. This example updates the List_Price field in the Dim_Products table to increase prices by 10 percent:

```
UPDATE Dim_Products SET List_Price = [List_Price]*1.1
```

Delete queries translated

Delete queries use the `DELETE` statement to delete rows in a data set. In this example, you're deleting all rows from the Employees table:

```
DELETE * FROM Employees
```

Creating crosstabs with the TRANSFORM statement

The `TRANSFORM` statement allows the creation of a crosstab data set that displays data in a compact view. The `TRANSFORM` statement requires three main components to work:

- The field to be aggregated
- The `SELECT` statement that determines the row content for the crosstab
- The field that will make up the column of the crosstab (the "pivot field")

The syntax is as follows:

```
TRANSFORM Aggregated_Field
SELECT Field1, Field2
FROM Table1
GROUP BY Select Field1, Field2
PIVOT Pivot_Field
```

For example, the following statement will create a crosstab that shows region and market on the rows and products on the columns, with revenue in the center of the crosstab:

```
TRANSFORM Sum(Revenue) AS SumOfRevenue
SELECT Region, Market
FROM PvTblFeed
GROUP BY Region, Market
PIVOT Product_Description
```

14

Using SQL-Specific Queries

SQL-specific queries are essentially action queries that cannot be run through the Access query grid. These queries must be run either in SQL view or via code (macro or VBA). There are several types of SQL-specific queries, each performing a specific action. In this section, we introduce you to a few of these queries, focusing on those that can be used in Access to shape and configure data tables.

Merging data sets with the UNION operator

The UNION operator is used to merge two compatible SQL statements to produce one read-only data set. Consider the following SELECT statement, which produces a data set (see Figure 14.7) that shows revenue by region and market:

```
SELECT Region, Market, Sum(Revenue) AS [Sales]
FROM PvTblFeed
GROUP BY Region, Market
```

FIGURE 14.7

This data set shows revenue by region and market.

Region	Market	Sales
MIDWEST	DENVER	$645,584.10
MIDWEST	KANSASCITY	$574,899.15
MIDWEST	TULSA	$628,407.41
NORTH	BUFFALO	$450,478.72
NORTH	CANADA	$776,247.78
NORTH	MICHIGAN	$678,708.11
NORTH	NEWYORK	$873,580.79
SOUTH	CHARLOTTE	$890,514.49
SOUTH	DALLAS	$467,086.11
SOUTH	FLORIDA	$1,450,397.76
SOUTH	NEWORLEANS	$333,452.80
WEST	CALIFORNIA	$2,254,751.64
WEST	PHOENIX	$570,254.17

A second SELECT statement produces a separate data set (see Figure 14.8) that shows total revenue by region:

```
SELECT Region, "Total" AS [Market], Sum(Revenue) AS [Sales]
FROM PvTblFeed
GROUP BY Region
```

FIGURE 14.8

This data set shows total revenue by region.

Region	Market	Sales
MIDWEST	Total	$1,848,890.66
NORTH	Total	$2,779,015.40
SOUTH	Total	$3,141,451.17
WEST	Total	$3,004,832.22

The idea is to bring together these two data sets to create an analysis that will show detail and totals all in one table. The UNION operator is ideal for this type of work, merging the results of the two SELECT statements. To use the UNION operator, simply start a new query, switch to SQL view, and enter the following syntax:

```
SELECT Region, Market, Sum(Revenue) AS [Sales]
FROM PvTblFeed
GROUP BY Region, Market
UNION
SELECT Region, "Total" AS [Market], Sum(Revenue) AS [Sales]
FROM PvTblFeed
GROUP BY Region
```

As you can see, the preceding statement is nothing more than the two SQL statements brought together with a UNION operator. When the two are merged (see Figure 14.9), the result is a data set that shows both details and totals in one table!

FIGURE 14.9

The two data sets have now been combined to create a report that provides summary and detail data.

Region	Market	Sales
MIDWEST	DENVER	$645,584.10
MIDWEST	KANSASCITY	$574,899.15
MIDWEST	Total	$1,848,890.66
MIDWEST	TULSA	$628,407.41
NORTH	BUFFALO	$450,478.72
NORTH	CANADA	$776,247.78
NORTH	MICHIGAN	$678,708.11
NORTH	NEWYORK	$873,580.79
NORTH	Total	$2,779,015.40
SOUTH	CHARLOTTE	$890,514.49
SOUTH	DALLAS	$467,086.11
SOUTH	FLORIDA	$1,450,397.76
SOUTH	NEWORLEANS	$333,452.80
SOUTH	Total	$3,141,451.17
WEST	CALIFORNIA	$2,254,751.64
WEST	PHOENIX	$570,254.17
WEST	SEATTLE	$179,826.42
WEST	Total	$3,004,832.22

14

NOTE

When a union query is run, Access matches the columns from both data sets by their position in the SELECT statement. That means two things: your SELECT statements must have the same number of columns, and the order of columns in both SELECT statements is important. Access will not make an attempt to match on column names. In fact, the column names in the two data sets don't have to match. As long as the columns have matching data types, Access will output a union of the two tables using the position of each column. The Column names from the first SELECT statement will be output in the resulting data set.

> **NOTE**
>
> Note that the UNION operator effectively performs a SELECT DISTINCT on the resulting data sets. This means that the UNION statement could very well eliminate duplicate rows where all the values in every field are identical between the two data sets. If you find that you're missing records when running a UNION query, consider using the UNION ALL operator. UNION ALL performs the same function as UNION, except it does not apply the SELECT DISTINCT and thus does not eliminate duplicate rows.

Creating a table with the CREATE TABLE statement

Often in your analytical processes, you'll need to create a temporary table in order to group, manipulate, or simply hold data. The CREATE TABLE statement allows you to do just that with one SQL-specific query.

Unlike a make-table query, the CREATE TABLE statement is designed to create only the structure or schema of a table. No records are ever returned with a CREATE TABLE statement. This statement allows you to strategically create an empty table at any point in your analytical process.

The basic syntax for a CREATE TABLE statement is as follows:

```
CREATE TABLE TableName
(<Field1Name> Type(<Field Size>), <Field2Name> Type(<Field Size>))
```

To use the CREATE TABLE statement, simply start a new query, switch to SQL view, and define the structure for your table.

In the following example, a new table called TempLog is created with three fields. The first field is a Text field that can accept 50 characters, the second field is a Text field that can accept 255 characters, and the third field is a Date field:

```
CREATE TABLE TempLog
([User] Text(50), [Description] Text, [LogDate] Date)
```

> **NOTE**
>
> Notice that in the preceding example, no field size is specified for the second text column. If the field size is omitted, Access will use the default field size specified for the database.

Manipulating columns with the ALTER TABLE statement

The ALTER TABLE statement provides some additional methods of altering the structure of a table behind the scenes. There are several clauses you can use with the ALTER TABLE statement, four of which are quite useful in Access data analysis: ADD, ALTER COLUMN, DROP COLUMN, and ADD CONSTRAINT.

> **NOTE**
>
> The ALTER TABLE statement, along with its various clauses, is used much less frequently than the SQL statements mentioned earlier in this chapter. However, the ALTER TABLE statement comes in handy when your analytical processes require you to change the structure of tables on the fly, helping you avoid any manual manipulations that may have to be done.
>
> It should be noted that there is no way to undo any actions performed using an ALTER TABLE statement. This obviously calls for some caution when using this statement.

Adding a column with the ADD clause

As the name implies, the ADD clause enables you to add a column to an existing table. The basic syntax is as follows:

```
ALTER TABLE <TableName>
ADD <ColumnName> Type(<Field Size>)
```

To use the ADD statement, simply start a new query in SQL view and define the structure for your new column. For instance, running the example statement shown here will create a new column called SupervisorPhone that is being added to a table called TempLog:

```
ALTER TABLE TempLog
ADD SupervisorPhone Text(10)
```

Altering a column with the ALTER COLUMN clause

When using the ALTER COLUMN clause, you specify an existing column in an existing table. This clause is used primarily to change the data type and field size of a given column. The basic syntax is as follows:

```
ALTER TABLE <TableName>
ALTER COLUMN <ColumnName> Type(<Field Size>)
```

To use the ALTER COLUMN statement, simply start a new query in SQL view and define changes for the column in question. For instance, the example statement shown here will change the field size of the SupervisorPhone field:

```
ALTER TABLE TempLog
ALTER COLUMN SupervisorPhone Text(13)
```

Deleting a column with the DROP COLUMN clause

The DROP COLUMN clause enables you to delete a given column from an existing table. The basic syntax is as follows:

```
ALTER TABLE <TableName>
DROP COLUMN <ColumnName>
```

14

To use the DROP COLUMN statement, simply start a new query in SQL view and define the structure for your new column. For instance, running the example statement shown here will delete the column called SupervisorPhone from the TempLog table:

```
ALTER TABLE TempLog
DROP COLUMN SupervisorPhone
```

Dynamically adding primary keys with the ADD CONSTRAINT clause

For many analysts, Access serves as an easy-to-use extract, transform, load (ETL) tool. That is, Access allows you to extract data from many sources, and then reformat and cleanse that data into consolidated tables. Many analysts also automate ETL processes with the use of macros that fire a series of queries. This works quite well in most cases.

There are, however, instances in which an ETL process requires primary keys to be added to temporary tables in order to keep data normalized during processing. In these situations, most people do one of two things: they stop the macro in the middle of processing to manually add the required primary keys, or they create a permanent table solely for the purpose of holding a table where the primary keys are already set.

There is a third option, though: the ADD CONSTRAINT clause allows you to dynamically create the primary keys. The basic syntax is as follows:

```
ALTER TABLE <TableName>
ADD CONSTRAINT ConstraintName PRIMARY KEY (<Field Name>)
```

To use the ADD CONSTRAINT clause, simply start a new query in SQL view and define the new primary key you're implementing. For instance, the example statement shown here will apply a compound key to three fields in the TempLog table:

```
ALTER TABLE TempLog
ADD CONSTRAINT ConstraintName PRIMARY KEY (ID, Name, Email)
```

Creating pass-through queries

A pass-through query sends SQL commands directly to a database server (such as SQL Server, Oracle, and so on). Often these database servers are known as the back end of the system, with Access being the client tool or front end. You send the command by using the syntax required by the particular server.

The advantage of pass-through queries is that the parsing and processing is actually done on the back-end server, not in Access. This makes them much faster than queries that pull from linked tables, particularly if the linked table is a very large one.

Here are the steps for building a pass-through query:

1. **On the Create tab of the Ribbon, click the Query Design command.**
2. **Close the Show Table dialog box.**
3. **Click the Pass-Through command on the Query Tools Design tab. The SQL design window appears.**

4. **Type a SQL statement that is appropriate for the target database system.** Figure 14.10 demonstrates a simple SQL statement.

FIGURE 14.10

To create a pass-through query, you must use the SQL window.

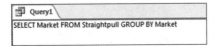

```
SELECT Market FROM Straightpull GROUP BY Market
```

5. **On the Query Tools Design tab, click the Property Sheet command.** The Property Sheet (shown in Figure 14.11) appears.

FIGURE 14.11

You must specify an ODBC connection string in the pass-through query's Property Sheet.

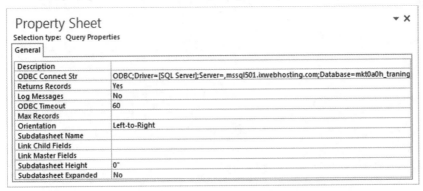

Property Sheet

Selection type: Query Properties

General

Description	
ODBC Connect Str	ODBC;Driver=[SQL Server];Server=,mssql501.ixwebhosting.com;Database=mkt0a0h_traning
Returns Records	Yes
Log Messages	No
ODBC Timeout	60
Max Records	
Orientation	Left-to-Right
Subdatasheet Name	
Link Child Fields	
Link Master Fields	
Subdatasheet Height	0"
Subdatasheet Expanded	No

6. **Enter the appropriate connection string for your server.** This is typically the ODBC connection string you normally use to connect to your server.

7. **Click Run.**

There are a few things you should be aware of when choosing to go the pass-through query route:

- You'll have to build the SQL statements yourself. Access provides no help—you can't use the QBD to build your statement.
- If the connection string of your server changes, you'll have to go back into the properties of the pass-through query and edit the ODBC connection string property. Alternatively, if you are using an existing DSN, you can simply edit the DSN configuration.
- The results you get from a pass-through are read only. You can't update or edit the returned records.

14

- You can only write queries that select data. This means you can't write update, append, delete, or make-table queries.
- Because you're hard-coding the SQL statements that will be sent to the server, including dynamic parameters (like a parameter query) is impossible because there is no way to get your parameters to the server after the SQL statement is sent.

Subqueries and Domain Aggregate Functions

IN THIS CHAPTER

Enhancing your analyses with subqueries

Using domain aggregate functions

Often, you'll carry out your analyses in layers, each layer of analysis using or building on the previous layer. This practice of building layers into analytical processes is actually very common. For instance, when you build a query using another query as the data source, you're layering your analysis. When you build a query based on a temporary table created by a make-table query, you're also layering your analysis.

All these conventional methods of layering analyses have two things in common:

- **They all add a step to your analytical processes.** Every query that has to be run in order to feed another query, or every temporary table that has to be created in order to advance your analysis, adds yet another task that must be completed before you get your final results.

- **They all require the creation of temporary tables or transitory queries, inundating your database with table and query objects that lead to a confusing analytical process, as well as a database that bloats easily.** This is where subqueries and domain aggregate functions can help.

Subqueries and domain aggregate functions allow you to build layers into your analyses within one query, eliminating the need for temporary tables or transitory queries.

The topic of subqueries and domain aggregate functions requires an understanding of SQL. Most beginning Access users don't have the foundation in SQL. If you fall into this category, press the pause button here and review Chapter 14 of this book. There, you'll get enough of a primer on SQL to continue this chapter.

ON THE WEB
The starting database for this walkthrough, `Chapter15.accdb`, can be downloaded from this book's website.

Enhancing Your Analyses with Subqueries

Subqueries (sometimes referred to as *subselect queries*) are select queries that are nested within other queries. The primary purpose of a subquery is to enable you to use the results of one query within the execution of another query. With subqueries, you can answer a multiple-part question, specify criteria for further selection, or define new fields to be used in your analysis.

The query shown in Figure 15.1 demonstrates how a subquery is used in the design grid. As you look at this, remember that this is one example of how a subquery can be used. Subqueries are not limited to being used as criteria.

FIGURE 15.1

To use a subquery in Query Design view, simply enter the SQL statement.

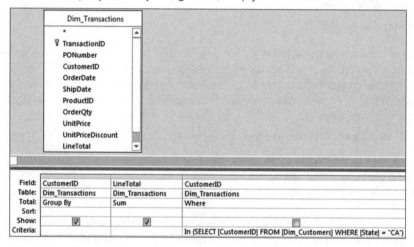

If you were to build the query in Figure 15.1 and switch to SQL view, you would see a SQL statement similar to this one. Can you pick out the subquery? Look for the second SELECT statement.

```
SELECT CustomerID, Sum(LineTotal) AS SumOfLineTotal
FROM Dim_Transactions
WHERE CustomerID IN
(SELECT [CustomerID] FROM [Dim_Customers] WHERE [State] = "CA")
GROUP BY CustomerID
```

> **NOTE**
> Subqueries must always be enclosed in parentheses.

The idea behind a subquery is that the subquery is executed first, and the results are used in the *outer query* (the query in which the subquery is embedded) as a criterion, an expression, a parameter, and so on. In the example shown in Figure 15.1, the subquery will first return a list of branches that belong to the California market. Then the outer query will use that list as criteria to filter out any employee who does not belong to the California market.

Why use subqueries?

Subqueries often run more slowly than a standard query using a join. This is because subqueries are either executed against an entire data set or evaluated multiple times, one time per each row processed by the outer query. This makes them slow to execute, especially if you have a large data set. So, why use them?

Many analyses require multistep processes that use temporary tables or transitory queries. Although there is nothing inherently wrong with temporary tables and queries, an excess amount of them in your analytical processes could lead to a confusing analytical process, as well as a database that bloats easily.

Even though using subqueries comes with a performance hit, it may be an acceptable trade for streamlined procedures and optimized analytical processes. You'll even find that as you become more comfortable with writing your own SQL statements, you'll use subqueries in on-the-fly queries to actually *save* time.

Subquery ground rules

There are a few rules and restrictions that you must be aware of when using subqueries:

- Your subquery must have, at a minimum, a SELECT statement and a FROM clause in its SQL string.
- You must enclose your subquery in parentheses.
- Theoretically, you can nest up to 31 subqueries within a query. This number, however, is based on your system's available memory and the complexity of your subqueries.
- You can use a subquery as an expression as long as it returns a single value.
- You can use the ORDER BY clause in a subquery only if the subquery is a SELECT TOP or SELECT TOP PERCENT statement.
- You can't use the DISTINCT keyword in a subquery that includes the GROUP BY clause.
- You must implement table aliases in queries in which a table is used in both the outer query and the subquery.

Creating subqueries without typing SQL statements

You may have the tendency to shy away from subqueries because you feel uncomfortable writing your own SQL statements. Indeed, many of the SQL statements necessary to perform the smallest analysis can seem daunting.

15

Imagine, for example, that you've been asked to provide the number of account managers who have a time in service greater than the average time in service for all account managers. Sounds like a relatively simple analysis, and it *is* simple when you use a subquery. But where do you start? Well, you could just write a SQL statement into the SQL view of a query and run it. But the truth is that not many Access users create SQL statements from scratch. The smart ones use the built-in functionalities of Access to save time and headaches. The trick is to split the analysis into manageable pieces:

1. **Find the average time in service for all account managers by creating the query shown in Figure 15.2.**

FIGURE 15.2

Create a query to find the average time in service for all account managers.

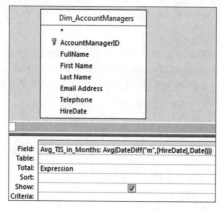

2. **Switch to SQL view (shown in Figure 15.3), and copy the SQL statement.**

FIGURE 15.3

Switch to SQL view and copy the SQL statement.

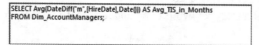

3. **Create a query that will count the number of account managers by time in service.** Figure 15.4 does just that.

FIGURE 15.4

Create a query to count the number of account managers by time in service.

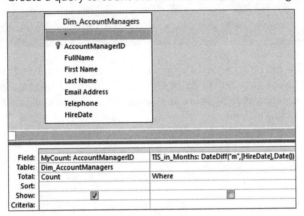

4. **Right-click in the Criteria row under the TIS_in_Months field and select Zoom.** The Zoom dialog box (shown in Figure 15.5) appears. The Zoom dialog box does nothing more than help you more comfortably work with text that is too long to be easily seen at one time in the query grid.

5. **With the Zoom dialog box open, paste the SQL statement you copied previously into the white input area.**

FIGURE 15.5

Paste the first SQL statement you copied into the Criteria row of the TIS_IN_ MONTHS field.

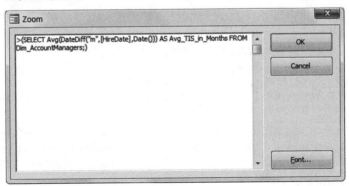

> **NOTE**
>
> Remember that subqueries must be enclosed in parentheses, so you'll want to enter parentheses around the SQL statement you just pasted. You'll also need to make sure you delete all carriage returns that were put in automatically by Access.

6. **Finish off the query by entering a greater than (>) symbol in front of your subquery and change the GROUP BY of the TIS_in_Months row to a WHERE clause. Click OK to accept your changes.** At this point, your query should look like the one shown in Figure 15.6.

FIGURE 15.6

Running this query will tell you there are 12 account managers that have a time in service greater than the company average.

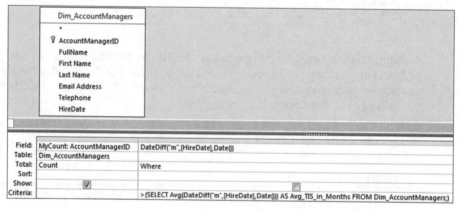

Now if you go to the SQL view of the query shown in Figure 15.6, you'll see the following SQL statement:

```
SELECT Count(AccountManagerID) AS MyCount
FROM Dim_AccountManagers
WHERE (((DateDiff("m",[HireDate],Date())))
>(SELECT Avg(DateDiff("m",[HireDate],Date())) AS Avg_TIS_in_Months
FROM Dim_AccountManagers;)));
```

The beauty is that you didn't have to type all this syntax. You simply used your knowledge of Access to piece together the necessary actions that needed to be taken in order to get to the answer. As you become more familiar with SQL, you'll find that you can create subqueries manually with no problems.

Using IN and NOT IN with subqueries

The IN and NOT IN operators enable you to run two queries in one. The idea is that the subquery will execute first, and then the resulting data set will be used by the outer query to filter the final output.

The example demonstrated in Figure 15.7 will first run a subquery that will select all customers based in California (CA). The outer query will then use the resulting data set as a criteria to return the sum of LineTotal for only those customers who match the customer numbers returned in the subquery.

FIGURE 15.7

This query uses the IN operator with a subquery, allowing you to run two queries in one.

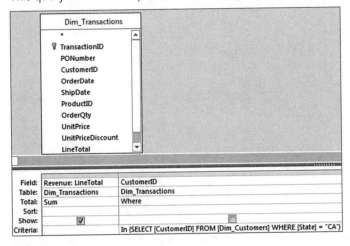

You would use NOT IN to go the opposite way and return the sum of LineTotal for those customers who don't match the customer numbers returned in the subquery.

Using subqueries with comparison operators

As its name implies, a *comparison operator* (=, <, >, <=, >=, <>, and so on) compares two items and returns True or False. When you use a subquery with a comparison operator, you're asking Access to compare the resulting data set of your outer query to that of the subquery.

15

For example, to return all customers who have purchases greater than the average purchase for all customers, you can use the query shown in Figure 15.8.

FIGURE 15.8

Use comparison operators to compare the resulting data set of your outer query to the results of the subquery.

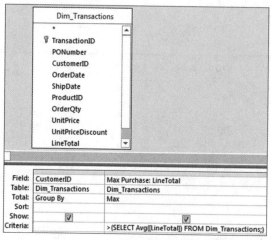

The subquery runs first, giving you the average purchase for all customers. This is a single value that Access then uses to compare the outer query's resulting data set. In other words, the maximum purchase for each customer is compared to the company average. If a customer's maximum purchase is greater than the company average, it's included in the final output; otherwise, it's excluded.

> **NOTE**
> A subquery that is used with a comparison operator must return a single value.

Using subqueries as expressions

In every example so far, you've used subqueries in conjunction with the WHERE clause, effectively using the results of a subquery as criteria for your outer query. However, you can also use a subquery as an expression, as long as the subquery returns a single value. The query shown in Figure 15.9 demonstrates how you can use a subquery as an expression in a calculation.

FIGURE 15.9

You're using a subquery as an expression in a calculation.

Field:	Market	Market Avg: UnitsSold	Vs Company Avg: [Market Avg]-(SELECT Avg(UnitsSold) FROM SalesByRegion;)
Table:	SalesByRegion	SalesByRegion	
Total:	Group By	Avg	Expression
Sort:			
Show:	☑	☑	☑
Criteria:			

This example uses a subquery to get the average units sold for the entire company; that subquery will return a single value. You're then using that value in a calculation to determine the variance between each market's average units sold and the average for the company. The output of this query is shown in Figure 15.10.

FIGURE 15.10

Your query result.

Market	Market Avg	Vs Company Avg
Asia	1,142	-612
Australia	1,119	-635
Northern Europe	2,647	893
South America	1,165	-589
Southern Europe	1,800	46
United Kingdom	2,591	837
United States	1,814	60

Using correlated subqueries

A *correlated query* is essentially a subquery that refers back to a column that is in the outer query. What makes correlated subqueries unique is that whereas standard subqueries are evaluated one time to get a result, a correlated subquery has to be evaluated multiple times—once for each row processed by the outer query. To illustrate this point, consider the following two SQL statements.

Uncorrelated subqueries

The following SQL statement is using an uncorrelated subquery. How can you tell? The subquery isn't referencing any column in the outer query. This subquery will be evaluated one time to give you the average revenue for the entire data set.

```
SELECT MainSummary.Branch_Number,
    (SELECT Avg(Revenue) FROM MainSummary)
    FROM MainSummary
```

Correlated subqueries

This following SQL statement is using a correlated subquery. The subquery is reaching back into the outer query and referencing the Branch_Number column, effectively forcing the subquery to be evaluated for every row that is processed by the outer query. The end result of this query will be a data set that shows the average revenue for every branch in the company. Figure 15.11 shows how the following SQL statement is represented in the query editor.

```
SELECT MainSummary.Branch_Number,
     (SELECT Avg(Revenue) FROM MainSummary AS M2
     WHERE M2.Branch_Number = MainSummary.Branch_Number) AS AvgByBranch
FROM MainSummary
GROUP BY MainSummary.Branch_Number
```

FIGURE 15.11

A correlated subquery.

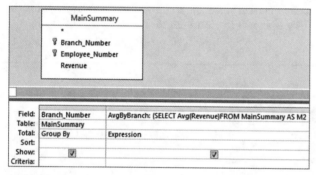

Using Aliases with Correlated Subqueries

Notice that in the correlated subquery, you're using the AS clause to establish a table alias of M2. The reason for this is that the subquery and the outer query are both utilizing the same table. By giving one of the tables an alias, you allow Access to distinguish exactly which table you're referring to in your SQL statement. Although the alias in this SQL statement is assigned to the subquery, you can just as easily assign an alias to the table in the outer query.

Note that the character M2 holds no significance. In fact, you can use any text string you like, as long as the alias and the table name combined do not exceed 255 characters.

To assign an alias to a table in Design view, simply right-click the field list and select Properties, as shown in the following figure.

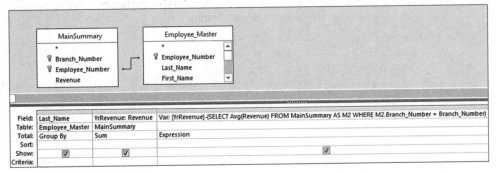

Field:	Branch_Number	AvgByBranch: (SELECT Avg(Revenue)FROM MainSummary AS M2
Table:	MainSummary	
Total:	Group By	Expression
Sort:		
Show:	☑	☑
Criteria:		

Next, edit the Alias property to the one you would like to use (see the following figure). You'll know that it took effect when the name on the Field List changes to your new alias.

Property Sheet ▾ ✕

Selection type: Field List Properties

General

Alias	M2
Source	

Using a correlated subquery as an expression

The example shown in Figure 15.9 used an uncorrelated subquery to determine the variance between each market's average units sold and the average units for the company.

You can apply the same type of technique to correlated subqueries. In the query demonstrated in Figure 15.12, a correlation for each branch number allows you to determine the variance between each employee's annual revenue and the average revenue for that employee's branch.

FIGURE 15.12

You can use a correlated subquery as part of an expression.

Field:	Last_Name	YrRevenue: Revenue	Var: [YrRevenue]-(SELECT Avg(Revenue) FROM MainSummary AS M2 WHERE M2.Branch_Number = Branch_Number)
Table:	Employee_Master	MainSummary	
Total:	Group By	Sum	Expression
Sort:			
Show:	☑	☑	☑
Criteria:			

15

Using subqueries within action queries

Action queries can be fitted with subqueries just as easily as select queries can. Here are a few examples of how you would use a subquery in an action query.

A subquery in a make-table query

This example illustrates how to use a subquery in a make-table query to create a new table containing data for all employees hired before January 1995:

```
SELECT E1.Employee_Number, E1.Last_Name, E1.First_Name
INTO OldSchoolEmployees
FROM Employee_Master as E1
WHERE E1.Employee_Number IN
      (SELECT E2.Employee_Number
      FROM Employee_Master AS E2
      WHERE E2.Hire_Date <#1/1/1995#)
```

A subquery in an append query

This example uses a subquery in an append query to add new customers to the CustomerMaster table from the LeadList:

```
INSERT INTO CustomerMaster (Customer_Number, Customer_Name, State )
SELECT CompanyNumber,CompanyName,State
FROM LeadList
WHERE CompanyNumber Not In
      (SELECT Customer_Number from CustomerMaster)
```

A subquery in an update query

This example uses a subquery in an update query to increase all prices in the PriceMaster table by 10% for only those branches in the South region:

```
UPDATE PriceMaster SET Price = [Price]*1.1
WHERE Branch_Number In
      (SELECT Branch_Number from LocationMaster WHERE Region = "South")
```

A subquery in a delete query

This example uses a subquery in a delete query to delete customers from the LeadList table if they already exist in the CustomerMaster table:

```
DELETE *
FROM LeadList
WHERE CompanyNumber In
      (SELECT Customer_Number from CustomerMaster)
```

Getting the Second Quartile of a Data Set with One Query

You can easily pull out the second quartile of a data set by using a top values subquery:

1. **Create a top values query that returns the top 25 percent of your data set.** You can specify that a query is a top values query by right-clicking the gray area above the white query grid and selecting Properties. In the Property Sheet dialog box, adjust the Top Values property to return the top *n*th value you need, as demonstrated in the following figure. For this example, use 25 percent.

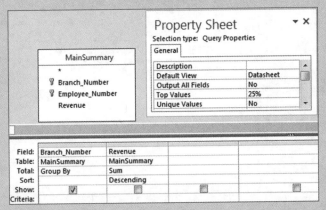

2. **Switch to SQL view (shown in the following figure), and copy the SQL string.**

```
SELECT TOP 25 PERCENT MainSummary.Branch_Number
FROM MainSummary
GROUP BY MainSummary.Branch_Number
ORDER BY MainSummary.Branch_Number, Sum(MainSummary.Revenue) DESC;
```

3. **Switch back to Design view and paste the SQL statement you just copied into the Criteria row of the Branch_Number field.** To do this, right-click inside the Criteria row of the Branch_Number field and select Zoom. Then paste the SQL statement inside the Zoom dialog box, as shown in the following figure.

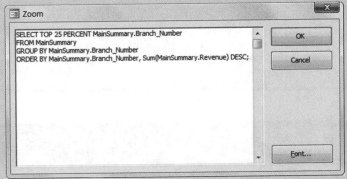

Continues

continued

4. **This next part is a little tricky. You need to perform the following edits on the SQL statement in order to make it work for this situation:**

- Because this subquery is a criteria for the Branch_Number field, you only need to select Branch_Number in the SQL statement; so, you can remove the line `Sum(MainSummary.Revenue) AS SumOfRevenue`.

- Delete all carriage returns.

- Place parentheses around the subquery and put the `NOT IN` operator in front of it all.

At this point, your Zoom dialog box should look like the one shown in the following figure.

5. **Switch to Design view.** If all went well, your query should look similar to the following figure.

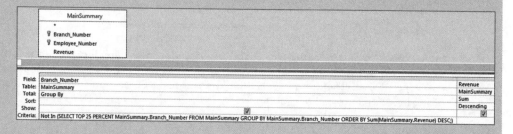

There you have it. Running this query will return the second quartile in the data set. To get the third quartile, simply replace `TOP 25 PERCENT` in the subquery with `TOP 50 PERCENT`; to get the fourth quartile, use `TOP 75 PERCENT`.

Domain Aggregate Functions

Domain aggregate functions enable you to extract and aggregate statistical information from an entire data set (a domain). These functions differ from aggregate queries in that an aggregate query groups data before evaluating the values, whereas a domain aggregate function evaluates the values for the entire data set; thus, a domain aggregate function will never return more than one value. To get a clear understanding of the difference between an aggregate query and a domain aggregate function, build the query shown in Figure 15.13.

FIGURE 15.13

This query shows you the difference between an aggregate query and a domain aggregate function.

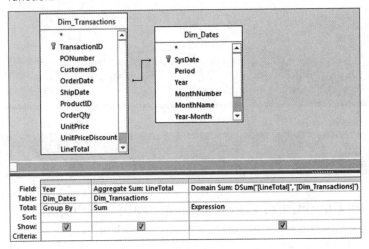

Run the query to get the results shown in Figure 15.14. You will notice that the Aggregate Sum column contains a different total for each year, whereas the Domain Sum column (the domain aggregate function) contains only one total (for the entire data set).

FIGURE 15.14

You can clearly see the difference between an aggregate query and a domain aggregate function.

Year	Aggregate Sum	Domain Sum
2011	$16,402,703	164564683.25
2012	$45,317,067	164564683.25
2013	$61,776,867	164564683.25
2014	$41,068,046	164564683.25

15

> **NOTE**
> Although the examples in this chapter show domain aggregate functions being used in query expressions, keep in mind that you can use these functions in macros, modules, or the calculated controls of forms and reports.

The Anatomy of Domain Aggregate Functions

There are 12 different domain aggregate functions, but they all have the same anatomy:

`FunctionName("[Field Name]","[Dataset Name]", "[Criteria]")`

- **FunctionName**: This is the name of the domain aggregate function you're using.

- **Field Name** (required): This expression identifies the field containing the data with which you're working.

- **Dataset Name** (required): This expression identifies the table or query you're working with; also known as the domain.

- **Criteria** (optional): This expression is used to restrict the range of data on which the domain aggregate function is performed. If no criteria is specified, the domain aggregate function is performed against the entire data set.

> **NOTE**
> You can't use parameters as expressions in domain aggregate functions.

Understanding the different domain aggregate functions

There are 12 different domain aggregate functions in Access, each performing a different operation. In this section, we take a moment to review the purpose and utility of each function.

DSum

The DSum function returns the total sum value of a specified field in the domain. For example, `DSum("[LineTotal]", "[Dim_Transactions]")` would return the total sum of LineTotal in the Dim_Transactions table.

DAvg

The DAvg function returns the average value of a specified field in the domain. For example, `DAvg("[LineTotal]", "[Dim_Transactions]")` would return the average LineTotal in the Dim_Transactions table.

DCount

The DCount function returns the total number of records in the domain. `DCount("*", "[Dim_Transactions]")`, for example, would return the total number of records in the Dim_Transactions table.

DLookup

The DLookup function returns the first value of a specified field that matches the criteria you define within the DLookup function. If you don't supply a criteria or if the criteria you supplied doesn't sufficiently identify a unique row, the DLookup function returns a random value in the domain. For example, DLookup("[Last_Name]","[Employee_Master]","[Employee_Number]='42620' ") would return the value in the Last_Name field of the record where the Employee_Number is 42620.

DMin and DMax

The DMin and DMax functions return the minimum and maximum values in the domain, respectively. DMin("[LineTotal]", "[Dim_Transactions]") would return the lowest LineTotal in the Dim_Transactions table, whereas DMax("[LineTotal]", "[Dim_Transactions]") would return the highest LineTotal.

DFirst and DLast

The DFirst and DLast functions return the first and last values in the domain, respectively. The following statement would return the first LineTotal in the Dim_Transactions statement:

```
DFirst("[LineTotal]", "[Dim_Transactions]")
```

The following statement would return the last LineTotal in the Dim_Transactions statement:

```
DLast("[LineTotal]", "[Dim_Transactions]")
```

Remember to use an ORDER BY clause to sort the field used in your DFirst or DLast function; otherwise, you will get a random value from that field.

DStDev, DStDevP, DVar, and DvarP

You can use the DStDev and DStDevP functions to return the standard deviation across a population sample and a population, respectively. Similarly, the DVar and the DVarP functions return the variance across a population sample and a population, respectively. DStDev("[LineTotal]", "[Dim_Transactions]") would return the standard deviation of all LineTotals in the Dim_Transactions table. DVar("[LineTotal]", "[Dim_Transactions]") would return the variance of all LineTotals in the Dim_Transactions table.

Examining the syntax of domain aggregate functions

Domain aggregate functions are unique in that the syntax required to make them work actually varies depending on the scenario. This has led to some very frustrated users who have given up on domain aggregate functions altogether. This section describes some general guidelines that will help you in building your domain aggregate functions.

Using no criteria

In this example, you're summing the values in the LineTotal field from the Dim_Transactions table (domain). Your field names and data set names must always be wrapped in quotes.

```
DSum("[LineTotal]","[Dim_Transactions]")
```

15

> **TIP**
>
> Note the use of brackets. Although they are not always required, it's generally a good practice to use brackets when identifying a field, a table, or a query.

Using text criteria

In this example, you're summing the values in the Revenue field from the PvTblFeed table (domain) where the value in the Branch_Number field is 301316. Note that the Branch_Number field is formatted as text. When specifying criteria that is textual or a string, your criteria must be wrapped in single quotes. In addition, your entire criteria expression must be wrapped in double quotes.

```
DSum("[Revenue]", "[PvTblFeed]", "[Branch_Number] = '301316' ")
```

> **TIP**
>
> You can use any valid WHERE clause in the criteria expression of your domain aggregate functions. This adds a level of functionality to domain aggregate functions, because they can support the use of multiple columns and logical operators such as AND, OR, NOT, and so on. An example would be:
>
> ```
> DSum("[Field1]", "[Table]", "[Field2] = 'A' OR [Field2] = 'B' AND [Field3] = 2")
> ```

If you're referencing a control inside a form or report, the syntax will change a bit:

```
DSum("[Revenue]", "[PvTblFeed]", "[Branch_Number] = ' " &
[MyTextControl] & " ' " )
```

Notice that you're using single quotes to convert the control's value to a string. In other words, if the value of the form control is 301316, then

```
"[System_Period] = '" &[MyTextControl] & "'"
```

is essentially translated to read

```
"[System_Period] = '301316'".
```

Using number criteria

In this example, you're summing the values in the LineTotal field from the Dim_Transactions table (domain) where the value in the LineTotal field is greater than 500. Notice that you aren't using the single quotes since the LineTotal field is an actual number field.

```
DSum("[LineTotal]", "[Dim_Transactions]", "[LineTotal] > 500 ")
```

If you're referencing a control inside a form or report, the syntax will change a bit:

```
DSum("[LineTotal]", "[Dim_Transactions]", "[LineTotal] >" [MyNumericControl])
```

Using date criteria

In this example, you're summing the values in the LineTotal field from the Dim_
Transactions table (domain) where the value in the OrderDate field is 07/05/2013:

```
DSum("[LineTotal]", "[Dim_Transactions]", "[OrderDate] = #07/05/2013# ")
```

If you're referencing a control inside a form or report, the syntax will change a bit:

```
DSum("[LineTotal]", "[Dim_Transactions]", "[OrderDate] = #" &
[MydateControl] & "#")
```

Notice that you're using pound signs to convert the control's value to a date. In other
words, if the value of the form control is 07/05/2013, then

```
"[Service_Date] = #" &[MydateControl]& "#"
```

is essentially translated to read

```
"[Service_Date] = #07/05/2013#".
```

Using domain aggregate functions

Like subqueries, domain aggregate functions aren't very efficient when it comes to performing large-scale analyses and crunching very large data sets. These functions are better
suited for use in specialty analyses with smaller subsets of data. Indeed, you'll most often
find domain aggregate functions in environments where the data set being evaluated is
predictable and controlled (for example, functions, forms, and reports). This is not to say,
however, that domain aggregate functions don't have their place in your day-to-day data
analysis. This section walks through some examples of how you can use domain aggregate
functions to accomplish some common tasks.

Calculating the percent of total

The query shown in Figure 15.15 will return products by group and the sum of LineTotal
for each product category. This is a worthwhile analysis, but you could easily enhance it by
adding a column that would give you the percent of total revenue for each product.

FIGURE 15.15

You want to add a column that shows the percent of total revenue for each product category.

Product_Category	Revenue
Bar Equipment	$1,806,137.90
Commercial Appliances	$8,634,337.05
Concession Equipment	$10,083,748.40
Fryers	$3,971,959.10
Ovens and Ranges	$58,399,471.75
Refrigerators and Coolers	$43,786,517.10
Warmers	$37,882,511.95

15

To get the percent of the total dollar value that each product makes up, you naturally would have to know the total dollar value of the entire data set. This is where a DSum function can come in handy. The following DSum function will return the total value of the data set:

```
DSum("[LineTotal]","[Dim_Transactions]")
```

Now you can use this function as an expression in the calculation that will return the percent of total for each product group. Figure 15.16 demonstrates how.

FIGURE 15.16

Use a DSum function as an expression in a calculation to get percent of total.

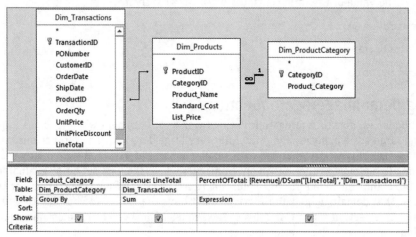

The result, shown in Figure 15.17, proves that this is a quick and easy way to get both total by group and percent of total with one query.

FIGURE 15.17

You retrieved both total by group and percent of total with one query.

Product_Category	Revenue	PercentOfTotal
Bar Equipment	$1,806,137.90	1.10%
Commercial Appliances	$8,634,337.05	5.25%
Concession Equipment	$10,083,748.40	6.13%
Fryers	$3,971,959.10	2.41%
Ovens and Ranges	$58,399,471.75	35.49%
Refrigerators and Coolers	$43,786,517.10	26.61%
Warmers	$37,882,511.95	23.02%

Creating a running count

The query in Figure 15.18 uses a DCount function as an expression to return the number of invoices processed on each specific invoice day.

FIGURE 15.18

This query will return all invoice dates and the number of invoices processed on each date.

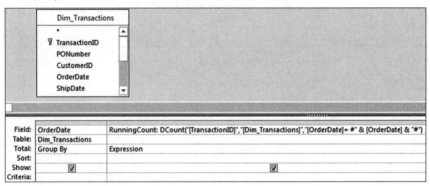

Take a moment to analyze what this DCount function is doing:

```
DCount("[TransactionID]","[Dim_Transactions]","[OrderDate]= #" &
[OrderDate] & "#")
```

This DCount function will get the count of invoices where the invoice date equals (=) each invoice date returned by the query. So, in the context of the query shown in Figure 15.18, the resulting data set shows each invoice date and its own count of invoices.

What would happen if you were to alter the DCount function to tell it to return the count of invoices where the invoice date equals or is earlier than (<=) each invoice date returned by the query, as follows?

```
DCount("[TransactionID]","[Dim_Transactions]","[OrderDate]<= #" &
[OrderDate] & "#")
```

The DCount function would return the count of invoices for each date *and* the count of invoices for any earlier date, thereby giving you a running count.

To put this into action, simply replace the = operator in the DCount function with the <= operator, as shown in Figure 15.19.

15

FIGURE 15.19

Use the <= operator in your DCount function to return the count of invoice dates that equals or is less than the date returned by the query.

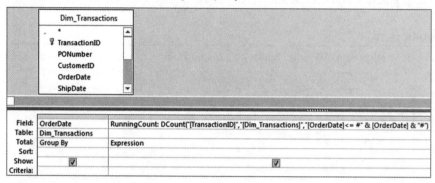

Figure 15.20 shows the resulting running count.

FIGURE 15.20

You now have a running count in your analysis.

OrderDate	RunningCount
7/1/2011	279
7/2/2011	283
7/3/2011	288
7/4/2011	290
7/5/2011	295
7/6/2011	299
7/7/2011	302
7/8/2011	305
7/9/2011	311
7/10/2011	314
7/11/2011	318
7/12/2011	322
7/13/2011	324
7/14/2011	331

TIP

You can achieve a running sum instead of a running count by using the DSum function.

Using a value from the previous record

The query in Figure 15.21 uses a DLookup function to return the revenue value from the previous record. This value is placed into a new column called "Yesterday."

FIGURE 15.21

This query uses a DLookup to refer to the previous revenue value.

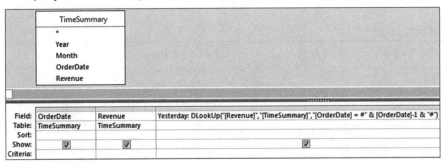

This method is similar to the one used when creating a running sum in that it revolves around manipulating a comparison operator in order to change the meaning of the domain aggregate function. In this case, the DLookup searches for the revenue value where the invoice date is equal to each invoice date returned by the query minus one (-1). If you subtract one from a date, you get yesterday's date!

```
DLookUp("[Revenue]","[TimeSummary]","[OrderDate] = #" & [OrderDate]-1 & "#")
```

> **TIP**
>
> If you add 1, you get the next record in the sequence. However, this trick won't work with textual fields. It only works with date and numeric fields. If you're working with a table that doesn't contain any numeric or date fields, create an AutoNumber field. This will give you a unique numeric identifier that you can use.

Running the query in Figure 15.21 yields the results shown in Figure 15.22.

FIGURE 15.22

You can take this functionality a step further and perform a calculation for the previous day.

OrderDate	Revenue	Yesterday
1/5/2008	$1,218.87	
1/6/2008	$29,280.65	1218.8734
1/7/2008	$34,418.48	29280.6534
1/8/2008	$34,437.67	34418.4828
1/9/2008	$41,319.75	34437.6745
1/12/2008	$37,923.82	
1/13/2008	$37,900.75	37923.8214
1/14/2008	$33,318.55	37900.7498
1/15/2008	$44,478.61	33318.5515
1/16/2008	$31,350.05	44478.6144

You can enhance this analysis by adding a calculated field that gives you the dollar variance between today and yesterday. Create a new column and enter

15

[Revenue]-NZ([Yesterday],0), as shown in Figure 15.23. Note that the Yesterday field is wrapped in an NZ function in order to avoid errors caused by null fields.

FIGURE 15.23

Enhance your analysis by adding a variance between today and yesterday.

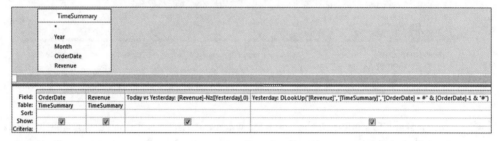

Figure 15.24 shows the result.

FIGURE 15.24

Another task made possible by domain aggregate functions.

OrderDate	Revenue	Today vs Yesterday	Yesterday
1/5/2008	$1,218.87	$1,218.87	
1/6/2008	$29,280.65	$28,061.78	1218.8734
1/7/2008	$34,418.48	$5,137.83	29280.6534
1/8/2008	$34,437.67	$19.19	34418.4828
1/9/2008	$41,319.75	$6,882.07	34437.6745
1/12/2008	$37,923.82	$37,923.82	
1/13/2008	$37,900.75	($23.07)	37923.8214
1/14/2008	$33,318.55	($4,582.20)	37900.7498
1/15/2008	$44,478.61	$11,160.06	33318.5515
1/16/2008	$31,350.05	($13,128.57)	44478.6144

Running Descriptive Statistics in Access

IN THIS CHAPTER

Determining rank, mode, and median

Pulling a random sampling from your data set

Calculating percentile ranking

Determining the quartile standing of a record

Creating a frequency distribution

*D*escriptive statistics allow you to present large amounts of data in quantitative summaries that are simple to understand. When you sum data, count data, and average data, you're producing descriptive statistics. It's important to note that descriptive statistics are used only to profile a data set and enable comparisons that can be used in other analyses. This is different from *inferential statistics*, in which you infer conclusions that extend beyond the scope of the data. To help solidify the difference between descriptive and inferential statistics, consider a customer survey. Descriptive statistics summarize the survey results for all customers and describe the data in understandable metrics, while inferential statistics infer conclusions such as customer loyalty based on the observed differences between groups of customers.

When it comes to inferential statistics, tools like Excel are better suited to handle these types of analyses than Access. Why? First, Excel comes with a plethora of built-in functions and tools that make it easy to perform inferential statistics—tools that Access simply does not have. Second, inferential statistics is usually performed on small subsets of data that can flexibly be analyzed and presented by Excel.

Running *descriptive statistics*, on the other hand, is quite practical in Access. In fact, running descriptive statistics in Access versus Excel is often the smartest option due to the structure and volume of the data set.

ON THE WEB
The starting database for this walkthrough, `Chapter16.accdb`, can be downloaded from this book's website.

Basic Descriptive Statistics

This section discusses some of the basic tasks you can perform using descriptive statistics.

Running descriptive statistics with aggregate queries

At this point in the book, you have run many Access queries, some of which have been aggregate queries. Little did you know that when you ran those aggregate queries, you were actually creating descriptive statistics. It's true. The simplest descriptive statistics can be generated using an aggregate query. For instance, the query in Figure 16.1 will output descriptive statistics around revenue generated by all sales reps.

FIGURE 16.1

Running this aggregate query will provide a useful set of descriptive statistics.

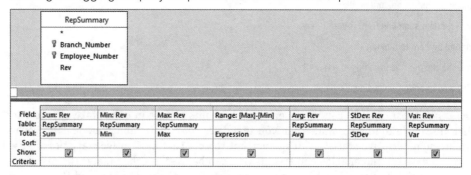

Similar to the descriptive statistics functionality found in Excel, the result of this query, shown in Figure 16.2, provides key statistical metrics for the entire data set.

FIGURE 16.2

Key statistical metrics for the entire data set.

Sum	Min	Max	Range	Avg	StDev	Var
$10,774,159	$86	$137,707	$137,621	$16,009	$21,059	$443,484,375

You can easily add layers to your descriptive statistics. In Figure 16.3, you're adding the Branch_Number field to your query. This will give you key statistical metrics for each branch.

As you can see in Figure 16.4, you can now compare the descriptive statistics across branches to measure how they perform against each other.

FIGURE 16.3

Add the Branch_Number field to your query to add another dimension to your analysis.

Field:	Branch_Number	Sum: Rev	Min: Rev	Max: Rev	Range: [Max]-[Min]	Avg: Rev	StDev: Rev	Var: Rev
Table:	RepSummary	RepSummary	RepSummary	RepSummary		RepSummary	RepSummary	RepSummary
Total:	Group By	Sum	Min	Max	Expression	Avg	StDev	Var
Sort:								
Show:	☑	☑	☑	☑	☑	☑	☑	☑
Criteria:								

RepSummary — * — Branch_Number — Employee_Number — Rev

FIGURE 16.4

You have a one-shot view of the descriptive statistics for each branch.

Branch_Number	Sum	Min	Max	Range	Avg	StDev	Var
101313	$444,631	$124	$78,824	$78,700	$22,232	$29,111	$847,454,523
101419	$124,597	$99	$46,645	$46,546	$20,766	$19,027	$362,039,701
102516	$63,228	$678	$36,387	$35,709	$21,076	$18,390	$338,192,979
103516	$101,664	$151	$31,428	$31,277	$6,778	$9,338	$87,200,338
173901	$107,216	$402	$33,136	$32,734	$13,402	$13,371	$178,773,758
201605	$69,818	$624	$27,657	$27,033	$8,727	$9,496	$90,165,337
201709	$96,853	$184	$42,778	$42,593	$6,918	$12,375	$153,131,218
201714	$288,714	$145	$57,803	$57,658	$12,553	$15,901	$252,833,070
201717	$450,524	$169	$61,521	$61,352	$34,656	$25,160	$633,007,891
202600	$151,338	$277	$58,473	$58,196	$18,917	$25,557	$653,147,704
202605	$242,527	$147	$62,042	$61,895	$16,211	$17,878	$219,627,725

Determining rank, mode, and median

Ranking the records in your data set, getting the mode of a data set, and getting the median of a data set are all tasks a data analyst will need to perform from time to time. Unfortunately, Access doesn't provide built-in functionality to perform these tasks easily. This means you'll have to come up with a way to carry out these descriptive statistics. In this section, you'll learn some of the techniques you can use to determine rank, mode, and median.

Ranking the records in your data set

You'll undoubtedly encounter scenarios in which you'll have to rank the records in your data set based on a specific metric such as revenue. Not only is a record's rank useful in presenting data, but it's also a key variable when calculating advanced descriptive statistics such as median, percentile, and quartile.

The easiest way to determine a record's ranking within a data set is by using a correlated subquery. The query shown in Figure 16.5 demonstrates how a rank is created using a subquery.

FIGURE 16.5

This query ranks employees by revenue.

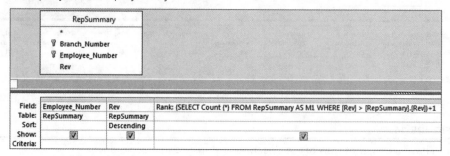

Take a moment to examine the subquery that generates the rank:

```
(SELECT Count(*) FROM RepSummary AS M1 WHERE [Rev] > [RepSummary]
.[Rev])+1
```

This correlated subquery returns the total count of records from the M1 table (this is the RepSummary table with an alias of M1), where the Rev field in the M1 table is greater than the Rev field in the RepSummary table. The value returned by the subquery is then increased by one. Why increase the value by one? If you don't, the record with the highest value will return 0 because zero records are greater than the record with the highest value. The result would be that your ranking starts with zero instead of one. Adding one effectively ensures that your ranking starts with one.

NOTE

Because this is a correlated subquery, this subquery is evaluated for every record in your data set, thereby giving you a different rank value for each record.

Correlated subqueries are covered in detail in Chapter 15.

Figure 16.6 shows the result.

TIP

This technique is also useful when you want to create a sequential number field within a query.

Getting the mode of a data set

The *mode* of a data set is the number that appears the most often in a set of numbers. For instance, the mode for {4, 5, 5, 6, 7, 5, 3, 4} is 5.

FIGURE 16.6

You've created a Rank column for your data set.

Employee_Number	Rank	Rev
64621	1	$137,707.14
4136	2	$111,681.81
5060	3	$106,299.32
56422	4	$102,239.87
56405	5	$83,525.72
160034	6	$78,823.82
60425	7	$77,452.50
3466	8	$76,789.52
52635	9	$76,684.54
52404	10	$76,532.26
2660	11	$75,600.22

Unlike Excel, Access doesn't have a built-in Mode function, so you have to create your own method of determining the mode of a data set. Although there are various ways to get the mode of a data set, one of the easiest is to use a query to count the occurrences of a certain data item and then filter for the highest count. To demonstrate this method, follow these steps:

1. **Build the query shown in Figure 16.7.** The results, shown in Figure 16.8, don't seem very helpful, but if you turn this into a top values query, returning only the top record, you would effectively get the mode.

FIGURE 16.7

This query groups by the Rev field and then counts the occurrences of each number in the Rev field. The query is sorted in descending order by Rev.

2. **Select the Query Tools Design tab and click the Property Sheet command.** The Property Sheet for the query appears.

3. **Change the Top Values property to 1, as shown in Figure 16.9.** You get one record with the highest count.

FIGURE 16.8

Almost there. Turn this into a top values query and you'll have your mode.

Rev	CountOfRev
$158.60	4
$145.02	3
$154.55	3
$185.27	3
$245.78	3
$151.03	3
$122.89	3
$309.11	3
$254.34	2
$650.24	2

FIGURE 16.9

Set the Top Values property to 1.

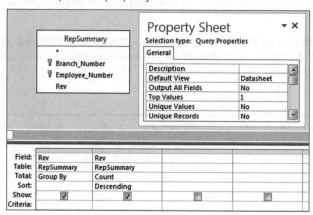

As you can see in Figure 16.10, you now have only one Rev figure—the one that occurs the most often. This is your mode.

FIGURE 16.10

This is your mode.

Rev	CountOfRev
$158.60	4

Getting the median of a data set

The *median* of a data set is the number that is the middle number in the data set. In other words, half the numbers have values that are greater than the median, and half have values that are less than the median. For instance, the median number in {3, 4, 5, 6, 7, 8, 9} is 6 because 6 is the middle number of the data set.

Access doesn't have a built-in `Median` function, so you have to create your own method of determining the median of a data set. An easy way to get the median is to build a query in two steps:

1. **Create a query that sorts and ranks your records.** The query shown in Figure 16.11 sorts and ranks the records in the RepSummary table.

FIGURE 16.11

The first step in finding the median of a data set is to assign a rank to each record.

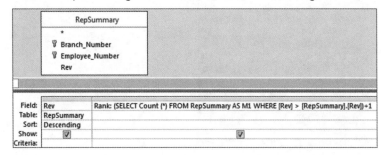

2. **Identify the middlemost record in your data set by counting the total number of records in the data set and then dividing that number by two.** This will give you a middle value. The idea is that because the records are now sorted and ranked,

the record that has the same rank as the middle value will be the median. Figure 16.12 shows the subquery that will return a middle value for the data set. Note that the value is wrapped in an Int function to strip out the fractional portion of the number.

The Middle Value subquery counts all the records in the data set and then divides that number by 2.

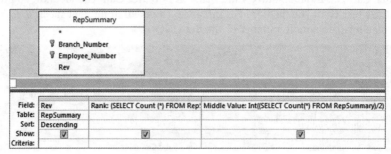

As you can see in Figure 16.13, the middle value is 336. You can go to record 336 to see the median.

Go to record 336 to get the median value of the data set.

Rev	Rank	Middle Value
$137,707.14	1	336
$111,681.81	2	336
$106,299.32	3	336
$102,239.87	4	336
$83,525.72	5	336
$78,823.82	6	336
$77,452.50	7	336
$76,789.52	8	336
$76,684.54	9	336
$76,532.26	10	336
$75,690.33	11	336
$75,489.77	12	336
$75,358.76	13	336
$74,653.99	14	336

If you want to return only the median value, simply use the subquery as a criterion for the Rank field, as shown in Figure 16.14.

FIGURE 16.14

Using the subquery as a criterion for the Rank field ensures that only the median value is returned.

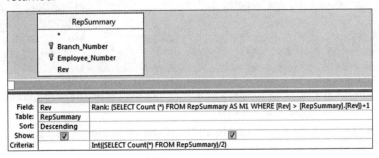

Pulling a random sampling from your data set

Although the creation of a random sample of data doesn't necessarily fall into the category of descriptive statistics, a random sampling is often the basis for statistical analysis.

There are many ways to create a random sampling of data in Access, but one of the easiest is to use the Rnd function within a top values query. The Rnd function returns a random number based on an initial value. The idea is to build an expression that applies the Rnd function to a field that contains numbers and then limit the records returned by setting the Top Values property of the query.

To demonstrate this method, follow these steps:

1. **Start a query in Design view on the Dim_Transactions table.**

2. **Create a Random ID field, as shown in Figure 16.15, and then sort the field (either ascending or descending will work).**

FIGURE 16.15

Start by creating a Random ID field using the Rnd function with the CustomerID field.

> **NOTE**
>
> The `Rnd` function won't work with fields that contain text or null values. Strangely enough, though, the `Rnd` function will work with fields that contain all numerical values even if the field is formatted as a Short Text field.
>
> If your table is made up of fields that contain only text, you can add an AutoNumber field to use with the `Rnd` function. Another option is to pass the field containing text through the `Len` function and then use that expression in your `Rnd` function—for example, `Rnd(Len([Mytext]))`.

3. **Select the Query Tools Design tab and click the Property Sheet command.** The Property Sheet for the query appears.

4. **Change the Top Values property to 1000, as shown in Figure 16.16.**

FIGURE 16.16

Limit the number of records returned by setting the Top Values property of the query.

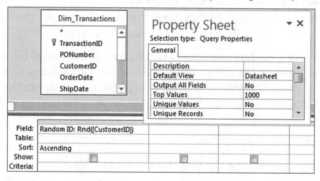

5. **Set the 'Show' row for the Random ID field to false, and add the fields you will want to see in your data set.**

6. **Run the query illustrated in Figure 16.17 to get a completely random sampling of data.**

> **CAUTION**
>
> Rerunning the query, switching the view state, or sorting the data set will result in a different set of random records. If you want to perform extensive analysis on an established set of random records that won't change, you'll need to run this query as a make-table query in order to create a hard table.

FIGURE 16.17

Running this query produces a sample of 1,000 random records.

Field:	CustomerID	ProductID	OrderDate	LineTotal	Rnd([CustomerID])
Table:	Dim_Transactions	Dim_Transactions	Dim_Transactions	Dim_Transactions	
Sort:					Ascending
Show:	☑	☑	☑	☑	☐
Criteria:					

Advanced Descriptive Statistics

When working with descriptive statistics, a little knowledge goes a long way. Indeed, basic statistical analyses often lead to more advanced statistical analyses. In this section, you build on the fundamentals you've just learned to create advanced descriptive statistics.

Calculating percentile ranking

A *percentile rank* indicates the standing of a particular score relative to the normal group standard. Percentiles are most notably used in determining performance on standardized tests. If a child scores in the 90th percentile on a standardized test, her score is higher than 90 percent of the other children taking the test. Another way to look at it is to say that her score is in the top 10 percent of all the children taking the test. Percentiles often are used in data analysis as a method of measuring a subject's performance in relation to the group as a whole—for instance, determining the percentile ranking for each employee based on annual revenue.

Calculating a percentile ranking for a data set is simply a mathematical operation. The formula for a percentile rank is (Record Count–Rank)/Record Count. The trick is getting all the variables needed for this mathematical operation.

Follow these steps:

1. **Build the query you see in Figure 16.18.** This query will start by ranking each employee by annual revenue. Be sure to give your new field an alias of "Rank."

2. **Add a field that counts all the records in your data set.** As you can see in Figure 16.19, you're using a subquery to do this. Be sure to give your new field an alias of "RCount."

FIGURE 16.18

Start with a query that ranks employees by revenue.

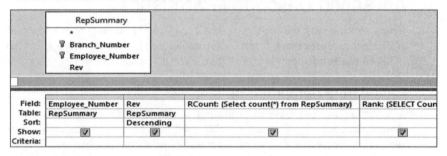

FIGURE 16.19

Add a field that returns a total data set count.

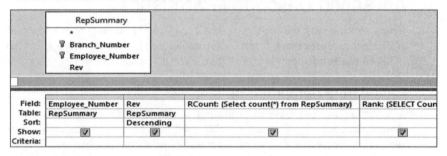

3. **Create a calculated field with the expression** `([RCount]-[Rank])/[RCount]`.
At this point, your query should look like the one shown in Figure 16.20.

FIGURE 16.20

The final step is to create a calculated field that will give you the percentile rank for each record.

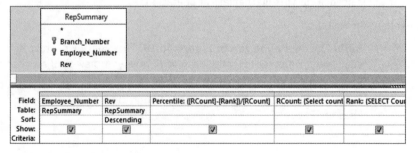

4. **Run the query.** Sorting on the Rev field will produce the results shown in Figure 16.21.

FIGURE 16.21

You've successfully calculated the percentile rank for each employee.

Rank ▾	Percentile ▾	Employee_Number ▾	Rev ▾	RCount ▾
1	99.85%	64621	$137,707.14	673
2	99.70%	4136	$111,681.81	673
3	99.55%	5060	$106,299.32	673
4	99.41%	56422	$102,239.87	673
5	99.26%	56405	$83,525.72	673
6	99.11%	160034	$78,823.82	673
7	98.96%	60425	$77,452.50	673
8	98.81%	3466	$76,789.52	673
9	98.66%	52635	$76,684.54	673
10	98.51%	52404	$76,532.26	673
11	98.37%	3660	$75,690.33	673
12	98.22%	1336	$75,489.77	673
13	98.07%	56416	$75,358.76	673
14	97.92%	55144	$74,653.99	673
15	97.77%	60334	$71,427.22	673

Again, the resulting data set enables you to measure each employee's performance in relation to the group as a whole. For example, the employee who is ranked 6th in the data set is the 99th percentile, meaning that this employee earned more revenue than 99 percent of the other employees.

Determining the quartile standing of a record

A *quartile* is a statistical division of a data set into four equal groups, with each group making up 25 percent of the data set. The top 25 percent of a collection is considered to be the first quartile, whereas the bottom 25 percent is considered to be the fourth quartile. Quartile standings typically are used for the purposes of separating data into logical groupings that can be compared and analyzed individually. For example, if you want to establish a minimum performance standard around monthly revenue, you could set the minimum to equal the average revenue for employees in the second quartile. This ensures that you have a minimum performance standard that at least 50 percent of your employees have historically achieved or exceeded.

Establishing the quartile for each record in a data set doesn't involve a mathematical operation; instead, it's a question of comparison. The idea is to compare each record's rank value to the quartile benchmarks for the data set. What are quartile benchmarks? Imagine that your data set contains 100 records. Dividing 100 by 4 would give you the first quartile benchmark (25). This means that any record with a rank of 25 or less is in the first quartile. To get the second quartile benchmark, you would calculate 100/4*2. To get the third, you would calculate 100/4*3, and so on.

Given that information, you know right away that you'll need to rank the records in your data set and count the records in your data set. Start by building the query shown in Figure 16.22. Build the Rank field the same way you did in Figure 16.18. Build the RCount field the same way you did in Figure 16.19.

FIGURE 16.22

Start by creating a field named Rank that ranks each employee by revenue and a field named RCount that counts the total records in the data set.

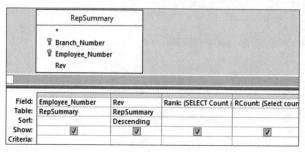

Once you've created the Rank and RCount fields in your query, you can use these fields in a Switch function that will tag each record with the appropriate quartile standing. Take a moment and look at the Switch function you'll be using:

```
Switch([Rank]<=[RCount]/4*1,"1st",[Rank]<=[RCount]/4*2,"2nd",
[Rank]<=[RCount]/4*3,"3rd",True,"4th")
```

This Switch function is going through four conditions, comparing each record's rank value to the quartile benchmarks for the data set.

 For more information on the Switch function, see Chapter 13.

Figure 16.23 demonstrates how this Switch function fits into the query. Note that you're using an alias of Quartile here.

As you can see in Figure 16.24, you can sort the resulting data set on any field without compromising your quartile standing tags.

FIGURE 16.23

Create the quartile tags using the Switch function.

RepSummary
*
☞ Branch_Number
☞ Employee_Number
Rev

Field:	Employee_Number	Rev	Quartile: Switch([Rank]<=[RCount]/4*1,"1st",[Rank]<=[RCount]/4*2,"2nd",[Rank]<=[RCount]/4*3,"3rd",True,"4th")
Table:	RepSummary	RepSummary	
Sort:		Descending	
Show:	☑	☑	☑
Criteria:			

FIGURE 16.24

Your final data set can be sorted any way without the danger of losing your quartile tags.

Employee_Number ▾	Rev ▾	Rank ▾	Quartile ▾	RCount ▾
104	$9,023.50	294	2nd	673
1044	$447.33	520	4th	673
1050	$179.74	614	4th	673
1054	$54,147.73	55	1st	673
106	$38,013.36	105	1st	673
113	$963.06	458	3rd	673
1130	$67,961.15	18	1st	673
1135	$1,477.21	429	3rd	673
1156	$192.07	602	4th	673
1245	$38,189.81	103	1st	673
1336	$75,489.77	12	1st	673
1344	$12,242.75	268	2nd	673
1416	$1,120.57	445	3rd	673
142	$1,622.30	421	3rd	673
1425	$42,118.02	89	1st	673

Creating a frequency distribution

A *frequency distribution* is a special kind of analysis that categorizes data based on the count of occurrences where a variable assumes a specified value attribute. Figure 16.25 illustrates a frequency distribution created by using the Partition function.

FIGURE 16.25

This frequency distribution was created using the Partition function.

Employees	Dollars
158	: 499
183	500: 5499
49	5500: 10499
43	10500: 15499
31	15500: 20499
34	20500: 25499
36	25500: 30499
22	30500: 35499
23	35500: 40499
13	40500: 45499
19	45500: 50499
15	50500: 55499
17	55500: 60499
10	60500: 65499
5	65500: 70499
4	70500: 75499
6	75500: 80499
1	80500: 85499

With this frequency distribution, you're clustering employees by the range of revenue dollars they fall in. For instance, 183 employees fall into the 500: 5499 grouping, meaning that 183 employees earn between 500 and 5,499 revenue dollars per employee. Although there are several ways to get the results you see here, the easiest way to build a frequency distribution is to use the Partition function:

```
Partition(Number, Range Start, Range Stop, Interval)
```

The Partition function identifies the range that a specific number falls into, indicating where the number occurs in a calculated series of ranges. The Partition function requires the following four arguments:

- **Number (required):** The number you're evaluating. In a query environment, you typically use the name of a field to specify that you're evaluating all the row values of that field.

- **Range Start (required):** A whole number that is to be the start of the overall range of numbers. Note that this number cannot be less than zero.

- **Range Stop (required):** A whole number that is to be the end of the overall range of numbers. Note that this number cannot be equal to or less than the Range Start.

- **Interval (required):** A whole number that is to be the span of each range in the series from Range Start to Range Stop. Note that this number cannot be less than one.

To create the frequency distribution you saw in Figure 16.25, build the query shown in Figure 16.26. As you can see in this query, you're using a Partition function to specify that you want to evaluate the Revenue field, start the series range at 500, end the series range at 100,000, and set the range intervals to 5,000.

FIGURE 16.26

This simple query creates the frequency distribution shown in Figure 16.25.

You can also create a frequency distribution by group by adding a Group By field to your query. Figure 16.27 demonstrates this by adding the Branch_Number field.

FIGURE 16.27

This query will create a separate frequency distribution for each branch number in your data set.

The result is a data set (shown in Figure 16.28) that contains a separate frequency distribution for each branch, detailing the count of employees in each revenue distribution range.

FIGURE 16.28

You've successfully created multiple frequency distributions with one query.

Branch_Number	Employees	Dollars
101313	3	: 499
101313	7	500: 5499
101313	2	5500: 10499
101313	1	15500: 20499
101313	1	20500: 25499
101313	1	25500: 30499
101313	1	45500: 50499
101313	1	60500: 65499
101313	1	70500: 75499
101313	2	75500: 80499
101419	2	: 499
101419	1	10500: 15499
101419	1	25500: 30499
101419	1	30500: 35499
101419	1	45500: 50499
102516	1	500: 5499

Part V

Working with Access Forms and Reports

Forms and reports are incredibly powerful components of the Access toolset. Access forms enable you to build user interfaces on top of database tables, providing a robust rapid application development platform for many types of organizations. Access reports allow you to easily integrate your database analysis with polished PDF-style reporting functionality, complete with grouping, sorting, and conditional formatting.

Chapters 17–19 show you everything you need to know in order to turn your simple database into a viable application with attractive interfaces that can be used for viewing, adding, editing, and deleting data.

Chapters 20 and 21 walk you through the steps for building Access reports, offering your users a flexible way of viewing summarized information in the desired level of detail, while enabling them to print their information in many different formats.

IN THIS PART

Chapter 17
Creating Basic Access Forms

Chapter 18
Working with Data on Access Forms

Chapter 19
Working with Form Controls

Chapter 20
Presenting Data with Access Reports

Chapter 21
Advanced Access Report Techniques

Creating Basic Access Forms

IN THIS CHAPTER

Working with form views

Understanding different types of forms

Adding controls to a form

Working with the Property Sheet

Forms provide the most flexible way for viewing, adding, editing, and deleting your data. They're also used for *switchboards* (forms with buttons that provide navigation), for dialog boxes that control the flow of the system, and for messages. Controls are the objects on forms, such as labels, text boxes, buttons, and many others. In this chapter, you learn how to create different types of forms. We also fill you in on the types of controls that are used on a form. This chapter also discusses form and control properties and how you determine the appearance and behavior of an Access interface through setting or changing property values.

The forms you add to an Access database are a critical aspect of the application you create. In most situations, users should not be permitted direct access to tables or query datasheets. It's far too easy for a user to delete valuable information or incorrectly input data into the table. Forms provide a useful tool for managing the integrity of a database's data. Because forms can contain VBA code or macros, a form can verify data entry or confirm deletions before they occur. Also, a properly designed form can reduce training requirements by helping the user understand what kind of data is required by displaying a message as the user tabs into a control. A form can provide default values or perform calculations based on data input by the user or retrieved from a database table.

ON THE WEB

In this chapter, you use tblProducts, tblCustomers, and other tables in `Chapter17.accdb`.

Working with Form Views

Forms have *views*. Views are different ways of interacting with the form, either as a developer or an end user. You can also restrict which views are available. To change a form's view, use the View drop-down list on the Home Ribbon. Following is a description of each view available and which property controls if you can see it:

- **Form view:** This is the most common way your end users will interact with your form. Showing a form in Form view is the equivalent of running your application. You don't do any design or layout work in Form view, only interacting with your data. The property Allow Form View can be set to No if you don't want a particular form used in this manner.

- **Datasheet view:** This is another view that allows the end user to interact with the data. It's less commonly used than Form view. It's similar in appearance to the table's Datasheet view, but you have more control over how the user interacts with the fields. The property Allow Datasheet View can be set to No to disable looking at the form in this view.

- **Design view:** This view is where most of the work designing the form is done. It shows the major areas of the form, like header, detail, and footer, as well as a major and minor grid to aid in control placement. The controls contain their name in this view as opposed to data in the other views. You can't disable Design view.

- **Layout view:** This is a hybrid between Form view and Design view. In Layout view, you see the data as it would be displayed on your form. You can even move among records. There are no gridlines and the major sections of the forms are not separated. You have limited ability to move controls around and change controls' properties. The Allow Layout View property can be set to No to disable this view.

In a typical design cycle, you work with the form in Design view, make minor adjustments to it in Layout view, and test it in Form or Datasheet view. To switch views, use the View control on the Home Ribbon, right-click the form's title bar if it's open, or right-click the form's icon in the Navigation pane if the form is closed. If the view you'd like to switch to isn't on the menu, switch to Design view and check the Allow properties in the Property Sheet.

Understanding Different Types of Forms

Use the Forms group on the Create tab of the Ribbon to add forms to your database. The commands in the Forms group, shown in Figure 17.1, let you create the following different types of forms and ways to work with Access forms:

FIGURE 17.1

Use the Forms group on the Create tab of the Ribbon to add new forms to your database.

- **Form:** Creates a new form that lets you enter information for one record at a time. You must have a table, query, form, or report open or selected to use this command. When you click the Form button with a table or query highlighted in the Navigation pane, Access binds the new form to the data source and opens the form in Layout view.

- **Form Design:** Creates a new blank form and displays it in Design view. The form isn't bound to any data source. You must specify a data source (table or query) and build the form by adding controls from the data source's field list.

- **Blank Form:** Instantly creates a blank form with no controls. Like Form Design, the new form is not bound to a data source, but it opens in Layout view.

- **Form Wizard:** Access features a simple wizard to help you get started building forms. The wizard asks for the data source, provides a screen for selecting fields to include on the form, and lets you choose from a number of very basic layouts for the new form.

- **Navigation Form:** The Access navigation form is a specialized form intended to provide user navigation through an application. Navigation forms are discussed in detail later in this chapter.

- **More Forms:** The More Forms button in the Forms group drops down a gallery containing a number of other form types.

  - **Multiple Items:** This is a simple tabular form that shows multiple records bound to the selected data source instead of the usual one-record-at-a-time display.

  - **Datasheet:** Creates a form that is displayed as a datasheet.

  - **Split Form:** Creates a split form, which shows a datasheet in the upper, lower, left, or right area of the form, and a traditional form in the opposite section for entering information on the record selected in the datasheet.

  - **Modal Dialog:** Provides a template for a modal dialog form. A modal dialog form (often called a *dialog box*) stays on the screen until the user provides information requested by the dialog or is dismissed by the user.

The options in the Forms group of the Create Ribbon all do the same thing—create a form. The difference is that each sets certain form properties to get a desired effect. You can set those properties yourself. For example, if you chose Form Design and restricted the views to only Datasheet View, it would be the same as choosing Datasheet on the More Forms menu. These controls are handy shortcuts, but don't worry if you pick the wrong one. You can change the properties to make the form look and behave exactly as you want.

If any of the terminology in the preceding bullets is new to you, don't worry—each of these terms is discussed in detail in this chapter. Keep in mind that the Access Ribbon and its contents are very context dependent, so every item may not be available when you select the Create tab.

Creating a new form

Like many other aspects of Access development, Access provides multiple ways of adding new forms to your application. The easiest is to select a data source, such as a table, and click the Form command on the Create tab of the Ribbon. Another is to use the Form Wizard and allow the wizard to guide you through the process of specifying a data source and other details of the new form.

Using the Form command

Use the Form command in the Forms group of the Ribbon to automatically create a new form based on a table or query selected in the Navigation pane.

> **NOTE**
>
> This process was called *AutoForm* in some previous versions of Access.

To create a form based on tblProducts, follow these steps:

1. **Select tblProducts in the Navigation pane.**
2. **Select the Create tab of the Ribbon.**
3. **Click the Form command in the Forms group.** Access creates a new form containing all the fields from tblProducts displayed in Layout view, shown in Figure 17.2. (The form shown in Figure 17.2 is included in the Chapter17.accdb example database as frmProducts_AutoForm.)

The new form is opened in Layout view, which is populated with controls, each of which is bound to a field in the underlying data source. Layout view gives you a good idea how the controls appear relative to one another, but it provides only limited ability to resize controls or move controls on the form. Right-click the form's title bar and select Design view to rearrange controls on the form.

The Form Design button in the Forms group also creates a new form, except that the form is not automatically bound to a table or query, no controls are added to the form's design surface, and the form is opened in Design view. Form Design is most useful when you're creating a new form that might not use all the fields in the underlying data source, and you want more control over control placement from the start.

Similarly, the Blank Form option opens a new empty form, but this time in Layout view. You add controls to the form's surface from the field list, but you have little control over control placement. The Blank Form option is most useful for quickly building a form with bound controls with little need for precise placement. A new blank form can be produced in less than a minute.

Using the Form Wizard

Use the Form Wizard command in the Forms group to create a form using a wizard. The Form Wizard visually walks you through a series of questions about the form that you want to create and then creates it for you automatically. The Form Wizard lets you select which fields you want on the form, the form layout (Columnar, Tabular, Datasheet, or Justified), and the form title.

FIGURE 17.2

Use the Form command to quickly create a new form with all the fields from a table or query.

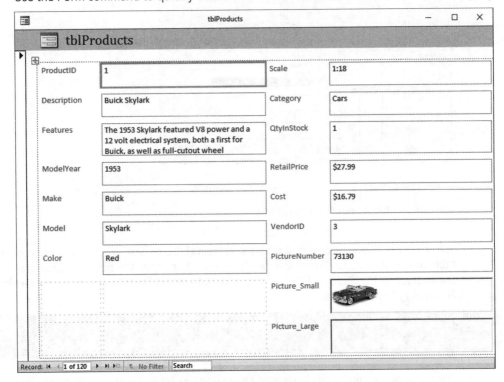

To start the Form Wizard based on tblCustomers, follow these steps:

1. **Select tblCustomers in the Navigation pane.**
2. **Select the Create tab of the Ribbon.**
3. **Click the Form Wizard button in the Forms group.** Access starts the Form Wizard, shown in Figure 17.3.

FIGURE 17.3

Use the Form Wizard to create a form with the fields you choose.

Add selected field

Add all fields   Remove all fields

Remove selected field

The wizard is initially populated with fields from tblCustomers, but you can choose another table or query with the Tables/Queries drop-down list above the field selection area. Use the buttons in the middle of the form to add and remove fields to the Available Fields and Selected Fields list boxes.

> **NOTE**
>
> You can also double-click any field in the Available Fields list box to add it to the Selected Fields list box.

The series of buttons at the bottom of the dialog box let you navigate through the other steps of the wizard. The types of buttons available here are common to most wizard dialog boxes:

- **Cancel:** Cancel the wizard without creating a form.
- **Back:** Return to the preceding step of the wizard.
- **Next:** Go to the next step of the wizard.
- **Finish:** End the wizard using the current selections and the default selections for any steps you don't complete.

> **CAUTION**
>
> If you click Next or Finish without selecting any fields, Access tells you that you must select fields for the form before you can continue.

Clicking Next opens the second wizard dialog box (shown in Figure 17.4) where you specify the overall layout and appearance of the new form.

FIGURE 17.4

Select the overall layout for the new form.

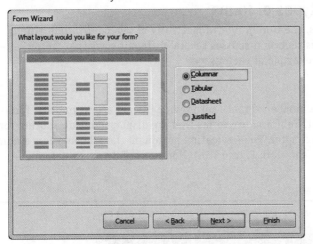

The Columnar layout is the default layout, but you can also choose the Tabular, Datasheet, or Justified options. Clicking Next takes you to the last wizard dialog box (shown in Figure 17.5), where you provide a name for the new form.

FIGURE 17.5

Saving the new form.

TIP

The main advantage of using the Form Wizard is that it binds the new form to a data source and adds controls for the selected fields. In most cases, however, you still have considerable work to do after the Form Wizard has finished.

Looking at special types of forms

When working with Access, the word *form* can mean any of several different things, depending on context. This section discusses several different ways that "forms" are used in Access and presents an example of each usage.

Navigation forms

Navigation forms include a number of tabs that provide instant access to other forms in a form/subform arrangement. Subforms are forms that are displayed inside another form and are discussed later in this chapter. The Navigation button on the Ribbon offers a number of button placement options (shown in Figure 17.6). Horizontal Tabs is the default.

FIGURE 17.6

The Navigation button provides a number of tab placement options.

Selecting the Horizontal Tabs placement in the Navigation drop-down list opens the new navigation form in Design view (see Figure 17.7). The new form includes a row of tabs along the top and a large area under the tabs for embedding subforms. You type the tab's label (like Products) directly into the tab, or add it through the tab's Caption property. As you complete the tab's label, Access adds a new, blank tab to the right of the current tab.

TIP

You can drag an existing form into the tab area of a navigation form to add it as a subform.

FIGURE 17.7

The navigation form features a large area for embedding subforms.

Horizontal tabs

Subfrom area

In Figure 17.7, the Horizontal Tabs option was selected when choosing a navigation form template, and a tab was named Products, which generates a new Add New tab. The alternatives to Horizontal Tabs (Vertical Tabs, Left; Vertical Tabs, Right; and so on) are shown in Figure 17.6.

The Product tab's Property Sheet (shown in Figure 17.8) includes the Navigation Target Name property on the Data tab, for specifying the Access form to use as the tab's subform. Select a form from the drop-down list in the Navigation Target Name property, and Access creates the association to the subform for you.

FIGURE 17.8

Use the Navigation Target Name property to specify the tab's subform.

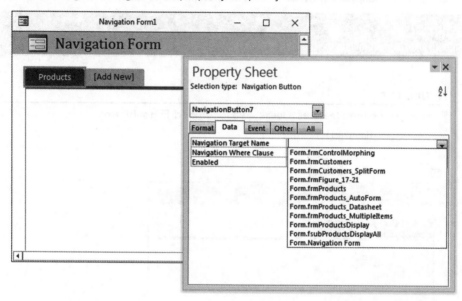

The completed navigation form is shown in Figure 17.9. The auto-generated navigation form makes extravagant use of screen space. There are a number of things that could be done to enhance this form, such as removing the navigation form's header section and reducing the empty space surrounding the subform. frmProducts, shown in Figure 17.9, is included in the Chapter17.accdb example database.

TIP

If you already know the name of the form you want to add to the navigation form, you can type it in a new tab. For example, if you type *frmProducts* in the new tab instead of just *Products*, frmProducts is automatically added as a subform. You can then edit the tab name to remove the frm prefix, if you prefer.

Multiple-items forms

Click the More Forms button in the Forms group of the Create Ribbon and then click the Multiple Items button to create a tabular form based on a table or query selected in the Navigation pane. A tabular form is much like a datasheet, but it's much more attractive than a plain datasheet.

Because the tabular form is an Access form, you can convert the default text box controls on the form to combo boxes, list boxes, and other advanced controls. Tabular forms display multiple records at one time, which makes them very useful when you're reviewing or updating multiple records. To create a multiple-items form based on tblProducts, follow these steps:

1. **Select tblProducts in the Navigation pane.**

2. **Select the Create tab on the Ribbon.**

3. **Click the More Forms button and click Multiple Items.** Access creates a new multiple-items form based on tblProducts displayed in Layout view (as shown in Figure 17.10).

FIGURE 17.9

A navigation form is a quick and easy way to provide basic navigation features.

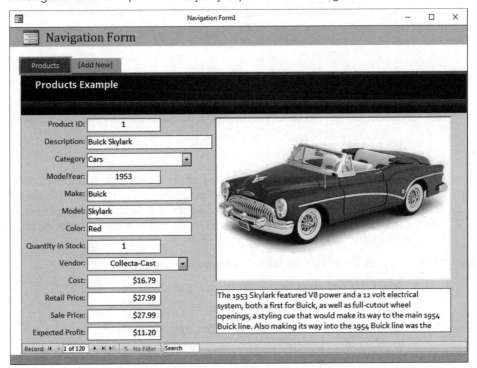

FIGURE 17.10

Create a multiple-items form when you want to see more than one record at a time.

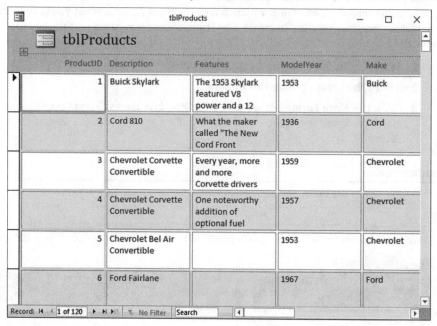

Split forms

Click the More Forms button in the Form group of the Create Ribbon and then click the Split Form button to create a split form based on a table or query selected in the Navigation pane. The split-form feature gives you two views of the data at the same time, letting you select a record from a datasheet in the lower section and edit the information in a form in the upper section.

To create a split form based on tblCustomers, follow these steps:

1. **Select tblCustomers in the Navigation pane.**
2. **Select the Create tab of the Ribbon.**
3. **Click the More Forms button and click Split Form.** Access creates a new split form based on tblCustomers displayed in Layout view (shown in Figure 17.11). Resize the form and use the splitter bar in the middle to make the lower section completely visible.

The Split Form Orientation property (on the Format tab of the form's Property Sheet) determines whether the datasheet is on the top, bottom, left, or right of the form area. The default is as shown in Figure 17.11, with the datasheet area on the bottom. frmCustomers_SplitForm is included in the Chapter17.accdb example database.

FIGURE 17.11

Create a split form when you want to select records from a list and edit them in a form. Use the splitter bar to resize the upper and lower sections of the form.

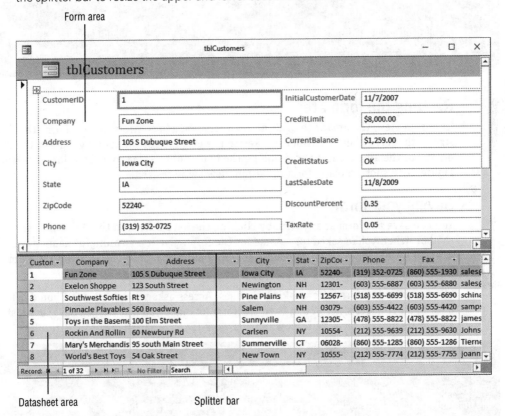

Datasheet forms

Click the More Forms button in the Forms group of the Create Ribbon and then click the Datasheet button to create a form that looks like a table or query's datasheet. A datasheet form is useful when you want to see the data in a row and column format but you want to limit which fields are displayed and editable.

To create a datasheet form based on tblProducts, follow these steps:

1. **Select tblProducts in the Navigation pane.**
2. **Select the Create tab of the Ribbon.**
3. **Click the More Forms button in the Forms group and then click Datasheet.** You can view any form you create as a datasheet by selecting Datasheet view from the View drop-down menu on the Ribbon. A datasheet form appears in Datasheet view by default when you open it.

> **TIP**
>
> Some forms have their Allow Datasheet View property set to No by default. The View drop-down doesn't show a Datasheet View option for those forms. You'll learn more about form properties in the "Introducing Properties" section, later in this chapter.

Resizing the form area

In Design view, the area with gridlines is where you add controls to your form. This is the size of the form when it's displayed. Resize the grid area of the form by placing the cursor on any of the area borders and dragging the border of the area to make it larger or smaller. Figure 17.12 shows a blank form in Design view being resized.

Saving your form

You can save the form at any time by clicking the Save button in the Quick Access toolbar. When you're asked for a name for the form, give it a meaningful name (for example, frmProducts, frmCustomers, or frmProductList). Once you've given the form a name, you won't be prompted the next time you click Save.

When you close a form after making changes, Access asks you to save it. If you don't save a form, all changes since you opened the form (or since you last clicked Save) are lost. You should frequently save the form while you work if you're satisfied with the results.

> **TIP**
>
> If you're going to make extensive changes to a form, you might want to make a copy of the form. For example, if you want to work on the form frmProducts, you can copy and then paste the form in the Navigation pane, giving it a name like frmProductsOriginal. Later, when you've completed your changes and tested them, you can delete the original copy.

FIGURE 17.12

Design view of a blank form. Resize the form area by dragging the bottom-right corner.

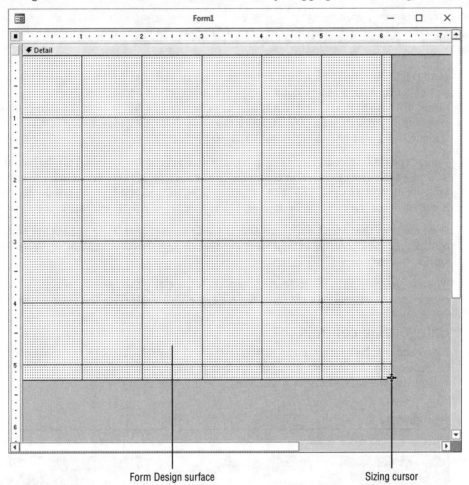

Form Design surface   Sizing cursor

Working with Controls

Controls and properties form the basis of forms and reports. It's critical to understand the fundamental concepts of controls and properties before you begin to apply them to custom forms and reports.

> **NOTE**
>
> Although this chapter is about forms, you'll learn that forms and reports share many common characteristics, including controls and what you can do with them. As you learn about controls in this chapter, you'll be able to apply nearly everything you learn when you create reports.

A control is any object on a form or report, such as a label or text box. These are the same sort of controls used in any Windows application, such as Access, Excel, web-based HTML forms, or those that are used in any language, such as VB.NET, C++, or C#. Although each language or product has different file formats and different properties, a text box in Access is similar to a text box in any other Windows product.

You enter data into controls and display data using controls. A control can be bound to a field in a table (when the value is entered in the control, it's also saved in some underlying table field), or data can be unbound and displayed in the form but not saved when the form is closed. A control can also be an object that doesn't hold data, such as a line or rectangle.

Some controls that aren't built into Access are developed separately—these are ActiveX controls. ActiveX controls extend the basic feature set of Access and are available from a variety of vendors.

Whether you're working with forms or reports, essentially the same process is followed to create and use controls. In this chapter, we explain controls from the perspective of a form.

Categorizing controls

Forms and reports contain many different types of controls. You can add these controls to forms using the Controls group on the Design tab, shown in Figure 17.13. Hovering the mouse over the control displays a ScreenTip telling you what the control is.

FIGURE 17.13

The Design tab lets you add and customize controls in a form's Design view.

Table 17.1 briefly describes the basic Access controls.

TABLE 17.1 Controls in Access Forms

Control	What It Does
Text box	Displays and allows users to enter or edit data.
Label	Displays static text that the user can't change.

Control	What It Does
Button	Also called a *command button*. Runs macros or VBA code when clicked.
Tab control	Displays a tabbed interface where each tab contains different controls.
Link	Creates a link to a web page, a picture, an e-mail address, or a program.
Web browser control	Adds a web browser to your form to display web pages.
Navigation control	Provides a tabbed interface that displays subforms. Selecting from the Navigation control on the Create Ribbon creates a form with this control.
Option group	Holds multiple option buttons, check boxes, or toggle buttons.
Insert page break	Usually used for reports and indicates a physical page break.
Combo box	A combination of a box and a list box. It includes a text box area at the top for entering text and a drop-down list box for selecting from a list.
Chart	Displays data in a graphical format.
Line	A graphical line of variable thickness and color, which is used for separation.
Toggle button	This is a two-state button—up or down—which usually uses pictures or icons instead of text to display different states.
Rectangle	A rectangle can be any color or size or can be filled in or blank; the rectangle is used to group related controls visually.
List box	A list of values that is always displayed on the form or report.
Check box	A two-state control, shown as a square that contains a check mark if it's on and an empty square if it's off. Before a check box's value is set, it appears as a grayed-out square.
Unbound object frame	Holds an OLE object or embedded picture that isn't tied to a table field and can include graphs, pictures, sound files, and video.
Attachment	Manages attachments for the Attachment data type. Attachment fields (see Chapter 3) provide a way to *attach* external files (such as music or video clips or Word documents) to Access tables.
Option button	Also called a *radio button*, this button is displayed as a circle with a dot when the option is on.
Subform/subreport	Displays another form or report within the main form or report.
Bound object frame	Holds an OLE object or embedded picture that is tied to a table field.
Image	Displays a bitmap picture with very little overhead.

17

The Use Control Wizards button, revealed by expanding the Controls group by clicking the More button in the lower-right corner of the group, doesn't add a control to a form. Instead, the Use Control Wizards button determines whether a wizard is automatically activated when you add certain controls. The option group, combo box, list box, subform/subreport, bound and unbound object frame, and command button controls all have wizards to help you when you add a new control. You can also use the ActiveX Controls button (also found at the bottom of the expanded Controls group) to display a list of ActiveX controls, which you can add to Access.

There are three basic categories of controls:

- **Bound controls:** These are controls that are bound to a field in the data source underlying the form. When you enter a value in a bound control, Access automatically updates the field in the current record. Most of the controls used for data entry can be bound. Controls can be bound to most data types, including Short Text, Date/Time, Number, Yes/No, OLE Object, and Long Text fields.

- **Unbound controls:** Unbound controls retain the entered value, but they don't update any table fields. You can use these controls for text label display, for controls such as lines and rectangles, or for holding unbound OLE objects (such as bitmap pictures or your logo) that are stored not in a table but on the form itself. Very often, VBA code is used to work with data in unbound controls and directly update Access data sources.

 Turn to Chapter 28 for details on using VBA to manipulate forms and controls and to work with unbound data.

- **Calculated controls:** Calculated controls are based on expressions, such as functions or calculations. Calculated controls are unbound because they don't directly update table fields. An example of a calculated control is = [SalePrice] - [Cost]. This control calculates a value based on two table fields for display on a form but is not bound to any table field. The value of an unbound calculated control may be referenced by other controls on the form or used in an expression in another control on the form or in VBA in the form's module.

Adding a control

You add a control to a form in a number ways:

- **By clicking a button in the Controls group on the Design tab of the Ribbon and drawing a new unbound control on the form:** Use the control's Control Source property to bind the new control to a field in the form's data source.

- **By dragging a field from the field list to add a bound control to the form:** Access automatically chooses a control appropriate for the field's data type and binds the control to the selected field.

- **By double-clicking a field in the field list to add a bound control to the form:** Double-clicking works just like dragging a field from the field list to the form. The only difference is that, when you add a control by double-clicking a field, Access decides where to add the new control to the form. Usually the new control is added to the right of the most recently added control, and sometimes below it.

- **By right-clicking a field in the field list and choosing Add Field to View:** Right-clicking places a bound control in the same location as if it were double-clicked.

- **By copying an existing control and pasting it to another location on the form:** Copying a control can be done in all the familiar ways: Click Copy on the Home tab of the Ribbon, right-click the control and choose Copy, or press Ctrl+C. Pasted controls are bound to the same field as the control that was copied.

Using the Controls group

When you use the buttons in the Controls group to add a control, you decide which type of control to use for each field. The control you add is *unbound* (not attached to the data in a table field) and has a default name such as Text21 or Combo11. After you create the control, you decide what table field to bind the control to, enter text for the label, and set any properties. You'll learn more about setting properties later in this chapter.

You can add one control at a time using the Controls group. To create three different unbound controls, perform these steps:

1. **With the form created earlier open in Design view, click the Text Box button in the Controls group.**

2. **Move the mouse pointer to the Form Design window, and click and drag the new control onto the form's surface in its initial size and position. Notice that a label control is added when you add a text box.**

3. **Click the Option button in the Controls group, and click and drag the new Option button onto the form's surface in its initial size and position.**

4. **Click the Check Box button in the Controls group and add it to the form, as you added the other controls.** When you're done, your screen should resemble Figure 17.14.

TIP

Clicking the Form Design window with a control selected creates a default-size control. If you want to add multiple controls of the same type, right-click the icon in the Controls group and choose Drop Multiple Controls, and then draw as many controls as you want on the form. Click the selector control (the arrow) to unlock the control and return to normal operation.

TIP

To remove the gridlines and grid points from the form's detail area, select Grid from the Size/Space control on the Arrange tab of the Ribbon while the form is in Design view. Most of the figures in this section don't show the grid so the edges of the controls are easier to see.

17

FIGURE 17.14

Unbound controls added from the Controls group.

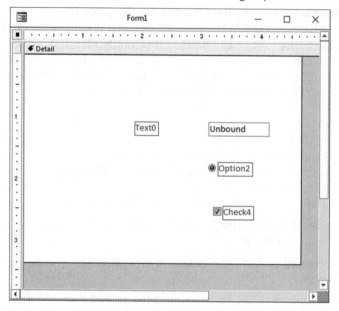

Using the field list

The field list displays a list of fields from the table or query the form is based on. Open the field list by clicking the Add Existing Fields button in the Tools group on the Design tab of the Ribbon (refer to Figure 17.13).

If you created a form using a method that automatically binds the form to a table or query, the field list for that table or query will be displayed. For this example, we created a form using the Blank Form button, which does not automatically bind the form to a data source. In this case, the field list only shows a Show All Tables link. Click the Show All Tables link to get a list of tables. Then click the plus sign next to tblProducts to show the fields in that table.

Drag Model from the field list and drop it onto the form to create a control bound to the Model field in tblProducts. You can select and drag fields one at a time or select multiple fields by using the Ctrl key or Shift key:

- **To select multiple contiguous fields,** click the first field, hold down the Shift key, and then click the last field that you want.
- **To select multiple noncontiguous fields,** click a field that you want, hold down the Ctrl key, and then click each additional field that you want.

> **NOTE**
> You can drag multiple fields only to a form that's already bound to a data source. Access prevents you from selecting multiple fields until at least one field has been added.

By default, the field list appears docked on the right of the Access window. The field list window is movable and resizable and displays a vertical scroll bar if it contains more fields than can fit in the window. Figure 17.15 shows the field list undocked and moved on top of the form.

FIGURE 17.15

Click Add Existing Fields in the Tools group to show the field list.

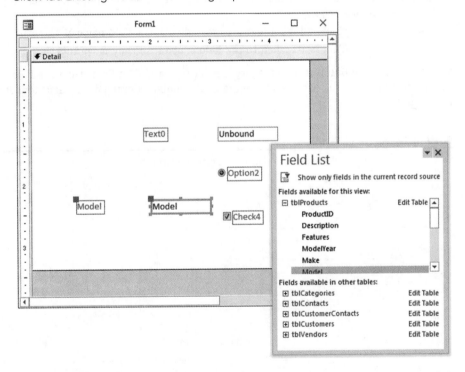

When Select is active in the control box, dragging a field from the field list to the Design window results in the default control type based on the data type of the field. Most often, the default is a bound text box. If you drag a Yes/No field from the field list window, Access adds a check box. Optionally, you can select the type of control by selecting a control from the Controls group and dragging the field from the field list to the Design window. For example, if you select Combo Box in the control box and drag a Short Text field to the

Design window, Access will create a combo box bound to that field instead of the default text box. This only works for controls that are appropriate for the field's data type. Any other type of control will result in the default control type.

You gain several distinct advantages by dragging a field from the field list window:

- The control is automatically bound to the field.
- Field properties inherit table-level formats, status bar text, and data validation rules and messages.
- The label control and label text are created with the field name as the caption.
- The label control is attached to the field control, so they move together.

Select and drag the Description, Category, RetailPrice, and Cost fields from the field list window to the form, as shown in Figure 17.16. Double-clicking a field also adds it to the form.

FIGURE 17.16

Drag fields from the field list to add bound controls to the form.

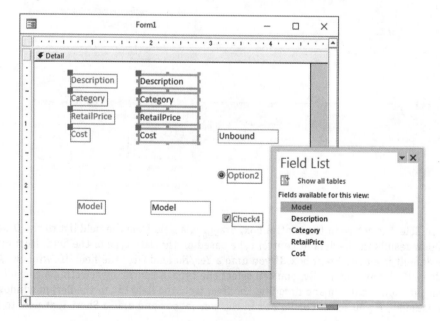

You can see four new pairs of controls in the form's Design view—each pair consists of a label control and a text box control (Access attaches the label control to the text box automatically). You can work with these controls as a group or independently, and you can select, move, resize, or delete them. Notice that each control has a label with a caption matching the field name, and the text box control displays the bound field name used in the text box. If you want to resize just the control and not the label, you must work with the two controls (label and associated text box) separately. You'll learn about working with labels attached to controls later in this chapter.

Close the field list by clicking the Add Existing Fields command in the Tools group of the Ribbon or by clicking the Close button on the field list.

> **TIP**
>
> In Access, you can change the type of control after you create it; then you can set all the properties for the control. For example, suppose that you add a field as a text box control and you want to change it to a list box. Right-click the control and select Change To from the shortcut menu to change the control type. However, you can change only from some types of controls to others. You can change almost any type of control to a text box control, while toggle button controls have more options and list box and combo box controls are interchangeable.

17

In the "Introducing Properties" section, later in this chapter, you learn how to change the control names, captions, and other properties. Using properties speeds the process of naming controls and binding them to specific fields. If you want to see the differences between bound and unbound controls, switch to Form view using the View command in the Views group of the Ribbon. The Description, Category, RetailPrice, Cost, and Model controls display data because they're bound to tblProducts. The other three controls don't display data because they aren't bound to any data source.

> **NOTE**
>
> As you add controls from the field list, Access builds the form's RecordSource property as a SQL statement. The RecordSource after adding these four fields is:
>
> ```
> SELECT tblProducts.Model, tblProducts.Description,
>     tblProducts.Category, tblProducts.RetailPrice,
>     tblProducts.Cost FROM tblProducts;
> ```
>
> If we had started with a form bound to a table or query, the RecordSource would have been set to the entire table or query and would not change as fields are added or removed.

Selecting and deselecting controls

After you add a control to a form, you can resize it, move it, or copy it. The first step is to select one or more controls. Depending on its size, a selected control might show from four to eight *handles* (small squares called *moving and sizing handles*) around the control—at the corners and midway along the sides. The move handle in the upper-left corner is larger than the other handles and you use it to move the control. You use the other handles to size the control. Figure 17.17 displays some selected controls and their moving and sizing handles.

FIGURE 17.17

Selected controls and their moving and sizing handles.

Moving handle   Sizing handle

The Select command (which looks like an arrow) in the Controls group must be chosen in order for you to select a control. If you use the Controls group to create a single control, Access automatically reselects the pointer as the default.

Selecting a single control

Select any individual control by clicking anywhere on the control. When you click a control, the sizing handles appear. If the control has an attached label, the move handle for the label also appears in the upper-left corner of the control. If you select a label control that is associated with another control, all the handles for the label control are displayed, and only the move handle appears in the associated control.

Selecting multiple controls

You select multiple controls in these ways:

- By clicking each control while holding down the Shift key
- By dragging the pointer through or around the controls that you want to select
- By clicking and dragging in the ruler to select a range of controls

Figure 17.17 shows the result of selecting the multiple bound controls graphically. When you select multiple controls by dragging the mouse, a rectangle appears as you drag the mouse. Be careful to drag the rectangle only through the controls you want to select. Any control you touch with the rectangle or enclose within it is selected. If you want to select labels only, make sure that the selection rectangle only touches the labels.

> **TIP**
>
> If you find that controls are not selected when the rectangle passes through the control, you may have the global selection behavior property set to Fully Enclosed. This means that a control is selected only if the selection rectangle completely encloses the entire control. Change this option by choosing File ⇨ Options. Then select Object Designers in the Access Options dialog box and set the Form/Report design view Selection behavior to Partially Enclosed.

> **TIP**
>
> By holding down the Shift or Ctrl key, you can select several noncontiguous controls. This lets you select controls on totally different parts of the screen. Click the form in Design view and then press Ctrl+A to select *all* the controls on the form. Press Shift or Ctrl and click any selected control to remove it from the selection.

Deselecting controls

Deselect a control by clicking an unselected area of the form that doesn't contain a control. When you do so, the handles disappear from any selected control. Selecting another control also deselects a selected control.

Manipulating controls

Creating a form is a multistep process. Once you've added controls to your form, you need to move them to their desired position and properly size them. The Arrange tab of the Ribbon (shown in Figure 17.18) contains commands used to assist you in manipulating controls.

Resizing a control

You *resize* controls using any of the smaller handles in the upper, lower, and right edges of the control. The sizing handles in the control corners let you drag the control larger or smaller in both width and height—and at the same time. Use the handles in the middle of the control sides to size the control larger or smaller in one direction only. The top and bottom handles control the height of the control; the left and right handles change the control's width.

FIGURE 17.18

The Arrange tab lets you work with moving and sizing controls, as well as manipulate the overall layout of the form.

When the mouse pointer touches a corner sizing handle of a selected control, the pointer becomes a diagonal double arrow. You can then drag the sizing handle until the control is the desired size. If the mouse pointer touches a side handle in a selected control, the pointer changes to a horizontal or vertical double-headed arrow. Figure 17.19 shows the Description control as it is being resized. Notice the double-headed arrow in the corner of the Description control.

FIGURE 17.19

Resizing a control.

When you double-click any of the sizing handles, Access resizes a control to best fit the text contained in the control. This feature is especially handy if you increase the font size and then notice that the text is cut off either at the bottom or to the right. For label controls, note that this best-fit sizing adjusts the size vertically and horizontally, though text controls are resized only vertically. This is because when Access is in Form Design mode, it can't predict how much of a field to display—the field name and field contents can be radically different. Sometimes, Access doesn't correctly resize the label and you must manually change its size.

17

Sizing controls automatically

The Size/Space drop-down on the Sizing & Ordering group of the Arrange tab of the Ribbon has several commands that help the arrangement of controls:

- **To Fit:** Adjusts control height for the font of the text they contain
- **To Tallest:** Makes selected controls the height of the tallest selected control
- **To Shortest:** Makes selected controls the height of the shortest selected control
- **To Grid:** Moves all sides of selected controls in or out to meet the nearest points on the grid
- **To Widest:** Makes selected controls the width of the widest selected control
- **To Narrowest:** Makes selected controls the width of the narrowest selected control

Moving a control

After you select a control, you can easily move it, using any of these methods:

- Click the control and hold down the mouse button; the cursor changes to a four-directional arrow. Drag the mouse to move the control to a new location.
- Click once to select the control and move the mouse over any of the highlighted edges; the cursor changes to a four-directional arrow. Drag the mouse to move the control to a new location.

- Select the control and use the arrow keys on the keyboard to move the control. Using this technique, a control changes by only 1 pixel at a time (or moves to the nearest gridline or grid point if Snap to Grid is selected in the Size/Space gallery on the Arrange tab of the Ribbon).
- Click and drag the move handle in the upper-left corner of the control. This differs from the other methods in that it will move the control or its label independently. The other methods move the control and label together.

Figure 17.20 shows a label control that is in the process of being separately moved to the top of the text box control.

FIGURE 17.20

Moving a control.

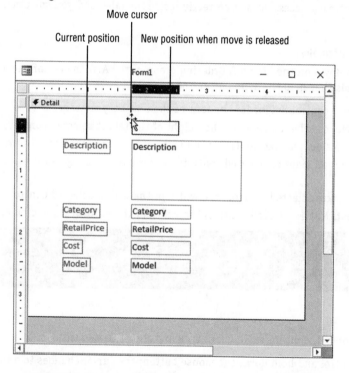

Press Esc before you release the mouse button to cancel a moving or a resizing operation. After a move or resizing operation is complete, click the Undo button on the Quick Access toolbar to undo the changes, if needed.

Aligning controls

You might want to move several controls so that they're all aligned. The Sizing & Ordering group's Align gallery on the Arrange tab of the Ribbon contains the following alignment commands:

- **To Grid:** Aligns the top-left corners of the selected controls to the nearest grid point
- **Left:** Aligns the left edge of the selected controls with the leftmost selected control
- **Right:** Aligns the right edge of the selected controls with the rightmost selected control
- **Top:** Aligns the top edge of the selected controls with the topmost selected control
- **Bottom:** Aligns the bottom edge of the selected controls with the bottommost selected control

You can align any number of selected controls by selecting an Align command. When you choose one of the Align commands, Access uses the control that's the closest to the desired selection as the model for the alignment. For example, suppose that you have three controls and you want to left-align them. They're aligned on the basis of the control farthest to the left in the group of the three controls.

Figure 17.21 shows several sets of controls. The first set of controls is not aligned. The label controls in the middle set of controls have been left-aligned while the text box controls in the right-side set have been right-aligned.

FIGURE 17.21

An example of unaligned and aligned controls on the grid.

Each type of alignment must be done separately. In this example, you can left-align all the labels or right-align all the text boxes at once.

By default, Access displays a series of small dots across the entire surface of a form while it's in Design view. The grid can assist you in aligning controls. Hide or display the grid by selecting the Grid command from the Size/Space gallery in the Sizing & Ordering group on the Arrange tab of the Ribbon. You can also hide or display the ruler using the Ruler command in the same gallery.

Use the Snap to Grid command in the Size/Space gallery to align controls to the grid as you draw or place them on a form. This also aligns existing controls to the grid when you move or resize them.

As you move or resize existing controls, Access lets you move only from grid point to grid point. When Snap to Grid is off, Access ignores the grid and lets you place a control anywhere on the form or report.

> **TIP**
>
> You can temporarily turn off Snap to Grid by pressing the Ctrl key before you create a control (or while sizing or moving it). You can change the grid's *fineness* (number of dots) from form to form by using the Grid X and Grid Y form properties. (Higher numbers indicate greater fineness.) You'll learn more about form properties in Chapter 18.

The Sizing & Ordering group on the Arrange tab of the Ribbon contains commands to adjust spacing between controls. The spacing commands adjust the distance between controls on the basis of the space between the first two selected controls. If the controls are across the screen, use horizontal spacing; if they're down the screen, use vertical spacing. The spacing commands are:

- **Equal Horizontal:** Makes the horizontal space between selected controls equal. You must select three or more controls in order for this command to work.
- **Increase Horizontal:** Increases the horizontal space between selected controls by one grid unit.
- **Decrease Horizontal:** Decreases the horizontal space between selected controls by one grid unit.
- **Equal Vertical:** Makes the vertical space between selected controls equal. You must select three or more controls in order for this command to work properly.
- **Increase Vertical:** Increases the vertical space between selected controls by one grid unit.
- **Decrease Vertical:** Decreases the vertical space between selected controls by one grid unit.

> **TIP**
>
> Aligning controls aligns only the controls themselves. If you want to align the text within the controls (also known as *justifying the text*), you must use the Font group on the Format tab of the Ribbon and click the Align Left, Align Right, or Center buttons.

Modifying the appearance of a control

To modify the appearance of a control, select the control and click commands that modify that control, such as the options in the Font or Controls group. Follow these steps to change the text color and font of the Description label:

1. **Click the Description label on the form.**

2. **In the Font group on the Format tab of the Ribbon, change the Font Size to** 14, **click the Bold button, and change the Font Color to** Blue.

3. **Resize the Description label so the larger text fits.** You can double-click any of the sizing handles to autosize the label.

To modify the appearance of multiple controls at once, select the controls and click commands to modify the controls, such as commands in the Font or Controls group. To change the text color and font of the Category, Retail Price, Cost, and Model labels and text boxes, follow these steps:

1. **Select the four remaining labels and four remaining text boxes by dragging a selection box through them.**

2. **In the Font group on the Format tab of the Ribbon, change the Font Size to** 14, **click the Bold button, and change the Font Color to** Blue.

3. **Resize the labels and text boxes so the larger text fits.** You can double-click any of the sizing handles to autosize the controls. As you click the commands, the controls' appearances change to reflect the new selections (shown in Figure 17.22). The fonts in each control increase in size, become bold, and turn blue. Any changes you make apply to all selected controls.

When multiple controls are selected, you can also move the selected controls together. When the cursor changes to the four-directional arrow, click and drag to move the selected controls. You can also change the size of all the controls at once by resizing one of the controls in the selection. All the selected controls increase or decrease by the same number of units.

Grouping controls

If you routinely change properties of multiple controls, you might want to group them together. To group controls together, select the controls by holding down the Shift key and clicking them or dragging the selection box through them. After the desired controls are selected, select the Group command from the Size/Space gallery on the Arrange tab of the Ribbon. When one control in a group is selected, all controls in that group are automatically selected, as shown in Figure 17.23.

FIGURE 17.22

Changing the appearance of multiple controls at the same time.

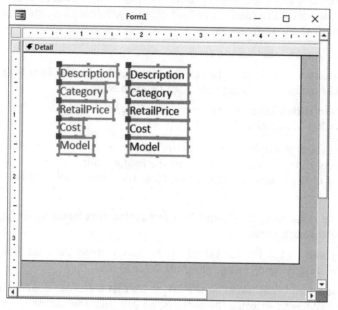

Double-click a control to select just one control in a group. After a single control in the group is selected, you can click any other control to select it. To reselect the entire group, click an empty area of the form, and then click any control in the group.

To resize the entire group, put your mouse on the side you want to resize. After the double arrow appears, click and drag until you reach the desired size. Every control in the group changes in size. To move the entire group, click and drag the group to its new location. With grouped controls, you don't have to select all the controls every time you change something about them.

To remove a group, select the group by clicking any field inside the group, and then select the Ungroup command from the Size/Space gallery of the Arrange tab of the Ribbon.

Changing a control's type

Although there are times you may want to use a check box to display a Boolean (yes/no) data type, there are other ways to display the value, such as a toggle button, as shown in Figure 17.24. A toggle button is raised if it's true and sunken if it's false.

FIGURE 17.23

Grouping multiple controls together.

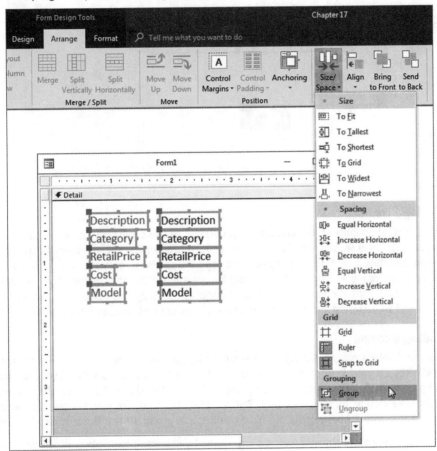

Use these steps to turn a check box into a toggle button:

1. **Open frmControlMorphing in Design view.**

2. **Select the Before label control (just the label control, not the check box).**

3. **Press Delete to delete the label control because it isn't needed.**

4. **Right-click the check box, and choose Change To ⇨ Toggle Button from the shortcut menu.**

5. **Resize the toggle button and click inside it to get the blinking cursor; then type** After **on the button as its caption (shown on the right of Figure 17.24).**

FIGURE 17.24

Turn a check box into a toggle button.

Copying a control

You can create copies of any control by copying it to the Clipboard and then pasting the copies where you want them. If you have a control for which you've entered many properties or specified a certain format, you can copy it and revise only the properties (such as the control's name and bound field name) to make it a different control. This capability is useful with a multiple-page form when you want to display the same values on different pages and in different locations or when copying a control from one form to another.

Deleting a control

You can delete a control simply by selecting it in the form's Design view and pressing the Delete key on your keyboard. The control and any attached labels will disappear. You can bring them back by immediately selecting Undo from the Quick Access toolbar (or using the keyboard shortcut for Undo, Ctrl+Z). You can also select Cut from the Clipboard group on the Home tab of the Ribbon, or Delete from the Records group on the Home tab of the Ribbon.

You can delete more than one control at a time by selecting multiple controls and pressing Delete. You can delete an entire group of controls by selecting the group and pressing Delete. If you have a control with an attached label, you can delete only the label by clicking the label itself and then selecting one of the delete methods. If you select the control, both the control and the label are deleted.

To delete only the label of the Description control, follow the next set of steps (this example assumes that you have the Description text box control in your Form Design window):

1. **Select the Description label control only.**
2. **Press Delete to remove the label from the form.**

Reattaching a label to a control

Later in this chapter, in the "Naming control labels and their captions" section, you'll learn about the special relationship between a control and its label. By default, Access controls include a label when the control is added to a form; this label moves around with the control as you reposition the control on the form. The "Naming control labels and their captions" section describes these behaviors and how to work with control labels. If you accidentally delete a label from a control, you can reattach it. To create and then reattach a label to a control, follow these steps:

1. **Click the Label button on the Controls group.**

2. **Place the mouse pointer in the Form Design window. The mouse pointer becomes a capital A.**

3. **Click and hold down the mouse button where you want the control to begin; drag the mouse to size the control.**

4. **Type** Description **and click outside the control.**

5. **Select the Description label control.**

6. **Select Cut from the Clipboard group on the Home tab of the Ribbon.**

7. **Select the Description text box control.**

8. **Select Paste from the Clipboard group on the Home tab of the Ribbon to attach the label control to the text box control.**

Another way to attach a label to a control is to click the informational icon next to the label, shown in Figure 17.25. This informational icon lets you know that this label is unassociated with a control. Select the Associate Label with a Control command from the menu, and then select the control you want to associate the label with.

FIGURE 17.25

Associating a label with a control.

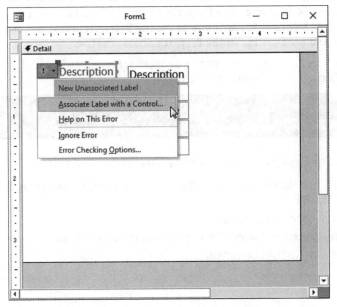

17

Introducing Properties

Properties are named attributes of controls, fields, or database objects that are used to modify the characteristics of a control, field, or object. Examples of these attributes are the size, color, appearance, or name of an object. A property can also modify the behavior of a control, determining, for example, whether the control is read-only or editable and visible or not visible.

Properties are used extensively in forms and reports to change the characteristics of controls. Each control on the form has properties. The form itself also has properties, as does each of its sections. The same is true for reports; the report itself has properties, as does each report section and individual control. The label control also has its own properties, even if it's attached to another control.

Everything that you do with the Ribbon commands—from moving and resizing controls to changing fonts and colors—can be done by setting properties. In fact, all these commands do is change properties of the selected controls.

Displaying the Property Sheet

Properties are displayed in a Property Sheet (sometimes called a *Property window*). To display the Property Sheet for the Description text box, follow these steps:

1. **Drag Description, Category, RetailPrice, Cost, and Model from the field list to a form's Design view (or use the form you created from a previous section if you haven't closed it).**

2. **Click the Description text box control to select it.**

3. **Click the Property Sheet command in the Tools group on the Design tab of the Ribbon, or press F4 to display the Property Sheet.** The screen should look like the one shown in Figure 17.26. In Figure 17.26, the Description text box control has been selected and the Data tab in the Property Sheet is active.

Because the Property Sheet is a window, it can be undocked, moved, and resized. It does not, however, have Maximize or Minimize buttons.

TIP

Double-click the title bar area of an undocked Property Sheet to return it to its most recent docked location.

There are several ways to display a control's Property Sheet if it isn't visible:

- Select a control and click the Property Sheet command in the Tools group on the Design tab of the Ribbon.
- Double-click the edge of any control.
- Right-click any control and select Properties from the shortcut menu.
- Press F4 while any control is selected.

FIGURE 17.26

Change an object's properties with the Property Sheet.

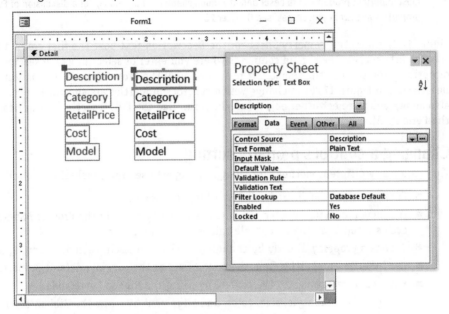

Getting acquainted with the Property Sheet

With the Property Sheet displayed, click any control in Design view to display the properties for that control. Select multiple controls to display similar properties for the selected controls. The vertical scroll bar lets you move among various properties.

The Property Sheet has an All tab that lets you see all the properties for a control. Or you can choose another tab to limit the view to a specific group of properties. The specific tabs and groups of properties are as follows:

- **Format:** These properties determine how a label or value looks: font, size, color, special effects, borders, and scroll bars.
- **Data:** These properties affect how a value is displayed and the data source it's bound to: control source, input masks, validation, default value, and other data type properties.
- **Event:** Event properties are named events, such as clicking a mouse button, adding a record, pressing a key for which you can define a response (in the form of a call to a macro or a VBA procedure), and so on.
- **Other:** Other properties show additional characteristics of the control, such as the name of the control or the description that displays in the status bar.

The number of properties available in Access has increased greatly since early versions of Access. The most important properties are described in various chapters of this book. For a discussion of Event properties and Event procedures, see Chapter 25.

Figure 17.26 shows the Property Sheet for the Description text box. The first column lists the property names; the second column is where you enter or select property settings or options. You can use the combo box near the top of the Property Sheet (displaying Description in Figure 17.26) to change which control's properties are shown. The combo box also allows you to select other objects on the form, like the Detail section, Form Header, or the Form itself.

Changing a control's property setting

There are many different methods for changing property settings, including the following:

- Enter or select the desired value in a Property Sheet.
- For some properties, double-clicking the property name in the Property Sheet cycles through all the acceptable values for the property.
- Change a property directly by changing the control itself, such as changing its size.
- Use inherited properties from the bound field or the control's default properties.
- Enter color selections for the control by using the Ribbon commands.
- Change label text style, size, color, and alignment by using the Ribbon commands.

You can change a control's properties by clicking a property and typing the desired value.

In Figure 17.27, you see a down arrow and a button with three dots to the right of the Control Source property entry area. Some properties display a drop-down arrow in the property entry area when you click in the area. The drop-down arrow tells you that Access has a list of values from which you can choose. If you click the down arrow in the Control Source property, you find that the drop-down list displays a list of all fields in the data source—a query of the tblProducts table. Setting the Control Source property to a field in a table creates a bound control.

Some properties have a list of standard values such as Yes or No; others display varying lists of fields, forms, reports, or macros. The properties of each object are determined by the control itself and what the control is used for.

A nice feature in Access is the ability to cycle through property choices by repeatedly double-clicking the choice. For example, double-clicking the Display When property on the Format tab alternately selects Always, Print Only, and Screen Only.

The Builder button contains an ellipsis (...) and opens one of the many builders in Access, including the Macro Builder, the Expression Builder, and the Code Builder. When you open a builder and make some selections, the property is filled in for you. You'll learn about builders later in this book.

Each type of object has its own Property Sheet and properties. These include the form itself, each of the form sections, and each of the form's controls. Once you've displayed the Property Sheet by clicking Property Sheet on the Design tab, you can change what the Property Sheet displays in two ways: by selecting the object on the form or by choosing the object from the Property Sheet's combo box. The Property Sheet will instantly change to show the properties for the selected object.

FIGURE 17.27

Setting a control's Control Source property.

Naming control labels and their captions

You might notice that each of the data fields has a label control and a text box control. Normally, the label's Caption property is the same as the text box's Name property. The text box's Name property is usually the same as the table's field name—shown in the Control Source property. Sometimes, the label's Caption is different because a value was entered into the Caption property for each field in the table.

When creating controls on a form, it's a good idea to use standard naming conventions when setting the control's Name property. Name each control with a prefix followed by a meaningful name that you'll recognize later (for example, txtTotalCost, cboState, lblTitle). Table 17.2 shows the naming conventions for form and report controls. You can find a complete, well-established naming convention online at www.xoc.net/standards.

TABLE 17.2 Form/Report Control Naming Conventions

Prefix	Object
frb	Bound object frame
cht	Chart (graph)
chk	Check box
cbo	Combo box
cmd	Command button
ocx	ActiveX custom control
det	Detail (section)
gft[n]	Footer (group section)
fft	Form footer section
fhd	Form header section
ghd[n]	Header (group section)
hlk	Hyperlink
img	Image
lbl	Label
lin	Line
lst	List box
opt	Option button
grp	Option group
pge	Page (tab)
brk	Page break
pft	Page footer (section)
phd	Page header (section)
shp	Rectangle
rft	Report footer (section)
rhd	Report header (section)
sec	Section
sub	Subform/subreport
tab	Tab control
txt	Text box
tgl	Toggle button
fru	Unbound object frame

The properties displayed in Figure 17.27 are the specific properties for the Description text box. The Control Source property is set to Description.

With bound controls, the Control Source property is the name of the table field to which the control is bound. In this example, Description refers to the field with the same name in tblProducts. An unbound control has no control source, whereas the control source of a calculated control is the actual expression for the calculation, as in the example =[SalePrice] - [Cost].

The Name property from the Other tab is simply the name of the field itself. When a control is bound to a field, Access automatically assigns the Name property to the bound field's name. Unbound controls are given names such as Field11 or Button13. However, you can give the control any name you want.

17

Working with Data on Access Forms

IN THIS CHAPTER

Viewing and modifying data in Form view

Editing form data

Printing Access forms

Understanding form properties

Adding form headers and footers

Adjusting a form's layout

Adding calculated controls to a form

Converting a form to a report

In Chapter 17, you learned about the tools necessary to create and display a form—Design view, bound and unbound controls, the Field List, and the Controls group on the Ribbon. In this chapter, you learn how to work with data on the form, view and change the form's properties, and use Layout view.

An Access application's user interface is made up of forms. Forms display and change data, accept new data, and interact with the user. Forms convey a lot of the personality of an application, and a carefully designed user interface dramatically reduces the training required of new users.

Most often, the data displayed on Access forms is bound (either directly or indirectly) to Access tables. Changes made to a form's data affect the data stored in the underlying tables.

ON THE WEB

In this chapter, you use tblProducts, tblSales, and tblContacts in the `Chapter18.accdb` database to provide the data necessary to create the examples.

Using Form View

Form view is where you actually view and modify data. The data in Form view is the same data shown in a table or query's Datasheet view, just presented a little differently. Form view presents the data in a user-friendly format, which you create and design.

 For more information on working in Datasheet view, see Chapter 5.

To demonstrate the use of the Form view, follow these steps to create a new form based on tblProducts:

1. **Select tblProducts in the Navigation pane.**
2. **Select the Create tab on the Ribbon.**
3. **Click the Form command in the Forms group.**
4. **Click the Form View button in the Views group of the Home tab to switch from Layout view to Form view.**

Figure 18.1 shows the newly created form displayed in Form view. This view shows the form's title bar with its caption and the form header at the top and the navigation controls at the bottom. The main part of the form in the center of the screen displays your data, one record at a time.

> **TIP**
>
> If the form contains more fields than can fit onscreen at one time, Access automatically displays a horizontal and/ or vertical scroll bar that you can use to see more of the data. You can also see the rest of the data by pressing the PgDn key. If you're at the bottom of a form, or the entire form fits on the screen without scrolling, and you press PgDn, you'll move to the next record.

The status bar at the bottom of the window displays the active field's Status Bar Text property that you defined when you created the table (or form). If no Status Bar Text exists for a field, Access displays "Form View" in the status bar. Generally, error messages and warnings appear in dialog boxes in the center of the screen (rather than in the status bar). The navigation controls and search box are found at the bottom of the form's window, and the view shortcuts are found in the status bar. These features let you move from record to record or quickly find data.

Looking at the Home tab of the Ribbon

The Home tab of the Ribbon tab (shown in Figure 18.2) provides a way to work with the data. The Home tab has some familiar objects on it, as well as some new ones. This section provides an overview of the Home tab. The individual commands are described in more detail later in this chapter.

FIGURE 18.1

A form in Form view.

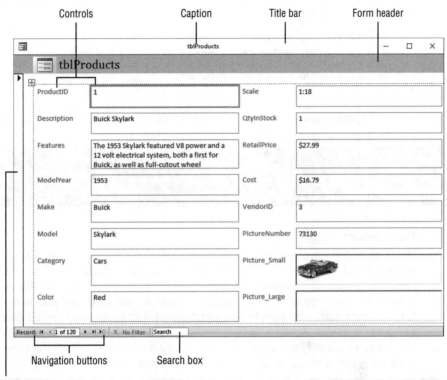

Controls   Caption   Title bar   Form header

Navigation buttons   Search box

Record selector

FIGURE 18.2

The Home tab of the Ribbon.

The Views group

At the far left is the Views group, which allows you to switch among the following views, which you can see by clicking the button's drop-down arrow.

- **Form view:** Allows you to manipulate data on the form
- **Datasheet view:** Shows the data in the row-and-column format

 Turn to Chapter 5 for information on Datasheet view.

- **Layout view:** Allows you to change the form's design while viewing data
- **Design view:** Allows you to make changes to the form's design

> **NOTE**
>
> All these commands may not be available on all forms. By setting the form's properties, you can limit which views are available. You'll learn more about form properties in the "Working with Form Properties" section, later in this chapter.

The Clipboard group

The Clipboard group contains the Cut, Copy, Paste, and Format Painter commands. These commands work like the same commands in other applications (like Word and Excel). The Clipboard is a resource provided by Windows and shared by virtually all Windows applications. Items you copy or cut from Excel, for example, can be pasted into Access if the context is appropriate. For example, you could copy a VBA procedure from an Excel worksheet and paste it into an Access VBA code module because the contexts are the same. But you can't copy an Excel spreadsheet and paste it into an Access form in Form view, because Form view has no way of working with an Excel spreadsheet.

> **TIP**
>
> Office has its own Clipboard that works with the Windows Clipboard by storing the copied content in additional, more Office-centric formats. Copy an Excel range, and the Office Clipboard will store that range in an Office format. Paste the range into a form in Design view, for instance, and an OLE control is automatically created.

The Paste command's drop-down arrow gives you three choices:

- **Paste:** Inserts whatever item has been copied to the Windows Clipboard into the current location in Access. Depending on the task you're working on, the pasted item might be plain text, a control, a table or form, or some other object.
- **Paste Special:** Gives you the option of pasting the contents of the Clipboard in different formats (text, CSV, records, and so on).
- **Paste Append:** Pastes the contents of the Clipboard as a new record—as long as a record with a similar structure was copied to the Clipboard. Obviously, Paste Append remains disabled for any operation that doesn't involve copying and pasting a database table record.

The other controls in the Clipboard group include:

- **Cut:** Removes the item from its current place in the application and puts it onto the Windows Clipboard. The item is not destroyed when removed from its current location; however, it must be pasted before a second item is copied to the Clipboard. (A cut or copied item overwrites whatever is on the Clipboard.)

- **Copy:** Copies the item or object to the Clipboard. Copy can be applied to plain text, but it also applies to controls on a form or report (with the form or report in Design view, of course), database records, entire tables, queries, other database objects, and so on. The Windows Clipboard accepts virtually anything that is copied to it.

- **Format Painter:** The Format Painter (the icon that looks like a paint brush) is a special tool to use when working with Access forms and reports in Design view. The concept of Format Painter is simple: you copy the format of an item (such as its font settings) and paint the formatting onto another item or group of items.

> **TIP**
>
> The Format Painter is a huge timesaver when working with many controls on a form or report. Set a control (such as a Text Box) to look exactly the way you want all the text boxes to look, select the text box, and then click (or double-click) the Format Painter. Then, as you click another text box, the first text box's formatting is applied to the second text box. Double-clicking the Format Painter "locks" it so that you can paint the format onto multiple items. (Click once on the Format Painter or press Esc to unlock it.)

The Sort & Filter group

The Sort & Filter group lets you change the order of the records and, based on your criteria, limit the records shown on the form.

The Records group

The Records group lets you save, delete, or add a new record to the form. It also contains commands to show totals, check spelling, freeze and hide columns, and change the row height and cell width while the form is displayed in Datasheet view.

The Find group

The Find group lets you find and replace data and go to specific records in the datasheet. Use the Select command to select a record or all records.

The Window group

The Window group contains two controls:

- **Size to Fit Form:** When you work with a form in Design view, Access "remembers" the size (height and width) of the form at the moment you save it. When working with the overlapping windows interface, a user may resize a form by dragging its borders to a new size and shape. The Size to Fit Form returns the form to the dimension set at design time.

18

- **Switch Windows:** Switch Windows provides a handy way to see all the objects (forms, reports, tables, and so on) that are currently open in the main Access windows. You can change to another object by selecting it from the drop-down list that appears when you click Switch Windows.

> **NOTE**
>
> When the current database's Document Window Options option is set to Tabbed Documents, the Home tab does not contain a Window group. With Tabbed Documents, all open Access objects are accessible through the tab interface, and the option to switch windows isn't necessary. To change the Document Window Options, choose File ⇨ Options and set the option in the Current Database area of the Access Options dialog box.

The Text Formatting group

The Text Formatting group lets you change the look of the datasheet in Datasheet view or Design view. Use these commands to change the font, font size, bold, italic, color, and so on. Use the Align Left, Align Right, and Center commands to justify the data in the selected column. Click the Gridlines option to toggle gridlines on and off. Use Alternate Row Color to change the colors of alternating rows, or make them all the same. When modifying text in a Long Text field with the Text Format property set to Rich Text, you can use these commands to change the fonts, colors, and so on.

Navigating among fields

Navigating a form is nearly identical to moving around a datasheet. You can easily move around the form by clicking the control that you want and making changes or additions to your data. Because the form window displays only as many fields as can fit onscreen, you need to use various navigational aids to move within your form or between records.

Table 18.1 displays the navigational keys used to move between fields within a form.

TABLE 18.1 Navigating in a Form

Navigational Direction	Keystrokes
Next field	Tab, right-arrow (→) key, down-arrow (↓) key, or Enter
Previous field	Shift+Tab, left-arrow (←) key, or up-arrow (↑) key
First field of current record	Home
First field of first record	Ctrl+Home
Last field of current record	End
Last field of last record	Ctrl+End
Next page	PgDn or Next Record
Previous page	PgUp or Previous Record

Moving among records in a form

Although you generally use a form to display one record at a time, you still need to move between records. The easiest way to do this is to use the Navigation buttons, shown in Figure 18.3.

The Navigation buttons are the six controls located at the bottom-left corner of the Form window. The two leftmost controls move you to the first record and the previous record in the form. The three rightmost controls position you on the next record, last record, or new record in the form. If you know the record number (the row number of a specific record), you can click the Current Record box, enter a record number, and press Enter to go directly to that record.

FIGURE 18.3

The Navigation buttons of a form.

Record: ◄ ◄ 1 of 120 ► ►I ►□

The record number displayed in the Navigation controls is just an indicator of the current record's position in the recordset and may change when you filter or sort the records. To the right of the record number is the total number of records in the current view. The record count may not be the same as the number of records in the underlying table or query. The record count changes when you filter the data on the form.

18

Changing Values in a Form

Earlier in this book, you learned datasheet techniques to add, change, and delete data within a table. These techniques are the same ones you use on an Access form. Table 18.2 summarizes these techniques.

TABLE 18.2   Editing Techniques

Editing Technique	Keystrokes
Move insertion point within a control	Press the right-arrow (→) and left-arrow (←) keys
Insert a value within a control	Position the insertion point and type new data
Select the entire contents of a control	Press F2
Replace an existing value with a new value	Select the entire field and enter a new value
Replace a value with the value of the preceding field	Press Ctrl+' (single quotation mark)
Replace the current value with the default value	Press Ctrl+Alt+Spacebar

Continues

TABLE 18.2 *(continued)*

Editing Technique	Keystrokes
Insert the current date into a control	Press Ctrl+; (semicolon)
Insert the current time into a control	Press Ctrl+: (colon)
Insert a line break in a Text control	Press Ctrl+Enter
Insert a new record	Press Ctrl++ (plus sign)
Delete the current record	Press Ctrl+– (minus sign)
Save the current record	Press Shift+Enter or move to another record
Toggle values in a check box or option button	Spacebar
Undo a change to the current control	Press Esc or click the Undo button
Undo a change to the current record	Press Esc or click the Undo button a second time after you Undo the current control

> **NOTE**
>
> The right-arrow (→) and left-arrow (←) keys work differently in Navigation mode than they do in Edit mode. The F2 key switches between Navigation mode and Edit mode. The only visual cue for the mode that you're in is that the insertion point is displayed in Edit mode. The arrow keys navigate between controls in Navigation mode and are used to select text in Edit mode.

Knowing which controls you can't edit

Some controls, including the following, can't be edited:

- **Controls displaying AutoNumber fields:** Access maintains AutoNumber fields automatically, calculating the values as you create each new record.
- **Calculated controls:** Access may use calculated controls in forms or queries. Calculated values are not actually stored in your table.
- **Locked or disabled fields:** You can set certain form and control properties to prevent changes to the data.
- **Controls in multiuser locked records:** If another user locks the record, you can't edit any controls in that record.

Working with pictures and OLE objects

Object Linking and Embedding (OLE) objects are objects not part of an Access database. OLE objects commonly include pictures but may be any number of other data types, such as links to Word documents, Excel spreadsheets, and audio files. You can also include video files such as MPG or AVI files.

In Datasheet view, you can't view a picture or an OLE object without accessing the OLE server (such as Word, Excel, or the Windows Media Player). In Design view, however, you can size the OLE control area to be large enough to display a picture, chart, or other OLE objects in Form view. You can also size Text Box controls on forms so that you can see the data within the field—you don't have to zoom in on the value, as you do with a datasheet field.

The Access OLE control supports many types of objects. As with a datasheet, you have two ways to enter OLE fields into a form:

- Copy the object (such as an MP3 file) to the Clipboard and paste it from the controls in the Clipboard group of the Ribbon.
- Right-click the OLE control and click Insert Object from the shortcut menu to display the Insert Object dialog box, shown in Figure 18.4. Use the Insert Object dialog box to add a new object to the OLE field, or add an object from an existing file. The Create from File option button adds a picture or other OLE object from an existing file.

FIGURE 18.4

The Insert Object dialog box.

When displaying a picture in an OLE control, set the Size Mode property to control how the image representing the OLE object is displayed. The settings for this property are:

- **Clip:** Keeps the image at its original size and cuts off parts of the picture that don't fit in the control.
- **Zoom:** Fits the image in the control and keeps it in its original proportion, which may result in extra white space.
- **Stretch:** Sizes an image to fit exactly between the frame borders. The stretch setting may distort the picture.

Entering data in the Long Text field

The Features field in the frmProducts form is a Long Text data type. This type of field contains up to 1GB of characters. The first four lines of data appear in the text box. When you click in this text box, a vertical scroll bar appears, allowing you to view all the data in the control.

Better yet, you can resize the control in the form's Design view if you want to make it larger to show more data. Another method for viewing more text in a Long Text field's text box is to press Shift+F2 with the text box selected. A Zoom dialog box is displayed, as shown in Figure 18.5, allowing you to see more data. The text in the Zoom dialog box is fully editable. You can add new text or change text already in the control.

FIGURE 18.5

The Zoom dialog box.

Entering data in the Date field

The SaleDate field in the frmSales_Layout form is a Date/Time data type. This field is formatted to accept and show date values. When you click in this text box, a Date Picker icon automatically appears next to it, as shown in Figure 18.6. Click the Date Picker to display a calendar from which you can choose a date.

FIGURE 18.6

Using the Date Picker control.

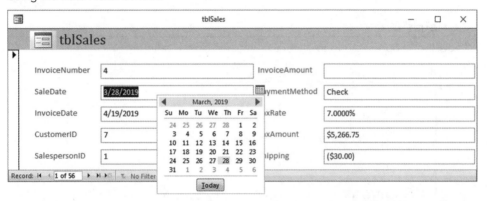

If the Date Picker doesn't appear, switch to Design view and change the control's Show Date Picker property to For Dates. Set the Show Date Picker property to Never, as shown in Figure 18.7, if you don't want to use the Date Picker.

18

FIGURE 18.7

Change the Show Date Picker property to Never to disable it.

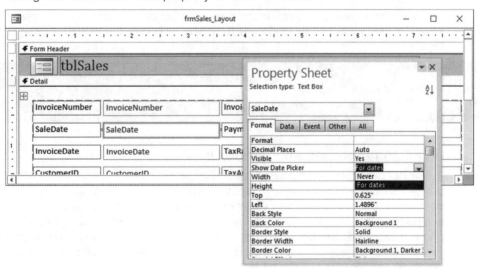

Using option groups

Option groups let you choose exactly one value from a number of possibilities. Option groups work best when you have a small number of mutually exclusive choices to select from. Figure 18.8 shows an option group next to the Follow-Up Date text box. Option groups most commonly contain option buttons but also work with toggle buttons and check boxes.

FIGURE 18.8

Using an option group to select a mutually exclusive value.

The easiest and most efficient way to create option groups is with the Option Group Wizard. You can use it to create option groups with multiple option buttons, toggle buttons, or check boxes. When you're through, all your control's property settings are correctly set. To create an option group, switch to Design view and select the Option Group button from the Design tab's Controls group. Make sure the Use Control Wizards command is selected in the Controls group.

Each element in an option group is assigned a number in its Option Value property. When an option group is bound to a field, the Option Value is stored in that field when the record is saved.

TIP

When creating an option group for a Yes/No field (which is actually stored as a number), set the Yes value to -1 and the No value to 0.

Using combo boxes and list boxes

Access has two types of controls—list boxes and combo boxes—for showing lists of data from which a user can select. The list box always displays as much of the list as possible, whereas the combo box has to be clicked to open the list. A combo box is a combination of a text box and a list box. The text box portion of a combo box is always visible, and the user can enter text into it just like any other text box. The user can also click the drop-down arrow to display the list box portion of the combo box and select an item rather than typing it.

Because combo boxes are a very efficient use of space on the surface of a form, you may want to use (for example) a combo box containing values from tblCustomers, as shown in Figure 18.9. The easiest way to do this is with the Combo Box Wizard. This wizard walks you through the steps of creating a combo box that looks up values in another table. To create a combo box, switch to Design view and select the Combo Box command from the Design tab's Controls group. Make sure the Use Control Wizards command is selected.

FIGURE 18.9

Using a combo box to select a value from a list.

After you create the combo box, examine the Row Source Type, Row Source, Column Count, Column Heads, Column Widths, Bound Column, List Rows, and List Width properties. Once you become familiar with setting these properties, you can right-click a text box, choose Change To ⇨ Combo Box, and set the combo box's properties manually.

Switching to Datasheet view

With a form open, switch to Datasheet view by using one of these methods:

- Click the Datasheet View command in the Home tab's Views group.
- Click the Datasheet View button in the View Shortcuts section at the bottom-right of the Access window.
- Right-click the form's title bar—or any blank area of the form—and choose Datasheet View from the shortcut menu.

The datasheet is displayed with the cursor on the same field and record that it occupied while in the form. Moving to another record and field and then redisplaying the form in Form view causes the form to appear with the cursor on the field occupied in Datasheet view.

To return to Form view—or any other view—select the desired view from the Views group, the View Shortcuts, or the shortcut menu.

> **NOTE**
>
> By default, a new form's Allow Datasheet View property is set to No. To be able to switch to Datasheet view, set this property to Yes.

Saving a record

Access automatically saves each record when you move to another record. Pressing Shift+Enter, selecting Save from the Records group on the Ribbon, or clicking Save on the Quick Access toolbar saves a record without changing the active record. Closing the form also saves a record.

> **CAUTION**
>
> Because Access automatically saves changes as soon as you move to another record, you may inadvertently change the data in the underlying tables. And, because you can undo only the most recent change, there is no easy way to revert to the record's previous state.

Printing a Form

You can print one or more records in your form exactly as they appear onscreen. (You learn how to produce formatted reports in Chapter 20.) The simplest way to print is to use the keyboard shortcut Ctrl+P to show the Print dialog box. The Print dialog box has several options to customize your printout:

- **Print Range:** Prints the entire form or only selected pages or records
- **Copies:** Determines the number of copies to be printed
- **Collate:** Determines whether copies are collated

You can also click the Properties button and set options for the selected printer or select a different printer. The Setup button allows you to set margins and print headings.

Printing a form is like printing anything else. Windows is a WYSIWYG ("What You See Is What You Get") environment, so what you see on the form is what you get in the printed hard copy. If you added page headers or page footers, they would be printed at the top or bottom of the page. The printout contains any formatting that you specified in the form (including lines, boxes, and shading) and converts colors to grayscale if you're using a black-and-white printer.

The printout includes as many pages as necessary to print all the data. Forms aren't typically designed to fit nicely onto the printed page, and you can end up with quite a few pages when you print one out. Access breaks up the printout as necessary to fit on each page.

The Print command under the File menu provides additional printing options:

- **Quick Print:** Prints the active form using the default printer with no opportunity to change any options
- **Print:** Shows the Print dialog box
- **Print Preview:** Shows what the printout will look like based on the current settings

> **TIP**
>
> In Print Preview mode, the Print Preview tab of the Ribbon is displayed (and all other tabs are hidden). Use the Ribbon commands to select different views, change print settings, and zoom in and out. Click Print to print the form to the printer. Click the Close Print Preview command on the right side of the Ribbon to return to the previous view.

Working with Form Properties

You use form properties to change the way the form is displayed and behaves. Property settings include the form's background color or picture, the form's width, and so on. Tables 18.3 through 18.5 cover some of the more important properties. Changing default properties is relatively easy: you select the property in the Property Sheet and type or select a new value.

> **ON THE WEB**
>
> The examples in this section use frmProducts from the `Chapter18.accdb` example database.

> **NOTE**
>
> The form selector is the area where the rulers meet while the form is in Design view. A small black square appears when the form is selected, as shown in Figure 18.10.

To set a form's properties, you have to show the Property Sheet for the form. Switch to Design or Layout view and display the form's Property Sheet in one of the following ways:

- Click the form selector so a small black square appears, and then click the Property Sheet button in the Design tab's Tools group.
- Click the Property Sheet command in the Design tab's Tools group, and then select Form from the drop-down at the top of the Property Sheet.
- Double-click the form selector.
- Right-click the form selector, either of the rulers, or in an empty area of the form and select Form Properties from the shortcut menu or by pressing F4 while the form is in Design or Layout view.

FIGURE 18.10

Using the form selector to display the form's Property Sheet.

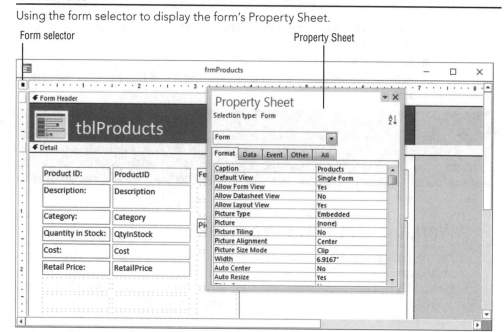

By default, the form's Property Sheet appears docked to the right side of the Access window. Because the Property Sheet is a window, it can be undocked, moved, and resized. In Figure 18.10, the Property Sheet has been undocked and dragged to a position overlying frmProducts. Notice that the Property Sheet window doesn't have Maximize or Minimize buttons or searching capabilities. There is a sort icon that toggles between the default order of the properties and an ascending alphabetical order.

 Chapter 17 has more information on working with the Property Sheet.

Changing the title bar text with the Caption property

Normally, a form's title bar (or its tab if you're using tabbed documents instead of overlapping windows) shows the name of the form after it's saved. The form's Caption property specifies the text displayed in the title bar when the form is in Form view. Follow these steps to change the title bar text:

1. **Click the form selector to make sure the form itself is selected.**

2. **Click the Property Sheet button in the Design tab's Tools group, or press F4 to open the Property Sheet.**

3. **Click the Caption property in the Property Sheet and enter** Products **in the property's text box, as shown in Figure 18.11.**

FIGURE 18.11

Change the Caption property in the form's Property Sheet.

Caption property   Selected object   Caption property value

4. **Click any other property or press Enter to move off of the Caption property.**

5. **Switch to Form view to see the form's new title bar text.** The caption you enter in the form's properties overrides the name of the saved form.

NOTE

Obviously, using a property to change a form's caption is a trivial exercise. This exercise is designed simply to show you how easily you can manipulate a form's appearance by changing its properties. As you work your way through this book, you'll encounter hundreds of examples of using the design tools provided by Access to enhance your application and make them more useful to your users.

Creating a bound form

A *bound form* is directly connected to a data source, such as a table or query. Bound forms usually automatically update data in the bound data source when the user moves to a new record in the form.

To create a bound form, you must specify a data source in the form's Record Source property. In Figure 18.11, the Data tab of the Property Sheet contains the properties controlling what and how data is displayed on the form. Although not shown here, the Record Source property is at the very top of the Property Sheet's Data tab.

The data source can be one of three choices:

- **Table:** The name of a table in the current database file. The table can be a local table (stored in the database itself) or can be linked to another Access database or an external data source such as SQL Server.
- **Query:** The name of a query that selects data from one or more database tables.
- **SQL Statement:** A SQL SELECT statement that selects data from a table or query.

When a form is unbound—the Record Source property is blank and the data is obtained with VBA code—you can't have bound controls on the form. (Bound controls have their Control Source property set to a field in a table.)

 For more information on adding bound controls with the Field List, see Chapter 17.

Specifying how to view the form

Access uses several properties to determine how a form is viewed. The Default View property determines how the data is displayed when the form is initially opened:

- **Single Form:** Displays one record at a time. Single Form is the default and displays one record per form page, regardless of the form's size.
- **Continuous Forms:** Shows more than one record at a time. Continuous Forms tells Access to display as many detail records as will fit onscreen. Figure 18.12 shows a continuous form displaying five records.
- **Datasheet:** Row and column view like a spreadsheet or the standard query Datasheet view.
- **Split Form:** Provides two views of the data at the same time, letting you select a record from a datasheet in the upper section and edit the information in the lower section of the split form.

There are three separate properties to allow the developer to determine if the user can change the default view. These include Allow Form View, Allow Datasheet View, and Allow Layout View. The default setting is Yes for Allow Form View and Allow Layout View and No for Allow Datasheet View. If you set the Allow Datasheet View property to Yes, the Datasheet view commands (in the Views group of the Ribbon, the form's View Shortcuts, and shortcut menu) will be available, and the data can be viewed as a datasheet. If you set the Allow Form View property to No, the Form view commands won't be available.

Removing the Record Selector

The Record Selectors property determines whether the Record Selector (the vertical bar shown in Figure 18.12 on the left side of a form) is displayed. The Record Selector is important in multiple-record forms or datasheets because it points to the current record. A right arrow in the Record Selector indicates the current record but changes to a pencil icon when the record is being edited. Though the Record Selector is important for datasheets, you probably won't want it for a single record form. To remove the Record Selector, change the form's Record Selectors property to No.

FIGURE 18.12

The Continuous Forms setting of the Default view property shows multiple records at once.

Pencil icon

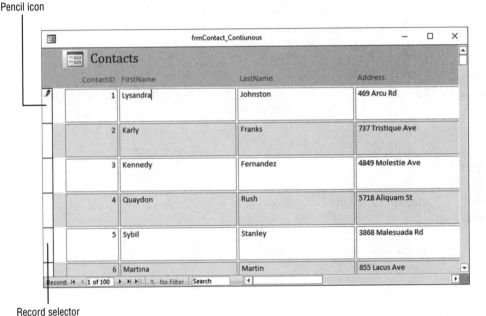

Record selector

Looking at other form properties

Tables 18.3 through 18.5 list the most commonly used form properties and offer a brief description of each. You'll learn more about most of these properties when they're used in examples in this chapter and other chapters throughout this book.

TABLE 18.3 **Form Format Properties**

Property	Description	Options
Caption	Text that is displayed in the form's title bar	Up to 2,048 characters
Default View	Determines the initial view when the form is opened	Single Form: One record per page (default)
		Continuous Forms: As many records per page as will fit
		Datasheet: Row and column view
		Split Form: Displays a datasheet in the upper portion and a form in the lower portion
Allow Form View	Form view allowed	Yes/No
Allow Datasheet View	Datasheet view allowed	Yes/No
Allow Layout View	Layout view allowed	Yes/No
Scroll Bars	Determines whether any scroll bars are displayed	Neither: No scroll bars are displayed
		Horizontal Only: Displays only a horizontal scroll bar
		Vertical Only: Displays only a vertical scroll bar
		Both: Displays both horizontal and vertical scroll bars
Record Selectors	Determines whether the Record Selector is displayed	Yes/No
Navigation Buttons	Determines whether navigation buttons are visible	Yes/No
Dividing Lines	Determines whether lines between form sections are visible	Yes/No
Auto Resize	Automatically resizes form to display a complete record	Yes/No
Auto Center	Centers form onscreen when it's opened	Yes/No

Property	Description	Options
Border Style	Determines the form's border style	None: No border or border elements (scroll bars, navigation buttons)
		Thin: Thin border, not resizable
		Sizable: Normal form settings
		Dialog: Thick border, title bar only, cannot be sized; use for dialog boxes
Control Box	Determines whether control menu (Restore, Move, and Size) is available	Yes/No
Min Max Buttons	Specifies whether the Min and Max buttons appear in the form's title bar	None: No buttons displayed in upper-right corner of form
		Min Enabled: Displays only Minimize button
		Max Enabled: Displays only Maximize button
		Both Enabled: Displays Minimize and Maximize buttons
Close Button	Determines whether to display Close button in upper-right corner and a Close menu item on the control menu	Yes/No
Width	Displays the value of the width of the form. Width can be entered or Access sets it as you adjust the width of the form	A number from 0 to 22 inches (55.87 cm)
Picture	Displays the name of the file used as the background of the entire form	Any valid image file name
Picture Type	Determines whether the form's picture is embedded, linked, or shared	Embedded: Picture is embedded in the form and becomes a part of the form
		Linked: Picture is linked to the form; Access stores the location of the picture and retrieves it every time the form is opened
		Shared: Picture is stored by Access and is available to other objects in the database

Continues

TABLE 18.3 *(continued)*

Property	Description	Options
Picture Size Mode	Determines how the form's picture is displayed	Clip: Displays the picture at its actual size
		Stretch: Fits picture to form size (nonproportional)
		Zoom: Fits picture to form size (proportional), which may result in the picture not fitting in one dimension (height or width)
		Stretch Horizontal: Fits picture to width of form, ignoring height dimension
		Stretch Vertical: Fits picture to height of form, ignoring width dimension
Picture Alignment	Determines the form's picture alignment	Top Left: Displays the picture in the top-left corner of the form
		Top Right: Displays the picture in the top-right corner of the form
		Center (default): Centers the picture
		Bottom Left: Displays the picture in the bottom-left corner of the form
		Bottom Right: Displays the picture in the bottom-right corner of the form
		Form Center: Centers the picture horizontally and vertically
Picture Tiling	Used when you want to overlay multiple copies of a small bitmap (for example, a single brick can become a wall)	Yes/No
Grid X	Displays setting for number of points per inch when X grid is displayed	A number from 1 to 64
Grid Y	Displays setting for number of points per inch when Y grid is displayed	A number from 1 to 64

Property	Description	Options
Layout for Print	Determines whether form uses screen fonts or printer fonts	Yes: Printer Fonts No: Screen Fonts
Subdatasheet Height	Determines the height of a subdatasheet when expanded	A number from 0 to 22 inches (55.87 cm)
Subdatasheet Expanded	Determines the saved state of all subdatasheets in a table or query	Yes: The saved state of subdatasheets is expanded. No: The saved state of subdatasheets is closed.
Palette Source	The palette for a form or report	(Default): Indicates the default Access color palette You can also specify other Windows palette files (PAL), ICO, BMP, DB, and WMF files.
Orientation	Determines view orientation	Right-to-Left: Appearance and functionality move from right to left. Left-to-Right: Appearance and functionality move from left to right.
Moveable	Determines whether the form can be moved	Yes/No
Split Form Orientation	Determines the look of a form in Split Form view	Datasheet on Top: Datasheet appears at the top of the form. Datasheet on Bottom: Datasheet appears at the bottom of the form. Datasheet on Left: Datasheet appears to the left of the form. Datasheet on Right: Datasheet appears to the right of the form.
Split Form Datasheet	Determines whether data can be edited in the datasheet of a Split Form	Allow Edits: Edits are allowed. Read Only: Data is read-only and cannot be changed.
Split Form Splitter Bar	Determines whether there's a splitter bar on a Split Form	Yes/No

18

Continues

TABLE 18.3 *(continued)*

Property	Description	Options
Save Splitter Bar Position	Determines whether the position of the Splitter Bar should be saved	Yes/No
Split Form Size	Size of the form part of the Split Form	Auto to let Access size the form or a number to set the actual size
Split Form Printing	Determines which section of a Split Form to print	Form Only: Prints the form portion Datasheet Only: Prints the datasheet section
Navigation Caption	Overrides the word *Record* in the form's navigation buttons	Up to 255 characters

TABLE 18.4 Form Data Properties

Property	Description	Options
Record Source	Specifies the source of data displayed on the form	Unbound: Blank Bound: The name of a table, query, or a SQL statement
Filter	Used to specify a subset of records to be displayed when a filter is applied to a form; can be set in the form properties, with a macro, or through VBA	Any string that is a valid SQL WHERE clause without the WHERE keyword
Filter On Load	Applies filter at form/report startup	Yes/No
Order By	Specifies the field(s) used to order the data in the view	Any string that is a valid SQL ORDER BY clause without the ORDER BY keywords
Order By On Load	Applies sort at form/report startup	Yes/No
Allow Filters	Determines whether a user will be able to display a filtered form	Yes/No
Allow Edits	Determines whether a user will be able to edit data, making the form editable or read only	Yes/No
Allow Deletions	Determines whether a user will be able to delete records	Yes/No

Property	Description	Options
Allow Additions	Determines whether a user will be able to add records	Yes/No
Data Entry	Determines whether form opens to a new blank record, not showing any saved records	Yes/No
Recordset Type	Used to determine whether multi-table forms can be updated	Dynaset: Only default table field controls can be edited.
		Dynaset (Inconsistent Updates): All tables and fields are editable.
		Snapshot: No fields are editable (same as read-only).
Record Locks	Used to determine default multiuser record locking on bound forms	No Locks: Locks record only as it's saved
		All Records: Locks entire form's records while using the form
		Edited Record: Locks only current record during an edit
Fetch Defaults	Determines whether default values should be retrieved.	Yes/No

TABLE 18.5 Form "Other" Properties

Property	Description	Option Definition
Pop Up	Form is a pop-up that floats above all other objects	Yes/No
Modal	User must close the form before doing anything else; disables other windows; when Pop Up set to Yes, Modal disables menus and toolbar, creating a dialog box	Yes/No
Cycle	Determines how Tab works in the last field of a record	All Records: Tabbing from the last field of a record moves to the next record.
		Current Record: Tabbing from the last field of a record moves to the first field of that record.
		Current Page: Tabbing from the last field of a record moves to the first field of the current page.

Continues

TABLE 18.5 *(continued)*

Property	Description	Option Definition
Ribbon Name	Name of custom Ribbon to apply on open	A valid Ribbon name (See Chapter 30)
Shortcut Menu	Determines whether shortcut (right-click) menus are available	Yes/No
Shortcut Menu Bar	Specifies the name of an alternate shortcut menu bar	A valid menu bar name
Fast Laser Printing	Prints rules instead of lines and rectangles	Yes/No
Tag	Allows you to store extra information about your form	A string up to 2048 characters long
Has Module	Allows you to show if your form has a class module; setting this property to No removes the VBA code module attached to the form.	Yes/No
Use Default Paper Size	Uses the default paper size when printing	Yes/No

Adding a Form Header or Footer

Although the form's Detail section usually contains the majority of the controls that display data, there are other sections in a form that you can add:

- **Form header:** Displayed at the top of each page when viewed and at the top when the form is printed
- **Form footer:** Displayed at the bottom of each page when viewed and at the bottom of the form when the form is printed

The form header and footer remain on the screen, while any controls in the Detail section can scroll up and down.

You select the header and footer options in the Header/Footer group on the Design tab of the Ribbon (with the form open in Design view, of course).

Working with Section Properties

The Form properties discussed in the previous section apply to the entire form. Each section of the form has its own set of properties that affect the appearance and behavior of the section. The three form sections—Detail, Form Header, and Form Footer—share the same properties, with a few exceptions.

The Visible property

The Visible property is a Yes/No property that determines if the section is shown or hidden. All three sections' visible properties are set to Yes by default. The Detail section should remain visible in all but the least conventional forms because that's where most of the controls will be. The Form Header and Form Footer sections may be hidden if they're not needed. Generally, the form header is used to display a title and possibly an image. Showing the form header on a continuous form helps the user stay oriented while using the form. The form footer is useful for showing summary or status information, like the current date and time.

The Height property

The Height property determines how tall the section is. The most common way to change the Height property is to grab the edge of the section with your mouse and drag up or down to decrease or increase the height. With the Property Sheet visible, you can see the Height property value change when you drag the edge and release it in its new location. If you want a specific height, change the Height property value instead of dragging the edge of the section.

The Back Color property

The Back Color property determines the color of the background of the controls. You can change the Back Color property by using the drop-down control on the Property Sheet. Access gives you many different built-in colors to choose from.

There's also a build button on the Property Sheet that displays the familiar color palette including Theme Colors and Standard Colors. The More Colors button at the bottom of the color palette allows you to specify any color you want.

Alternatively, you can type in the color you want. The Back Color property accepts a six-digit hexadecimal number. Hexadecimal consists of the numbers 0 through 9 and the letters A through F (16 choices in all). You precede the hexadecimal number with a pound sign (#), such as #000000 for black and #FFFFFF for white. This method of setting Back Color is useful if you're trying to match a color and you already know that color's hexadecimal code.

Many developers prefer to keep the Back Color property of the Detail section set to plain white. It's important that the color of the Detail section doesn't distract the user from the purpose of the form. However, a conservative Back Color can add depth to your form and provide a consistent brand across all your forms.

The Special Effect property

The Special Effect property can be set to Flat, Raised, or Sunken. Flat is the default value, and Raised and Sunken provide a beveled effect at the edges of the section.

18

The Display When property

The Display When property can be set to Always, Screen Only, or Print Only. This allows you to hide or show a section when printing. You may want to show the Form Header and Form Footer sections on the screen, but only get the Detail section if the form is printed. You can achieve this by setting the Display When properties of the Form Header and Form Footer to Screen Only and then by leaving the Detail section set to the default, Always.

The printing properties

Most of the remaining section properties, such as Auto Height, Can Grow, and Can Shrink, are more applicable to reports than forms. They allow you to dynamically control the height of sections based on the data those sections contain. They have no effect on how your form displays on the screen and are rarely used.

Changing the Layout

In this section, you'll learn how to change a form's layout using Layout view. You'll add, move, and resize controls, as well as change a few other characteristics while viewing the form's data.

With a form open in Layout view, select the Arrange tab in the Form Layout Tools area of the Ribbon. The Arrange tab includes controls for selecting a form's initial layout, including the default positions of controls on the form. Figure 18.13 shows the Arrange tab after selecting a number of controls on the form. Different controls are enabled or disabled based on what is selected.

FIGURE 18.13

The Arrange tab of the Ribbon for Layout view.

Changing a control's properties

In previous versions of Access, you had to make changes to the form in Design view. In Layout view, you can change these properties while looking at data instead of empty controls. Click the Property Sheet command in the Form Layout Tools Design tab's Tools group to display the Property Sheet for the selected control.

 For more information on changing control properties with the Property Sheet, see Chapter 17.

Setting the tab order

You may notice that when you use the Tab key to move from control to control, the cursor jumps around the screen. The route taken by the Tab key may seem strange, but that's the original order in which the controls were added to the form.

The tab order of the form is the order in which the focus moves from control to control as you press Tab. The form's default tab order is always the order in which the controls were added to the form. Moving controls around on the form means you'll need to change the form's tab order. Even though you may make heavy use of the mouse when designing your forms, most data-entry people use the keyboard, rather than the mouse, to move from control to control.

Select Tab Order from the Design tab's Tools group when you're in Design view to display the Tab Order dialog box, shown in Figure 18.14. This dialog box shows the controls in the form arranged in the current tab order. Controls such as labels, lines, and other non-data controls don't appear in the Tab Order dialog box.

FIGURE 18.14

The Tab Order dialog box.

The Tab Order dialog box lets you select one or more rows at a time. Multiple contiguous rows are selected by clicking the first control and dragging to select multiple rows. After highlighting rows, the selected rows can be dragged to their new positions in the tab order.

The Tab Order dialog box has several buttons at the bottom. Auto Order places the controls in order from left to right and from top to bottom, according to their position in the form. This button is a good starting place when the tab order is very disorganized. The OK button applies the changes to the form, while the Cancel button closes the dialog box without changing the tab order.

Each control has two properties related to the Tab Order dialog box. The Tab Stop property determines whether the cursor stops at the control when you press the Tab key. The default is Yes. Changing the Tab Stop property to No does not remove the control from the tab order, but the control is skipped when you reach its position by tabbing through the form. When you set the tab order in the Tab Order dialog box, you're setting each control's Tab Index property. Moving the fields around in the Tab Order dialog box changes the Tab Index properties of those (and other) controls.

CAUTION

Setting a control's Tab Stop property to No does not make the control read-only. The user can still select the control and change its value.

Modifying the format of text in a control

To modify the formatting of text within a control, select the control by clicking it, and then select a formatting style to apply to the control. The Format tab of the Ribbon (shown in Figure 18.15) contains additional commands for changing the format of a control.

FIGURE 18.15

The Format tab of the Ribbon for Layout view.

To change the fonts for the Category control, make sure you're in Layout view, and then follow these steps:

1. **Select the Category Text Box control in the form by clicking it.**

2. **Change Font Size to 14, and then click the Bold button in the Format tab's Font group.** The control may not automatically resize when changing certain font properties. If you see only a portion of the text box, the control may require resizing to display all the text.

Using the Field List to add controls

The form's Field List displays a list of fields from the table or query on which the form is based. Use the Add Existing Fields button on the Design tab to open it if the Field List is not currently visible. Drag fields from the Field List to the form's surface to add bound controls to the form. Select and drag them one at a time, or select multiple fields by using the Ctrl key or Shift key. The Field List in Layout view works the same as the Field List in Design view, which is described in detail in Chapter 17.

Click the Add Existing Fields command in the Design tab's Controls group to display the Field List, shown in Figure 18.16. By default, the Field List appears docked on the right of the Access window. This window is movable and resizable and displays a vertical scroll bar if it contains more fields than can fit in the window.

FIGURE 18.16

Adding fields from the Field List in a form's Layout view.

Access adds a control that's appropriate for the data type of the bound field. For example, dragging a text field to the form's surface adds a text box, while an OLE data field adds a Bound OLE Object control.

To add fields from the Field List to a new form, follow these steps:

1. **Select the Create tab on the Ribbon, and then select the Blank Form command in the Forms group to open a new form in Layout view. The new form is not bound to any data source.**

2. **If the Field List isn't displayed, select the Design tab of the Ribbon, and then select Add Existing Fields from the Tools group.**

3. **Double-click the ProductID and Cost fields in the Field List to add them to the form.**

> **TIP**
>
> You can select noncontiguous fields in the list by clicking each field while holding down the Ctrl key. The selected fields can be dragged (as part of the group) to the form's design surface. However, this technique does not work until the form is already bound to a data source—that is, until at least one field has been added.

Converting a Form to a Report

To save a form as a report, open the form in Design view and choose File ⇨ Save As. The entire form is saved as the report. If the form has headers or footers, these are used as the report's Header and Footer sections. If the form has page headers or page footers, these are used as the report's Page Header and Page Footer sections. You can now use the report in Design view, adding groups and other features without having to re-create the general layout all over again. You'll learn more about reports in Chapters 20 and 21.

Working with Form Controls

IN THIS CHAPTER

Setting properties for Access forms and controls

Creating a calculated control

Using subforms in Access

Reviewing basic techniques for designing forms

Learning advanced Access forms techniques

Working with Tab controls in Access forms

Collecting information with dialog boxes

Creating a form from scratch

*U*ser interface is a term you hear frequently in discussions about computer software. In virtually all applications built with Microsoft Access, the user interface consists of a series of Access forms. If you intend to develop successful Access applications, you need to understand Access forms inside and out.

This chapter helps you improve your understanding of forms. First, we show you some common controls and their properties. These controls are the building blocks out of which forms are built. We also show you some powerful ways to take advantage of subforms. We devote one section of the chapter to presenting a grab bag of forms-related programming techniques that will help you create forms that elicit the best performance from Access and your computer. Then we present a step-by-step tutorial for creating a form from scratch.

ON THE WEB
This chapter uses examples in the `Chapter19.accdb` database and other files available for download on this book's website.

Setting Control Properties

The building blocks of Access forms are known as *controls*. The Controls group on the Design tab of the Ribbon contains more than a dozen different types of controls from which you can build forms, including labels, text boxes, option groups, option buttons, toggle buttons, check boxes, combo boxes, list boxes, and other controls. This chapter doesn't discuss every type of Access form control in detail, but it does document the most commonly used controls found in Access applications.

Each control on an Access form has a set of properties that determines the control's appearance and behavior. In Design view, you manipulate a control's property settings through its Property Sheet. To display the Property Sheet, do one of the following:

- Right-click the object and select Properties from the shortcut menu.
- Select the object and click the Property Sheet button on the Ribbon.
- Press F4 with the object selected.

Once the Property Sheet is open, clicking any other control in the form displays the selected control's property settings. Figure 19.1 shows the Property Sheet for the command button named cmdNew on the Customers form (frmCustomers) in the Chapter19.accdb application.

FIGURE 19.1

The Property Sheet for the cmdNew command button.

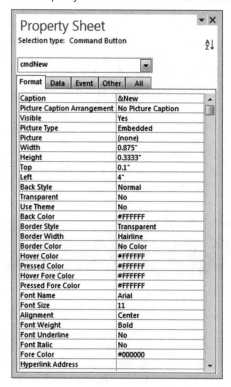

Property Sheet	
Selection type: Command Button	
cmdNew	

Format | Data | Event | Other | All

Caption	&New
Picture Caption Arrangement	No Picture Caption
Visible	Yes
Picture Type	Embedded
Picture	(none)
Width	0.875"
Height	0.3333"
Top	0.1"
Left	4"
Back Style	Normal
Transparent	No
Use Theme	No
Back Color	#FFFFFF
Border Style	Transparent
Border Width	Hairline
Border Color	No Color
Hover Color	#FFFFFF
Pressed Color	#FFFFFF
Hover Fore Color	#FFFFFF
Pressed Fore Color	#FFFFFF
Font Name	Arial
Font Size	11
Alignment	Center
Font Weight	Bold
Font Underline	No
Font Italic	No
Fore Color	#000000
Hyperlink Address	

The form itself also has its own set of properties. If you display the Property Sheet in Design view before selecting a specific control, Access lists the form's properties in the Property Sheet, as indicated by the selection type "Form" in the Property Sheet's title bar (see Figure 19.2). To display the form's properties in the Property Sheet after first displaying a control's properties, click a completely blank area in the form design window (outside the form's defined border).

FIGURE 19.2

The Property Sheet for the Customers form.

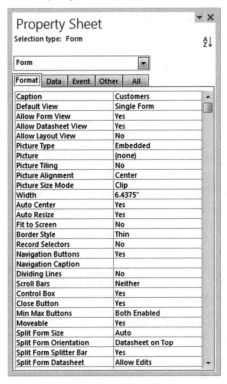

Customizing default properties

Whenever you create a control from the Ribbon, the control is created with a default set of property values. This may seem obvious, but what you may not know is that you can set many of these default values yourself. For example, if you want all list boxes in your form to be flat rather than sunken, it's more efficient to change the default Special Effect property to Flat before you design the form, instead of changing the Special Effect property for every list box individually.

To set control defaults, select a tool in the Controls group of the Design tab and then set properties in the Property Sheet without adding the control to the form. Notice that the title in the Property Sheet is "Selection type: Default <ControlType>." As you set the control's properties, you're actually setting the default properties for that type of control for the current form. Instead of adding the control to the form, select another control (such as the Select control in the upper-left corner of the Controls group) to "lock down" the default settings. Then, when you reselect the control you want, you'll see that the control's default properties have been set the way you wanted. When you save the form, the property defaults you've set for the form's controls are saved along with the form.

Looking at common controls and properties

In this section, we describe the most common controls needed to build an Access application and the properties that control their appearance and behavior. We don't list every control or property, but the controls and properties described here will give you a solid understanding of form development, and many of the properties are shared by other controls. Many properties work together to achieve a specific result, and the Property Sheet lists these related properties together.

The Text Box control

The Text Box control is the workhorse of controls when it comes to displaying data. The data in this control is always a String data type, even when it looks like a number or a date. The most important properties of the Text Box control determine how data is entered and displayed.

The Format property

The Format property determines the format of the data displayed. The choices available under Format are determined by the data type of the underlying field. For instance, Text Boxes bound to date fields show date formats, and Text Boxes bound to numeric fields show numeric formats. Unbound Text Boxes show all available formats.

When an appropriate Format is set, the Decimal Places property controls how many digits are displayed to the right of the decimal point.

The Format property does not affect the underlying value, only its display. If you set a Text Box to only display two decimal places and you enter three decimal places, the three decimals will be stored in the date, but only two will be displayed in the Text Box.

Properties that control appearance

The Back Style and Back Color properties control how the background of the Text Box is displayed. Setting Back Style to Transparent allows anything underneath the control to show through. A Back Style of Normal colors the background according to the Back Color property.

The Border Style, Border Width, and Special Effect properties control how the edges of the Text Box appear. Set Border Style to Transparent to show no border, or choose one of the other combinations of solid lines, dashes, and dots. When Border Style is set to something other than Transparent, the Border Width property controls the thickness of the border. There are several options for Special Effect that give your Text Boxes a more polished appearance.

Properties that control data appearance

Font Name and Font Size control the font of the data in the Text Box. While these properties can be set in the Property Sheet, they're more often set using the Format tab of the Ribbon.

The Text Align property can be set to General, Left, Center, Right, or Distribute. The General setting determines the most appropriate alignment for the data type displayed. Distribute attempts to fill the entire width of the Text Box with the data by increasing the spacing between characters.

The Font Underline and Font Italic properties are Yes/No options that determine if the data is shown with an underline or in an italicized font, respectively. Bold is the most common setting for the Font Weight property, but several other options allow a great deal of control of the boldness of the data.

The Fore Color property controls the color of the font. It's not simply a color name, however. It's actually a number that represents the value of the text color in the control. The easiest way to set this property is to use the Font Color command on the Format tab of the Ribbon.

Data entry properties

The Text Format property can be set to Plain Text or Rich Text. Rich Text is a format that allows you to apply formatting to the characters during data entry. When you enter data in a Text Box whose Text Format property is set to Rich Text, certain controls on the Ribbon are enabled that are disabled for Plain Text. The data is stored with HTML tags that define the formatting that is applied. If you set a bound control's Text Format property to Rich Text, make sure the underlying field is also Rich Text.

The Input Mask property can be set to limit how data is entered. There are several built-in input masks, such as Phone Number and Social Security Number, that can be used to encourage the user to enter data correctly. You can also create your own input masks—for instance, if your company uses part numbers that are in a well-defined format.

The Default Value property is used to populate a Text Box with a defined value when a new record is created. In addition to hard-coded values, calculations can be used to create a different Default Value depending on the values of other controls.

The Validation Rule and Validation Text properties can be used to ensure that the user has entered data that is appropriate for the Text Box. For instance, you may want to limit the entry of a date into a text box to only a certain range of dates. The Validation Rule property can be set to show a message when data falls outside a range. If a rule is broken, Validation Text is used to give the user more information about what is expected in the Text Box.

19

The Command Button control

Just as the Text Box control is the workhorse of data entry, the Command Button control is the go-to control for user actions. Command Buttons are used to run macros or VBA code. Common actions associated with the Command Button are showing another form, navigating to another record, or automating another Office application.

Properties that control appearance

The Command Button control has many of the same appearance-related properties as the Text Box control. And they work in much the same way. In addition, the Command Button has the Picture Type and Picture properties that allow you to specify an image to be shown as a button.

The Hover Color, Hover Fore Color, Pressed Color, and Pressed Fore Color properties control the appearance of the Command Button when the user hovers over it or when the user clicks it. They can be used to provide a visual indicator of where the user's mouse is and give the user confidence that the correct button was pressed.

Default action properties

The Default property is a Yes/No property. When set to Yes, the user can press Enter anywhere on the form and get the same effect as clicking the Command Button. A Command Button with the Default property set to Yes is a useful to tool to speed data entry on a form.

The Cancel property is also a Yes/No property and is closely related to the Default property. When set to Yes, the user can press Esc anywhere on the form and get the same effect as clicking the Command Button. Generally, a Command Button designated as Cancel should perform an action consistent with cancelling the current operation or closing the form.

> **TIP**
>
> Only one Command Button can be designated as Default. Similarly, only one Command Button can be designated as Cancel. Setting either of these properties to Yes will set the property for all other Command Buttons on the form to No.

The Combo Box and List Box controls

The Combo Box and List Box controls are used to display a list to the user to aid in data entry. The List Box control shows as many items as the size of the control will allow while the Combo Box must be clicked to display the list. The Combo Box gets its name because it is intended to be a combination of a Text Box and a List Box. The user can either enter text directly into the Text Box part of a Combo Box or select an item from the List Box portion. Properties unique to Combo Boxes and List Boxes control how the data is displayed and what actions the user can take with the list.

List content properties

The Row Source property determines what data is displayed in the list. The list data generally comes from a Table, Query, or SQL statement. It can also be a list of values typed directly into Row Source at design time or assigned at run time. The Row Source Type property determines what options are available for the Row Source property. When Row Source Type is set to `Value List`, the form designer can type a list of values into Row Source. When Row Source Type is set to `Table/Query`, Row Source can be a table name, query name, or SQL statement. The third option for Row Source Type is `Field List`. When Row Source Type is set to `Field List`, Row Source can be a table name, query name, or SQL statement, just like when it's set to `Table/Query`. The difference is that the control will display a list of the field names rather than the values.

The Bound Column property determines the "value" of the control. List Boxes and Combo Boxes can show more than one column of data in the list. When two or more columns are shown, Bound Column determines which column's data will be stored in the field for bound controls or saved for later use in unbound controls.

List display properties

The Column Count property determines how many columns exist (but not necessarily displayed) in the list. If this property's value does not equal the number of columns in the data (defined by the Row Source property), some data may not be shown or blank columns may be shown. The Column Widths property holds a semicolon-delimited list of values that represent the width of each column. If the property is left blank or if fewer column widths are entered than specified in Column Count, Access guesses how wide to make the unspecified columns. The Column Heads property is a Yes/No property that determines if column headings are displayed at the top of the list.

The List Rows property is a number that specifies how many list items to show. If there are more list items than specified in List Rows, a vertical scroll bar appears for the user to scroll down to see more list items. The List Width property determines how wide the list is. You can use a wide list with a relatively narrow Combo Box as a very efficient use of space on your form. List Rows and List Width are not properties associated with the List Box control. The List Box control shows as many rows as will fit and is as wide as the control itself.

List selection properties

For Combo Boxes, the Validation Rule, Validation Text, and Input mask properties work the same as they do for Text Boxes. List Boxes do not have these properties because the user is restricted to selecting items in the list.

The Limit To List property of the Combo Box control is a Yes/No property. A setting of `Yes` forces the user to type or select only values that are in the list, making the Combo Box work the same as a List Box. A setting of `No` allows the user to either select an item from the list or type an unlisted value in the Combo Box.

19

The Multi Select property that applies to List Boxes determines how the user can select multiple items in the List Box. A value of None means that multiple selection is not allowed. A value of Simple means that items are selected or deselected one at a time by clicking them. A value of Extended means that items can be selected one at a time by holding down the Ctrl key and clicking the time or in blocks by holding down the Shift key and clicking the last item in the block.

The Check Box and Toggle Button controls

The Check Box and Toggle Button controls are most commonly bound to Yes/No fields. A check mark in a Check Box control and a depressed Toggle Button are Yes values. An empty Check Box and a raised Toggle Button are No values. The Triple State property is unique to these two controls. When Triple State is set to Yes, the Check Box or Toggle Button can represent three values: Yes, No, and Null. Triple State is useful when you want to track whether the user has positively set the field to Yes or No.

The Option Group control

An Option Group isn't really a control at all. In fact, it's a group of separate, but related, controls. The group contains a Frame control and one or more Option Button controls. When you create an Option Group, you also have the option of using Check Box controls or Toggle Button controls instead of Option Buttons. Check Boxes and Toggle Buttons that are part of an Option Group behave differently than the same controls that are not part of an Option Group. Controls that are part of an Option Group are mutually exclusive—that is, selecting one of the controls automatically deselects the others in the group.

The Frame Control determines the value that is stored in the database. It has a Control Source property that identifies which field it's bound to. It also has a Default Value property that works the same as the Default Value property in other types of controls. The option controls within the Frame don't have these properties.

The option controls have an Option Value property. This property determines the actual value that is inherited by the Frame control and eventually stored in a field or saved for future use. By default, Access assigns the numbers 1, 2, 3, and so on to the option controls in the order in which they appear in the Frame.

> **TIP**
> You can change the Option Value property, but be careful not to assign the same number to two different controls.

The Web Browser control

The Web Browser control is a mini web browser on your form. You can use it to display data that the user completing the form might find useful, like a map or product photos kept on a web server. The key property of the Web Browser control is the Control Source property.

Control Source takes a formula of sorts. A proper Control Source value is an equal sign followed by the URL of a website enclosed in double quotes. For example, `="http://www.wiley.com"` will display that web page in the Web Browser control. Generally, the Control Source property is changed with VBA based on other data entered in the form.

Creating a Calculated Control

Unbound controls may use an expression as their Control Source property. As the form loads, Access evaluates the expression and populates the control with the value returned by the expression. The following example demonstrates creating an unbound calculated control:

1. **Select the Create tab of the Ribbon, and then click the Form Design command in the Forms group.** A new form appears in Design view.

2. **If the Field List is not visible, click the Add Existing Fields command on the Form Design Tools Design tab and click the Show all tables link.**

3. **From tblProducts, drag RetailPrice and Cost from the Field List onto the form's surface.**

4. **Click Text Box in the Controls group, and draw a new text box on the form.**

5. **Set the Name property to** txtCalculatedProfit **and set its Control Source property to** =[RetailPrice]-[Cost].

7. **Change the Format property to Currency and its Decimal Places to Auto.**

8. **Change the label's Caption property to** Net Profit:.

9. **Switch to Form view to test the expression.** Your form should look similar to Figure 19.3. txtCalculatedProfit shows the difference between the RetailPrice and Cost.

FIGURE 19.3

Creating a calculated control.

19

Working with Subforms

Subforms are indispensable for displaying information from two different tables or queries on the screen together. Typically, subforms are used where the main form's record source has a one-to-many relationship with the subform's record source—that is, many records in the subform are associated with one record in the main form.

Access uses the LinkMasterFields and LinkChildFields properties of the Subform control to choose the records in the subform that are related to each record in the main form. Whenever a value in the main form's link field changes, Access automatically queries the subform again.

When creating a subform, you might want to display subform aggregate information in the master form. For example, you might want to display the count of the records in the subform somewhere on your main form. For an example of this technique, see the txtItemCount control in frmCustomerSales in Chapter19.accdb. In this case, the Control Source expression in the txtItemCount control is

```
="(" & [subfPurchases].[Form]![txtItemCount] & " items)"
```

(Note that the equal sign needs to be included.) The result of this expression is shown in Figure 19.4.

FIGURE 19.4

Aggregate data from a subform can be displayed on the main form.

Before you can put aggregate data in the master form, its value must be found in the subform. To do this, place a text box wherever you want in the subform, and set its Visible property to No (False) so that it's hidden. Put an aggregate expression, such as = Count([ProductID]), into the Control Source property of the hidden control.

In the main form, insert a new text box with Control Source set to the following value:

> =[*Subform1*].Form![*Name-of-Aggregate-Control*]

where *Subform1* is the name of the control on the main form that contains the embedded subform and *Name-of-Aggregate-Control* is the name of the control on the subform that contains the aggregate data. The name of the control, Subform1 in this example, is not necessarily the name of the Form object that the control contains. When you add .Form to the name of the control, you refer to the underlying form, and you don't need to know its object name.

The control on the main form updates each time you change its value in the subform.

Form Design Tips

Following is a grab bag of form design tips that you might find handy. We hope they inspire you to come up with many more on your own!

Using the Tab Stop property

From time to time, you might place a control on a form that is intended to trigger a fairly drastic result, such as deleting a record or printing a long report. If you want to reduce the risk that the user might activate this control by accident, you might want to make use of the Tab Stop property, which specifies whether you can use the Tab key to move the focus to the control.

For example, suppose you've placed a command button named cmdDelete on a form that deletes the current record. You don't want the user to click this button by mistake. Modify the Tab Stop property of cmdDelete to No to remove the button from the form's tab order (the default is Yes). A user will have to explicitly click the button to activate it, and the user won't be able to accidentally choose it while entering data.

19

Tallying check boxes

If you ever need to count the number of True values in a Check Box control, consider using the following expression:

> Sum(Abs([*CheckBoxControl*]))

Abs converts every –1 to 1, and the Sum function adds them up. To count False values, use the following expression:

> Sum([*CheckBoxControl*] + 1)

Each True value (–1) is converted to 0 and each False value (0) is converted to 1 before being summed.

Setting up combo boxes and list boxes

Combo boxes and list boxes are powerful tools in your form-building toolbox, but they can be complicated to set up. When you build combo boxes and list boxes, it's important to keep in mind the distinction between Control Source (the table or query field to and from which the control saves and loads data) and Row Source (the source of the data displayed in the list). Because combo and list boxes support multiple columns, they allow you to easily relate data from another table without basing your form on a query that joins the tables. This technique, which involves a bound Combo Box or List Box control that stores an ID number but displays names in a list, is used in the Organization combo box in the form named frmContacts_Northwind in Chapter19.accdb.

For example, suppose you're creating a form to display information about your clients and customers (your "contacts"), and you want to identify the organization with which these contacts are associated. In a well-designed database, you store only an organization ID number with each contact record, while you store the organization's name and other information in a separate table. You want your form to include a combo box that displays organization names and addresses in the list but stores organization ID numbers in the field. (For an example of this technique, see frmContacts_Northwind in Chapter19.accdb.)

To accomplish your design goal, create a multiple-column combo box. Set the Control Source to the OrgID field (the field in the Contacts table that contains the organization ID number for each contact person). Set the Row Source Type property of the combo box to Table/Query. You could base the list on a table, but you want the list of names to be sorted; instead, set the Row Source property to a query that includes OrgID numbers in the first field, and organization names sorted ascending in the second field. The best way to do this is using the Query Builder for the Row Source property to create a SQL statement; alternatively, you can create and save a query to provide the list. In the frmContacts_Northwind example (the Organization combo box), the Row Source query is as follows:

```
SELECT Organizations.OrgID, Organizations.Name,
Organizations.AddressLine1, Organizations.AddressLine2,
Organizations.City, Organizations.State,
Organizations.ZipCode, Organizations.Country
FROM Organizations ORDER BY Organizations.Name
```

Because you're interested in seeing all this data listed in the combo box, set the Column Count property to 8 (the number of fields in the SELECT statement). You hide the OrgID column in a minute, but you need it in the combo box Row Source because it contains the data that's saved by the control when a row is selected by the user. This column is identified by the combo box's Bound Column property (set to 1 by default). The bound column containing ID numbers doesn't have to be visible to the user. The Column Widths property contains a semicolon-separated list of visible column widths for the columns in the drop-down list. Access uses default algorithms to determine the widths of any columns for which you don't explicitly choose a width. If you choose a width of 0 for any column, that column is hidden from the user on the screen, but it isn't hidden from the rest of your forms, VBA code, or macros. In this case, you set the property to the following:

```
0";1.4";1.2";0.7";0.7";0.3;0.5";0.3"
```

This indicates to Access that you want the first column to be invisible and sets explicit column widths for the other columns.

The second column—in this case, the organization name—is the one against which the user's text input is matched. The first visible column in the combo box is always used for this purpose. Figure 19.5 shows the resulting drop-down list. Although this is a rather extreme example of loading a combo box with data, it effectively illustrates the power of the Access Combo Box control.

FIGURE 19.5

The drop-down list for the Organization combo box.

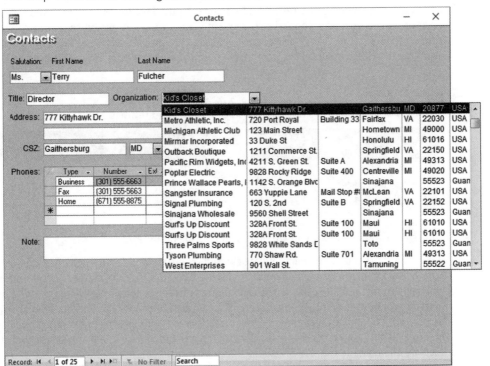

When working with combo boxes, if you set the Limit To List property to Yes, the user is required to choose from only the entries in the drop-down list. You can then construct an event procedure for the control's NotInList event to handle what should happen if a user enters a value not in the list. You might want to open a form into which the user can enter new information; or perhaps you want to display a message box that instructs the user what procedure to follow to add data.

Tackling Advanced Forms Techniques

Access contains many powerful and exciting features in its forms design and user interface capabilities. As you now know, the forms in your applications are the main component of the user interface. To a large extent, a user's perception of an application's ease of use and strength is determined by the attractiveness and effectiveness of its user interface. Microsoft has provided Access forms with significant capabilities to control the user interface. Many of these features have been in Access for a very long time but haven't been discovered by many developers.

Using the Page Number and Date/Time controls

Forms often include the current date and time. Many developers add this information to a form or report with an unbound text box, and the Date() function to return this information to the unbound text box. Access simplifies this process with the Date and Time command in the Header/Footer group on the Design tab of the Ribbon (see Figure 19.6).

FIGURE 19.6

These commands simplify adding the date to forms and reports.

Figure 19.6 shows the Ribbon when a form is in Design view.

When the Date and Time command is selected, the Date and Time dialog box (shown in Figure 19.7) appears, asking how you want the date and time formatted. After you make your selections and click OK, Access adds a form header containing the date and time formatted as you requested. If you change your mind about how the date or time should be formatted, you can always change the Format property of the text box added by this command. The date and time shown in the header reflects when the form was opened, not necessarily the current time.

The Header/Footer group includes other commands for adding a logo (virtually any image file) and a title to the form header area. Using the Header/Footer controls in an application gives all the forms a consistent appearance (see Figure 19.8, which is frmDialog in the sample database).

FIGURE 19.7

Tell Access how you want the date to appear.

FIGURE 19.8

The header and footer controls provide a consistent look to your Access forms.

Using the Image control

A subtle and often overlooked performance issue in Access applications occurs when static images are added to forms. Images are often added to Access forms as OLE objects, which means that a certain amount of memory and disk space is required to maintain the image's connection to its parent application. This overhead is used even when the image is a company logo or other graphic that will not be changed or edited at run time.

19

Access simplifies this process and provides a great deal more flexibility with the Image control. The Image control places an image frame onto a form or report but doesn't burden the image object with the overhead associated with OLE objects. The Image control accepts virtually any type of image data type recognized by Windows (BMP, PCX, ICO, DIB, GIF, WMF, JPG, PNG, TIF, and so on) and enables you to specify the path to the image file at run time in its Picture property. The Image control also accepts image data stored in an Access table, although it doesn't provide the flexibility of in-place editing.

Morphing a control

Surely one of the most frustrating problems when building Access forms is the need to specify the control type when a control is added to a form. For example, consider the issues involved when you add a list box to an Access form; specify the Control Source, Row Source Type, Row Source, and other properties; and then discover there's not enough room on the form for the list box. In this case, it seems the only solution is to remove the list box, add a combo box, and reset all the properties, even though the properties for the combo box are identical for the list box you just removed.

In Access, you can change a control to any other compatible type. For example, a text box can be changed to a label, list box, or combo box. Simply right-click the control and select the Change To command from the shortcut menu to see the options. Figure 19.9 shows the options for changing a Text Box control.

FIGURE 19.9

Access lets you change the type of a control without losing the properties you've already set.

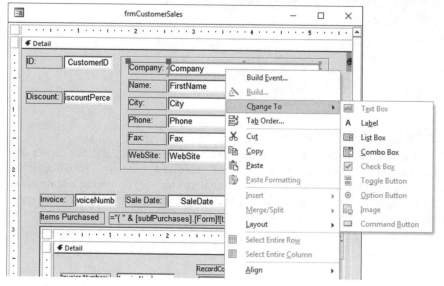

The choices you see in the shortcut menu are specific for the type of control you're changing. For example, an option button can be changed to a check box or toggle button but not to a text box.

Using the Format Painter

Access includes a Format Painter that functions much like the same feature in Word. When creating a form, you set the appearance of a control (such as its border, font, and special effects, like sunken or raised) and then click the Format Painter button on the Font group on the Design tab of the Ribbon to copy the properties to a special internal buffer. When you click another control of the same type, the appearance characteristics of the selected control are transferred to the second control. In Figure 19.10, the format properties of one text box are about to be "painted" onto the Phone text box. (The little paint brush adjacent to the mouse pointer tells you that you're in Paint mode.)

FIGURE 19.10

The Format Painter makes it easy to "paint" the appearance of a control onto other controls on a form.

You can lock the Format Painter by double-clicking its button on the Ribbon. Note that not all properties are painted onto the second control. The size, position, and data properties of the control are not affected by the Format Painter; only the most basic formatting properties are influenced by the Format Painter.

Offering more end-user help

All Microsoft Office programs feature ScreenTip help—those little notes that appear when you hover the mouse over a control or button.

You add ScreenTips to Access forms by adding the help text to the control's ControlTip Text property (see Figure 19.11). By default, the text in a ScreenTip doesn't wrap, but you can add a new line character by pressing Ctrl+Enter in the ControlTip Text property wherever you want the break to appear.

FIGURE 19.11

ScreenTips help make your applications easier to use.

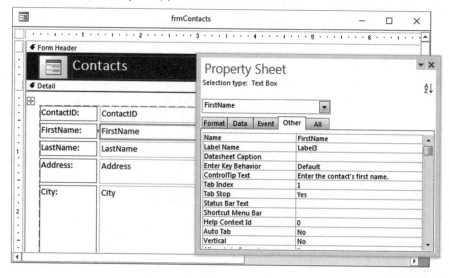

In general, you should use ScreenTips consistently throughout an application. After your users become accustomed to ScreenTips, they expect them on all but the most obvious controls.

Adding background pictures

Attractive forms are always valuable additions to Access applications. It's difficult to add color or graphics to forms without obscuring the data contained on the form. Access makes it easy to add a graphic to the background of a form, much as a watermark might appear on expensive bond paper. The picture can contain a company logo, text, or any other graphic element. The picture is specified by the form's Picture property and can be embedded in the form or linked to an external file. If the picture is linked, the graphic displayed on the form changes anytime the external file is edited.

The picture can also be positioned at any of the form's four corners or centered in the middle of the form. Although the picture can be clipped, stretched, or zoomed to fit the dimensions of the form, you can't modify the picture to make it smaller (other than editing the image file, of course). Figure 19.12 shows a small background picture of an automobile positioned in the upper-right corner of frmCustomerSales.

FIGURE 19.12

A small BMP file has been added to frmCustomerSales as the Picture property.

To add a picture to your form, open the form in Design view and show the Property Sheet. If the Property Sheet is not already showing the form's properties, choose Form from the combo box. Click the builder button for the Picture property to choose which picture to include on the form. Change the Picture Tiling, Picture Alignment, and Picture Size Mode properties to display the picture in different ways.

You can even make controls on a form transparent so that the form's background picture shows through the controls (see Figure 19.13). In this case (frmEmployees_Background), the Back Style property of each Label control is set to Transparent, letting the form's background picture show through.

FIGURE 19.13

Transparent Label controls allow the background picture to show through.

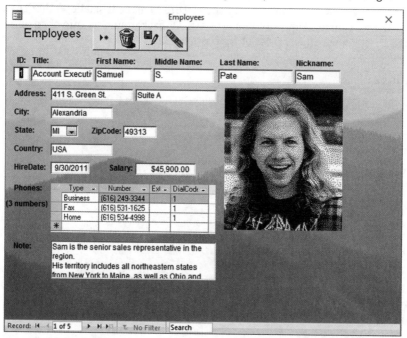

It's easy to overdo the background picture added to Access forms, but, when carefully used, background pictures can make forms easier for users to understand.

> **CAUTION**
>
> Background pictures added to a form noticeably slow down the form's appearance on the screen. Generally speaking, you should use a background picture only when the benefit provided by the picture outweighs the unavoidable performance degradation caused by the picture's presence.

Limiting the records shown on a form

Usually, the records that a form shows are determined by the Record Source property. To show fewer records, change the underlying query or SQL statement. However, sometimes you want to show a subset of records by default and still allow the user to see all the records if she chooses.

With the Filter property of the form, you can define a filter that limits the records shown. For example, on a form based on order, you may want to show only orders that haven't shipped yet but still allow the user to see any order. By setting the Filter property to

[Shipped Date] Is Null and setting the Filter On Load property to Yes, the form will open filtered only to records with no Shipped Date. The status bar of the form indicates that a filter is applied, as shown in Figure 19.14.

FIGURE 19.14

The status bar indicates that the form has a filter applied.

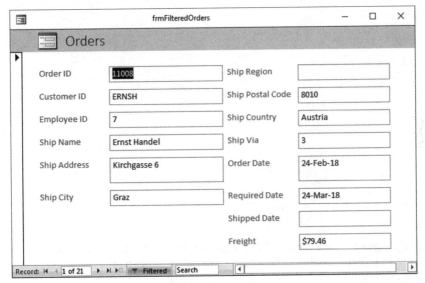

The user can click the Filtered button on the status bar to remove the filter and see all records. The button caption will change to Unfiltered. Another click of the button reapplies the filter.

Using the Tab Control

A Tab control provides several pages, each accessed through a tab at the top, bottom, or side of the dialog box. Figure 19.15 shows frmCustomers, a perfect example of a tabbed Access form. frmCustomers contains a Tab control with three pages, allowing the form to contain many more controls than possible without the Tab control. Each of the tabs along the top of the form reveals a different page of the form's data. Each page contains many controls. Figure 19.15 shows buttons, labels, and text boxes. Each control on the page behaves independently of all other controls on the form and can be accessed through Access VBA code as an independent unit.

FIGURE 19.15

The Tab control allows a form to host a large amount of data.

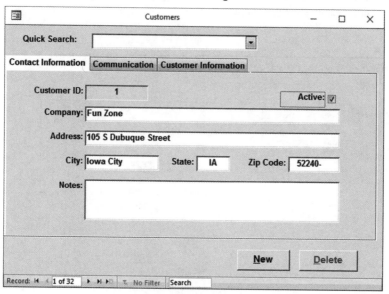

As you might guess, the Tab control is fairly complex. It includes its own properties, events, methods, and object collections. You have to know and understand these items before you can effectively use the Tab control in your applications.

> **NOTE**
> Developers often use the term *tab* when referring to the pages of a tabbed dialog box. In this chapter, the terms *page* and *tab* are used interchangeably.

A Tab control consists of a number of tabs. From the user interface, the quickest and easiest way to add or delete a page is to right-click the control and select the appropriate command from the shortcut menu (see Figure 19.16).

The Tab control contains some unique properties, some of which are described in Table 19.1. Use these properties to tailor the Tab controls in your applications to suit the needs of your users.

FIGURE 19.16

The Tab control's shortcut menu contains relevant commands.

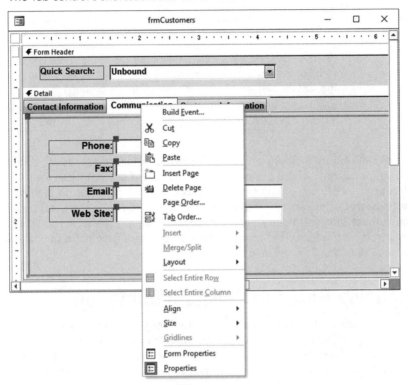

TABLE 19.1   Important Tab Control Properties

Property	Description
Caption	Applies to each page in the Tab control. Provides the text that appears on the tab.
Multi Row	Applies to the Tab control. Determines whether the tabs appear as a single row or as multiple rows. You can't specify how many tabs appear in each row. Instead, Access adds as many rows as necessary to display all tabs, given their respective widths.
Style	By default, tabs appear as tabs. The alternative (Buttons) forces the tabs to appear as command buttons.
Tab Fixed Height	This value determines the height (in inches or centimeters, depending on the units of measurement settings in Windows Settings) of the tabs on the control. When the Tab Fixed Height is set to 0, the tab height is determined by the size of the font specified for the Tab control.

Continues

19

TABLE 19.1   *(continued)*

Property	Description
Tab Fixed Width	This value determines the width (in inches or centimeters) of the tabs on the control. Text that is too wide to fit on the tab when the Tab Fixed Width value is set is truncated. When the Tab Fixed Width is set to 0, the width of the tab is determined by the font size selected for the Tab control and the text specified in the tab's Caption property.
Picture	Applies to each page on the Tab control. The Picture property specifies an image (BMP, ICO, or built-in picture) to display on the tab.

A Tab control can contain virtually any type of control, including text boxes, combo and list boxes, option buttons, check boxes, and OLE objects. A Tab control can even include other Tab controls! Although a form can contain multiple Tab controls, it's probably not a good idea to overload the user by putting more than one Tab control on a form. After all, the reason you use Tab controls in an application is to simplify the form by fitting multiple pages of controls within a single control. In most cases, there is no point in challenging the user with more than one Tab control on a form.

Using Dialog Boxes to Collect Information

The dialog box is one of the most valuable user-interface components in Windows applications. When properly implemented, dialog boxes provide a way to extend the available screen space on the computer. Instead of having to place every text box, option button, and other user input control on the main form, dialog boxes provide a handy way to move some of these controls to a convenient pop-up device that is on the screen only when needed.

Dialog boxes usually collect a certain type of information, such as font attributes or hard-copy parameters. Dialog boxes are a valuable way to prefilter or qualify user input without cluttering the main form. Or use a dialog box to allow the user to enter query criteria before running a query that populates a form or report or to gather information that is added to a report's header or footer area.

Although they are forms, dialog boxes typically don't look like or behave as other forms in the application do. Dialog boxes often pop up over the user's work. When properly implemented, dialog boxes also provide a means to simply cancel the query without breaking anything on the user's workspace.

A simple query form implemented as a dialog box is shown in Figure 19.8. This simple form asks for a zip code that is used to query the database for contact information.

The relevant properties of this dialog box are outlined in Table 19.2.

TABLE 19.2 Property Settings for Dialog Forms

Property	Setting	Purpose
Scroll Bars	Neither	Not needed
Navigation Buttons	No	Not needed
Pop Up	Yes	Keeps the form on top of other forms in the application
Modal	Yes	Prevents the user from working with another part of the application until the dialog box is removed
Record Selectors	No	Not needed
Border Style	Dialog	Specifies wide borders that can't be resized. Also removes Minimize and Maximize buttons
Shortcut Menu	No	Not needed

After these changes have been made, you have a form that's always on top of the user's work and won't leave the screen until the user clicks the Run Query or Cancel button.

There are a couple rules you should follow when constructing dialog boxes. These rules ensure that your dialog boxes conform to the generally accepted behavior for Windows dialog boxes.

Designing the query

When the user clicks Run Query, Access runs a query named qryDialog. The qryDialog query has a special criterion that uses the value in the form's only text box to limit the records shown. Here's the SQL statement for qryDialog:

```
SELECT Contacts.FirstName, Contacts.LastName Contacts.City,
    Contacts.State, Contacts.ZipCode FROM Contacts WHERE
    (((Contacts.ZipCode)=[Forms]![frmDialog]![txtZipCode]));
```

The WHERE clause references txtZipCode, a special type of parameter query. (See Chapter 13 for more on parameter queries.) The parameter uses a special syntax to reference a control on a form. As long as the form is open, the query can retrieve that value and insert it as criteria for the query. If the form is not open, Access won't understand what [Forms]![frmDialog] means, and it will prompt you for a value as if it were a standard parameter query.

Setting up the command buttons

When a command button is added to a form, Access presents a wizard to help you define the actions for the button. The Run Query action was selected for the Run Query button, as shown in Figure 19.17.

19

FIGURE 19.17

Assigning an action to a command button.

On the next screen of the wizard, qryDialog was selected as the query to run. Now when the button is clicked, that query will execute and use the form's text box as a criterion.

The Cancel button was similarly set up, except that Close Form was selected from the Form Operations category on the wizard.

Adding a default button

There should be a button on the form that's automatically selected if the user presses the Enter key while the dialog box is open. The default button doesn't have to be selected by the user to be triggered; Access automatically fires the default button's Click event as the user presses the Enter key.

For example, the user enters 22152 in the zip code text box and presses Enter. Unless a default button is specified, the input cursor simply moves to the next control. If you've designated the Run Query button as the dialog box's default, Access interprets the Enter key press as a Click event for the Run Query button.

Set the Run Query's Default property to Yes to make it the default for this dialog box. Only one button on a form can have its Default property set to Yes—if you move to the Cancel button and set its Default property to Yes, Access silently changes the Run Query's Default property to No.

Normally, the designated default button is on the left of the form. If you've arranged the command buttons vertically on a form, the top button should be the default.

You should select a button that won't cause trouble if accidentally triggered as the default for a form. For example, to avoid the risk of losing data, it's probably not a good idea to set a button that performs a delete action query as the default. In this case, you might decide to make the Cancel button the default.

Setting a Cancel button

The Cancel button on a form is automatically selected if the user presses the Esc key while the form is open. In most cases, you simply want the dialog box to disappear if the user hits the Esc key while the dialog box is open.

Set a button's Cancel property to designate it as the form's Cancel button. In this example, cmdCancel has been designated as the dialog box's Cancel button. As with the default button, only one button on a form can be the Cancel button. Access triggers the Cancel button's On Click event whenever the user presses the Esc key.

Removing the control menu

After you've designated default and Cancel buttons, you have no need for the control menu button in the upper-left corner of the form. Set the form's Control Box property to No to hide the control menu button. When the control menu box is removed, the user will have to use the Cancel or Run Query buttons to remove the form from the screen.

Designing a Form from Scratch

In this section, you'll create an invoice entry form from scratch and apply much of what you learned from this chapter and previous chapters. The main focus of this form will be to record sales, so tblSales will provide many of the fields you use.

Creating the basic form

To create the form, follow these steps:

1. **On the Create tab of the Ribbon, click Form Design.**

2. **On the Form Design Tools Design tab, click Add Existing Fields. The Field List pane appears.** The Add Existing Fields button is a toggle, so if it makes the Field List pane disappear, click it again to bring it back.

3. **From tblSales, double-click InvoiceNumber, SaleDate, InvoiceDate, CustomerID, SalespersonID, PaymentMethod, and TaxRate to add these fields to the form.** Don't worry about the placement of these controls just yet. At this point, your form should look similar to Figure 19.18.

4. **Save the form as frmInvoiceEntry.**

Your new form, frmInvoiceEntry, is a working form that's bound to tblSales. You can view the form in Form view and cycle through all the records in tblSales. It's nice to get something working so quickly, but you have some work to do to make it user friendly. The most glaring omission is that there's no way to identify the product being sold. Also, entering CustomerID and SalespersonID would require the user to have an outstanding memory (or very few customers and salespeople). Note that the frmInvoiceEntry form included in Chapter19.accdb is the final version of the form and has a few more features than the form at this stage.

19

FIGURE 19.18

Placing controls on a new form.

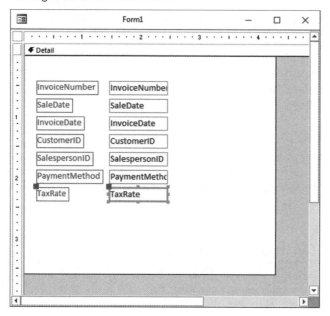

Creating a subform

Next, you'll add a subform so the user can enter products and quantities. The best way to add a subform is to create the form to be used as a subform on its own prior to adding it to the main form. To create the subform, follow these steps:

1. **From the Create tab on the Ribbon, click Form Design to create a new form.**

2. **From the tblSalesLineItems table, add the SalesLineItemID, InvoiceNumber, ProductID, Quantity, DiscountPercent, and SellingPrice fields to the subform.** This subform will be displayed as a datasheet on the main form, so it's not important that this form look pretty. It is important that the fields are in the order you want them to appear in the datasheet.

3. **Right-click the ProductID text box and choose Combo Box from the Change To menu.** This converts the ProductID control to a combo box so the user can select a product more easily.

4. **Change the Row Source property of ProductID to the following SQL statement:**

   ```
   SELECT ProductID, Description FROM tblProducts ORDER BY Description;
   ```

5. **Change the Column Count property to** 2, **the Column Widths property to** 0";1", **and the Bound Column property to** 1. The Column Widths property determines how wide the columns are in the drop-drown list. By setting the first column width to zero, the first column is hidden. The Bound Column property determines which field is stored in the table. In this case, the first field (ProductID) is stored in the table. This is a very typical way to select values on a form. The user sees the user-friendly Description field, but the database-friendly ProductID field is stored.

6. **Change the label from ProductID to** Product. Also, change the DiscountPercent label to **Discount%** and the SellingPrice label to **Price**.

7. **Change the Default View property of the Form to Datasheet.** That's the view you'll want when you display the subform on the main form.

8. **Save the form as sfrmInvoiceEntryLines, and compare what you have to Figure 19.19.**

FIGURE 19.19

A subform for invoice lines.

Adding the subform

To add the subform to the main form, follow these steps:

1. **Open frmInvoiceEntry in Design view.**

2. **Draw a Subform/Subreport control across the bottom of the form.** The SubForm Wizard will appear as shown in Figure 19.20.

FIGURE 19.20

Selecting an existing form as a subform.

3. **Choose Use an Existing Form and select sfrmInvoiceEntryLines, and then click Next.**

4. **On the next screen of the SubForm Wizard, choose the first option for linking the forms, as shown in Figure 19.21, and click Next.**

FIGURE 19.21

Linking a subform to a main form.

5. **Keep the default name on the final screen of the wizard and click Finish.**

6. **Delete the label that was automatically created for the subform.**

> **NOTE**
>
> When you add a subform, Access does a good job of guessing how the main form and subform are linked. In the fourth step and in Figure 19.21, you accepted the guess that Access made for the link. That step of the wizard actually sets two properties of the subform: Link Master Fields and Link Child Fields.
>
> The Link Master Fields property contains the name of the field on the main form that links to the subform. Similarly, the Link Child Fields property contains the name of the field on the subform. In the example in this section, both properties contain the field InvoiceNumber. InvoiceNumber is a field on both the main form and the subform that ties the two together.
>
> If Access guesses wrong, you can easily change these properties by typing in the proper field names or by clicking the build button next to one of the properties and selecting the proper fields from a list.

Now that you've added a subform to your main form, you have a rather messy-looking form. Don't worry—we're going to spruce it up. The subform displays inside the main form in Design view even though we'll be displaying it in Datasheet view when we show the main form. The subform is fully editable while inside the main form.

In general, the best way to create a form in Access is to follow three steps:

1. **Add all the controls and subforms you want to the form.**

2. **Set the form and control properties that affect the behavior of the form.**

3. **Position the controls on the form and set the properties that affect the appearance of the form.**

You can do the second two steps in the opposite order, but you'll find it easier to save fine-tuning the form's appearance until after you have the form working correctly.

Changing the form's behavior

The next step in the form design is to get the form working properly. You need to change some properties of the form and its controls to get the desired behavior.

Setting the form properties

Change the following form properties to the values given:

- **Caption:** New Invoice Entry
- **Allow Datasheet View:** No
- **Allow Layout View:** No
- **Record Selectors:** No
- **Navigation Buttons:** No
- **Control Box:** No
- **Data Entry:** Yes
- **Cycle:** Current Record

19

These are typical property settings for a data entry form. The purpose of the form is to enter a new invoice, so hiding the record navigation aspects of the form makes sense. The Data Entry property ensures that the form shows a new record when it's opened. Setting the Cycle property to Current Record disables the default behavior of moving to the next record when the user leaves the last field. By disabling that behavior, you can control when the record is saved.

Looking up values during data entry

On the subform, we converted the ProductID text box to a combo box so that the user would be selecting from a list of descriptions rather than a list of numbers. On the main form, there are more fields where we can use the same technique: CustomerID, SalespersonID, PaymentMethod, and TaxRate. In these cases, it'll be easier for the user entering the invoice to select from a name or other description rather than an ID. To convert the CustomerID text box into a combo box, follow these steps:

1. **Right-click the CustomerID text box and choose Combo Box from the Change To menu.**

2. **Change the Row Source property to** `SELECT CustomerID, Company FROM tblCustomers ORDER BY Company;`.

3. **If necessary, change the Limit To List property to** `Yes`.

4. **Change the Column Count property to 2 and the Column Widths property to 0";1".**

Change the properties of the other controls similarly. The Row Source property of each control is shown in Table 19.3. Be sure to change the Column Count property based on the number of fields returned in the SQL statement.

TABLE 19.3 **Row Source Properties**

Control Name	Row Source Property
CustomerID	SELECT CustomerID, Company FROM tblCustomers ORDER BY Company;
SalespersonID	SELECT SalespersonID, SalespersonName FROM tblSalesperson ORDER BY SalespersonName;
PaymentMethod	SELECT PaymentType FROM tblPaymentType;
TaxRate	SELECT TaxLocation, TaxRate FROM tblTaxRates ORDER BY TaxRate DESC;

The CustomerID and SalespersonID fields store a foreign key from another table just as ProductID did on the subform. The PaymentMethod and TaxRate fields are a little different. For example, the PaymentMethod control doesn't store a foreign key to tblPaymentType. Instead, it stores text, and tblPaymentType simply stores common payment types. Similarly, tblTaxRates stores some common tax rates to choose from. For both PaymentMethod and TaxRate, ensure the Limit To List property is set to No so the user can enter whatever value is appropriate.

Note also that the value from tblTaxRates that we want to store in the tblSales table is from the second column. To store the proper value, change the Bound Column property of TaxRate to 2. Since the PaymentMethod only has one column and you want to show both columns for TaxRate, leave the Column Widths property blank for both controls. When Column Widths is blank, Access displays all columns and chooses a width that's best for the data.

Saving the record

The last area of form behavior is saving the record. Earlier, you set the Cycle property to Current Record to prevent the record from changing when the user leaves the last field. You can control the flow of the form through command buttons. To create a command button to save the record, follow these steps:

1. **From the Controls group of the Design tab of the Ribbon, select the Button control and place it on the form.**
2. **On the Command Button Wizard's first screen, select Record Navigation and Go to Next Record, and then click Next.**
3. **On the next screen of the wizard, check the Show All Pictures check box and choose the Save Record picture, and then click Next.**
4. **On the last screen of the wizard, name the button** cmdSave **and click Finish.**

Using a Command Button to go to the next record automatically saves the current record. It provides a more familiar interface to saving than simply leaving the last field. It also displays a new, empty record ready for more data entry.

You should also provide a way for the user to cancel entering the invoice. Add another command button to the form and choose Undo Record from the Record Operations group in the wizard. Choose the default picture for Undo and name the button *cmdCancel*.

Finally, you'll need to add a button that allows the user to close the form. You set the Control Box property to No so that the X at the top right of the form is hidden. Add a button to the form that uses the Close Form action from the Form Operations category. Name the button *cmdClose*.

19

Changing the form's appearance

The last step is to make the form pretty. On the main form, change the width and placement of the controls and position the command buttons near the bottom right. On the subform, make the width of the SalesLineItemID and InvoiceNumber columns zero by dragging the right border of each column all the way to the left. To drag the border of these columns, you'll need to view the form in Form view. Figure 19.22 shows the placement of the controls.

FIGURE 19.22

Controls placed on a form.

Finally, change the tab order of the controls on the form. Click the Tab Order control on the Design tab of the Ribbon to show the Tab Order dialog box, as shown in Figure 19.23. Once the tab order is set, change the Tab Stop property of the InvoiceNumber control to No. The invoice number is an AutoNumber field, so the user doesn't need access to that field.

FIGURE 19.23

Setting the tab order of controls.

Presenting Data with Access Reports

IN THIS CHAPTER

Looking at the different types of Access reports

Creating reports with the Report Wizard

Creating a report from scratch

Improving a report's appearance

R eports provide a great way to view and print data from your database. You can display information highly summarized, with a lot of detail, or anywhere in between, and you can view or print your information in many different formats. You can add multilevel totals, statistical comparisons, and pictures and graphics to a report.

In this chapter, you learn to use the Report Wizard as a starting point. You also learn how to create reports from scratch and discover what types of reports you can create with Access.

> **ON THE WEB**
> In this chapter, you create new reports using the Report Wizard and by creating a blank report without using a wizard. You use tables created in previous chapters. The `Chapter20.accdb` database file on the book's website contains the completed reports described in this chapter.

Introducing Reports

Reports present a customized view of your data. Report output is viewed onscreen or printed to provide a hard copy of the data. Very often, reports provide summaries of the information contained in the database. Data can be grouped and sorted in any order and can be used to create totals that perform statistical operations on data. Reports can include pictures and other graphics as well as memo fields. If you can think of a report you want, Access probably supports it.

Identifying the different types of reports

Three basic types of reports are used by most businesses:

- **Tabular reports:** Print data in rows and columns with groupings and totals. Variations include summary and group/total reports.
- **Columnar reports:** Print data and can include totals and graphs.
- **Mailing label reports:** Create labels that work with a variety of manufacturers.

Tabular reports

Tabular reports are similar to a table displaying data in rows and columns. Figure 20.1 is a typical tabular report (rptProductsSummary) displayed in Print Preview.

FIGURE 20.1

A tabular report (rptProductsSummary) displayed in Print Preview.

| | | rptProductsSummary | | | | — □ × |

Products Summary
Collectible Mini Cars

Category	Product I	Description	Qty in Stock	Retail Price	Cost	Profit
Cars						
	1	Buick Skylark	1	$27.99	$16.79	$11.20
	2	Cord 810	1	$39.99	$23.99	$16.00
	3	Chevrolet Corvette Con	1	$25.99	$15.59	$10.40
	4	Chevrolet Corvette Con	1	$21.99	$13.19	$8.80
	5	Chevrolet Bel Air Conve	1	$34.99	$20.99	$14.00
	6	Ford Fairlane	1	$31.99	$19.19	$12.80
	7	Buick T-Type	1	$32.99	$19.79	$13.20
	8	Pontiac Vibe	1	$19.99	$11.99	$8.00
	9	Pontiac Fiero GT	1	$23.14	$13.88	$9.26
	10	Chrysler Crossfire	1	$27.99	$16.79	$11.20
	11	Ford Saleen Mustang	1	$0.00	$0.00	$0.00
	12	Chevrolet Camaro 35th	1	$33.00	$19.80	$13.20
	13	Ford Coupe 2-Door	1	$27.99	$16.79	$11.20
	14	Ford Mustang	1	$27.99	$16.79	$11.20
	15	Ford Convertible	1	$23.99	$14.39	$9.60
	16	Volkswagen Beetle	1	$21.99	$13.19	$8.80
	18	Aston-Martin Mark II	1	$44.99	$26.99	$18.00

5/27/2018 9:56:02 AM   Page 1 of 7

Page: ◄ ◄ 1 ► ► ⁒ No Filter

Unlike forms or datasheets, tabular reports often group data by one or more fields. Often, tabular reports calculate and display subtotals or statistical information for numeric fields in each group. Some reports include page totals and grand totals. You can even have multiple snaked columns so that you can create directories (such as telephone books). These types of reports often use page numbers, report dates, or lines and boxes to separate information. Reports may have color and shading and display pictures, business graphs, and memo fields. A special type of summary tabular report has all the features of a detail tabular report but omits record details.

Columnar reports

Columnar reports generally display one or more records per page, but they do so vertically. Columnar reports display data very much as a data entry form does, but they're used strictly for viewing data and not for entering it. Figure 20.2 shows part of a columnar report (rptProducts) in Print Preview.

FIGURE 20.2

A columnar report showing report controls distributed throughout the entire page.

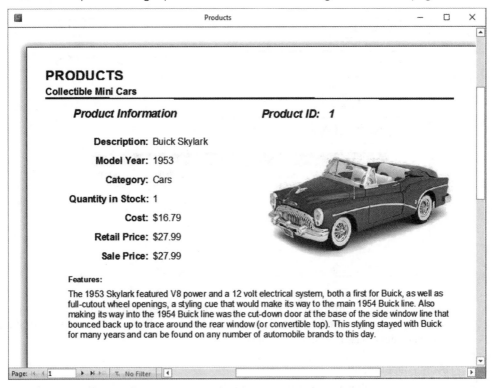

Another type of columnar report displays one main record per page (like a business form) but can show many records within embedded subreports. An invoice is a typical example. This type of report can have sections that display only one record and at the same time have sections that display multiple records from the "many" side of a one-to-many relationship—and even include totals.

Figure 20.3 shows an invoice report (rptInvoice) from the Collectible Mini Cars database system in Report view.

FIGURE 20.3

An invoice report (rptInvoice).

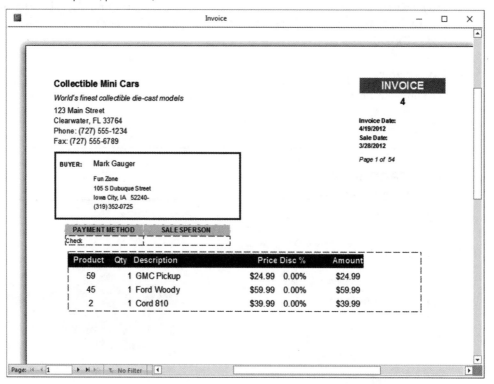

In Figure 20.3, the information in the top portion of the report is on the "main" part of the report, whereas the product details near the bottom of the figure are contained in a subreport embedded within the main report.

Mailing label reports

Mailing labels (shown in Figure 20.4) are also a type of report. Access includes a Label Wizard to help you create this type of report. The Label Wizard enables you to select from a long list of label styles. Access accurately creates a report design based on the label style you select. You can then open the report in Design mode and customize it as needed.

FIGURE 20.4

rptCustomerMailingLabels, a typical mailing label report.

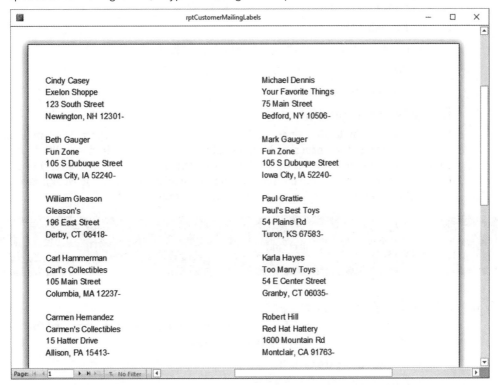

Distinguishing between reports and forms

The main difference between reports and forms is the intended output. Whereas forms are primarily for data entry and interaction with the users, reports are for viewing data (either onscreen or in hard-copy form). Calculated fields can be used with forms to display an amount based on other fields in the record. With reports, you typically perform calculations on groups of records, a page of records, or all the records included in the report. Anything you can do with a form—except input data—can be duplicated by a report. In fact, you can save a form as a report and then refine it in the Report Design window.

20

Creating a Report, from Beginning to End

The report process begins with your desire to view data, but in a way that differs from a form or datasheet display. The purpose of the report is to transform raw data into a meaningful set of information. The process of creating a report involves several steps:

1. **Define the report layout.**
2. **Assemble the data.**
3. **Create the report with the Access Report Wizard.**
4. **Print or view the report.**
5. **Save the report.**

Defining the report layout

You should begin by having a general idea of the layout of your report. You can define the layout in your mind, on paper, or interactively using the Report Designer. When laying out a report, consider how the data should be sorted (for example, chronologically or by name), how the data should be grouped (for example, by invoice number or by week), and how the size of the paper used to print the report will constrain the data.

> **NOTE**
>
> An Access report often is expected to duplicate an existing paper report or form used by the application's consumers. In that case, the layout is already defined.

Assembling the data

After you have a general idea of the report layout, assemble the data needed for the report. Access reports use data from two primary sources:

- A single database table
- A recordset produced by a query

You can join tables in a query and use the query's recordset as the record source for your report. A query's recordset appears to an Access report as if it were a single table.

As you learned in Chapter 8, you use queries to specify the fields, records, and sort order of the records stored in tables. Access treats a recordset's data as if it were a single table (for processing purposes) in datasheets, forms, and reports. When the report is run, Access matches data from the recordset or table against the bound controls specified in the report and uses the data available at that moment to produce the report.

> **NOTE**
>
> Reports don't follow the sort order specified in an underlying query. Reports are sorted at the report level. It's a waste of time to sort data in a query that is used solely to populate a report because the data is re-sorted and rearranged by the report itself.

In the following example, you use data from tblProducts to create a relatively simple tabular report.

Creating a report with the Report Wizard

Access enables you to create virtually any type of report. Some reports, however, are easier to create than others, especially when the Report Wizard is used as a starting point. Like form wizards, the Report Wizard gives you a basic layout for your report, which you can then customize.

The Report Wizard simplifies laying out controls by stepping you through a series of questions about the report that you want to create. In this chapter, you use the Report Wizard to create tabular and columnar reports.

Creating a new report

The Ribbon contains several commands for creating new reports for your applications. The Create tab of the Ribbon includes the Reports group, which contains several options such as Report, Labels, and Report Wizard. For this exercise, click the Report Wizard button. The first screen of the Report Wizard (shown in Figure 20.5) appears.

FIGURE 20.5

The first screen of the Report Wizard after selecting a data source and fields.

In Figure 20.5, tblProducts has been selected as the data source for the new report. You can do this by selecting table tblProducts in the Navigation pane before clicking the Report Wizard button or by selecting tblProducts from the Tables/Queries drop-down list. Under the Tables/Queries drop-down list is a list of available fields. When you click a field in this list and click the right-pointing arrow, the field moves from the Available Fields list to the report's Selected Fields list. For this exercise, select Product ID, Category, Description, QtyInStock, RetailPrice, and Cost, in that order.

TIP

Double-clicking any field in the Available Fields list adds it to the Selected Fields list. You can also double-click any field in the Selected Fields list to remove it from the box.

You're limited to selecting fields from the original record source you started with. You can select fields from other tables or queries by using the Tables/Queries drop-down list in the Report Wizard. As long as you've specified valid relationships so that Access properly links the data, these fields are added to your original selection and you use them on the report. If you choose fields from unrelated tables, a dialog box asks you to edit the relationship and join the tables. Or you can return to the Report Wizard and remove the fields.

After you've selected your data, click Next to go to the next step in the wizard.

Selecting the grouping levels

The next dialog box enables you to choose which field(s) to use for grouping data. Figure 20.6 shows the Category field selected as the data grouping field for the report. The field selected for grouping determines how data appears on the report, and the grouping fields appear as group headers and footers in the report.

FIGURE 20.6

Specifying the report's grouping.

Groups are most often used to combine data that is logically related. This example groups products by product category because users will want to see products in the same category adjacent to each other for comparison purposes. Another example is choosing to group invoice data on CustomerID so that each customer's sales history appears as a group on the report. You use CustomerID because it's a unique field and you won't get two customers grouped together. Then you can use the report's group headers and footers to display the customer name and any other information specific to each customer.

The Report Wizard lets you specify as many as four group fields for your report. You use the Priority buttons to change the grouping order on the report. The order you select for the group fields is the order of the grouping hierarchy.

Select the Category field as the grouping field and click the > button to specify a grouping based on category values. Notice that the picture changes to show Category as a grouping field, as shown in Figure 20.6. Each of the other fields (ProductID, Description, QtyInStock, RetailPrice, and Cost) selected for the report will appear in the Category group's details section.

Defining the group data

After you select the group field(s), click the Grouping Options button at the bottom of the dialog box to display the Grouping Intervals dialog box, which enables you to further define how you want groups displayed on the report.

For example, you can choose to group by only the first character of the grouping field. This means that all records with the same first character in the grouping field are grouped. If you group a customers table on CustomerName, and then specify grouping by the first character of the CustomerName field, a group header and footer appears for all customers whose name begins with the same character. This specification groups all customer names beginning with the letter *A*, another group for all records with customer names beginning with *B*, and so on.

The Grouping Intervals drop-down displays different values for various data types:

- **Text:** Normal, 1st Letter, 2 Initial Letters, 3 Initial Letters, 4 Initial Letters, 5 Initial Letters
- **Numeric:** Normal, 10s, 50s, 100s, 500s, 1000s, 5000s, 10000s, 50000s, 100000s
- **Date:** Normal, Year, Quarter, Month, Week, Day, Hour, Minute

Normal means that the grouping is on the entire field. In this example, use the entire Category field.

Notice that the grouping options simplify creating reports grouped by calendar months, quarters, years, and so on. This means that you can easily produce reports showing sales, payroll, or other financial information needed for business reporting.

If you displayed the Grouping Intervals dialog box, click the OK button to return to the wizard, and then click the Next button to move to the sorting screen of the wizard.

20

Selecting the sort order

By default, Access automatically sorts grouped records in an order meaningful to the grouping field(s). For example, after you've chosen to group by Category, Access arranges the groups in alphabetical order by Category. However, you can't be sure of the order of the records within the group, so it's a good idea to specify a sort within each group. For example, your users might want to see the product records sorted by Retail Price in descending order so that the most expensive products appear near the top for each category group.

In this example, Access sorts data by the Category field. Select Description from the first drop-down. Figure 20.7 shows the sorting step of the wizard.

FIGURE 20.7

Selecting the field sorting order.

You can only select sorting fields that haven't been chosen for grouping. The fields chosen in this dialog box affect only the sorting order in the data displayed in the report's Detail section. Select ascending or descending sort by clicking the button to the right of each sort field.

Selecting summary options

Near the bottom of the sorting screen of the Report Wizard is a Summary Options button. Clicking this button displays the Summary Options dialog box (shown in Figure 20.8), which provides additional display options for numeric fields. All the numeric and currency fields selected for the report are displayed and may be summed. Additionally, you can display averages, minimums, and maximums. For this example, select Sum for QtyInStock and Avg for both RetailPrice and Cost.

FIGURE 20.8

Selecting the summary options.

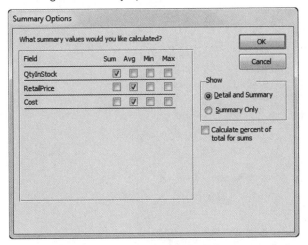

You can also decide whether to show or hide the data in the report's Detail section. If you select Detail and Summary, the report shows the detail data, whereas selecting Summary Only hides the Detail section and shows only totals in the report.

Finally, checking the Calculate Percent of Total for Sums box adds the percentage of the entire report that the total represents below the total in the group footer. For example, if you have three products and their totals are 15, 25, and 10, respectively, 30%, 50%, and 20% shows below their total (that is, 50)—indicating the percentage of the total sum (100%) represented by their sum.

Clicking the OK button in this dialog box returns you to the sorting screen of the Report Wizard. There you can click the Next button to move to the next wizard screen.

Selecting the layout

The next step in the Report Wizard affects the look of your report. The Layout area enables you to determine the basic layout of the data. The Layout area provides three layout choices that tell Access whether to repeat the column headers, indent each grouping, and add lines or boxes between the detail lines. As you select each option, the picture on the left changes to show how the choice affects the report's appearance.

You can choose between Portrait and Landscape layout for the report in the Orientation area. Finally, the Adjust the Field Width So All Fields Fit on a Page check box enables you to cram a lot of data into a little area. (A magnifying glass may be necessary!)

For this example, choose Stepped and Portrait, as shown in Figure 20.9. Then click the Next button to move to the next wizard screen.

20

FIGURE 20.9

Selecting the page layout.

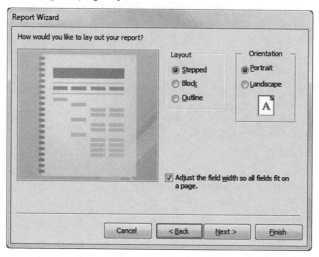

Opening the report design

The final Report Wizard screen contains a text box for you to enter a title for the report. This title appears only once, at the very beginning of the report, not at the top of each page. The report title also serves as the new report's name. The default title is the name of the table or query you initially specified as the report's data source. The report just created in the Chapter20.accdb example is named rptProducts_Wizard.

> **NOTE**
>
> The Chapter20.accdb file contains all of the reports described in this chapter. If you follow along to create your own reports, simply choose a different name in the last step so you don't overwrite the examples.

Next, choose one of the option buttons at the bottom of the dialog box:

- Preview the report
- Modify the report's design

For this example, leave the default selection intact to preview the report. Click Finish and the report displays in Print Preview (see Figure 20.10).

FIGURE 20.10

rptProducts_Wizard displayed in Print Preview.

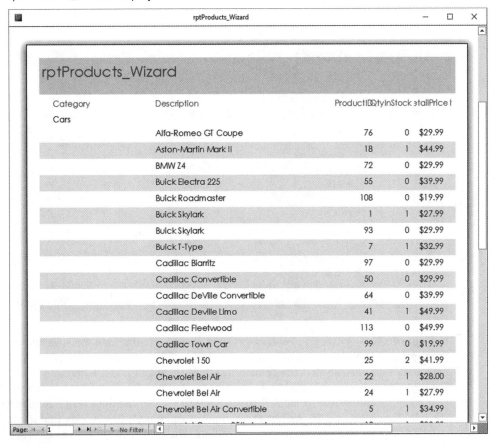

Adjusting the report's layout

There are a few small issues with the report shown in Figure 20.10. The Access Report Wizard has chosen the fonts and overall color scheme, which may not be what you had in mind. Also, the column headings on the right side overlap, and the Cost column was made very narrow.

The Report Wizard displays the new report in Print Preview. Right-click the report's title bar and select Layout View from the shortcut menu. The new report in Layout view is shown in Figure 20.11.

20

FIGURE 20.11

FIGURE 20.11

Layout view is useful for resizing controls in a columnar report.

In Figure 20.11, the Category column has been shrunk to eliminate some wasted space, the Description column has been widened to the left to fill that space, the remaining columns have been separated so that the column headings show and aren't all pushed together, and the QtyInStock header was shortened to just Qty. You may find it difficult to the select the Cost column because Access made it so narrow. First, move the RetailPrice column to the left. Then click just to the left of the report's right edge. Or you may find it easier to switch to Design mode to resize the Cost column. Working with controls in Layout view for a report is identical to working with them in Layout view for a form. To shrink a column, for example, drag the right edge of the control to the left.

Choosing a theme

After you adjust the layout, you can use controls in the Themes group on the Design tab of the Ribbon to change the report's colors, fonts, and overall appearance. The Themes button opens a gallery containing several dozen themes (see Figure 20.12).

FIGURE 20.12

Choosing a theme for the report.

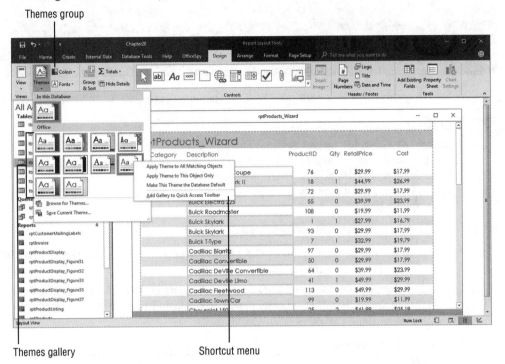

Themes group

Themes gallery   Shortcut menu

Themes are an important concept in Access 2019. A theme sets the color scheme, selected font face, font colors, and font sizes for Access 2019 forms and reports. As you hover the mouse over the theme icons in the gallery, the report open in Layout view behind the gallery instantly changes to show you how the report would look with the selected theme.

Each theme has a name, like Office, Facet, Organic, and Slice. Theme names are useful when you want to refer to a particular theme in the application's documentation or in an e-mail or other correspondence. Themes are stored in a file with a THMX extension, in the `Program Files\Microsoft Office\root\Document Themes 19` folder. Themes apply to all the Office 2019 documents (Word, Excel, and Access), making it easy to determine a style to apply to all of a company's Office output.

As the shortcut menu in Figure 20.12 indicates, you can apply the selected theme just to the current report (Apply Theme to this Object Only), all reports (Apply Theme to All Matching Objects), or all forms *and* reports in the application (Make This Theme the Database Default). There's even an option to add the theme as a button to the Quick Access toolbar, an extremely useful option for selectively applying the theme to other objects in the database.

20

For the purposes of this exercise, the Wisp theme was selected for the products report.

Creating new theme color schemes

Access 2019 provides several default themes, with each theme consisting of a set of complementary colors, fonts, and font characteristics. In addition, you can set up entirely new color and font themes and apply them to your forms and reports. Creating a custom color theme is a great way to apply a company's corporate color scheme to the forms and reports in an application.

With a form or report open in Design view, follow these steps:

1. **Click the Colors button in the Themes group on the Design tab of the Ribbon.**
   The color theme list opens.

2. **Select the Customize Colors command at the bottom of the list of color themes.**
   The Create New Theme Colors dialog box (shown in Figure 20.13) appears, showing the currently selected color theme.

FIGURE 20.13

Setting up a custom color theme.

Modifying a color theme requires a considerable amount of work. As you can see from Figure 20.13, each color theme includes 12 different colors. Each of the 12 buttons on the Create New Theme Colors dialog box opens a color palette (shown in Figure 20.14) where you select a theme element's color, such as the color for the Text/Background – Light 2 element.

FIGURE 20.14

Selecting a theme element's color.

3. **When the color customization is complete, assign a name for the custom color theme and click Save.** When you close the Create New Theme Colors dialog box, you'll see that the custom color theme has been applied to the form or report currently open in Design view. If you want to apply the new color theme to all the forms or reports in the application, open the color theme list, right-click the name of a custom color theme at the top of the list (see Figure 20.15), and select Apply Color Scheme to All Matching Objects. If you have a report open in Design view, the theme will be applied to all reports in the application. If, on the other hand, you have a form open in Design view, all the forms in the application receive the new color theme.

20

FIGURE 20.15

Applying a color theme to all matching objects in an application.

Even after applying a color theme, you can adjust the colors of individual items on a report (or form, for that matter). Open the report in Design view, select the item to change, and choose its new color(s) in the Property Sheet.

Although not described or shown here, a similar dialog box is available (Create New Theme Fonts) in the Fonts drop-down list in the Themes group on the Design tab. The Create New Theme Fonts dialog box enables you to set up a custom font theme (heading and body fonts) to apply to forms and reports. Creating custom font themes works just like adding your own color themes to an application. Save the theme with a name you'll recognize, and apply the font theme to forms and reports as needed.

Using the Print Preview window

Figure 20.16 shows the Print Preview window in a zoomed view of rptProducts_Wizard. To open a report in Print Preview, right-click the report in the Navigation pane and choose Print Preview. This view displays your report with the actual fonts, shading, lines, boxes, and data that will be used on the report when printed to the default printer. Clicking the left mouse button on the report's surface toggles the view between a zoomed view and an entire page view.

FIGURE 20.16

Displaying rptProducts_Wizard in the zoomed preview mode.

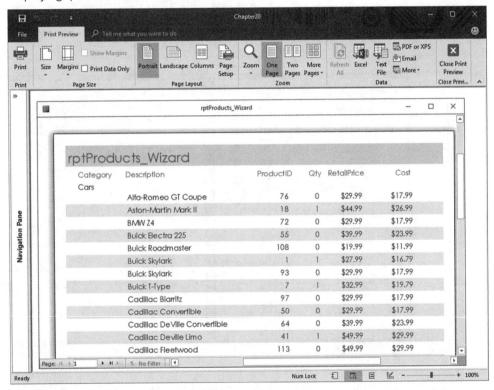

The Ribbon transforms to display controls relevant to viewing and printing the report. The Print Preview tab of the Ribbon includes controls for adjusting the size, margins, page orientation (Portrait or Landscape), and other printing options. The print options are stored with the report when you save the report's design. The Print Preview tab also includes a Print button for printing the report, and another button for closing Print Preview and returning to the report's previous view (Design, Layout, or Report view).

You can move around the page by using the horizontal and vertical scroll bars or use the Page controls (at the bottom-left corner of the window) to move from page to page. The Page controls include navigation buttons to move from page to page or to the first or last page of the report. You can also go to a specific page of the report by entering a value in the text box between the Previous Page and Next Page controls.

Right-clicking the report and selecting the Multiple Pages option, or using the controls in the Zoom group on the Print Preview tab of the Ribbon, lets you view more than one page of the report in a single view. Figure 20.17 shows a view of the report in the Print Preview's two-page mode. Use the navigation buttons (in the lower-left section of the Print Preview window) to move between pages, just as you would to move between records in a datasheet.

FIGURE 20.17

Displaying multiple pages of a report in Print Preview's page preview mode.

If, after examining the preview, you're satisfied with the report, click the Print button on the Ribbon to print the report. If you're dissatisfied with the design, click the Close Print Preview button to switch to the Report Layout window and make further changes.

Publishing in alternate formats

An important feature of the Print Preview tab is the ability to output the Access report in a number of common formats, including PDF, XPS (XML Paper Specification), HTML, and other formats.

Clicking the PDF or XPS button in the Data group on the Print Preview tab of the Ribbon opens the Publish as PDF or XPS dialog box (shown in Figure 20.18). This dialog box provides options for outputting in standard PDF format or in a condensed version (for use in a web context). You also specify the destination folder for the exported file.

FIGURE 20.18

Access 2019 provides powerful options for publishing reports.

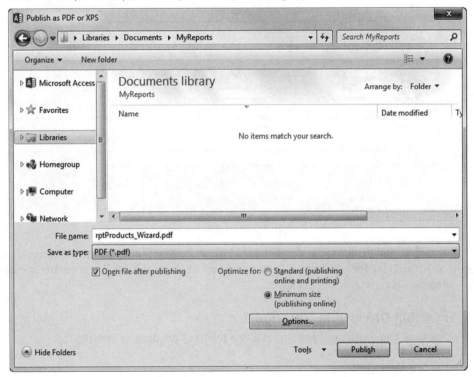

The PDF or XPS view of an Access report is indistinguishable from the report when viewed in Access. The PDF format is used far more frequently than XPS.

Viewing the report in Design view

Right-clicking the report's title bar and selecting Design View opens the report in Design view. As shown in Figure 20.19, the report design reflects the choices you made using the Report Wizard.

20

FIGURE 20.19

The report in Design view.

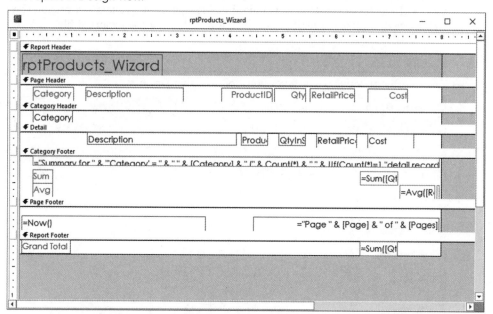

Return to the Print Preview mode by clicking Print Preview on the shortcut menu or by choosing Print Preview in the Views group on the Home tab. We'll discuss Design view in greater detail later in this chapter.

Printing or viewing the report

The final step in the process of creating a report is printing or viewing it.

Printing the report

There are several ways to print your report:

- **Choose File ⇨ Print in the main Access window (with a report highlighted in the Navigation pane).** The Backstage area appears with the following options:
    - Quick Print. This sends the report to the default printer immediately.
    - Print. This shows the print dialog box allowing you to make certain changes prior to printing.
    - Print Preview. This displays the report in print preview mode.
- **Click the Print button on the Print Preview tab of the Ribbon.** The print dialog is shown.

Viewing the report

You can view a report in four different views: Design view, Report view, Layout view, and Print Preview. The Design and Layout views are used to build a report and are similar to Design and Layout views for forms. Most of the work in this chapter is done in Design view.

You begin working with a new report by selecting a table or query to serve as the new report's data source. Click the Report button on the Create tab of the Ribbon. By default, the new report appears in Layout view, as shown in Figure 20.20.

FIGURE 20.20

Layout view of a new report based on tblProducts.

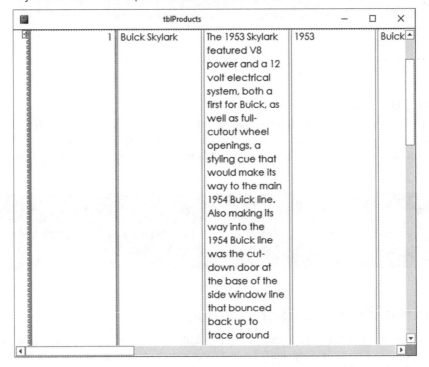

Layout view enables you to see the relative positions of the controls on the report's surface, as well as the margins, page headers and footers, and other report details.

The main constraint of Layout view is that you can't make fine adjustments to a report's design unless you switch to Design view. Layout view is primarily intended to allow you to adjust the relative positions of controls on the report and is not meant for moving individual controls around on the report.

20

While in Layout view, you can also right-click any control and select Properties from the shortcut menu. The Property Sheet allows you to modify the settings for the selected control.

Figure 20.21 shows the Ribbon while a report is open in Layout view. Not surprisingly, the options on the Ribbon are mostly involved with adjusting the appearance of the controls on the report.

FIGURE 20.21

The Ribbon while a report is open in Layout view.

Saving the report

Save the report design at any time by choosing File ⇨ Save or File ⇨ Save As from the Report Design window or by clicking the Save button on the Quick Access toolbar. The first time you save a report (or any time you select Save As), a dialog box enables you to select or type a name.

> **TIP**
>
> You might find it useful to save a copy of a report before beginning maintenance work on the report. Reports tend to be pretty complicated, and it's easy to make a mistake on a report's design and not remember how to return the report to its previous state. A backup provides a valuable safeguard against accidental loss of a report's design.

Banded Report Design Concepts

Access reports support a *banded* approach to design. The banded report design is an important concept in Access development. In an Access report, data is processed one record at a time. Individual fields may be placed in different places on a report and can even appear more than once in a report, if needed.

Many first-time Access developers are confused by a report's appearance in Design view. They might expect it to work similar to how forms are built. However, because Access processes report data one record at a time, Design view is meant to help you specify how each row is laid out on the printed page. In addition, Design view shows you elements such as a page's header and footer, as well as areas occupied by group headers and footers. Each area occupied by controls plays a part in the report's appearance when printed.

Reports are divided into *sections,* known as *bands* in most report-writing software packages. (In Access, these are simply called *sections.*) Access processes each record in the underlying data set, processing each section in order and deciding (for each record) whether to process fields or text in that section. For example, the report footer section is processed only after the last record is processed in the recordset.

Figure 20.22 shows rptProductsSummary in Print Preview. Notice that the data on the report is grouped by Category (Cars, Trucks, and so on). Each group has a *group header* containing the category name. Each group also has a footer displaying summary information for the category. The *page header* contains column descriptions (Category, Product ID, Description, and so on).

FIGURE 20.22

A portion of rptProductsSummary, a grouped report containing summary data.

Group header   Page header

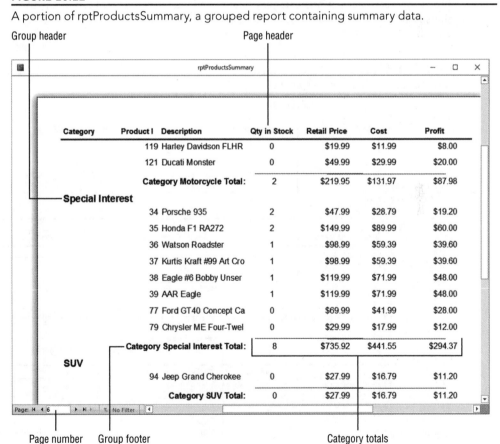

Page number   Group footer   Category totals

The following Access sections are available:

- **Report header:** Prints only at the beginning of the report; used for the title page
- **Page header:** Prints at the top of each page
- **Group header:** Prints before the first record of a group is processed
- **Detail:** Prints each record in the table or recordset
- **Group footer:** Prints after the last record of a group is processed
- **Page footer:** Prints at the bottom of each page
- **Report footer:** Prints only at the end of a report after all records are processed

Figure 20.23 shows rptProductsSummary open in Design view. As you can see, the report is divided into as many as seven sections. The group section displays data grouped by categories, so you see the sections Category Header and Category Footer. Each of the other sections is also named based on where it displays on the report.

FIGURE 20.23

rptProductsSummary in Design view.

You can place any type of text or Text Box controls in any section, but Access processes the data one record at a time. It also takes certain actions (based on the values of the group fields or current section of the page being processed) to make the bands or sections active. The example in Figure 20.23 is typical of a report with multiple sections. As you learned, each section in the report has a different purpose and different triggers.

> **NOTE**
> Page and report headers and footers are added as pairs. To add one without the other, remove any controls in the section you don't want and resize the section to a height of 0 or set its Visible property to No.

> **CAUTION**
> If you remove a header or footer section, you also lose the controls in those sections.

The Report Header section

Controls in the Report Header section are printed only once, at the beginning of the report. A common use of a Report Header section is as a cover page or a cover letter or for information that needs to be communicated only once to the user of the report.

To use the Report Header section as a title page, set the Force New Page property in the Report Header section to After Section. This will cause the controls in the Report Header section to be printed on their own page.

> **NOTE**
> If you place a data field in the report header, it will display data from the first record only.

The Page Header section

Controls in the Page Header section normally print at the top of every page. If a report header on the first page is not on a page of its own, the information in the Page Header section prints just below the report header information. Typically, page headers contain column headers in group/total reports. Page headers often contain a title for the report that appears on every page.

The Page Header section shown in Figure 20.23 contains a horizontal line below the Label controls. Each Label control can be moved or sized individually. You can also change special effects (such as color, shading, borders, line thickness, font type, and font size) for each control.

20

Both the Page Header and Page Footer properties can be set to one of four settings (found in the Report's properties, not the section properties):

- **All Pages:** The section (either page header or page footer) prints on every page.
- **Not with Rpt Hdr:** The section does not print on the page with the report header.
- **Not with Rpt Ftr:** The report footer is forced onto its own page when either Page Header or Page Footer is set to Not with Rpt Ftr. The section with this setting does not print on that page.
- **Not with Rpt Hdr/Ftr:** The report footer is forced onto its own page. The section does not print on that page, nor does it print on the page with the report header.

The Group Header section

A Group Header section normally displays the name of the group, such as Trucks or Motorcycles. Access knows that all the records in a group have been displayed in a Detail section when the group name changes. In this example, the detail records are all about individual products. The Category control in the Category Header tells you that the products within the group belong to the indicated category (Trucks or Motorcycles). Group Header sections immediately precede Detail sections.

You can have multiple levels of group headers and footers. In this report, for example, the data is only for categories. However, in some reports you might have groups of information with date values. You could group your sections by year or by month and year, and within those sections by another group such as category.

> **NOTE**
>
> To set group-level properties such as Group On, Group Interval, Keep Together, or something other than the default, you must first set the Group Header and Group Footer property (or both) to Yes for the selected field or expression. You learn about these later in the chapter.

The Detail section

The Detail section processes *every* record in the data and is where each value is printed. The Detail section frequently contains calculated fields such as profit that is the result of a mathematical expression. In this example, the Detail section simply displays information from the tblProduct table except for the last control. The profit is calculated by subtracting the cost from the RetailPrice.

> **TIP**
>
> You can tell Access whether you want to display a section in the report by changing the section's Visible property in the Report Design window. Turning off the display of the Detail section (or excluding selected group sections) displays a summary report with no detail or with only certain groups displayed.

The Group Footer section

You use the Group Footer section to calculate summaries for all the detail records in a group. In the Products Summary report, the expression =Sum([RetailPrice]-[Cost]) adds a value calculated from all the records within a category. The value of this Text Box control is automatically reset to 0 every time the group changes.

 You learn more about expressions in Chapter 9 and summary text boxes in Chapter 21.

> **TIP**
>
> You can change the way summaries are calculated by changing the Running Sum property of the text box in the Report Design window. A Running Sum of No will only show the value of the current record and is the default setting. A value of Over Group will accumulate the amounts for that control over every record in the group. A value of Over All accumulates the values for that control over every record in the report.

The Page Footer section

The Page Footer section usually contains page numbers or control totals. In very large reports, such as when you have multiple pages of detail records with no summaries, you might want page totals, as well as group totals. For the Products Summary Report, the page number is printed by combining some literal text and the built-in page number controls. These controls show Page *x* of *y*, where *x* is the current page number and *y* is the total number of pages in the report. A Text Box control with the following expression in the Control Source property can be used to display page-number information that keeps track of the page number in the report:

```
="Page " & [Page] & " of " & [Pages]
```

You can also print the date and the time the report was printed. You can see the page number text box in the Page Footer section in Figure 20.23. The Page Footer in rptProductsSummary also contains the current date and time at the left side of the Page Footer section.

The Report Footer section

The Report Footer section is printed once at the end of the report after all the detail records and group footer sections are printed. Report footers typically display grand totals or other statistics (such as averages or percentages) for the entire report. The report footer for the Products Summary report uses the expression =Sum with each of the numeric fields to sum the amounts.

> **NOTE**
>
> When there is a report footer, the Page Footer section is printed after the report footer.

20

The report writer in Access is a two-pass report writer, capable of preprocessing all records to calculate the totals (such as percentages) needed for statistical reporting. This capability enables you to create expressions that calculate percentages as Access processes those records that require foreknowledge of the grand total.

Creating a Report from Scratch

Most often, you'll probably use the Report Wizard or one of the other shortcuts to create a report that you will then modify to suit your needs. In this section, we'll skip all the shortcuts and build a report from scratch in order to better understand how all the pieces fit together.

It may be obvious, but it bears mentioning that the data in a printed report is static and only reflects the state of data in the database at the moment the report is printed. For this reason, every report should have a "printed" date and time somewhere on the report (often in the report header or page footer area) to document exactly when the report was printed.

> **NOTE**
>
> Access lets you create a report without first binding it to a table or query, but you'll have no bound controls on the report. This capability can be used to work out page templates with common text headers or footers, such as page numbering or the date and time, which can serve as models for other reports. You can add controls later by changing the underlying control source of the report.

Throughout the rest of this chapter, you learn the tasks necessary to create the Product Display report (a part of a page is shown in Figure 20.24). In these sections, you design the basic report, assemble the data, and place the data in the proper positions.

> **TIP**
>
> As with almost every task in Access, there are many ways to create a report without wizards. It is important, however, to follow some type of methodology, because creating a good report involves a fairly consistent approach. You should create a checklist that is a set of tasks that will result in a good report every time. As you complete each task, check it off your list. When you're done, you'll have a great-looking report. The following section outlines this approach.

FIGURE 20.24

The Product Display report.

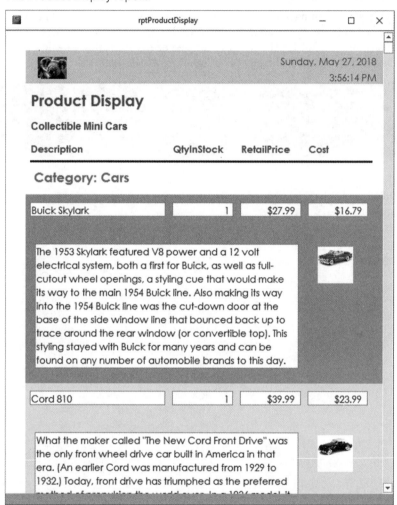

Creating a new report and binding it to a table

The first step is to create a new, empty report and bind it to tblProducts.

Creating a blank report is quite easy:

1. **Select the Create tab of the Ribbon.**
2. **Click the Blank Report button in the Reports group.** Access opens a blank report in Layout view and either positions a Field List dialog box on top of the new report

(see Figure 20.25) or docks the Field List on the right side of the application window. Click Show all tables on the Field List to see the available tables.

At this point, you have two different paths for adding controls to the report: continue working in Layout view or switch to Design view. Each of these techniques has advantages, but for the purposes of this exercise, we'll use Design view because it better demonstrates the process of building Access reports.

> **NOTE**
> The figures in this section that show Design view have the gridlines turned off so they're easier to see. Gridlines are on by default and are useful when you're laying out a report. To turn the grid on or off, select Report Design Tools ⇨ Arrange ⇨ Size/Space ⇨ Grid.

FIGURE 20.25

A blank report in Layout view.

3. **Right-click the report's title bar, and select Design view from the shortcut menu.** The Report window transforms to the traditional Access banded Report Designer, as shown in Figure 20.26. This figure also shows the Field List open on tblProducts, allowing you to add fields from the list to the appropriate section on the new report.

In Figure 20.26, the Description field has been dragged onto the Detail section of the report.

FIGURE 20.26

Building the new report in Design view.

Defining the report page size and layout

As you plan your report, consider the page-layout characteristics, as well as the kind of paper and printer you want to use for the output. As you make these decisions, you use several dialog boxes and properties to make adjustments. These specifications work together to create the desired output.

Select the Page Setup tab of the Ribbon to select the report's margins, orientation, and other overall characteristics. Figure 20.27 shows a portion of the Access screen with the Page Setup tab selected and the Margins option open.

FIGURE 20.27

Setting a report's margins.

Notice that the Page Setup tab includes options for setting the paper size, the report's orientation (Portrait or Landscape), its margins, and other details. Dropping down either the Size or Margins option reveals a gallery containing common settings for each of these options.

rptProductDisplay is to be a portrait report, which is taller than it is wide. You want to print on letter size paper (8½ x 11 inches), and you want the left, right, top, and bottom margins all set to 0.25 inch. In Figure 20.27 notice that the Narrow margins option is selected, which specifies exactly 0.25 inch for all four margin settings.

If the margins you need for your particular report are not shown in the Margins options, click Page Setup in the Page Layout group to open the Page Setup dialog box. This dialog box enables you to specify the margins, orientation, and other page-layout specifications.

To set the right border for the Product Display report to 7½ inches, follow these steps:

1. **Click the right edge of the report body (where the white page meets the gray background).** The mouse pointer changes to a double-headed arrow.

2. **Drag the edge to the 7½-inch mark.**

NOTE
Your units of measure may be different, depending on the regional settings in Windows settings.

If the ruler isn't displayed in the Report Designer, click Ruler from the Size/Space drop-down on the Arrange tab.

NOTE
You can also change the Width property in the Property Sheet for the report.

TIP
If you run your report and every other page is blank, it's a sign that the width of your report exceeds the width of your page. To fix this problem, decrease the left and right margin size or reduce the report's width. Sometimes, when you move controls around, you accidentally make the report width larger than you originally intended. For example, in a portrait report, if your left margin plus report width plus right margin is greater than 8½ inches, you'll see blank pages. If you're unable to reduce the report's width, it's because there are controls in the way. Locate the offending controls and move or resize them.

Placing controls on the report

Access takes full advantage of drag-and-drop capabilities of Windows. The method for placing controls on a report is no exception:

1. **Click the Add Existing Fields button in the Tools group on the Design tab of the Ribbon.** The Field List window appears.

2. **Choose a control in the Controls group on the Design tab if you want to use something other than the default control types for the fields.**

3. **Select each field that you want on your report and then drag them to the appropriate section of the Report Design window.** Select multiple fields by holding down the Ctrl key as you click fields in the Field List. Depending on whether you choose one or several fields, the mouse pointer changes shape to represent your selection as you drag fields onto the report.

The fields appear in the detail section of the report, as shown in Figure 20.28. Notice that for each field you dragged onto the report, there are two controls. When you use the drag-and-drop method of placing fields, Access automatically creates a Label control with the field name attached to the Text Box control to which the field is bound.

20

FIGURE 20.28

The report with several fields added.

> **NOTE**
>
> Access always creates a Bound Object Frame control for an OLE-type object found in a table, such as for the Picture_Small field in Figure 20.28. Also notice that the Detail section automatically grows taller to fit all the controls. Note that the Text Box control for the Features field is different from the other Text Box controls because it is bound to a Long Text field.

Controls are needed for information to be displayed in the page header section. Before you do this, however, you must resize the page header to make room for them.

Resizing a section

To make room on the report for the title information in the page header, you must resize it. You resize by using the mouse to drag the bottom of the section you want to resize. The mouse pointer turns into a vertical double-headed arrow as it's positioned over the bottom of a report section. Drag the section border up or down to make the section smaller or larger.

Resize the Page Header section to make it about ¾-inch high by dragging the bottom margin of the page header downward. Use the Controls group on the Design tab of the Ribbon to drag labels to the report. Add two labels to the Page Header section, and enter **Product Display** as the Caption property of one label, and **Collectible Mini Cars** for the other.

The labels you just added are unattached; they aren't related to any other controls on the report. When you drag a field from the Field List, Access adds not only a control to contain the field's data but also a label to provide an identifier for the control. Labels that you drag from the Controls group on the Ribbon are unattached and not related to any control on the report.

You may notice the Page Header section expanding to accommodate the Label controls that you dragged into the section. All the fields needed for the Product Display report are now placed in their appropriate sections.

> **TIP**
>
> To create a multiple-line label entry, press Ctrl+Enter to force a line break where you want it in the control.

> **TIP**
>
> If you enter a caption that is longer than the space in the Property Sheet, the contents scroll as you type. Otherwise, you can open a Zoom box that gives you more space to type by pressing Shift+F2.

Modifying the appearance of text in a control

To modify the appearance of the text in a control, select the control and select a formatting style to apply to the label by clicking the appropriate button on the Format tab.

To make the titles stand out, follow these steps to modify the appearance of label text:

1. **Click the newly created report heading Product Display label in the Page Header section.**
2. **Select the Format tab of the Ribbon, and click the Bold button in the Font group.**
3. **From the Font Size drop-down list, select 18.**
4. **Repeat for the Collectible Mini Cars label, using a 12 pt font and Bold.** The size of the labels may not fit their displayed text. To tighten the display or to display all the text when a label isn't big enough, double-click any of the sizing handles, and Access chooses an appropriate size for the label.

Figure 20.29 shows these labels added, resized, and formatted in the report's Page Header section.

20

FIGURE 20.29

Adding unbound labels to the report.

Working with Text Box controls

So far, you've added controls bound to fields in the tables and unbound Label controls used to display titles in your report. There is another type of Text Box control that is typically added to a report: unbound text boxes that are used to hold expressions such as page numbers, dates, or a calculation.

Adding and using Text Box controls

In reports, Text Box controls serve two purposes:

- They enable you to display stored data from a particular field in a query or table.
- They display the result of an expression.

Expressions are calculations that can use other controls as their operands, Access functions (either built in or user defined), or a combination of the two.

Entering an expression in a Text Box control

Expressions enable you to create a value that is not already in a table or query. They can range from simple functions (such as a page number) to complex mathematical computations.

Chapter 9 discusses expressions in greater detail.

A *function* is a small program that, when run, returns a single value. The function can be one of many built-in Access functions or it can be user defined.

The following steps show you how to use an unbound Text Box control to add a page number to your report:

1. **Click in the middle of the Page Footer section, and resize the page footer so that it's ½ inch in height.**

2. **Drag a Text Box control from the Controls group on the Design tab of the Ribbon and drop it into the Page Footer area.** Make the text box about three-quarters of the height of the Page Footer section and about ¾-inch wide.

3. **Select the text box's attached label and change its contents to say** Page:.

4. **Select the Text Box control (it says "Unbound") and enter** = Page **directly into the text box.** Alternatively, you could open the Property Sheet (press F4) and enter = [Page] as the text box's Control Source property.

5. **Drag the new Text Box control until it's near the right edge of the report's page, as shown in Figure 20.30.** You may want to also move the text box's label so that it's positioned close to the text box. The upper-left handle on the label moves the label independently of the text box.

> **TIP**
>
> You can always check your result by clicking Print Preview in the Views group on the Design tab of the Ribbon and scrolling down to the Page Footer section to check the page number.

FIGURE 20.30

Adding a page-number expression in a Text Box control.

Sizing a Text Box control or Label control

You select a control by clicking it. Depending on the size of the control, from three to seven sizing handles appear—one on each corner except the upper-left corner and one on each side. Moving the mouse pointer over one of the sizing handles changes the mouse pointer to a double-headed arrow. When the pointer changes, click the control and drag it

20

to the size you want. Notice that, as you drag, an outline appears indicating the size the Label control will be when you release the mouse button.

If you double-click any of the sizing handles, Access resizes a control to best fit for text in the control. This feature is especially handy if you increase the font size and then notice that the text no longer fits the control.

Note that, for Label controls, the *best-fit sizing* resizes both vertically and horizontally, although text controls resize only vertically. The reason for this difference is that in Report Design mode, Access doesn't know how much of a field's data you want to display. Later on, the field's name and contents might be radically different. Sometimes Label controls are not resized correctly, however, and have to be adjusted manually.

TIP

You can also choose Arrange ⊏⊃ Size/Space ⊏⊃ To Fit to change the size of the Label control's text automatically.

Before continuing, you should check how the report is progressing. You should also save the report frequently as you make changes to it. You could send a single page to the printer, but it's probably easier to view the report in Print Preview. Right-click the report's title bar, and select Print Preview from the shortcut menu. Figure 20.31 shows a print preview of the report's current appearance. The page header information is at the very top of the page, and the first product record appears below the header.

As you move the mouse over the print preview, the cursor changes to a magnifying glass. Click any portion of the view to zoom in so that you can closely examine the report's layout. Only one record per page appears on the report because of the vertical layout. In the next section, you move the controls around and create a more horizontal layout.

Deleting and cutting attached labels from Text Box controls

To create a more horizontal report, you must move the text-box labels from the Detail section to the Page Header section and reposition the Text Box controls to a tabular layout. Once moved, these controls appear as headings above each column of data and are repeated on each page of the report.

You can easily delete one or more attached controls in a report. Simply select the desired controls and press Delete. However, if you want to *move* the label to the Page Header section (instead of simply deleting it), you can cut the label instead of deleting it. When removing attached controls, there are three choices:

- Delete only the Label control.
- Cut the Label control to the Clipboard.
- Delete or cut the Label control and the Text Box control.

Oddly enough, you can't simply drag a label from the Detail section to the Page Header section. Dragging an attached label from the Detail section drags its text box along with it. You must cut the label from the Detail section and paste it into the Page Header section.

FIGURE 20.31

A print preview of the report so far.

Controls in page header

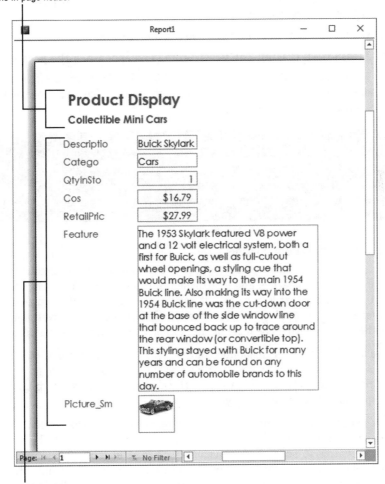

Controls in detail section

If you select the Label control and cut it by pressing Ctrl+X, only the Label control is removed. If you select the Text Box control and cut or delete it, the Label and Text Box controls are removed. To cut an attached Label control (in this case, the label attached to the Description text box), follow these steps:

1. **Click the Close Print Preview button on the Ribbon to exit Print Preview mode.**

2. **Select the Description label in the Detail section.**

3. **Press Ctrl+X (Cut).** After you've cut the label, you may want to place it somewhere else. In this example, place it in the Page Header section.

20

Pasting labels into a report section

It's as easy to cut labels from controls placed in the Detail section and paste them into the page header as it is to delete the labels and create new ones in the page header. Regardless, you now paste the label you cut in the previous steps:

1. **Click anywhere in or on the Page Header section.**
2. **Press Ctrl+V (Paste). The Description label appears in the page header.**
3. **Repeat for the Quantity in Stock and Cost labels.** If you accidentally selected the data Text Box control and both controls are cut or deleted, click the Undo button, or press Ctrl+Z, to undo the action.

> **TIP**
>
> If you want to delete only the Text Box control and keep the attached Label control, right-click the Label control and select Copy from the shortcut menu. Next, to delete the Text Box control and the Label control, select the Text Box control and press the Delete key. Finally, right-click anywhere on the form and select Paste from the shortcut menu to paste only the copied Label control to the report.

Moving Label and Text Box controls

Before discussing how to move Label and Text Box controls, it's important to review a few differences between attached and unattached controls. When an attached label is created automatically with a Text Box control, it's called a *compound control*. In a compound control, whenever one control in the set is moved, the other control moves along with it. This means that moving either the label or the text box also moves the related control.

To move both controls in a compound control, select either of the pair of controls with the mouse. As you move the mouse pointer over either of the objects, the pointer turns into a hand. Click the controls and drag them to their new location. As you drag, an outline for the compound control moves with your pointer.

To move only one of the controls in a compound control, drag the desired control by its moving handle (the large square in the upper-left corner of the control). When you click a compound control, it looks like both controls are selected, but if you look closely, you see that only one of the two controls (Text Box or Label) is selected (as indicated by the presence of both moving and sizing handles). The unselected control displays only a moving handle. A pointing finger indicates that you've selected the move handles and can now move one control independently of the other. To move either control individually, select the control's move handle and drag it to its new location.

> **TIP**
>
> To move a label that isn't attached, simply click any border (except where there is a handle) and drag it.

To make a group selection, click with the mouse pointer anywhere outside a starting point and drag the pointer through (or around) the controls you want to select. A gray, outlined rectangle appears, showing the extent of the selection. When you release the mouse button, all controls the rectangle surrounds are selected. You can then drag the group of controls to a new location.

Make sure you also resize all the controls as shown in the figure. Change the size and shape of the Features Long Text field and the OLE picture field Picture. The OLE picture field displays as a rectangle with no field name in Design view. (It's the bottommost control above the footer in Figure 20.32.)

FIGURE 20.32

Rearranging the controls on the report.

Place all the controls in their proper position to complete the report layout. Figure 20.32 shows one possible layout of the controls. You make a series of group moves by selecting several controls and positioning them close to where you want them. Then, if needed, you can fine-tune their position by dragging individual controls.

Use Figure 20.32 as a guide to placing controls on the report.

At this point, you're about halfway done. The screen should look something like Figure 20.32. Remember that these screenshots are taken with the Windows screen resolution set to 1,920 x 1080. If you're using a lower resolution or you have large fonts turned on in the Windows Display Properties (in Windows Settings), you have to scroll the screen to see the entire report.

These steps complete the rough design for this report. There are still properties, fonts, and sizes to change. When you make these changes, you have to move controls around again. Use the designs in Figure 20.32 only as a guideline. How it looks to *you*, as you refine the look of the report in the Report window, determines the final design.

Modifying the appearance of multiple controls

The next step is to apply bold formatting to all the Label controls in the Page Header section directly above the section separator. The following steps guide you through modifying the appearance of text in multiple Label controls:

1. **Select all Label controls in the bottom of the Page Header section by clicking them one at a time while holding down the Shift key.** Alternatively, click in the vertical ruler immediately to the left of the labels in the Page Header. Access selects all controls to the right of where you clicked in the vertical ruler. There are four Label controls to select (refer to Figure 20.32).

   Alternatively, you can drag a bounding box around the Label controls in the page header.

2. **Click the Bold button on the Format tab.** After you make the final modifications, you're finished, except for fixing the picture control. To do this, you need to change properties, which you do in the next section.

> **NOTE**
>
> This may seem to be an enormous number of steps because the procedures were designed to show you how laying out a report design can be a slow process. Remember, however, that when you click away with the mouse, you don't realize how many steps you're doing as you visually design the report layout. With a WYSIWYG (What You See Is What You Get) layout tool like the Access Report Designer, you might need to perform many tasks, but it's still easier and faster than programming. Figure 20.32 shows the final version of the design layout as seen in this chapter. In the next section, you continue to improve this report layout.

Changing Label and Text Box control properties

To change the properties of a Text Box or Label control, you need to display the control's Property Sheet. If it isn't already displayed, perform one of these actions to display it:

- Double-click the border of the control (anywhere except a sizing handle or move handle).
- Select a control and press F4.
- Right-click the control with the mouse and select Properties.
- Press F4 to open the Property Sheet, and use the drop-down list at the top of the window to select the form or control on the form.

The Property Sheet enables you to look at and edit a control's property settings. Using tools on the Format tab of the Ribbon, such as the font drop-downs and text-formatting buttons, also changes the property settings of a control. Clicking the Bold button in the Format tab, for example, sets the control's Font Weight property to Bold. It's usually easier and more intuitive to use the controls on the Format tab of the Ribbon, but many properties are not accessible through the Ribbon. Plus, objects often have more options available through the Property Sheet.

The Size Mode property of an OLE object (bound object frame), with its options of Clip, Stretch, and Zoom, is a good example of a property that is available only through the Property Sheet.

The Image control, which is a bound object frame, presently has its Size Mode property set to Zoom, which is the default. With Size Mode set to Clip, the picture is displayed in its original size and Access either cuts off the picture at the edge of its control or shows extra space around the image. With Size Mode set to Stretch, the image will fit the control frame but may be distorted if the control frame has a different aspect ratio than the image. A Size Mode of Zoom keeps the image's aspect ratio and fits the image inside the control frame. You may find that extra space is shown around the image, but it's usually a good trade-off so the image isn't distorted.

You might consider changing the Border Style property to Transparent. When set to Transparent, no boxes are drawn around the picture and the picture blends into the report's surface.

The labels for Features and Pictures aren't needed because a user will surely know what data is being presented without them. Select each label and press the Delete key to remove them. Next, resize the Feature control as shown and reposition the Image control to the right of the Feature control.

These steps complete the changes to your report so far. A print preview of the first few records appears in Figure 20.33. If you look at the pictures, notice how the picture is properly displayed and the product's Features text box now appears across the bottom of each Detail section.

20

FIGURE 20.33

The report displayed in Print Preview.

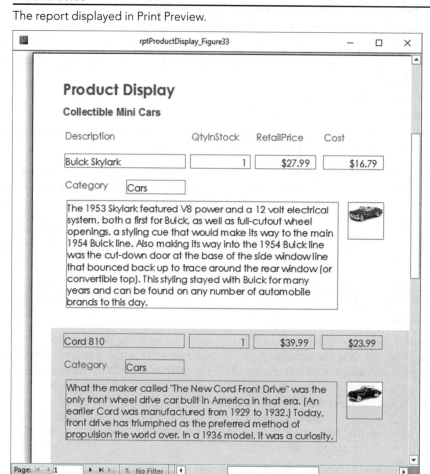

Growing and shrinking Text Box controls

When you print or print-preview controls that can have variable text lengths, Access provides options for enabling a control to grow or shrink vertically, depending on the exact contents of a record. The Can Grow and Can Shrink properties determine whether a Text Box control resizes its vertical dimension to accommodate the amount of text contained in its bound field. Although these properties are usable for any text control, they're especially helpful for Text Box controls.

Table 20.1 explains the acceptable values for these two properties.

TABLE 20.1 Text Box Control Values for Can Grow and Can Shrink

Property	Value	Description
Can Grow	Yes	If the data in a record uses more lines than the control is defined to display, the control resizes to accommodate additional lines.
Can Grow	No	If the data in a record uses more lines than the control is defined to display, the control does not resize. Rather, it truncates the data in the control.
Can Shrink	Yes	If the data in a record uses fewer lines than the control is defined to display, the control resizes to eliminate blank space. The Can Shrink property of all controls in the section must be set to Yes before the section can shrink.
Can Shrink	No	If the data in a record uses fewer lines than the control is defined to display, the control does not resize to eliminate blank space.

To change the Can Grow settings for a Text Box control, follow these steps:

1. **Select the Features Text Box control.**

2. **Display the Property Sheet.**

3. **Click the Can Grow property and make sure it's set to Yes.** If it's not, select Yes from the drop-down.

> **NOTE**
>
> The Can Grow and Can Shrink properties are also available for report sections. Use a section's Property Sheet to modify these values. Setting a report section's Can Grow and Can Shrink affects only the section, not the controls contained within the section. However, you must set the section's Can Grow to Yes to allow the control within the section to grow. If the section's Can Grow is not set, the control can only expand as far as the section's border permits.

The report is starting to look good, but you may want to see groups of like data together and determine specific orders of data. To do this, you use sorting and grouping.

Sorting and grouping data

You can often make the data on the report more useful to users by grouping the data in informative ways. Suppose that you want to list your products first by category and then by description within each category. To do this, you use the Category and Description fields to group and sort the data.

Creating a group header or footer

Grouping on a field in the report's data adds two new sections—Group Header and Group Footer—to the report. In the following steps, you use the group header to display the name of the product category above each group of records. You won't use the Category group footer in this example because there are no totals by category or other reasons to use a group footer.

Follow these steps to create a Category group header:

1. **Click the Group & Sort button in the Grouping & Totals group on the Design tab of the Ribbon.** The Group, Sort, and Total pane appears at the bottom of the screen.

2. **Click the Add a Group button in the Group, Sort, and Total area.**

3. **Select Category from the Field List.** Access adds Group on Category with A on Top in the Group, Sort, and Total area. Access adds Category Header and Category Footer sections to the report's design as soon as you select the Category field for grouping. The Category Header section appears between the Page Header and Detail sections. If you define a group footer, it appears below the Detail section, and above the Page Footer section. If a report has multiple groupings, each subsequent group becomes the one closest to the Detail section. The groups defined first are farthest from the Detail section.

The Group Properties pane (displayed when you click the More button on the group) displays a sentence with each option separated by a comma. The options are drop-down lists or clickable text for setting the property. The options sentence for the Category group contains these choices:

- **Group on Category:** Determines the field on which to group. You can change this field even after you've set the group field by selecting a different field from the drop-down.

- **With A on top:** Determines the sort order. In this case it's alphabetical. Select With Z on Top to reverse the sort.

- **By entire value:** Groups are separated based on the value in the field. You can also group on the first character of the field, the first two characters of the field, or any number of characters that you type into the Characters box in the drop-down.

- **With no totals:** Determines what totals are displayed in the group header or footer. You can select which field to total and the type of total to display.

- **With title:** Allows you to specify a title for the group.

- **With a header section:** Displays the group header section. Choose Without a Header Section to hide the header.

- **Without a footer section:** Hides the group footer section. Choose With a Footer Section to display the footer.

- **Do not keep together on one page:** Allows the group to be continued on the next page if there is too much information for the current page. Choose Keep Whole Group Together on One Page to start a new page when there is too much information for the current page. Choose Keep Header and First Record Together on One Page to start a new page only when there isn't enough room for the first record.

Click the Less button to hide these options once set. The preceding options are shown for a grouping on the Category field, which is a text field. Other field types have some of the same options and some different options. Date fields show these options:

- **From oldest to newest:** Instead of With A on Top as with text fields, date fields are sorted from oldest to newest. Choose From Newest to Oldest to reverse the sort.
- **By quarter:** Allows you to group by the entire date, by day, by week, by month, by quarter, by year, or by a custom date or time increment.

The other date field options are the same as for text fields and are not repeated here. Numeric fields show these options:

- **From smallest to largest:** Determines the numeric sort. Choose From Largest to Smallest to reverse the order.
- **By entire value:** Group by each numeric value individually or by 5s, 10s, 100s, 1,000s, or by a custom interval.

Sorting data within groups

Sorting enables you to determine the order in which the records are displayed on the report, based on the values in one or more controls. This order is important when you want to view the data in your tables in a sequence other than that of your input. For example, new products are added to tblProducts as they're needed on an invoice. The physical order of the database reflects the date and time a product is added. Yet, when you think of the product list, you probably expect it to be in alphabetical order by Product ID, and you want to sort it by Description or the cost of the product. By sorting in the report itself, you don't have to worry about the order of the data. Although you can sort the data in the table by the primary key or in a query by any field you want, there are good reasons to do it in the report. This way, if you change the query or table, the report is still in the correct order.

In the case of the products report, you want to display the records in each category group sorted by description. Follow these steps to define a sort order based on the Description field within the Category grouping:

1. **Click the Grouping button on the Design tab of the Ribbon to display the Group, Sort, and Total area, if it isn't already open.** You should see that the Category group already exists in the report.

2. **Click the Add a Sort button in the Group, Sort, and Total area.**

3. **Select Description in the Field List.** Notice that Sort by defaults to With A on Top. The Group, Sort, and Total section should now look like Figure 20.34.

4. **Close the Group, Sort, and Total area by clicking the X in the upper-right corner.**

20

FIGURE 20.34

The Group, Sort, and Total area completed.

Although you used a field in this example, you can also sort (and group) with an expression. To enter an expression, click the Add a Sort or Add a Group button in the Group, Sort, and Total area, and then click the Expression button at the bottom of the Field List. The Expression Builder dialog box opens, enabling you to enter any valid Access expression, such as in `=[RetailPrice]-[Cost]`.

To change the sort order for fields in the Field/Expression column, simply click the drop-down arrow to the right of the With A on Top button (see Figure 20.34) to display the Sort Order list. Select With Z on Top from the sort options that appear.

Removing a group

To remove a group, display the Group, Sort, and Total area, select the group or sort specifier to delete, and then press the Delete key. Any controls in the group header or footer will be removed.

Hiding a section

Access also enables you to hide headers and footers so that you can break data into groups without having to view information about the group itself. You can also hide the Detail section so that you see only a summary report. To hide a section, follow these steps:

1. **Click the section you want to hide.**
2. **Display the section's Property Sheet.**
3. **Click the Visible property and select No from the drop-down list in the property's text box.**

> **NOTE**
>
> Sections are not the only objects in a report that can be hidden; controls also have a Visible property. This property can be useful for expressions that trigger other expressions.

Sizing a section

Now that you've created the group header, you might want to put some controls in the section, move some controls around, or even move controls between sections. Before you start manipulating controls within a section, you should make sure the section is the proper height.

To modify the height of a section, drag the top border of the section below it. For example, if you have a report with a page header, Detail section, and a page footer, change the height of the Detail section by dragging the top of the Page Footer section's border. You can make a section larger or smaller by dragging the bottom border of the section.

For this example, change the height of the group header section to ½ inch by following these steps:

1. **Move your mouse pointer to the bottom of the Category Header section.** The pointer changes to a horizontal line split by two vertical arrows.

2. **Select the top of the Detail section (which is also the bottom of the Category Header section).**

3. **Drag the selected band lower until three dots appear in the vertical ruler and release the mouse button when you have the band positioned.** The gray line indicates where the top of the border will be when you release the mouse button.

Moving controls between sections

You now want to move the Category control from the Detail section to the Category Header section. You can move one or more controls between sections simply by dragging the control with your mouse from one section to another or by cutting it from one section and pasting it to another section:

1. **Select the Category control in the Detail section and drag it up to the Category Header section, as shown in Figure 20.35.** You should now perform the following steps to complete the report design.

FIGURE 20.35

Completing the Group Header section.

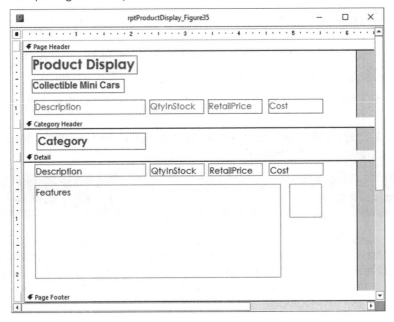

2. **Delete the Category label from the group header.**

3. **Set the Border Style property of the Category control and all the controls in the Page Header to Transparent.**

4. **Change the font size, bold, and font color of the Category control to visually distinguish it from the records below it.** Figure 20.35 shows the placement of the controls on the completed report design.

> **TIP**
>
> Access names the group header and footer sections automatically. To change this name, select the group header in the Property Sheet and change the Name property to something more appropriate. For example, change the Name property from GroupHeader0 to CategoryHeader so that it's easier to identify.

Adding page breaks

Access enables you to force page breaks based on groups. You can also insert forced breaks within sections, except in Page Header and Page Footer sections.

In some report designs, it's best to have each new group begin on a different page. You can achieve this effect easily by using the Force New Page property of a group section, which enables you to force a page break every time the group value changes.

The four Force New Page property settings are:

- **None:** No forced page break (the default)
- **Before Section:** Starts printing the current section at the top of a new page every time there is a new group
- **After Section:** Starts printing the next section at the top of a new page every time there is a new group
- **Before & After:** Combines the effects of Before Section and After Section

To force a page break before the Category group:

1. **Click anywhere in the Category header, or click the Category Header bar above the section.**

2. **Display the Property Sheet and select Before Section in the Force New Page property's drop-down list.**

> **TIP**
>
> Alternatively, you can set the Force New Page property to After Section in the Category Footer section.

Sometimes, you want to force a page break—but not on the basis of a grouping. For example, you might want to split a report title across several pages. The solution is to use the Page Break control from the Controls group of the Ribbon. Drag the Page Break control and drop it on the report where you want a page break to occur each time the page prints.

NOTE

Be careful not to split a control and show it over two pages. Place page breaks above or below controls without overlapping them.

Improving the Report's Appearance

As you near completion of testing your report design, you should also test the printing of your report. Figure 20.36 shows the first page of the Product Display report. There are a number of things still to do to complete the report.

FIGURE 20.36

The report is pretty plain and uninteresting at this point.

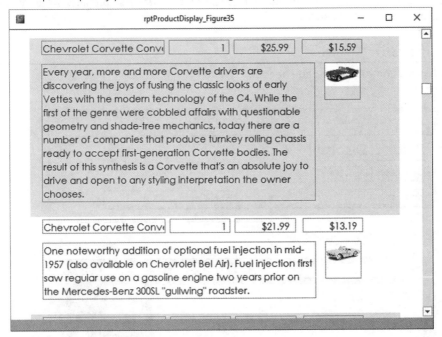

The report is pretty boring and plain. If your goal is to just look at the data, this report is done. However, you need to do more before you're really done.

Although the report has good, well-organized data, it isn't of professional quality. To make a report more visually appealing, you generally add a few graphic elements like lines and rectangles, and possibly some special effects such as shadows or sunken areas. You want to make sure sections have distinct areas separate from each other using lines or colors. Make sure controls aren't touching each other (because text might eventually touch if a value is long enough). Make sure text is aligned with other text above or below and to the right or left.

Adjusting the page header

The page header contains several large labels positioned far apart from each other. The column headers are small and just hanging there. They could be made one font size larger. The entire page header should be separated from the Detail section by a horizontal line.

If you wanted to add some color to your report, you could make the report name a different color. Be careful not to use too many colors unless you have a specific theme in mind, though. Most serious business reports use one or two colors, and rarely more than three with the exception of graphs and charts. Furthermore, colors are not much use when printed on black-and-white printers.

Figure 20.37 shows these changes. The Product Display label has been changed to a blue background color with white foreground text. This is done by first selecting the control and then selecting Blue for the background. They've also been placed under each other and left aligned. The rectangle around each of the controls was also properly sized by double-clicking each control's sizing handles.

FIGURE 20.37

Adjusting controls in the page header.

The next step is to add a nice thick line separating the Page Header section from the Category Group Header section:

1. **Select the Line tool in the Controls group of the Ribbon.**
2. **Drag a line below the Description and QtyInStock labels, as shown in Figure 20.37.**
3. **Select the line and change the Border Width property to 2 pt on the line's Property Sheet.**

Creating an expression in the group header

Figure 20.37 also shows that the Category field has been replaced by an expression. If you place the value of the category in the Group Header section, it looks out of place and may not be readily identifiable. Most data values should have some type of label to identify what they are.

The expression =`"Category: "` & [Category] displays Category: followed by a space and the value of the Category field (such as Category: Cars) in the text box. The & symbol (the concatenation operator) joins strings. Make sure you leave a space after the colon or the value won't be separated from the label.

You may find that Access complains about a circular reference on the Category text box after you change the control's Control Source. This happens because the name of the control is Category, and the text box is bound to a field named Category. Access doesn't understand that [Category] in the expression you entered as the Control Source actually refers to the field, not the text box. (A text box's value can't be based on the text box's contents—that's the definition of *circular reference*.) The solution is to rename the text box to txtCategory to distinguish it from its bound field.

> **CAUTION**
>
> When you create a bound control, it uses the name of the data field as the default control name. Using the control in an expression without changing the name of your control causes circular references. You must manually rename the control to something other than the original field name. This is another reason why a simple naming convention, such as prefixing text boxes with *txt*, is such a good idea. You'll avoid a lot of nagging problems by adopting a naming convention for the controls on your Access reports.

Follow these steps to complete the expression and rename the control:

1. **Select the Category control in the Category Group Header section and display the Property Sheet for the control.**
2. **Change the Control Source property to** ="Category: " & [Category].
3. **Change the Name property to** txtCategory.

20

The final formatting step for the Category Header is to change the Border Style property of the txtCategory control to Transparent. You have visually distinguished this control by changing the font, and a border is unnecessary.

Creating a report header

The Report Header section is printed only once for the entire report. The report header is the logical place to put things such as the report's title, a logo, and the print date and time. Having this information in the report header makes it easy for any user of the report to know exactly what's in the report and when the report was printed.

With the report open in Design view, the Ribbon includes a Design tab. Within the Header/Footer group on the Design tab are a number of controls that help you add important features to the report's header and footer.

For example, click the Logo button, and Access opens the Insert Picture dialog box (shown in Figure 20.38) for browsing to an image file to insert as the report's logo. Virtually any image file (JPG, GIF, BMP, and so on) is a candidate for inclusion as the report's logo.

FIGURE 20.38

Browsing to an image file to use as the report's logo.

The Title button in the Header/Footer group adds the report's name as the report header's title and positions the edit cursor within the title label to make it easy for you to adjust the report's title.

Finally, the Date and Time button opens the Date and Time dialog box (shown in Figure 20.39). Specify the date and time format you'd like to use for the Date control by selecting the Date and Time control in the Header/Footer group on the Design tab of the Ribbon.

FIGURE 20.39

Specifying the date and time format.

The completed report in Print Preview is shown in Figure 20.40. The report header in this figure was created in less than a minute using the tools built into Access 2019.

20

FIGURE 20.40

The completed report in Print Preview.

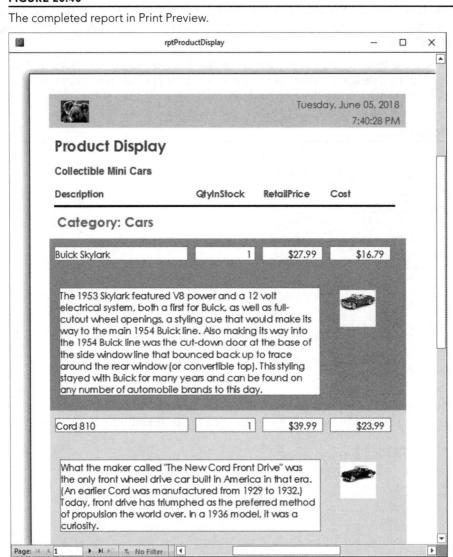

As you close the report, Access will prompt you to save the report if you have not yet done so.

Advanced Access Report Techniques

IN THIS CHAPTER

Organizing reports to present the data in a logical manner

Producing more attractive reports

Providing additional information about the report

Learning other approaches to enhance your presentation

In Chapter 20, you created attractive and useful reports by following a few simple steps. For most of your reporting needs, Access' default reports will do just fine. Sometimes, however, you want more than the basic report layout. Perhaps you're trying to mimic an existing paper report. Or maybe you're trying to develop a consistent style in your organization that's different than the Access default report.

In this chapter, we show you some advanced techniques for changing the organization of your reports and adding interesting formatting and some tips for avoiding blank reports and working with controls.

 See Chapter 20 for information on the basic process of building Access reports.

ON THE WEB

All the examples in this chapter can be found in the `Chapter21.accdb` sample database on this book's website. Please note that many of the figures in this chapter appear with the report Design view grid turned off to make the report design details easier to see.

> **NOTE**
>
> This chapter uses data from the Northwind Traders example database. The Northwind data is ideally suited for the example report described in this chapter and is a good model for most Access databases. The techniques described in the following sections should be adaptable to any well-designed database without too much trouble.

Grouping and Sorting Data

To be most useful, the data on a report should be well organized. Grouping data that's similar can reduce the amount of data presented, which makes it easier to find specific data. As you'll see in this section, the Access Report Builder offers a fair degree of flexibility in this regard.

 Grouping and sorting were introduced in Chapter 20. This section expands on that information and provides more examples.

Grouping alphabetically

Reports should be used to display data in a meaningful way. That usually means there is some level of data manipulation or summarization happening on the report. A report displaying every sale made by every employee arranged in a tabular format can be difficult to read. Anything you do to reduce the overload of tabular reports can make the data more meaningful.

> **NOTE**
>
> The report rptSalesJanuaryAlpha is the basic report with no sorting and grouping. It's a good place to start if you'd like to follow the examples. The reports rptSalesJanuaryAlpha1 and rptSalesJanuaryAlpha2 show the completed reports.

The Group, Sort, and Total pane (which is opened by clicking the Group & Sort button in the Grouping & Totals group on the Design tab) controls how data is grouped on Access reports. Sorting alphabetically by company name arranges the records in alphabetical order based on the first character of the company name, while grouping by company name creates a separate group for each company.

Clicking the Add a Group button in the Group, Sort, and Total pane opens a list from which you choose a field to use for grouping data on the report. In Figure 21.1, both CompanyName and OrderDate have been selected, with CompanyName being grouped first and then OrderDate sorted within the company groups.

Typically, data is grouped on the entire contents of a field or combination of fields. Simply grouping on the CompanyName field means that all records for Bottom-Dollar Markets appear together as a group and all the records for Ernst Handel appear together as another group. You can, however, override the default and group based on *prefix characters* by changing the Group On property in the Group, Sort, and Total pane.

FIGURE 21.1

Alphabetical grouping is easy.

Notice the More button in the CompanyName sorting bar in Figure 21.1. Clicking the More button reveals the sorting details you want to apply to the CompanyName field (see Figure 21.2). By default, text fields such as CompanyName are sorted alphabetically by the field's entire contents. You can change this behavior to alter how Access applies grouping to the field's data (see Figure 21.3).

FIGURE 21.2

Many options are available for grouping and sorting.

FIGURE 21.3

Modifying a text-based grouping.

When you select by first character, the Group Interval property tells Access how many characters to consider when grouping on prefix characters. In this case, the grouping interval is set to 1, meaning, "Consider only the *first* character when grouping." You could choose to group by the first character, the first two characters, or any number of characters in the field, depending on your requirements.

Notice also that the CompanyName field is set to ascending sort (with *A* on top), which causes alphabetic grouping starting at names beginning with *A* and progressing to names beginning with *Z*. With this combination of properties, all companies starting with *A* will be grouped together, those beginning with *B* will be in another group, and so on.

The report for this example (rptSalesJanuaryAlpha1, shown in Figure 21.4) shows purchases during the month of January, sorted by company name. The order date, the order ID, and the sales person are shown across the page. The result of the sorting and grouping specification in Figure 21.1 is shown in Figure 21.4.

FIGURE 21.4

Sorting and grouping a report by company name.

Sorting and grouping can yield useful information. For example, you can easily see that Bottom-Dollar Markets placed three orders in January, one with salesperson Steven Buchanan, one with Robert King, and one with Nancy Davolio.

Let's assume you want to refine the rptSalesJanuaryAlpha1 report by labeling the groups with the letters of the alphabet. That is, all customers beginning with *A* (Antonio Moreno Taqueria and Around the Horn) are in one group, all customers beginning with *B* (Blondel père et fils, Bon app', and Bottom-Dollar Markets) are in another group, and so on. Within each group, the company names are sorted in alphabetical order. The sales to each customer are further sorted by order date.

To emphasize the alphabetical grouping, a text box containing the first character for each group has been added to the report (see rptSalesJanuaryAlpha2 in Figure 21.5). Although the data set in this example is rather small, in large reports such headings can be useful.

FIGURE 21.5

An alphabetic heading for each customer group makes the rptSalesJanuaryAlpha2 report easier to read.

Northwind Sales: January

Company Name	Order Date	Order ID	Sales Person
A			
Antonio Moreno Taquería	24-Jan-19	10365	Janet Leverling
Around the Horn	12-Jan-19	10355	Michael Suyama
B			
Blondel père et fils	19-Jan-19	10360	Margaret Peacock
Bon app'	22-Jan-19	10362	Janet Leverling
Bottom-Dollar Markets	17-Jan-19	10358	Steven Buchanan
	25-Jan-19	10367	Robert King
	30-Jan-19	10371	Nancy Davolio
C			
Chop-suey Chinese	30-Jan-19	10370	Michael Suyama
D			
Die Wandernde Kuh	04-Jan-19	10348	Margaret Peacock
	15-Jan-19	10356	Michael Suyama
Drachenblut Delikatessen	23-Jan-19	10363	Margaret Peacock
E			
Eastern Connection	23-Jan-19	10364	Nancy Davolio
Ernst Handel	08-Jan-19	10351	Nancy Davolio
	26-Jan-19	10368	Andrew Fuller
F			

To add the text box containing the alphabetic character, follow these steps:

1. **Right-click the report's title bar and choose Design View.**

2. **Choose Group & Sort from the Design tab of the Ribbon.** The Group, Sort, and Total pane appears.

3. **Add a Group for CompanyName.**

4. **Click More, and ensure that With a Header Section is selected. This action adds a band for a group based on the CompanyName information (see Figure 21.6).**

5. **Select By First Character instead of the default By Entire Value.**

6. **Expand the CompanyName group header and add an unbound text box to the CompanyName group header.**

7. **Set the text box's Control Source property to the following expression:**

   `=Left$([CompanyName],1)`

8. **Delete the label and set the other text box properties (Font, Font Size, and so on) appropriately.**

9. **While you're grouping on the first character of the company name, you still need to ensure that company names are sorted correctly.** Click Add a Sort and select the CompanyName field again. Click More to ensure that the entire field is going to be sorted, and that no header section will be added.

10. **Finally, add a sort for OrderDate so that multiple orders for the same company are in order.** When you're done, the report in Design view should appear as shown in Figure 21.6.

Notice the CompanyName group header that was added by the Group Header setting in the Group, Sort, and Total pane. The unbound text box in the CompanyName Header displays the expression used to fill it.

This little trick works because all the rows within a CompanyName group have the first character in common. Using the `Left$()` function to peel off the first character and use it as the text in the text box in the group header provides an attractive, useful heading for the CompanyName groups.

Grouping on date intervals

Many reports require grouping on dates or date intervals (day, week, or month). For example, Northwind Traders may want a report of January sales grouped on a weekly basis so that week-to-week patterns emerge.

Fortunately, the Access report engine includes just such a feature. An option in the Group, Sort, and Total pane enables you to quickly and easily group report data based on dates or date intervals. Just as we grouped data based on prefix characters in an earlier example, we can group on dates using the group's Group On property. Figure 21.7 shows the January sales report grouped by each week during the month. This report is named rptSalesJanuaryByWeek.

FIGURE 21.6

rptSalesJanuaryAlpha2 in Design view.

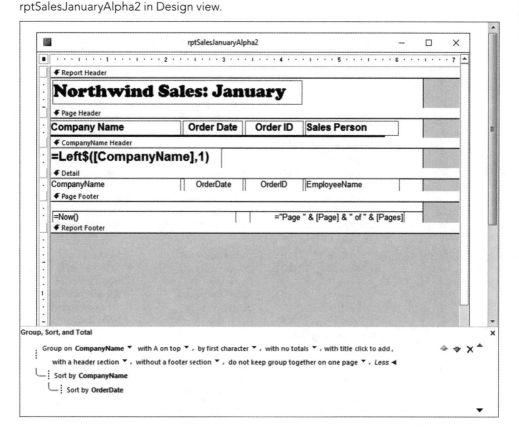

This report is easy to set up. Open the Group, Sort, and Total pane again and establish a group for the OrderDate field. Select With a Header Section from the header drop-down (click More if you don't see the header drop-down) and select By Week from the drop-down list shown in Figure 21.8. Notice that Access is smart enough to present Group On options (Year, Quarter, Month, Week, and so on) that make sense for Date/Time fields like OrderDate. Selecting Week from this list instructs Access to sort the data on the OrderDate, grouped on a week-by-week basis. Note, though, that you still need to sort by the entire value of the OrderDate to ensure that they're in sequential order within the week.

FIGURE 21.7

The January sales data grouped by each week during the month.

The label at the top of the group identifying the week (the first one reads Week begin-ning 1/1/2019:) is the product of the following expression in an unbound text box in the OrderDate group header:

```
="Week beginning " & [OrderDate] & ":"
```

See the Design view of rptSalesJanuaryByWeek in Figure 21.9. Notice the unbound text box in the OrderDate group header. This text box contains the value of the order date that Access used to group the data in the OrderDate grouping.

FIGURE 21.8

OrderDate is a Date/Time field, so the grouping options are relevant for date and time data.

FIGURE 21.9

The Design view of rptSalesJanuaryByWeek. Notice the expression in the OrderDate group header.

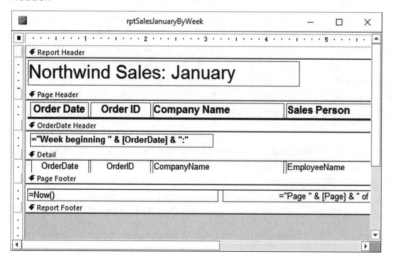

Hiding repeating information

A simple way to improve a tabular report is to reduce the amount of repeated information on the report. Figure 21.10 shows a typical tabular report (rptTabularBad) produced by Access, based on a simple query of the Northwind Traders data.

21

FIGURE 21.10

Simple tabular reports can be cluttered and boring.

The report in Figure 21.10 was produced with the Access Report Wizard, selecting the tabular report format and all defaults. The query underlying this report selects data from the Customers, Orders, and Employees tables in `Chapter21.accdb` and is shown in Figure 21.11. Notice that the data returned by this query is restricted to the month of January 2019. Also, the first and last names of employees are concatenated as the Name field.

The query in Figure 21.11 (qrySalesJanuary) is used as the basis of several examples in this chapter.

You can significantly improve the report in Figure 21.10 simply by hiding repeated information in the Detail section. As soon as Andrew Fuller's name is given, there's no need to repeat it for every sale that Andrew made in January 2019. The way the data is arranged on rptTabularBad, you have to search for where one employee's sales data ends and another employee's data begins.

Making the change to hide the repeated values is very easy:

1. **Open the report in Design view.**

2. **In the Detail section, select the EmployeeName field containing the employee's first and last names.**

3. **Open the Property Sheet for the Name field (see Figure 21.12).**

FIGURE 21.11

The simple query underlying rptTabularBad.

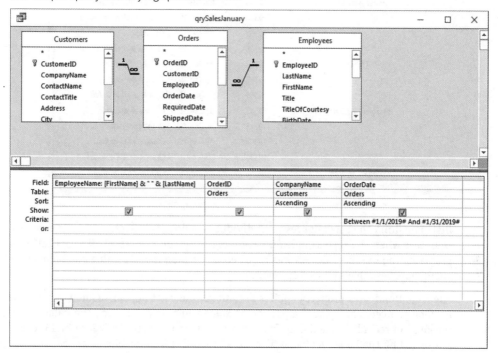

4. **Change the Hide Duplicates property to Yes.** The default is No, which directs Access to display every instance of every field.

5. **Switch to Print Preview mode and enjoy the new report layout (shown in Figure 21.13).** The report shown in Figure 21.13 is rptTabularGood.

FIGURE 21.12

The default property values sometimes lead to unsatisfactory results.

Distinguishing the sales figures for individual employees in Figure 21.13 is much easier than it is when the repeating information is printed on the report. Notice that no fancy programming or report design was required. A simple property-value change resulted in a much more readable and useful report.

The Hide Duplicates property applies only to records that appear sequentially on the report. As soon as Access has placed a particular Name value on the report, the name won't be repeated in records immediately following the current record. In Figure 21.13, the records are sorted by the EmployeeName field, so all records for an employee appear sequentially as a group. If the report were sorted by another field (for example, OrderID or OrderDate), the Hide Duplicates property set on the Name field would apply only to those instances where the employee's name coincidentally appeared together in multiple records.

The Hide Duplicates property can be applied to multiple controls within a report. As long as you understand that Hide Duplicates only hides subsequent duplicate values within a detail section, you should be able to achieve the results you expect. (Note, though, that you may occasionally run into unexpected results if only one of the multiple fields changes.)

Hiding a page header

Sometimes you need to display a page header or footer on just the first page of a report. An example is a terms and conditions clause in the header of the first page of an invoice. You want the terms and conditions to appear only on the first page of the invoice but not on subsequent pages.

FIGURE 21.13

Hiding repeated information results in a more attractive report.

Name	Order ID	Order Date	Company Name
			rptTabularGood — □ ×

Northwind Sales: January

Name	Order ID	Order Date	Company Name
Andrew Fuller	10345	01-Jan-19	QUICK-Stop
	10368	26-Jan-19	Ernst Handel
Janet Leverling	10346	02-Jan-19	Rattlesnake Canyon Gro
	10352	09-Jan-19	Furia Bacalhau e Frutos
	10362	22-Jan-19	Bon app'
	10365	24-Jan-19	Antonio Moreno Taqueríε
Laura Callahan	10354	11-Jan-19	Pericles Comidas clásic
	10366	25-Jan-19	Galería del gastrónomo
	10369	29-Jan-19	Split Rail Beer & Ale
Margaret Peacock	10347	03-Jan-19	Familia Arquibaldo
	10348	04-Jan-19	Die Wandernde Kuh
	10360	19-Jan-19	Blondel père et fils
	10363	23-Jan-19	Drachenblut Delikatesse
Michael Suyama	10350	08-Jan-19	La maison d'Asie

 Some of the examples in this chapter use Visual Basic for Applications (VBA). VBA is discussed more fully in Chapters 24–29.

To hide the header after the first page, add an unbound Text Box control to the report with its Control Source property set to the expression =HideHeader(). Delete the text box's label. The HideHeader() function returns a null string, making the text box invisible.

NOTE

You can't actually set the control's Visible property to No; if you did, the control wouldn't be able to respond to events.

The HideHeader() function is as follows:

```
Function HideHeader() As String

    'Set the visible property of the header
    Me.Section("PageHeader0").Visible = False
    HideHeader = vbNullString

End Function
```

The invisible text box can be placed virtually anywhere on the first page but is most logically located in the page footer. The assumption is that, because the page header is the first item printed on the page, you'll always get the first page header. Once the page footer containing the invisible text box has been processed, the page header's Visible property will be set to False, and the page header will not be seen on any other pages in the report.

Starting a new page number for each group

Sometimes a report will contain a number of pages for each group of data. You might want to reset page numbering to 1 as each group prints so that each group's printout will have its own page-numbering sequence. For example, assume you're preparing a report with sales data grouped by region. Each region's sales may require many pages to print, and you're using the Force New Page property to ensure that grouped data doesn't overlap on any page. But how do you get the page numbering within each group to start at 1?

The report's Page property, which you use to print the page number on each page of a report, is a read/write property. This means that you can reset Page at any time as the report prints. Use the group header's Format event to reset the report's Page property to 1. Every time a group is formatted, Page will be reset to 1 by the following code:

```
Private Sub GroupHeader0_Format(Cancel As Integer, FormatCount As Integer)
  Me.Page = 1
End Sub
```

Use the Page property to display the current page number in the page header or footer as usual. For example, include the following expression in an unbound text box in the page footer:

```
= "Page " & [Page]
```

The report named rptResetPageEachGroup is included in Chapter21.accdb and shows this technique. Unfortunately, it's not nearly as easy to count the pages within a group so that you could put a "Page x of y" in the page footer, where y is the number of pages within the group.

Formatting Data

In addition to sorting and grouping data, you can make reports more useful by formatting them to highlight specific information. Numbering the entries or using bullets can make things stand out, as can using lines or spaces to separate parts of the report. Ensuring that the elements on the report are positioned in a consistent manner is important as well; you might have all the necessary data in a report, but poor presentation can leave a negative impression on the users. The techniques discussed in this section will help you produce reports that are more professional looking.

Creating numbered lists

By default, the items contained on an Access report are not numbered. They simply appear in the order dictated by the settings in the Group, Sort, and Total pane.

Sometimes it would be useful to have a number assigned to each entry on a report or within a group on a report. You might need a number to count the items in a list or uniquely identify items in the list. For example, an order details report might contain an item number for each item ordered, plus a field for items ordered, showing how many things were ordered.

The Access Running Sum feature provides a way to assign a number to each item in a list on an Access report. For example, the Northwind Traders sales management has asked for a report showing the sum of all purchases by each customer during the month of January, sorted in descending order so that the top purchaser appears at the top. Oh, yes—and they want a number assigned to each line in the report to provide a ranking for the Northwind customers.

The query to implement this request is shown in Figure 21.14 (qryCustomerPurchasesJanuary). This query sums the purchases by each customer for the month of January 2019. Because the Purchases column is sorted in descending order, the customers buying the most product will appear at the top of the query results set. The OrderDate field is not included in the query results and is used only as the query's selection criterion (notice the *Where* in the Total row).

FIGURE 21.14

An interesting query that sums data and sorts the query results in descending order of the sum.

Although you could do much of this work at run time using VBA to programmatically sum the values returned by the query or a SQL statement in the report's Record Source property, you should always let the Access query engine perform aggregate functions. All Access queries are optimized when you save the query. You're guaranteed that the query will run as fast as possible—much faster than a filter based on a SQL statement in a report's Record Source property.

> **TIP**
>
> The Access Query Builder's aggregate functions perform flawlessly. Furthermore, ACE will perform the aggregate function exactly the same way every time the query is run. There is no reason you should be tempted to manually sum data when the query will do it for you.

The basic report (rptUnNumberedList) prepared from the data provided by qryCustomerPurchasesJanuary is shown in Figure 21.15. All sorting options have been removed from the Group, Sort, and Total pane to permit the records to arrange themselves as determined by the query.

FIGURE 21.15

A straightforward report (rptUnNumberedList) produced with data from qryCustomerPurchasesJanuary.

To add a Ranking column to the report, use the Running Sum property of an unbound text box to sum its own value over each item in the report. When the Running Sum property is set to Over Group, Access adds 1 to the value in this text box for each record displayed in the Detail section of the report (Running Sum can also be used within a group header or footer). The alternate setting (Over All) instructs Access to add 1 each time the text box appears in the entire report. Add an unbound text box to the left of the CompanyName text box on the report, with an appropriate header in the Page Header area. Set the Control Source property for the text box to =1 and the Running Sum property to Over All. Figure 21.16 shows how the Rank text box is set up on rptNumberedList.

 Chapter 20 discusses how to move labels from the Detail section to another section.

When this report (rptNumberedList) is run, the Rank column is filled with the running sum calculated by Access (see Figure 21.17). Once again, the data in this report is the same as in other report examples. The main difference is the amount of manipulation done by the query before the data arrives at the report and the additional information provided by the running sum.

FIGURE 21.16

The value in the unbound text box named txtRank will be incremented by 1 for each record in the report.

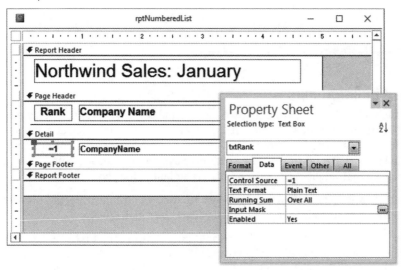

Reports can contain multiple running sum fields. You could, for example, keep a running sum to show the number of items packed in each box of a multiple-box order while another running sum counts the number of boxes. The running sum starts at zero, hence the need to initialize it to 1 in the Control Source property on the Property Sheet.

You can also assign a running sum within each group by setting the Running Sum property of the unbound text box to Over Group instead of Over All. In this case, the running sum will start at zero for each group. So, be sure to set the Control Source property of a group's running sum to 1.

FIGURE 21.17

The Rank column provides a ranking for each customer in order of purchases during January.

Creating bulleted lists

You can add bullet characters to a list instead of numbers, if you want. Instead of using a separate field for containing the bullet, however, you can simply concatenate the bullet character to the control's Record Source property—a much easier solution. Access will "glue" the bullet character to the data as it's displayed on the report, eliminating alignment problems that might occur with a separate unbound text box.

The design of rptBullets is shown in Figure 21.18. Notice the bullet character in the txtCompanyName text box as well as in the Property Sheet for this text box.

The bullet is added by exploiting a Windows feature. Position the text insertion character in the Control Source property for the CompanyName field, hold down the Alt key, and type **0149** on the numeric keypad. Windows inserts the standard Windows bullet character, which you see in the Property Sheet. Looking at Figure 21.18, you can see that the bullet character is inserted correctly into the text box on the report. The expression you use in the Control Source property is the following:

```
= "•" & Space$(2) & [CompanyName]
```

where the bullet is inserted by the Alt+0149 trick.

You can produce the same effect by using the following expression in the text box:

```
= Chr(149) & Space$(2) & [CompanyName]
```

This expression concatenates the bullet character—returned by Chr (149)—with the data in the CompanyName field.

FIGURE 21.18

The bullet character is added to the Control Source property of the txtCompanyName text box.

 This particular trick only works if the character set (such as Arial) assigned to the control (Label or Text Box) includes a bullet character as the 149th ASCII character. Not all fonts accessible by Access applications include a bullet character, but popular typefaces such as Arial do tend to include this character.

The report now appears as shown in Figure 21.19 (with some summary information at the top that will be addressed later in this chapter). You can increase or decrease the number in the Space$() function to pad the white space between the bullet and the text. Because the bullet character and CompanyName field have been concatenated together in the text box, they'll be displayed in the same typeface. Also, adding the bullet character to the text box containing the company name guarantees that the spacing between the bullet and first character of the company name will be consistent in every record. When using proportionally spaced fonts such as Arial, it can sometimes be difficult to get precise alignment between report elements. Concatenating data in a text box eliminates spacing problems introduced by proportionally spaced characters. Note, though, that if the amount of text in the text box exceeds a single row, subsequent rows will not be indented.

You might want to add other special characters to the control. For a complete display of the characters available in the font you've chosen for the Text Box control, run Charmap.exe, the Windows Character Map application (see Figure 21.20). Be sure to select the font you've chosen for the Text Box control. The only constraint on the characters you use on an Access report is that the font used in the text boxes on the report must contain the specified characters. Not all Windows TrueType character sets include all the special characters, like bullets.

FIGURE 21.19

Use a Windows feature to insert the bullet in front of the CompanyName field.

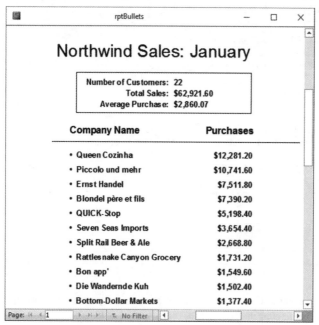

Charmap is easy to use. Select a font from the drop-down list at the top of the dialog box, and the main area fills with the font's default character set. Some character sets are incredibly large. For example, the Arial Unicode MS font includes more than 53,000 different characters, including traditional and simplified Chinese, Japanese Kanji, and Korean Hangul character sets.

Most characters in a Windows font are accessible through the Chr$() function. The page footer of rptBullets includes a text box filled with characters specified by the Chr$() function. For example, the smiley face character in the Wingdings font is specified with Chr$(74). Some of the characters displayed by Charmap are identified only by their hexadecimal values. If the decimal value is not given, the hexadecimal value can be used with `Chr$()` by using the `CLng()` function to convert the hex value to integer: `Chr$(CLng("&H00A9"))` displays the familiar copyright symbol (©) when used to set the contents of a control set to the Arial font.

FIGURE 21.20

Charmap is a useful tool for exploring Windows font sets.

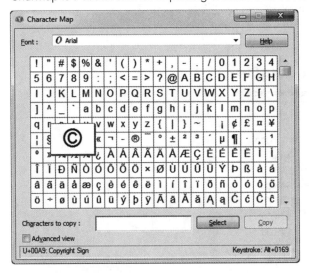

Adding emphasis at run time

You can show or hide a control for a particular record by setting its Visible property. This can be useful if you only want to show a field in certain conditions and hide it otherwise. You can even use the value of another control as your condition. You hide a control, of course, by setting its Visible property to `False` (or `No`) at design time. Only when the information contained in the control is needed do you reset the Visible property to `True`.

An example might be a message to the Northwind Traders customers that a certain item has been discontinued and inventory is shrinking. If you were to show this message for every item in the Northwind catalog, the report would be very cluttered and you would lose the effect of highlighting discontinued items. But by only showing the stock count message on discontinued items, you might encourage buyers to stock up on the item.

Figure 21.21 shows rptPriceList in Print Preview mode. (You may have to right-click the report name and select Print Preview from the shortcut menu.) Notice that the Guaraná Fantástica beverage product appears in italics, the price is bold italics, and the `Only 20 units in stock!` message appears to the right of the product information.

Figure 21.22 reveals part of the secret behind this technique. The visible unit price text box is actually unbound. This is the text box used to display the unit price to the user.

Another text box is bound to the UnitPrice field in the underlying recordset, but it's hidden by setting its Visible property to No. Just to the left of the hidden UnitPrice field is a hidden check box representing the Discontinued field. txtMessage, which contains the Only x units in stock! message, is also hidden.

FIGURE 21.21

Can you tell Guaraná Fantástica is on sale?

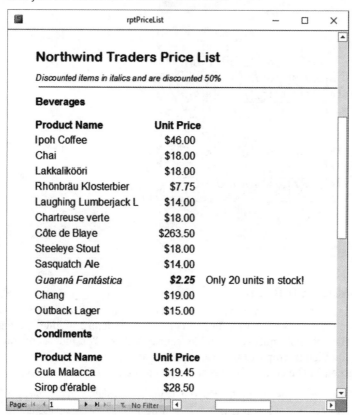

Use the Detail section's Format event to switch the Visible property of txtMessage to True whenever Discontinued contains a true value. The code is shown here:

```
Private Sub Detail1_Format(Cancel As Integer, _
    FormatCount As Integer)

    Me.txtProductName.FontItalic = Me.Discontinued.Value
    Me.txtPrice.FontItalic = Me.Discontinued.Value
    Me.txtPrice.FontBold = Me.Discontinued.Value
```

```
'Cut price in half for discontinued
Me.txtPrice = Me.UnitPrice * IIf(Me.Discontinued.Value, 0.5, 1)
Me.txtMessage.Visible = Me.Discontinued.Value

End Sub
```

FIGURE 21.22

rptPriceList in Design view reveals how this effect is implemented.

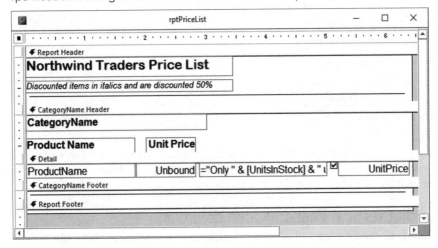

In this procedure, Me is a shortcut reference to the report. You must explicitly turn off the italics, bold, and other font characteristics when the product is not discontinued; otherwise, once a discontinued product has been printed, all products following the discontinued product will print with the special font attributes. The font characteristics you set in a control's Property Sheet are just the initial settings for the control. If you change any of those properties at run time, they stay changed until modified again. Similarly, txtMessage must be hidden after it's been displayed by setting its Visible property to False, or in this case the value of Discontinued.

Avoiding empty reports

If Access fails to find valid records to insert into the Detail section of a report, all you'll see is a blank Detail section when the report is printed. To avoid this problem, attach code to the report's NoData event that displays a message and cancels the print event if no records are found.

The NoData event is triggered when Access tries to build a report and finds no data in the report's underlying recordset. Using NoData is easy:

```
Private Sub Report_NoData(Cancel As Integer)

    MsgBox "There are no records for this report."
```

```
        Cancel = True

    End Sub
```

The `Cancel = True` statement instructs Access to stop trying to show the report. The user will see the dialog box shown in Figure 21.23 and will avoid getting a report that can't be printed. (Open rptEmpty in `Chapter21.accdb` for this example.)

FIGURE 21.23

Inform the user that there are no records to print.

Because the `NoData` event is tied to the report itself, don't look for it in any of the report's sections. Simply add this code as the report's `NoData` event procedure, and your users will never wonder why they're looking at a blank report.

Inserting vertical lines between columns

You can easily add a vertical line to a report section whose height is fixed (like a group header or footer). Adding a vertical line to a section that can grow in height (like a Detail section on a grouped report) is more difficult. It's particularly difficult to get a vertical line between columns of a report (see rptVerticalLines in Figure 21.24). If you simply add a vertical line to the right side of a section of a snaking columns report, the line will appear to the right of the rightmost column on the page. You have to be able to specify where vertical lines will appear on the printed page.

Reports using snaking columns are discussed in the "Adding Even More Flexibility" section later in this chapter.

Although you add most controls at design time, sometimes you have to explicitly draw a control as the report is prepared for printing. The easiest approach in this case is to use the report's Line method to add the vertical line at run time. The following subroutine, triggered by the Detail section's `Format` event, draws a vertical line 3½ inches from the left printable margin of the report:

```
    Private Sub Detail_Format(Cancel As Integer, FormatCount As Integer)
      Dim X1 as Single
      X1 = 3.5 * 1440
      Me.Line (X1, 0)-(X1, 32767)
    End Sub
```

The syntax of the `Line` method is as follows:

```
object.Line (X1, Y1) - (X2, Y2)
```

The `Line` method requires four arguments. These arguments (X1, X2, Y1, and Y2) specify the top and bottom (or left and right, depending on your perspective) coordinates of the line. Notice that all calculated measurements on a report must be specified in twips. (There are 1,440 twips per inch or 567 twips per centimeter.) In this case, X1 and X2 are the same value, and we're forcing the line to start at the very top of the Detail section (0) and to extend downward for 32,767 twips.

FIGURE 21.24

Vertical lines in rptVerticalLines help segregate data.

You might wonder why we're using 32,767 as the Y2 coordinate for the end of the line. Access will automatically "clip" the line to the height of the Detail section. Because the Line control doesn't contain data, Access won't expand the Detail section to accommodate the line you've drawn in code. Instead, Access draws as much of the 32,767-twip line as needed to fill the Detail section, and then it stops. The maximum value for Y2 is 32,767.

The same procedure could be used to draw horizontal lines for each section on the report. In the report example (rptVerticalLines) in the database accompanying this chapter

(Chapter21.accdb), we've added Line controls to the report instead. Using the Line control when the height of the report section is fixed (for example, in the group header and footer) is faster than drawing the line for each of these sections.

> **NOTE**
>
> When a report is double-clicked in the Navigation pane, it opens in Report view by default. To see certain techniques, like the vertical line technique, you must switch to Print Preview.

Adding a blank line every *n* records

Detail sections chock-full of dozens or hundreds of records can be difficult to read. It's easy to lose your place when reading across columns of figures and when the rows are crowded together on the page. Wouldn't it be nice to insert a blank row every fourth or fifth record in a Detail section? It's much easier to read a single row of data in a report (rptGapsEvery5th in Chapter21.accdb) where the records have been separated by white space every fifth record (see Figure 21.25).

FIGURE 21.25

Using white space to break up tabular data can make it easier to read.

rptGapsEvery5th

Northwind Traders Order Details

Product ID	Unit Price	Quantity	Discount
11	$14.00	12	0%
42	$9.80	10	0%
72	$34.80	5	0%
14	$18.60	9	0%
51	$42.40	40	0%
41	$7.70	10	0%
51	$42.40	35	15%
65	$16.80	15	15%
22	$16.80	6	5%
57	$15.60	15	5%
65	$16.80	20	0%
20	$64.80	40	5%
33	$2.00	25	5%
60	$27.20	40	0%
31	$10.00	20	0%
39	$14.40	42	0%

Page: 1   No Filter

Access provides no way to insert a blank row in the middle of a Detail section. You can, however, trick Access into inserting white space in the Detail section now and then with a little bit of programming and a couple of hidden controls.

Figure 21.26 reveals the trick behind the arrangement you see in Figure 21.25. An empty, unbound text box named txtSpacer is placed below the fields containing data in the Detail section. To the left of txtSpacer is another unbound text box named txtCounter.

FIGURE 21.26

This report trick uses hidden unbound text boxes in the Detail section.

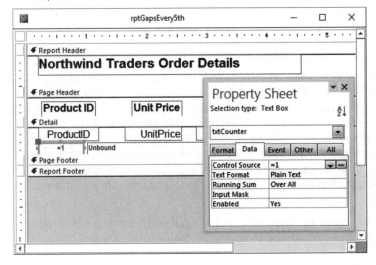

Set the properties in Table 21.1 for txtSpacer, txtCounter, and the Detail sections.

TABLE 21.1   Properties for the "Blank Line" Example

Control	Property	Value
txtSpacer	Visible	Yes
	Can Shrink	Yes
txtCounter	Visible	No
	Running Sum	Over All
	Control Source	=1
Detail1	Can Shrink	Yes

These properties effectively hide the unbound txtSpacer and txtCounter controls, and permit these controls and the Detail section to shrink as necessary when the txtSpacer Text

Box control is empty. Even though txtSpacer is visible to the user, Access shrinks it to 0 height if it contains no data. The txtCounter control never needs any space because its Visible property is set to No, hiding it from the user.

The last step is to enter the following code as the Detail section's Format event procedure:

```
Private Sub Detail1_Format(Cancel As Integer, _
  FormatCount As Integer)

If Me.txtCounter.Value Mod 5 = 0 Then
  Me.txtSpacer.Value = Space$(1)
Else
  Me.txtSpacer.Value = Null
End If


End Sub
```

The Format event occurs as Access begins to format the controls within the Detail section. The value in txtCounter is incremented each time a record is added to the Detail section. The Mod operator returns whatever number is left over when the value in txtCounter is divided by 5. When txtCounter is evenly divisible by 5, the result of the txtCounter Mod 5 expression is 0, which causes a space character to be assigned to txtSpacer. In this situation, because txtSpacer is no longer empty, Access increases the height of the Detail section to accommodate txtSpacer, causing the "empty" space every fifth record to be printed in the Detail section. You never actually see txtSpacer because all it contains is an empty space character.

txtCounter can be placed anywhere within the Detail section of the report. Make txtSpacer as tall as you want the blank space to be when it's revealed on the printout.

Even-odd page printing

If you've ever prepared a report for two-sided printing, you may have encountered the need for knowing whether the data is being printed on the even side of the page or the odd side of the page. Most users prefer the page number to be located near the outermost edge of the paper. On the odd-numbered page, the page number should appear on the right edge of the page, while on the even-numbered side, the page number must appear on the left side of the page. How, then, do you move the page number from side to side?

Assuming the page number appears in the Page Footer section of the report, you can use the page footer's Format event to determine whether the current page is even or odd, and align the text to the left or right side of the text box accordingly.

The basic design of rptEvenOdd is shown in Figure 21.27. Notice that txtPageNumber is made almost as wide as the report—much wider than needed to display its data. Also, the Text Align property is set to Right. The Format event will determine whether the text is aligned to the right or left, so it doesn't matter if you set Text Align to Right or Left at design time.

FIGURE 21.27

txtPageNumber is the same width as the report.

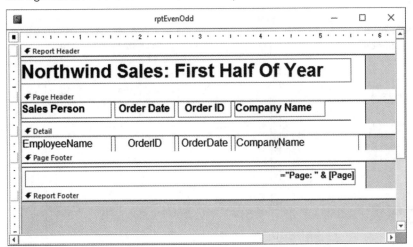

The Page Footer Format event procedure adjusts the Text Align property of txtPageNumber to shift the page number all the way to the left or right side of the text box depending on whether the page is even or odd:

```
Private Sub PageFooter1_Format(Cancel As Integer, _
    FormatCount As Integer)

    Const byALIGN_LEFT As Byte = 1
    Const byALIGN_RIGHT As Byte = 3

    If Me.Page Mod 2 = 0 Then
        Me.txtPageNumber.TextAlign = byALIGN_LEFT
    Else
        Me.txtPageNumber.TextAlign = byALIGN_RIGHT
    End If

End Sub
```

In this event procedure, any time the expression Me.Page Mod 2 is zero (meaning the page number is even), the Text Align property is set to Left. On odd-numbered pages, Text Align is set to Right.

Figure 21.28 shows that Page 1, an odd numbered page, is shown on the right side, and Page 2, an even numbered page, is shown on the left.

FIGURE 21.28

txtPageNumber jumps from right to left.

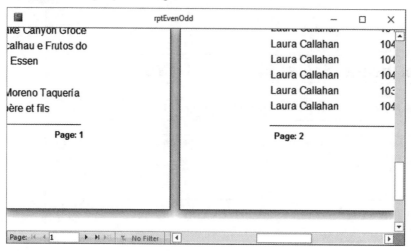

Using different formats in the same text box

On some reports, you may want the format of certain fields in a record to change according to the values in other fields on the report. A good example is a journal voucher report in a multicurrency financial system in which the voucher detail debit or credit amount format varies according to the number of decimal places used to display the currency value.

Unfortunately, a control in a Detail section of a report can have only one format specified in its Property Sheet. Use the following trick to set the format property at run time. The FlexFormat() function, which is stored in the MFunctions module and used in rptFlex-Format, uses the lDecimals argument to return a string specifying the desired format:

```
Public Function FlexFormat(lDecimals As Long) As String

    FlexFormat = "#,##0." & String(lDecimals, "0")

End Function
```

The String function returns text that has lDecimal number of characters and all the characters are 0. If lDecimals is 2, for example, FlexFormat returns "#,##0.00".

Assume that the field to be dynamically formatted has its Control Source set to [Amount]. The format of the Amount text box should vary depending on the value of the CurrDecPlaces field in the same record. CurrDecPlaces is a Long Integer data type. To use FlexFormat, change the Control Source property of the Amount text box to the following:

```
=Format([Amount],FlexFormat([CurrDecPlaces]))
```

The Amount text box will be dynamically formatted according to the value contained in the CurrDecPlaces text box. This trick may be generalized to format fields other than currency fields. By increasing the number of parameters of the user-defined formatting function, the formatting can be dependent on more than one field, if necessary.

Centering the title

Centering a report title directly in the middle of the page is often difficult. The easiest way to guarantee that the title is centered is to stretch the title from left margin to right margin, and then click the Center button in the Text Formatting group of the Home tab.

Aligning control labels

Keeping text boxes and their labels properly aligned on reports is sometimes difficult. Because a text box and its label can be independently moved on the report, all too often the label's position must be adjusted to bring it into alignment with the text box.

You can eliminate text box labels completely by including the label text as part of the text box's record source. Use the concatenation character to add the label text to the text box's control source:

```
= "Product: " & [ProductName]
```

Now, whenever you move the text box, both the label and the bound record source move as a unit. The only drawback to this technique is that you must use the same format for the text box and its label.

Micro-adjusting controls

The easiest way to adjust the size or position of controls on a report in tiny increments is to hold down either the Shift or Ctrl key and press the arrow key corresponding to Table 21.2.

TABLE 21.2   Micro-Adjustment Keystroke Combinations

Key Combination	Adjustment
Ctrl+Left Arrow	Move left
Ctrl+Right Arrow	Move right
Ctrl+Up Arrow	Move up
Ctrl+Down Arrow	Move down
Shift+Left Arrow	Reduce width
Shift+Right Arrow	Increase width
Shift+Up Arrow	Reduce height
Shift+Down Arrow	Increase height

Another resizing technique is to position the cursor over any of the sizing handles on a selected control and double-click. The control automatically "sizes to fit" the text contained within the control. This quick method can also be used to align not only labels but also text boxes to the grid.

Adding Data

When you're looking at data through forms, you can usually assume that the data is current. However, with printed reports, you don't always know how old the data is. Adding little touches like when the report was printed can help increase the confidence the user has in the report. This section shows you some techniques that enable you to add additional information to the report to let the users know something of its origin.

Adding more information to a report

You probably know that the following expression in an unbound text box prints the current page and the number of pages contained in the report:

```
="Page " & [Page] & " of " & [Pages]
```

Both Page and Pages are report properties that are available at run time and can be included on the report.

But consider the value of adding other report properties on the report. Most of the report properties can be added to unbound text boxes as long as the property is enclosed in square brackets. For the most part, these properties are only of value to you as the developer, but they may also be useful to your users.

For example, the report's Name, Record Source, and other properties are easily added the same way. Figure 21.29 demonstrates how unbound text boxes can deliver this information to a report footer or some other place on the report.

The inset in the lower part of Figure 21.29 shows the information provided by adding the four text boxes to this report. Very often, the user is not even aware of the name of a report—the only text the user sees associated with reports is the text that appears in the title bar (in other words, the report's Caption property). If a user is having problems with a report, it might be helpful to display the information you see in Figure 21.29 in the report footer.

Adding the user's name to a bound report

An unbound text box with its Control Source set to an unresolved reference will cause Access to pop up a dialog box requesting the information necessary to complete the text box. For example, an unbound text box with its Control Source set to the following displays the dialog box you see in the middle of Figure 21.30 when the report is run:

```
=[What is your name?]
```

FIGURE 21.29

rptMoreInfo demonstrates how to add more information to your reports.

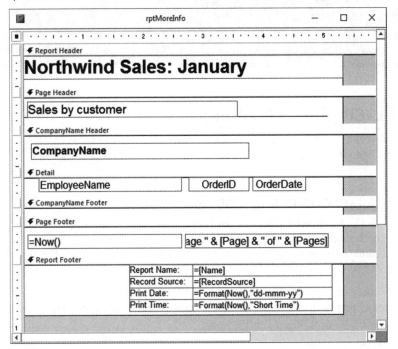

FIGURE 21.30

Use an unbound text box to capture useful information.

Access displays a similar Parameter dialog box for each parameter in a parameter query. The text entered into the text box is then displayed on the report. (rptUserName in Chapter21.accdb on this book's companion website demonstrates this technique.)

The unbound text box on the report can be referenced by other controls on the report. The Enter Parameter Value dialog box appears before the report is prepared for printing, which means that the data you enter into the dialog box can be used in expressions, calculations, or the VBA code behind the report.

> **TIP**
>
> VBA includes the `ENVIRON()` function, which can be used to get the user's name automatically. Use `ENVIRON("USERNAME")` in a VBA function and refer to that function in a text box's Control Source to display the user's name without prompting for it. The username returned by `ENVIRON()` is easily changed by the user, so don't use it where identity is critical.

Adding Even More Flexibility

As you've probably discovered by now, reporting in Access is a very large topic. We've included a few additional techniques that will help you make your reports even more flexible to users.

Displaying all reports in a combo box

The names of all the top-level database objects are stored in the MSysObjects system table. You can run queries against MSysObjects just as you can run queries against any other table in the database. It's easy to fill a combo box or list box with a list of the report objects in an Access database.

Choose Table/Query as the Row Source Type for the list box and put this SQL statement in the Row Source of your list box to fill the box with a list of all reports in the database:

```
SELECT DISTINCT [Name] FROM MSysObjects
WHERE [Type] = -32764
ORDER BY [Name];
```

The `-32764` identifies report objects in MSysObjects, one of the system tables used by Access. The results are shown in Figure 21.31.

> **NOTE**
>
> Reports don't have to be open for this technique to work. MSysObjects knows all the objects in the database, so no reports will escape detection using this technique.

If you're using a naming convention for your database objects, use a prefix to show only the reports you want. The following code returns only those reports that begin with tmp:

```
SELECT DISTINCTROW [Name] FROM MSysObjects
WHERE [Type] = -32764 AND Left([Name], 3) = "tmp"
ORDER BY [Name];
```

Because MSysObjects stores the names of all database objects, you can return the names of the other top-level database objects as well. Just substitute the -32764 as the type value in the preceding SQL statement with the Table 21.3 values to return different database object types.

FIGURE 21.31

frmAllReports displays the reports in Chapter21.accdb.

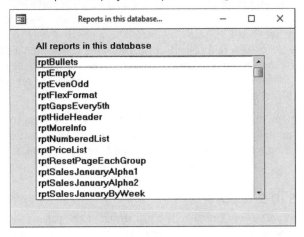

TABLE 21.3 **Access Object Types and Values**

Object	Type Value
Local Tables	1
Linked tables (except tables linked using ODBC)	6
Linked tables using ODBC	4
Forms	−32768
Modules	−32761
Macros	−32766
Queries	5
Reports	−32764

To view the MSysObjects table, select the Show System Objects check box in the Navigation Options dialog box (which you can get to by right-clicking the Navigation pane's title bar, and selecting Navigation Options from the shortcut menu). MSysObjects does *not* have to be visible for this trick to work.

NOTE

Although Microsoft says that MSysObjects and the type values are not supported and are, therefore, prone to change at any time, Access has used the same type values for many, many years. It's unlikely Microsoft will drop the MSysObjects table or change the type values, but this trick is not guaranteed to work indefinitely.

Fast printing from queried data

A report that is based on a query can take a long time to print. Because reports and forms can't share the same recordset, once a user has found the correct record on a form, it's a shame to have to run the query over again to print the record on a query. A way to "cache" the information on the form is to create a table (we'll call it tblCache) containing all the fields that are eventually printed on the report. Then, when the user has found the correct record on the form, copy the data from the form to tblCache, and open the report. The report, of course, is based on tblCache.

The query is run only once to populate the form. Copying the data from the form to tblCache is a very fast operation, and multiple records can be added to tblCache as needed. Because the report is now based on a table, it opens quickly and is ready to print as soon as the report opens.

Using snaking columns in a report

When the data displayed on a report doesn't require the full width of the page, you may be able to conserve the number of pages by printing the data as snaking columns, as in a dictionary or phone book. With snaking columns, less space is wasted and fewer pages need to be printed. Other benefits are that more information is available at a glance and that many people find snaking columns more aesthetically pleasing than simple blocks of data.

For the examples in this section, we need a query that returns more data than we've been using up to this point. Figure 21.32 shows the query used to prepare the sample reports in this section.

FIGURE 21.32

This query returns more detailed information than we've been using.

This query returns the following information: CompanyName, OrderID, OrderDate, ProductName, UnitPrice, and Quantity for the period from January 1, 2019, to March 31, 2019.

The initial report design for rptSalesQ1 is shown in Design view in Figure 21.33. This rather complex report includes a group based on the order ID for each order placed by the company, as well as a group based on the company itself. This design enables us to summarize data for each order during the quarter, as well as for the company for the entire quarter.

FIGURE 21.33

Notice how narrow the records in this report are.

The same report in Print Preview mode is shown in Figure 21.34. Notice that the report really doesn't make good use of the page width available to it. In fact, each record of this report is only 3¼ inches wide.

Setting a report to print as snaking columns is actually part of the print setup for the report, not an attribute of the report itself. With the report in Design view, click the Columns button on the Report Design Tools Page Setup tab of the Ribbon to open the Page Setup dialog box (shown in Figure 21.35) with the Columns tab selected. Change the Number of Columns property to 2. As you change Number of Columns from 1 to 2, the Column Layout area near the bottom of the Layout tab becomes active, showing you that Access has selected the Across, Then Down option to print items across the page first, and then down the page. Although this printing direction is appropriate for mailing labels, it's not what we want for our report. Select the Down, Then Across option to direct Access to print the report as snaking columns (see Figure 21.35).

FIGURE 21.34

The report makes poor use of the available page width.

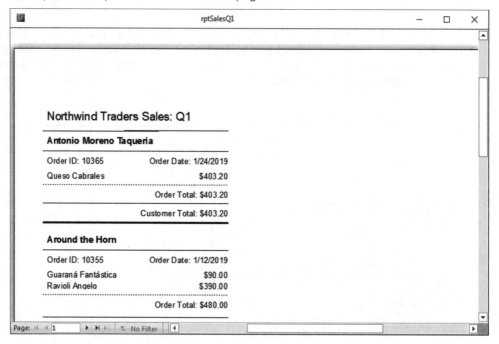

FIGURE 21.35

Only a few changes are needed to produce snaking columns.

When working with snaking columns, make sure the proper Column Layout option is selected. If you neglect to set the Column Layout to Down, Then Across, the snaking columns will be laid out horizontally across the page. This common error can cause a lot of confusion because the report won't look as expected (see Figure 21.36). The reports shown in Figures 21.36 and 21.37 are the same with the exception of the Column Layout setting.

FIGURE 21.36

The wrong Column Layout setting can be confusing.

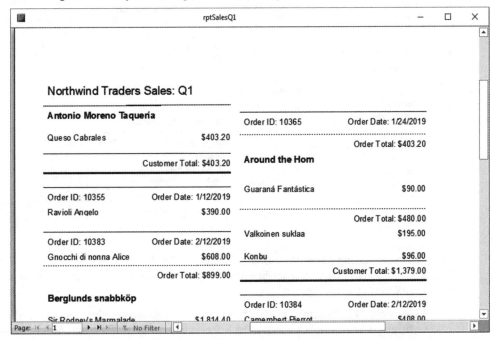

As long as the Same as Detail check box is *not* checked in the Page Setup dialog box, Access intelligently adjusts the Column Spacing and other options to accommodate the number of items across that you've specified for the report. With Same as Detail checked, Access will force the columns to whatever width is specified for the columns in Design view, which might mean that the number of columns specified in the Number of Columns parameter won't fit on the page.

Figure 21.37 clearly demonstrates the effect of changing the report to a snaking two-column layout using the Down, Then Across layout option. Before the change, this report required 17 pages to print all the data. After this change, only nine pages are required.

FIGURE 21.37

Snaking columns conserve page space and provide more information at a glance.

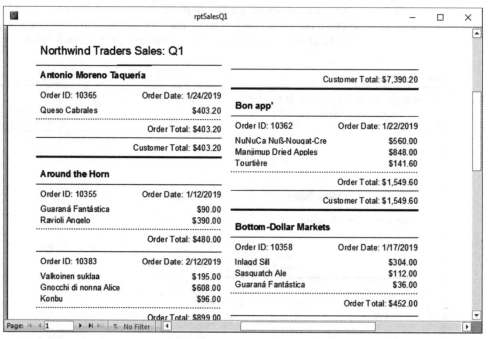

You may be wondering about the other print options in the Page Setup dialog box (refer to Figure 21.35). Here is a short description of each of the relevant settings on the Columns tab of the Page Setup dialog box:

- **Number of Columns:** Specifies the number of columns in the report. You should be aware that Number of Columns affects only the Detail section, Group Header section, and Group Footer section of the report. The Page Header section and Page Footer section are not duplicated for each column. When designing a multi-column report, you must keep the width of the design area narrow enough to fit on the page when multiplied by the number of columns you've selected. Most often, printing a report in landscape mode helps the width required for more than one column in a report.

- **Row Spacing:** Additional vertical space allowed for each detail item. Use this setting if you need to force more space between detail items than the report's design allows.

- **Column Spacing:** Additional horizontal space allowed per column. Use this setting if you need to force more space between columns in the report than the design allows.

- **Column Size – Same as Detail:** The column width and detail height will be the same as on the report in Design view. This property is useful when you need to fine-tune the column placement on a report (for example, when printing the data onto preprinted forms). Making adjustments to the report's design will directly influence how the columns print on paper.

- **Column Size – Width and Height:** The width and height of a column. These options are handy when printing onto preprinted forms to ensure that the data falls where you want it to.

- **Column Layout:** How the items are to be printed: either Across, Then Down or Down, Then Across.

In addition to these properties, be sure to take note of the New Row Or Col property for the CompanyName Header section (see Figure 21.38). The values for New Row Or Col are None, Before Section, After Section, and Before & After. You use New Row Or Col to force Access to, for example, start a new column immediately after a group footer or detail section has printed (see Figure 21.39). Depending on your reports and their data, New Row Or Col may provide you with the flexibility necessary to make reports more readable.

FIGURE 21.38

Headers (and footers) have properties that can be used to control actions when the grouping value changes.

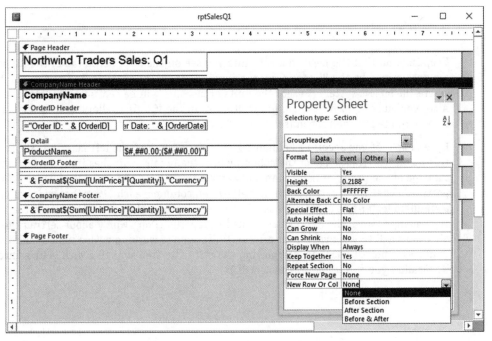

FIGURE 21.39

The New Row Or Col property forces Access to start a column before or after a section.

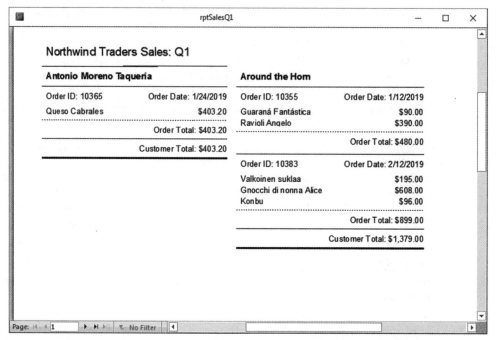

Keep in mind that the measurement units you see on the Page Setup tab of the Ribbon are determined by the Windows international settings. For example, in Germany or Japan where the metric system is used, the units of measure will be centimeters instead of inches. Also, you must allow for the margin widths set in the Margins gallery, accessed from the Page Setup tab of the Ribbon (see Figure 21.40).

For example, if you specify a Column Size Width of 3.5" and the left margin is set to 1", this means the right edge of the column will actually fall 4½ inches from the left physical edge of the paper, or more than halfway across an 8-x-11-inch sheet of paper printed in portrait mode. These settings will not allow two columns, each 3½ inches wide, to print on a standard letter-size sheet of paper. In this case, you might consider reducing the left and right margins until the 3½-inch columns fit properly. (Don't worry about setting the margins too small to work with your printer. Unless you're working with a nonstandard printer, Windows is pretty smart about knowing the printable area available with your printer and won't allow you to set margins too small.)

FIGURE 21.40

All report page settings must consider the margin widths.

Exploiting two-pass report processing

In Chapter 20, we mention that Access uses a two-pass approach when formatting and printing reports. We'll now explore what this capability means to you and how you can exploit both passes in your applications.

The main advantage of two-pass reporting is that your reports can include expressions that rely on information available anywhere in the report. For example, placing a control with the Sum() function in a header or footer means that Access will use the first pass to accumulate the data required by the function, and then use the second pass to process the values in that section before printing them.

Another obvious example is putting an unbound text box in the footer of a report containing the following expression:

```
="Page " & [Page] & " of " & [Pages]
```

The built-in Pages variable (which contains the total number of pages in the report) isn't determined until Access has completed the first pass through the report. On the second pass, Access has a valid number to use in place of the Pages variable.

The biggest advantage of two-pass reporting is that you're free to use aggregate functions that depend on the report's underlying record source. Group headers and footers can include information that can't be known until the entire record source is processed.

There are many situations where aggregate information provides valuable insight into data analysis. Consider a report that must contain each salesperson's performance over the last year measured against the total sales for the sales organization, or a region's sales figures against sales for the entire sales area. A bookstore might want to know what portion of its inventory is devoted to each book category.

Figure 21.41 shows such a report. The Number of Customers, Total Sales, and Average Purchase information at the top of this report (rptSummary) are all part of the report header. In a one-pass report writer, the data needed to perform these calculations would not appear until the bottom of the page, after all the records have been processed and laid out.

FIGURE 21.41

The summary information is part of the report's header.

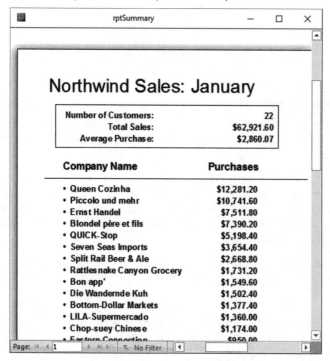

A glance at rptSummary in Design view (see Figure 21.42) reveals that the text boxes in the report header are populated with data derived from these mathematical expressions:

```
Number of Customers: =Count([CompanyName])
Total Sales: =Format(Sum([Purchases]),"Currency")
Average Purchase: =Format(Sum([Purchases])/ _
    Count([CompanyName]), "Currency")
```

FIGURE 21.42

rptSummary in Design view.

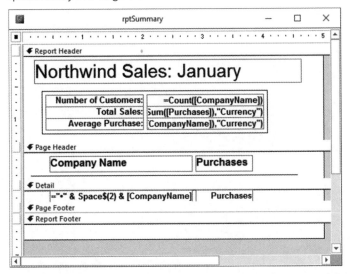

The Count() and Sum() functions both require information that isn't available until the entire report has been processed in the first pass. As long as Access can find the arguments provided to these functions (CompanyName and Purchases) in the underlying recordset, the calculations proceed without any action by the user.

Assigning unique names to controls

If you use the Report Wizard or drag fields from the Field List when designing your reports, Access assigns the new text boxes the same names as the fields in the recordset underlying the report. For example, if you drag a field named Discount from the Field List, both the Name and Control Source properties of the text box are set to Discount.

If another control on the report references the text box, or if you change the Control Source of the text box to a calculated field, such as:

```
=IIf([Discount]=0,"N/A",[Discount])
```

you'll see #Error when you view the report. This happens because Access can't distinguish between the control named Discount and the field in the underlying recordset named Discount.

You must change the Name property of the control to something like txtDiscount so that Access can tell the difference between the control's name and the underlying field.

Part VI

Microsoft Access Programming Fundamentals

P art VI introduces macro programming and explains the art and science of Visual Basic for Applications (VBA).

Long maligned as weaker or inferior to VBA, macros were often relegated to second-class citizenship in many Access developer tool-kits. However, as you'll read later in this chapter, Microsoft introduced *embedded macros*, an efficient technique for auto-mating many tasks in forms and reports. Chapter 23 takes a look at data macros, which enable you to perform important data-management tasks at the table level.

Starting with Chapter 24, Part VI turns your attention to automation with VBA. VBA provides functionality that goes far beyond simply opening forms and reports and con-trolling the user interface.

IN THIS PART

Chapter 22
Using Access Macros

Chapter 23
Using Access Data Macros

Chapter 24
Getting Started with Access VBA

Chapter 25
Mastering VBA Data Types and Procedures

Chapter 26
Understanding the Access Event Model

Chapter 27
Debugging Your Access Applications

Part VI

Microsoft Access
Programming Fundamentals

Using Access Macros

IN THIS CHAPTER

Getting acquainted with macros

Understanding macro security

Working with multi-action macros

Using submacros for actions that are frequently required

Making decisions with conditions

Using temporary variables

Handling errors and debugging your macros

Understanding embedded macros

Comparing macros to VBA

Macros have been a part of Access since the beginning. As Access evolved as a development tool, the Visual Basic for Applications (VBA) programming language became the standard in automating Access database applications. Macros in versions prior to Access 2007 lacked variables and error handling, which caused many developers to abandon macros altogether. Access today has these, which make macros a much more viable alternative to VBA than in previous versions. If you're creating a database to be used on the Web, or if you aren't a VBA guru but you still want to customize the actions that your application executes, then building structured macros is the answer.

ON THE WEB

This chapter uses a database named `Chapter22.accdb`. If you haven't already downloaded it from this book's website, you'll need to do so now. This database contains the tables, forms, reports, and macros used in this chapter.

An Introduction to Macros

A *macro* is a tool that allows you to automate tasks in Access. It's different from Word's Macro Recorder, which lets you record a series of actions and play them back later. (It's also different from Word in that Word macros are actually VBA code, whereas Access macros are something very different.) Access macros let you perform defined actions and add functionality to your forms and reports. Think of macros as a simplified, step-wise programming language. You build a macro as a list of actions to perform, and you decide when you want those actions to occur.

Building macros consists of selecting actions from a drop-down list and then filling in the action's *arguments* (values that provide information to the action). Macros let you choose actions without writing a single line of VBA code. The macro actions are a subset of commands VBA provides. Most people find it easier to build a macro than to write VBA code. If you're not familiar with VBA, building macros is a great stepping-stone to learning some of the commands available to you while providing added value to your Access applications.

Suppose you want to build a main form with buttons that open the other forms in your application. You can add a button to the form, build a macro that opens another form in your application, and then assign this macro to the button's Click event. The macro can be a stand-alone item that appears in the Navigation pane, or it can be an embedded object that is part of the event itself (see the "Embedded Macros" section, later in this chapter).

Creating a macro

A simple way to demonstrate how to create macros is to build one that displays a message box that says "Hello World!" To create a new stand-alone macro, click the Macro button on the Macros & Code group on the Create tab of the Ribbon (shown in Figure 22.1).

FIGURE 22.1

Use the Macro button on the Create tab to build a new stand-alone macro.

Clicking the Macro button opens the macro builder (shown in Figure 22.2). Initially, the macro builder is almost featureless. The only thing in the Macro Builder is a drop-down list of macro actions.

To the right of the Macro Builder you may see the Action Catalog. There are dozens of different macro actions, and knowing which action to use for a particular task can be an issue. The Action Catalog provides a tree view of all available macro actions and helps you know which action is needed to perform a particular task.

Select MessageBox from the drop-down list in the macro builder. The macro builder changes to display an area where you input the arguments (Message, Beep, Type, and Title) associated with the MessageBox action.

Set the arguments as follows:

- **Message:** Hello World!
- **Beep:** No
- **Type:** None
- **Title:** A Simple Macro

FIGURE 22.2

The macro builder displaying the Macro Builder and Action Catalog.

Macro window   Action catalog

Your screen should look similar to Figure 22.3. The Message argument defines the text that appears in the message box and is the only argument that is required and has no default. The Beep argument determines whether a beep is heard when the message box appears. The Type argument sets which icon appears in the message box: None, Critical, Warning?, Warning!, or Information. The Title argument defines the text that appears in the message box's title bar.

FIGURE 22.3

The Hello World! macro uses the MessageBox action to display a message.

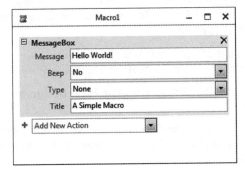

To run the macro, click the Run button in the Tools group of the Design tab of the Ribbon. (The Run button looks like a big red exclamation point at the far left of the Ribbon.) When you create a new macro or change an existing macro, you'll be prompted to save the macro. In fact, you must save the macro before Access runs it for you. When prompted, click Yes to save it, provide a name (such as "mcrHelloWorld"), and click OK. The macro runs and displays a message box with the arguments you specified (shown in Figure 22.4).

FIGURE 22.4

Running the Hello World! macro displays a message box.

You can also run the macro from the Navigation pane. Close the macro builder and display the Macros group in the Navigation pane. Double-click the mcrHelloWorld macro to run it. You'll see the same message box that displayed when you ran the macro from the design window.

Notice that the message box always appears near the middle of the screen and blocks you from working with Access until you click OK. These are built-in behaviors of the message box object and are identical in every regard to a message box displayed from VBA code.

When you're satisfied with the Hello World! macro, click the Close button in the upper-right corner of the macro builder to return to the main Access window.

Assigning a macro to an event

When you're creating macros, you probably don't want end users using the Navigation pane to run them—or worse, running them from the macro builder. Macros are intended for you to automate your application without writing VBA code. In order to make an application easy to use, assign your macros to an object's event.

The most common event to which you might assign a macro is a button's Click event. Follow these steps to create a simple form with a button that runs mcrHelloWorld:

1. **Select the Create tab on the Ribbon, and then click the Form Design button in the Forms group.**

2. **On the Form Design Tools Design tab of the Ribbon, deselect the Use Control Wizards option in the Controls group.** For this example, you don't want to use a wizard to decide what this button does.

3. **Click the Button control and draw a button on the form.**

4. **Set the button's Name property to cmdHelloWorld.** Press F4 to open the button's Property Sheet if it isn't visible on the screen.

5. **Set the button's Caption property to Hello World!.** This is the text that appears on the face of the button.

6. **Click the drop-down list in the button's** `On Click` **event property, and select mcrHelloWorld from the list (shown in Figure 22.5).**

FIGURE 22.5

Set any object's event property to the macro to trigger that macro when that event occurs.

22

TIP

You aren't limited to the button's `Click` event. If you want a macro to run every time a form loads, set the `On Load` event property of the form to the macro's name. Select the Event tab on any object's Property Sheet to see the available events.

That's all there is to creating and running a macro. Just select the action, set the action arguments, and assign the macro to an event property.

NOTE

Historically, there has been quite a bit of confusion about the names of events and their associated event properties. An event is always an action, such as `Click`, while its event property is `OnClick` or `On Click`. Conceptually, they're almost the same thing, but in technical terms, an event (like `Click` or `Open`) is an action supported by an Access object (like a form or command button), and an event procedure (`OnClick` or `OnOpen`) is how the event is attached or bound to the object.

Understanding Macro Security

The Hello World! macro we built in the last section is as harmless as they come. But not all macros are harmless. You can do almost anything in a macro that you can do in the Access user interface. Some of those things, like running a delete query, can cause data loss. Access has built-in a security environment that helps you prevent unwanted, harmful macros from being run.

When you run forms, reports, queries, macros, and VBA code in your application, Access uses the Trust Center to determine which commands may be unsafe and which unsafe commands you want to run. From the Trust Center's perspective, macros and VBA code are "macros" and shouldn't be trusted by default. Unsafe commands could allow a malicious user to hack into your hard drive or other resource in your environment. A malicious user could possibly delete files from your hard drive, alter the computer's configuration, or generally wreak all kinds of havoc in your workstation or even throughout your network environment.

Each time a form, report, or other object opens, Access checks its list of unsafe commands. By default, when Access encounters one of the unsafe commands, it blocks the command from execution. To tell Access to block these potentially unsafe commands, you must enable sandbox mode.

Enabling sandbox mode

Sandbox mode allows Access to block any of the commands in the unsafe list it encounters when running forms, reports, queries, macros, data access pages, and Visual Basic code. Here's how to enable it:

1. **Open Access, click the File button, and select Options.** The Access Options dialog box appears.

2. **Select the Trust Center tab, and then click Trust Center Settings.** The Trust Center dialog box appears.

3. **Select the Macro Settings tab (shown in Figure 22.6).**

4. **Select either Disable All Macros without Notification or Disable All Macros with Notification.**

FIGURE 22.6

Enabling sandbox mode.

5. **Restart Access to apply the security change.**

The Macro Settings tab provides four levels of macro security:

- **Disable All Macros without Notification:** All macros and VBA code are disabled and the user isn't prompted to enable them.
- **Disable All Macros with Notification:** All macros and VBA code are disabled and the user is prompted to enable them.
- **Disable All Macros Except Digitally Signed Macros:** The status of the macro's digital signature is validated for digitally signed macros. For unsigned macros, a prompt displays advising the user to enable the macro or to cancel opening the database.
- **Enable All Macros (Not Recommended; Potentially Dangerous Code Can Be Run):** Macros and VBA code are not checked for digital signatures and no warning displays for unsigned macros.

A *digital signature* (contained within a *digital certificate*) is an encrypted secure file that accompanies a macro or document. It confirms that the author is a trusted source for the macro or document. Digital signatures are generally implemented within large organizations that are willing to fund the expense of purchasing and maintaining digital signatures. You, or your organization's IT department, can obtain a digital certificate through a commercial certification authority, like VeriSign, Inc., or Thawte. Search `http://msdn .microsoft.com` for "Microsoft Root Certificate Program Members" to obtain information on how to obtain a digital certificate.

The default, and generally the best choice, is Disable All Macros with Notification. During the development and maintenance cycles, you'll want all the code and macros in the application to execute without interrupting you with permissions dialog boxes. The next section describes Trusted Locations. You can put your development database in a trusted location to avoid having to enable unsigned code, but still be protected from other databases you may open.

If you or your organization has acquired a digital certificate, you can use it to sign your Access projects:

1. **Open the Access database to digitally sign; then access any module to open the Visual Basic Editor.**
2. **Choose Tools ➪ Digital Signature from the Visual Basic Editor menu.** The Digital Signature dialog box opens, as shown in Figure 22.7.
3. **Click Choose to display the Select Certificate dialog box and select a certificate from the list.**
4. **Select the certificate to add to the Access project.**
5. **Click OK to close the Select Certificate dialog box, and click OK again to close the Digital Signature dialog box and save the security setting.**

FIGURE 22.7

Digitally signing an Access project.

> **NOTE**
>
> Don't sign your Access project until the application has been thoroughly tested and you don't expect to make any further changes to it. Modifying any of the code in the project invalidates the digital signature.

> **TIP**
>
> To prevent users from making unauthorized changes to the code in your project, be sure to lock the project and apply a project password.

The Trust Center

The Trust Center is where you can find security and privacy settings for Access. To display the Trust Center, click the File button and click Options to open the Access Options dialog box. Select the Trust Center tab, and then click Trust Center Settings.

Here's a description of each section and what it controls:

- **Trusted Publishers:** Displays a list of trusted publishers—publishers where you clicked Trust All Documents from This Publisher when encountering a potentially unsafe macro—for Office. To remove a publisher from this list, select the publisher and click Remove. Trusted publishers must have a valid digital signature that hasn't expired.

- **Trusted Locations:** Displays the list of trusted locations on your computer or network. From this section, you can add, remove, or modify folders on your computer that will always contain trusted files. Any file in a trusted location can be opened without being checked by the Trust Center. You can also choose not to allow network locations and to disable all Trusted Locations and accept signed files.

- **Trusted Documents:** When Trusted Documents is selected, the name of the Access application is added to a special area in the system registry on the user's computer. Then, each time the application is used, it is recognized as a *trusted document*, and all the macros, code, and other elements of the application are enabled without interrupting the user's workflow.

- **Trusted Add-In Catalogs:** The Trusted Add-In Catalogs section allows you to add, remove, or modify the SharePoint catalogs you trust.
- **Add-ins:** Lets you to set up how Access handles add-ins. You can choose whether add-ins need to be digitally signed from a trusted source and whether to display a notification for unsigned add-ins. You can also choose to disable all add-ins, which may impair functionality.
- **ActiveX Settings:** Lets you set the security level for ActiveX controls.
- **Macro Settings:** Lets you set the security setting for macros not in a trusted location. (For more information on Macro Settings, see the previous section on sandbox mode.)
- **Message Bar:** Lets you set whether to display the message bar that warns you about blocked content, or to never show information about blocked content.
- **Privacy Options:** Lets you choose how Microsoft Office Online communicates with your computer. You can set options to use Microsoft Office Online for help, show featured links at startup, download files to determine system problems, and sign up for the Customer Experience Improvement Program.

Multi-action Macros

The true power of macros comes from performing multiple actions at the click of a button. Creating a macro that runs a series of action queries is better than double-clicking each action query in the Navigation pane—you may forget to run one or you may run them out of proper sequence.

For this next example, Chapter22.accdb contains two delete queries that remove data from two different tables: tblContacts_Backup and tblProducts_Backup. Chapter22.accdb also includes two append queries that copy records from tblContacts and tblProducts to the backup tables.

The mcrBackupContactsAndProducts macro (also found in the Chapter 22.accdb sample database) automates the running of these four queries so that we have the ability to back up the data in the tblContacts table and the tblProducts table.

Table 22.1 shows the macro actions and action arguments for mcrBackupContactsAndProducts (a portion of which is shown in Figure 22.8).

> **NOTE**
>
> If all the actions don't appear in the Action drop-down list, click the Show All Actions command in the Show/Hide group on the Macro Tools Design tab of the Ribbon. Some macro actions require a trusted database or enabling macros through your security settings. Also, some macro actions are considered unsafe because they modify data in the database or perform actions that may cause damage to the application if used incorrectly. Macro actions that are considered unsafe are indicated by a warning icon (which looks like a yellow triangle containing an exclamation point) in the macro designer. By default, Access only displays trusted macro actions that run regardless of the security settings.

FIGURE 22.8

mcrBackupContactsAndProducts archives data from the live tables into the backup tables.

TABLE 22.1 mcrBackupContactsAndProducts

Action	Action Argument	Action Argument Setting
DisplayHourglassPointer	Hourglass On	Yes
SetWarnings	Warnings On	No
Echo	Echo On	No
	Status Bar Text	Step 1: Deleting Data
OpenQuery	Query Name	qryDeleteContactsBackup
	View	Datasheet
	Data Mode	Edit
OpenQuery	Query Name	qryDeleteProductsBackup
	View	Datasheet
	Data Mode	Edit
Echo	Echo On	No
	Status Bar Text	Step 2: Appending Data
OpenQuery	Query Name	qryAppendContactsBackup
	View	Datasheet
	Data Mode	Edit
OpenQuery	Query Name	qryAppendProductsBackup
	View	Datasheet
	Data Mode	Edit

Action	Action Argument	Action Argument Setting
Echo	Echo On	Yes
	Status Bar Text	\<Leave Blank\>
SetWarnings	Warnings On	Yes
DisplayHourglassPointer	Hourglass On	No
MessageBox	Message	Contacts and Products have been archived.
	Beep	Yes
	Type	Information
	Title	Finished Archiving

The heart of the macro is the four OpenQuery actions that run the four action queries. qryDeleteContactsBackup and qryDeleteProductsBackup clear the contents of tblContacts_Backup and tblProducts_Backup so that the current data can be copied into them. qryAppendContactsBackup and qryAppendProductsBackup append data from tblContacts and tblProducts into the backup tables.

As you look at Figure 22.8, you will note the warning icons next to a few of the actions in the macro (specifically SetWarnings and Echo). These icons simply indicate that the associated actions are potentially unsafe and may require a closer look.

Here's a closer look at the actions this macro performs:

- DisplayHourglassPointer: This action changes the cursor to an hourglass or a pointer using the Hourglass On argument. For macros that may take a while to run, set this argument to Yes at the beginning of the macro and to No at the end of the macro. Be sure not to forget to set Hourglass Off at the conclusion of the macro; otherwise, the hourglass cursor stays on indefinitely.

- SetWarnings: This action turns the system messages on or off using the Warnings On argument. When running action queries, you'll be prompted to make sure you want to run the action query, asked whether it's okay to delete these 58 records, and then asked again for the next action query. Set Warnings On to No at the beginning of the macro to turn these messages off. Setting Warnings On to No has the effect of automatically clicking the default button of the warning (usually OK or Yes). Don't forget to set warnings back to Yes at the end of the macro. Once warnings are turned off, the user won't get confirmation messages from Access on important actions like record deletions until warnings are re-enabled.

- Echo: In effect, the Echo command "freezes" the screen so that the user isn't aware of activities performed by the macro. Set the Echo On argument to No if you want to hide the results of the macro or Yes if you want to show the results. Set the Status Bar Text argument to give the user an indication of what's happening. This is useful in longer-running macros to know where in the process the macro is.

22

Be sure to restore the Echo On status to Yes at the end of the macro so that Access resumes its normal appearance. If Echo On is not set back to Yes, the user may think the application has "locked up" because of a problem.

■ OpenQuery: This action is the heart of the mcrBackupContactsAndProducts macro. OpenQuery opens a select or crosstab query or runs an action query. The Query Name argument contains the name of the query to open or run. The View argument lets you pick the view—Datasheet, Design, Print Preview, and so forth—for a select or crosstab query. The Data Mode argument lets you choose from Add, Edit, or Read Only to limit what users can do in a select query. The View and Data Mode arguments are ignored for action queries.

> **NOTE**
>
> You could easily build this macro just using the four OpenQuery actions, but running it would be cumbersome, requiring the user to watch the macro run through each query and be ready to confirm each query action. The DisplayHourglassPointer, SetWarnings, Echo, and MessageBox actions serve to eliminate the need for user interaction and let the user know when the macro has completed its activity.

Submacros

When automating your application with macros, you might easily get carried away filling the Navigation pane with a bunch of little macros for opening every form and every report. If you have a series of actions that are performed in a number of places, ideally you only want one copy, so that you need to make changes only in one place. *Submacros* give you that capability: You define the series of actions in one place as a submacro, and then invoke that submacro wherever it's needed.

The macro action drop-down list contains Submacro as an entry. While working on a macro, selecting Submacro from the action list adds an area to the macro where you can input the actions associated with the submacro.

Without using submacros, you'd have to create three separate macros to automate a main menu form with three buttons that open frmContacts, frmProducts, and frmSales. Using submacros, just create a single top-level macro that contains three submacros. Each of the submacros opens one form. Only the top-level macro appears in the Navigation pane. Table 22.2 shows the submacro names, the actions, and submacro actions for mcrMainMenu.

TABLE 22.2 mcrMainMenu

Submacro	Action	Action Argument	Action Argument Setting
OpenContacts	OpenForm	Form Name	frmContacts
		View	Form
		Filter Name	<Leave Blank>

Submacro	Action	Action Argument	Action Argument Setting
		Where Condition	\<Leave Blank\>
		Data Mode	\<Leave Blank\>
		Window Mode	Normal
OpenProducts	OpenForm	Form Name	frmProducts
		View	Form
		Filter Name	\<Leave Blank\>
		Where Condition	[ProductID]=3
		Data Mode	Read Only
		Window Mode	Dialog
OpenSales	OpenForm	Form Name	frmSales
		View	Layout
		Filter Name	qrySales2012
		Where Condition	\<Leave Blank\>
		Data Mode	Edit
		Window Mode	Icon

Figure 22.9 shows the creation of mcrMainMenu in progress. The developer has selected Submacro from the Add New Action list, provided a name (OpenContacts) for the submacro, and filled in its properties.

FIGURE 22.9

Adding a second submacro to a macro.

> **TIP**
>
> The Add New Action drop-down displays a list of available actions sorted alphabetically. However, the first four items—Comment, Group, If, and Submacro—are shown at the top of the list rather than in their proper place. These four items are really program flow elements and are separated from the items considered actions.

Next, the developer selected Submacro a second time from the Add New Action list, and provided OpenProduct as its name. None of the arguments for the second submacro has been filled in.

The confusing thing about submacros is that you see two Add New Action lists in Figure 22.9. One is at the very bottom of the main macro, while the second is inside the second submacro. The submacro that is currently being developed (OpenProducts) is enclosed in a lightly shaded box, while the completed submacro (OpenContacts) at the top of the main macro is not contained in a box.

> **NOTE**
>
> In Figure 22.9, notice the small minus sign to the left of Submacro in the first line of the macro. The minus sign is there to show you that the submacro is currently expanded so that you can see all the steps in the submacro. Clicking the minus sign collapses the macro to a single line, which lets you view more of the macro and its actions in a single glance. Several figures in this chapter show macros with portions collapsed (identifiable by the small plus sign to the left), so don't be confused if portions of a macro illustrated in a figure appear to be missing.

To implement a macro using submacros, create a form (frmMainMenu) with three buttons—in this case, cmdContacts, cmdProducts, and cmdSales. Then set the On Click event properties of these buttons as follows (see Figure 22.10):

Button Name	On Click Event Property
cmdContacts	mcrMainMenu.OpenContacts
cmdProducts	mcrMainMenu.OpenProducts
cmdSales	mcrMainMenu.OpenSales

Open frmMainMenu in Form view and click the Contacts button; frmContacts opens and displays all the records. Click the Products button to display frmProducts, which only displays one record. Click the Sales button to display frmSales in a minimized state, which displays the sales made in 2012.

To see why these forms open differently, take a look at the action arguments for the OpenForm action:

- Form Name: This argument is the name of the form you want the macro to open.
- View: This argument lets you select which view to open the form in: Form, Design, Print Preview, Datasheet, PivotTable, PivotChart, or Layout. For this example,

frmContacts and frmProducts open in Form view, while frmSales opens in Layout view.

- **Filter Name**: This argument lets you select a query or a filter saved as a query to restrict and/or sort the records for the form. For this example, this argument is set to qrySales2012 for the OpenSales macro. qrySales2012 is a query that outputs all the fields in the table and only displays sales between 1/1/2012 and 12/31/2012. This query also sorts the records by SaleDate.

- **Where Condition**: This argument lets you enter a SQL Where clause or expression that selects records for the form from its underlying table or query. For this example, this argument is set to [ProductID]=3 for the OpenProducts submacro, which only shows one record when you open frmProducts.

- **Data Mode**: This argument lets you choose the data-entry mode for the form. Select Add to only allow users to add new records, Edit to allow adding and editing of records, or Read Only to allow only viewing of records. This setting only applies to forms opened in Form view or Datasheet view, and overrides settings of the form's AllowEdits, AllowDeletions, AllowAdditions, and DataEntry properties. To use the form's setting for these properties, leave this argument blank. For this example, frmProducts opens in read-only mode, while frmContacts and frmSales allow editing.

- **Window Mode**: This argument lets you choose the window mode for the form. Select Normal to use the form's properties. Select Hidden to open the form with its Visible property set to No. Select Icon to open the form minimized. Select Dialog to open the form with its Modal and PopUp properties set to Yes and Border Style property set to Dialog. For this example, frmContacts opens normally, frmProducts opens as a dialog box, and frmSales opens minimized.

FIGURE 22.10

The submacro names appear after the macro object in the event property drop-down list.

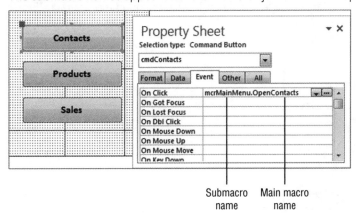

Submacro name   Main macro name

For more information on form properties, see Chapter 17.

> **NOTE**
> When you run a macro with submacros from the Navigation pane, only the first submacro executes.

If you're careful in planning your macros, you can create one top-level macro object for each form or report and use submacros for each action you want to perform in the form or report. Submacros let you limit the number of macros that appear in the Navigation pane and make managing numerous macros much easier.

Conditions

Submacros let you put multiple groups of actions in a single macro object, but a *condition* specifies certain criteria that must be met before the macro performs the action. The `If` macro action also takes a Boolean expression. If the expression evaluates to False, No, or 0, the action will not execute. If the expression evaluates to any other value, the action is performed.

Opening reports using conditions

To demonstrate conditions and the `If` macro action, frmReportMenu (shown in Figure 22.11), contains three buttons and a frame control (fraView) with two option buttons: Print and Print Preview. Clicking Print sets the frame's value to 1; clicking Print Preview sets the frame's value to 2.

FIGURE 22.11

frmReportMenu uses a frame to select the view in which to open the Contacts, Products, and Sales reports.

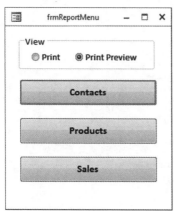

The macro that opens the reports uses submacros, as well as the If macro action. Table 22.3 shows the submacro names, conditions, actions, and action arguments for mcrReportMenu (a portion of which is shown in Figure 22.12), which opens one of three reports. The Filter Name and Where Condition arguments are blank for each OpenReport action.

TABLE 22.3 mcrReportMenu

Submacro Name	If Macro Action Condition	Action	Action Argument	Action Argument Setting
OpenContacts	[Forms]![frmReport Menu]![fraView]=1	OpenReport	Report Name	rptContacts_ Landscape
			View	Print
			Window Mode	Normal
	[Forms]![frmReport Menu]![fraView]=2	OpenReport	Report Name	rptContacts_ Landscape
			View	Print Preview
			Window Mode	Normal
OpenProducts	[Forms]![frmReport Menu]![fraView]=1	OpenReport	Report Name	rptProducts
			View	Print
			Window Mode	Normal
	[Forms]![frmReport Menu]![fraView]=2	OpenReport	Report Name	rptProducts
			View	Print Preview
			Window Mode	Normal
OpenSales	[Forms]![frmReport Menu]![fraView]=1	OpenReport	Report Name	rptSales_ Portrait
			View	Print
			Window Mode	Normal
	[Forms]![frmReport Menu]![fraView]=2	OpenReport	Report Name	rptSales_ Portrait
			View	Print Preview
			Window Mode	Normal

22

FIGURE 22.12

mcrReportMenu uses an If action to open reports in Print or Print Preview view.

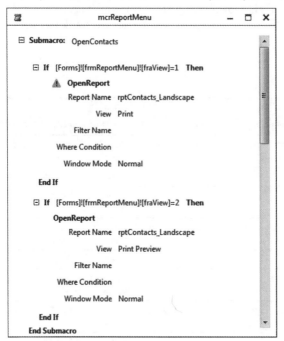

To implement this macro, set the On Click event properties of the buttons (cmdContacts, cmdProducts, and cmdSales) on frmReportMenu as follows:

Button Name	On Click Event Property
cmdContacts	mcrReportMenu.OpenContacts
cmdProducts	mcrReportMenu.OpenProducts
cmdSales	mcrReportMenu.OpenSales

The If macro action in mcrReportMenu has two expressions that look at fraView on frm-ReportMenu to determine whether Print or Print Preview is selected:

- [Forms]![frmReportMenu]![fraView]=1: Print view selected
- [Forms]![frmReportMenu]![fraView]=2: Print Preview view selected

If Print is selected on frmReportMenu, the OpenReport action with the View arguments set to Print executes. If Print Preview is selected on frmReportMenu, the OpenReport action with the View arguments set to Print Preview executes. This structure is set up for each submacro in mcrReportMenu.

Multiple actions in conditions

If you want to run multiple actions based on a condition, add multiple actions within the
If and End If actions. Figure 22.13 illustrates this concept.

FIGURE 22.13

Multiple actions within If and End If actions execute as a group.

The If macro action lets you selectively run actions based on other values in your application. Use the If macro action to reference controls on forms or reports and other objects
and determine which actions to execute.

Temporary Variables

In previous versions of Access, you could use variables only in VBA code. Macros were
limited to performing a series of actions without carrying anything forward from a
previous action. Beginning with Access 2007, three new macro actions—SetTempVar,
RemoveTempVar, and RemoveAllTempVars—let you create and use temporary variables
in your macros. You can use these variables in conditional expressions to control which
actions execute, or to pass data to and from forms or reports. You can even access these
variables in VBA to communicate data to and from modules.

Enhancing a macro you've already created

A simple way to demonstrate how to use variables in macros is to enhance the Hello World!
example created earlier in this chapter (see "Creating a macro"). Table 22.4 shows the macro
actions and action arguments for mcrHelloWorldEnhanced (shown in Figure 22.14).

TABLE 22.4 mcrHelloWorldEnhanced

Action	Action Argument	Action Argument Setting
SetTempVar	Name	MyName
	Expression	InputBox("Enter your name.")
MessageBox	Message	="Hello " & [TempVars]![MyName] & "."
	Beep	Yes
	Type	Information
	Title	Using Variables
RemoveTempVar	Name	MyName

FIGURE 22.14

mcrHelloWorldEnhanced uses the SetTempVar action to get a value from the user and display it in a message box.

The SetTempVar action has two arguments: Name and Expression. The Name argument (MyName in this example) is simply the name of the temporary variable. The Expression argument is what you want the value of the variable to be. In this example, the InputBox() function prompts the user for his name.

The MessageBox action's Message argument contains the following expression:

```
="Hello " & [TempVars]![MyName] & "."
```

This expression concatenates the word Hello with the temporary variable MyName, created in the SetTempVar action of the macro. When referring to a temporary variable created with the SetTempVar action, use the following syntax:

```
[TempVars]![VariableName]
```

For more information on string concatenation using the ampersand (&), see Chapter 9.

The `RemoveTempVar` action removes a single temporary variable from memory—in this example, `MyName`. You can have only 255 temporary variables defined at one time. These variables stay in memory until you close the database, unless you remove them with `RemoveTempVar` or `RemoveAllTempVars`. It's a good practice to remove temporary variables when you're done using them.

> **CAUTION**
>
> Using the `RemoveAllTempVars` action removes all temporary variables created with the `SetTempVar` action. Unless you're sure you want to do this, use the `RemoveTempVar` action instead.

Temporary variables are global. Once you create a temporary variable, you can use it in VBA procedures, queries, macros, or object properties. For example, if you remove the `RemoveTempVar` action from mcrHelloWorldEnhanced, you can create a text box on a form and set its `Control Source` property as follows to display the name the user entered:

```
=[TempVars]![MyName]
```

Using temporary variables to simplify macros

Using temporary variables, you can sometimes eliminate steps from a macro. You can get the form or report name from another control on a form. With a temporary variable, you eliminate the need for creating a structure of multiple `OpenForm` or `OpenReport` actions. You can also use more than one variable in a macro.

For this example, use `frmReportMenuEnhanced` (shown in Figure 22.15), which contains the same `fraView` shown in Figure 22.12 but adds a combo box (cboReport), which contains a list of reports to run. The Run Report command button executes mcrReportMenuEnhanced, which doesn't use submacros to decide which report to open.

FIGURE 22.15

frmReportMenuEnhanced uses a combo box to select which report to open.

Table 22.5 shows the conditions, actions, and action arguments for mcrReportMenuEnhanced (shown in Figure 22.16), which opens one of three reports.

TABLE 22.5 mcrReportMenuEnhanced

Condition	Action	Action Argument	Action Argument Setting
	SetTempVar	Name	ReportName
		Expression	[Forms]![frmReportMenuEnhanced]![cboReport]
	SetTempVar	Name	ReportView
		Expression	[Forms]![frmReportMenuEnhanced]![fraView]
[TempVars]![ReportView]=1	OpenReport	Report Name	=[TempVars]![ReportName]
		View	Print
		Window Mode	Normal
[TempVars]![ReportView]=2	OpenReport	Report Name	=[TempVars]![ReportName]
		View	Print Preview
		Window Mode	Normal
	RemoveTempVar	Name	ReportName
	RemoveTempVar	Name	ReportView

The first two SetTempVar actions in mcrReportMenuEnhanced set the values of the temporary variables—ReportName and ReportView—from cboReport and fraView on frmReportMenuEnhanced. The OpenReport actions use the temporary variables in the Condition column and for the ReportName argument. When using temporary variables as a setting for an argument, you must use an equal (=) sign in front of the expression:

```
=[TempVars]![ReportName]
```

There are still two OpenReport actions in this macro. Certain arguments—such as View—don't allow the use of temporary variables in expressions. Because one of your variables is a setting for the report's view, you still have to use the Condition column to decide which view to open the report in.

The last two RemoveTempVar lines remove the temporary variables—ReportName and ReportView—from memory. Because these variables probably won't be used later on in the application, it's important to remove them.

You can use temporary variables to store values to use later on in the macro, or anywhere in the application. Just remember that you have only 255 temporary variables to use, so don't forget to clean up after yourself by removing them from memory once you're finished using them.

FIGURE 22.16

mcrReportMenuEnhanced uses temporary variables to open the report in Print or Print Preview view.

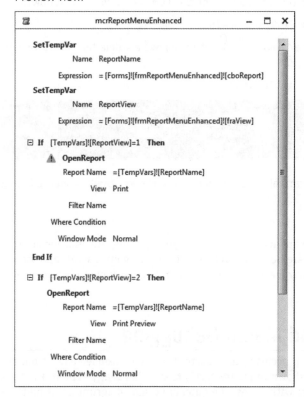

Using temporary variables in VBA

You may start out using macros to automate your application, but over time, you may begin using VBA code to automate and add functionality to other areas. What do you do with the temporary variables you've already implemented with macros? Well, you don't have to abandon them; instead, you can use them directly in your VBA code.

To access a temporary variable in VBA, use the same syntax used in macros:

```
X = [TempVars]![VariableName]
```

If you don't use spaces in your variable names, you can omit the brackets:

```
X = TempVars!VariableName
```

Use the previous syntax to assign a new value to an existing temporary variable. The only difference is to put the temporary variable on the left side of the equation:

```
TempVars!VariableName = NewValue
```

Use the `TempVars` object to create and remove temporary variables in VBA. The `TempVars` object contains three methods: `Add`, `Remove`, and `RemoveAll`. To create a new temporary variable and set its value, use the `Add` method of the `TempVars` object as follows:

```
TempVars.Add "VariableName", Value
```

Use the `Remove` method of the `TempVars` object to remove a single temporary variable from memory:

```
TempVars.Remove "VariableName"
```

> **TIP**
>
> When adding or removing temporary variables in VBA, remember to put the temporary variable's name in quotation marks.

To remove all the temporary variables from memory, use the `RemoveAll` method of the `TempVars` object as follows:

```
TempVars.RemoveAll
```

Any VBA variables you create are available to use in your macros, and vice versa. Any variables you remove in VBA are no longer available to use in your macros, and vice versa. Using temporary variables, your macros and VBA code no longer have to be independent from each other.

Error Handling and Macro Debugging

Prior to Access 2007, if an error occurred in a macro, the macro stopped execution, and your user saw an ugly dialog box (shown in Figure 22.17) that didn't really explain what was going on. If he was unfamiliar with Access, he quickly became disgruntled using the application. The lack of error handing in macros is one main reason many developers use VBA instead of macros to automate their applications.

A common error that's easy to demonstrate is the divide-by-zero error. For the next example, mcrDivision (shown in Figure 22.18) contains two temporary variables—MyNum and MyDenom—set with the `InputBox()` function asking for a numerator and denominator. The `MessageBox` action shows the result—`[TempVars]![MyNum] & " divided by " & [TempVars]![MyDenom]`—in a message box, and the `RemoveTempVar` actions remove the variables from memory.

FIGURE 22.17

Errors in macros cause the macro to cease operation.

FIGURE 22.18

mcrDivision divides the numerator by the denominator and generates an error when the denominator is zero.

Run the macro and enter **1** for the numerator and **2** for the denominator; the macro runs and displays a message box saying 1 divided by 2 is 0.5. Run the macro again and enter **0** in the denominator; a divide-by-zero error occurs, and the macro stops running.

Without error handling, the two `RemoveTempVar` actions won't run and won't remove the temporary variables from memory.

If an error occurs in another macro—such as a string of action queries—any queries after an error occurs won't run. Adding error handling to your macros allows you to choose what to do when an error occurs while a macro's running.

The OnError action

The `OnError` action lets you decide what happens when an error occurs in your macro. This action has two arguments: `Go to` and `Macro Name`. The `Go to` argument has three settings, and the `Macro Name` argument is used only with one of these settings, described as follows:

- **Next:** This setting records the details of the error in the `MacroError` object but does not stop the macro. The macro continues with the next action.
- **Macro Name:** This setting stops the current macro and runs the macro in the `Macro Name` argument of the `OnError` action.
- **Fail:** This setting stops the current macro and displays an error message. This is the same as not having error handling in the macro.

The VBA equivalents of these settings are as follows:

```
On Error Resume Next        'Next
On Error GoTo LABELNAME     'Macro Name
On Error GoTo 0             'Fail
```

The simplest way to add error handling to a macro is to make `OnError` the first action and set the `Go to` argument to `Next`. This will cause your macro to run without stopping, but you won't have any clue which actions ran and which ones didn't.

Instead, create an error-handling structure. Table 22.6 shows the macro names, actions, and action arguments for mcrDivisionErrorHandling (shown in Figure 22.19).

TABLE 22.6 mcrDivisionErrorHandling

Submacro Name	Action	Action Argument	Action Argument Setting
	OnError	Go to	Macro Name
		Macro Name	ErrorHandler
	SetTempVar	Name	MyNum
		Expression	InputBox("Enter Numerator.")
	SetTempVar	Name	MyDenom
		Expression	InputBox("Enter Denominator.")

Submacro Name	Action	Action Argument	Action Argument Setting
	MessageBox	Message	=[TempVars]![MyNum] & " divided by " & [TempVars]![MyDenom] & " is " & [TempVars]![MyNum]/ [TempVars]![MyDenom]
		Beep	Yes
		Type	Information
		Title	Division Example
	RunMacro	Macro Name	mcrDivisionErrorHandling. Cleanup
ErrorHandler	MessageBox	Message	="The following error occurred: " & [MacroError]. [Description]
		Beep	Yes
		Type	Warning?
		Title	="Error Number: " & [MacroError].[Number]
	ClearMacroError		
	RunMacro	Macro Name	mcrDivisionErrorHandling. Cleanup
Cleanup	RemoveTempVar	Name	MyNum
	RemoveTempVar	Name	MyDenom

The first OnError action in the macro lets Access know to move to the submacro ErrorHandler when an error occurs. If an error occurs (by entering 0 as the denominator), the macro stops and moves to the ErrorHandler submacro. The ErrorHandler submacro displays a message box—using the MacroError object (described in the next section) to display the error's description in the Message and the error's number in the Title, using the following expressions:

```
[MacroError].[Description]
[MacroError].[Number]
```

After the error handler's message box, the ClearMacroError action clears the MacroError object. The RunMacro action moves execution to the macro's Cleanup submacro. The Cleanup section of the macro removes the temporary variables.

FIGURE 22.19

mcrDivisionErrorHandling uses the OnError action to display a user-friendly error message and remove the temporary variables.

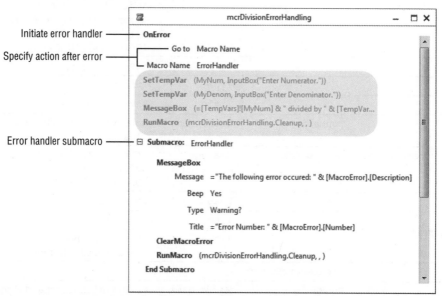

> **NOTE**
>
> There's no Resume functionality in macro error handling. If you want to run additional code after the error-handling actions, you must use the RunMacro action in the error-handling submacro to run another macro or place the actions in the error handler.

The RunMacro action also appears after the MessageBox action in the main section of the macro. Because you're using submacros, the macro stops after it reaches the ErrorHandler submacro. In order to force the cleanup of the temporary variables, use the RunMacro action to run the Cleanup submacro. Otherwise, you'd have to put the RemoveTempVar actions in the main section and in the ErrorHandler section of the macro.

The MacroError object

The MacroError object contains information about the last macro error that occurred. It retains this information until a new error occurs or you clear it with the ClearMacroError action. This object contains a number of read-only properties you can access from the macro itself or from VBA. These properties are as follows:

- ActionName: This is the name of the macro action that was running when the error occurred.

- `Arguments`: The arguments for the macro action that was running when the error occurred.
- `Condition`: This property contains the condition for the macro action that was running when the error occurred.
- `Description`: The text representing the current error message—for example, Divide by Zero or Type Mismatch.
- `MacroName`: Contains the name of the macro that was running when the error occurred.
- `Number`: This property contains the current error number—for example, 11 or 13.

Use the `MacroError` object as a debugging tool or to display messages to the user, who can then relay that information to you. You can even write these properties to a table to track the errors that occur in your macros. Use this object within an `If` action to customize what actions execute based on the error that occurs. When used in combination with the `OnError` action, it gives you additional functionality by handling errors, displaying useful messages, and providing information to you and the user.

Debugging macros

Trying to figure out what's going on in a macro can be difficult. The `OnError` action and `MacroError` object make debugging Access macros easier than in previous versions. There are other tools and techniques that are useful when debugging macros. Use the following list as a guideline for troubleshooting macros:

- **Single Step:** Click the Single Step button in the Tools group on the Macro Tools Design tab of the Ribbon to turn on Single Step mode. At this point, when you run the macro (while still in design mode) the Macro Single Step dialog box activates. The Macro Single Step dialog box (shown in Figure 22.20) lets you see the macro name, condition, action name, arguments, and error number of a macro action before the action executes. From this dialog box, click Step to execute the action, Stop All Macros to stop the macro from running, or Continue to finish the macro with Single Step mode turned off.
- **MessageBox:** Use the `MessageBox` macro action to display values of variables, error messages, control settings, or whatever else you want to see while the macro is running. To see the value of a combo box on a form, set the `Message` argument as follows:

  ```
  [Forms]![frmReportMenuEnhanced]![cboReport]
  ```

- **StopMacro:** Use the `StopMacro` action to stop the macro from executing. Insert this action at any point in the macro to stop it at that point. Use this in conjunction with the debug window to check values.
- **Debug window:** Use the debug window to look at any values, temporary variables, or properties of the `MacroError` object after you stop the macro. Press Ctrl+G to display the code window after you stop the macro. Just type a question mark (?)

22

and the name of the variable or expression you want to check the value of, and press Enter. Here are some examples of expressions to display in the Debug window:

```
? TempVars!MyNum
? MacroError!Description
? [Forms]![frmReportMenuEnhanced]![cboReport]
```

FIGURE 22.20

Use the Macro Single Step dialog box to step through a macro.

These techniques are similar to ones you'd use when debugging VBA code. You can step through sections of code, pause the code and look at values in the debug window, and display message boxes to display variables or errors that occur. Granted, you don't have all the tools available—such as watching variables and `Debug.Print`—but at least you have the new `MacroError` object to provide the information you need to figure out what's going wrong.

 For more information on error handling and debugging VBA code see Chapter 27.

Embedded Macros

An *embedded macro* is stored in an event property and is part of the object to which it belongs. When you modify an embedded macro, you don't have to worry about other controls that might use the macro because each embedded macro is independent. Embedded macros aren't visible in the Navigation pane and are only accessible from the object's Property Sheet.

As an example, let's say you want to add a command button to a form that opens a report. You could use a global macro (one that's in the Navigation pane) to open the report, or you could add an embedded macro to the command button.

Embedded macros are trusted. They run even if your security settings prevent the running of code. Using embedded macros allows you to distribute your application as a trusted application because embedded macros are automatically prevented from performing unsafe operations.

Using embedded macros instead of code accomplishes two things:

- It allows you to quickly create a distributable application.
- It allows users not familiar with VBA code to customize buttons created with wizards.

Follow these steps to create an embedded macro that opens frmContacts:

1. **Select the Create tab on the Ribbon, and then click the Form Design button in the Forms group.**
2. **On the Form Design Tools Design tab of the Ribbon, deselect the Use Control Wizards option in the Controls group, if necessary.** For this example, you don't want to use a wizard to decide what this button does.
3. **Click the Button control and draw a new button on the form.**
4. **Set the button's Name property to cmdContacts and the Caption property to Contacts.**
5. **Display the Property Sheet for cmdContacts, select the Event tab, and then click the On Click event property.**
6. **Click the builder button—the button with the ellipsis (...).** The Choose Builder dialog box (shown in Figure 22.21) appears.

FIGURE 22.21

Use the builder button in the event property to display the Choose Builder dialog box to create an embedded macro.

7. **Choose Macro Builder and click OK to display the macro builder (shown in Figure 22.22).**

FIGURE 22.22

An embedded macro doesn't have a name. The title bar displays the control and the event in which the macro is embedded.

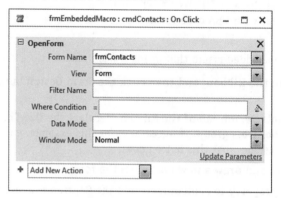

8. **Add the OpenForm action to the macro, and then set the** Form Name **argument to frmContacts.**

9. **Close the embedded macro, and click OK when you're prompted to save the changes and update the property.** The On Click event property of cmdContacts now displays [Embedded Macro].

Using an embedded macro has some advantages over using an event procedure containing VBA code. If you copy the button and paste it on another form, the embedded macro goes with it. You don't have to copy the code and paste it as a separate operation. Similarly, if you cut and paste the button on the same form (for example, moving it onto a tab control), you don't have to reattach the code to the button.

Embedded macros offer another improvement to macros in previous versions. If you automate your application with embedded macros and import a form or report into another database (or just copy the control within the same database), you don't have to worry about importing or copying the associated macros. By using embedded macros, all the automation moves with the form or report. This makes maintaining and building applications easier.

Macros versus VBA Statements

In Access, macros often offer an ideal way to take care of many details, such as running reports and forms. You can develop applications and assign actions faster using a macro because the arguments for the macro actions are displayed with the macro (in the bottom portion of the macro builder). You don't have to remember complex or difficult syntax.

Several actions you can accomplish with VBA statements are better suited for macros. The following actions tend to be more efficient when they're run from macros:

- Using macros against an entire set of records with action queries—for example, to manipulate multiple records in a table or across tables (such as updating field values or deleting records)
- Opening and closing forms
- Running reports

> **NOTE**
> The VBA language supplies a `DoCmd` object that accomplishes many macro actions. Under the surface, `DoCmd` runs a macro task to accomplish the same result provided by a macro action. You could, for example, specify `DoCmd` `.Close` to run the `Close` macro action and close the currently active form.

22

Choosing between macros and VBA

Although macros sometimes prove to be the solution of choice, VBA is the tool of choice at other times. You'll probably want to use VBA rather than macros when you want to:

- **Create and use your own functions.** In addition to using the built-in functions in Access, you can create and work with your own functions by using VBA code.
- **Use automation to communicate with other Windows applications or to run system-level actions.** You can write code to see whether a file exists before you take some action, or you can communicate with another Windows application (such as a spreadsheet), passing data back and forth.
- **Use existing functions in external Windows Dynamic Link Libraries (DLLs).** Macros don't enable you to call functions in other Windows DLLs.
- **Work with records one at a time.** If you need to step through records or move values from a record to variables for manipulation, code is the answer.
- **Create or manipulate objects.** In most cases, you'll find that creating and modifying an object is easiest in that object's Design view. In some situations, however, you may want to manipulate the definition of an object in code. With a few VBA statements, you can manipulate virtually any and all objects in a database, including the database itself.
- **Display a progress meter on the status bar.** If you need to display a progress meter to communicate progress to the user, VBA code is the answer.

Converting existing macros to VBA

After you become comfortable with writing VBA code, you may want to rewrite some of your application macros as VBA procedures. As you begin this process, you quickly realize how mentally challenging the effort can be as you review every macro in your various macro libraries. You can't merely cut the macro from the macro builder and paste it into a module window. For each condition, action, and action argument for a macro, you must analyze the task it accomplishes and then write the equivalent statements of VBA code in your procedure.

Fortunately, Access provides a feature that converts macros to VBA code automatically. On the Tools group of the Design tab of the Ribbon, there is a Convert Macros to Visual Basic button. This option enables you to convert a macro to a module in seconds.

> **NOTE**
>
> Only macros that appear in the Navigation pane can be converted to VBA. Macros that are embedded in a form or report must be converted manually.

To try the conversion process, convert the mcrHelloWorldEnhanced macro used earlier in this chapter. Follow these steps to run the conversion process:

1. **Click the Macros group in the Navigation pane.**

2. **Open mcrHelloWorldEnhanced in Design view.**

3. **Click the Convert Macros to Visual Basic button on the Design tab.** The Convert Macro dialog box (shown in Figure 22.23) appears.

FIGURE 22.23

The Convert Macro dialog box.

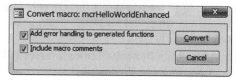

4. **Select the options that include error handling and macro comments, and click Convert.** When the conversion process completes, the Visual Basic Editor (VBE) is displayed and the `Conversion Finished!` message box appears.

5. **Click OK to dismiss the message box.**

6. **In the VBE, open the Project Explorer from the View menu (Ctrl+R) and double-click the module named Converted Macro-mcrHelloWorldEnhanced.** The code and Project Explorer are shown in Figure 22.24.

When you open the VBE for the new module, you can view the procedure created from the macro. Figure 22.24 shows the mcrHelloWorldEnhanced function that Access created from the mcrHelloWorldEnhanced macro.

At the top of the function, Access inserts four comment lines for the name of the function. The `Function` statement follows the comment lines. Access names the function, using the macro library's name (mcrHelloWorldEnhanced).

FIGURE 22.24

The newly converted module.

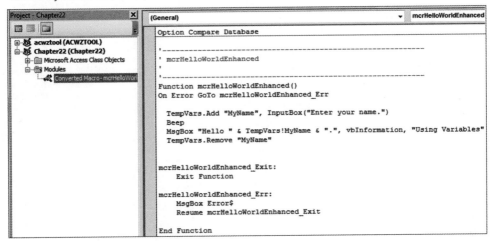

When you specify that you want Access to include error processing for the conversion, Access automatically inserts the On Error statement as the first command in the procedure. The On Error statement tells Access to branch to other statements that display an appropriate message and then exit the function.

The statement beginning with TempVars.Add is the actual code that Access created from the macro. Each line of the macro is converted into a line of VBA code, including the TempVars object, the Beep method, and the MsgBox function.

If you're new to VBA and want to learn code, a good starting point is converting your macros to modules. Just save your macros and modules, and then look at the VBA code to become familiar with the syntax. The macro features in Access 2019 make it harder to decide whether to use macros or VBA.

Using Access Data Macros

IN THIS CHAPTER

Creating data macros

Understanding table events

Understanding data macro limitations

For a long time, macros were considered the poor cousins of VBA statements. Although in many ways VBA and macros were equivalent in their capabilities, macros have always been considered inferior to VBA for handling an application's logic.

The problems with traditional Access macros were considerable:

- **Macros existed as separate database objects, so keeping track of the macro's effect on a particular form was often difficult.** Because there was no direct connection between a form (or a report, for that matter) and a macro, it was easy to break the macro by deleting or renaming it. VBA code encapsulated within the form's code module never had this problem.

- **There was no way to trap or handle errors in macros.** In versions of Access prior to 2007, macros would simply stop running and display an error dialog box if something unexpected happened. These interruptions were not welcomed by users, particularly because there was, most often, nothing a user could do to correct the problem or prevent it from happening again. VBA code has always featured strong error handling and could often provide a default value or instruct the user what to do in the event of a problem.

- **Macros were unable to work with code.** There was no way for a macro to loop through a recordset—for example, to sum field values or detect out-of-range data. VBA code is well suited for data management tasks and includes all the looping constructs necessary to iterate over recordsets.

In Access 2019, those concerns are all but a distant memory. Macros now offer error handling and temporary variables during a macro's execution. Access 2019 also offers embedded macros. As discussed in Chapter 22, embedded macros eliminate the objection that macros were always external to the form or report they serviced. Chapter 22 also demonstrates that macros in Access 2019 allow for error handling.

This chapter specifically covers data macros, which add yet another reason macros in Access 2019 are a more attractive option than ever before.

If you haven't done so, you'll want to explore Chapter 22. There, you'll get the foundation needed to better understand the terms and features you'll see in this chapter.

Introducing Data Macros

A data macro is logic you attach to a table to enforce business rules at the table level. In some ways, a data macro is similar to a validation rule, except that a validation rule is rather unintelligent. Validation rules can't modify data or determine whether corrective action is needed. Data macros are specifically provided to allow you to manage data-oriented activity at the table level.

Data macros are intended to make it easier to ensure consistent data handling throughout your application. Because data macros are applied at the table level, the exact same action happens each time the table's data is updated. Although the subset of actions available to data macros is considerably smaller than standard macros, when carefully crafted and implemented, data macros are a powerful addition to Access applications.

NOTE

Data macros are especially handy in split database applications (applications where the tables live in a separate Access file from the forms and reports). Because the macros are attached to the tables, they continue to work even if someone links to the tables in some other way than the designed front-end application.

Understanding Table Events

There are five different macro-programmable table events: BeforeChange, BeforeDelete, AfterInsert, AfterUpdate, and AfterDelete.

To see these events in the Ribbon, open the Chapter23.accdb database and open tblProducts in Datasheet view. On the Ribbon, you'll see a Table tab. Select that tab and you'll see the events shown in Figure 23.1: BeforeChange, BeforeDelete, AfterInsert, AfterUpdate, and AfterDelete.

These events are designated as "before" and "after" events. The "before" events occur before changes are made to the table's data, while the "after" events indicate that successful changes have been made.

FIGURE 23.1

Every Access table includes five data-oriented events that can be selected when in Datasheet view.

"Before" events

The "before" events (BeforeChange and BeforeDelete) are very simple and support only a few macro actions. They support the program flow constructs (Comment, Group, and If) and just the LookupRecord data block. The only macro data actions they provide are ClearMacroError, OnError, RaiseError, SetLocalVar, SetField, and StopMacro.

The BeforeChange event is similar to the BeforeUpdate event attached to forms, reports, and controls. As its name implies, BeforeChange fires just before the data in a table is changed by the user, a query, or VBA code.

BeforeChange gives you a chance to look at new values in the current record and make changes if needed. By default, references to a field within a BeforeChange or BeforeDelete data macro automatically refer to the current record.

BeforeChange is an excellent opportunity to validate user input before committing values to a table. A simple example is shown in Figure 23.2. In this case, the default value of the Description field in tblProducts_BeforeChange is set to Description. If the user fails to change the Description field while adding a new record to the table, the BeforeChange event updates the field to "Please provide description."

FIGURE 23.2

Using BeforeChange to update a field.

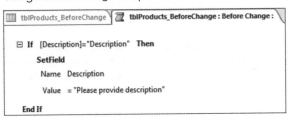

The BeforeChange event can't interrupt the user with a message box or stop the record from updating in the underlying table. All BeforeChange can do is set a field's value or set a local macro variable's value before the record is added or updated in the table.

BeforeChange fires for both updates to existing records and new record insertions into the table. Access provides the IsInsert property that tells the macro whether the current change is the result of inserting a new record or is because a record is being updated.

Figure 23.3 illustrates how IsInsert can be used within an If block to ensure the BeforeChange fired as the result of a new record inserted into the table.

FIGURE 23.3

Using IsInsert to determine if BeforeChange fired as the result of adding a new record.

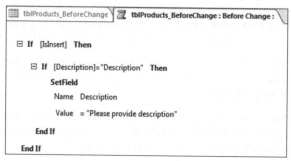

Figure 23.3 also illustrates that program-flow blocks (like If) can be nested. The outer If block checks the value of IsInsert, while the inner If conditionally sets the Description field value.

The BeforeDelete event is parallel in almost every regard to BeforeChange, so no examples are given here. Use BeforeDelete to verify that conditions are appropriate for deletion. As with BeforeChange, the BeforeDelete event can't prevent a record's deletion, but it can set a local variable or raise an error if conditions warrant.

"After" events

The "after" events (AfterUpdate, AfterInsert, and AfterDelete) are more robust than their "before" counterparts. Each of these events supports the entire family of data macro actions (DeleteRecord, SetField, SendEmail, and so on), so it's likely that you'll frequently use these events as the basis of your data macros.

Figure 23.4 shows a typical use of the AfterInsert event. The AfterInsert event fires whenever a new record is added to a table. The new record has already been committed to the table, and AfterInsert is used to update a table named tblProductActivityLog.

FIGURE 23.4

Using `AfterInsert` to add a record to tblProductActivityLog.

In Figure 23.4, notice that three fields (ProductActivity, ProductID, and ProductDescription) in tblProductActivityLog are being updated as part of a `CreateRecord` data block. The ProductID is an AutoNumber field in tblProducts_AfterInsert. The `CreateRecord` block has already added the record to the table, so the new record's ProductID value is available to this data macro. Therefore, when the `SetField` macro action updates the ProductID field in tblProductActivityLog, the new product record's ID is successfully added to the log table.

The `AfterInsert` data macro runs whenever a record is added to the table. Similar data macros can be added to the table's `AfterUpdate` and `AfterDelete` to log other changes to the table.

The most useful aspect of the "after" events is that they can use the `ForEachRecord` macro block to iterate over recordsets provided by tables or queries. This capability makes these events ideal for scanning a table for consistency, adding a record to a log table, or performing some other compute-intensive updates.

Using the Macro Builder for Data Macros

Data macros use the same macro builder used to create embedded and user interface macros. Once you master the macro builder, you'll use it for all macro development and macro management. The primary difference is that the Action Catalog (described in the next section) contains different actions, depending on the context.

Adding data macros to a table is quite easy. In fact, an Access table doesn't even have to be in Design view—you can add data macros to a table displayed as a datasheet, if you like. The data macros you construct for a table are in effect immediately, so you can easily work on a macro and observe how well the macro works without compiling or switching between Design view and Datasheet view.

In the `Chapter23.accdb` database, start by opening tblProducts in Datasheet view. On the Ribbon, you'll select the Table tab to expose the table's data events (see Figure 23.1).

Click the After Update command to open the macro builder (shown in Figure 23.5). Initially, at least, there's not much to look at.

FIGURE 23.5

The macro builder for the table's `AfterUpdate` event.

The large blank area to the left is the macro design area. This is where you place macro actions. On the right side is the Action Catalog, a hierarchical list of all macro actions currently available. The only indication of which table event is being programmed is in the main Access window caption and in the tab above the macro design area.

With a macro open in the design area, the Ribbon contains several tools you use when working with the macro. Notice that you can collapse or expand macro sections, save the macro currently under construction, and close the macro builder.

You'll notice that the Ribbon you see in Figure 23.6 is exactly the same seen when working with embedded or standard macros. However, some options are not available to you. All the items in the Tools group, for example, are grayed out. This is because data macros don't provide the option of single-stepping through macro actions or converting to VBA code. Data macros are intended to be relatively simple, short, and to the point, rather than large and complex.

Incidentally, if your table is in Design view, you can get to the data macro builder by selecting the Create Data Macros command from the Design tab (see Figure 23.6).

FIGURE 23.6

FIGURE 23.6

Selecting a table event when a table is in Design view.

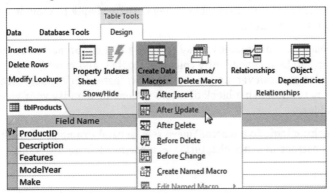

In either case, the macro builder opens as shown in Figure 23.5. When the Access tabbed interface is used, the table's name and selected event appear in the macro builder's tab. If the overlapping windows interface is selected, this information appears in the Access main window's caption.

In Figure 23.6, notice the Create Named Macro option. A *named macro* is just like a data macro attached to a table event. The only difference is that a named macro is *free floating* and not specifically tied to a particular event. A named macro is meant to be called from an event macro and typically implements logic that is common to a table's fields. Consider the business rule described earlier. If more than one data macro in a table might change a product's wholesale cost, you might create a named macro to handle updating the RetailPrice field. The named macro could then be called by any of the table's other data macros so that every macro within the table handles the update in the same way.

Understanding the Action Catalog

The Action Catalog on the right side of the macro builder serves as the repository of macro actions you add to your data macros. The contents of the Action Catalog depend entirely on which table event has been selected, so its appearance varies considerably while you work with Access macros.

Program flow

At the top of the Action Catalog in Figure 23.5 are certain program flow constructs you apply to your macros. When working with data macros, the only program flow constructs available are comments, groups, and `If` blocks.

Comments help document your macros and should be used if the macro's logic is not easily understood. Macro comments are not executable—they're there simply to provide some text describing the goings-on in the macro.

A group (also called a *macro group*) provides a way to wrap a number of macro actions as a named entity. The group can be independently collapsed, copied, and moved around within a macro. A macro group is not, however, an executable unit; instead, it's simply meant to provide a convenient way to establish a block of macro actions to simplify your view of the macro in the macro builder.

The `If` block adds branching logic to a macro. You've seen several examples of the VBA `If...Then...Else` construct in other chapters, and a macro `If` is no different.

Data blocks

If you go back and look at Figure 23.5 again, you'll see Data Blocks under the Program Flow constructs. Each of the data block constructs includes an area for adding one or more macro actions. A data block construct performs all the macro actions as part of its operation. In other words, you typically set up the data block you want to perform (for example, `EditRecord`) and then add the actions you want to execute as part of the block.

Data blocks may also be nested. You could, for example, set up a `ForEachRecord` and then run the `CreateRecord` block, adding records to another table with data contained in the records returned by the `ForEachRecord`.

The data blocks macro actions are:

- `CreateRecord`: The `CreateRecord` action provides a way to add a record to the current table (which is rarely done) or to another table (which is more typical). An example of using `CreateRecord` is building a log of all changes to the tblProducts table (similar to Figure 23.4). The `CreateRecord` macro action can add a new record to a table, populating fields in the record with data passed from the current table. The reason `CreateRecord` is not often used to add a record to the current table is that recursion can occur. Adding a new record to the current table triggers events such as `AfterInsert` (described in earlier in this chapter), which may run the `CreateRecord` action again and again.

- `EditRecord`: As its name implies, `EditRecord` provides a way to change the content of an existing record in the current, or another, table. `EditRecord` is ideal for situations such as adjusting inventory levels when a product is sold or returned or calculating sales tax or shipping costs when the quantity field has been provided.

- `ForEachRecord`: The `ForEachRecord` action is a looping construct. Given the name of a table or query, `ForEachRecord` can perform an operation on every record in the recordset. The action can be an update using the `SetField` action (described in the next section), can copy data, or can perform a mathematical operation on the data in the recordset. The `ForEachRecord` block has a macro action included within the block to make it easy to specify the action you want this block to perform. And you can stack multiple macro actions within the `ForEachBlock` to perform more-complex operations.

- `LookupRecord`: The `LookupRecord` action is quite simple and easy to understand. `LookupRecord` returns a record found in a table and provides a macro action area for specifying the actions you want to perform on the returned record.

> **NOTE**
>
> The `CreateRecord`, `EditRecord`, and `ForEachRecord` blocks will be available only when you're building "after" macro events. This means they'll be available only when creating `AfterInsert`, `AfterUpdate`, and `AfterDelete` data macros. The "before" events are meant to be very fast and lightweight, so they don't provide for CPU-intensive operations such as adding or editing new records.

Data actions

The next group of actions in the Action Catalog is the Data actions; these are the *actions* a data macro can take. You've already read that a data macro consists of one or more actions that are executed as a single unit in response to a table event. You need a good understanding of the variety of macro actions available to data macros.

Here are the data macro actions:

> **NOTE**
>
> Not all these actions are available to every table event. `BeforeChange` and `BeforeDelete` (described in the "'Before' events" section, earlier in this chapter) support only a subset of these actions because many actions are computationally intensive (such as updating or adding records), and the "before" events are meant to be very fast and lightweight.

- `DeleteRecord`: As its name implies, `DeleteRecord` deletes a record in a table (without confirmation from the user). Obviously, `DeleteRecord` must be used carefully to prevent deleting valuable data from the application. A typical use of `DeleteRecord` would be as part of an archiving operation, where data in a table is copied into another table (perhaps a linked SQL Server table) and then deleted from the current table.

- `CancelRecordChange`: `EditRecord` and `CreateRecord` both make irrevocable changes to a record. `CancelRecordChange`, in conjunction with an `If` block, allows a data macro to cancel the changes made by `EditRecord` and `CreateRecord` before the changes are committed to the database.

- `ExitForEachRecord`: The `ForEachRecord` loops through a recordset returned from a table or query, enabling the data macro to make changes to the recordset's data or scan the data for "interesting" values. There are many situations where a data macro may need to escape from a `ForEachRecord` loop before it has run to the end of its recordset. For example, consider a data macro that searches for a certain value in a table, and once the value is found, there is no need to continue the loop. The `ExitForEachRecord` action is typically executed as part of an `If` block (also discussed in the next section) and is executed only when a certain condition is true.

- `LogEvent`: Every Access 2019 application includes a hidden USysApplicationLog table (this table is hidden by virtue of the USys prefix in its name). USysApplicationLog is used to record data macro errors and can be used to log other information as well. The `LogEvent` macro action is specifically designed to add a record to USysApplicationLog from a data macro. The only field in USysApplicationLog that can be written using `LogEvent` is Description, a memo type field. The other fields in USysApplicationLog (Category, Context, DataMacroInstanceID, ErrorNumber, ObjectType, and SourceObject) are provided by the macro itself.

- `SendEmail`: This macro action, obviously, sends an e-mail using the default Windows e-mailer (usually Outlook). The arguments for `SendEmail` are To, CC, BCC, Subject, and Body. `SendEmail` is quite useful in certain situations, such as automatically dispatching an e-mail when an error condition occurs, or when a product's inventory level falls below some threshold.

- `SetField`: The `SetField` action updates the value of a field in a table. The arguments to `SetField` include the table and field names and the new value to assign to the field. `SetField` is not available to `BeforeChange` and `BeforeDelete` table events.

- `SetLocalVar`: Access 2019 macros are able to use local variables for passing values from one part of a macro to another. For example, you might have a macro that looks up a value in a table and passes the value as a variable to the next macro action. `SetLocalVar` is an all-purpose variable declaration and assignment action that creates a variable and assigns a value to it.

- `StopMacro`: The `StopMacro` action interrupts the currently executing macro, causing it to terminate and exit. Most often used in conjunction with an `If` data block, or in the destination of an `OnError` macro action, there are no arguments to `StopMacro`.

- `StopAllMacros`: This macro action is parallel to `StopMacro`, except that it applies to all currently executing macros. Macros may run asynchronously because table events might launch multiple macros at one time, or a macro might call a named macro as part of its execution.

- `RunDataMacro`: This macro action is very simple. Its only argument is the name of some other data macro that Access runs. `RunDataMacro` is useful in situations where a certain data macro performs some task that another data macro finds useful. Instead of duplicating the macro's actions, it's simpler just to call the macro and allow it to perform its actions as a single operation.

- OnError: The OnError macro action is the heart of Access macro error handling. OnError is a directive that tells Access what to do in the event an error occurs during a macro's execution. The first argument (GoTo) is required and is set to either Next, Macro Name, or Fail. Next directs Access to simply ignore the error and continue execution at the macro action following the action that caused the error.
- Unless another OnError is positioned within the data macro, OnError GoTo Next tells Access to ignore all errors in the data macro and continue execution regardless of whatever errors occur. The Macro Name directive names a macro you want to jump to in the event of an error. The destination of Macro Name is a named macro, which is just a collection of macro actions not attached to a table event. The Macro Name destination could be a named macro within the current table or in another table.
- RaiseError: The RaiseError macro action passes an error up to the user interface layer. An example is using RaiseError on a BeforeChange event to validate data before it's committed to the database. RaiseError passes an error number and description to the application, adding the error details to USysApplicationLog.
- ClearMacroError: Once an error has been handled by the RaiseError macro action or by the OnError GoTo macro action, the ClearMacroError action can be used to reset the macro error object and prepare Access for the next error.

Creating Your First Data Macro

Now that you have some orientation on the macro builder and the Action Catalog, it's time to create your first data macro.

For this walkthrough, let's assume that your company uses a standard markup of 66.66 percent on its products. This means that a product's wholesale cost is multiplied by 1.6666 to yield the default selling price of an item. Your company has found that a 66.66 percent markup provides the margin necessary for you to offer volume discounts, special sales, and significant discounts to selected buyers while remaining profitable.

The problem to be solved with a data macro is updating the retail price of a product anytime the product's cost is changed. Although this could be done quite easily with code or a macro behind Access forms, consider the issue if there were dozens of different forms where the product's cost might be changed. The same code or macro would have to be added in many different places, contributing to development and maintenance costs. Also, there is always the chance that one or more forms would not be updated should your company ever decide on a different approach for setting the default retail price of its products.

Using a data macro attached directly to the tblProducts table, for example, simplifies development and maintenance of the application's forms and reports. Because the business rule (multiplying cost by 1.66) is enforced at the data layer, every form, report, and query using the tblProducts table's data benefits from the data macro.

1. **Open the tblProducts table in Datasheet view.**
2. **Select the Table tab on the Ribbon, and choose the `BeforeChange` event.** At this point, Access will activate the macro builder.
3. **Double-click or drag the Group program flow action onto the macro's design surface.** Here, you're creating a new macro group. Give the macro group a name as shown in Figure 23.7.

FIGURE 23.7

Add a Group to the macro and give it a name.

4. **While in the newly created group, double-click the Comment program flow action to place a comment onto the macro's design surface.** With this comment, enter some friendly text describing what you're doing here (see Figure 23.8).

FIGURE 23.8

Add a Comment describing the actions taken in this macro.

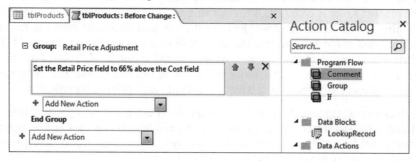

5. **Now double-click the `If` program flow action to place a new logic check onto the macro's design surface.** As you can see in Figure 23.9, you're evaluating the Cost field to ensure the value is greater than zero. This check will ensure the rest of the macro only triggers if the conditions you specified are met.

FIGURE 23.9

The `If` block conditionally executes macro actions based on logic you provide.

6. **If the condition we specified evaluates to true, we want to edit the record. In that case, double-click the SetField action to add it to the If block.** Here, you need to identify the field you want edited and the value you want to use. Figure 23.10 illustrates that we want to set the [RetailPrice] field to the value returned by [Cost]*1.66.

7. **At this point, the logic for our macro is complete. The last step is to click the Save command to finalize your data macro (see Figure 23.11).**

To test the macro, simply open tblProducts and enter a positive value in the Cost field of any record (as demonstrated in Figure 23.12). The RetailPrice field will (as soon as you move to another record) calculate per the actions provided by the `BeforeChange` data macro you just created.

FIGURE 23.10

Adding the SetField action tells Access to change the record if the condition specified is true.

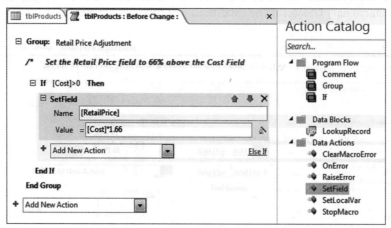

FIGURE 23.11

Click Save to finalize the macro and have it take effect.

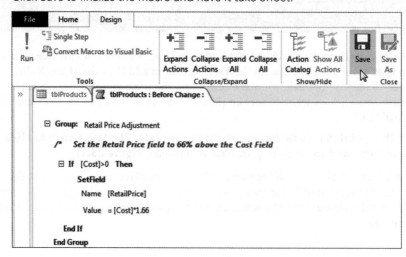

FIGURE 23.12

Entering a positive cost will now automatically update the RetailPrice field.

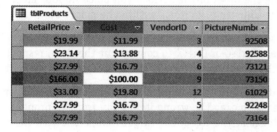

Again, this data macro will be in full effect even when edits are made via an Access form.

Managing Macro Objects

At this point, you should have a solid sense of how the macro builder works. In this section, let's dig deeper and explore some of the options for managing macro objects once they're added to a macro's design.

Collapsing and expanding macro items

Notice in Figure 23.11 that each macro item is accompanied by a collapse/expand button to the left of its name in the designer. These buttons allow you to view or hide parts of the macro. In Figure 23.13, you see the same macro with the Group level collapsed.

Collapsing items helps when you need to review large macros and want to see only a subset of the macro at one time. Note that you can also use the Collapse/Expand commands found in the Ribbon.

FIGURE 23.13

You can collapse and expand your macro items to simplify the surface of the macro builder.

Moving macro items

You may find it necessary to change the order of the actions you place in your macro. Access provides several methods for adjusting the items within the macro builder.

Macro items (blocks, actions, and so on) can be copied and pasted within the macro. Simply click any given macro item and press Ctrl+C or Ctrl+X to copy or cut the item, respectively, and then place your cursor in another location within the macro builder and press Ctrl+V.

Alternatively, macro items can be dragged into a new position with the mouse. This process is a little tricky because it's very easy to drag the wrong item away from its proper position. Carefully position the mouse pointer near the top of the target item, click with the mouse, and drag the item to its new location.

Access also provides the convenient up and down arrows (see Figure 23.14) that allow you to quickly move any macro item where you need it.

FIGURE 23.14

The order of macro items can be changed by using the up and down arrows next to the target item, by clicking and dragging items, or by copying and pasting.

Saving a macro as XML

A completely hidden feature of Access data macros is the ability to copy them from the macro builder and paste them into a text editor as XML. Access internally stores macros as XML, and copying a macro actually means copying its XML representation.

There are a couple of reasons you may want to save a macro as XML:

- **To e-mail the macro to someone.**
- **To archive it as a backup.** Because each table contains only one copy of each event macro (AfterUpdate, for example), there's no easy way to set aside a copy of the macro before embarking on changes to the macro's logic.

Figure 23.15 shows the XML of the same macro you see in Figure 23.14 pasted into Windows Notepad.

FIGURE 23.15

Saving a macro as XML.

To get the XML, simply go into the macro builder, press Ctrl+A to select all the actions, and then press Ctrl+C to copy all the actions. At this point, you can paste into an e-mail message, Notepad, or some other text editor.

The XML saved in a text file can be pasted right into the macro builder surface, and Access will display it as usual. The paste action works exactly as it does in Word or a plain text editor. The pasted macro actions appear exactly where the cursor is when the paste is initiated.

Recognizing the Limitations of Data Macros

As powerful as they are, data macros can't do everything. For example, data macros have no user interface at all. Data macros can't display a message box and can't open a form or report. Your ability to communicate with the user interface from a data macro is very limited, so data macros can't be used to notify users of problems or changes to data in tables. Displaying a user interface (such as a message box) would extract a serious performance penalty, particularly during bulk updates or inserts. Data macros are meant to run invisibly, with the highest possible performance.

Data macros are attached directly to Access tables and not to individual fields. If you have a situation where more than a few fields must be monitored or updated, the macro may become quite complex. Using the If block construct is a good way to conditionally execute blocks of macro statements.

The macro builder supports only one macro at a time. You must come to a stopping point on the current macro before closing it and opening another data macro.

Similarly, the macro builder is modal. You can't leave the macro builder without closing and saving (or not saving) the current macro. This restriction makes it difficult to view a table's data when working on a data macro's logic. As always, careful planning is a good idea when considering adding a data macro to a table.

Data macro execution doesn't occur on the back end in a split-database paradigm. Although the data macro resides in the table in the back-end database, the data macro is only executed in the front end.

Data macros can't work on multi-value or attachment fields. If it's important to use logic to control these data types, you must use traditional user interface macros or VBA.

Access 2019 data macros are not supported on linked tables. If the table in an Access database is linked to SQL Server, you can't write data macros for the table. You must use traditional user interface macros or VBA code for this purpose.

Data macros can't call VBA procedures. One of the primary objectives for data macros was to make them portable to SharePoint when an Access application was upsized to a web application. Any calls to VBA procedures were sure to fail because there was no way to convert VBA to JavaScript in the SharePoint environment. Although Access web applications have been deprecated and can no longer be created, data macros retain the limitation of not being able to call VBA procedures.

Data macros don't support transactions. Every field and record update is executed immediately, and there's no way to roll back multiple table changes.

Finally, data macros are not compatible with versions of Access earlier than 2010. Anyone using Access 2007 (with Service Pack 1 installed) will be able to open and read tables containing data macros, but they will not be able to write to those tables.

Getting Started with Access VBA

IN THIS CHAPTER

Working with VBA

Reviewing VBA terminology

Understanding VBA code basics

Creating your first procedure

Adding branching constructs

Learning looping constructs

Understanding objects and collections

Exploring the Visual Basic Editor

Most Access developers use macros now and then. Although macros provide a quick and easy way to automate an application, writing Visual Basic for Applications (VBA) modules is the best way to create applications. VBA provides data access, looping and branching, and other features that macros simply don't support—or at least not with the flexibility most developers want. In this chapter, you learn how to use VBA to extend the power and usefulness of your applications.

ON THE WEB

Download the database file `Chapter24.accdb` from this book's website.

The Limitations of Macros

The biggest limitation of Access macros is that they can only be used in Access applications. If your application will always be in Access and a macro does the job you need it to do, then a macro is an excellent way to extend your application. In recent versions of Access, macros have become even more powerful, adding variables and simple error handling. Plus, there are two areas where macros can't be beat: data macros in tables and embedded macros on forms and controls. The ability to embed macros in tables and forms make macros much more attractive than in versions prior to Access 2007.

Continues

continued

However, there are reasons why you might choose VBA over Access macros. For one, VBA code is portable to Word, Excel, Outlook, Visio, and even Visual Studio .NET (with changes). It's impossible to tell where an Access application might end up. Sometimes Access applications are upsized and upgraded to SQL Server and Visual Studio .NET and converting VBA to Visual Basic .NET is easier than converting macros. Another reason is that during development of an application, you might encounter a situation that becomes too complex for a macro to handle. There is virtually no limit to what you can do in VBA and if you start with VBA, you know your application won't outgrow it.

VBA is a very powerful, portable, useful language, and VBA skills are applicable in many situations other than building Access applications.

Introducing Visual Basic for Applications

Visual Basic for Applications (VBA) is the programming language built into Microsoft Access. VBA is shared among all the Office applications, including Word, Excel, Outlook, PowerPoint, and even Visio. If you aren't already a VBA programmer, learning the VBA syntax and how to hook VBA into the Access event model is a definite career builder.

VBA is a key element in most professional Access applications. Microsoft provides VBA in Access because VBA provides significant flexibility and power to Access database applications. Without a full-fledged programming language like VBA, Access applications would have to rely on the somewhat limited set of actions offered by Access macros. Although macro programming also adds flexibility to Access applications, VBA is much easier to work with when you're programming complex data-management features or sophisticated user-interface requirements.

 If you want more information on macros, including converting macros to VBA code, turn to Chapter 22.

If you're new to programming, try not to become frustrated or overwhelmed by the seeming complexity of the VBA language. As with any new skill, you're much better off approaching VBA programming by taking it one step at a time. You need to learn exactly what VBA can do for you and your applications, along with the general syntax, statement structure, and how to compose procedures using the VBA language.

This book is chock-full of examples showing you how to use the VBA language to accomplish useful tasks. Each of the procedures you see in this book has been tested and verified to work correctly. If you find that a bit of code in this book doesn't work as expected, take the time to ensure that you've used the example code exactly as presented in this book. Often, the most difficult problems implementing any programming technique stem from simple errors, such as misspelling or forgetting to include a comma or parentheses where required.

What's in a Name?

The name Visual Basic is a source of endless confusion for people working with Microsoft products. Microsoft has applied the name Visual Basic to a number of different products and technologies. For more than a decade, Microsoft marketed a stand-alone product named Visual Basic that was, in many ways, comparable to and competitive with Access. Visual Basic was folded into Visual Studio in its very first version. In 1995, Microsoft added the Visual Basic for Applications (VBA) programming language to Access, Word, and Excel in Microsoft Office (although it was called *Access Basic* until Access 2000). The name Visual Basic for Applications was chosen because the VBA syntax is identical in Access, Word, and Excel.

Although the VBA language used in Access is very similar to Visual Basic .NET, they aren't exactly the same. You can do some things with VB .NET that can't be done with Access VBA, and vice versa.

In this book, the expressions *VBA* and *Visual Basic* refer to the programming language built into Access and should not be confused with the Microsoft VB .NET product.

NOTE

A programming language is much like a human language. Just as humans use words, sentences, and paragraphs to communicate with one another, a computer language uses words, statements, and procedures to tell the computer what you expect it to do. The primary difference between human and computer languages is that a computer language follows a strict format. Every word and sentence must be precisely composed because a computer doesn't understand context or nuance. Every task must be carefully defined for the computer, using the syntax supported by the programming language.

Understanding VBA Terminology

Before we plunge into our VBA coverage, here's a review of some basic VBA terminology:

- **Keyword:** A word that has special meaning in VBA. For example, in the English language, the word *now* simply indicates a point in time. In VBA, Now is the name of a built-in VBA function that returns the current date and time.

- **Statement:** A single VBA word or combination of words that constitutes an instruction to be performed by the VBA engine.

- **Procedure:** A collection of VBA statements that are grouped together to perform a certain task. You might, for example, write a complex procedure that extracts data from a table, combines the data in a particular way, and then displays the data on a form. Or, you might write three smaller procedures, each of which performs a single step of the overall process.

  There are two types of VBA procedures: *subs* (subroutines) and *functions:*

  - **Subroutines** execute the statements within them and they stop when they reach the end.

24

- **Functions** execute the statements within them and return a value, such as the result of a calculation.
- **Module:** Procedures are stored in *modules*. If statements are like sentences and procedures are like paragraphs, then modules are the chapters or documents of the VBA language. A module consists of one or more procedures and other elements combined as a single entity within the application.
- **Variable:** Variables are nothing more than a little piece of the computer's memory that you reserve for your application and that you name so you can refer to it later. You temporarily store data in variables until your application needs them. In virtually all VBA programs, you create and use variables to hold values such as customer names, dates, and numeric values manipulated by the VBA code.

VBA is appropriately defined as a *language*. And just as with any human language, VBA consists of a number of words, sentences, and paragraphs, all arranged in a specific fashion. Each VBA sentence is a *statement*. Statements are aggregated as *procedures*, and procedures live within *modules*. A *function* is a specific type of procedure—one that returns a value when it's run. For example, Now() is a built-in VBA function that returns the current date and time, down to the second. You use the Now() function in your application whenever you need to capture the current date and time, such as when assigning a timestamp value to a record.

Starting with VBA Code Basics

Each statement in a procedure is an instruction you want Access to perform.

There are an infinite number of different VBA programming statements that could appear in an Access application. Generally, however, VBA statements are fairly easy to read and understand. Most often, you'll be able to understand the purpose of a VBA statement based on the keywords (such as DoCmd.OpenForm) and references to database objects in the statement.

Each VBA statement is an instruction that is processed and executed by the VBA language engine built into Access. Here's an example of a typical VBA statement that opens a form:

```
DoCmd.OpenForm "frmMyForm", acNormal
```

Notice that this statement consists of an action (OpenForm) and a noun (frmMyForm). Most VBA statements follow a similar pattern of action and a reference either to the object performing the action or to the object that's the target of the action.

DoCmd is a built-in Access object that performs numerous tasks for you. Think of DoCmd as a little robot that can perform many different jobs. The OpenForm that follows DoCmd is the task you want DoCmd to run, and frmMyForm is the name of the form to open. Finally, acNormal is a modifier that tells DoCmd that you want the form opened in its "normal" view. The implication is that there are other view modes that may be applied to opening a form; these modes include Design (acDesign) or Datasheet (acFormDS) view, and Print Preview (acPreview, when applied to reports).

Creating VBA Programs

Access has a wide variety of tools that enable you to work with tables, queries, forms, and reports without ever having to write a single line of code. At some point, you might begin building more sophisticated applications. You might want to "bulletproof" your applications by providing more intensive data-entry validation or implementing better error handling.

Some operations can't be accomplished through the user interface, even with macros. You might find yourself saying, "I wish I had a way to ..." or "There just has to be a function that will let me ...." At other times, you find that you're continually putting the same formula or expression in a query or filter. You might find yourself saying, "I'm tired of typing this formula into ..." or "I mistyped the formula in this ...."

For situations such as these, you need the horsepower of a high-level programming language such as VBA. VBA is a modern, structured programming language offering many of the programming structures available in most programming languages. VBA is *extensible* (capable of calling Windows API routines) and can interact through ActiveX Data Objects (ADO), through Data Access Objects (DAO), and with any Access or VBA data type.

Getting started with VBA programming in Access requires an understanding of its event-driven environment.

Modules and procedures

In this section, you'll create a simple procedure. First, we'll take you through the steps to create the procedure, including creating a module, inputting the statements, and running the procedure. Then, we'll describe each of the elements of the procedure in greater detail. The procedure you'll create in this section displays the result of squaring a number.

To create the SquareIt procedure, follow these steps:

1. **Select the Create tab of the Ribbon, and click the Module button in the Macros & Code group.** The Visual Basic Editor (VBE) will open with a blank *code pane*, as shown in Figure 24.1.

2. **In the code pane, type the following statements:**

```
Sub SquareIt()

    Dim lNumber As Long

    lNumber = 2
```

24

```
    MsgBox lNumber & " squared is " & lNumber ^ 2

End Sub
```

FIGURE 24.1

Creating a module presents a blank code pane.

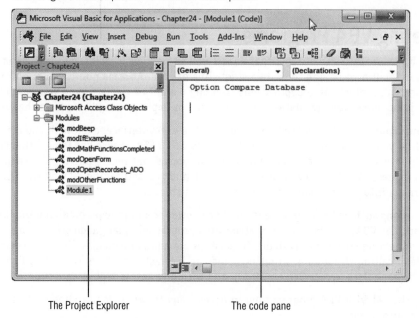

The Project Explorer   The code pane

3. **Place your cursor anywhere inside the code you just typed and choose Run Sub/Userform from the Run menu.** You should see a message box similar to Figure 24.2.

4. **Click OK to dismiss the message box and return to the VBE.**

5. **Choose File ⇨ Save and name the module when prompted (see Figure 24.3).**

If you followed the preceding steps, you created a procedure and ran it. Congratulations! In the next several sections, we'll discuss each of these steps in more detail.

Modules

The first step you performed in the previous steps was creating a new module. Modules are containers that hold your procedures. In this example, we created a *standard module*. The other type of module you can create is called a *class module*.

FIGURE 24.2

Running the code displays a message box.

Standard modules

Standard modules are independent from other Access objects, like forms and reports. Standard modules store code that is used from anywhere within your application. These procedures are often called *global* or *public* because they're accessible to all elements of your Access application.

Use public procedures throughout your application in expressions, macros, event procedures, and other VBA code. To use a public procedure, you simply type its name in another procedure in your application.

TIP

Procedures *run*; modules *contain*. Procedures are executed and perform actions. Modules, on the other hand, are simple containers, grouping procedures and declarations together. A module can't be run; instead, you run the procedures contained *within* the module.

Standard modules are stored in the Modules section of the Navigation pane. Form and report modules (see the next section) are attached to their hosts and are accessed through the Form Property Sheet or Report Property Sheet.

FIGURE 24.3

Saving the database prompts you to save any unsaved modules.

TIP
Generally speaking, you should group related procedures into modules, such as putting all of an application's data conversion routines into a single module. Logically grouping procedures make maintenance much easier because there is a single place in the application for all the procedures supporting a particular activity. Plus, most modules contain procedures that are related in some way.

Class modules

The other type of module is called a *class module*. A *class* defines how an *object* behaves. You can create your own classes, called *custom classes*, but the most common class module you'll use is a class module that's bound to a form or report.

In the previous example, you created a standard module using the Ribbon. For class modules that are bound to a form or report, the module is created automatically by Access whenever you add VBA code to the form or report.

The most important difference between standard modules and class modules is that class modules support events. Events respond to user actions and run VBA code that's contained within the event procedure.

The Access event module and event procedures are discussed in Chapter 26.

Module sections

You may have noticed that when you created the module, there was already code in it. Depending on the options you have set for your environment, Access will insert code into new modules automatically.

The area above the first procedure in a module is called the *declaration section*. The declaration section is used to store options and variables that will apply to every procedure in the module. Two common option declarations are Option Compare Database and Option Explicit. Option Compare Database determines how two strings are compared to each other and directs VBA to use the same comparison method that the database uses. The other options for comparing strings are Option Compare Text and Option Compare Binary. Basically, Option Compare Text doesn't care whether the letters are uppercase or lowercase, and Option Compare Binary does care. It's a little more complicated than that, but Option Compare Database is usually the best option.

Option Explicit directs VBA to warn you if you have undeclared variables. By setting this option, you're telling VBA that you intend to explicitly declare any variables that you'll use. You'll learn more about declaring variables later.

Everything below the declarations section is known as the *procedure section* or *code section*. This section contains the subprocedures and functions of the module. It's important to understand the differences between these two sections because you can't put statements that belong in the declaration section into the code section, nor can you put code in the declaration section. If you do, the VBE will let you know that it's not allowed.

Procedures and functions

The next step you completed after creating a module to hold your procedure was to create the procedure itself. It's a simple procedure that does some simple math and displays the result. Each statement is structured according to the language's *syntax*, meaning that the spelling of keywords and the order of the words in the statement is important.

Subprocedures

A subprocedure (or *sub*) is the simplest type of procedure in a VBA project. A subprocedure is nothing more than a container for VBA statements that typically perform a task such as opening a form or report or running a query.

Subprocedures have two required statements: Sub procname and End Sub. If those were the only two statements you had, it would be a valid subprocedure, but it would be pretty uninteresting because it wouldn't do anything. In our example, the procedure is started with the Sub SquareIt() statement. The procedure ends with the End Sub statement.

When determining the name of your procedure, there are a few rules that you must follow. The most important rules to remember are that the name must begin with a letter,

24

can't contain most punctuation, and can't be more than 255 characters long. Rules aside, you should pick names for your procedures that describe what they do in a way that will be obvious to you when you read them later. Procedure names like GetData() will likely be hard to understand later, but ReadDataFromEmployeeTable() will be crystal clear. You probably don't want to push the 255-character limit on procedure names, but don't be afraid to make long, descriptive names.

Variable declaration

The first statement in our simple subprocedure is a *variable declaration statement*. It starts with the Dim keyword, which is short for dimension. The variable's name, lNumber, comes next. Variable names follow the same rules as procedure names, described in the previous section. The As keyword follows the name, which is followed by the data type. In this case, lNumber was declared as a Long Integer data type.

 Variables and data types are discussed extensively in Chapter 25.

Variables hold data that you can use later in your procedure. When you declare a variable with the Dim keyword, you're telling VBA to reserve a spot in the computer's memory to store that data. The amount of memory that VBA will reserve depends on the data type. In this example, you told VBA to hold enough memory to store a Long Integer, or 32 bits of memory.

The As datatype portion of the variable declaration statement is optional. You could declare lNumber with the statement:

```
Dim lNumber
```

When you omit the data type, VBA will determine an appropriate data type when you assign a value to the variable. That may seem like a handy service VBA is providing, but it's not a very good practice. VBA will assign a data type to the variable based on the first time you use it, but it doesn't know all the plans you have in mind for that variable. It may end up assigning a data type that's too small for what you need. Having VBA assign data types is also slower than if you assign them as you write the code.

> **TIP**
>
> If you're new to VBA, don't get too hung up on which data type to use for your variables. Use String for text, Long for numbers without decimals, Double for numbers with decimals, and Boolean for true/false values. You can get a lot done with just those four data types.

Variable assignment

By declaring a variable with the Dim statement, you've reserved a place in memory where you can store data for later use. The next line in the procedure stores the number 2 in the variable lNumber. Here's what that line looks like in the procedure:

```
lNumber = 2
```

Assigning values to variables is easy. There are really only two things you need to remember:

- **You must assign a value that is appropriate for the variable's data type.** In this case, you're storing a number without a decimal in a variable declared as Long. If you tried to store data that isn't appropriate for the variable's data type, VBA would do its best to convert the value into the appropriate data type. If you tried to store the value 8.26, for example, in a Long variable, VBA would convert it to 8 by truncating the number to remove the decimals. If VBA were unable to convert the data, you'd get an error.

- **The variable name goes on the left of the equal sign, and the value goes on the right.** Everything on the right of the equal sign is evaluated before it's assigned to the variable. For this example, there's not much to evaluate because it's simply the number 2. Consider the following statement, which computes the product of two numbers and assigns it to a variable:

```
dProduct = 3 * 6.1
```

In that statement, 3 is multiplied by 6.1, and the result, 18.3, is assigned to the variable. That's still pretty straightforward, but consider yet another example:

```
bIsEqual = dProduct = 18.3
```

In this statement, bIsEqual is a variable declared as Boolean, and dProduct is a variable declared as Double. But there are two equal signs. The first equal sign is the assignment operator—setting a variable equal to a value. Any other equal signs (there's only one other, in this case) are comparison operators. Comparison operators return True or False. If dProduct were equal to 18.3, then bIsEqual would get the value True. Everything to the right of the first equal sign (the assignment operator) is evaluated first, and the result is assigned to the variable.

Functions

A function is very similar to a subprocedure, with one major exception: a function returns a value when it ends. A simple example is the built-in VBA Now() function, which returns the current date and time. Now() can be used virtually anywhere your application needs to use or display the current date and time. An example is including Now() in a report header or footer so that the user knows exactly when the report was printed.

Now() is just one of several hundred built-in VBA functions. As you'll see throughout this book, the built-in VBA functions provide useful and very powerful features to your Access applications.

In addition to built-in functions, you might add custom functions that return values required by your applications. An example is a data transformation routine that performs a mathematical operation (such as currency conversion or calculating shipping costs) on an input value. It doesn't matter where the input value comes from (table, form, query, and so

24

on). The function always returns exactly the correct calculated value, no matter where the function is used.

Within the body of a function, you specify the function's return value by assigning a value to the function's name (and, yes, it does look pretty strange to include the function's name within the function's body). You then can use the returned value as part of a larger expression. The following function calculates the square footage of a room:

```
Function SquareFeet(dHeight As Double, _
    dWidth As Double) As Double

    'Assign this function's value:
    SquareFeet = dHeight * dWidth

End Function
```

This function receives two parameters: dHeight and dWidth. Notice that the function's name, SquareFeet, is assigned a value within the body of the function. The function is declared as a Double data type, so the return value is recognized by the VBA interpreter as a Double.

The main thing to keep in mind about functions is that they return values. The returned value is often assigned to a variable or control on a form or report, as in these two examples:

```
dAnswer = SquareFeet(dHeight, dWidth)

Me!txtAnswer = SquareFeet(dHeight, dWidth)
```

If the function (or subroutine, for that matter) requires information (such as the Height and Width in the case of the SquareFeet function), the information is passed as arguments within the parentheses in the function's declaration.

 Arguments (also called *parameters*) are discussed in more detail in Chapter 25.

Working in the code window

Unlike designing a table or dropping controls in the sections of a report, a module's code pane is a very unstructured place to work. VBA code is simply text, and there aren't a lot of visual cues to tell you how to write the code or where to put particular pieces of the code. In this section, we'll describe some features of the code window and some techniques to keep your code organized and readable.

White space

In the code already presented in this chapter, you may have noticed some indentation and some blank lines. In the programming world, this is known as *white space*. White space consists of spaces, tabs, and blank lines. With very few exceptions, VBA ignores white space. The following two procedures are identical as far as the VBA compiler is concerned:

```
Function BMI(dPounds As Double, lHeight As Long) As Double

    BMI = dPounds / (lHeight ^ 2) * 703

End Function
```

```
Function BMI(dPounds As Double, lHeight As Long) As Double
BMI = dPounds / (lHeight ^ 2) * 703
End Function
```

In the first function, a blank line was inserted after the Function statement, and another blank line was inserted before the End Function statement. Also, a tab was inserted before the single statement within the procedure. All the white space elements were removed in the second function. Despite the difference in appearance, the VBA compiler reads the two functions identically, and the two functions return the same result.

In some programming languages, white space is important and meaningful. That isn't the case for VBA. The purpose of white space is to make your code more readable. Different programmers format their code with white space in different ways. Whatever formatting conventions you choose to use, the most important thing is to be consistent. Consistency in formatting will help you read and understand your code more easily, even if you're reading months or years later.

Line continuation

The VBE window can expand to be as wide as your screen. Sometimes your statements are so long that they extend beyond the window even when it's as wide as it can be. VBA provides a way to continue the current line onto the next line. When used with long statements, this can help make your code more readable. The line continuation characters are a space followed by an underscore. When the VBA compiler sees a space and an underscore at the end of the line, it knows that the next line is a continuation of the current one. Figure 24.4 shows a simple procedure with one very long statement. The statement extends beyond the code pane window, and you must scroll to read it.

Use the line continuation characters to break the long statement into multiple lines. This will allow you to see the whole statement. The statement in Figure 24.4 could be rewritten as the following statement:

```
Function GetDatedFooter() As String

    GetDatedFooter = "This report was printed on " _
        & Format(Now, "dd-mmm-yyyy") & _
        " and changes made to the data after that " & _
        "date won't be reflected."

End Function
```

24

FIGURE 24.4

A long statement extends beyond the code window.

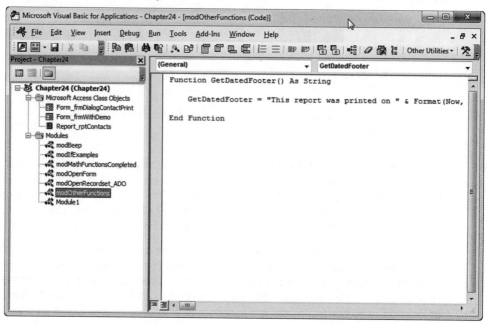

The underscore is typically referred to as the *line continuation character*, but the space that comes before it is equally important. You need both characters, space and underscore, to continue a line. The line continuation character can't be used in the middle of a string. Notice in the preceding example that the long string is broken up into four smaller strings and concatenated together with ampersands. To spread a long string over multiple lines, it must be broken up so that the line continuation character can be used.

Multi-statement lines

Another way to improve the readability of your code is by putting two or more statements on one line. VBA uses the colon to separate statements on the same line. If you have a lot of short statements that are taking up a lot of vertical space in the code pane, you can put a few of them on the same line to clean up the code. In the following example, many simi-lar statements are grouped together:

```
i = 12: j = 45: k = 32
l = 87: m = 77: n = 2
o = 89: p = 64: q = 52
```

Those nine statements are assigning numbers to nine different variables. If they were writ-ten out one after the other, they would eat up a lot of the code window. By putting three statements on each line, less space is wasted. This technique is useful when you have small statements that are all doing roughly the same operation. If your statements are long or diverse, it actually hinders the readability of the code and should be avoided.

IntelliSense

Suppose that you know you want to use a specific command, but you can't remember the exact syntax. Access includes four features (collectively known as *IntelliSense*) to help you find the proper keyword and determine the correct parameters as you create each line of code:

- **Complete Word:** Any time you're in a code pane, you can press Ctrl+spacebar to get a list of keywords. The list automatically scrolls to the keyword that matches what you've already typed. If there is only one match, you don't see the list and the word is simply completed for you. Figure 24.5 shows what happens when you type "do" and press Ctrl+spacebar.

FIGURE 24.5

Complete Word shows a list of keywords.

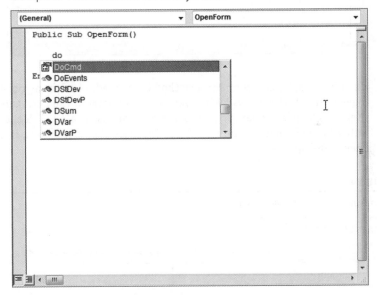

If you were to type "doc" instead of just "do," the keyword DoCmd would be completed rather than a list because there is only one keyword that starts with doc.

- **Auto List Members:** Auto List Members is a drop-down list that is automatically displayed when you type the beginning of a keyword that has associated objects, properties, or methods. For example, if you enter DoCmd.openf, a list of the possible options displays, as shown in Figure 24.6. Scroll through the list box and press Enter to select the option you want or continue typing to narrow the selections in the list.

FIGURE 24.6

Access Auto List Members help in a module.

In this example, the OpenForm method is selected. (Actions associated with an object are called *methods*.) After you choose an item in the list, more Auto List Members help is displayed. Or, if parameters are associated with the keyword, the other type of module help, Auto Quick Info (see the next bullet), is displayed, as shown in Figure 24.7.

FIGURE 24.7

Access Auto Quick Info help in a module.

■ **Auto Quick Info:** Auto Quick Info guides you through all the options (called *parameters*) for the specific item. The bold word (FormName) is the next parameter available for the OpenForm method. Figure 24.7 shows that there are many parameters available for the OpenForm command. The parameters are separated by commas. As each parameter is entered, the next parameter is highlighted in bold. The position of parameters is significant; they can't be rearranged without causing problems. Press the Esc key to hide Auto Quick Info help.

Not every parameter is required for every VBA command. Parameters surrounded by square brackets (such as View in Figure 24.7) are optional. Access provides reasonable defaults for all optional arguments that are omitted from the statement using the command.

■ **Auto Constants:** Auto Constants is a drop-down list that displays when you're on a parameter that requires a built-in constant. In Figure 24.7, the Auto Quick Info shows that the second parameter is View and is described as [View As acFormView = acNormal]. The brackets around the parameter indicate that it's an optional parameter. acFormView is a family of built-in constants that you can use for this parameter. The default constant, acNormal, is used if you omit this parameter. Figure 24.8 shows the list of acFormView constants available. Simply select the one you want and type a comma. The constant and the comma are inserted into the statement, and you're ready for the next parameter.

FIGURE 24.8

Access Auto Constants help in a module.

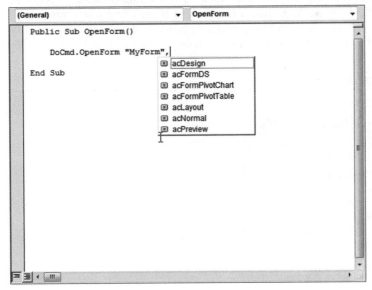

TIP

You can split the code window into two independent edit panes by dragging down the splitter bar (the little horizontal bar at the very top of the vertical scroll bar at the right edge of the code window). Splitting the window enables simultaneous editing of two sections of code. Each section of a split VBA code window scrolls independently, and changes you make in one pane of a split window show up in the other pane. Double-click the splitter bar to return the window to its former state, or grab the splitter bar with the mouse and drag it to the top of the code editor window to close the second edit pane. (Word and Excel feature a similar splitter button, making it very easy to edit different parts of the same Word document or Excel worksheet.)

Compiling procedures

After code has been written, you should compile it to complete the development process.

The compilation step converts the English-like VBA syntax to a binary format that is easily executed at run time. Also, during compilation, all your code is checked for incorrect syntax and other errors that will cause problems when the user works with the application.

If you don't compile your Access applications during the development cycle, Access compiles the code whenever a user opens the application and begins using it. In this case, errors in your code might prevent the user from using the application, causing a great deal of inconvenience to everyone involved.

Compile your applications by choosing Debug ⇨ Compile from the VBE's menu. An error window appears if the compilation is not successful. Figure 24.9 shows the result of an unsuccessful compile due to a misspelling of a variable name. It doesn't tell you that you misspelled a variable; rather, it reports that it can't find where you declared a particular variable. That can mean that you simply forgot to declare it, but it usually means you spelled it differently in the code from how you spelled it in the declaration statement.

FIGURE 24.9

The compiler reports errors.

Saving a module

Modules differ from other Access objects in that there isn't an explicit way to save a newly created, individual module. New modules that are created don't display in the Navigation pane until they're saved, and the modules that are displayed there open in the VBE when double-clicked.

Modules are saved by saving the database and responding to the prompts that Access displays. In the VBE, choose File ➪ Save to save the database. You'll be prompted to save all unsaved modules and other unsaved objects. You aren't prompted to save modules that have already been saved, even if they've been changed. Those modules are simply saved with the name you provided previously.

Class modules that are attached to a form or report are saved when the form or report is saved.

Understanding VBA Branching Constructs

The real power of any programming language is its capability to make a decision based on a condition that might be different each time the user works with the application. VBA provides two ways for a procedure to execute code conditionally: branching and looping.

Branching

Often, a program performs different tasks based on some value. If the condition is true, the code performs one action. If the condition is false, the code performs a different action. An application's capability to look at a value and, based on that value, decide which code to run is known as *branching* (or *conditional processing*).

The procedure is similar to walking down a road and coming to a fork in the road; you can go to the left or to the right. If a sign at the fork points left for home and right for work, you can decide which way to go. If you need to go to work, you go to the right; if you need to go home, you go to the left. In the same way, a program looks at the value of some variable and decides which set of code should be processed.

VBA offers two sets of conditional processing statements:

- `If...Then...Else...End If`
- `Select Case...End Select`

24

The If keyword

The `If` keyword can be used in a few different ways, but they all check a condition and, based on the evaluation, perform an action. The condition must evaluate to a Boolean value (`True` or `False`). If the condition is true, the program moves to the line following the `If` statement. If the condition is false, the program skips to the statement following the `Else` statement, if present, or the `End If` statement if there is no `Else` clause.

The If...Then construct

An `If` statement can take a few different forms. The first form is the `If...Then` construct. It is a one line statement where the condition and the action are all in the same statement. In the following example, the `sState` variable is set if the `sCity` variable contains certain data:

```
If sCity = "Dallas" Then sState = "Texas"
```

VBA first evaluates `sCity = "Dallas"` and determines if the conditional is true or false. If it's true (that is, if `sCity` has been assigned the value `Dallas`), the portion of the statement after the `Then` keyword is executed. In this case, the `sState` variable is assigned the value `Texas`. If the conditional is false, the program moves on to the next line in the procedure and the `sState` variable doesn't change.

The If...End If construct

The next form is the `If...End If` construct. This construct, and the ones that follow, are commonly known as *If blocks* because they can contain more than one line of code (a block of code), unlike the `If...Then` construct that can only execute one line. The previous example can be rewritten as an `If...End If`:

```
If sCity = "Dallas" Then
    sState = "Texas"
End If
```

This example is exactly the same as the one before it. If the conditional statement is true, the single line in the `If` block is executed. The difference is when the conditional is false. In that case, the program braches to the line immediately following the `End If` statement and program execution continues.

The benefit of the `If...End If` construct is that you can execute multiple statements when a conditional is true. In the next example, two variables are assigned values when the conditional is true:

```
If sCity = "Dallas" Then
    sState = "Texas"
    dTaxRate = 0.075
End If
```

If the conditional is true, both statements are executed. Otherwise, the program branches to the line just below `End If` and continues executing.

The If...Else...End If construct

In the previous examples, one or more statements are executed when the conditional is true and nothing happens when the conditional is false. The `Else` keyword can be included in an `If` block to identify statements that should run when the conditional is false:

```
If sCity = "Dallas" Then
    sState = "Texas"
    dTaxRate = 0.075
Else
    sState = "Michigan"
    dTaxRate = 0.05
End If
```

When the conditional is true, the first two statements are executed (setting `sState` to Texas and `dTaxRate` to `0.075`). Then the program branches to the line below `End If` and continues executing. The two statements between `Else` and `End If` aren't executed.

If the conditional is false, however, the program branches to the statement below the `Else` statement and skips the first two. It's very common to see a construct like this that executes certain lines of code when a condition is met and certain other lines when it's not.

You must use an `If` block to use an `Else` statement. `Else` statements do not work with the first construct (the `If...Then` construct).

The If...ElseIf...End If construct

The final `If` construct is yet another `If` block type of construct. Instead of only one conditional, there are multiple conditionals. The `ElseIf` statement defines as many other conditionals as you need:

```
If sCity = "Dallas" Then
    sState = "Texas"
    dTaxRate = 0.075
ElseIf sCity = "Detroit" Then
    sState = "Michigan"
    dTaxRate = 0.05
Else
    sState = "Oregon"
    dTaxRate = 0.0625
End If
```

The program flows through an `If...ElseIf...EndIf` construct much like it does through the others. If the first conditional is true, the statements in the first section are executed and the program branches to the line just below the `End If`. If the first conditional is false, the program branches to the second conditional (the first `ElseIf`) and tests that conditional. If none of the conditionals is true, the statements in the `Else` section are executed. The `Else` statement is optional when using `ElseIf`. If you omit the `Else` statement and none of the conditionals is true, no statements in the `If` block are executed.

24

Nested If statements

Nesting statements refers to putting statements inside a block of other statements. In the case of `If`, nesting means that one `If` block is inside another `If` block:

```
If sState = "Michigan" Then
    If sCity = "Detroit" Then
        dTaxRate = 0.05
    ElseIf sCity = "Kalamazoo" Then
        dTaxRate = 0.045
    Else
        dTaxRate = 0
    End If
End If
```

The outer `If` block tests the `sState` variable. If that condition is true, the inner `If` block is executed, and the `sCity` variable is tested. If the conditional in the outer `If` block is false, the program branches to the line below the `End If` statement that matches the `If` statement being evaluated. Proper indenting, though not required, is helpful to see which `Else` and `End If` statements go with which `If` statements.

Boolean values and conditionals

`If` statements are wonderful, and you'll see them in almost every piece of code you write. However, there are two situations in which they're misused. Consider this code fragment:

```
If bIsBuyer = True Then
    bIsInPurchasing = True
Else
    bIsInPurchasing = False
End If
```

This is a simple `If...Else...End If` construct where the conditional checks to see if the Boolean variable `bIsBuyer` is `True`. Based on the result of that conditional, another Boolean variable is set to `True` or `False`. There's nothing wrong with the code—it will compile and run just fine—but there is a way to simplify the code and make it more readable. First, comparing a Boolean variable to `True` or `False` is unnecessary because the variable already is true or false. The first line can be simplified to:

```
If bIsBuyer Then
```

Assuming `bIsBuyer` is `True`, then in the first example, the compiler evaluates `bIsBuyer = True`, which reduces to `True = True`, and of course that returns `True`. In the simpler example, `bIsBuyer` is evaluated and returns `True`. Because `bIsBuyer` is a Boolean variable, comparing it to a Boolean value is redundant.

The second simplification step is to remove the `If` statement altogether. Whenever you're setting a Boolean value in an `If` block, you should consider whether the Boolean value can be set directly:

```
bIsInPurchasing = bIsBuyer
```

This one line of code does the same things as the five lines we started with. If bIsBuyer is True, bIsInPurchasing will also be True. If bIsBuyer is False, bIsInPurchasing will also be False. There may be situations in which you need to set one variable to the opposite of the other. VBA provides the Not keyword to convert Booleans from True to False and vice versa:

```
bIsInPurchasing = Not bIsTruckDriver
```

The variable bIsTruckDriver is evaluated as either true or false and the Not keyword returns the opposite. If bIsTruckDriver is True, bIsInPurchasing will be assigned the value False.

When you have many conditions to test, the If...Then...ElseIf...Else conditions can get rather unwieldy. A better approach is to use the Select Case...End Select construct.

The Select Case...End Select statement

VBA offers the Select Case statement to check for multiple conditions. Following is the general syntax of the Select Case statement:

```
Select Case Expression

    Case Value1
        [Action to take when Expression = Value1]

    Case Value2
        [Action to take when Expression = Value2]

    Case ...

    Case Else
        [Default action when no value matches Expression]

End Select
```

Notice that the syntax is similar to that of the If...Then statement. Instead of a Boolean condition, the Select Case statement uses an expression at the very top. Then, each Case clause tests its value against the expression's value. When a Case value matches the expression, the program executes the block of code until it reaches another Case statement or the End Select statement. VBA executes the code for only one matching Case statement.

NOTE

If more than one Case statement matches the value of the test expression, only the code for the first match executes. If other matching Case statements appear after the first match, VBA ignores them.

24

Figure 24.10 shows `Select...Case` used by frmDialogContactPrint to decide which of several reports to open.

FIGURE 24.10

Using the `Select Case` statement.

The code in Figure 24.10 shows that the expression in the `Select Case` statement is `Me![grpTypeOfPrint]`. This expression represents a group of option buttons on the form. When evaluated, it returns a 1, 2, or 3 depending on which option button is selected. The value in each `Case` statement is then compared to the expression's value and, if there is a match, any statements between the matching `Case` statement and the next `Case` statement (or the `End Select` statement) are executed.

Using the `Case Else` statement is optional, but it's always a good idea. The `Case Else` clause is always the last `Case` statement of `Select Case` and is executed when none of the `Case` values matches the expression at the top of the `Select Case` statement.

The `Case` statement can be inequality comparisons by incorporating the `Is` keyword:

```
Select Case dTaxRate
    Case Is < 0.03
        MsgBox "Low taxes"
    Case Is > 0.07
        MsgBox "High taxes"
    Case Else
        MsgBox "Average taxes"
End Select
```

By including the `Is` keyword, you can make a comparison in the `Case` statement. In this example, the dTaxRate variable is evaluated in the `Select Case` statement. In the first `Case` statement, the value is compared to `0.03` and if it's lower, the code under that `Case` statement is executed. If dTaxRate is in between 0.03 and 0.07, the Case Else statement will be executed because neither of the first two Case statements would be true.

The Case statement also accepts multiple values. You can separate multiple values in the same Case statement with a comma. You can also specify a range of values using the To keyword. The following example shows both of these techniques:

```
Select Case dSalesAmt
  Case 0.99, 1.99
    dCommissionPct = 0.1
  Case 2 To 4.99
    dCommissionPct = 0.15
  Case Is >= 5
    dCommissionPct = 0.17
End Select
```

Looping

Another powerful process that VBA offers is *looping*, the capability to execute a single statement or a group of statements over and over. The statement or group of statements is repeated until some condition is met.

VBA offers two types of looping constructs:

- Do...Loop
- For...Next

Do...Loop constructs are used when you need to repeat a statement or group of statements and you don't know how many times you need to repeat them. For...Next constructs are used when you already know how many times to repeat the statements.

Loops are commonly used to process records within a recordset, change the appearance of controls on forms, and a number of other tasks that require repeating the same VBA statements multiple times.

The Do...Loop statement

Do...Loop is used to repeat a group of statements *while* a condition is true or *until* a condition is true. This statement is one of the most commonly used VBA looping constructs:

```
Do [While | Until Condition]
    [VBA statements]
    [Exit Do]
    [VBA statements]
Loop
```

Alternatively, the While (or Until) may appear at the bottom of the construct:

```
Do
    [VBA statements]
    [Exit Do]
```

```
        [VBA statements]
    Loop [While | Until Condition]
```

Notice that Do...Loop has several options. The While clause causes the VBA statements within the Do...Loop to execute as long as the condition is true. Execution drops out of the Do...Loop as soon as the condition evaluates to false.

The Until clause works in just the opposite way. The code within the Do...Loop executes only as long as the condition is false.

Placing the While or Until clause at the top of the Do...Loop means that the loop never executes if the condition is not met. Placing the While or Until at the bottom of the loop means that the loop executes at least once because the condition is not evaluated until after the statements within the loop have executed the first time.

Exit Do immediately terminates the Do...Loop. Use Exit Do as part of a test within the loop:

```
    Do While Condition1
        [VBA statements]
        If Condition2 Then Exit Do
        [VBA statements]
    Loop
```

Exit Do is often used to prevent endless loops. An endless loop occurs when the condition's state (true or false) never changes within the loop.

In case you're wondering, Condition1 and Condition2 in this example may be the same. There is no requirement that the second condition be different from the condition used at the top of the Do...Loop.

Figure 24.11 illustrates how a Do loop may be used. In this particular example, a recordset has been opened, and each record is processed within the Do loop. In this example, the last name field is printed in the Immediate window, but the data is not modified or used in any way.

The While and Until clauses provide powerful flexibility for processing a Do...Loop in your code.

The For...Next statement

Use For...Next to repeat a statement block a set number of times. The general format of For...Next is:

```
    For CounterVariable = Start To End
        [VBA Statements]
        [Exit For]
        [VBA Statements]
    Next CounterVariable
```

FIGURE 24.11

Using the Do...Loop statement.

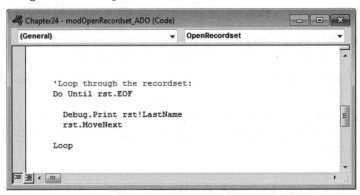

The following procedure uses the built-in Beep function to emit a sound a set number of times. The For...Next loop determines the number of beeps:

```
Sub BeepWarning()
    Dim lBeep As Long
    Dim lBeepCount As Long
    lBeepCount = 5
    For lBeep = 1 To lBeepCount
        Beep
    Next lBeep
End Sub
```

In this procedure, lBeep is the counter variable, 1 is the start, and lBeepCount is the end. When the program reaches the For line, lBeep is set to 1. As long as lBeep is less than or equal to lBeepCount, the statements inside the For...Next block are executed. When the Next line is reached, lBeep is increased by one and again compared to lBeep-Count. If lBeep is still less than or equal to lBeepCount, the loop is executed again. When lBeep becomes greater than lBeepCount, the loop is complete, and the remaining code in the procedure is executed.

An alternate form of For...Next is:

```
For CounterVariable = Start To End Step StepValue
    [Statement block]
Next CounterVariable
```

The only difference here is that the StepValue is added to the first statement. The Step keyword followed by an increment causes the counter variable to be incremented by the step value each time the loop executes. For example, if Start is 10 and End is 100 and StepValue is 10, the counter variable starts at 10 and increments by 10 each time the loop executes. As you saw in the previous example, when Step is omitted, the default is to increment CounterVariable by 1.

24

Most of the time, a For...Next loop counts upward, starting at an initial value and incrementing the counter variable by the amount specified by the step value. In some cases, however, you might need a loop that starts at a high start value and steps downward to an end value. In this case, use a negative number as the step value. The Step keyword is required when looping backward. If you omit it, the For statement will see that *CounterVariable* is greater than End and the loop won't be executed.

For Each...Next is a special implementation of For...Next for looping through collections. For Each...Next is discussed in the next section.

Up until this point, you've been working with simple variables such as Booleans, Longs, and Strings. The following section explains the special syntax to use when working with objects instead of simple variables.

Working with Objects and Collections

Very often, you have to work with objects such as the controls on a form or a recordset object containing data extracted from the database. VBA provides several constructs specifically designed to work with objects and collections of objects.

An object primer

Although VBA for Access is not strictly an object-oriented language, it's often referred to as *object based*. Many of the things you work with in Access are objects and not just simple numbers and character strings. Generally speaking, an *object* is a complex entity that performs some kind of job within an Access application. Access uses *collections* to aggregate similar objects as a single group.

For example, when you build an Access form, you're creating a Form object. As you add controls to the form, you're creating objects and adding them to the form's Controls collection. Even though you might add different types of controls (such as buttons and text boxes) to the form, the form's Controls collection contains all the controls you've added to the form.

You'll see many examples of working with individual objects and collections of objects in this book. Understanding how objects differ from simple variables is an important step to becoming a proficient Access developer.

Each type of Access object includes its own properties and methods, and shares many other properties (such as Name) and methods with many other Access objects.

Collections are usually named by taking the name of the objects they contain and making it plural. The Forms collection contains the Form object. The Reports collection contains the Report object. There are exceptions, however, such as the Controls collection. While the Controls collection does contain Control objects, each Control object is also another type of object. A Control object can be a Textbox object, a Combobox object, or any one of several more specific object types.

Collections have just a few properties. These are the two most important properties associated with Access collections:

- Count: The number of items contained with the collection. A collection with a Count of 0 is empty. Collections can contain virtually any number of items, but performance degrades when the Count becomes very large (in excess of 50,000 objects).
- Item: Once you have objects stored in a collection, you need a way to reference individual objects in the collection. The Item property points to a single item within a collection.

The following example demonstrates setting a property on just one item in a collection:

```
MyCollection.Item(9).SomeProperty = Value
```

or:

```
MyCollection.Item("ItemName").SomeProperty = Value
```

where *MyCollection* is the name assigned to the collection, *SomeProperty* is the name of a property associated with the item, and *Value* is the value assigned to the property.

NOTE

The Forms and Reports collections are a little unusual in that they only contain Form and Report objects that are currently open. By contrast, the TableDefs collection contains all the tables in the database regardless of whether they are open.

This short example demonstrates a few important concepts regarding collections:

- **There are different ways to reference the items stored in a collection.** In most cases, each item stored in a collection (such as a form's Controls collection) has a name and can be referenced using its name:

  ```
  MyForm.Controls("txtLastName").FontBold = True
  ```

  As a consequence, each object's name within a collection must be unique. You can't, for example, have two controls with the same name on an Access form.

  The alternate way to reference an object in a collection is with a number that indicates the item's ordinal position within the collection. The first item added to a collection is item 0 (zero), the second is item 1, and so on.

- **Collections have default properties.** You may have noticed that the last code fragment didn't use the Item property to get at the txtLastName control. The Item property is the default property for most collections and is often omitted. The following two lines of code are the same:

  ```
  MyForm.Controls.Item(1).Text = "Name"

  MyForm.Controls(1).Text = "Name"
  ```

24

- **A collection might contain many thousands of objects.** Although performance suffers when a collection contains tens of thousands of objects, a collection is a handy way to store an arbitrary number of items as an application runs. You'll see several examples of using collections as storage devices in this book.

> **NOTE**
> The period that exists between an object and its properties or methods is commonly known as the *dot operator*. The dot operator gives you access to an object's properties and methods.

Properties and methods

Objects have properties and methods. They also have events, which we'll discuss thoroughly in Chapter 26.

Properties

Properties let you read and change simple values that are the characteristics of the object. The Label object has a Caption property. The Caption property is the string that is displayed in the label. The Label object also has Height and Width properties that hold numbers determining the object's size. These are examples of properties that hold simple values.

Properties can also return other objects. As you've seen, the Form object has a Controls property. But isn't Controls a collection object? Yes, it is. And for each collection object, there is a property that returns it. When you write MyForm.Controls.Count, you're using the Controls property of MyForm to get access to the Controls collection object. Fortunately, the Access object model is so well designed that you don't have to worry about what is a simple property and what is a property returning an object. When you see two dot operators in a single statement, you can be sure you're accessing another object. Typing a dot operator after a simple value property won't give you any options.

Methods

You can also access an object's methods through the dot operator. Methods differ from properties because they don't return a value. Methods can generally be put into two categories:

- Methods that change more than one property at once
- Methods that perform an action external to the object

The first type of method changes two or more properties at once. The CommandButton object has a method called SizeToFit. The SizeToFit property changes the Height property, the Width property, or both so that all the text in the Caption property can be displayed.

The second type of method performs some action outside its parent object. It usually also changes a few properties on the way. The Form object has an Undo method. The Undo method has to go outside of the form and read the undo stack from Access to determine what the last action was. When this method is called after a text box is changed, the text box's Text property is changed back to its previous value.

The With statement

The With statement enables you to access an object's properties and methods without typing the object's name over and over. Any properties or methods used between With and End With automatically refer to the object specified in the With statement. Any number of statements can appear between the With and End With statements, and With statements can be nested. Properties and methods will refer to the object in the innermost With block that contains them.

For example, consider the code using the following For...Next looping construct. This code loops through all members of a form's Controls collection, examining each control. If the control is a command button, the button's font is set to 12 point, bold, Times New Roman:

```
Private Sub cmdOld_Click()
  Dim i As Integer
  Dim MyControl As Control

  For i = 0 To Me.Controls.Count - 1
    Set MyControl = Me.Controls(i) 'Grab a control
    If TypeOf MyControl Is CommandButton Then
      'Set a few properties of the control:
      MyControl.FontName = "Times New Roman"
      MyControl.FontBold = True
      MyControl.FontSize = 12
    End If
  Next
End Sub
```

Don't be confused by the different expressions you see in this example. The heart of this procedure is the For...Next loop. The loop begins at zero (the start value) and executes until the i variable reaches the number of controls on the form minus one. (The controls on an Access form are numbered beginning with zero. The Count property tells you how many controls are on the form.) Within the loop, a variable named MyControl is pointed at the control indicated by the i variable. The If TypeOf statement evaluates the exact type of control referenced by the MyControl variable.

Within the body of the If...Then block, the control's properties (FontName, FontBold, and FontSize) are adjusted. You'll frequently see code such as this when it's necessary to manipulate all the members of a collection.

Notice that the control variable is referenced in each of the assignment statements. Referencing control properties one at a time is a fairly slow process. If the form contains many controls, this code executes relatively slowly.

24

An improvement on this code uses the `With` statement to isolate one member of the `Controls` collection and apply a number of statements to that control. The following code uses the `With` statement to apply a number of font settings to a single control:

```
Private Sub cmdWith_Click()
  Dim i As Integer

  Dim MyControl As Control

  For i = 0 To Me.Controls.Count - 1
    Set MyControl = Me.Controls(i)   'Grab a control
    If TypeOf MyControl Is CommandButton Then
      With MyControl
        'Set a few properties of the control:
        .FontName = "Arial"
        .FontBold = True
        .FontSize = 8
      End With
    End If
  Next
End Sub
```

The code in this example (`cmdWith_Click`) executes somewhat faster than the previous example (`cmdOld_Click`). Once Access has a handle on the control (`With MyControl`), it's able to apply all the statements in the body of the `With` without having to fetch the control from the controls on the form as in `cmdOld_Click`.

In practical terms, however, it's highly unlikely that you'll notice any difference in execution times when using the `With` construct as shown in this example. However, when working with massive sets of data, the `With` statement might contribute to overall performance. In any case, the `With` statement reduces the wordiness of the subroutine and makes the code much easier to read and understand. It also saves tons of typing when you're changing a lot of properties of an object.

Think of the `With` statement as if you're handing Access a particular item and saying "Here, apply all these properties to *this* item." The previous example said, "Go get the item named *x* and apply this property to it" over and over again.

The For Each statement

The code in `cmdWith_Click` is further improved by using the `For Each` statement to traverse the `Controls` collection. `For Each` walks through each member of a collection, making it available for examination or manipulation. The following code shows how `For Each` simplifies the example:

```
Private Sub cmdForEach_Click()
  Dim MyControl As Control
```

```
   For Each MyControl In Me.Controls
      If TypeOf MyControl Is CommandButton Then
         With MyControl
            .FontName = "MS Sans Serif"
            .FontBold = False
            .FontSize = 8
         End With
      End If
   Next
End Sub
```

The improvement goes beyond using fewer lines to get the same amount of work done. Notice that you no longer need an integer variable to count through the Controls collection. You also don't have to call on the Controls collection's Count property to determine when to end the For loop. All this overhead is handled silently and automatically for you by the VBA programming language.

The code in this listing is easier to understand than in either of the previous procedures. The purpose of each level of nesting is obvious and clear. You don't have to keep track of the index to see what's happening, and you don't have to worry about whether to start the For loop at 0 or 1. The code in the For...Each example is marginally faster than the With...End With example because no time is spent incrementing the integer value used to count through the loop, and Access doesn't have to evaluate which control in the collection to work on.

On the Web

The Chapter24.accdb example database includes frmWithDemo (see Figure 24.12), which contains all the code discussed in this section. Each of the three command buttons along the bottom of this form uses different code to loop through the Controls collections on this form, changing the font characteristics of the controls.

FIGURE 24.12

frmWithDemo is included in Chapter24.accdb.

24

Exploring the Visual Basic Editor

To be a productive Access developer, you need to know your way around the Visual Basic Editor (VBE). This section explores the features of the VBE and how to use them.

The Immediate window

When you write code for a procedure, you might want to try the procedure while you're in the module, or you might need to check the results of an expression. The Immediate window (shown in Figure 24.13) enables you to try your procedures without leaving the module. You can run the module and check variables.

FIGURE 24.13

The Immediate window.

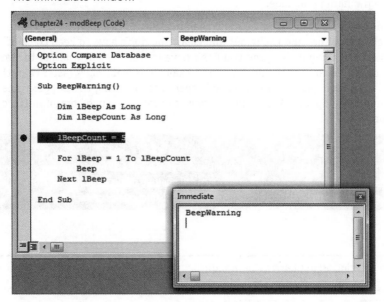

Press Ctrl+G to view the Immediate window, or choose View ⇨ Immediate Window in the VBA code editor.

> **NOTE**
>
> Notice that the VBE window doesn't use the Ribbon. Instead, the code window appears much as it has in every version of Access since Access 2000. Therefore, in this book, you'll see references to the code window's toolbar and menu whenever we describe working with Access VBA modules. Don't confuse references to the code editor's toolbar with the main Access window's Ribbon.

Running the `BeepWarning` procedure is easy. Simply type **BeepWarning** into the Immediate window and press Enter. You might hear five beeps or only a continuous beep because the interval between beeps is short.

 The Immediate window is an excellent debugging tool. Debugging VBA code is discussed in Chapter 27.

The Project Explorer

The Project Explorer is a window within the VBE that displays all the modules in your project, both standard modules and form and report modules. It provides an easy way to move between modules without going back to the main Access application.

To view the Project Explorer, press Ctrl+R or choose View ➪ Project Explorer from the VBE's menu. By default, the Project Explorer is docked to the left side of the VBE window, as shown in Figure 24.14.

FIGURE 24.14

The Project Explorer shows all the modules in your database.

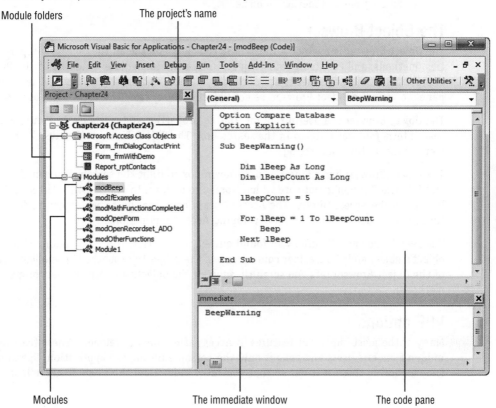

Module folders

The project's name

Modules   The immediate window   The code pane

The Project Explorer shows your project at the top of a collapsible list. The project name is the same as the database name without the ACCDB extension. Beneath the project name is one or more folders. In Figure 24.14, you can see that our project has a folder for Microsoft Access Class Objects and one for Modules. The Class Objects folder holds class modules that are associated with a form or report, while the Modules folder holds standard modules.

There are three icons at the top of the Project Explorer:

- **View Code:** Clicking View Code puts the focus into the code pane—the large area where you write and edit VBA code. It offers little advantage over just moving your mouse and clicking in the code pane.

- **View Object:** Clicking View Object displays the object associated with the module. If you're in a module associated with a form or report, that form or report will be displayed. It's a handy shortcut for moving back to the main Access window. This button has no effect on standard modules.

- **Toggle Folders:** Modules are displayed in folders by default. To remove the folders and display all the modules as one list, click Toggle Folders. Click it again to return to folder view. With proper naming conventions, showing folders in the Project Explorer is unnecessary. If you prefix all your standard modules with *mod*, they'll all be grouped together in either view.

The Object Browser

The Object Browser is a window in the VBE that lets you see all the objects, properties, methods, and events in your project. Unlike the Immediate window and the Project Explorer, the Object Browser is not docked by default and usually covers up the entire code pane. To view the Object Browser, select Object Browser from the View menu or press F2.

The Object Browser is a useful tool for finding properties and methods. In Figure 24.15, the search term *font* was entered in the search box. The Object Browser displays all the elements that contain that string.

The Object Browser has a Libraries drop-down box to limit the search. You can also search "All Libraries" if you're not sure which library to look in. In Figure 24.15, the search was limited to the Access library. The Access library contains the Access object model and is the library you'll use the most when developing Access applications.

The search shown in Figure 24.15 found quite a few entries. The Class column shows the object's name, and the Member column shows the property or method. The bottom section of the Object Browser lets you scroll through all the objects and see all their properties and methods.

VBE options

Many of the most important features in Access affect only developers. These features are hidden from end users and benefit only the person building the application. Spend some time exploring these features so that you fully understand their benefits. You'll soon settle on option settings that suit the way you work and the kind of assistance you want as you write your VBA code.

FIGURE 24.15

Search the Object Browser to find properties and methods.

Search box   Library drop-down

Search results   Object list   Member information   Member list

The Editor tab of the Options dialog box

The Options dialog box contains several important settings that greatly influence how you interact with Access as you add code to your applications. These options are accessed by choosing Tools ⇨ Options from the VBE menu. Figure 24.16 shows the Editor tab of the Options dialog box.

FIGURE 24.16

The Editor tab of the Options dialog box.

Auto Indent

Auto Indent causes code to be indented to the current depth in all successive lines of code. For example, if you indented the current line of code with two tabs, the next line of code that you create when you press Enter will automatically be indented the same amount.

Auto Syntax Check

When the Auto Syntax Check option is selected, Access checks each line of code for syntax errors as you enter it in the code editor and displays a message box when it finds one. Many experienced developers find this behavior intrusive and prefer to keep this option disabled. With Auto Syntax Check disabled, lines with syntax errors are colored red, but no message box is displayed. The benefit of the message box is that it gives you a little more information about the error it found, although often these messages are hard to understand.

Require Variable Declaration

This setting automatically inserts the Option Explicit directive into all new VBA modules in your Access application. This option is *not* selected by default. It's almost universally accepted that Option Explicit should be used and this option should be enabled. Any modules created before this option is set will not be updated to include Option Explicit. The good news is, you can simply type the directive into those modules.

Chapter 25 discusses variable declaration and the Option Explicit declaration in more detail.

TIP

When you get used to having Option Explicit set on every module (including standard and class modules), the instances of rogue and unexplained variables (which, in reality, are almost always misspellings of declared variables) disappear. With Option Explicit set in every module, your code is easier to debug and maintain because the compiler catches every single misspelled variable.

Auto List Members

This option pops up a list box containing the members of an object's hierarchy in the code window. In Figure 24.6, the list of the DoCmd object's members appeared as soon as we typed the period following DoCmd in the VBA statement. You select an item from the list by continuing to type it in or scrolling the list and pressing the spacebar.

Auto Quick Info

When Auto Quick Info has been selected, Access pops up syntax help (refer to Figure 24.7) when you enter the name of a procedure (function, subroutine, or method) followed by a period, space, or opening parenthesis. The procedure can be a built-in function or subroutine or one that you've written yourself in Access VBA.

Auto Data Tips

The Auto Data Tips option displays the value of variables when you hold the mouse cursor over a variable with the module in break mode. Auto Data Tips is an alternative to setting a watch on the variable and flipping to the Debug window when Access reaches the break point.

Debugging Access VBA is described in Chapter 27.

The Project Properties dialog box

All the code components in an Access application—including all the modules, procedures, variables, and other elements—are aggregated as the application's VBA project. The VBA language engine accesses modules and procedures as members of the project. Access manages the code in your application by keeping track of all the code objects that are included in the project, which is different and separate from the code added into the application as runtime libraries and wizards.

Each Access project includes a number of important options. The Project Properties dialog box (shown in Figure 24.17) contains a number of settings that are important for developers. Open the Project Properties dialog box by choosing Tools ➪ *Project Name* Properties (where *Project Name* is the name of your database's project).

24

FIGURE 24.17

The Project Properties dialog box contains a number of interesting options.

Project Name

Certain changes in an application's structure require Access to recompile the code in the application. For example, changing the code in a standard module affects all statements in other modules using that code, so Access must recompile all the code in the application. Until the code is recompiled, Access "decompiles" the application by reverting to the plain-text version of the code stored in the ACCDB file and ignoring the compiled code in the ACCDB. This means that each line of the code must be interpreted at run time, dramatically slowing the application.

Sometimes insignificant modifications, such as changing the name of the project itself, are sufficient to cause decompilation. This happens because of the hierarchical nature of Access VBA. Because all objects are "owned" by some other object, changing the name of a high-level object might change the dependencies and ownerships of all objects below it in the object hierarchy.

Access maintains a separate, independent project name for the code and executable objects in the application. Simply changing the name of the ACCDB file is not enough to decompile the code in an Access application. By default, the project name is the same as the name of the ACCDB, but it's not dependent on it. You can assign a unique name to the project with the Project Name text box in the General tab of the Project Properties dialog box.

Project Description

The Project Description is, as its name implies, a description for the project. Because this area is so small, it isn't possible to add anything of significance that might be helpful to another developer.

Conditional Compilation Arguments

Compiler directives instruct the Access VBA compiler to include or exclude portions of code, depending on the value of a constant established in the module's declarations section. Code lines that begin with # are conditionally compiled.

One of the limitations of using compiler directives is that the constant declaration is local to the module. This means that you have to use the #Const compiler directive to set up the constant in every module that includes the #If directive. This limitation can make it difficult to remove all the #Const compiler directives to modify the code at the conclusion of development.

For example, consider a situation in which you want to use conditional compilation to include certain debugging statements and functions during the development cycle. Just before shipping the application to its users, you want to remove the compiler directives from the code so that your users won't see the message boxes, status bar messages, and other debugging information. If your application consists of dozens of forms and modules, you have to make sure you find every single instance of the #Const directive to make sure you successfully deactivated the debugging code. (This is why it's such a good idea to apply a naming convention to the identifiers you use with the #Const directive.)

Fortunately, Access provides a way for you to set up "global" conditional compilation arguments. The General tab of the Project Properties dialog box contains the Conditional Compilation Arguments text box, where you can enter arguments to be evaluated by the conditional compilation directives in your code.

As an example, assume you've set up the following sort of statements in all the modules in your application:

```
#If CC_DEBUG2 Then
   MsgBox "Now in ProcessRecords()"
#End If
```

Instead of adding the constant directive (#Const CC_DEBUG2 = True) to every module in the application, you might enter the following text into the Conditional Compilation Arguments text box:

```
CC_DEBUG2 = -1
```

This directive sets the value of CC_DEBUG2 to -1 (True) for all modules (global and form and report class modules) in the application. You need to change only this one entry to CC_DEBUG2=0 to disable the debugging statements in all modules in the application.

> **NOTE**
>
> You don't use the words *true* or *false* when setting compiler constants in the Project Properties dialog box, even though you do use these values within a VBA code module. You must use −1 for true and 0 for false in the Project Properties dialog box.

Separate multiple arguments with colons—for example: CC_DEBUG1=0 : CC_DEBUG2=-1.

Project protection

The Protection tab contains a Lock Project for Viewing check box that, when checked, asks for a password when you (or someone else) tries to open the module. You must supply a password (and confirm it) when using this option. Don't forget your password, because there's no official way to get it back.

Mastering VBA Data Types and Procedures

IN THIS CHAPTER

Naming and declaring variables

Looking at the VBA data types

Understanding the scope and lifetime of variables

Using constants

Looking at arrays

Working with subs and functions

Building functions

A ll VBA applications require *variables* to hold data while the program executes. Variables are like a white board where important information can be temporarily written and read later on by the program. For example, when a user inputs a value on a form, you may need to use a variable to temporarily hold the value until it can be permanently stored in the database or printed on a report. Simply put, a variable is the name you've assigned to a particular bit of data in your application. In more technical terms, a variable is a named area in memory used to store values during program execution.

Variables are transient and do not persist after an application stops running. And, as you'll read in the "Understanding variable scope and lifetime" section later in this chapter, a variable may last a very short time as the program executes or may exist as long as the application is running.

In most cases, you assign a specific data type to each of the variables in your applications. For example, you may create a string variable to hold text data such as names or descriptions. A currency variable, on the other hand, is meant to contain values representing monetary amounts. You shouldn't try to assign a text value to a currency variable because a runtime error may occur as a result.

The variables you use have a dramatic effect on your applications. You have many options when it comes to establishing and using variables in your Access programs. Inappropriately using a variable can slow an application's execution or potentially cause data loss.

This chapter contains everything you need to know about creating and using VBA variables. The information in this chapter helps you use the most efficient and effective data types for your variables while avoiding the most common problems related to VBA variables.

Using Variables

One of the most powerful concepts in programming is the variable. A *variable* is a temporary storage location for some value and is given a name. You can use a variable to store the result of a calculation, hold a value entered by the user, or read from a table, or you can create a variable to make a control's value available to another procedure.

To refer to the result of an expression, you use a variable's name to store the result. To assign an expression's result to a variable, you use the = operator. Here are some examples of expressions that assign values to variables:

```
counter = 1

counter = counter + 1

today = Date()
```

Figure 25.1 shows a simple procedure using several different variables. Although this is a very simple example of using variables, it effectively demonstrates the basics of using VBA variables:

FIGURE 25.1

Variable declarations appear at the top of VBA procedures.

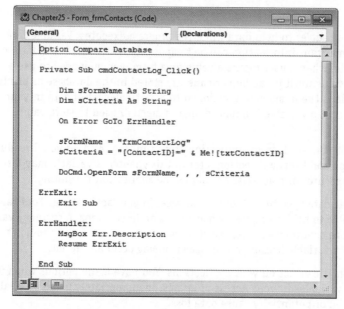

- The `Dim` keyword establishes the new variables—sFormName and sCriteria—within a procedure.
- You provide a meaningful name for the variable as part of the `Dim` statement. In Figure 25.1, the variable names are sFormName and sCriteria, indicating how the variables are used by the procedure.
- The `Dim` statement includes the data type of the new variable. In Figure 25.1, both variables are declared as the `String` data type.
- Different techniques can be used to assign a value to a variable. Figure 25.1 uses the = operator to assign a literal value—frmContactLog—to sFormName. Notice that frmContactLog is surrounded by quotation marks, making it a *literal* value. A value pulled from the txtContactID text box on the form is combined with a literal string—" [ContactID] ="—and assigned to the sCriteria variable. The data assigned to variables should always be appropriate for the variable's data type.
- Variables are manipulated with a variety of operators. Figure 25.1 uses the VBA concatenation operator (&) to combine [ContactID] = and the value in txtContactID.

There are a number of ways to perform each of the tasks you see in Figure 25.1. For example, as you'll read in the "Declaring variables" section later in this chapter, the `Dim` statement is not the only way to establish a variable. And, as you'll see throughout this book, the = operator is not the only way to assign a value to a variable. Also, you don't need to use a variable like sCriteria to temporarily hold the value generated by combining two values. The two values can just as easily be combined on the fly within the DoCmd.OpenForm statement:

```
DoCmd.OpenForm "frmContactLog", _
    "[ContactID] = " & Me![txtContactID]
```

Very few rules govern how you declare and use your variables. You should always strive for readability in your VBA code. In the small example shown in Figure 25.1, you can easily see that sFormName holds the name of a form, especially because it's used as part of the DoCmd.OpenForm statement.

Naming variables

Every programming language has its own rules for naming variables. In VBA, a variable name must meet the following conditions:

- It must begin with an alphabetical character.
- It must have a unique name. The variable's name cannot be used elsewhere in the procedure or in modules that use the variables.
- It must not contain spaces or punctuation characters (except underscore).
- It must not be a reserved word, such as Sub, Module, or Form.
- It must be no longer than 255 characters.

25

Although you can make up almost any name for a variable, most programmers adopt a standard convention for naming variables. Some common practices include the following:

- Using a mix of uppercase and lowercase characters, as in `TotalCost`.
- Using all lowercase characters, as in `counter`.
- Separating the parts of a variable's name with underscores, as in `Total_Cost`.
- Preceding the name with the data type of the value. A variable that stores a number (a Long Integer in this case) might be called `lCounter`, while a variable holding a string might be named `sLastName`.

The "Using a naming convention with variables" section later in this chapter goes into greater detail about the benefits of a naming convention.

> **NOTE**
>
> One source of endless confusion to Access developers is the fact that Access object names (tables, queries, forms, and so on) may contain spaces, while variable names never include spaces. One reason not to use spaces in Access object names is to eliminate confusion when mixing different naming conventions within a single application. You're really better off being consistent in how you apply names to your Access objects, variables, procedures, and other application entities.

> **TIP**
>
> When creating variables, you can use uppercase, lowercase, or both to specify the variable or call it later. VBA variables are not case sensitive. This means that you can use the `TodayIs` variable later without having to worry about the case that you used for the name when you created it; `TODAYIS`, `todayis`, and `tOdAyIs` all refer to the same variable. The VBE automatically changes any explicitly declared variables to the case that was used in the declaration statement (the `Dim` statement).

When you need to use the contents of a variable, you simply reference its name. When you specify the variable's name, the computer program goes into memory, finds the variable, and gets its contents for you. This process means, of course, that you need to be able to remember and correctly reference the name of the variable.

Declaring variables

There are two principle ways to add variables to your applications. The first method—called *implicit declaration*—is to let VBA automatically create the variables for you. As with most things that are not carefully controlled, you'll find that letting VBA prepare your variables for you is not a particularly good idea and can lead to performance issues in, and problems debugging, your programs (see the "Comparing implicit and explicit variables" section later in this chapter).

Implicit declaration means that VBA automatically creates an `Empty` variable for each identifier it recognizes as a variable in an application. In the following, there are two implicitly declared variables—`sFirstName` and `sLastName`. In this example, two variables

(sFirstName and sLastName) are assigned the text contained in two text boxes
(txtFirstName and txtLastName), and a third variable (sFullName) is assigned the
combination of sFirstName and sLastName, with a space between them:

```
Private Sub Combine_Implicit()

    sFirstName = Me.txtFirstName.Text
    sLastName = Me.txtLastName.Text
    sFullName = sFirstName & Space(1) & sLastName

End Sub
```

The second approach is to *explicitly* declare them with one of the following keywords: Dim,
Static, Private, or Public (or Global). The choice of keyword has a profound effect on
the variable's scope within the application and determines where the variable can be used
in the program. (Variable scope is discussed in the "Understanding variable scope and lifetime" section later in this chapter.)

> **TIP**
>
> To force explicit variable declaration, type the directive **Option Explicit** at the top of each module. Better yet,
> check Require Variable Declaration in the VBE Options dialog box, and all new modules will automatically include the
> Option Explicit directive.

The syntax for explicitly declaring a variable is quite simple:

```
Dim VariableName As DataType
Static VariableName As DataType
Private VariableName As DataType
Public VariableName As DataType
```

In each case, the name of the variable and its data type are provided as part of the declaration. VBA reserves the amount of memory required to hold the variable as soon as the declaration statement is executed. Once a variable is declared, you can't change its data type,
although you can easily convert the value of a variable and assign the converted value to
another variable.

The following example shows the Combine_Implicit sub rewritten to use explicitly
declared variables:

```
Private Sub Combine_Explicit()

  Dim sFirstName As String
  Dim sLastName As String
  Dim sFullName As String

  sFirstName = Me.txtFirstName.Text
  sLastName = Me.txtLastName.Text
  sFullName = sFirstName & Space(1) & sLastName

End Sub
```

25

So, if there's often very little difference between using implicit and explicit variables, why bother declaring variables at all? The following code demonstrates the importance of using explicitly declared variables in your applications:

```
Private Sub Form_Load()

    sDepartment = "Manufacturing"
    sSupervisor = "Joe Jones"
    sTitle = "Senior Engineer"

    'Dozens of lines of code go here

    Me.txtDepartment = sDepartment
    Me.txtSupervisor = sSuperviser
    Me.txtTitle = sTitle

End Sub
```

In this example code, the txtSupervisor text box on the form is always empty and is never assigned a value. A line near the bottom of this procedure assigns the value of an implicitly declared variable named Superviser to the txtSupervisor text box. Notice that the name of the variable (Superviser) is a misspelling of the intended variable (Supervisor). Because the source of the assignment appears to be a variable, VBA simply creates a new variant named Superviser and assigns its value (which is, literally, Nothing) to the txtSupervisor text box. And, because the new Superviser variable has never been assigned a value, the text box always ends up empty. Misspellings such as this are very common and easy to overlook in long or complex procedures.

Furthermore, the code shown in this example runs fine and doesn't produce a VBA error. Because this procedure uses implicit variable declaration, Access doesn't raise an error because of the misspelling, and the problem isn't detected until someone notices the text box is always empty. Imagine the problems you'd encounter in a payroll or billing application if variables went missing because of simple spelling errors!

When you declare a variable, Access sets up a location in the computer's memory for storing a value for the variable ahead of time. The amount of storage allocated for the variable depends on the data type you assign to the variable. More space is allocated for a variable that will hold a currency amount (such as $1,000,000) than for a variable that will never hold a value greater than, say, 255. This is because a variable declared with the Currency data type requires more storage than another variable declared as a Byte data type. (Data types are discussed later in this chapter, in the "Working with Data Types" section.)

Even though VBA doesn't require you to declare your variables before using them, it does provide various declaration commands. Getting into the habit of declaring variables is good practice. A variable's declaration assures that you can assign only a certain type of data to it—always a numeric value or only characters, for example. In addition, you attain real performance gains by pre-declaring variables.

The Dim keyword

To declare a variable, you use the `Dim` keyword. (*Dim* is an abbreviation of the archaic *Dimension* programming term—because you're specifying the dimension of the variable.) When you use the `Dim` keyword, you must supply the variable name that you assign to the variable. Here's the format for a `Dim` statement:

```
Dim [VariableName] [As DataType]
```

The following statement declares the variable lBeeps as a Long Integer data type:

```
Dim lBeeps As Long
```

Notice that the variable name follows the `Dim` statement. In addition to naming the variable, use `As Data Type` to specify a data type for the variable. The data type is the kind of information that will be stored in the variable—String, Long, Currency, and so on. The default data type is Variant; it can hold any type of data.

Table 25.1 in the next section lists all the data types available.

When you use the `Dim` statement to declare a variable in a procedure, you can refer to that variable only within that procedure. Other procedures, even if they're stored in the same module, don't know anything about the variable declared within a procedure. Such a variable is often described as *local* because it's declared *locally* within a procedure and is known only by the procedure that owns it. (You can read more about variable scope in the "Understanding variable scope and lifetime" section later in this chapter.)

Variables also can be declared in the declarations section of a module. Then all the procedures in the module can access the variable. Procedures *outside* the module in which you declared the variable, however, can't read or use the variable.

The Public keyword

To make a variable available to all modules in the application, use the Public keyword when you declare the variable. Figure 25.2 illustrates declaring a public variable.

25

FIGURE 25.2

Declaring a public variable.

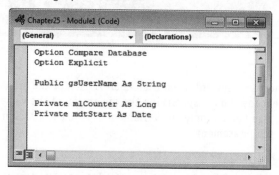

Although you can declare a public variable in any module, the best practice for declaring public variables is to declare them all in a single standard module that's used only to store public variables. Public variables, while necessary in some cases, should be limited. Because any procedure in your project can change a public variable's value, it can be difficult to find which procedure is making an unwanted change. With all the publically declared variables in one place, it's easy to locate them, and it's easy to see if you're using too many and may need to rethink your code structure.

The Private keyword

The declarations section in Figure 25.2 shows the use of the `Private` keyword to declare variables. Technically, there is no difference between `Private` and `Dim` when used in the declarations section of a module, but using `Private` at the module level to declare variables that are available to only that module's procedures is a good idea. The `Private` keyword ensures that all procedures in the module can access the variable, but all procedures in other modules cannot. Declaring private variables contrasts with:

- Dim, which *must* be used at the procedure level
- Public, the other method of declaring variables in modules, making understanding your code easier

TIP

You can quickly go to the declarations section of a module while you're working on code in a form's module by selecting (General) in the Object drop-down list in the code editor. The Procedure drop-down list will change to (Declarations). (Refer to the Module window combo boxes in Figure 25.2.) The Declarations item is not available when a control, or the form, is selected in the Object drop-down list.

When you declare a variable, you use the As clause to specify a data type for the new variable. Because Access is a database development system, it's not surprising that variable data types are similar to field data types in an Access database table.

Working with Data Types

When you declare a variable, you also specify the data type for the variable. Each variable has a data type. The data type of a variable determines what kind of information can be stored in the variable.

A string variable—a variable with a data type of String—can hold any character that you can type on a keyboard, plus a few others. Once created, a string variable can be used in many ways: comparing its contents with another string, pulling characters out of the string, and so on. If you have a variable defined as a String, however, you cannot use it to do mathematical calculations.

Table 25.1 describes the 12 fundamental data types supported by VBA.

TABLE 25.1 VBA Data Types

Data Type	Range	Description
Boolean	True or False	2 bytes
Byte	0 to 255	1-byte binary data
Currency	−922,337,203,685,477,5808 to 922,337,203,685,477,5807	8-byte number with fixed decimal point
Decimal	+/−79,228,162,514,264,337,593,543,950,335 with no decimal point +/−7.9228162514264337593543950335 with 28 places to the right of the decimal; smallest nonzero number is +/−0.0000000000000000000000000001	14 bytes
Date	01 Jan 100 00:00:00 to 31 Dec 9999 23:59:59	8-byte date/time value

Continues

25

TABLE 25.1 *(continued)*

Data Type	Range	Description
Double	−1.79769313486231E308 to −4.94065645841247E−324 for negative values and 4.94065645841246544E−324 through 1.79769313486231570E+308 for positive values	8-byte floating-point number
Integer	−32,768 to 32,767	2-byte integer
Long	−2,147,483,648 to 2,147,483,647	4-byte integer
Object	Any object reference	4 bytes
Single	−3.402823E38 to −1.401298E−45 for negative values and 1.401298E−45 to 3.402823E38 for positive values	4-byte floating-point number
String (fixed length)	1 to approximately 65,400	Length of string
String (variable length)	0 to approximately 2,000,000,000	10 bytes plus length of string
Variant (with characters)	0 to approximately 2,000,000,000	22 bytes plus length of string
Variant (with numbers)	Any numeric value up to the range of the Double data type (see earlier in this table)	16 bytes

Most of the time, you use the String, Date, Long, and Currency or Double data types. The Integer data type is no longer used by VBA. It's still in the language for backward compatibility, but behind the scenes VBA converts all Integer variables to Long variables. You don't save any memory using Integer, and you might experience a very small performance hit, because VBA actually has to do the conversion. On top of that, you limit yourself to a smaller range of numbers with no memory savings. In short, never use the Integer data type.

When you want to assign the value of an Access field to a variable, you need to make sure that the type of the variable can hold the data type of the field. Table 25.2 shows the corresponding VBA data types for Access field types. Some Access data types can't be stored in a VBA variable.

TABLE 25.2   Access and VBA Data Types

Access Field Data Type	VBA Data Type
Attachment	—
AutoNumber (Long Integer)	Long
AutoNumber (Replication ID)	—

Access Field Data Type	VBA Data Type
Currency	Currency
Calculated	—
Date/Time	Date
Long Text	String
Number (Byte)	Byte
Number (Integer)	Integer
Number (Long Integer)	Long
Number (Single)	Single
Number (Double)	Double
Number (Replication ID)	—
OLE object	String
Short Text	String
Hyperlink	String
Yes/No	Boolean

Now that you understand variables and their data types, you're ready to learn how to use them when writing procedures.

Comparing implicit and explicit variables

The default data type for VBA variables is Variant. This means that, unless you specify otherwise, every variable in your application will be a Variant. As you read earlier in this chapter, although useful, the Variant data type is not very efficient. Its data storage requirements are greater than the equivalent simple data type (a String, for instance), and the computer spends more time keeping track of the data type contained in a Variant than for other data types.

Here's an example of how you might test for the speed difference when using implicitly declared Variant variables and explicitly declared variables. This code is found behind frmImplicitTest in Chapter25.accdb:

```
'Use a Windows API call to get the exact time:
Private Declare Function GetTickCount _
    Lib "kernel32" () As Long

Private Sub cmdGo_Click()

  Dim i As Integer
  Dim j As Integer
  Dim snExplicit As Single
```

25

```
Me.txtImplicitStart.Value = GetTickCount()

For o = 1 To 10000
  For p = 1 To 10000
    q = i / 0.33333
  Next p
Next o

Me.txtImplicitEnd.Value = GetTickCount()

Me.txtImplicitElapsed.Value = _
Me.txtImplicitEnd.Value - Me.txtImplicitStart.Value

DoEvents 'Force Access to complete pending operations

Me.txtExplicitStart.Value = GetTickCount()

For i = 1 To 10000
  For j = 1 To 10000
    snExplicit = i / 0.33333
  Next j
Next i

Me.txtExplicitEnd.Value = GetTickCount()

Me.txtExplicitElapsed.Value = _
  Me.txtExplicitEnd.Value - Me.txtExplicitStart.Value
DoEvents

  End Sub
```

In this small test, the loop using implicitly declared variables required approximately 2.5 seconds to run, while the loop with the explicitly declared variables required only 2.3 seconds. This is a performance enhancement of approximately 10 percent just by using explicitly declared variables.

The actual execution time of this—or any—VBA procedure depends largely on the relative speed of the computer and the tasks the computer is executing at the time the procedure is run. Desktop computers vary a great deal in CPU, memory, and other resources, making it quite impossible to predict how long a particular bit of code should take to execute.

> **NOTE**
>
> The example in this section uses the `GetTickCount` Windows API function. An Application Programming Interface, or API, is a way for a program (Windows, in this case) to expose certain features to your program. API function details are outside the scope of this book, but the Windows API is well documented, and many examples are available online.

Forcing explicit declaration

Access provides a simple *compiler directive* that forces you to always declare the variables in your applications. The Option Explicit statement, when inserted at the top of a module, instructs VBA to require explicit declaration of all variables in the module. If, for example, you're working with an application containing a number of implicitly declared variables, inserting Option Explicit at the top of each module results in a check of all variable declarations the next time the application is compiled.

Because explicit declaration is such a good idea, it may not come as a surprise that Access provides a way to automatically ensure that every module in your application uses explicit declaration. The Editor tab of the Options dialog box (shown in Figure 25.3) includes a Require Variable Declaration check box. This option automatically inserts the Option Explicit directive at the top of every module created from this point in time onward.

FIGURE 25.3

Requiring variable declaration is a good idea in most Access applications.

The Require Variable Declaration option doesn't affect modules already created. This option applies only to modules created *after* this option is selected, so you'll have to type the Option Explicit statement yourself in existing modules. Require Variable Declaration is not set by default in current versions of Access. You must set this option yourself to take advantage of having Access add Option Explicit to all your modules.

Using a naming convention with variables

Like most programming languages, applications written in VBA tend to be quite long and complex, often occupying many thousands of lines of code. Even simple VBA programs may require hundreds of different variables. VBA forms often have dozens of different controls on them, including text boxes, command buttons, option groups, and other controls. Keeping track of the variables, procedures, forms, and controls in even a moderately complicated VBA application is a daunting task.

One way to ease the burden of managing the code and objects in an application is through the use of a naming convention. A *naming convention* applies a standardized method of supplying names to the objects and variables in an application.

The most common naming convention used in Access applications uses a one- to four-character prefix (a *tag*) attached to the base name of the objects and variables in a VBA application. The tag is generally based on the type of control for controls and the type of data the variable holds or the scope for variables. For example, a text box containing a person's last name might be named txtLastName, while a command button that closes a form would be named cmdClose or cmdCloseForm.

The names for variables follow a similar pattern. The string variable holding a customer name might be named sCustomer, and a Boolean variable indicating whether the customer is currently active would be bActive.

Using a naming convention is not difficult. Most of the code in this book uses one-character prefixes for variables and three-character prefixes for control names. The actual naming convention you use is not important. The important point is that you use the convention consistently. As you write more VBA code, the right convention for you will become obvious. Table 25.3 shows one naming convention.

TABLE 25.3 A Sample Naming Convention

Control/Data Type	Prefix	Example
Control: Text Box	txt	txtFirstName
Control: Label	lbl	lblFirstName
Control: Command Button	cmd	cmdClose
Control: Frame	frm	frmOptions
Control: Combo Box	cbx	cbxCustomers
Control: List Box	lbx	lbxProducts
Control: Check Box	chk	chkActive
Control: Option Button	opt	optFemale
Type: Byte	bt	btCounter
Type: Boolean	b	bActive
Type: Integer	i	iCounter
Type: Long	l	lCustomerID
Type: Single	sn	snTaxRate

Control/Data Type	Prefix	Example
Type: Double	d	dGrossPay
Type: Currency	c	cNetSales
Type: Date	dt	dtHired
Type: Object	o	oControl
Type: String	s	sLastName
Type: Variant	v	vCompany
Scope: Local	None	sState
Scope: Private	m	msState
Scope: Public	g	gsState

One benefit to using shorter prefixes for variables and longer prefixes for controls is that it becomes easy to tell them apart when you're reading your code. Also note that more commonly used data types get the one-character prefixes. You'll typically use Booleans more often than Bytes, so a shorter prefix for Booleans saves typing.

Some developers don't use any prefixes for variables. There's nothing wrong with that. There are some advantages to using prefixes, however. The first advantage is that you can identify the data type at the point you're using the variable. It's easy to see that a statement like sCustomer = chkActive may cause a problem. You know sCustomer is a String data type, and chkActive, being a check box control, returns a Boolean value. Another advantage is variable name uniqueness. Recall that the variable naming rules state that all variable names must be unique and that you can't use reserved keywords for variable names. That means that you can't have a Boolean variable named Print that determines whether to print a report. By using a prefix, bPrint does not violate any rules.

Including an additional prefix for the scope conveys similar advantages. Knowing the scope of the variable in the portion of code you're working helps debug the code when things go wrong. It also allows you to use similar variables with different scopes. For example, you could have a private module-level variable mbIsEnabled that applies to all the code in your module and still have a local procedure-level variable bIsEnabled for use in only that procedure.

One final advantage to a naming convention that uses a mix of uppercase and lowercase letters is that you can detect spelling errors in your variable names very quickly. VBA will change the case of the variable name to match the case you use when you declare it. If you declare a variable using Dim sFirstName As String and later type **sfirstname = "Larry"** (all lowercase), as soon as you complete that line of code, your variable will change to sFirstName = "Larry". That immediate feedback will help you catch spelling errors before they become problems.

25

Understanding variable scope and lifetime

A variable is more than just a simple data repository. Every variable is a dynamic part of the application and may be used at different times during the program's execution. The declaration of a variable establishes more than just the name and data type of the variable. Depending on the keyword used to declare the variable and the placement of the variable's declaration in the program's code, the variable may be visible to large portions of the application's code. Alternatively, a different placement may severely limit where the variable can be referenced in the procedures within the application.

Examining scope

The visibility of a variable or procedure is called its *scope*. A variable that can be seen and used by any procedure in the application is said to have *public scope*. A variable that is available to any procedure in one module is scoped *private* to that module. A variable that is usable by a single procedure is said to have scope that is *local* to that procedure.

There are many analogies for public and private scope. For example, a company is likely to have a phone number that is quite public (the main switchboard number) and is listed in the phone book and on the company's website; each office or room within the company might have its own extension number that is private within the company. A large office building has a public street address that is known by anyone passing by the building; each office or suite within that building will have a number that is private within that building.

Variables declared within a procedure are local to that procedure and can't be used or referenced outside that procedure. Most of the listings in this chapter have included a number of variables declared within the procedures in the listings. In each case, the `Dim` keyword was used to define the variable. `Dim` is an instruction to VBA to allocate enough memory to contain the variable that follows the `Dim` keyword. Therefore, `Dim lMyInt As Long` allocates less memory (4 bytes) than `Dim dMyDouble As Double` (8 bytes).

The `Public` (or `Global`) keyword makes a variable visible throughout an application. `Public` can be used only at the module level and can't be used within a procedure. Most often, the `Public` keyword is used only in standard (stand-alone) modules that are not part of a form. Figure 25.4 illustrates variables declared with three very different scopes. This code can be found in the `modScope` module in `Chapter25.accdb`.

Every variable declared in the declarations section of a standard module is private to that module unless the `Public` keyword is used. `Private` restricts the visibility of a variable to the module in which the variable is declared. In Figure 25.4, the `gsAppName` variable declared with `Public` scope at the top of the module will be seen everywhere in the application while the `mbIsComplete` variable declared in the next statement is accessible only within the module. The `sMessage` variable is declared inside a procedure, so only that procedure can see it.

Misunderstanding variable scope is a major cause of serious bugs in many Access applications. It's entirely possible to have two same-named variables with different scopes in an Access VBA project. When ambiguity exists, Access always uses the "closest" declared variable.

FIGURE 25.4

Variable scope is determined by the variable's declaration.

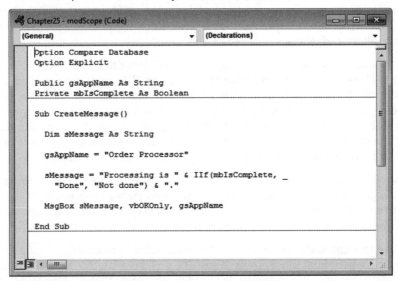

```
Chapter25 - modScope (Code)

(General)                              ▼    (Declarations)                    ▼

Option Compare Database
Option Explicit

Public gsAppName As String
Private mbIsComplete As Boolean

Sub CreateMessage()

  Dim sMessage As String

  gsAppName = "Order Processor"

  sMessage = "Processing is " & IIf(mbIsComplete, _
    "Done", "Not done") & "."

  MsgBox sMessage, vbOKOnly, gsAppName

End Sub
```

Consider two variables named MyVariable. One of these variables is global (Public) in scope, while the other is a module-level variable declared with the Private keyword. In any procedure Access uses one or the other of these variables. In a module where MyVariable is *not* declared, Access uses the public variable. The private variable is used only within the module containing its declaration.

The problem comes when multiple procedures use a variable with the same name as the multiple-declared MyVariable. Unless the developer working on one of these procedures has diligently determined which variable is being used, a serious error may occur. All too easily, a procedure might change the value of a public variable that is used in dozens of places within an application. If even one of those procedures changes the public variable instead of a more local variable, a very difficult-to-resolve bug occurs.

Determining a variable's lifetime

Variables are not necessarily permanent citizens of an application. Just as their visibility is determined by the location of their declaration, their *lifetime* is determined by their declaration as well. A variable's lifetime determines when it's accessible to the application.

By default, local variables exist only while the procedure is executing. As soon as the procedure ends, the variable is removed from memory and is no longer accessible. As already discussed, the scope of procedure-level variables is limited to the procedure and cannot be expanded beyond the procedure's boundaries.

25

A variable declared in the declarations section of a form's module exists as long as the form is open regardless of how it's declared (Public, Private, Dim, and so on). All the procedures within the form's module can use the module-level variables as often as they need, and they all share the value assigned to the variable. When the form is closed and removed from memory, all its variables are removed as well.

The greatest variable lifetime is experienced by the variables declared as Public in standard modules. These variables are available as soon as the VBA application starts up, and they persist until the program is shut down and removed from memory. Therefore, public variables retain their values throughout the application and are accessible to any of the procedures within the program. Private variables (declared with the Private keyword) declared at the top of standard modules endure throughout the application, but following the rules of variable scope, they're accessible only from within the module.

There is one major exception to the general rule that procedure-level variables persist only as long as the procedure is running. The Static keyword makes a procedure-level variable persist between calls to the procedure. Once a value has been assigned to a static variable, the variable retains its value until it's changed in another call to the procedure.

An alternative to using static variables is to declare a global or module-level variable and use it each time a particular procedure is called. The problem with this approach is that a global or module-level variable is accessible to other procedures that are also able to modify its value. You can experience undesirable side-effect bugs by unwittingly changing the value of a widely scoped variable without realizing what has happened. Because of their procedure-limited scope, static variables are one way to avoid side-effect bugs.

Incidentally, declaring a procedure with the Static keyword makes all variables in the procedure static as well. In the following listing, both variables—lStatic and lLocal— in the StaticTest sub are static, in spite of their local declarations within the procedure. The Static keyword used in the procedure's heading makes both variables static in nature:

```
Private Static Sub StaticTest()

    'Both variables are static because of the
    ' 'Static' keyword in the procedure declaration
    Static lStatic As Long
    Dim lLocal As Long

    lStatic = lStatic + 1
    lLocal = lLocal + 1

    Me.txtLocal.Value = lLocal
    Me.txtStatic.Value = lStatic

End Sub
```

Deciding on a variable's scope

Now that you know how declaring a variable affects its scope and lifetime, you may be wondering how you decide what scope to make a particular variable. The answer is easy: always limit the scope of your variables as much as possible. That means that most of your variables will be at the procedure level and declared with the Dim keyword. If you find that you need to retain the value of a variable for the next time you call the procedure, change the Dim to Static. By doing that, you'll increase the lifetime but not the scope. Limiting the scope reduces the number of places that a variable can change, which makes it easier to track down problems when they occur.

If another procedure in the same module needs to use a variable, pass that variable to the other procedure as a parameter. Parameters are discussed later in this chapter. When passed as a parameter, the variable is local to the procedure it's declared in and local to the procedure it's passed to, but no other procedures can see it. If the value of your variable changes unexpectedly, you have only two procedures to debug to find out why.

Sometimes you find yourself passing variables from procedure to procedure within the same module. When more than a few procedures in a module have the same variable passed to them, it may be time to declare that variable as Private to the module.

The next level of variable scope is when a procedure outside the module needs to use a variable. It's tempting to make the variable global with the Public keyword at this point, but in trying to follow the rule to keep the variable's scope as limited as possible, there are a couple of other considerations. First, consider whether that other procedure belongs in the module with the variable. Modules should be designed to contain related procedures, and it's possible this "outsider" procedure should be moved. If that's not the case, consider passing the variable to the other procedure as a parameter. If you were to pass a module-level variable to a procedure outside the module, the variable would be available to any procedure in its own module and only the one other procedure it was passed to. The scope of such a variable is starting to grow but is still as limited as you can make it.

Global variables, declared in standard module with the Public keyword, should be kept to a minimum. However, almost all projects have at least one global variable. The name of your application, your application's version, and a Boolean flag that determines if the current user of the application has special permissions are all good examples of data to store in global variables.

Using constants

Constants differ from variables in one major respect: a constant's value never changes. The value is assigned to the constant when it's declared, and attempts to change that value in code will result in an error.

25

Declaring constants

Constants are declared with the Const keyword. The format of a constant declaration is as follows:

```
[Public | Private] Const constname [As type] = constvalue
```

Using constants improves the readability of your code. Constants can also aid in error-proofing your code if you use the same value in more than one place. Figure 25.5 shows a procedure, found in modConstants, that uses a constant.

FIGURE 25.5

Constants are declared with the Const keyword.

If the procedure in Figure 25.5 did not use a constant for the discount rate, it might contain a line that looks like this:

```
dFinalPrice = dFullPrice * (1 - 0.15)
```

Because of the variable names, you might be able to decipher that 0.15 is a discount rate. By using a constant like dDISCOUNT, its purpose is obvious to anyone reading the code.

The scope and lifetime of a constant are very similar to variables. Constants declared inside a procedure are available only within that procedure. Constants declared with the Private keyword in a module are available to all the procedures in that module and none of the procedures in other modules. Global constants, declared with the Public keyword, are available throughout the project. The values of constants never change, so the Static keyword is not available, and unnecessary, when declaring constants.

Using a naming convention with constants

It's a good practice to use the same naming convention for constants that you use with variables. Prefixing a constant's name with a g for public constants and an m for private constants allows you to know the scope of the constant at the point of use. Also including a prefix identifying the data type of the constant helps keep your constant names unique and prevents errors, such as using a String constant in a mathematical operation.

In Figure 25.5, the constant name is all uppercase except for the prefix. There is no requirement to use uppercase with constants. Constants can be declared with any combination of uppercase and lowercase letters. The rules regarding naming variables and procedures also apply to constants. However, the all-uppercase convention is used by many developers:

```
dFinalPrice = dFullPrice * (1 - dDISCOUNT)
```

In the preceding line, it's easy to see what's a variable and what's a constant by using a proper-case naming scheme for variables and an uppercase naming scheme for constants.

Unlike variables, using global constants poses no risk to the maintainability of your code. Constant values never change, so there's no need to track down which procedures use them. Like variables, it's a good practice to put all globally scoped constants in a single module used only for global variables and constants. If you see a module named modGlobals in a project, it's a good bet the developer is using that convention.

Eliminating hard-coded values

Numbers used in a procedure are sometimes referred to as *magic numbers*. The term doesn't imply that the numbers have any special powers, but that another developer reading your code may not be able to determine where the number came from. To the other developer— or to you reading your own code months or years later—the numbers seem to appear magically, without explanation. Many developers strive to remove any magic numbers from their code except the numbers 0 and 1 and numbers being assigned to variables. This keeps the code well organized and easy to maintain.

In the following code, a rewrite of the procedure in Figure 25.5, the magic numbers have been removed and replaced with constants:

```
Sub DiscountedAmount2()

    Dim dFullPrice As Double
    Dim dFinalPrice As Double

    Const dDISCOUNT As Double = 0.15
    Const dDISCTHRESHOLD As Double = 5000
    Const sPROMPT As String = "The price is "

    dFullPrice = 8000

    If dFullPrice > dDISCTHRESHOLD Then
        dFinalPrice = dFullPrice * (1 - dDISCOUNT)
```

25

```
    Else
      dFinalPrice = dFullPrice
    End If

    MsgBox sPROMPT & dFinalPrice

  End Sub
```

If you want to change the message that's displayed, the discount rate, or the discount threshold, you don't have to look through the code to find where those values are used. All the important values used in the procedure can be found in the declarations section's Const statements. Changing the values in the Const statements changes them anywhere they're used in the procedure. The line If dFullPrice > dDISCTHRESHOLD Then is easily understood as a comparison of the full price to a discount threshold. You can get carried away removing magic numbers from your code. The best practice is to use a constant for any number that's used more than once and to read your code as if you're reading it for the first time and deciding if a descriptive comment name is a better choice over a magic number.

Working with arrays

An array is a special type of variable. One array variable actually holds multiple pieces of data. Instead of reserving one block of memory, like a variable, an array reserves several blocks of memory. The size of an array can be fixed or dynamic. With dynamic arrays, you can increase or decrease the size in a procedure. The code in this section can be found in the modArrays module in Chapter25.accdb.

Fixed arrays

When you declare a fixed array, you specify the size in the Dim statement, and that size cannot be changed later. The simplest way to declare a fixed array is by putting the upper bound index in parentheses after the variable name:

```
    Dim aCustomers(10) as Long
```

In this example, aCustomers is an array that can hold 11 long integers, perhaps from a CustomerID field. Why 11? By default, the lower bound of arrays declared in this way is zero. That means a value can be stored at aCustomers(0), aCustomers(1), all the way up to aCustomers(10).

Another way to declare a fixed array is to specify both the lower and upper bound indices. It's a good practice to include the lower bound in the declaration statement even if you intend to use the default. Use the To keyword to specify the lower and upper bound indices of an array:

```
    Dim aCustomers(1 to 10) as Long
```

Unlike the previous example, this array has only enough room to hold ten long integers. Long integers use 8 bytes of memory, and declaring this array reserves 80 bytes to hold all ten values. The memory is used when the array is declared, so even if you never assign any values to the array, nothing else can access that memory. If you're having performance problems or your application is using a lot of memory, one place you can look is your arrays to make sure they're not larger than you need. However, with modern computers, 80 bytes here and there probably isn't an issue.

Assigning values to an array is just like assigning them to any other variable except that you must specify in which index you want the variable. The following procedure assigns floating-point numbers (Doubles) to an array in a loop:

```
Sub ArrayAssignment()

    Dim aCustomers(1 To 5) As Double

    aCustomers(1) = 0.2
    aCustomers(2) = 24.6
    aCustomers(3) = 7.1
    aCustomers(4) = 99.9
    aCustomers(5) = 14.7

End Sub
```

Just as with assigning values to variables, the array name goes on the left of the equal sign, and the value goes on the right. Unlike variables, however, each assignment includes the index of the array that is being assigned the value.

> **TIP**
>
> VBA includes a directive for setting the default lower bound for arrays where the lower bound is not specified. The `Option Base` directive determines the default lower bound. Including `Option Base 1` at the top of the module forces the lower bound to 1. Arrays declared with both a lower and upper bound ignore the `Option Base` directive. The `Option Base` directive applies only to the module in which it's declared.

Reading values from an array will look familiar. Like reading values from variables, you simply use the variable name. With arrays, you always must include the index you want to read. The following procedure stores five random numbers in an array, multiplies those numbers by 10, and finally prints the numbers to the Immediate window:

```
Sub ArrayRandom()

    Dim aRandom(1 To 5) As Double
    Dim i As Long

    For i = 1 To 5
        aRandom(i) = Rnd
    Next i

    For i = 1 To 5
        aRandom(i) = aRandom(i) * 10
```

25

```
    Next i

    For i = 1 To 5
      Debug.Print aRandom(i)
    Next i

  End Sub
```

Because array indexes increase by one, `For...Next` loops are a common way to access all the elements in an array.

The arrays we've looked at so far are known as *one-dimensional arrays*. One-dimensional arrays are like lists—they have many rows, but only one column. You can also have two-dimensional arrays. Two-dimensional arrays are like tables—they have many rows and columns. Declare a two-dimensional array using a comma to separate the bounds of the first dimension from the bounds of the second dimension:

```
    Dim aContact(1 to 10, 1 to 3) As String
```

The `aContact` array has 30 places to store data. This array might be used to store three pieces of data for ten contacts. Reading and writing to a two-dimensional array requires that you specify the index for both dimensions:

```
    Sub TwoDArray()

      Dim aPotus(1 To 2, 1 To 3)
      Dim i As Long

      aPotus(1, 1) = "George"
      aPotus(1, 2) = "Washington"
      aPotus(1, 3) = "1789-1797"
      aPotus(2, 1) = "John"
      aPotus(2, 2) = "Adams"
      aPotus(2, 3) = "1797-1801"

      For i = 1 To 2
        Debug.Print aPotus(i, 1) & Space(1) & aPotus(i, 2) & Space(1) & _
          "was President in the years" & Space(1) & aPotus(i, 3)
      Next i

    End Sub
```

NOTE

You can specify dimensions beyond two, but those arrays can get very difficult to manage. If you need to store that much data, consider a user-defined type or a custom class module.

Dynamic arrays

Dynamic arrays are declared without any indices and can be resized later in the procedure. Other than the lack of index numbers, they're declared in the same way as fixed arrays:

```
Dim aProductIDs() as Long
```

With a dynamic array declaration, no memory is allocated until the array is initialized by providing dimensions. You can't assign values to this array until it's initialized. To initialize a dynamic array, use the ReDim keyword:

```
ReDim aProductIDs(1 to 100)
```

Note that the data type is not included in the ReDim statement. The data type is set when the array is declared and cannot be changed. Use a dynamic array when you don't know the size of array you'll need until run time. In this example, all the open forms' names in a database are put into an array. Since you can't know which forms will be open, declare a dynamic array and resize it when the procedure executes:

```
Sub FormArray()

   Dim aForms() As String
   Dim frm As Form
   Dim lFrmCnt As Long
   Dim i As Long

   If Application.Forms.Count > 0 Then
     ReDim aForms(1 To Application.Forms.Count)

     For Each frm In Application.Forms
       lFrmCnt = lFrmCnt + 1
       aForms(lFrmCnt) = frm.Name
     Next frm

     For i = LBound(aForms) To UBound(aForms)
       Debug.Print aForms(i) & " is open."
     Next i
   End If

End Sub
```

The Forms.Count property is used to size the dynamic array. Then a For...Each loop puts each open form's name into a different index in the array. Finally, the procedure loops through the array and prints each form's name to the Immediate window.

If you know the size of the array at design time, it's best to create a fixed array. If you must use a dynamic array, you'll get the best performance by determining the array size you need and issuing a ReDim statement to resize the array. There are times, however,

25

where you don't know how many elements you'll need until you start filling the array. VBA provides the `Preserve` keyword to resize a dynamic array without losing any of the data that's already in the array. Using `ReDim` without `Preserve` resizes the array, as you've seen, but the array is re-initialized and any existing data is lost:

```
ReDim Preserve aCustomerIDs(1 to x) As Long
```

The `Preserve` keyword makes a new array of the new size and then copies all the data from the old array to the new one. Even for moderately sized arrays, this can be a performance killer. Use `Preserve` only when there is no other option.

Array functions

VBA provides several useful functions to use with arrays. We don't have room to cover all of them, but we'll cover the most used and most interesting.

Boundary functions

VBA provides two functions, `LBound` and `UBound`, to determine the size of an array. `LBound` returns the lower bound, and `UBound` returns the upper bound. These functions are most useful when used to loop through all the elements of an array:

```
For i = LBound(aContacts) To UBound(aContacts)
   Debug.Print aContacts(i)
Next i
```

If `aContacts` is declared as `Dim aContacts(1 to 5) As String`, the `LBound` will return 1 and `UBound` will return 5. The real benefit comes when you revise the code to `Dim aContacts(1 to 6) As String`. If you had hard-coded the boundaries in the `For...Next` loop, you would've needed to change the upper bound in two places. By using `LBound` and `UBound`, you only have to make the change in the `Dim` statement.

For two-dimensional arrays, `LBound` and `UBound` require a second argument for the dimension. The following example is a typical method for looping through all the elements of a two-dimensional array:

```
For i = LBound(aBounds, 1) To UBound(aBounds, 1)
   For j = LBound(aBounds, 2) To UBound(aBounds, 2)
      Debug.Print aBounds(i, j)
   Next j
Next i
```

The Array function

The `Array` function allows you to create an array by supplying all the values for the array in one statement. The array returned by the `Array` function is known as a *variant array*—a Variant data type holding an array. To return the results of the `Array` function to a variable, that variable must be declared as a Variant. The syntax for the `Array` function is:

```
Array(ParamArray ArgList() as Variant)
```

The `ParamArray` keyword indicates that there can be one or more arguments, but the number is not known ahead of time. The arguments of the `Array` function are separated by commas, with each argument becoming an element of the array:

```
Sub ArrayFunction()

    Dim vaRates As Variant
    Dim i As Long

    vaRates = Array(0.05, 0.055, 0.06, 0.065, 0.07)

    For i = LBound(vaRates) To UBound(vaRates)
      Debug.Print vaRates(i)
    Next i

End Sub
```

In the preceding example, the `vaRates` variable is a Variant containing an array with five elements (the five numbers from the `Array` function). Since the variable is a Variant, you don't specify the size of the array beforehand. The number of arguments in the `Array` function determines the size. Because of this, the lower and upper bounds are determined by VBA. The default lower bound is zero, and the default upper bound is one less than the number of arguments in the `Array` function. For `vaRates` in the preceding example, the bounds would be 0 to 4. The lower bound of an array returned by the `Array` function is determined by the `Option Base` directive, if one exists, at the top of the module.

> **NOTE**
>
> The `Array` function returns a variant array—a Variant containing an array. You can also declare an array of Variants. An array of Variants is a fixed or dynamic array whose data type is Variant. A variant array and an array of Variants are two different types of arrays.

The Split function

The `Split` function converts text into a Variant array. VBA can't know the size of the array the `Split` function will return, so the variable holding the array must be declared as a Variant. The `Split` syntax is as follows:

```
Split(string_expression, [delimiter], [limit], [compare])
```

The first argument is the string you want to split into an array. The `delimiter` argument tells the `Split` function on which characters to split the string. The `limit` argument determines how large the resulting array is. Once the array reaches the limit defined, `Split` stops splitting the string even if more delimiters are present:

```
Sub TheSplitFunction()

    Dim vaWords As Variant
    Dim i As Long
```

25

```
vaWords = Split("Now is the time.", Space(1))

For i = LBound(vaWords) To UBound(vaWords)
  Debug.Print vaWords(i)
Next i

End Sub
```

The vaWords variable will be a variant array containing four elements: Now, is, the, and time. The delimiter—in this case, a single space—is not included in the elements. The period at the end *is* included, making the last element time. (with a period) rather than time (without a period).

The Join function

The Join function is the opposite of Split. Join takes an array and returns a string. The syntax for Join is:

```
Join(source_array, [delimiter])
```

The first argument is the one-dimensional array to be converted into a String. The source_array can be any data type that VBA can convert into a String, even numbers and dates. The delimiter is the character or characters to be inserted between the elements of the array:

```
Sub TheJoinFunction()

  Dim sResult As String
  Dim aWords(1 To 5) As String

  aWords(1) = "The"
  aWords(2) = "quick"
  aWords(3) = "brown"
  aWords(4) = "fox"
  aWords(5) = "jumped"

  sResult = Join(aWords, Space(1))

  Debug.Print sResult

End Sub
```

The sResult variable will contain the String The quick brown fox jumped. Each element of the array is concatenated together with the delimiter inserted between them, in this case a single space.

Understanding Subs and Functions

The code in a VBA application lives in containers called *modules*. As you learned in Chapter 24, modules exist behind the forms and reports in an Access application, as well as in stand-alone modules. The modules themselves contain many procedures, variable and constant declarations, and other directives to the VBA engine.

The code within the modules is composed of procedures. There are two main types of procedures in VBA: *subroutines* or *subprocedures* (often called *subs*) and *functions*.

The general rules for procedures include the following:

- **You must give the procedure a unique name within its scope (see "Understanding variable scope and lifetime," earlier in this chapter).** Although it isn't a good idea—because of the chance of confusing the VBA engine or another person working with your code—it is possible to have more than one procedure with the same name, as long as the name is unique within each procedure's scope.
- **The name you assign to a procedure can't be the same as a VBA keyword.**
- **A procedure and a module cannot have the same name.** This is one place where a naming convention can be very useful. If you always prefix module names with bas or mod, you don't run the risk of an error occurring from having a procedure and module with the same name.
- **A procedure can't contain other procedures within it.** A procedure can, however, call another procedure and execute the code in the other procedure at any time.

Because of the rules governing procedure scope, you can't have two public procedures both named MyProcedure, although you can have two private procedures, both named MyProcedure, or one public procedure named MyProcedure and one private procedure named MyProcedure, but not in the same module. The reason it's a bad idea to use the same procedure name for multiple procedures, even when the procedures have different scopes, should be obvious.

The following sections cover some of the specifics regarding VBA procedures. Planning and composing the procedures in your modules is the most time-consuming part of working with VBA, so it's important to understand how procedures fit into the overall scheme of application development.

Subroutines and functions both contain lines of code that you can run. When you run a subroutine or function, you *call* it. *Calling*, *running*, and *invoking* are all terms meaning *to execute* (or run) the statements (or lines of code) within the procedure or function. All

25

these terms can be used interchangeably (and they will be, by different developers). No matter how you invoke a VBA procedure—using the Call keyword, referencing the procedure by its name, or running it from the Immediate window—they all do the same thing, which is to cause lines of code to be processed, run, executed, or whatever you want to call it.

The only real difference between a procedure and a function is that, when it's called, a function returns a value—in other words, it generates a value when it runs and makes the value available to the code that called it. You can use a Boolean function to return a True or False value indicating, for example, where the operation the procedure performed was successful. You can see if a file exists, if a value was greater than another value, or anything you choose. Functions return dates, numbers, or strings; functions can even return complex data types such as recordsets.

A subroutine does not return a value. However, although a function directly returns a value to a variable created as part of the function call, there are other ways for functions and subroutines to exchange data with form controls or declared variables in memory.

Understanding where to create a procedure

You create procedures in one of two places:

- **In a standard VBA module:** You create a subroutine or function in a standard module when the procedure will be shared by code in more than one form or report or by an object other than a form or report. For example, queries can use functions to handle very complex criteria.
- **Behind a form or report:** If the code you're creating will be called only by a single procedure or form, the subroutine or function should be created in the form or report's module.

> **NOTE**
> A *module* is a container for multiple subroutines and functions.

Calling VBA procedures

VBA procedures are called in a variety of ways and from a variety of places. They can be called from events behind forms and reports, or they can be placed in modules and called simply by using their name or by using the Call statement. Here are some examples:

```
SomeSubRoutineName

Call SomeSubRoutineName

Somevalue = SomeFunctionName
```

Only functions return values that may be assigned to variables. Subroutines are simply called, do their work, and end. Although functions return a single value, both subroutines and functions can place values in tables, in form controls, or even in public variables available to any part of your program. You can see several examples of different ways to use subroutines and functions throughout this chapter.

The syntax used for calling subroutines with parameters changes depending on how you call the procedure. For example, when using the `Call` keyword to call a subroutine that includes arguments, the arguments must be enclosed in parentheses:

```
Call SomeSubRoutineName(arg1, arg2)
```

However, when the same procedure is called without the `Call` keyword, it requires no parentheses:

```
SomeSubRoutineName arg1, arg2
```

Also, using the `Call` keyword with a function tells Access your code is not capturing the function's return value:

```
Call SomeFunctionName
```

Or, when arguments are required:

```
Call SomeFunctionName(arg1, arg2)
```

In this case, the function is treated as if it is a subroutine.

> **TIP**
>
> The `Call` keyword has been in the BASIC programming language since the beginning. There's no advantage to using `Call`, and most developers have stopped using it altogether.

Creating subs

Conceptually, subroutines are easy to understand. A *subroutine* (usually called a *sub* and sometimes called a *subprocedure*) is a set of programming statements that is executed as a unit by the VBA engine. VBA procedures can become complex, so this elementary description of subroutines is quickly overwhelmed by the actual subroutines you'll compose in your Access applications.

Figure 25.6 shows a typical subroutine. Notice the `Sub` keyword that begins the routine, followed by the name of the subroutine. The declaration of this particular subroutine includes the `Private` keyword, which restricts the availability of this subroutine to the module containing the subroutine.

25

FIGURE 25.6

A typical subroutine in an Access application.

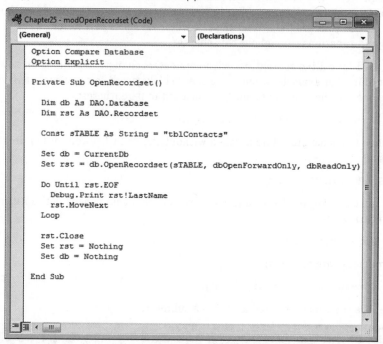

```vba
Chapter25 - modOpenRecordset (Code)

(General)                              (Declarations)

Option Compare Database
Option Explicit

Private Sub OpenRecordset()

    Dim db As DAO.Database
    Dim rst As DAO.Recordset

    Const sTABLE As String = "tblContacts"

    Set db = CurrentDb
    Set rst = db.OpenRecordset(sTABLE, dbOpenForwardOnly, dbReadOnly)

    Do Until rst.EOF
        Debug.Print rst!LastName
        rst.MoveNext
    Loop

    rst.Close
    Set rst = Nothing
    Set db = Nothing

End Sub
```

The subroutine you see in Figure 25.6 contains most of the components you'll see in almost every VBA sub or function:

- **Declaration:** All procedures must be *declared* so that VBA knows where to find them. The name assigned to the procedure must be unique within the VBA project. The Sub keyword identifies this procedure as a subroutine.

- **Terminator:** All procedures must be terminated with the End keyword followed by the type of procedure that is ending. In Figure 25.6, the terminator is End Sub. Functions are terminated with End Function.

- **Declarations area:** Although variables and constants can be declared anywhere in the body of the procedure (as long as it's before they're used), good programming conventions require variables and constants to be declared near the top of the procedure where they'll be easy to find.

- **Statements:** A VBA procedure can contain many statements. Usually, however, you'll want to keep your VBA procedures small to make debugging as painless as possible. Very large subroutines can be difficult to work with, and you'll avoid problems if you keep them small. Instead of adding too many features and operations in a single procedure, place operations in separate procedures, and call those procedures when those operations are needed.

At the conclusion of a subroutine, program flow returns to the code or action that originally called the sub. The subroutine shown in Figure 25.6 may be called from a form's Load event, so control is returned to that event.

As an example of a useful VBA subroutine, the next several paragraphs describe building an event procedure for a control on an Access form. This procedure retrieves a value from one of the cboCustomerID combo box columns and uses it to find a record. The RowSource of the cboCustomerID combo box is a SQL statement that returns the CustomerID and the Company fields. Here's the SQL statement:

```
SELECT DISTINCT tblCustomers.CustomerID, tblCustomers.Company
FROM tblCustomers
INNER JOIN tblSales
ON tblCustomers.CustomerID = tblSales.CustomerID
ORDER BY tblCustomers.Company;
```

The tblCustomers table is inner-joined with the tblSales table so that only those customers with an invoice are displayed in the combo box. The DISTINCT keyword is used so that each customer is only returned once.

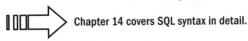 Chapter 14 covers SQL syntax in detail.

The objective of this exercise is to learn about procedures, but it also serves to teach you some additional VBA commands. The code is added to the form as the cboCustomerID_AfterUpdate event.

To create an event procedure in a form, follow these steps:

1. **Select the cboCustomerID control in frmSales Design view.**
2. **Press F4 to display the Property Sheet for the control.**
3. **Click in the After Update event property in the Event tab of the Property Sheet and select [Event Procedure] from the event's drop-down list.**
4. **Click the builder button (...) to open the VBA code editor.**
5. **Enter the following code into the cboCustomerID_AfterUpdate event procedure, as shown in Figure 25.7.** The following code goes between Private Sub cboCustomerID_AfterUpdate() and End Sub in the VBA code editor:

```
Me.txtCustomerID.SetFocus

If Not IsNull(Me.cboCustomerID.Value) Then
    DoCmd.FindRecord Me.cboCustomerID.Value
End If

Me.txtInvoiceDate.SetFocus
```

6. **Select Compile Chapter25 from the Debug menu in the code editor to check your syntax.**
7. **Close the VBA window and return to the frmSales form.**

25

The code first moves the focus to the txtCustomerID text box to make that field the current field. The Me. refers to the current form and substitutes in this example for Forms!frmSales!.

The first If statement checks to make sure a Customer ID was selected by making sure the current value of the combo box's bound column—CustomerID—is not null.

The heart of the procedure is the FindRecord method of the DoCmd object. FindRecord searches through the recordset and returns a record that matches the arguments. There are several arguments to FindRecord, but we supply only the first, FindWhat. The FindWhat argument is what FindRecord searches for through the records. In this case, it's searching for Me.cboCustomerID.Value. The other arguments to FindRecord are optional, and we have accepted the defaults. By setting the focus to Me.txtCustomerID, we made that field the current field. By default, FindRecord only searches in the current field, and setting the current field before calling FindRecord achieves our aims.

The final line of code sets the focus to the txtInvoiceDate text box. When the user locates a record, it's a good practice to set the focus to a good starting point for navigating through the record. While not required, it provides a good user experience.

Figure 25.7 shows the procedure created in the code editor after entering the procedure described earlier. After you finish entering these statements, click the Save button on the toolbar to save your code before closing the VBA window.

FIGURE 25.7

The frmSales cboCustomerID_AfterUpdate event procedure in the VBA code window.

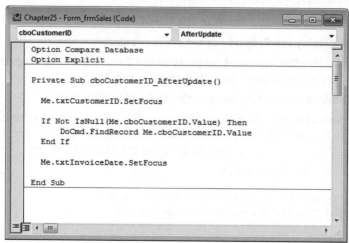

The procedure behind this form runs each time the user selects a different customer in cboCustomerID. This code shows the first invoice for that customer.

Creating Functions

Functions differ from subroutines in that functions return a value. In the examples in this section, you'll see functions that calculate the extended price (quantity × price) for a line item, create a function to calculate the total of all the taxable line items, and then apply the current tax rate to the total.

Although functions can be created behind individual forms or reports, usually they're created in standard modules. This first function will be created in a new module that you'll name modSalesFunctions. Putting this function in a standard module makes it available to all parts of the applications. To do this, follow these steps:

1. **Select the Modules tab in the Navigation pane.**

2. **Right-click the modSalesFunctions module and select Design View from the shortcut menu.** The VBA window is displayed with the title modSalesFunctions (Code) in the title bar.

3. **Move to the bottom of the module, and enter the following code:**

```
Public Function CalcExtendedPrice( _
    lQuantity As Long, _
    cPrice As Currency, _
    dDiscount As Double _
    ) As Currency

    Dim cExtendedPrice As Currency

    cExtendedPrice = lQuantity * cPrice

    CalcExtendedPrice = cExtendedPrice * (1 - dDiscount)

End Function
```

The first statement declares the variable cExtendedPrice as the Currency data type. cExtendedPrice is used in an intermediate step in the function. The next line of code performs a calculation assigning the product of two variables, lQuantity and cPrice, to the cExtendedPrice variable. You might notice that the lQuantity and cPrice variables are not declared within the function; these variables are explained in the next section, "Handling parameters."

Finally, the last line of code performs one more calculation to apply any discount to cExtendedPrice. The function's name is treated as if it were a variable and is assigned the value of the calculation. This is how a function gets the value that it returns to the calling program.

Now that you've entered the function, you can use it in various ways, as described in the following sections.

25

Handling parameters

Now, the question you should be asking is: Where did the lQuantity, cPrice, and dDiscount variables come from? The answer is simple. They're the parameters passed from another procedure, as you may have already guessed.

Parameters (often called *arguments*) passed to a procedure are treated like any other variable by the procedure. Parameters have a name and a data type and are used as a way to send information to a procedure. Parameters are often used to get information back from a procedure, as well.

The following table shows the names and data types of the arguments used in the CalcExtendedPrice function:

Parameter Name	Data Type
lQuantity	Long
cPrice	Currency
dDiscount	Double

These parameter names can be anything you want them to be. Think of them as variables you would normally declare. All that's missing is the Dim statement. They don't have to be the same name as the variables used in the call to the function. Very often, you'll pass the names of fields in a table or controls on a form or variables created in the calling procedure as parameters to a procedure.

The completed CalcExtendedPrice function is shown in Figure 25.8. Notice how this function's parameters are defined in the function's declaration statement. The parameters are separated by continuation characters (a space followed by an underscore) to make the code easier to read.

Calling a function and passing parameters

Now that you've completed the function, it's time to test it.

Normally, a function call comes from a form or report event or from another procedure, and the call passes information as parameters. The parameters passed to a procedure are often variables or data taken from a form's controls. You can test this function by going to the Immediate window and using hand-entered values as the parameters.

Follow these steps to test the function:

1. **Press Ctrl+G to display the Immediate window.**

2. **Enter** ? CalcExtendedPrice(5, 3.50, .05)**.** This statement passes the values as 5, 3.50, and .05 (5 percent) to the lQuantity, dPrice, and dDiscount parameters, respectively. CalcExtendedPrice returns 16.625 using those values, as shown in Figure 25.9.

FIGURE 25.8

The completed CalcExtendedPrice function.

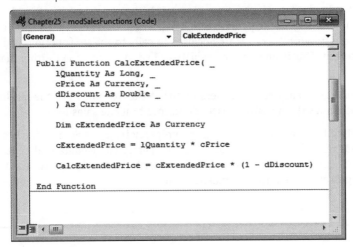

FIGURE 25.9

Testing the CalcExtendedPrice function in the Immediate window.

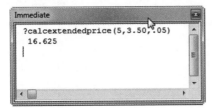

3. **Close the Immediate window and the VBA window to return to the Database window.**

The next task is to use the function to calculate the extended price (price multiplied by quantity) of each item included in a sales invoice. You can add a call to the function from the Amount box on fsubSalesLineItems. This is a subform embedded on frmSales. Follow these steps:

1. **Display the frmSales form in Design view.**

2. **Click into the fsubSalesLineitems subform.**

3. **Click into the txtAmount control in the subform.**

4. **Display the Property Sheet and enter the following into the Control Source property on the Data tab, as shown in Figure 25.10:** =CalcExtendedPrice (Nz(txtQuantity,0),Nz(txtPrice,0),Nz(txtDiscountPercent,0)).

This expression passes the values from three controls—txtQuantity, txtPrice, and txtDiscountPercent—in the subform to the CalcExtendedPrice function in the module and returns the value back to the control source of the txtAmount control each time the line is recalculated or any of the parameters change. The references to txtQuantity, txtPrice, and txtDiscountPercent are enclosed in calls to the Nz function, which converts null values to zero. This is one way to avoid Invalid use of null errors that would otherwise occur.

The sales form (frmSales) enforces a business rule that the extended price is recalculated any time the user changes the quantity, price, or discount on the sales form.

In Figure 25.10, notice that the Control Source property for txtAmount simply calls the CalcExtendedPrice function. The call does not specify the module that contains the function. Because CalcExtendedPrice was declared with the Public keyword, Access easily finds it and passes the required arguments to it.

FIGURE 25.10

Adding a function call to the Control Source of a control.

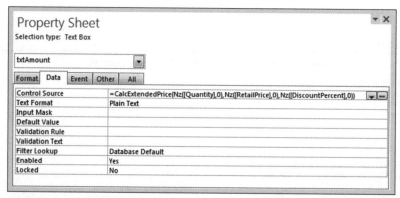

> **TIP**
>
> The CalcExtendedPrice example illustrates an important aspect of Access development: add a public function in a single location anywhere in the application's code and use the function anywhere it's needed. The ability to reuse a procedure in multiple places reduces maintenance. Changing the single instance of the function is reflected everywhere the public procedure is used.

Creating a function to calculate sales tax

In the Collectible Mini Cars application, whenever you add a line item to a sales invoice, you specify whether the item is taxable. The sales form adds up the extended prices for all the taxable line items to determine the sales tax for the sale. This total can then be multiplied by the tax rate to determine the tax.

The Collectible Mini Cars sales form (frmSales) includes a Text Box control for the tax amount. You can simply create an expression for the control's value such as:

```
=fSubSalesLineitems.Form!txtTaxableTotal * txtTaxRate
```

This expression references txtTaxableTotal in the subform (fSubSalesLineitems) and multiplies it by the tax rate (txtTaxRate) from the main form (frmSales).

However, although this expression displays the tax amount, the expression entered into the txtTaxAmount control would make the txtTaxAmount control read-only because it contains an expression. You wouldn't be able to override the calculated amount if you wanted to. The tax applied to a sale is one of the fields that needs to be changed once in a while for specific business purposes.

Better than using a hard-coded expression is creating a function to calculate a value and then place the value of the calculation in the control. This way, you can simply type over the calculated value if needed.

You can enter the following lines of code to the AfterUpdate events behind the txtQuantity, txtPrice, txtDiscountPercent, and chkTaxable controls. This way, each time one of those controls' values is changed, the tax is recalculated after the contact's tax rate is retrieved on the frmSales form:

```
txtTaxAmount = _
    fSubSalesLineitems.Form!txtTaxableTotal * txtTaxRate
```

Actually, better would be to place this statement in the AfterUpdate event of fsubSalesLineitems. This way, the tax is recalculated each time a value is updated in any record of this form. Because fsubSalesLineitems is displayed as a datasheet, the AfterUpdate event fires as soon as the user moves to another line in fsubSalesLineitems.

Although you can use a simple expression that references controls on forms and subforms, this technique works only behind the form containing the code. Suppose you also need to calculate tax in other forms or in reports. There's a better way than relying on a form.

This is an old developer's expression: "Forms and reports lie; tables never lie." This means that the controls of a form or report often contain expressions, formats, and VBA code that may make a value seem to be one thing when the table actually contains a completely different value. The table containing the data is where the real values are stored, and it's where calculations and reports should retrieve data from.

You can easily use VBA code to extract data from a table, use the data in a complex calculation, and return the result to a control on a form, on a report, or to another section of code.

Figure 25.11 shows the completed CalcTax function.

25

The function is called from the AfterUpdate event behind the frmSalesLineitems subform. The CalcTax function calculates the sum of the taxable line items from the tblSalesItems table. The SQLstatement is combined with a bit of ADO code to determine the total. The calculated total amount is then multiplied by the dTaxPercent parameter to calculate the tax. The tax is set to the cReturn variable, which is set to CalcTax (the name of the expression) at the end of the function.

An important feature of this example code is that it combines data extracted from a database table (Quantity, RetailPrice, DiscountPercent) with data passed as parameters (dTaxPercent, lInvoiceNum). All the extraction and calculations are automatically performed by the code, and the user is never aware of how the tax amount is determined.

FIGURE 25.11

The CalcTax function.

> **TIP**
>
> Functions and subroutines are important to the concept of reusable code within an application. You should try to use functions and subroutines and pass them parameters whenever possible. A good rule is this: the first time you find yourself copying a group of code, it's time to create a procedure or function.

Simplifying Code with Named Arguments

Another feature of Access VBA is the use of named arguments for procedures. Without named arguments, the arguments passed to procedures must appear in the correct left-to-right order. With named arguments, you provide the name of each parameter passed to a subroutine or function, and the subroutine or function uses the argument based on its *name* rather than on its *position* in the argument list. If you use named arguments, you can omit optional arguments from the list entirely.

Assume your application includes the function shown here:

```
Function PrepareOutput(sStr1 As String, sStr2 As String, _
    sStr3 As String) As String

    PrepareOutput = sStr1 & Space(1) & sStr2 & Space(2) & sStr3

End Function
```

This function, of course, does nothing more than concatenate sStr1, sStr2, and sStr3 and return it to the calling routine. The next example shows how this function may be called from another procedure:

```
Private Sub cmdForward_Click()

  Me.txtOutput.Value = PrepareOutput( _
      Me.txtFirstName.Value, _
      Me.txtLastName.Value, _
      Me.txtHireDate.Value)

    End Sub
```

The arguments required by PrepareOutput() must be passed in the same order they're listed in the procedure declaration. The results of this function are shown in Figure 25.12. The text in the Function Output text box on this form shows the arguments in the order in which they appear in the text boxes on the left side of this form.

FIGURE 25.12

frmNamedArguments demonstrates using named arguments in VBA procedures.

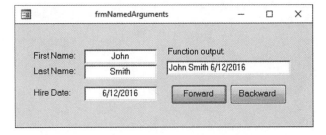

Each argument can be specified by its name as you pass it to functions. Naming arguments makes them position independent.

Examine the code in the following listing to see how named arguments work:

```
Private Sub cmdBackward_Click()

  Me.txtOutput.Value = PrepareOutput( _
      sStr2:=Me.txtLastName.Value, _
```

```
            sStr3:=Me.txtFirstName.Value, _
            sStr1:=Me.txtHireDate.Value)

        End Sub
```

The thing to notice in cmdBackward_Click is that the arguments are not passed to
PrepareOutput() in the order specified by the procedure's argument list. As long as the
name used for an argument matches an argument in the PrepareOutput argument list,
Access VBA correctly uses the arguments in PrepareOutput().

> **NOTE**
>
> The Chapter25.accdb example database includes the frmNamedArguments you see in Figure 25.12 and
> Figure 25.13. The two buttons below the Function Output text box pass the text from the First Name, Last Name, and
> Hire Date text boxes to the PrepareOutput() function using positional and named arguments.

FIGURE 25.13

PrepareOutput() is able to use arguments submitted in any order as long as they're
named.

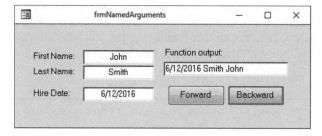

Understanding the Access Event Model

IN THIS CHAPTER

Mastering Access event programming

Reviewing common events

Understanding event sequences

When working with a database system, you may perform the same tasks repeatedly. Instead of doing the same steps each time, you can automate the process with VBA macros.

Database management systems continually grow as you add records to a form, build new queries, and create new reports. As the system grows, many of the database objects are saved for later use—for a weekly report or monthly update query, for example. You tend to create and perform many tasks repetitively. Every time you add contact records, you open the same form. Likewise, you print the same form letter for contacts that have purchased a vehicle in the past month.

You can add VBA code throughout your application to automate these tasks. The VBA language offers a full array of powerful commands for manipulating records in a table, controls on a form, or just about anything else. This chapter continues the previous chapters' discussions of working with procedures in forms, reports, and standard modules.

This chapter focuses on the Access event model, a vitally important aspect of Access development. As you'll see in this chapter, Access provides a wide variety of events to trigger your code in response to user actions.

Programming Events

An Access event is the result or consequence of some user action. An Access event occurs when a user moves from one record to another in a form, closes a report, or clicks a command button on a form. Even moving the mouse generates a continuous stream of events.

Access applications are event driven, and Access objects respond to many types of events. Access events are hooked into specific object properties. For example, checking or unchecking a check box triggers a MouseDown, a MouseUp, and a Click event. These events are hooked into the check box through the OnMouseDown, OnMouseUp, and OnClick properties, respectively. You use VBA to compose event procedures that run whenever the user clicks the check box.

Access events can be categorized into seven groups:

- **Windows (form, report) events:** Opening, closing, and resizing
- **Keyboard events:** Pressing or releasing a key
- **Mouse events:** Clicking or pressing a mouse button
- **Focus events:** Activating, entering, and exiting
- **Data events:** Changing the current row, deleting, inserting, or updating
- **Print events:** Formatting and printing
- **Error and timing events:** Happening after an error has occurred or some time has passed

In all, Access supports more than 50 different events that can be harnessed through VBA event procedures.

Of these types of events, by far the most common are the keyboard and mouse events on forms. As you'll see in the following sections, forms and most controls recognize keyboard and mouse events. In fact, exactly the same keyboard and mouse events are recognized by forms and controls. The code you write for a mouse-click event on a command button is exactly the same sort of code that you might write for the mouse-click on a form.

In addition, most Access object types have their own unique events. The following sections discuss the most commonly programmed events. Many ActiveX controls you might use in your Access applications may have their own unique and special events. When using an unfamiliar control or a new type of object in your Access applications, be sure to check out what events and properties are supported by the control or object.

Understanding how events trigger VBA code

You can create an event procedure that runs when a user performs any one of the many different events that Access recognizes. Access responds to events through special form and control properties. Reports have a similar set of events, tailored to the special needs and requirements of reports.

Figure 26.1 shows the Property Sheet for frmProducts. This form has many event properties. Each form section (page header, form header, detail, page footer, form footer) and every control on the form (labels, text boxes, check boxes, and option buttons, for example) has its own set of events.

FIGURE 26.1

The Property Sheet for frmProducts with the Event tab open.

In Figure 26.1, notice that the Property Sheet is open on the Event tab. Access forms include 52 events, and each form section includes a number of events, as well as each control on the form. As you select a form section or a control on the form, the Event tab in the Property Sheet changes to show you the events for that object.

In Figure 26.1, all the events with existing event procedures contain [Event Procedure], which indicates that the property has associated VBA code that executes whenever this event is triggered. The events may also contain [Embedded Macro], the name of a non-embedded macro, or the name of a function.

Creating event procedures

In Access, you execute event procedures through an object's event properties.

Access provides event properties you use to tie VBA code to an object's events. For example, the On Open property is associated with a form or report opening on the screen.

You add an event procedure to a form or report by selecting the event property (Before Update, for this example) in the object's Property Sheet. If no event procedure currently exists for the property, a drop-down arrow and builder button appear in the property's box, as shown in the Before Update event property in Figure 26.1.

The drop-down arrow exposes a list that contains the single item [Event Procedure]. Selecting this option and then clicking the builder button takes you to the VBA code editor with an event procedure template already in place (see Figure 26.2).

FIGURE 26.2

An empty event procedure template for the form's BeforeUpdate event.

Notice the general format of the event procedure's declaration:

```
Private Sub Object_Event()
```

The *Object* portion of the procedure's name is the name of the object raising the event, while the *Event* portion is the specific event raised by the object. In Figure 26.2, the object is Form, and the event is BeforeUpdate. Some events support arguments, which appear within the parentheses at the end of the declaration.

In case you're wondering, you can't change the name or the arguments of an event procedure and expect it to continue working. Access VBA relies on the Object_Event naming convention to tie a procedure to an object's event.

Identifying Common Events

Certain events are raised by many different Access objects. Microsoft has taken great care that these events behave exactly the same way, regardless of the object raising them. Table 26.1 lists several of the events most commonly used by Access developers. Most of these events apply to forms and all the different controls you might add to an Access form.

TABLE 26.1 Events Common to Multiple Object Types

Event	Event Type	When the Event Is Triggered
Click	Mouse	When the user presses and releases (clicks) the left mouse button on an object
DblClick	Mouse	When the user presses and releases (clicks) the left mouse button twice on an object
MouseDown	Mouse	When the user presses the mouse button while the pointer is on an object
MouseMove	Mouse	When the user moves the mouse pointer over an object
MouseUp	Mouse	When the user releases a pressed mouse button while the pointer is on an object
MouseWheel	Mouse	When the user spins the mouse wheel
KeyDown	Keyboard	When the user presses any key on the keyboard when the object has focus or when the user uses a SendKeys macro action
KeyUp	Keyboard	When the user releases a pressed key or immediately after the user uses a SendKeys macro action
KeyPress	Keyboard	When the user presses and releases a key on an object that has the focus or when the user uses a SendKeys macro action

Not surprisingly, these events are all associated with the mouse and the keyboard because these are the user's primary means of inputting information and giving directions to an application. Not every object responds to every one of these events, but when an object responds to any of these events, the event exhibits exactly the same behavior.

> **TIP**
>
> Many developers simply copy and paste VBA code from one event procedure to the same event procedure on another object. For example, you might want to do some fancy formatting on a text box when the user clicks into the box. You can copy the code performing the fancy formatting into another control's Click event procedure to get the same effect without having to retype the code. Even though you'll have to fix up the pasted code with the second text box's name, it's much less work than retyping the entire procedure.

Access supports many different events. In fact, one of Access's fundamental strengths is the wide variety of events available to developers. You can control virtually every aspect of an Access application's behavior and data management through event procedures. Although Microsoft makes no formal distinction between types of events, the following sections categorize events and event procedures into groups based on the type of object (forms, reports, and so on) that raise the events within the group.

> **TIP**
>
> Access supports a rich event model. Not many Access developers master every Access event, nor is there need to. Virtually all Access developers learn and use the events that are important for the applications they're building and then learn other events as they go. You don't need to worry about memorizing all these events; instead, just be aware that Access supports many different types of events and that they're there when you need them.

Form event procedures

When working with forms, you can create event procedures based on events at the form level, the section level, or the control level. If you attach an event procedure to a form-level event, whenever the event occurs, the action takes effect against the form as a whole (such as when you move to another record or leave the form).

To have your form respond to an event, you write an event procedure and attach it to the event property in the form that recognizes the event. Many properties can be used to trigger event procedures at the form level.

> **NOTE**
>
> When we refer to *form events*, we're talking about events that happen to the form as a whole, not about an event that can be triggered by a specific control on a form. Form events execute when moving from one record to another or when a form is being opened or closed. We cover control events in the "Control event procedures" section later in this chapter.

Essential form events

Access forms respond to many events. You'll never write code for most of these events, because of their specialized nature. There are, however, some events that you'll program over and over again in your Access applications. Table 26.2 lists some of the most fundamental and important Access form events. Not coincidentally, these are also the most commonly programmed Access form events.

Table 26.2 lists a number of events that deal with the form as a whole, such as when it's opened or closed.

TABLE 26.2 Essential Form Events

Event	When the Event Is Triggered
Open	When a form is opened, but the first record is not yet displayed
Load	When a form is loaded into memory
Resize	When the size of a form changes
Unload	When a form is closed and the records unload, but before the form is removed from the screen
Close	When a form is closed and removed from the screen
Activate	When an open form receives the focus, becoming the active window
Deactivate	When a different window becomes the active window, but before the current window loses focus
GotFocus	When a form with no active or enabled controls receives the focus
LostFocus	When a form loses the focus
Timer	When a specified time interval passes; the interval (in milliseconds) is specified by the Timer Interval property
BeforeScreenTip	When a ScreenTip is activated

Form mouse and keyboard events

Access forms also respond to a number of mouse and keyboard events, as shown in Table 26.3.

TABLE 26.3 Form Mouse and Keyboard Events

Event	When the Event Is Triggered
Click	When the user presses and releases (clicks) the left mouse button
DblClick	When the user presses and releases (clicks) the left mouse button twice on a form
MouseDown	When the user presses the mouse button while the pointer is on a form
MouseMove	When the user moves the mouse pointer over an area of a form
MouseUp	When the user releases a pressed mouse button while the pointer is on a form
MouseWheel	When the user spins the mouse wheel
KeyDown	When the user presses any key on the keyboard when a form has focus or when the user uses a SendKeys macro action
KeyUp	When the user releases a pressed key or immediately after the user uses a SendKeys macro action
KeyPress	When the user presses and releases a key on a form that has the focus or when the user uses a SendKeys macro

In addition, the Key Preview property is closely related to form keyboard events. This property (which is found only in forms) instructs Access to allow the form to see keyboard events before the controls on the form. By default, the controls on an Access form receive events before the form. For example, when you click a button on a form, the button—not the form—sees the click, even though the form supports a Click event. This means that a form's controls mask key events from the form, and the form can never respond to those events. You must set the Key Preview property to Yes (true) before the form responds to any of the key events (KeyDown, KeyUp, and so on).

Form data events

The primary purpose of Access forms is to display data. Not surprisingly then, Access forms have a number of events that are directly related to a form's data management. You'll see these events programmed over and over again in this book, and you'll encounter event procedures written for these events virtually every time you work on an Access application. These events are summarized in Table 26.4.

TABLE 26.4 **Form Data Events**

Event	When the Event Is Triggered
Current	When you move to a different record and make it the current record
BeforeInsert	After data is first entered into a new record, but before the record is actually created
AfterInsert	After the new record is added to the table
BeforeUpdate	Before changed data is updated in a record
AfterUpdate	After changed data is updated in a record
Dirty	When a record is modified and in an unsaved state
Undo	When a user has returned a form to a clean state (the record has been set back to an unmodified state); the opposite of Dirty
Delete	When a record is deleted, but before the deletion takes place
BeforeDelConfirm	Just before Access displays the Delete Confirm dialog box
AfterDelConfirm	After the Delete Confirm dialog box closes and confirmation has happened
Error	When a runtime error is produced
Filter	When a filter has been specified, but before it is applied
ApplyFilter	After a filter is applied to a form

The Current event fires just after the data on a form is refreshed. Most often this occurs as the user moves the form to a different record in the recordset underlying the form. The

`Current` event is often used to perform calculations based on the form's data or to format controls. For example, if a certain numeric or date value is outside an expected range, the `Current` event can be used to change the text box's Back Color property so the user notices the issue.

The `BeforeInsert` and `AfterInsert` events are related to transferring a new record from the form to an underlying data source. `BeforeInsert` fires as Access is about to transfer the data, and `AfterInsert` is triggered after the record is committed to the data source. For example, you could use these events to perform a logging operation that keeps track of additions to a table.

The `BeforeUpdate` and `AfterUpdate` events are frequently used to validate data before it's sent to the underlying data source. As you'll see later in this chapter, many form controls also support `BeforeUpdate` and `AfterUpdate`. A control's update is triggered as soon as the data in the control is changed.

> **TIP**
>
> A form's `Update` event fires much later than the `BeforeInsert` or `AfterInsert` events. The `Update` event occurs just as the form prepares to move to another record. Many developers use the form's `BeforeUpdate` event to scan all the controls on the form to ensure that all the data in the form's controls is valid. A form's `BeforeUpdate` event includes a `Cancel` parameter that, when set to `True`, causes the update to terminate. Canceling an update is an effective way to protect the integrity of the data behind an Access application.

> **TIP**
>
> Users often want to be notified of pending updates before they move off a record to another record. By default, Access forms automatically update a form's underlying data source as the user moves to another record or closes the form. The `Dirty` event fires whenever the user changes any of the data on a form. You can use the `Dirty` event to set a module-level Boolean (true/false) variable (let's call it `bIsDirty`) so that other controls on the form (such as a Close button) know that pending changes exist on the form. If `bIsDirty` is `True` when the Close button is clicked or when the `BeforeUpdate` event fires, you can display an `Are you sure?` message box to confirm the user's intention to commit the changes to the database.

Control event procedures

Controls also raise events. Control events are often used to manipulate the control's appearance or to validate data as the user makes changes to the control's contents. Control events also influence how the mouse and keyboard behave while the user works with the control. A control's `BeforeUpdate` event fires as soon as the focus leaves the control (more precisely, `BeforeUpdate` fires just before data is transferred from the control to the recordset underlying the form, enabling you to cancel the event if data validation fails), whereas a form's `BeforeUpdate` does not fire until you move the form to another record. (The form's `BeforeUpdate` commits the entire record to the form's data source.)

This means that a *control's* BeforeUpdate is good for validating a single control while the *form's* BeforeUpdate is good for validating multiple controls on the form. The form's BeforeUpdate would be a good place to validate that values in two different controls are in agreement with each other (such as a zip code in one text box and the city in another text box), instead of relying on the BeforeUpdate in each of the controls.

You create event procedures for control events in exactly the same way you create procedures for form events. You select [Event Procedure] in the Property Sheet for the event and then add VBA code to the event procedure attached to the event. Table 26.5 shows each control event property, the event it recognizes, and how it works. As you review the information in Table 26.5, keep in mind that not every control supports every type of event.

TABLE 26.5 Control Events

Event	When the Event Is Triggered
BeforeUpdate	Before changed data in the control is updated to the underlying recordset
AfterUpdate	After changed data is transferred to the form's recordset
Dirty	When the contents of a control change
Undo	When the control is returned to a clean state
Change	When the contents of a text box change or a combo box's text changes
Updated	When an ActiveX object's data has been modified
NotInList	When a value that isn't in the list is entered into a combo box
Enter	Before a control receives the focus from another control
Exit	Just before the control loses focus to another control
GotFocus	When a nonactive or enabled control receives the focus
LostFocus	When a control loses the focus
Click	When the left mouse button is pressed and released (clicked) on a control
DblClick	When the left mouse button is pressed and released (clicked) twice on a control or label
MouseDown	When a mouse button is pressed while the pointer is on a control
MouseMove	When the mouse pointer is moved over a control
MouseUp	When a pressed mouse button is released while the pointer is on a control
KeyDown	When any key on the keyboard is pressed when a control has the focus or when a SendKeys macro action is used
KeyPress	When a key is pressed and released on a control that has the focus or when a SendKeys macro action is used
KeyUp	When a pressed key is released or immediately after a SendKeys macro is used

> **NOTE**
>
> The `Click` event is most commonly associated with clicking the left mouse button on a control. However, several other actions will trigger this event. Other actions that will trigger a `Click` event include pressing the spacebar when the control has the focus, pressing the Enter key when the control's Default property is set to `Yes`, pressing Esc when the control's Cancel property is set to `Yes`, and pressing the control's access key (the underlined letter in the control's caption, if it has one).

Report event procedures

Just as with forms, reports also use event procedures to respond to specific events. Access reports support events for the overall report itself and for each section in the report. Individual controls on Access reports do not raise events.

Attaching an event procedure to the report runs code whenever the report opens, closes, or prints. Each section in a report (header, footer, and so on) also includes events that run as the report is formatted or printed.

Several overall report event properties are available. Table 26.6 shows the Access report events. As you can see, the list of report events is much shorter than the form event list.

TABLE 26.6 **Report Events**

Event	When the Event Is Triggered
Open	When the report opens but before printing
Close	When the report closes and is removed from the screen
Activate	When the report receives the focus and becomes the active window
Deactivate	When a different window becomes active
NoData	When no data is passed to the report as it opens
Page	When the report changes pages
Error	When a runtime error is produced in Access

Even though users do not interact with reports as they do with forms, events still play a vital role in report design. Opening a report containing no data generally yields erroneous results. The report may display a title and no detail information. Or, it may display #error values for missing information. This situation can be a little scary for the user. Use the NoData event to inform the user that the report contains no data. NoData fires as a report opens and there is no data available in the report's RecordSource. Use the NoData event procedure to display a message box describing the situation to the user and then cancel the report's opening. Figure 26.3 shows a typical NoData event procedure.

FIGURE 26.3

Running a NoData event procedure when there is no data for a report.

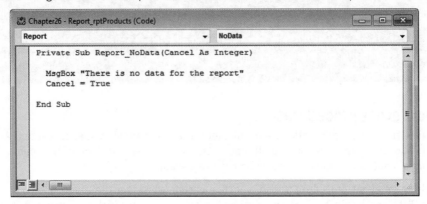

The Report_NoData event illustrated in Figure 26.3 first displays a message box to advise the user that the report contains no data. Then the event procedure cancels the report's opening by setting the Cancel parameter to True. Because the Cancel parameter is set to True, the report never appears on the screen and is not sent to the printer.

Many Access events are accompanied by parameters, such as the Cancel parameter you see in Figure 26.3. In this case, setting Cancel to True instructs Access to simply ignore the process that triggered the event and to prevent the triggering of subsequent events. Because NoData was triggered as part of the report's opening process, setting Cancel to True prevents the report from being sent to the printer or being displayed on the screen. You'll see many examples of event property procedure parameters throughout this book.

Report section event procedures

In addition to the event properties for the report itself, Access offers three specialized event properties to use with report sections. Table 26.7 shows each event and how it works.

TABLE 26.7   Report Section Events

Event	When the Event Is Triggered
Format	When the section is pre-formatted in memory before being sent to the printer. This is your opportunity to apply special formatting to controls within the section.
Print	As the section is sent to the printer. It is too late to format controls in a report section when the Print event fires.
Retreat	After the Format event but before the Print event. Occurs when Access has to back up past other sections on a page to perform multiple formatting passes. Retreat is included in all sections except headers and footers.

Use the Format event to apply special formatting to controls within a section before the section is printed. Format is useful, for example, to hide controls you don't want to print because of some condition in the report's data. The event procedure runs as Access lays out the section in memory but before the report is sent to the printer.

You can set the On Format and On Print event properties for any section of the report. However, On Retreat is not available for the page header or page footer sections. Figure 26.4 shows the Property Sheet's Event tab for a report. Notice that the drop-down list at the top of the Property Sheet shows that the report is selected, so the events in the Event tab relate to the report itself and not an individual control on the report.

FIGURE 26.4

Specifying an event procedure for a report's On No Data event.

In addition to the NoData event, the Format event is frequently used. Figure 26.5 shows how to add code to a report section's Format event to control the visibility of controls on the report.

The Detail0_Format event procedure illustrated in Figure 26.5 first checks the value of the txtQtyInStock control. If the value of txtQtyInStock is less than 10, lblLowStock is displayed; otherwise, the warning control is hidden.

TIP

Access names the sections of reports by appending a digit to the type of section, such as Detail0. You can rename these sections by changing the Name property of the section.

FIGURE 26.5

Running an event procedure to display or hide a control on a report.

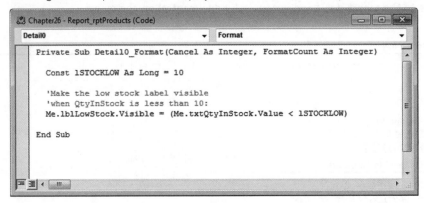

You'll see many examples of using events and event procedures to manipulate forms, reports, and controls throughout this book.

Paying Attention to Event Sequence

Sometimes even a fairly simple action on the part of the user raises multiple events in rapid succession. As an example, every time the user presses a key on the keyboard, the KeyDown, KeyPress, and KeyUp events are raised, in that order. Similarly, clicking the left mouse button fires the MouseDown and MouseUp events, as well as a Click event. It's your prerogative as a VBA developer to decide which events you program in your Access applications.

Events don't occur randomly. Events actually fire in a predictable fashion, depending on which control is raising the events. Sometimes the trickiest aspect of working with events is keeping track of the order in which events occur. It may not be intuitive, for example, that the Enter event occurs before the GotFocus event (see Table 26.5) or that the KeyDown event occurs before the KeyPress event (see Table 26.3).

Looking at common event sequences

Here are the sequences of events for the most frequently encountered form scenarios:

- **Opening and closing forms:**
  - **When a form opens:** Open (form) → Load (form) → Resize (form) → Activate (form) → Current (form) → Enter (control) → GotFocus (control)
  - **When a form closes:** Exit (control) → LostFocus (control) → Unload (form) → Deactivate (form) → Close (form)
- **Changes in focus:**
  - **When the focus moves from one form to another:** Deactivate (form1) → Activate (form2)
  - **When the focus moves to a control on a form:** Enter → GotFocus
  - **When the focus leaves a form control:** Exit → LostFocus
  - **When the focus moves from control1 to control2:** Exit (control1) → LostFocus (control1) → Enter (control2) → GotFocus (control2)
  - **When the focus leaves the record in which data has changed, but before entering the next record:** BeforeUpdate (form) → AfterUpdate (form) → Exit (control) → LostFocus (control) → Current (form)
  - **When the focus moves to an existing record in Form view:** BeforeUpdate (form) → AfterUpdate (form) → Current (form)
- **Changes to data:**
  - **When data is entered or changed in a form control and the focus is moved to another control:** BeforeUpdate → AfterUpdate → Exit → LostFocus
  - **When the user presses and releases a key while a form control has the focus:** KeyDown → KeyPress → KeyUp
  - **When text changes in a text box or in the text box portion of a combo box:** KeyDown → KeyPress → Change → KeyUp
  - **When a value that is not present in the drop-down list is entered into a combo box's text area:** KeyDown → KeyPress → Change → KeyUp → NotInList → Error
  - **When data in a control is changed and the user presses Tab to move to the next control:**
    - Control1: KeyDown → BeforeUpdate → AfterUpdate → Exit → LostFocus
    - Control2: Enter → GotFocus → KeyPress → KeyUp
  - **When a form opens and data in a control changes:** Current (form) → Enter (control) → GotFocus (control) → BeforeUpdate (control) → AfterUpdate (control)
  - **When a record is deleted:** Delete → BeforeDelConfirm → AfterDelConfirm

- **When the focus moves to a new blank record on a form and a new record is created when the user types in a control:** Current (form) → Enter (control) → GotFocus (control) → BeforeInsert (form) → AfterInsert (form)
- **Mouse events:**
  - **When the user presses and releases (clicks) a mouse button while the mouse pointer is on a form control:** MouseDown → MouseUp → Click
  - **When the user moves the focus from one control to another by clicking the second control:**
    - Control1: Exit → LostFocus
    - Control2: Enter → GotFocus → MouseDown → MouseUp → Click
  - **When the user double-clicks a control other than a command button:** MouseDown → MouseUp → Click → DblClick → MouseUp

Writing simple form and control event procedures

Writing simple procedures to verify a form or control's event sequence is quite easy. Use the preceding information to determine which event should be harnessed in your application. Unexpected behavior often can be traced to an event procedure attached to an event that occurs too late or too early to capture the information that is needed by the application.

The Chapter26.accdb example database includes a form named frmEventLogger that prints every event for a command button, a text box, and a toggle button in the Debug window. The form is not bound to a recordset, so the list of events will be slightly different than for a bound form. It is provided to demonstrate just how many Access events are triggered by minor actions. For example, clicking the command button one time, and then tabbing to the text box and pressing one key on the keyboard fires the following events:

- cmdButton_MouseDown
- cmdButton_MouseUp
- cmdButton_Click
- cmdButton_KeyDown
- cmdButton_Exit
- cmdButton_LostFocus
- txtText1_Enter
- txtText1_GotFocus
- txtText1_KeyPress
- txtText1_KeyPress
- txtText1_KeyUp
- txtText1_KeyDown
- txtText1_KeyPress
- txtText1_Change
- txtText1_KeyUp

You'll have to open the code editor and display the Immediate window to see these events displayed. From anywhere in the Access environment, press Ctrl+G and the code editor instantly opens with the Immediate window displayed. Then, Alt+Tab back to the main Access screen, open the form, and click the various controls and type something into the text box. You'll see a long list of event messages when you use Ctrl+G to return to the Immediate window.

Obviously, these are far more events than you'll ever want to program. Notice that, on the command button, both the MouseDown and MouseUp events fire before the Click event. Also, a KeyDown event occurs as the Tab key is pressed, and then the command button's Exit event fires before its LostFocus event. (The focus, of course, moves off the command button to the text box as the Tab key is pressed.)

Also, notice that the text box raises more than one KeyPress event. The first is the KeyPress from the Tab key, and the second is the KeyPress that occurs as a character on the keyboard is pressed. Although it may seem strange that the Tab key's KeyPress event is caught by a text box and not by the command button, it makes sense when you consider what is happening under the surface. The Tab key is a directive to move the focus to the next control in the tab sequence. Access actually moves the focus before passing the KeyPress event to the controls on the form. This means that the focus moves to the text box, and the text box receives the KeyPress raised by the Tab key.

Keep in mind that you write code only for events that are meaningful to your application. Any event that does not contain code is ignored by Access and has no effect on the application.

Also, it's entirely likely that you'll occasionally program the wrong event for a particular task. You may, for example, be tempted to change the control's appearance by adding code to a control's Enter event. (Many developers change a control's BackColor or ForeColor to make it easy for the user to see which control has the focus.) You'll soon discover that the Enter event is an unreliable indicator of when a control has gained focus. The GotFocus and LostFocus events are specifically provided for the purpose of controlling the user interface, while the Enter and Exit events are more "conceptual" in nature and are not often programmed in Access applications.

This small example helps explain, perhaps, why Access supports so many different events. Microsoft has carefully designed Access to handle different *categories* of events, such as data or user-interface tasks. These events provide you with a rich programming environment. You'll almost always find exactly the right control, event, or programming trick to get Access to do what you need.

Opening a form with an event procedure

Most applications require multiple forms and reports to accomplish the application's business functions. Instead of requiring the users of the application to browse the database container to determine which forms and reports accomplish which tasks, an application generally provides a switchboard form to assist users in navigating throughout the application. The switchboard provides a set of command buttons labeled appropriately to suggest the purpose of the form or report it opens. Figure 26.6 shows the switchboard for the Collectible Mini Cars application.

FIGURE 26.6

Using a switchboard to navigate through the forms and reports of an application.

The Collectible Mini Cars switchboard includes five command buttons. Each command button runs an event procedure when the button is clicked. The Products button (cmdProducts), for example, runs the event procedure that opens frmProducts. Figure 26.7 shows the Property Sheet for cmdProducts. Figure 26.8 shows the VBA code for the Click event of cmdProducts.

FIGURE 26.7

Specifying an event procedure for a control event.

FIGURE 26.8

Using an event procedure to open a form.

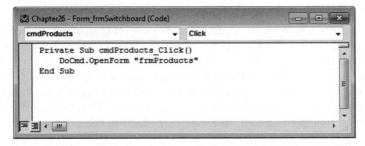

Running an event procedure when closing a form

Sometimes, you'll want to perform some action when you close or leave a form. For example, you might want Access to keep a log of everyone using the form, or you might want to close the form's Print dialog box every time a user closes the main form.

To automatically close frmDialogProductPrint every time frmProducts is closed, create an event procedure for the frmProducts Close event. Figure 26.9 shows this event procedure.

FIGURE 26.9

Running an event procedure when a form closes.

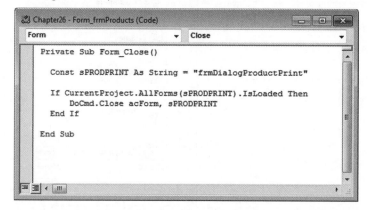

The Form_Close event illustrated in Figure 26.9 first checks to see if frmDialogProductPrint is open. If it is open, the statement to close it executes. Although trying to close a form that isn't currently open doesn't cause an error, it's a good idea to check to see if an object is available before performing an operation on the object.

Using an event procedure to confirm record deletion

Although you can use the Delete button on the Records group of the Home tab of the Ribbon to delete a record in a form, a better practice is to provide a Delete button on the form. A Delete button is more user-friendly because it provides a visual cue to the user as to how to delete a record. Plus, a command button affords more control over the delete process because you can include code to verify the deletion before it's actually processed. Or you might need to perform a referential integrity check to ensure that deleting the record doesn't cause a connection to the record from some other table in the database to be lost.

Use the MsgBox() function to confirm a deletion. cmdDelete's event procedure uses MsgBox() to confirm the deletion, as shown in Figure 26.10.

FIGURE 26.10

Using the MsgBox() function to confirm a deletion.

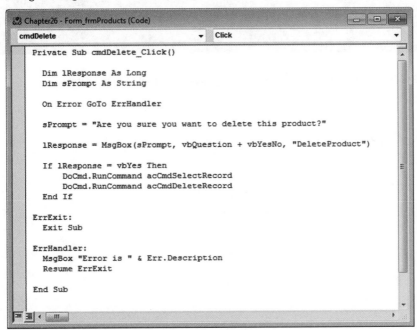

When the cmdDelete_Click() event procedure executes, Access displays a message box prompt, as shown in Figure 26.11. Notice that the message box includes two command buttons: Yes and No. Access displays the prompt and waits for the user to make a selection. The record is deleted only when the user confirms the deletion by clicking the Yes button.

FIGURE 26.11

A confirmation dialog box before deleting a record.

> **CAUTION**
>
> Before the `RunCommand acCmdDeleteRecord` statement executes, it automatically checks to see if deleting the record violates referential integrity rules that you've set up in the Relationships diagram. If a violation occurs, an Access error message displays and the deletion is canceled.

 See Chapter 4 for more information on setting up referential integrity in a database.

Debugging Your Access Applications

IN THIS CHAPTER

Organizing VBA code

Testing an application

Debugging the traditional way: with `MsgBox` and `Debug.Print`

Taking advantage of the debugging tools in Access

Trapping unexpected errors

M any Access applications rely on significant amounts of VBA code in forms and reports and as stand-alone modules. Because of its power and flexibility, VBA is used for all aspects of application development, from communicating with the user to massaging and transforming data on its way from tables and queries to forms and reports.

Like with any programming language, debugging an error in VBA or a problem in an application can be difficult and time-consuming. Depending on how well organized the code is and whether simple conventions, such as providing descriptive names for variables and procedures, were followed, tracking down even a small coding bug can be a frustrating experience.

Fortunately, Access provides a full complement of debugging tools to make your life easier. These tools not only save time by helping you pinpoint where a coding error occurs but can help you better understand how the code is organized and how execution passes from procedure to procedure.

> **NOTE**
>
> This chapter largely ignores the errors caused by poor design: misrepresentation of data caused by ill-designed queries, update and insert anomalies caused by inappropriate application of referential integrity rules, and so on. For the most part, these problems occur because of issues such as failing to conform to proper design disciplines, misunderstanding Access query design, and so on. What we can help you with, however, are the bugs that creep into your VBA code, particularly those bugs that cause noticeable problems with the data or user interface in your applications.

ON THE WEB

This chapter is a departure from the other example files you've used in the book. The sample database file (`Chapter27.accdb`) contains the basic example code shown throughout this chapter. The code in `Chapter27.accdb` does not necessarily do anything useful. It's provided mostly as a "test bench" for practicing with the Access debugging tools rather than as a good example of practical VBA code.

Organizing VBA Code

The first step in debugging your code is to avoid coding errors in the first place. It shouldn't come as any surprise that your coding habits have a lot to do with the type and amount of errors you encounter in your applications. Often, the adoption of simple coding conventions eliminates all but the toughest syntactical and logical errors in VBA code. Some of these conventions are described elsewhere in this book but are repeated here as a helpful reminder:

- **Use a naming convention.** Naming conventions for procedures, variables, and constants don't have to be complicated. But a consistently applied naming convention can help you spot errors that might otherwise slip through the cracks. Trying to assign a value to a constant, using a `String` variable in a mathematical operation, and passing improperly typed arguments to a function are examples of problems that a naming convention can help you avoid.

- **Limit scopes for variables.** Your variables should have the smallest scope possible that still allows your program to work efficiently and effectively. Create your variables at the procedure level by default and only increase the scope when the logic of your code requires it. Keep your globally scoped variables in their own module. When the list of global variables starts to get too big, consider refactoring your code.

- **Use constants.** Constants are a great way to add readability to your code and prevent errors. When you use a constant like `dDISCOUNT_THRESHOLD`, your intent is immensely more obvious than when you have a magic number like `5000`. Try to remove all magic numbers from your code and put them in descriptively named constants. Even if you don't succeed in getting all of them, your code will be more robust and error-proof than if you spread numbers around liberally.

- **Keep your procedures short.** In general, a procedure should do one thing. If you find your procedures are getting too long to fit on one screen, consider breaking the procedure into multiple procedures and calling each of them from the main procedure. There are certainly cases in which procedures will do more than one thing. However, you'll find your code much easier to manage when you have many simple procedures as opposed to a few giant ones.

- **Keep your modules clean.** There is virtually no limit to the number of modules you can have in your project. All the procedures in a module should be related in some way. Modules behind forms and reports will contain event procedures for their parent object but should only contain other procedures that support those event procedures. Keeping only related procedures in a module will also give you more confidence that private variables in that module won't be misused.

- **Use comments when necessary.** Comments can be an important part of the code in your project. If you have too many comments, however, nobody will ever read them, and they'll quickly become out of date as your code changes. Use well-named procedures, variables, and constants to make your code self-documenting. Use comments when you've coded something a little out of the ordinary or to explain why you took one approach to a problem over another. Comments should not describe what the code does, but why the code does it.

- **Don't repeat yourself.** Much of the code you write will seem repetitive, particularly when you're coding the events on a form with a lot of controls. If it seems like you're writing the same code over and over, consider moving the code to separate procedures and passing in arguments from the event procedure. If a change is required, you'll only have to change the code in one place, saving you time and preventing errors.

- **Compile often.** Compile your project after you've written or changed several lines of code. Don't wait until the entire module or project is written to compile. Catching syntax errors while you're writing code enables you to fix those errors easily. You'll have a lot of the information about what your procedure does and where it's used when you're writing it, which makes it the best time to catch errors.

Testing Your Applications

Testing Access applications is an ongoing process. Each time you switch a form or report from Design view to Normal view or leave the VBA Editor to run a bit of code, you're testing your application. Every time you write a line of code and move to another line, the VBA syntax parser checks the code you just wrote. Each time you change a property in a form or report and move your cursor to another property or another control, you're testing the property you've changed.

Testing is the time to see if your application runs the way you intend, or even if it runs at all. When you run an application and it doesn't work, you've found a bug. Fixing problems in code is referred to as *debugging*.

> **NOTE**
> This term dates back to the earliest electro-mechanical computers. Legend has it that a moth shorted out an electrical circuit. The late Admiral Grace Hopper, an early pioneer in computing, coined the term *debugging* to describe the process of removing the moth.

When you run a report and no data appears, you've had to check the report's RecordSource property to ensure that the report is pulling the correct data. You may have viewed the data in a query or table to see if the data source is the problem. If you run a form and you see #Name or #Error in individual controls, you've learned to check the control's ControlSource property. Perhaps you have an incorrect reference to a table field or you spelled something wrong and Access is unable to evaluate the reference.

Maybe you have too many parentheses in an expression or you've used a control name in a formula that conflicts with an Access keyword. Each time you had this problem, you may have asked someone with more experience than you what the problem was, or perhaps you looked it up online or in a book, or you researched the syntax of the formula.

Most problems with query, form, and report design are pretty obvious. You know you have a problem when a query returns the wrong data, or a form or report fails to open or displays an error message as it opens. Behind the scenes, Access does a great deal to help you notice and rectify problems with your application's design. When you run forms and reports, Access often reports an error if it finds something seriously and obviously wrong.

It's much more difficult for Access to help you with incorrectly written code. Very often, a problem in VBA code exists for months or even years before a user notices it. Even poorly written code can run without throwing errors or exhibiting obvious problems. However, determining exactly where a bug exists in VBA code—and figuring out what to do to repair the bug—can be very challenging. When you create VBA code, you're pretty much on your own when it comes to detecting and resolving problems. Fortunately, a wide variety of tools have been built into the editor to help you.

> **TIP**
>
> Testing and debugging takes quite a bit of time. Many good developers easily spend a third of their time designing a program, another third writing code, and another third testing and debugging. Having someone other than the developer test a program's operation is a good idea. A person who is unfamiliar with an application is more likely to do something the developer never expected, leading to new and surprising bugs and instability issues.

Testing functions

Functions return values, and that makes them easier to test than other types of procedures. A good developer will write a separate procedure to test each function to make sure the output is what's expected. Testing your function when it's written will expose any problems at a time when the problem is easiest to fix. If a function contains an error and that error propagates to a control on a form, it may be harder to track down. Writing tests also forces you to think through the logic of your functions from different angles.

VBA provides the Debug.Assert method to aid in writing tests. The following example procedure computes a discount on an invoice. There are several factors that determine whether a discount is given. See if you can identify them as you read the code:

```
Function InvoiceDiscountAmount( _
    sCustomerID As String, _
    cInvoiceTotal As Currency, _
    dtInvoice As Date _
    ) As Currency
```

```
Dim cReturn As Currency

Const dDISCOUNT_THRESHOLD As Double = 10000
Const dDEFAULT_DISCOUNT As Double = 0.1

cReturn = 0

If cInvoiceTotal >= dDISCOUNT_THRESHOLD Then
  cReturn = cInvoiceTotal * dDEFAULT_DISCOUNT
ElseIf IsDiscountCustomer(sCustomerID) Then
  cReturn = cInvoiceTotal * dDEFAULT_DISCOUNT
ElseIf IsLastDayOfMonth(dtInvoice) Then
  cReturn = cInvoiceTotal * dDEFAULT_DISCOUNT
End If

InvoiceDiscountAmount = cReturn

End Function
```

There are three situations that will result in a discount. If the invoice is over a certain amount, if the customer is flagged as getting a discount, or if it's the last day of the month, the default discount is applied to the invoice. Comparing the invoice total to the threshold is fairly straightforward. In order to make the code clean and readable, the other two conditions were moved to their own functions. Those functions are shown here:

```
Private Function IsDiscountCustomer(sCustomerID As String) As Boolean

  Dim rsCustomer As ADODB.Recordset
  Dim conn As ADODB.Connection
  Dim sSql As String

  Set conn = CurrentProject.Connection
  sSql = "SELECT GetsDiscount FROM Customers " & _
    "WHERE CustomerID = '" & sCustomerID & "'"

  Set rsCustomer = conn.Execute(sSql)

  If Not rsCustomer.EOF Then
    IsDiscountCustomer = rsCustomer.Fields(0).Value
  End If

End Function

Private Function IsLastDayOfMonth(dtDate As Date) As Boolean

  'The zeroth day of the next month is the last
  'day of the current month
  IsLastDayOfMonth = (dtDate = DateSerial(Year(dtDate), Month(dtDate), 0))

End Function
```

Now that the functions are written, we can write a test procedure to see if it works as expected. We know the three conditions that should result in a discount, and we'll test the combinations of those. The Debug.Assert method will halt the code if a test doesn't pass. For illustration purposes, there is an error in the IsLastDayOfMonth function. We'll fix that error shortly. Figure 27.1 shows the test procedure after it has been run.

FIGURE 27.1

Debug.Assert halts code when a test fails.

```
Chapter27 - modInvoiceFunctions (Code)

(General)                                          TEST_InvoiceDiscountAmount

    Private Sub TEST_InvoiceDiscountAmount()

      Dim vaCustomer As Variant 'holds the customers to test
      Dim vaTotal As Variant 'hold invoice totals to test
      Dim vaDate As Variant 'holds invoice dates to test
      Dim i As Long, j As Long, k As Long
      Dim cDiscount As Currency

      'First element gets a discount, second doesn't
      vaCustomer = Array("ALFKI", "ANATR")
      vaTotal = Array(10000, 9999)
      vaDate = Array(#1/31/2019#, #2/1/2019#)

      For i = LBound(vaCustomer) To UBound(vaCustomer)
        For j = LBound(vaTotal) To UBound(vaTotal)
          For k = LBound(vaDate) To UBound(vaDate)

            cDiscount = InvoiceDiscountAmount(vaCustomer(i), vaTotal(j), vaDate(k))

            'only last elements of all array get no discount
            If i = UBound(vaCustomer) And _
               j = UBound(vaTotal) And _
               k = UBound(vaDate) Then

              Debug.Assert cDiscount = 0

            Else

              Debug.Assert cDiscount = vaTotal(j) * 0.1

            End If
          Next k
        Next j
      Next i

    End Sub
```

To test the function, three arrays were created containing information to pass to the function. The vaCustomer array contains one customer that gets a discount and one customer that doesn't. These customers were selected by inspecting the Customers table. The vaTotal array contains an invoice total amount that gets a discount and one that doesn't. The first value is the amount of the threshold (and should pass), and the second value is one less than the threshold (and should fail). Picking values around the value that defines pass/fail is called picking *edge cases*. The last array contains a date that should pass (because it's the last day of the month) and a date that shouldn't.

The procedure contains three nested loops so that all eight combinations of data are passed to the function. Only when the last element of each array is the current element should there be no discount (that is, when ANATR, 9999, and #2/1/2019# are passed to the function). The If statement checks to see if each loop is referencing the last element. If they are, Debug.Assert compares the calculated discount to zero. If any loop is not referencing the last element, then Debug.Assert compares the calculated discount to 10 percent of the invoice total.

Running the test procedure caused execution to stop on the Debug.Assert line. Checking the values of i, j, and k, we can see that the combination of "ANATR", 9999, and #2/1/2019# resulted in a calculated discount of zero, but our test says it should have been 999.9. We know there is a problem in our function—now we just have to find it.

Upon closer inspection of the IsLastDayOfMonth function, we see that it should have read:

```
IsLastDayOfMonth = (dtDate = DateSerial(Year(dtDate), Month(dtDate) + 1, 0))
```

We forgot to include the +1 to advance the month to the next month. After correcting the error and rerunning TEST_InvoiceDiscountAmount, the code runs without error. Debug.Assert stops the code only when a test doesn't pass. If everything is fine, nothing happens. You may want to include a MsgBox or Debug.Print statement at the end of your tests to give you a visual cue that the test procedure completed.

In this example, it took almost as long to write the test as it did to write the three functions. However, if we hadn't caught the error, it could have caused many worse problems in the form where the function was used. The erroneous procedure would have returned no discount when one was warranted. It's easy to imagine that the user would not notice the error, and the result would be an unhappy customer. Another benefit of testing functions in this way is that any changes to the function can be tested using the same test procedure. If the tests pass, we know our changes haven't violated the business rules of our application.

Compiling VBA code

After you create a subprocedure or function and want to make sure that all your syntax is correct, you should compile your procedures by choosing Debug ⇨ Compile *Project Name* from the VBA code editor window menu (where *Project Name* is the name of the project set in the Project dialog box, accessed from the Tools menu). Figure 27.2 shows the Debug menu opened in the editor window.

FIGURE 27.2

The Debug menu in the VBA code editor window contains valuable debugging tools.

The compile action checks your code for errors and also converts the programs to a form that your computer can understand. If the compile operation is not successful, an error window appears, as shown in Figure 27.3.

FIGURE 27.3

Viewing a compile error.

This level of checking is more stringent than the single-line syntax checker. Variables are checked for proper references and type. Each statement is checked for all proper parameters. All text strings are checked for proper delimiters, such as the quotation marks. Figure 27.3 illustrates a typical compile-time error. In this case, the name of a method (GetOption) has been misspelled, and the compiler is unable to resolve the misspelled reference.

Access compiles all currently uncompiled procedures, not just the one you're currently viewing. If you receive a compiler error, immediately modify the code to rectify the problem, and then try to compile the procedure again. If there are further compiler errors, you'll see the next error.

> **TIP**
>
> After compiling your application, you can't choose Debug ➪ Compile (it's grayed out). Before implementing an application, you should make sure that your application is compiled.

Your database is named with a standard Windows name, such as Chapter27.accdb, but Access uses an internal project name to reference the VBA code in your application. You'll see this name when you compile your database. When the database file is first created, the project name and the Windows filename will be the same. The project name isn't changed when you change the Windows filename of the ACCDB file. You can change the project name by choosing Tools ➪ *Project Name* Properties (where *Project Name* is the current internal project name).

Compiling your database only makes sure that you have no syntax errors. The compiler can check only for language problems by first recognizing the VBA statement and then checking to see that you specify the correct number of options and in the right order. The VBA compiler can't detect logical errors in your code, and it certainly can't help with errors that compile but occur while the code is executing (known as *runtime errors*).

> **TIP**
>
> If you find your database file getting unusually large, you should compact your database (see Chapter 31 for more on compacting). Every time you make a change to your program, Access stores both the changes and the original version. When you compile your program, it may double in size as the compiled and uncompiled versions of your code are stored. Compacting the database can reduce the size of the database by as much as 80 percent to 90 percent, because it eliminates all previous versions internally.

Traditional Debugging Techniques

Two widely used debugging techniques have been available since Access 1.0. The first is to insert MsgBox statements to display the value of variables, procedure names, and so on. The second common technique is to insert Debug.Print statements to output messages to the Immediate window.

Using MsgBox

Figure 27.4 shows an example of a message box displaying a long SQL statement to enable the developer to verify that the statement was properly composed by the application. The example in Figure 27.4 is found in the `modUsingMsgBox` module in the `Chapter27.accdb` example database and is shown here:

```
Public Function UsingMsgBox()
  Dim db As DAO.Database
  Dim rs As DAO.Recordset
  Dim sSQL As String

  Set db = CurrentDb

  sSQL = "SELECT DISTINCTROW OrderDetails.OrderID, " _
    & "OrderDetails.ProductID, " _
    & "Products.ProductName, " _
    & "OrderDetails.UnitPrice, " _
    & "OrderDetails.Quantity, " _
    & "OrderDetails.Discount, " _
    & "CCur(OrderDetails.UnitPrice*Quantity) AS ExtendedPrice " _
    & "FROM Products INNER JOIN OrderDetails " _
    & "ON Products.ProductID = OrderDetails.ProductID " _
    & "ORDER BY OrderDetails.OrderID;"

  MsgBox "sSQL: " & sSQL

  Set rs = db.OpenRecordset(sSQL, dbOpenForwardOnly)

  rs.Close
  Set rs = Nothing


End Function
```

FIGURE 27.4

The MsgBox statement makes a satisfactory debugging tool (with some limitations).

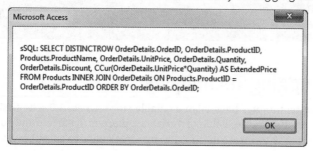

Microsoft Access

sSQL: SELECT DISTINCTROW OrderDetails.OrderID, OrderDetails.ProductID, Products.ProductName, OrderDetails.UnitPrice, OrderDetails.Quantity, OrderDetails.Discount, CCur(OrderDetails.UnitPrice*Quantity) AS ExtendedPrice FROM Products INNER JOIN OrderDetails ON Products.ProductID = OrderDetails.ProductID ORDER BY OrderDetails.OrderID;

OK

The MsgBox keyword stops code execution and displays a string in a box that must be cleared before code execution continues. Here are the advantages of using the MsgBox statement:

- The MsgBox statement is easy to use and occupies only a single line of code.
- The MsgBox statement can output many types of data.
- The message box itself pops up right on the user interface, and you don't have to have the Immediate window open or flip to the Immediate window to view the message box.
- MsgBox halts code execution, and because you know where you've put the MsgBox statements, you know exactly where the code is executing.

There are also some problems associated with MsgBox statements:

- There is nothing about the MsgBox statement to prevent it from popping up in front of an end user, causing all kinds of confusion and other problems.

> **CAUTION**
>
> It's a good idea to remove all debugging statements from your code before shipping to end users. Search your code for MsgBox and Debug.Print to make sure all debugging statements have been removed.

- Message boxes are modal, which means you can't flip to the code editor window or Immediate window (discussed in the "Running code with the Immediate window" section) to examine the value of variables or examine the code underlying the application.
- It's difficult to get the text out of a message box. You can't copy the text or select parts of it. Other than reading the text in a message box, about the only other action you can do is print the screen.

Compiler Directives

A refinement of the MsgBox technique is to use compiler directives to suppress the MsgBox statements, unless a special type of constant has been set in the code or within the Access environment. Examine the code in the following figure. Notice the #Const compiler directive above the MsgBox statement and the #If and #End If directives surrounding the MsgBox statement.

Continues

continued

```
Chapter27 - modCompilerDirective (Code)
(General)                                    FillRecordset2
#Const DEBUG1 = False

Public Sub FillRecordset2()
   Dim db As DAO.Database
   Dim rs As DAO.Recordset
   Dim sSQL As String

   Set db = DBEngine.Workspaces(0).Databases(0)

   sSQL = "SELECT DISTINCTROW OrderDetails.OrderID, " _
      & "OrderDetails.ProductID, " _
      & "Products.ProductName, " _
      & "OrderDetails.UnitPrice, " _
      & "OrderDetails.Quantity, " _
      & "OrderDetails.Discount, " _
      & "CCur(OrderDetails.UnitPrice*Quantity) AS ExtendedPrice " _
      & "FROM Products INNER JOIN OrderDetails " _
      & "ON Products.ProductID = OrderDetails.ProductID " _
      & "ORDER BY OrderDetails.OrderID;"


   #If DEBUG1 Then
      MsgBox "sSQL: " & sSQL
   #End If

   Set rs = db.OpenRecordset(sSQL, dbOpenDynaset)

   rs.Close
   Set rs = Nothing
   Set db = Nothing

End Sub
```

All the keywords beginning with the pound sign (#) are seen only by the VBA compiler. These keywords (#Const, #If, #Else, and #End If) constitute directives to the VBA compiler to include (or exclude) certain statements in the compiled version of your project.

(Conditional compilation using compiler directives is introduced in Chapter 24.)

The #Const directive you see in the preceding figure can appear anywhere in the module as long as it's placed above the #If directive. The logical place for the #Const is in the module's declaration section, since #Const values are global to the module. In the figure, the compiler constant is set to False, which means the statements between #If and #End If won't be compiled into the application's VBA project. In this case, the MsgBox statement isn't processed and doesn't appear in the user interface. Setting the #Const directive's value to True displays the MsgBox statement when the code is run.

Compiler directives also can be used for statements other than MsgBox. You could, for example, use compiler directives to conditionally compile features, additional help, or other capabilities into an application. Compiler directives are particularly effective for suppressing MsgBox statements that are used for debugging purposes and must be squelched before giving the application to users. You can easily reactivate MsgBox statements by setting the #Const statement to True.

Perhaps the biggest impediment to using compiler constants is that the #Const statement is module-level in scope. A compiler constant declared in one module is not seen by other modules in the application. This means that you must add compiler constants to every module in which you want to employ conditional compilation.

Access provides the Conditional Compilation Arguments text box in the General tab of the application's Project Properties dialog box (Tools ➪ *Application Name* Properties) to get around this constraint. As shown in the following figure, you use the Conditional Compilation Arguments text box to specify any number of compiler constants that apply to the entire application. These settings make it very easy to toggle conditional compilation from a single location in the application, instead of changing the #Const statements in every module.

Conditional Compilation Arguments and other settings set in the Project Properties dialog box are relevant only to the current application. Unlike the options you set in the Options dialog box (accessible from the Tools menu), the Project Properties settings are not shared among multiple Access applications.

In the preceding figure, notice that the value assigned to the Conditional Compilation Argument is numeric. Assigning zero to a Conditional Compilation Argument sets the argument's *logical* value to False; any nonzero value is interpreted as True. You can't use the words *True* and *False* in the Conditional Compilation Arguments text box. Setting the value to 0 (False) means that you can leave all the conditional compilation directives in your code. Setting the value to False effectively disables them, allowing your code to execute as if they don't exist.

If you're confused about the conflicting terminologies applied to the VBA conditional compilation feature, you're not alone. In a VBA code module, you assign conditional compilation constants using the #Const keyword, yet in the Project Properties dialog box, you set Conditional Compilation Arguments. Also, you assign the True and False keywords to conditional compilation constants in a VBA module, but use -1 and 0 to assign True and False, respectively, to Conditional Compilation Arguments.

Continues

continued

This is one place where the terminology and syntax used for the same purpose are quite different in different parts of an Access VBA project.

In case you're wondering, the name you apply to a compiler constant is anything you want it to be. The example in this section uses gDEBUG1 merely as a convenience, but it could have been MyCompilerConstant, Betty, DooDah, or any other valid constant name.

Using Debug.Print

The second commonly used debugging technique is using Debug.Print to output messages to the Immediate window. (Print is actually a method of the Debug object.) Figure 27.5 shows how the sSQL variable appears in the Immediate window.

FIGURE 27.5

Use Debug.Print to output messages to the Immediate window.

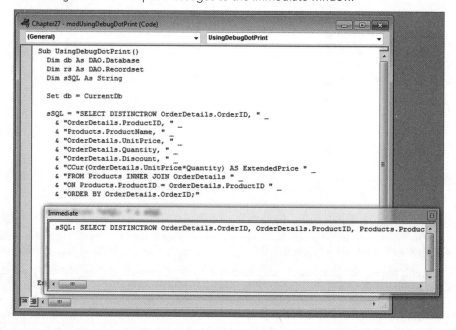

The following code can be found in the modUsingDebugDotPrint module in Chapter27 .accdb. It's almost identical to the code in modUsingMsgBox, except that instead of using MsgBox to inspect the variable, it uses Debug.Print:

```
Sub UsingDebugDotPrint()
    Dim db As DAO.Database
    Dim rs As DAO.Recordset
    Dim sSQL As String
```

```
Set db = CurrentDb

sSQL = "SELECT DISTINCTROW OrderDetails.OrderID, " _
    & "OrderDetails.ProductID, " _
    & "Products.ProductName, " _
    & "OrderDetails.UnitPrice, " _
    & "OrderDetails.Quantity, " _
    & "OrderDetails.Discount, " _
    & "CCur(OrderDetails.UnitPrice*Quantity) AS ExtendedPrice " _
    & "FROM Products INNER JOIN OrderDetails " _
    & "ON Products.ProductID = OrderDetails.ProductID " _
    & "ORDER BY OrderDetails.OrderID;"

Debug.Print "sSQL: " & sSQL

Set rs = db.OpenRecordset(sSQL, DB_OPEN_DYNASET)

rs.Close
Set rs = Nothing
Set db = Nothing


End Sub
```

Unlike the MsgBox statement, you don't have to do anything special to suppress the
Debug.Print output from the user interface. The output of Debug.Print only goes to
the Immediate window, and because end users never see the Immediate window, you don't
have to worry about a user encountering debug messages.

The problems with Debug.Print are obvious from Figure 27.5. Long strings don't wrap
in the Immediate window. Also, the Immediate window must be visible in order for you
to view its output. But these limitations are relatively harmless, and you'll frequently use
Debug.Print in your applications.

> **NOTE**
>
> Some people have reported that excessive numbers of Debug.Print statements can slow an application. Even
> though the Immediate window is not visible, Access executes the Debug.Print statements that it finds in its
> code. You may want to consider surrounding each Debug.Print statement with the compiler directives described
> in the "Compiler Directives" sidebar to remove them from the end user's copy of the application.

Using the Access Debugging Tools

Access features a full complement of debugging tools and other capabilities. You use these tools
to monitor the execution of your VBA code, halt code execution on a statement so that you can
examine the value of variables at that moment in time, and perform other debugging tasks.

Running code with the Immediate window

Open the Immediate window (also called the Debug window) by choosing View ➪ Immediate Window or by pressing Ctrl+G. You can open the Immediate window any time (for example, while you're working on a form's design). You'll sometimes find it useful to test a line of code or run a procedure (both of which are supported by the Immediate window) while you're working on a form or report.

The Immediate window is shown in Figure 27.6. The Immediate window permits certain interactivity with the code and provides an output area for Debug.Print statements. The basic debugging procedures include stopping execution so that you can examine code and variables, dynamically watching variable values, and stepping through code.

FIGURE 27.6

Get to know the Immediate window. You'll use it a lot in Access.

One of the most basic uses of the Immediate window is to run code, such as built-in functions, or subroutines and functions that you've written. Figure 27.7 shows several examples that have been run in the Immediate window.

FIGURE 27.7

Running code from the Immediate window is a common practice.

The first example in Figure 27.7 shows how to run a subprocedure (UsingDebugDotPrint) that's been added to the VBA project. This subprocedure includes a Debug.Print statement that returns a long SQL statement, and that output is shown below the procedure name when the Enter key is pressed.

In the second example, the built-in Now() function has been run from the Immediate window, returning the current date and time. The question mark (?) in front of the Now()

function name is a shortcut for the Print keyword. Instead of typing ?Now, you can type **Print Now**. Both the question mark and the Print keyword are a directive to the Immediate window to display (or print) the value returned by the Now() function.

The third example in Figure 27.7 shows calling a function (IsLastDayOfMonth) from the Immediate window. As with Now(), the question mark is used to direct VBA to return the value from the function. The one required argument is passed, and the result is shown below the function call. This function was changed from Private to Public for this example, as only Public functions can be called from the Immediate window.

Suspending execution with breakpoints

You suspend execution by setting a *breakpoint* in the code. When Access encounters a breakpoint, execution immediately stops, allowing you to switch to the Immediate window to set or examine the value of variables.

Setting a breakpoint is easy. Open the code window and click the gray Margin Indicator bar to the left of the statement on which you want execution to stop (see Figure 27.8). Alternatively, position the cursor on the line and click the Breakpoint toolbar button. The breakpoint itself appears as a large brown dot in the gray bar along the left edge of the code window and as a brown highlight behind the code. The text of the breakpoint statement appears in a bold font.

FIGURE 27.8

Setting a breakpoint is easy.

Removing a breakpoint involves nothing more than clicking the breakpoint indicator in the Margin Indicator bar. Breakpoints are also automatically removed when you close the application.

When execution reaches the breakpoint, Access halts execution and opens the module at the breakpoint (see Figure 27.9). You now use the Immediate window (see the preceding section) to examine the values of variables and perform other operations, or use any of the other debugging tools described in this section. Neither the code window nor the Immediate window is modal, so you still have full access to the development environment.

FIGURE 27.9

Execution stops on the breakpoint.

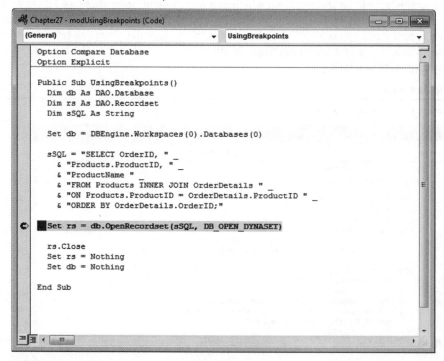

Figure 27.10 illustrates two techniques for viewing the values of variables while execution is stopped at a breakpoint. The Locals window contains the names and current values of all the variables in the current procedure. You open the Locals window by choosing Locals Window from the View menu. If you want to see the value of a variable in a slightly different format, use the Print command (?) in the Immediate window to display the variable's value.

FIGURE 27.10

Variables are in scope when in break mode.

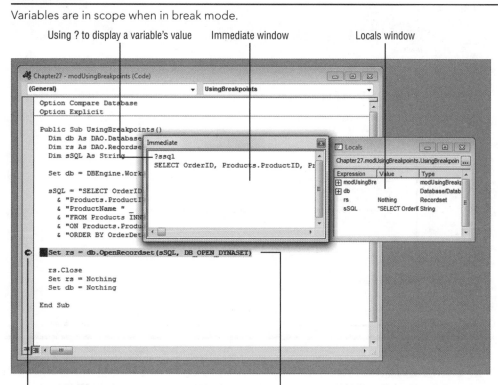

Using ? to display a variable's value   Immediate window   Locals window

27

Current position indicator arrow   Code at breakpoint

Using Stop Statements Instead of Setting Breakpoints

An alternative to setting breakpoints is to use `Stop` statements. The `Stop` statement halts execution but is more permanent than a breakpoint. A `Stop` statement, like any other VBA statement, persists from session to session until explicitly removed. You can, however, surround the `Stop` statement with conditional compilation expressions and toggle their action by changing the value assigned to a conditional compilation constant. The following figure illustrates using the `Stop` statement.

Using `Stop` is a bit dangerous, however. Because `Stop` is an executable statement, unless it's carefully controlled with compiler directives, deleted, or commented out, your application will, literally, *stop executing* in front of a user. You're probably better off using regular breakpoints than `Stop` statements in most situations.

Continues

continued

```
Chapter27 - modUsingStopStatements (Code)

(General)                                    ▼    UsingStopStatements                ▼

Option Compare Database
Option Explicit

Public Function UsingStopStatements()
    Dim db As DAO.Database
    Dim rs As DAO.Recordset
    Dim sSQL As String

    Set db = DBEngine.Workspaces(0).Databases(0)

    sSQL = "SELECT OrderID, " _
        & "Products.ProductID, " _
        & "ProductName " _
        & "FROM Products INNER JOIN OrderDetails " _
        & "ON Products.ProductID = OrderDetails.ProductID " _
        & "ORDER BY OrderDetails.OrderID;"

    Set rs = db.OpenRecordset(sSQL, DB_OPEN_DYNASET)

⇨   Stop

End Function
```

The most fundamental operation at a breakpoint is to walk through the code, one statement at a time, enabling you to view what's happening to the application's logic and variables. After you've reached a breakpoint, you use a few keystroke combinations to control
the execution of the application. You're able to step through code one statement at a time,
automatically walk through the local procedure, or step over the procedure and continue
execution on the "other side" of the procedure.

In Figure 27.11, a breakpoint has been inserted near the top of the UsingBreakpoints()
subroutine. When execution reaches this statement a breakpoint asserts itself, allowing you
to take control of program execution.

In Figure 27.12, the break has occurred, and we've clicked the Step Into button (or pressed
F8). The Step Into button executes the current statement and moves to the next statement
in the program's flow of execution. In this case, the db variable is set, and the current line
becomes the statement that sets the sSql variable (indicated by a yellow highlight and
an arrow in the left margin). At this point, the sSql assignment statement has not been
executed, and the value of sSql is an empty string. Press F8 again to execute the sSql
assignment statement and move the current line to the next line. After sSql is set, you can
see the value of sSql in the Immediate window by using ?sSql or by opening the Locals
window (described in the "Looking at variables with the Locals window" section, later in
this chapter).

FIGURE 27.11

Insert a breakpoint near the location of the code you want to step through.

FIGURE 27.12

Step Into executes one line at a time.

Consecutive clicks on the Step Into button (or pressing F8) executes the code one state-ment at a time. If a statement includes a call to a child procedure, you'll be taken to that procedure, and each of its lines will execute one at a time. If you want, you can use the Step Over button (or press Shift+F8) to execute all the code in the child routine (not one line at a time) but continue in the calling procedure one line at a time. If you've previously debugged the child routine and you're sure it contains no errors, there is no reason to walk through its code. The code in the called routine is actually executed when you click the Step Over button, changing any variables involved.

When you're satisfied that you don't need to continue walking through the code in the child procedure, click the Step Out button (or press Ctrl+F8) to complete the procedure. The Step Out button is handy if you've stepped into a called routine and you're sure there's nothing interesting going on in it.

One very nice feature in the Access VBA window is the Auto Data Tips option in the Editor tab in the Options dialog box (see Chapter 25 for more on VBE Options). With this option selected, you're able to view the value of any variable in a ScreenTip-like window by hover-ing the mouse pointer over the variable's name in the module window (see Figure 27.13).

FIGURE 27.13

Auto Data Tips are a powerful tool for debugging.

The Auto Data Tips display you see by hovering the mouse over a variable is very dynamic. The value shown in Auto Data Tips changes whenever the variable is assigned a new value. Because hovering the mouse is easy to do, you don't have to use the Immediate window to view every variable in your code. You can hover over any variable in the procedure, not just on the current line. In Figure 27.13, the mouse is over the sSql variable in the line with the execution pointer (the first argument of OpenRecordset).

> **NOTE**
> The Auto Data Tips option must be selected in the Editor tab in order for the data tip you see in Figure 27.13 to appear.

> **TIP**
> Figure 27.13 shows an Auto Data Tip for a variable with a very long string. You can't see the whole value using this method. You can, however, see the last part of the screen by holding down the Ctrl key while you hover over a variable.

One very nice feature of breakpoints is that the execution pointer (the yellow arrow in the left margin) is movable. You can use the mouse to reposition the pointer to another statement within the current procedure. For example, you can drag the pointer to a position above its current location to re-execute several lines of code.

You can easily reposition the execution pointer in such a way that your code's execution is invalid, such as moving it into the body of an If...Then...Else statement, or into the middle of a loop. Also, moving the pointer to a position *lower* in the code may mean that variables aren't set correctly or an important bit of code is ignored. Overall, though, the ability to easily re-execute a few lines of code is a valuable debugging aid.

Looking at variables with the Locals window

The Locals window (View ➪ Locals Window) shows all variables that are currently in scope, saving you from having to examine each variable one at a time. The variable's name, its data type, and its current value are displayed.

Notice the items in the Locals window in Figure 27.14. Any line in the Locals window that begins with a plus sign will unfold to reveal more information. For example, you can set a breakpoint on the rs.Close statement near the bottom of the UsingBreakpoints procedure to halt execution so that you can examine the results of the rs assignment statement. Unfolding the rs entry in the Locals window reveals all the properties of the rs object and its contents (see Figure 27.14).

FIGURE 27.14

Use the Locals window to examine the values of complex objects.

One powerful feature of the Locals window is that you can set the values of simple variables (numeric, string, and so on) by clicking the Value column in a variable's row and typing in a new value for the variable. This makes it very easy to test how various combinations of variable values affect your application.

In the preceding section, we tell you how to move the execution point within a procedure by dragging the yellow arrow with the mouse. By changing the value of a variable and moving the execution point to different places in the procedure, you can verify that the code executes as expected. Directly manipulating variables is much easier than other methods of testing the effect of outliers and unexpected values.

> **NOTE**
> The Locals window shows only module-level variables under the name of the module. Globally scoped variables are not shown in the Locals window. You have to use the Immediate window or the Auto Data Tips to inspect global variables.

Setting watches with the Watches window

The Locals window can be overrun with variables in a large application or in an application with many variables in scope. The Watches window enables you to specify just which variables you want to monitor as you single-step through your code. The value of a watched variable changes dynamically as the code runs. (You need to be at some kind of breakpoint to actually see the values.) The advantage of using the Watches window is that the variables displayed don't have to be from the local procedure. In fact, the variables in the Watch window can be from any part of the application.

Setting a watch requires a few more steps than using the Locals window or setting a breakpoint:

1. **Choose View ⇨ Watch Window to display the Watches window.**

2. **Choose Debug ⇨ Add Watch or right-click anywhere in the Watches window and select Add Watch from the shortcut menu.** The Add Watch dialog box (see Figure 27.15) appears.

3. **Enter the name of the variable or any other expression in the Expression text box.**

FIGURE 27.15

The Add Watch dialog box includes some powerful options.

The Add Watch dialog box includes some important options. In addition to the name of a variable or expression (an expression might be something like Len(sSql) = 0), there are options for specifying the module and procedure within the module to watch. In Figure 27.15, the Add Watch dialog box is set up to watch the sSql variable, but only with the UsingBreakpoints procedure in the modUsingBreakpoints module. If a variable named sSql exists in any other procedure or any other module, you can't see it here.

At the bottom of the Add Watch dialog box are the following options:

- **Watch Expression:** The variable's value will dynamically change in the Watch window. You must use an explicit breakpoint or `Stop` statement in order to observe the value of the watched variable.

- **Break When Value Is True:** This option asserts a break whenever the value of the watched variable or expression becomes `True`. If you set the expression to `Len(sSql) = 0`, a breakpoint occurs whenever the value of the `sSql` variable changes to an empty string.

- **Break When Value Changes:** This directive causes Access to halt execution whenever the value of the variable or expression changes. Obviously, this setting can generate a *lot* of breakpoints, but it can be useful if a variable is changing unexpectedly and you can't figure out where.

CAUTION

Use watches wisely. You don't want to be breaking into program execution too frequently, or you'll never get through the code. On the other hand, you don't want to overlook some important change in the value of a variable because you didn't set a watch appropriately.

Figure 27.16 shows the Watches window in action. This watch window contains the `rs` variable that is expandable and the `sSql` variable showing the string assigned.

FIGURE 27.16

The Watches window reveals all of a variable's details.

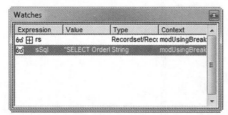

TIP

The Watches window can "float" or be docked at any side of the VBA editor window. If you don't like the Watches window's current position, use its title bar to drag it to another location. As you drag the window to a docking position, a gray rectangle appears where Access thinks you want to dock the window. Just release the mouse button when you have the window positioned in its new location, and Access will either dock the window or leave it floating freely, as you directed. The Watches window will be in the same position the next time you open the VBA editor window.

If you don't like the "docking" behavior, right-click anywhere within the body of the Watches window and deselect the Dockable option.

Using conditional watches

Although watching variables in the Locals window or Watches window can be entertaining, you can spend a lot of unproductive time hoping to see something unexpected happen. You'll probably find it much more efficient to set a *conditional watch* on a variable, and instruct the VBA engine to break when the condition you've established is met.

The Add Watch dialog box (see Figure 27.17) accepts a Boolean (True or False) expression, such as rs.Fields("OrderID").Value=10251 in the text box near the top. You specify where in the application (which procedures and which modules) the expression is applied, and you tell Access what you want the VBA engine to do when the expression is evaluated. For our purposes, we want execution to break when the loop reaches a record whose OrderID field is equal to 10251—that is, when the preceding expression is True.

FIGURE 27.17

A conditional watch halts execution when the expression rs.Fields("OrderID").Value=10251 is True.

Running the FillRecordset1 procedure in the modSQLStatement module with this watch set will cause the code to stop on the Loop statement. At this point, you can inspect the other values in the recordset via the Locals window or write some statements in the Immediate window to investigate a problem.

The conditional watches you set up through the Add Watch dialog box are added to the Watches window. The watch expression appears in the Watches window's Expression column.

You can use conditional watches in other ways, too, such as using compound conditions (X = True And Y = False), and forcing a break whenever a value changes from the value set in the Expression text box. The small example illustrated in Figure 27.17 only hints at the capabilities possible with conditional watches.

> **TIP**
>
> The Watches window is more than a static display. If needed, you can click an item in the Expression column and change a watched expression. For example, let's say you set up a watch containing an expression as `TotalSale > 100` and directed the watch to assert a breakpoint as soon as this expression becomes `True`. You may find that the breakpoint occurs much too often for your testing purposes. Instead of deleting the watch expression and starting over, you can easily modify the expression, replacing 100 with 200 or any other value you'd like to try.

You can have as many watches as you want, but, as with all other debugging tools, the watches are removed when you exit Access.

> **TIP**
>
> If, while working with conditional watches, you find a particular expression useful, you may want to write it down for future use.

Using the Call Stack window

The last debugging tool we'll examine is a bit more difficult to understand because it involves "multiple dimensions" of execution. In many Access applications, you'll have procedures that call other procedures that call still other procedures. To our knowledge, there is no practical limit on the number of procedures that can be sequentially called in a VBA project. This means you may have a "tree" of procedures many levels deep, one level of which is causing problems in your application. This situation is particularly true in the case of an application that has been modified many times, or when little thought was given to optimizing how the code in the application is used.

Even so, some very carefully designed applications end up with deeply nested code, making it difficult to understand how all the code ties together.

Imagine a function that performs a common operation (such as calculating shipping costs) in an application. As a general rule, rather than include this function in every module in the application, you'll put the function into a single module, declare it with the `Public` keyword so that it's recognized and used by the entire application, and then call it from whichever procedure needs a shipping costs calculation.

Furthermore, imagine that this application has many such functions and subroutines, each calling the other, depending on the application's logic at that moment. Finally, imagine that a user reports that the shipping fee appears to be incorrectly calculated under some conditions but not others.

You could single-step through all the code in the application, hoping to discover the cause of the erroneous shipping fee. However, this approach wouldn't be efficient. You'd be much better off setting a conditional watch on an important variable within the shipping fee function, forcing the code to break when the condition is `True`. Then open the Call Stack window, by choosing Call Stack from the View menu (see Figure 27.18), to view the path that the VBA engine has taken to reach this particular point in the code.

The bottom entry in the Call Stack window (`Chapter27.modCallStack1.Procedure1`) indicates that `Procedure1` (contained in module `modCallStack1`) was the first function called. The entry above it (`Chapter27.modCallStack2.Procedure2`) indicates that `Procedure1` called `Procedure2` (contained in `modCallStack2`) and so on. You can quite easily trace the path that the VBA code has taken to reach the current breakpoint.

FIGURE 27.18

The Call Stack window shows you how the execution point reached its current position.

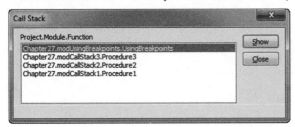

Double-click any of the items listed in the Call Stack to be taken to the statement that sent execution to the next procedure. Using the Call Stack window in conjunction with conditional watches enables you to stop code wherever relevant and to diagnose how code has executed up to the breakpoint.

Trapping Errors in Your Code

You can test and debug your code to your heart's content, but you still won't find every possible bug. All projects of a significant size contain bugs that the developers were not able to uncover during the testing and debugging phase of development. As a developer, it's your job to ensure that your program handles unexpected problems gracefully.

Understanding error trapping

When VBA encounters an error in your code, it *raises an error*. A number of things happen when an error is raised, most notably the VBA engine looks for an `On Error` statement and the `Err` object is created. You include the `On Error` keywords in your code when you want VBA to act in a certain way when an error occurs.

On Error Resume Next

An `On Error Resume Next` statement instructs VBA to ignore any errors in the statements that follow it and continue executing as if the error never happened. This can be a very dangerous statement. If statements in your code rely on prior statements being executed successfully, the errors will pile up and can cause a mess. Used judiciously, however, `On Error Resume Next` can be very useful.

VBA contains an object called a `Collection` that can hold multiple items. When items are added to a collection, the key associated with that item must be unique. If you try to add a key that already exists, an error will occur. You can use this feature of the `Collection` object with `On Error Resume Next` to get a unique list of items:

```
Sub IgnoringErrors()

    Dim colUnique As Collection
    Dim vaFruit As Variant
    Dim i As Long

    vaFruit = Array("Apple", "Pear", "Orange", "Apple", "Grape", "Pear")
    Set colUnique = New Collection

    For i = LBound(vaFruit) To UBound(vaFruit)
      On Error Resume Next
        colUnique.Add vaFruit(i), vaFruit(i)
      On Error GoTo 0
    Next i

    For i = 1 To colUnique.Count
      Debug.Print colUnique.Item(i)
    Next i

End Sub
```

In the preceding procedure, there is an array that contains duplicates. To get a list of items in the arrays without the duplicates, each item is added to a collection, and that item's name is also used as the key (the second argument to the `Add` method). When VBA encounters the `colUnique.Add` statement for an item that already exists in the collection, it raises an error. The `On Error Resume Next` statement above that line instructs VBA to ignore the error and continue processing. The duplicate item does not get added and only unique items end up in the collection.

This procedure demonstrates how a known error can be suppressed to your advantage. The very next line after the line that will generate an error instructs VBA to treat errors normally. Resetting the error handler in this way ensures that you don't suppress errors unintentionally. It's also a good practice to indent any statements between the `On Error` statements to provide a visual cue about which errors should be suppressed.

CAUTION

`On Error Resume Next` suppresses all errors that would otherwise cause the code to stop. While it can be useful to suppress particular errors, it doesn't know the difference between the error that you want to ignore and the error that you unintentionally coded. Be sure to carefully debug the statements covered by `On Error Resume Next`.

On Error Goto 0

In the preceding example, you used On Error Resume Next to ignore any errors. If you don't tell it otherwise, VBA will continue ignoring errors for the rest of the subroutine, which may not be what you want. In that example, the On Error GoTo 0 statement was used a few lines later to reset the error handler to the default. If no On Error statement were included in the code, VBA would break on any error and display a message. The On Error GoTo 0 statement does the same thing. Typically, it's used with On Error Resume Next to return the error handler back to the default state after intentionally suppressing a particular error.

On Error GoTo Label

The most common use of On Error is to direct the program flow to a label in your procedure. Labels are special statements that provide anchors in your code. Labels are text followed by a colon and cannot be indented. When VBA raises an error after On Error GoTo Label, the program branches to the line just below the label and continues executing:

```
Sub BranchError()

    Dim x As Long

    On Error GoTo ErrHandler

    x = 1 / 0

    Debug.Print x

ErrHandler:
    MsgBox "An error occurred"

End Sub
```

In this simple example, an error is generated by attempting to divide by zero. When the error is raised, VBA branches to the line below ErrHandler:, displays a message box, and continues on to the End Sub statement. The Debug.Print statement is never executed.

The Resume keyword

We've seen how Resume Next can be used with On Error to ignore certain errors. Resume can also be used on its own. Used alone, Resume branches the program back to the line that caused the error and the error is re-raised. This is useful when you want to handle errors but have the option of inspecting the line that caused the error, but it can cause an infinite loop of raising errors and resuming if you're not careful.

Resume can also be used with a label to branch program execution elsewhere. Generally, Resume Label branches to a part of the code that performs clean-up duty and exits the procedure. A label is a special line in VBA code that ends with a colon (:). Labels are like bookmarks or anchors in your code—they're places that you can jump to, such as when using a `Resume` statement:

```
Sub ErrorResumeOptions()

    Dim x As Long
    Dim lResp As Long

    On Error GoTo ErrHandler

    x = 1 / 0

    Debug.Print x

ErrExit:
    Exit Sub

ErrHandler:
    lResp = MsgBox("Do you want to inspect the error?", vbYesNo)
    If lResp = vbYes Then
        Stop
        Resume
    Else
        Resume ErrExit
    End If

End Sub
```

Like the previous example, this code intentionally raises an error by attempting to divide by zero. The error handler is called, and the program is branched to the `ErrHandler:` label. Inside the error handler, the user is asked whether she would like to inspect the error. Clicking `No` on the message box executes the `Resume ErrExit` statement, and execution is branched to that label where `Exit Sub` is executed. Clicking `Yes` first executes a `Stop` statement. Without the `Stop` statement, `Resume` would send program execution back to the line that caused the error, the error would be raised again, and the program would head back to the error handler. `Stop` allows the developer to step through the code line-by-line, first executing `Resume` to see what line caused the error and then inspecting variables to diagnose the problem.

The Err object

In addition to raising an error and branching based on `On Error`, VBA also creates an `Err` object that contains information about the error. In fact, the `Err` object is always present, even when no error has been raised. When VBA encounters an error, regardless of whether there is error handling in place, the `Number` property of the `Err` object is set to the number of the error that occurred. When no error has been encountered, `Number` is zero.

The `Err` object also has a Description property. The error number may not be meaningful to you, but the Description property generally helps you identify the error.

Including error handling in your procedures

Some procedures are so trivial that error handling is not needed. For all other procedures, you should include some error handling to avoid having your users thrust into the VB Editor when an unexpected error occurs.

Your error handling technique should include an `On Error GoTo Label` statement near the top of the procedure, suspension of the error handling in the code when needed, an exit label that cleans up any in-process variables, and an error handling label that displays the error and controls program flow.

Here'a a typical procedure with error handling:

```
Sub ATypicalErrorHandler()

    Dim statements

    On Error GoTo ErrHandler

    Multiple statements

    On Error Resume Next
      Intentional errors to ignore
    On Error GoTo ErrHandler

    Multiple statements

ErrExit:
    Clean up code
    Exit Sub

ErrHandler:
    MsgBox Err.Description, vbOKOnly
    If gbDebugMode Then
      Stop
      Resume
    Else
      Resume ErrExit
    End If

End Sub
```

The procedure starts with `On Error GoTo ErrHandler`, which directs the program to the `ErrHandler` label if an unexpected error occurs. In the middle of the procedure is an example of stopping the error handler using `On Error Resume Next` to trap an intentional error. The error handler is restarted after the statements with the intentional errors. Above the error handling section, the clean-up and exiting statements are executed. If there are no errors, this code will be run and the procedure will complete without running the error handling code.

The error handling section displays a message using the Description property of the Err object. There is a global variable, gbDebugMode, that the developer can set to True during debugging and False when the application is sent to the users. If gbDebugMode is True, the program stops and the developer can step through the code to investigate the error. Otherwise, the ErrExit portion of the code is executed and the user sees only the message box.

Part VII

Advanced Access Programming Techniques

A ccess is all about managing data. Once you become familiar with VBA, it's a natural progression to want to use code to manage your data. Access provides multiple ways to access and manipulate data via VBA.

Chapters 28 and 29 give you all the tools you'll need access and control your data with code, including learning about the DAO and ADO object models.

Chapter 30 teaches you how to change the Ribbon in Access to give your application increased ease-of-use and a more professional look.

Chapter 31 explains the processes you'll need to know to make your Access application ready to ship to your users.

Finally, if you're in a SharePoint environment, chapter 32 will introduce you to the skills required to integrate Access with SharePoint.

IN THIS PART

Chapter 28
Accessing Data with VBA

Chapter 29
Advanced Data Access with VBA

Chapter 30
Customizing the Ribbon

Chapter 31
Preparing Your Access Application for Distribution

Chapter 32
Integrating Access with SharePoint

Accessing Data with VBA

IN THIS CHAPTER

Working with Access data

Looking at DAO objects

Examining the ADO object model

Updating a table with VBA code

Data access and data management are at the core of any database application. Although you can do a decent job building applications with bound forms and reports, using Visual Basic for Applications (VBA) code to access and manipulate data directly provides far greater flexibility than a bound application can. Anything that can be done with bound forms and controls can be done with a bit of VBA code using ActiveX data objects (ADO) or data access objects (DAO) to retrieve and work with data.

The VBA language offers a full array of powerful commands for manipulating records in a table, providing data for controls on a form, or just about anything else. This chapter provides some in-depth examples of working with procedures that use DAO or SQL and ADO to manipulate database data.

ON THE WEB

In the `Chapter28.accdb` database, you'll find a number of forms to use as a starting point and other completed forms to compare to the forms you change in this example.

Working with Data

The first thing to note when discussing data access objects is that the DAO and ADO object models are separate from the Access object model. DAO and ADO represent the objects managed and "owned" by the Access database engines (ACE or Jet), which are software components installed along with Office. In the past, Excel (with the MSQuery add-on) and Visual Basic (the stand-alone application development product) could directly use the Jet database engine or access it through open database connectivity (ODBC) or Microsoft Query.

Using Access VBA enables you to manipulate your database objects behind the scenes, giving you a great amount of flexibility within your applications. Access provides two different object models for working with data: DAO and ADO.

DAO is the default data management library for working with data in Access. It is included in all new projects as part of the Microsoft Office Access database engine Object Library. The DAO object model is a rich and complex hierarchy that is optimized for working with Access data (or more specifically, data in the ACE format). Unless there is something about a project that would benefit from using ADO, most Access developers use DAO to manipulate their data.

ADO is based on Microsoft's ActiveX technology, which provides the basis for independent objects that perform complex tasks without input from their hosts. Unlike DAO's rich hierarchy, the ADO object model is flat and sparse. Only a few objects are needed to perform virtually all data access tasks in Access applications. ADO is most commonly used when your project includes external data.

As you learn about and work with DAO and ADO in your VBA code, you might find that DAO feels like you're manipulating your data directly and that ADO feels like you're just passing SQL statements. That's because DAO was built specifically to manipulate ACE data and ADO is meant to be able to work with any compatible database.

Working with DAO and ADO in VBA procedures provides you with much greater flexibility than dealing strictly with forms and reports bound to queries and tables. As you'll see in the rest of this chapter, relatively few lines of code perform complex operations on data, such as updating or deleting existing records, or adding new records to tables. Using VBA code means that an application can respond to current conditions on a form, such as missing or incorrect values. It's quite easy to perform ad hoc queries against data that would otherwise require complex queries with many parameters.

Entire books—*big* books—have been written on the topics covered in this chapter. All we can do in this chapter is provide you with some fundamental examples of using DAO and ADO in Access applications, and, coupled with the material in the other chapters in this book, you should be well prepared to incorporate VBA-based data management in your Access applications.

> **NOTE**
>
> ADO and DAO are not equivalent in every regard. Both syntaxes enable you to add to or modify the data in tables, build recordsets, work with data in recordsets, and populate forms with data. However, ADO has a distinct edge when it comes to working with external data sources. As you'll soon see, ADO requires a provider that defines the data source used by the ADO objects in an application. ADO providers are specific to the data source, such as SQL Server or Access. The provider endows the ADO objects with special abilities (such as the ability to test the connection to the data source), depending on the underlying data sources. DAO, on the other hand, is a more generic data access syntax and is not specific to any one data source. DAO also natively understands the newer Access data types, like the Attachment data type.

Although Access is not strictly object oriented, it is most certainly object *based*. The remainder of this chapter describes the object models you use in VBA code to perform data-management tasks in your Access applications. An *object model* is simply the arrangement of the objects that perform the data-management tasks. A sound understanding of the DAO and ADO object models is an essential requirement when using VBA code to manage Access data.

Many of the objects described in this chapter contain a collection of zero or more objects. A *collection* is a container holding all the members of a certain type of object. (A collection is, itself, an object.)

A collection is like a stack of baseball cards. Each card in the stack is different from all the other cards, but all baseball cards have certain characteristics (like size, the statistics printed on the back, and so on) in common. In Access, a *recordset* object (either ADO or DAO) contains a collection of *field* objects. Every recordset object shares certain characteristics with all other recordset objects, and every field object is similar to all other fields in certain ways.

The name of a collection is almost always the plural of the object type within the collection. Therefore, a `Fields` collection contains a number of different `Field` objects.

> **NOTE**
>
> It's important to know when a term applies to an object of the same name or is just the name of a general category of database items. In this book, a capitalized word like *Field* refers to a `Field` object, in contrast to *field* (lowercase), which is a generic reference to any field in any table. Similarly, *Fields* means a `Fields` collection, while *fields* refers to a number of different fields.

Each object comes with a collection of properties and methods. Each property or method provides you with a way to define the object or represents an action you use to direct the object to perform its job.

An object's `Properties` collection is made up of a number of `Property` objects. Each `Property` object has its *own* set of properties. Properties can be referenced directly, created through the Access interface, or created by a user and added to the `Properties` collection. You generally refer to a property in this way: *ObjectName.PropertyName*. For example, to refer to the `Name` property of a field, the syntax would be as follows:

```
MyField.Name
```

Methods are a little different. A method is an *action* an object can perform or is an action performed *on* an object. The purpose of a data access object is to manipulate or display data in a database; therefore, each object must have some way to act upon that data. You can't add or delete methods in the objects. (This is one of the several ways that Access is not truly object oriented.) You can only invoke the method on the object. For example, the following code places the record pointer of the recordset MyRecordset at the next record:

```
MyRecordset.MoveNext
```

Like properties, every object has a set of methods applicable to that object.

If you ever need to know more about an object, use the Object Browser (see Figure 28.1). Open the Object Browser from within the VBA Editor by pressing F2 or by choosing View ⇨ Object Browser from the menu in the VBA Editor window. The Object Browser lets you examine each object's methods and properties and the arguments you can expect when using them. The Object Browser is used by all Microsoft applications that feature VBA as their language engine.

28

FIGURE 28.1

The Object Browser provides a view into an object's properties and methods.

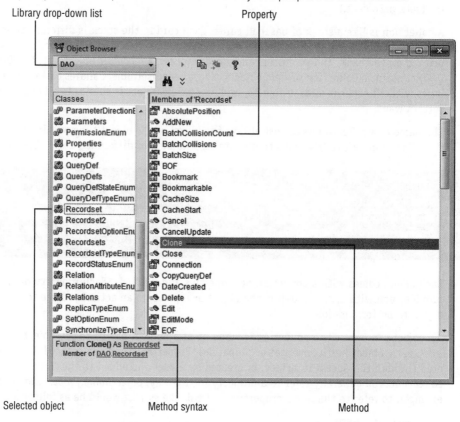

Library drop-down list   Property

Selected object   Method syntax   Method

The Object Browser is easy to use. Select a library (DAO, for example) from the drop-down list in the upper-left corner; then scroll through the object list on the left side of the browser to find an object of interest. Selecting an object fills the right-side list with the object's properties, methods, and events (if applicable). Clicking a property, method, or event reveals the item's syntax in the area below the lists.

Although the Object Browser doesn't show specific code examples, very often seeing the syntax associated with the property, method, or event may be enough to get you started writing VBA code, or to clarify the object's details.

Understanding DAO Objects

DAO is the default Access data access object model. DAO has been included in Access since the very beginning and Microsoft has been updating DAO to keep pace with changes in the Access database engine.

DAO objects are arranged in a hierarchical fashion. Certain objects are subordinate to other objects, and they can't exist without an instance of their parent object. The top-level DAO object is DBEngine, and all other DAO objects are descendants of DBEngine (see Figure 28.2).

Each of the most frequently used DAO objects is described later in this section.

Generally speaking, the DAO hierarchy closely follows the arrangement of Access database objects. For example, an Access table (which is a TableDef object) contains fields (each of which is a Field object). A field has a set of properties you use to specify the details of its data type, the default value, validation rules, and so on.

FIGURE 28.2

The DAO object model.

> **NOTE**
> For clarity's sake, the set of properties associated with each DAO object is left out of Figure 28.2. But you can safely assume that every object in Figure 28.2 includes a number of properties.

Each DAO object also has a collection of properties appropriate for its object type. A `TableDef` object may have some properties in common with a `QueryDef`, but each object has properties that are unique to its object type. While both `QueryDef` and `TableDef` objects have a `Name` property, only a `QueryDef` has a `SQL` property. The same is true of methods. Each DAO object has actions that only it can perform. For example, an action query defined by a `QueryDef` has an `Execute` method, but a `TableDef` does not. Learning which properties and methods apply to each DAO object is perhaps the biggest challenge facing Access developers.

> **NOTE**
>
> As you read the following sections, you'll notice that details have been omitted from the discussions of each type of data access object. Because of the numerous properties and methods associated with each DAO object, and the many ways these objects are used in Access applications, it's not possible to present a detailed description of the entire DAO object model in a single chapter. Instead, examples of specific ways to use DAO (and ADO) are given throughout this book. Please refer to the index to find the chapters and sections in this book that discuss particular data access objects.

> **NOTE**
>
> Access 2007 introduced ACE (Microsoft Access Engine), a new database engine for the Office products. ACE is why Access 2007 through 2019 support advanced features such as attachment and multi-value fields. Because of the new data types, ACE required an updated version of DAO (called ACEDAO) to support the new capabilities. The biggest differences between DAO and ACEDAO are the introduction of the `Recordset2` and `Field2` objects and new properties and methods required to support the features introduced with Access 2007. The examples in this chapter use ACEDAO, but the data access model is referred to as DAO for simplicity. The Access 2003 MDB format only supports DAO 3.6, not ACEDAO.

The DAO DBEngine object

The `DBEngine` object, the object representing the ACE engine, is at the very top of the DAO hierarchy. It isn't a member of any collection, and all collections are children of `DBEngine`. There is only one instance of this object, and it's one of the few data access objects that you can't create yourself. You open the `DBEngine` object when you start Access and issue a DAO operation. It has relatively few properties and methods. For property changes to take effect, they must be issued *before* a data access object operation has been performed; otherwise, you'll receive an error. Because `DBEngine` is at the top of the hierarchy, you almost always begin a DAO code sequence with `DBEngine`.

The DAO Workspace object

A `Workspace` object represents an open, active session for each user working with Access. All databases are opened within a workspace, either as a default database session or one that has been created using the `CreateWorkspace` method of the `DBEngine` object.

Security is also implemented from `Workspace` objects (but, only for the MDB file format). The security methods available to `Workspace` objects allow you to create your own security interfaces and routines. If necessary, you can create users or groups using the `CreateUser` or `CreateGroup` methods of the `Workspace` object.

The DAO Database object

A `Database` object represents an open Access file. Access is able to directly open a number of different database formats. When you work directly with the ACE or Jet database engines, your database could be any number of sources, such as another ACCDB or an ODBC data source. The distinguishing feature is how you set your database object variables.

The following code refers to the currently open Access database:

```
Dim daDb As DAO.Database
Set daDb = CurrentDb
```

`CurrentDb` is a method of the Access `Application` object, which represents the entire Access environment and all its objects. `CurrentDb` is a fast, easy way to access the database that the user is currently working with.

It's also possible to open an Access database *outside* the current database:

```
Dim daDb As DAO.Database
Set daDb = OpenDatabase("C:\Northwind.mdb")
```

Notice that the `OpenDatabase` method accepts the path to an existing MDB or ACCDB file. The `OpenDatabase` method may fail, depending on whether the external Access database is available or whether its current state prevents opening from another Access application.

If you mix DAO and ADO in your project, be sure to prefix DAO object type declarations with DAO so that Access is clear as to which library to use when setting up the object. If you only use DAO, you don't need to use the library name (simply `Dim daDb As Database` in the preceding example), but some developers include it for clarity. The examples in this book will generally include the library name prefix.

28

The DAO TableDef object

The DAO `TableDef` object represents a table in an Access database. The table may be local to the current database or linked to an external source. The following procedure (which is included in the `Chapter28.accdb` example database) creates a new table named MyTempTable, adds three text fields to it, and adds the table to the current database's `TableDefs` collection:

```
Public Sub CreateNewTableDef()

    Dim daDb As DAO.Database
    Dim daTdf As DAO.TableDef

    Const sTABLENAME As String = "MyTempTable"

    Set daDb = Application.CurrentDb

    'Delete an existing table, but ignore the error
    'if table doesn't exist
    On Error Resume Next
      daDb.TableDefs.Delete sTABLENAME
    On Error GoTo 0

    ' Create a new TableDef object:
    Set daTdf = daDb.CreateTableDef(sTABLENAME)

    With daTdf
        ' Create fields and append them to the TableDef
        .Fields.Append .CreateField("FirstName", dbText)
        .Fields.Append .CreateField("LastName", dbText)
        .Fields.Append .CreateField("Phone", dbText)
    End With

    ' Append the new TableDef object to the current database:
    daDb.TableDefs.Append daTdf

    daDb.Close
    Set daDb = Nothing

End Sub
```

Running this code in the `Chapter28.accdb` database creates a new table named MyTempTable, a permanent addition to the database. Notice that the `CreateNewTableDef` procedure deletes this table if it exists, before creating it as a new `TableDef`. Access won't be able to append the new `TableDef` object to its `TableDefs` collection if a table with the same name already exists in the database.

The CreateNewTableDef procedure includes two statements that control how Access handles errors in this code. Chapter 27 discusses the VBA error handling statements and explains why you'd use `On Error Resume Next` and `On Error GoTo 0` in a procedure such as this.

`TableDef` objects are stored in the `TableDefs` collection. The following procedure displays the names of all `TableDef` objects (including hidden and system tables) in the current database:

```
Public Sub DisplayAllTableDefs()

  Dim daDb As DAO.Database
  Dim daTdf As DAO.TableDef

  Set daDb = CurrentDb

  With daDb

    Debug.Print .TableDefs.Count & _
      " TableDefs in " & .Name

    For Each daTdf In .TableDefs
       Debug.Print , daTdf.Name
    Next daTdf
  End With

  daDb.Close
  Set daDb = Nothing

End Sub
```

The DAO QueryDef object

A `QueryDef` object represents a saved query in an Access database. Using VBA code, you can point a `QueryDef` object variable at an existing query (or create a new query) and change the query's SQL statement, populate parameters used by the query, and execute the query. The query could be a select query that returns a recordset or an action query that modifies code in the tables underlying the query.

Creating a `QueryDef` in code is similar to creating a `TableDef` except that the new `QueryDef` doesn't have to be explicitly appended to the database's `QueryDefs` collection.

28

The CreateNewQueryDef procedure shown here creates a new QueryDef that queries records from the Customers table:

```
Public Sub CreateNewQueryDef()

    Dim daDb As DAO.Database
    Dim daQdf As DAO.QueryDef

    Const sQRYNAME As String = "MyQueryDef"

    Set daDb = CurrentDb

    Set daQdf = daDb.CreateQueryDef(sQRYNAME, _
      "SELECT * FROM tblCustomers;")

    daDb.Close
    Set daDb = Nothing

End Sub
```

In fact, as soon as the CreateQueryDef method is executed, Access adds the new QueryDef to the database. You must explicitly delete the QueryDef if you don't want it to appear in the Navigation pane:

```
CurrentDb.TableDefs.Delete "QueryDefName"
```

You could, if desired, create a QueryDef without a name. In this case, the new QueryDef is not saved and does not show up in the Navigation pane. This technique might be useful, for instance, if you're filling a combo box or list box with data and you don't want to create a permanent QueryDef because the criteria changes every time the code is executed.

One time-honored advanced Access technique is dynamically changing an existing QueryDef object's SQL statement. Once the SQL property has been changed, the query returns the recordset specified by the new SQL statement:

```
Public Sub ChangeQueryDefSQL()

    CurrentDb.QueryDefs("MyQueryDef").SQL = _
      "SELECT * FROM tblProducts;"

End Sub
```

Notice that the ChangeQueryDefSQL procedure doesn't declare any object variables, such as daDb or daQdf, to refer to the Database or QueryDef. Instead, the procedure uses CurrentDb to refer to the Database and accesses the SQL property directly on the object returned by the QueryDefs property. It is advisable to use object variables for longer procedures, but for short procedures like this one, using CurrentDb directly is easier and can actually improve readability.

It's very easy to populate a DAO `Recordset` object directly from a `QueryDef` (see the next section for more on the `Recordset` object):

```
Public Function GetRecordset() As DAO.Recordset

    Dim daRs As DAO.Recordset
    Dim daQdf As DAO.QueryDef

    Set daQdf = CurrentDb.QueryDefs("MyQueryDef")

    'Open Recordset from QueryDef.
    Set daRs = daQdf.OpenRecordset(dbOpenSnapshot)

    daRs.MoveLast
    Debug.Print "Number of records = " & daRs.RecordCount

    Set GetRecordset = daRs

End Sub
```

The locally declared `Recordset` object (daRs) is assigned to the function just before the function ends. This is one way for a procedure to build recordsets without having to duplicate the code setting up the recordset and running the `QueryDef` every place a recordset is needed by an application.

The DAO Recordset object

`Recordset` objects are the primary way to manipulate data in code. Using a `Recordset` object's methods you can update, edit, and delete records, move forward and backward within the recordset, or jump to specific records.

A `Recordset` object can be one of five types; the type you specify depends on your needs. Table 28.1 describes the different types of recordsets.

TABLE 28.1 Recordset Types

Type	Description
Table	Data from a single, native Access table and not a linked table or query.
Dynaset	Data from any table or query that can be updated, added to, or deleted from. This is the most common type used.
Snapshot	Similar to Dynaset, but the records are read-only. If you know you only want to read the data, this can be faster than Dynaset.
Forward Only	Identical to Snapshot (read-only), but you can only move forward through the records. If you only want to loop through the records and read data, this type is the fastest.
Dynamic	Used for ODBCDirect Workspaces, which are outside the scope of this book.

28

You specify the type of recordset using the dbOpenTable, dbOpenDynaset, dbOpenSnapshot, and dbOpenForwardOnly constants as arguments of the OpenRecordset method of a Database object. The following example shows how to open a Snapshot-type recordset based on a SQL string:

```
Dim daDb As DAO.Database
Dim daRs As DAO.Recordset
Dim sSql As String
sSql = "SELECT * FROM tblCustomers;"
Set daDb = CurrentDb
Set daRs = daDb.OpenRecordset(sSql, dbOpenSnapshot)
```

If you don't explicitly choose a type of Recordset, Access uses what it believes to be the most efficient method. The Dynaset-type recordset is the most commonly used because it's the most versatile. The other types restrict what you can do with the recordset in exchange for better performance.

Navigating recordsets

Recordsets wouldn't be much use if all you could do is open and close them. Depending on context, the word *recordset* means several different things:

- The rows of data returned by a query
- The data bound to an Access form
- The object filled with data as the result of a DAO operation

In all cases, however, a recordset is a data structure containing rows and columns of data. The rows, of course, are *records*, while the columns are *fields*.

It makes sense that DAO provides ways to *navigate* through a recordset. When viewing a table or query results as a datasheet, you can use the vertical and horizontal scroll bars or arrow keys to move up and down, left and right, through the Datasheet view of the recordset. It's not surprising, then, that Recordset objects support methods for moving through the records contained in a recordset.

The following procedure, RecordsetNavigation, demonstrates the fundamental recordset navigation methods:

```
Public Sub RecordsetNavigation()

    Dim daDb As DAO.Database
    Dim daRs As DAO.Recordset

    Set daDb = CurrentDb
    Set daRs = daDb.OpenRecordset("tblCustomers", dbOpenTable)

    Debug.Print daRs!CustomerID, daRs!Company

    daRs.MoveNext
    Debug.Print daRs!CustomerID, daRs!Company
```

```
daRs.MoveLast
Debug.Print daRs!CustomerID, daRs!Company

daRs.MovePrevious
Debug.Print daRs!CustomerID, daRs!Company

daRs.MoveFirst
Debug.Print daRs.Fields("CustomerID").Value, _
  daRs.Fields("Company").Value

daRs.Close
Set daRs = Nothing
Set daDb = Nothing

End Sub
```

This procedure begins by setting a variable to the current database and opening a
Recordset object populated with data from tblCustomers. It immediately displays the
CustomerID and Company from the very first record; then it moves around the recordset a
few rows at a time, displaying the CustomerID and Company for each record along the way.
It ends by returning to the first record and displaying its data. The output produced by
RecordsetNavigation is shown in Figure 28.3.

28

FIGURE 28.3

Demonstrating recordset navigation.

Obviously, this is a trivial example meant to demonstrate how easily recordsets can be navi-
gated. As a developer, you're free to work with any record in the recordset, moving up and
down the rows as needed.

Recordsets support the concept of a *current record pointer.* Only one record at a time within
a recordset is *current.* When you make changes to a recordset or navigate through its rows,
your code affects only the current record.

The RecordsetNavigation procedure also demonstrates two methods for referencing
individual fields within a record: using the bang operator (!) and the Fields collection.

After moving to a row, individual fields are referenced as members of the recordset. Access works on just one record at a time, so any reference to a field evaluates to the field within the current record.

Detecting the recordset end or beginning

The MovePrevious and MoveNext methods move the current record pointer one row through the recordset. If the pointer is at the very first or very last record, these methods move the pointer off the beginning or end of the recordset without raising an error. When you're navigating a recordset, you need to be sure the current record pointer is resting on a valid record before referencing data or executing an action on the record.

The Recordset object supports two Boolean properties, EOF and BOF, that indicate when the current record pointer is at the end or beginning (respectively) of the recordset. (EOF and BOF are acronyms for *end of file* and *beginning of file*.) EOF and BOF are both False when the record pointer is on a valid record. EOF is True only when the record pointer has moved past the last record in the recordset, and BOF is True only when the record pointer has moved backward before the first record in the recordset. EOF and BOF are both True *only* when the recordset contains no records at all.

The Use_EOF_BOF procedure illustrates using EOF and BOF:

```
Public Sub Use_EOF_BOF()

    Dim daDb As DAO.Database
    Dim daRs As DAO.Recordset
    Dim sSql As String

    sSql = "SELECT * FROM tblCustomers" _
      & " WHERE State = 'NY'" _
      & " ORDER BY Company;"

    Set daDb = CurrentDb
    Set daRs = daDb.OpenRecordset(sSql, dbOpenDynaset)

    If daRs.BOF And daRs.EOF Then
        Debug.Print "No records to process"
        Exit Sub
    End If

    Do Until daRs.EOF
        Debug.Print daRs!Company
        daRs.MoveNext
    Loop

    daRs.MoveLast

    Do Until daRs.BOF
        Debug.Print daRs!Company
        daRs.MovePrevious
```

```
        Loop

        daRs.Close
        Set daRs = Nothing
        Set daDb = Nothing

    End Sub
```

In this example, if both BOF and EOF are True, a message is printed and the procedure is exited. If there are records, the code loops through them forward then backward, printing as it goes. The Do Until block of statements is a common way to loop through a recordset.

Counting records

It's often very useful to know how many records are in a recordset before beginning operations that may take a long time. A user may unwisely select criteria that return too many records to handle efficiently, and you may want your code to alert them before processing a large recordset. Fortunately, Recordset objects provide a RecordCount property that tells you exactly how many records are present in the recordset. The following UseRecordCount subroutine uses the RecordCount property to display the total records as the recordset is processed:

```
    Public Sub UseRecordCount()

        Dim adRs As ADODB.Recordset
        Dim lCnt As Long

        Set adRs = New ADODB.Recordset
        adRs.ActiveConnection = CurrentProject.Connection
        adRs.CursorType = adOpenStatic

        adRs.Open "SELECT * FROM tblCustomers;"

        Do While Not adRs.EOF
          lCnt = lCnt + 1
          Debug.Print "Record " & lCnt & " of " & adRs.RecordCount
          adRs.MoveNext
        Loop

        adRs.Close
        Set adRs = Nothing

    End Sub
```

RecordCount is a convenient way to determine whether a recordset contains any records at all. The only issue with RecordCount is that, on large recordsets, RecordCount penalizes performance. The Recordset object actually counts the number of records it contains, halting execution until the count is complete.

A much faster way to detect an empty recordset is determining whether EOF and BOF are both True:

```
If daRs.BOF And daRs.EOF Then
    Debug.Print "No records to process"
    Exit Sub
End If
```

If BOF and EOF are both True, the cursor is both before the first record and after the last record at the same time. That only can happen when there are no records.

The DAO Field objects (recordsets)

Field objects within recordsets represent a column of data from a table or returned by a query. Recordset Field objects differ from their TableDef and QueryDef counterparts in that they actually contain a data value. Each TableDef object contains a Fields collection containing the data held within the table represented by the TableDef.

You'll see many, many references to DAO (and ADO) fields in this book, so there isn't much to discuss at this point. In the meantime, it's enough to know that the DAO Field object supports many more properties than are visible in the Access Table Designer. The Chapter28.accdb example database includes the following procedure that enumerates all the "valid" properties of the Company field in tblCustomers:

```
Public Sub DisplayFieldProperties()

    Dim daDb As DAO.Database
    Dim daTdf As DAO.TableDef
    Dim daFld As DAO.Field
    Dim daProp As DAO.Property

    Set daDb = CurrentDb
    Set daTdf = daDb.TableDefs("tblCustomers")

    Set daFld = daTdf.Fields("Company")

    Debug.Print "Properties in Company field:"

    For Each daProp In daFld.Properties

      On Error Resume Next
        Debug.Print Space(2) & daProp.Name & " = " & daProp.Value
      On Error GoTo 0
    Next daProp

    daDb.Close

End Sub
```

Not every property associated with a `Field` object is *valid* at a particular time. Some properties are set only after the field contains data or when the field is involved in an index. For example, the `Value` property of the `Field` object cannot be referenced directly from code. Instead, you set or get the value of a field only through the field's membership in a `Recordset` object. The `On Error Resume Next` statement allows this code to run, in spite of invalid properties. The errors that may occur when invalid properties are referenced by this code are ignored.

Understanding ADO Objects

The ADO object model is shown in Figure 28.4. As you can see, the ADO object model is flatter and simpler than the DAO model and includes only a few objects. Notice that the ADO object model is not hierarchical. Each object stands alone and is not subordinate to another object in the model.

FIGURE 28.4

The ADO object model.

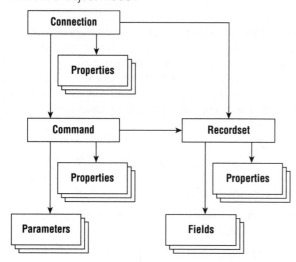

Using ADO objects requires a reference to the ADO library. Figure 28.5 shows the References dialog box (opened by choosing Tools ⇨ References in the VBA Editor window) with the ADO library (Microsoft ActiveX Data Objects) selected. The exact version of the ADO library installed on your machine may vary, and, in fact, there may be more than one ADO library in the References dialog box. Select the highest-numbered library if you want to use the latest version available to Access. You may want to select a lower-numbered library to maintain compatibility with an existing system.

FIGURE 28.5

Referencing the ADO library.

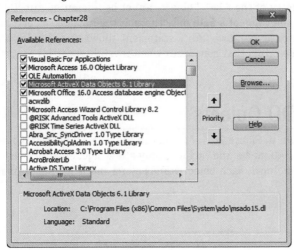

In the following code examples, all the ADO object variables are referenced as ADODB object types. Although not entirely necessary, prefixing object type names with a library reference clears up any ambiguity that Access might have regarding the type of object referenced by the VBA statements. For example, both ADO and DAO support a `Recordset` object. Unless the object type declaration is prefixed with either ADODB or DAO, Access may misunderstand *which* type of recordset is referenced in a VBA statement.

The ADO Connection object

As its name suggests, the `Connection` object provides a connection to a data source. Having access to a data source is necessary for any data operation, so the `Connection` object is required in virtually any scenario involving ADO.

After the ADO library has been referenced, creating a `Connection` object is simple (the ADO library is referenced as ADODB in VBA code):

```
Dim adConn as ADODB.Connection
Set adConn = New ADODB.Connection
```

The `Connection` must be opened before it can be used. The following statement is the easiest way to open an ADO `Connection`:

```
adConn.Open CurrentProject.Connection
```

In this case, the `Connection` connects to the current database. As you'll soon see, a `Connection` object requires a number of properties to be set before it can successfully open, but opening a `Connection` on the current database's `Connection` property provides all those settings. `CurrentProject.Connection` is actually a long string (specifically, a *connection string*) that includes all the information needed about the current database. A typical `Connection` property setting is as follows:

```
Provider=Microsoft.ACE.OLEDB.12.0;User ID=Admin;
Data Source=C:\...\Chapter28.accdb;
Mode=Share Deny None;Extended Properties="";
Jet OLEDB:System database=C:\...\Microsoft\Access\System.mdw;
Jet OLEDB:Registry Path=Software\...\Access Connectivity Engine;
Jet OLEDB:Database Password="";
Jet OLEDB:Engine Type=6;
Jet OLEDB:Database Locking Mode=1;
Jet OLEDB:Global Partial Bulk Ops=2;
Jet OLEDB:Global Bulk Transactions=1;
Jet OLEDB:New Database Password="";
Jet OLEDB:Create System Database=False;
Jet OLEDB:Encrypt Database=False;
Jet OLEDB:Don't Copy Locale on Compact=False;
Jet OLEDB:Compact Without Replica Repair=False;
Jet OLEDB:SFP=False;
Jet OLEDB:Support Complex Data=True;
Jet OLEDB:Bypass UserInfo Validation=False;
Jet OLEDB:Limited DB Caching=False;
Jet OLEDB:Bypass ChoiceField Validation=False
```

28

NOTE

Line breaks have been added to the preceding code for clarity, and some lines have been shortened.

This is actually considerably more than the `Connection` object actually needs, but Microsoft wanted to make sure nothing was missing.

Notice the `Data Source` portion of the `ConnectionString` property. This is the part that points to a specific ACCDB file. Changing this path means the `Connection` object can open virtually any Access database as long as the path is valid and points to an ACCDB file.

The following procedure opens a `Connection` against the current database, prints the `Connection` object's `Provider` property, and then closes and discards the `Connection` object:

```
Public Sub OpenConnection()

    Dim adConn As ADODB.Connection

    Set adConn = New ADODB.Connection
    adConn.Open CurrentProject.Connection
```

```
            ' Connection is open
            Debug.Print adConn.Provider

            adConn.Close
            Set adConn = Nothing

     End Sub
```

When working with ADO, it's very important to close an object (if the object supports a Close method) and set it to Nothing when your code is done with the object. ADO objects tend to stay in memory once they've been opened and must be explicitly closed and discarded (set to Nothing) to clear them from memory. If an ADO object is not properly terminated, it may remain in memory causing problems for users.

A Connection object requires the provider information and the data source. The provider specifies which ADO provider (essentially a driver) to attach to the Connection object. For example, there are providers for SQL Server databases: one for the Jet database engine and another for the ACE database engine. Each provider knows how to connect to a different type of data and endows the Connection object with features specific to the data source.

The downside to the Connection object, and one that causes a lot of problems for Access developers, is that you must know the correct syntax to use for the ConnectionString property. Fortunately, there are many sites on the internet that list connection strings for virtually every data provider.

The ADO Command object

The second major ADO topic is the Command object. As its name implies, a Command object executes a command against the data source opened through a Connection. The command can be as simple as the name of an Access query or as complex as a long SQL statement that selects dozens of fields and includes WHERE and ORDER BY clauses. In fact, the Command object is the most common way to execute SQL Server stored procedures from Access applications.

As you'll see later in this chapter, the output from executing a Command object can be directed into a recordset. The data in the recordset can then be used to populate a form or controls such as text boxes, combo boxes, and list boxes.

There are many ways to use Command objects. The following procedure is just one example of using a Command object. In this case, the Command object populates a recordset with data taken directly from tblCustomers. (Recordsets are discussed in the next section.) The following procedure, ExecuteCommand, is included in modADO_Commands in the Chapter28.accdb example database:

```
     Public Sub ExecuteCommand()

            Dim adRs As ADODB.Recordset
            Dim adCmd As ADODB.Command
```

```
    Const sTABLE As String = "tblCustomers"

    Set adRs = New ADODB.Recordset
    Set adCmd = New ADODB.Command

    adCmd.ActiveConnection = CurrentProject.Connection
    adCmd.CommandText = sTABLE

    Set adRs = adCmd.Execute

    Debug.Print adRs.GetString

    adRs.Close
    Set adRs = Nothing
    Set adCmd = Nothing

End Sub
```

Notice the following actions in this procedure:

- A Recordset and a Command object are both declared and instantiated.
- The Command object's ActiveConnection property is set to the current project's Connection property.
- The Command object's CommandText property is set to the name of a table in the database.
- The recordset is populated by setting it to the value returned when the Command object is executed.

Notice the use of the recordset's GetString method. GetString is a handy way to output everything that's in the recordset. Figure 28.6 shows the output from ExecuteCommand in the Immediate window.

FIGURE 28.6

GetString is a convenient way to see what's in a recordset.

The Immediate window is thoroughly discussed in Chapter 27.

This little example illustrates the basics of what you need to know about ADO `Command` objects. A `Command` object must be attached to an available `Connection` through its `ActiveConnection` property. The `ActiveConnection` can be a connection string or an open `Connection` object. It doesn't make any difference where the `Connection` is pointing—an Access or SQL Server database, Oracle, or any other data source. The `Command` object uses the `Connection`'s special knowledge of the data source to get at the data.

`Command` objects are most valuable when working with parameterized queries. Each `Command` object includes a `Parameters` collection containing, naturally, `Parameter` objects. Each parameter corresponds to a parameter required by the query or stored procedure referenced by the `Command`'s `CommandText` property.

Very often the `CommandText` property is set to a SQL statement that includes parameters:

```
SELECT * FROM tblCustomers
WHERE State = 'NY' OR State = 'NJ';
```

You'll see examples of using the ADO `Command` object to populate recordsets and perform actions on data throughout this book.

The ADO Recordset object

`Recordset` is a very versatile ADO object. Most often, it's populated by executing a `Command` or directly through its `Open` method. `Open_ADO_Recordset` illustrates how easily the `Recordset` object opens an Access table:

```
Public Sub Open_ADO_Recordset()

    Dim adRs As ADODB.Recordset

    Set adRs = New ADODB.Recordset

    adRs.Open "SELECT * FROM tblCustomers;", _
      CurrentProject.Connection

    Debug.Print adRs.GetString

    adRs.Close
    Set adRs = Nothing

End Sub
```

In this example, the recordset is populated by selecting records from the Customers table using a SQL statement. The SQL statement could include `WHERE` or `ORDER BY` clauses to filter and sort the data as it's selected.

An alternative way to write this procedure is to use a separate statement for assigning the `ActiveConnection` property:

```
Public Sub Open_ADO_Rs_Connection()

    Dim adRs As ADODB.Recordset

    Set adRs = New ADODB.Recordset
    adRs.ActiveConnection = CurrentProject.Connection

    adRs.Open "SELECT * FROM tblCustomers;"

    Debug.Print adRs.GetString

    adRs.Close
    Set adRs = Nothing

End Sub
```

Many developers prefer the approach in `Open_ADO_Rs_Connection` because it's easier to see exactly what's happening to the `Recordset` object and where its properties are being set. Although these very small procedures are easily understood, in larger code segments finding all the references to an object like `adRs` can be challenging, especially when the VBA statements become long and complex.

As with the other ADO objects, a `Recordset` object must be declared and instantiated. Like the `Command` object, if the `Open` method is used to populate a `Recordset` object, an open connection must be provided as an argument to the `Open` method.

`Recordset` objects are used in many different places in this book. Depending on context, the most commonly used `Recordset` methods include `Open`, `Close`, `MoveFirst`, `MoveNext`, `MovePrevious`, and `MoveLast`.

 Open_ADO_Recordset and Open_ADO_Rs_Connection are included in modADO_Recordsets in the `Chapter28.accdb` example database.

Writing VBA Code to Update a Table

Updating data in a table by using a form is easy. You simply place controls on the form for the fields of the table that you want to update. For example, Figure 28.7 shows frmSales. The controls on frmSales update data in tblSales, tblSalesLineitems, and tblSalesPayments because these fields are directly bound to controls on frmSales.

28

FIGURE 28.7

Using a form to update data in tables.

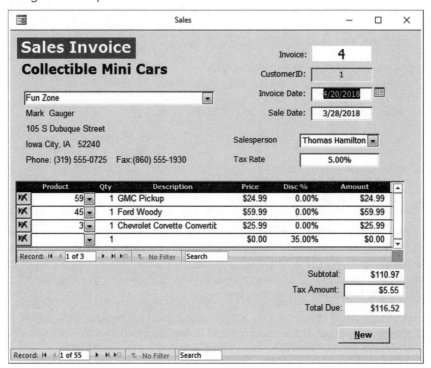

Sometimes, however, you want to update a field in a table that isn't displayed on the form. When information is entered in frmSales, for example, the field for the last sales date (LastSalesDate) in tblCustomers should be updated to reflect the most recent date on which the contact purchased a product. When you enter a new sale, the value for the LastSalesDate field is the value of the txtSaleDate control on frmSales.

Because the contact's last sales date refers to the txtSaleDate control on frmSales, you don't want the user to have to enter it twice. Theoretically, you could place the LastSalesDate field as a calculated field that is updated after the user enters the Sale Date, but displaying this field would be confusing and is irrelevant to the items for the current sale.

The best way to handle updating the LastSalesDate field in tblCustomers is to use a VBA procedure. You can use VBA code to update individual fields in a record, add new records, or delete records.

Updating fields in a record using ADO

Use the AfterUpdate event procedure to update LastSalesDate (see Figure 28.8).

FIGURE 28.8

Using ADO to update a table.

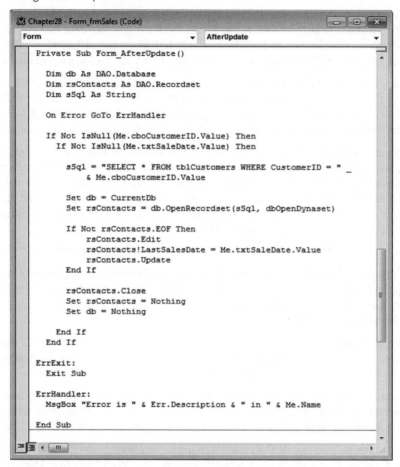

```
Private Sub Form_AfterUpdate()

    Dim db As DAO.Database
    Dim rsContacts As DAO.Recordset
    Dim sSql As String

    On Error GoTo ErrHandler

    If Not IsNull(Me.cboCustomerID.Value) Then
      If Not IsNull(Me.txtSaleDate.Value) Then

        sSql = "SELECT * FROM tblCustomers WHERE CustomerID = " _
            & Me.cboCustomerID.Value

        Set db = CurrentDb
        Set rsContacts = db.OpenRecordset(sSql, dbOpenDynaset)

        If Not rsContacts.EOF Then
            rsContacts.Edit
            rsContacts!LastSalesDate = Me.txtSaleDate.Value
            rsContacts.Update
        End If

        rsContacts.Close
        Set rsContacts = Nothing
        Set db = Nothing

      End If
    End If

ErrExit:
    Exit Sub

ErrHandler:
    MsgBox "Error is " & Err.Description & " in " & Me.Name

End Sub
```

Variables are declared in the top portion of the code using `Dim` statements. You can declare a variable anywhere as long as it's declared before you use it. It's good practice to declare all your variables together at the top. The variables for the database and the recordset use the library as the prefix (DAO in this case). This file contains both DAO and ADO code, so it's necessary to specify which library to use. If only DAO were used, you could just use, for example, `Dim db As Database` and most programmers omit the library in that case.

The next line of code uses `On Error` to tell VBA to jump to the `ErrHandler` label if it encounters any errors. Without error handling, the user would be thrust into the VBE if an error occurred. The two labels near the bottom, `ErrExit` and `ErrHandler` complete the error handling. This is very common method of including error handling in your code. You set the `On Error` near the top of the program, the error handler label near the bottom of the code, and an Exit Sub statement just above the error handler label. If no error occurs, the Exit Sub statement is executed before the MsgBox statement.

The next two lines start two nested If blocks. The meat of our code is inside these blocks. They check to make sure that a customer has been chosen and a sale date has been entered. If either of those are blank, the rest of the code will fail. The IsNull function will return True if those values aren't set and the Not operator turns True to False and vice versa.

You've already seen how to open recordsets in the previous sections. The actual writing of data occurs in the five-line If block. It first checks to see that we're not at the end of the file. The SQL statement is designed to return one record (the customer with a certain ID). If no records are returned, rsContacts.EOF will be True, and the code that updates will be skipped.

The three lines that write the date include the Edit method, an assignment statement, and the Update method. Calling the Edit method tells DAO that you intend to change data on the current record. The assignment statement changes the LastSalesDate field's value to the value in the sale date text box. Once data has been changed, you call Update to write the data and tell DAO that you're done editing. You can have as many assignment statements between Edit and Update as you like.

Finally, the code closes the recordset and releases the memory held for the two DAO variables.

One major difference between a table open in Datasheet view and a recordset is that a recordset provides no visual representation of the data it contains. A datasheet provides you with rows and columns of data and even includes column headings so you know the names of the fields in the underlying table.

A recordset exists only in memory. There is no easy way to visualize the data in a recordset. As a developer you must always be aware of the field names, row count, and other data attributes that are important to your application.

When you are working with datasheets and recordsets, only one record is active. In a datasheet the active record is indicated by a color difference in the row. Recordsets have no such visual aid, so you must always be aware of which record is current in a recordset.

Before you change data in any of the recordset's fields, you need to make sure that you're in the record you want to edit. When a recordset opens, the current record is the first record in the set. If the recordset contains no records, the recordset's EOF property is True. In this example, the SQL statement was designed to return only one record. But if you're dealing with a recordset with multiple records, you need to navigate so that the record you want to change is the current record.

Updating a calculated control

In the frmSales example, the txtTaxAmount control displays the tax to collect at the time of the sale. The tax amount's value is not a simple calculation. The tax amount is determined by the following items:

- The sum of the item amounts purchased that are taxable
- The customer's tax rate in effect on the sale date
- The value in txtOtherAmount and whether the txtOtherAmount is a taxable item

When the user changes information for the current sale, any one or all three of these factors can change the tax amount. The tax amount must be recalculated whenever any of the following events occur in the form:

- Adding or updating a line item
- Deleting a line item
- Changing the buyer to another customer
- Changing txtTaxLocation
- Changing txtOtherAmount

You use VBA procedures to recalculate the tax amount when any of these events occurs.

Recalculating a control when updating or adding a record

Figure 28.9 shows the code for adding or updating a line item on frmSales.

A single event can handle recalculating the tax amount when new line items are added or when a line item is changed—when an item's price or quantity is changed, for example. In any case, you can use the subform's AfterUpdate event to update the sales tax. AfterUpdate occurs when a new record is entered or when any value is changed for an existing record.

The Form_AfterUpdate procedure for fsubSalesLineitems executes when a line item is added to the subform or when any information is changed in a line item. The Form_AfterUpdate procedure recalculates the tax amount control (txtTaxAmount) on frmSales. The dTaxRate variable holds the customer's tax rate (the value of txtTaxRate on frmSales), and cTaxAmount stores the value returned by the CalcTax() function. CalcTax() calculates the actual tax amount. When the After_Update procedure calls CalcTax(), it passes two parameters: the value of dTaxRate and the current line item's invoice number (Me.InvoiceNumber). Figure 28.10 shows the CalcTax() function.

28

FIGURE 28.9

Recalculating a field after a form is updated.

```
Chapter28 - Form_fsubSalesLineitems (Code)

Form                              ▼   AfterUpdate                    ▼

  Private Sub Form_AfterUpdate()

      Dim dTaxRate As Double
      Dim cTaxAmount As Currency

      dTaxRate = CDbl(Nz(Forms!frmSales!txtTaxRate, 0))

      cTaxAmount = CalcTax(dTaxRate, Me.InvoiceNumber.Value)

      Forms!frmSales!txtTaxAmount = cTaxAmount


    UpdateTaxRate Me.Parent, _
      CDbl(Nz(Me.Parent.txtTaxRate.Value, 0)), _
      Me.InvoiceNumber.Value


  End Sub
```

FIGURE 28.10

CalcTax() uses DAO to determine sales tax.

```
Chapter28 - modSalesFunctions (Code)

(General)                         ▼   CalcTax                        ▼

    Public Function CalcTax(dTaxPercent As Double, _
      lInvoiceNum As Long) As Currency

        Dim db As DAO.Database
        Dim rs As DAO.Recordset
        Dim sSql As String

        sSql = "SELECT Sum(CalcExtendedPrice(Nz([Quantity],0), " _
            & "Nz([RetailPrice],0), Nz([DiscountPercent],0))) AS SubTotal " _
            & "FROM tblSalesLineItems " _
            & "WHERE [InvoiceNumber] = " & lInvoiceNum

        Set db = CurrentDb
        Set rs = db.OpenRecordset(sSql, dbOpenForwardOnly)

        If Not rs.EOF Then
            CalcTax = rs!Subtotal * dTaxPercent
        End If

        rs.Close
        Set rs = Nothing
        Set db = Nothing

    End Function
```

928

`CalcTax()` creates a recordset that sums the quantities and prices for the taxable items in tblSalesLineItems for the current sale. The function receives two parameters: the tax rate (`dTaxPercent`) and the invoice number (`lInvoiceNum`). The code checks to see whether the recordset returned a record. If the recordset is at the end of the file (`EOF`), the recordset did not find any line items for the current sale—and `CalcTax` returns 0. If the recordset does contain a record, the return value for `CalcTax` is set to the recordset's Subtotal field times the tax rate (`dTaxPercent`).

At the end of a procedure that calls `CalcTax`, shown in Figure 28.11, txtTaxAmount is set to the `cTaxAmount` value.

When the Buyer, Tax Location, or Tax Rate controls are changed in frmSales, you use the `AfterUpdate` event for the individual control to recalculate the tax amount. Figure 28.11 shows the code for the `txtTaxRate_AfterUpdate` event.

FIGURE 28.11

Recalculating a control after a control is updated.

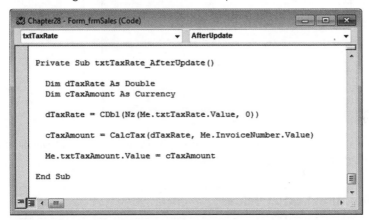

The logic implemented in `txtTaxRate_AfterUpdate` is identical to the logic in `fsub-SalesLineitems_AfterUpdate`. In fact, you can use the same code for the Buyer and Tax Location controls as well. The only difference between the code in Figure 28.9 and the code in Figure 28.11 is that the procedure in Figure 28.9 runs whenever a change occurs in the sales line items subform, whereas the code in Figure 28.11 runs whenever a change is made to txtTaxRate on the main form.

Checking the status of a record deletion

Use the form's `AfterDelConfirm` event to recalculate the txtTaxAmount control when deleting a line item. The form's `AfterDelConfirm` event (shown in Figure 28.12) is similar to the code for the subform's `AfterUpdate` event. Notice, however, that txtTaxAmount on the main sales form is set by this procedure, even though this code runs in fsubSalesLineitems subform embedded on frmSales.

Access always confirms deletions initiated by the user. Access displays a message box asking the user to confirm the deletion. If the user affirms the deletion, the current record is removed from the form's recordset and temporarily stored in memory so that the deletion can be undone if necessary. The `AfterDelConfirm` event occurs after the user confirms or cancels the deletion. If the `BeforeDelConfirm` event isn't canceled, the `AfterDelConfirm` event occurs after the delete confirmation dialog box is displayed. The `AfterDelConfirm` event occurs even if the `BeforeDelConfirm` event is canceled.

FIGURE 28.12

Recalculating a control after a record is deleted.

The `AfterDelConfirm` event procedure returns status information about the deletion. Table 28.2 describes the deletion status values.

TABLE 28.2   Deletion Status Values

Status value	Description
`acDeleteOK`	Deletion occurred normally.
`acDeleteCancel`	Deletion canceled programmatically.
`acDeleteUserCancel`	User canceled deletion.

The `Status` argument for the `AfterDelConfirm` event procedure can be set to any of these values within the procedure. For example, if the code in the `AfterDelConfirm` event procedure determines that deleting the record may cause problems in the application, the `Status` argument should be set to `acDeleteCancel`:

```
If <Condition_Indicates_a_Problem> Then
    Status = acDeleteCancel
```

```
      Exit Sub
   Else
      Status = acDeleteOK
   End If
```

The `Status` argument is provided to enable your VBA code to override the user's decision to delete a record if conditions warrant such an override. In the case that `Status` is set to `acDeleteCancel`, the copy of the record stored in the temporary buffer is restored to the recordset, and the delete process is terminated. If, on the other hand, `Status` is set to `acDeleteOK`, the deletion proceeds and the temporary buffer is cleared after the user moves to another record in the recordset.

Eliminating repetitive code

The examples in this section result in three procedures containing nearly identical code. If the code needs to be modified, you will have to modify it in the `Form_AfterDelConfirm` and `Form_AfterUpdate` events of the subform and the `txtTaxRate_AfterUpdate` event of the main form. If your modifications are not identical or if you simply forget to modify the code in one of the procedures, you can introduce errors into the project.

When you find yourself writing the same, or very similar, code in multiple event procedures, the best practice is to move the code to a standard module and call it from the event procedures. We can't simply copy the code to a standard module because, while very similar, the code isn't exactly the same. The differences in the code, for example how txtTaxRate is referenced, need to be handled in parameters to the new procedure:

```
Public Sub UpdateTaxRate(frmMain As Form, _
   dTaxRate As Double, _
   lInvoiceNumber As Long)

   Dim cTaxAmount As Currency

   cTaxAmount = CalcTax(dTaxRate, lInvoiceNumber)

   frmMain.txtTaxAmount.Value = cTaxAmount

End Sub
```

This procedure is placed in the modSalesFunctions module. Instead of having similar code in three event procedures, each of those event procedures calls this procedure. If any changes are necessary, only this procedure needs to be updated. The following code shows how to call this procedure from the subform's `Form_AfterUpdate` event and the main form's `txtTaxRate_AfterUpdate` event:

```
Private Sub txtTaxRate_AfterUpdate()

   UpdateTaxRate Me, CDbl(Nz(Me.txtTaxRate.Value, 0)), _
      Me.InvoiceNumber.Value

End Sub
```

28

```
Private Sub Form_AfterUpdate()

    UpdateTaxRate Me.Parent, _
        CDbl(Nz(Me.Parent.txtTaxRate.Value, 0)), _
        Me.InvoiceNumber.Value

End Sub
```

From the main form, the Me keyword is passed (referring to the form itself), and the other parameters are taken from controls on the form. From the subform, Me.Parent is used to refer to the main form to retrieve the necessary values.

Adding a new record

You can add a record to a table just as easily as updating a record. Use the AddNew method to add a new record to a table. The following shows an ADO procedure for adding a new customer to tblCustomerContacts:

```
Public Sub AddNewContact(sFirstName As String, sLastName As String)

    Dim db As DAO.Database
    Dim rs As DAO.Recordset

    Set db = CurrentDb
    Set rs = db.OpenRecordset("tblCustomerContacts", dbOpenDynaset)

    With rs
        .AddNew    'Add new record

        'Add data:
        .Fields("LastName").Value = sLastName
        .Fields("FirstName").Value = sFirstName

        .Update    'Commit changes
    End With

    rs.Close
    Set rs = Nothing
    Set db = Nothing

End Sub
```

As you see in this example, using the AddNew method is similar to using the Edit method to edit recordset data. AddNew creates a buffer for a new record. After executing AddNew, you assign values to fields in the new record. The Update method adds the new record to the end of the recordset and then to the underlying table.

Deleting a record

To remove a record from a table, you use the ADO method `Delete`. The following code shows an ADO procedure for deleting a record from tblCustomerContacts:

```
Public Sub DeleteContact(ContactID As Long)

    Dim db As DAO.Database
    Dim rs As DAO.Recordset
    Dim sSql As String


    sSql = "SELECT * FROM tblCustomerContacts " _
        & "WHERE ID = " & ContactID & ";"

    Set db = CurrentDb
    Set rs = db.OpenRecordset(sSql, dbOpenDynaset)

    With rs
        If Not .EOF Then
            .Delete    'Delete the record
        End If
    End With

    rs.Close
    Set rs = Nothing
    Set db = Nothing
```

28

> **NOTE**
>
> Notice that you don't follow the `Delete` method with `Update`. As soon as the `Delete` method executes, the record is permanently removed from the recordset.

Deleting records doesn't trigger the deletion confirmation dialog box. Generally speaking, changes made to data with code are not confirmed because confirmation would interrupt the user's workflow. This means that, as the developer, you're responsible for making sure that deletions are appropriate before proceeding. Once the record is deleted, there is no way to undo the change to the underlying table. Access does, however, still enforce referential integrity. If you attempt to delete a record that violates referential integrity, you'll get an error.

Deleting related records in multiple tables

When you write code to delete records, you need to be aware of the application's relationships. The table containing the record that you're deleting may be participating in a one-to-many relationship with another table.

Take a look at the relationships diagram (see Figure 28.13) for the tables used in the frm-Sales example. tblSales has two dependent tables associated with it: tblSalesLineItems and tblSalesPayments.

FIGURE 28.13

Examining the tables of a one-to-many relationship.

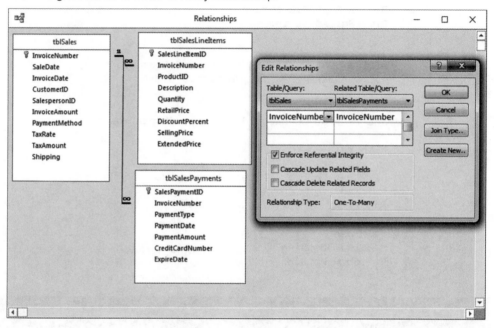

The Edit Relationships dialog box shows how the relationship is set up between tblSales and tblSalesLineItems. The relationship type is a one-to-many (1:M) and referential integrity is enforced. A one-to-many relationship means that each record in the parent table (tblSales) may have one or more records in the child table (tblSalesLineItems). Each record in the parent table must be unique—you can't have two sales records with exactly the same InvoiceNumber, SalesDate, and other information.

 Relationships between tables are discussed in Chapter 4.

In a one-to-many relationship each child record (in tblSalesLineItems) *must* be related to one record (and *only* one record) in the parent table (tblSales). But each sales record in tblSales may be related to more than one record in tblSalesLineItem.

When you enforce referential integrity on a one-to-many relationship, you're telling Access that a record in tblSales *can't* be deleted if records with the same invoice number value exist in tblSalesLineItems. If Access encounters a delete request that violates referential integrity, Access displays an error message and the delete will be canceled, unless cascading deletes have been enabled in the Edit Relationships dialog box (refer to Figure 28.13).

As you'll recall from Chapter 4, you have the option of setting Cascade Update Related Fields and Cascade Delete Related Records in the Edit Relationships dialog box. By default, these options are not enabled—and for good reason. If cascading deletes is turned on, when you use VBA code to delete a sales record, all the related records in tblSalesLineItems and tblSalesPayments are also deleted. Depending on the situation, this may or may not be a good thing. In the case of a canceled sales order, there is probably no harm done by deleting the unsold sales line items. However, when working on a canceled order where payment has been made, deleting the customer's payment history may be an issue. Surely, they'll expect a refund of payments made on the order, but Access just deleted the payment records.

In most cases, you're far better off using an Active field (Yes/No data type) to indicate a parent record's status. The Active field is set to Yes when the order is placed, and only set to No when the order has been canceled or completed. You might also consider adding a CancellationDate field to tblSales and set it to the date on which an order is canceled. If CancellationDate is null, the order has not been canceled.

When you write code to delete a record, you need to first check to see whether there are any one-to-many relationships between the table containing the record to delete and any other tables in the database. If there are dependent tables, the records in the dependent tables need to be deleted before Access allows you to delete the record in the parent table.

Fortunately, you can write a single procedure to delete records in both the dependent table(s) and the parent table. Figure 28.14 shows the code for the cmdDelete command button in frmSales.

The cmdDelete_Click event procedure deletes records in tblSalesPayments, tblSalesLineItems, and tblSales that have an invoice number matching the current invoice number.

The first statement in cmdDelete_Click (If Me.NewRecord Then) uses the NewRecord property to see whether the current sales record is new. If the record is new, Me.Undo rolls back changes to the record. If the current record is not new, the procedure displays a message box to confirm that the user really wants to delete the record. If the user clicks the Yes button, the procedure deletes the record from the tables.

Two constants, sSQL_DELPMTS and sSQL_DELLINE, hold the SQL statements for locating and deleting records in tblSalesPayments and tblSalesLineItems, respectively, with an invoice number that matches the invoice number on frmSales. The invoice number is concatenated to the end of the constants, and they're passed as a parameter to the Execute method of CurrentDb. You can pass either the name of a query or a SQL statement as a parameter to the Execute method. The Execute method simply runs the specified query or SQL statement.

28

FIGURE 28.14

Using ADO code to delete multiple records.

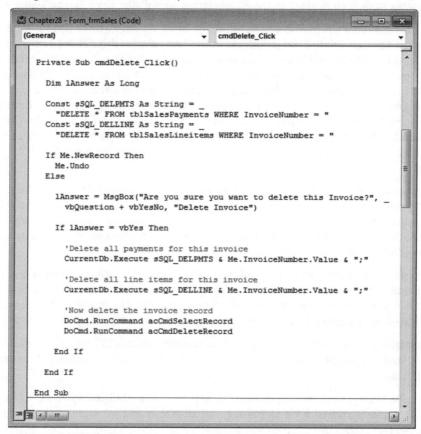

```
Chapter28 - Form_frmSales (Code)

(General)                                    cmdDelete_Click

    Private Sub cmdDelete_Click()

      Dim lAnswer As Long

      Const sSQL_DELPMTS As String = _
        "DELETE * FROM tblSalesPayments WHERE InvoiceNumber = "
      Const sSQL_DELLINE As String = _
        "DELETE * FROM tblSalesLineItems WHERE InvoiceNumber = "

      If Me.NewRecord Then
        Me.Undo
      Else

        lAnswer = MsgBox("Are you sure you want to delete this Invoice?", _
          vbQuestion + vbYesNo, "Delete Invoice")

        If lAnswer = vbYes Then

          'Delete all payments for this invoice
          CurrentDb.Execute sSQL_DELPMTS & Me.InvoiceNumber.Value & ";"

          'Delete all line items for this invoice
          CurrentDb.Execute sSQL_DELLINE & Me.InvoiceNumber.Value & ";"

          'Now delete the invoice record
          DoCmd.RunCommand acCmdSelectRecord
          DoCmd.RunCommand acCmdDeleteRecord

        End If

      End If

    End Sub
```

> **NOTE**
>
> If the query or SQL statement contains a WHERE clause and the Execute method does not find any records that meet the WHERE condition, no error occurs. If the query or SQL statement contains invalid syntax or an invalid field or table name, however, the Execute method fails and an error is raised.

After the tblSalesPayments and tblSalesLineItems records are deleted, the tblSales record can then be deleted.

Advanced Data Access with VBA

IN THIS CHAPTER

Using a combo box to find a record on a form

Using the form's filter options

Using parameter queries to filter a form

I n the previous few chapters, you learned the basics of Access programming, reviewed some built-in VBA functions, and experienced the various VBA logical constructs. You learned about DAO and ADO and how to access data in tables and queries through recordsets. You also learned a lot about forms and queries.

In this chapter, you use all this knowledge and learn how to display selected data in forms or reports using a combination of techniques involving forms, Visual Basic code, and queries.

ON THE WEB

In the Chapter29.accdb database, you'll find several forms to use as a starting point, and other completed forms to compare to the forms you change in this example. All the examples use a modified version of frmProducts or tblProducts.

Adding an Unbound Combo Box to a Form to Find Data

When viewing an Access form, you often have to page through hundreds or even thousands of records to find the record or set of records you want to work with. You can teach your users how to use the Access "find" features, what to do to see other records, and so on, but this defeats the purpose of a programmed application. If you build an application, you want to make it easier for your users to be productive with your system, not teach them how to use the tools built into Access.

Figure 29.1 shows a form based on frmProducts that has an additional control at the top: a combo box that is not bound to any data in the form. The unbound combo box is used to directly look up a record in tblProducts and then display the record in the form using a bit of code. This chapter shows several ways to build this combo box and use it as a quick way to find records in the form.

FIGURE 29.1

The frmProductsExample1 form with an unbound combo box.

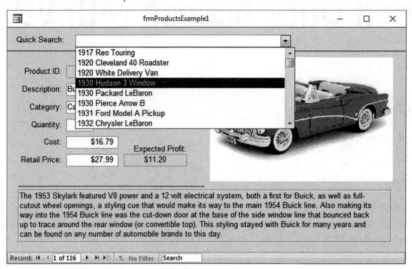

The design for the combo box is shown in Figure 29.2. Notice that the Control Source property is empty. This indicates that the combo box is not bound to any field in a table and is used only by the form, not to change data in the underlying database.

FIGURE 29.2

The Property Sheet for the unbound combo box control.

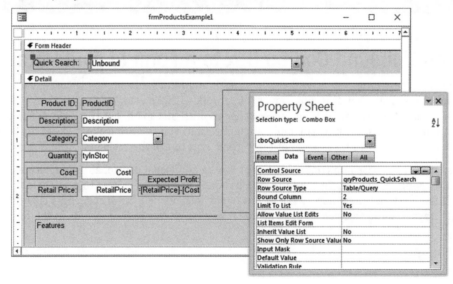

The combo box contains two columns selected by the query shown in Figure 29.3. The first column, LongDescription, concatenates ModelYear and Description from tblProducts. The second column is the ProductID field in tblProducts. The ProductID column serves as the bound column for the combo box and is the value returned by the combo box when a row is selected in the combo box. The second column's width is 0, which hides the column when the combo box list is pulled down.

> **NOTE**
>
> In the code examples that follow, you'll see references to `cboQuickSearch.Value`. Keep in mind that the value of the combo box comes from the bound column (and not necessarily the displayed information) and in this case is the Product ID of the item selected in the combo box.

FIGURE 29.3

The query behind the Row Source property of cboQuickSearch.

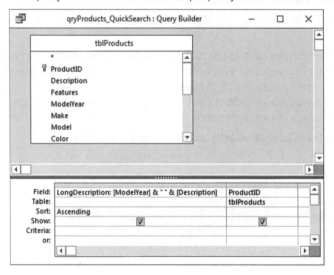

This combo box is used for several of the examples in this chapter. Next, you see how to find records in a variety of ways using the combo box and the code behind it.

Using the FindRecord method

Let's take a look at how the quick search combo box on frmProductsExample1 works. Selecting a product from cboQuickSearch fires the `AfterUpdate` event. Code in the `AfterUpdate` event procedure performs the search on the form, and the form instantly displays the selected record.

The `FindRecord` method locates a record in the form's bound recordset. This is equivalent to using the magnifying glass on the Ribbon to find a record in a datasheet.

When performing a search on a datasheet, you begin by clicking the column you want to search, perhaps LastName. Next, you click the magnifying glass (Find button) on the Ribbon to open the Find and Replace dialog box and enter the name you want to find in the recordset. Access knows to use the LastName field because that's the column you selected in the datasheet. When you enter **Smith** as the search criteria, Access moves the datasheet record pointer to the first row that contains Smith in the LastName field.

When you use code to search through the contents of a bound Access form, you actually perform these same steps using VBA statements.

Perform the following steps to create an `AfterUpdate` event procedure behind the combo box:

1. **Display frmProductsExample1 in Design view, click cboQuickSearch, and then press F4 to display the Property Sheet.**

2. **Select the Event tab and select the AfterUpdate event.**

3. **Click the drop-down arrow in the AfterUpdate event property and select Event Procedure.**

4. **Click the Builder button that appears in the right side of the property.** The procedure appears in a separate VBA code window. The event procedure template (`Private Sub cboQuickSearch_AfterUpdate()...End Sub`) is automatically created in the form's code module. As you've learned, whenever you create an event procedure, the names of the control and event are part of the subprocedure.

5. **Enter the four lines of code exactly as shown in Figure 29.4.**

FIGURE 29.4

Using the `FindRecord` method to find a record.

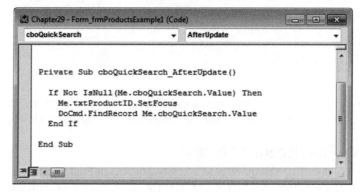

The first line checks to make sure that cboQuickSearch contains a value; i.e., it isn't null. If cboQuickSearch is null, the program flows to the `End If` statement, and no search takes place. If cboQuickSearch has a value, the code inside the `If` block is executed, starting with this statement:

```
Me.txtProductID.SetFocus
```

This statement moves the cursor to the txtProductID control. Just as you need to manually move the cursor to a column in a datasheet in order to use the Find icon on the Ribbon, you must place the cursor in the bound control you want to use as the search's target. In this case, you're moving the cursor to the control containing the ProductID value because the search will look for a particular ProductID in the form's bound recordset.

The next statement in the `If` block is:

```
DoCmd.FindRecord Me.cboQuickSearch.Value
```

In this statement, the `FindRecord` method uses the combo box's value (which is the selected item's Product ID) to search for the selected product's record. Access matches the value in cboQuickSearch with the ProductID in the recordset bound to the form.

The first value found by the `FindRecord` method is determined by a series of parameters, including whether the case is matched and whether the search is forward, backward, or the first record found. Enter **DoCmd.FindRecord** in the code window and press the spacebar to see all available options. The `FindRecord` method finds only one record at a time, while allowing all other records to be viewed.

Using a bookmark

The `FindRecord` method is a good way to search when the control you want to use to find a record is displayed on the form. It's also a good way if the value being searched for is a single value. A *bookmark* is another way of finding a record.

frmProductsExample2 contains the code for this example.

Figure 29.5 shows the combo box's `AfterUpdate` event procedure. This code uses a bookmark to locate the record in the form's recordset matching the search criteria.

29

FIGURE 29.5

Using a `RecordsetClone` bookmark to find a record.

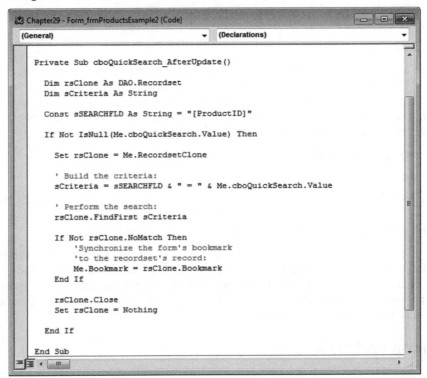

The first several lines are:

```
Dim rsClone As DAO.Recordset
Dim sCriteria As String

Const sSEARCHFLD As String = "[ProductID]"

If Not IsNull(Me.cboQuickSearch.Value) Then

    Set rsClone = Me.RecordsetClone
```

The first three lines declare a recordset named `rsClone`, a string named `sCriteria`, and a constant named `sSEARCHFLD` that is set to the name of the field to search. These will be used later in the code. Next, the procedure checks whether cboQuickSearch has a value, which means the user selected something in the combo box. The following line sets the recordset to a copy of the form's bound recordset (the `RecordsetClone`).

A `RecordsetClone` is exactly what its name implies: an in-memory clone of the form's recordset that you can use when searching for records. If you used the form's bound recordset instead, your search will move the current record away from the record displayed in the form. If the search target is not found in the form's bound recordset, the form ends up positioned at the last record in the bound recordset, which is sure to confuse users.

The `Recordset` object's `FindFirst` method requires a search string containing criteria to look up in the recordset. By searching the clone, you can control when the bound recordset changes the current record.

The criteria string can be as complicated as needed. The following statement concatenates [ProductID] (our constant), an equal sign, and the value of cboQuickSearch:

```
sCriteria = sSEARCHFLD & " = " & Me.cboQuickSearch.Value
```

Assuming the value of cboQuickSearch is 17, sCriteria is now:

```
[ProductID] = 17
```

NOTE

The criteria string works only because ProductID is a numeric field. If it were text, quotes would be required around the value, as in:

```
sCriteria = sSEARCHFLD & " = '" & Me.cboQuickSearch.Value & "'"
```

so that the criteria would actually be:

```
[ProductID] = '17'
```

In this example, we have a lot of control over the criteria string because we're using a combo box's value. In other cases, we may get parts of the criteria string from a text box where a user could type virtually anything he wants. If, for instance, he included an apostrophe in a text box that was used in a criteria string, we would have a situation known as an *embedded quote* (a quote inside a quoted string).

Fortunately, embedded quotes are easy to avoid. If you need a quote inside a quoted string, you simply use two quotes. For example, if you search for the name O'Mally, it would look like this:

```
sCriteria = "[LastName] = 'O''Mally'"
```

Note the two quotes in `O''Mally` that get converted to one quote when the criteria string is processed. To accomplish this with a text box, use the `Replace` function to replace one quote with two quotes:

```
sCriteria = "[LastName] = " & _
   Replace(Me.txtLastName, String(2, "'"), _
   String(1, "'"))
```

TIP

Creating criteria in code is sometimes a complicated process. The objective is to build a string that could be copied into a query SQL window and run as is. Often, the best way to create a criteria string is to build a query, switch to SQL view, and copy the SQL into a VBA code window. Then, break the code's `WHERE` clause into field names and control values, inserting concatenation operators and delimiters as needed around string and date values.

29

After the criteria string is completed, use the recordset's `FindFirst` method to search for the record in the `RecordsetClone`. The following line uses the `FindFirst` method of the recordset, passing the criteria string as the argument:

```
rsClone.FindFirst sCriteria
```

> **NOTE**
>
> You don't have to create an `sCriteria` variable and then set the criteria string to it. You can simply place the criteria after the `rsClone.FindFirst` method, like this:
>
> `rsClone.FindFirst "ProductID = " & Me.cboQuickSearch.Value`
>
> However, when you have complex criteria, it may be easier to create the criteria separately from the command that uses the criteria string so you can debug the string separately in the query editor.

The next lines are used to determine whether the record pointer in the form should be moved. Notice the `Bookmark` property referenced in the following code block. A *bookmark* is a stationary pointer to a record in a recordset. The `FindFirst` method positions the recordset's bookmark on the found record.

```
If Not rsClone.NoMatch Then
   Me.Bookmark = rsClone.Bookmark
End If
```

If no record is found, the recordset's `NoMatch` property is `True`. Because you want to set the bookmark if a record *is* found, you need the computer equivalent of a double negative. Essentially, it says if there is "not no record found," then the bookmark is valid. Why Microsoft chose `NoMatch` instead of `Match` (which would reduce the logic to `If rsClone.Match Then...`) is a mystery to everyone.

If a matching record is found, the form's bookmark (`Me.Bookmark`) is set to the found recordset's bookmark (`rsClone.Bookmark`) and the form repositions itself to the bookmarked record. This doesn't filter the records—it merely positions the form's bookmark on the first record matching the criteria. All other records are still visible in the form.

The last lines of code simply close the recordset and remove it from memory.

> **NOTE**
>
> Criteria can be as complex as you need them to be, even involving multiple fields of different data types. Remember that strings must be delimited by single quotes (not double quotes, because double quotes surround the entire string), dates are delimited by pound signs (#), and numeric values are not delimited.

Using the `FindFirst` or `Bookmark` method is preferable to using `FindRecord` because it allows for more complex criteria and doesn't require the control being searched to be visible. You don't have to move the cursor to a different control to use the recordset's `FindFirst` method.

Filtering a Form

Although using the `FindRecord` or `FindFirst` methods allow you to quickly locate a record meeting the criteria you want, it still shows all the other records in a table or query recordset and doesn't necessarily keep all the records together. Filtering a form lets you view only the record or set of records you want, hiding all non-matching records.

Filters are good when you have large recordsets and want to view only the subset of records matching your needs.

You can filter a form with code or with a query. We cover both approaches in this section.

Filtering with code

Figure 29.6 shows the `cboQuickSearch_AfterUpdate` event containing the two lines of code necessary to create and apply a filter to a form's recordset. Each form contains a `Filter` property that specifies how the bound records are filtered. By default, the `Filter` property is blank, and the form shows all the records in the underlying recordset.

FIGURE 29.6

Code for filtering and clearing a filter behind a form.

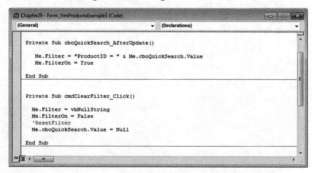

The first line of code sets the form's `Filter` property:

```
Me.Filter = "ProductID = " & Me.cboQuickSearch.Value
```

Notice that this is exactly the same string used as the criteria passed to the recordset's `FindFirst` property.

The second line of code (`Me.FilterOn = True`) turns on the filter. You can put all the criteria that you want in a filter property, but unless you explicitly set the `FilterOn` property to `True`, the filter is never applied to the form's recordset. The filter hides all the records that do not meet the criteria, showing only the records meeting the filter's value:

```
Me.FilterOn = True
```

Whenever you turn on a filter, it's useful to provide a way to turn off the filter. There is a small button (cmdClearFilter) next to the combo box on frmProductsExample3. This button turns off the filter and sets the form's `Filter` property to an empty string (`vbNullString`). The second procedure shown in Figure 29.6 is the button's `Click` event procedure:

```
Private Sub cmdClearFilter_Click()

    Me.Filter = vbNullString
    Me.FilterOn = False
    Me.cboQuickSearch.Value = Null

End Sub
```

> **CAUTION**
>
> If you create a form filter and then save the form design with the filter set, the filter is saved with the form. The next time the form is opened, the filter is active. It's a good practice to set the form's `Filter` property to an empty string as the form closes. The following code uses the form's `Close` event procedure to clear the filter:
>
> ```
> Private Sub Form_Close()
>     Me.Filter = vbNullString
>     Me.FilterOn = False
> End Sub
> ```
>
> Other than the line to clear the combo box, this code is identical to the code in `cmdClearFilter_Click`. In order to have a cleaner code base, it's a good idea to move the repetitive code into its own procedure. The two event procedures and the new procedure with the repetitive code are shown here:
>
> ```
> Private Sub cmdClearFilter_Click()
>
>     ResetFilter
>     Me.cboQuickSearch.Value = Null
>
> End Sub
> Private Sub Form_Close()
>
>     ResetFilter
>
> End Sub
> Private Sub ResetFilter()
>
>     Me.Filter = vbNullString
>     Me.FilterOn = False
>
> End Sub
> ```
>
> Instead of duplicate code, both event procedures call `ResetFilter`.

Filtering with a query

You might want to have one form control another. Or you might want a recordset to display selected data based on ad hoc criteria entered by the user. For example, each time a report is run, a dialog box is displayed, and the user enters a set of dates or selects a product or customer. One way to do this is to use a parameter query.

Creating a parameter query

A *parameter query* is any query that has criteria that references a variable, a function, or a control on a form. Normally, you enter a value such as **SMITH**, **26**, or **6/15/18** in a criteria entry area. But you can also enter a variable (also known as a prompt) such as **[Enter the Last Name]** or a reference to a control on a form such as **Forms!frmProducts![cboQuickFind]**.

ON THE WEB

The Chapter29.accdb database contains a parameter query named qryProductParameterQuery.

The simplest way to create a parameter query is to create a select query, specify the query's criteria, and run the query to make sure it works. Then change the criteria to the following:

```
Like [<some prompt>] & "*"
```

or:

```
Like "*" & [<some prompt>] & "*"
```

where <some prompt> is the question you want to ask the user. Figure 29.7 shows a parameter query that prompts the user whenever the query is run to enter the Product Category.

FIGURE 29.7

Creating a simple parameter query.

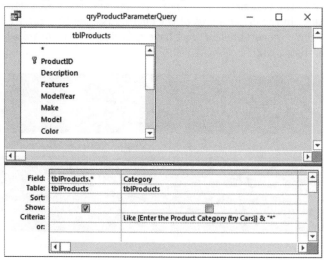

Anytime the query is run, even if it's used as the record source for a form or report or the row source for a list or combo box, the parameter dialog box is displayed—and depending on what's entered, the query criteria filters the query results. Figure 29.8 shows the parameter dialog box open, asking for the product category value required by the query.

FIGURE 29.8

Running the parameter query.

You may remember learning that the `Like` operator allows for wildcard searches. For example, if you want to filter the query records for any product category that starts with "car" (or "CAR"), you enter **CAR** in the parameter dialog box. Without the parameter, you would have to enter `Like "CAR*"` in the criteria area of the query. Also, because the wildcard (*) is included as part of the parameter, users don't have to include the wildcard when they respond to the parameter dialog box.

> **TIP**
>
> You can use the wildcards * (anything in and after this position) and ? (one character in this position) with a `Like` operator in any query or SQL string.

> **NOTE**
>
> If SQL Server Compatible Syntax (ANSI 92) is selected (choose File ⇨ Options, then select the Object Designers tab) or if ADO is being used to run the SQL statement, the wildcards are % (anything in and after this position) and _ (one character in this position).

A consequence of adding the asterisk to the parameter is that, if the user doesn't enter a parameter value, the criteria evaluates to `"LIKE *"`, and the query returns all records except the nulls. Leaving the asterisk out of the criteria expression results in no returned records if the user fails to provide a product category.

Figure 29.9 shows the Query Parameters dialog box (opened by right-clicking the query's upper area and selecting Parameters from the shortcut menu). You use the Query Parameters dialog box to specify parameters that require special consideration, such as date/time entries or specially formatted numbers. One text entry has been entered in the Query Parameters dialog box to show how it works. You enter the parameter text and choose the parameter's data type.

FIGURE 29.9

The Query Parameters dialog box.

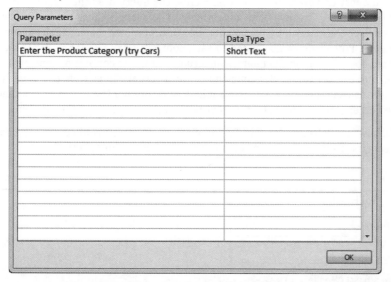

TIP

If you want to add more-complex parameters, such as a range of dates, use an expression such as `Between [Enter the Start Date] and [Enter the End Date]` as a criterion in a date field. This would display two separate parameter dialog boxes and then filter the date value appropriately.

Unfortunately, Access parameter queries don't provide a way to supply default values for parameters. Your best bet is to always include the asterisk in your criteria expression so that if the user closes the parameter dialog box without entering a value, the query will return all records because the criteria expression will resolve to `Like "*"`.

> **CAUTION**
>
> You can only use `Like "*"` with text fields. For numeric fields, you can set the criteria to `[My Prompt]` OR `([My Prompt] IS NULL)`. Just be certain that both occurrences of `My Prompt` are typed identically. (Copy and paste is a good idea.) You can also use this technique with text fields if you want to return all the records including those with null values.

Creating an interactive filter dialog box

The problem with parameter queries is that they're only suitable for simple parameters. The users have to know exactly what to type into the parameter dialog box, and if they enter the parameter incorrectly, they won't see the results they expect. Also, using parameter queries for entering complex criteria is fairly difficult.

A better technique is to create a simple form, place controls on the form, and reference the controls from a query as parameters. In other words, the query uses the form's controls to get its parameter values. This is a huge advantage to the users because the controls can help the user select the criteria by presenting lists or drop-down menus of the acceptable parameter values. Plus, code can be added to each control's `AfterUpdate` event to validate the user's input to ensure that the query will actually run. The content of controls like combo boxes or list boxes can be dynamic and contain actual values from the underlying tables. This means that the criteria controls might contain only the names of customers who've placed orders, or product categories actually in the database at the moment.

Figure 29.10 shows frmFilterProducts in Design view. cboCategory is filled with the data from qryCategories, which sorts the records in tblCategories in alphabetical order.

FIGURE 29.10

Creating a dialog box for selecting records.

cboCategory's Default Value property is set to Cars because this is the most commonly used criteria for the Products form. In this case, Limit To List is set to Yes because we want to force users to select only from the categories actually in tblCategories.

Figure 29.11 shows qryProducts_FormParameter. This query selects all fields in tblProducts based on the category retrieved from cboCategory on frmFilterProducts. Notice the criteria expression in the Category column:

```
= [Forms]![frmFilterProducts]![cboCategory]
```

As the query runs, it automatically retrieves the criteria value from cboCategory. The combo box returns Cars, unless the user has chosen a different category.

FIGURE 29.11

Creating a query that references a form control.

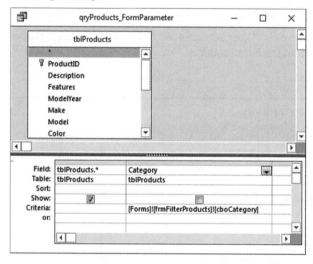

In normal operation, the user selects a product category from frmFilterProducts and clicks OK. Code behind the button opens frmProductsExample4, which is bound to qryProducts_FormParameter. The criteria for the Category field in qryProducts_FormParameter looks up the selected value in cboCategory on frmFilterProducts, and magically frmProductsExample4 opens with just the selected product category loaded.

The only issue facing developers working with tightly integrated database objects like this (in this case, frmFilterProducts, qryProducts_FormParameter, and frmProductsExample4) is that it may not be obvious that the objects work together. Removing or modifying any of these objects might break the workflow or cause problems for the users.

You might choose to use a naming convention that implies the relationship between the two forms and the query, such as giving each item the same name, but with different prefixes. Or, you could use the custom groups in the Navigation pane and add the objects to a single group. Very often things that are obvious to you—the original designer and developer—may not be as clear to someone else, so it pays to take advantage of simple techniques that help document your applications.

> **CAUTION**
>
> Running qryProducts_FormParameter when frmFilterProducts is not open will result in the query prompting the user to enter a value. When frmFilterProducts is not open, Access can't figure out what the criteria [Forms] ! [frmFilterProducts] ! [cbCategory] means because there is not a form named frmFilterProducts loaded. In this situation, Access assumes the parameter is a prompt and displays an input box.

Linking the dialog box to another form

The frmFilterProducts dialog box (refer to Figure 29.10) does more than just create a value that can be referenced from a query. It also contains code to open frmProductsExample4.

Figure 29.12 shows the cmdCancel_Click and cmdOK_Click event procedures behind the Cancel and OK buttons found on frmFilterProducts.

FIGURE 29.12

Creating a dialog box that opens a form.

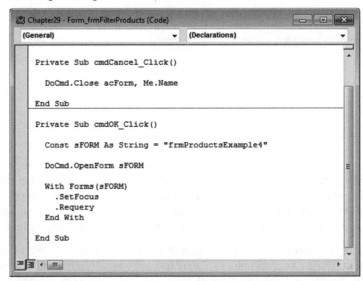

The cmdOK_Click event procedure code opens frmProductsExample4, sets the focus on it, and then re-queries the form to make sure that the latest selection is used on the form. The SetFocus method is necessary to move focus to the form that is opened. The Requery method isn't strictly required, because a form automatically re-queries its record source the first time it's opened. However, if the form is already opened—for example, if you use the dialog box a second time to search for another record—the `Requery` method ensures that the form displays fresh data.

Although not implemented in frmFilterProducts, the `cmdOK_Click` event procedure could also contain a `DoCmd.Close` statement to close the dialog box after it has opened frmProductExample4. Or, you may elect to keep the dialog box open to make it easy for users to select another product category to view.

Using the With Keyword

The `With` keyword is used to save execution time by not referencing the controls on the form explicitly (that is, directly)—for example, `Forms!frmProductsExample4.SetFocus`. This syntax requires Access to search alphabetically through the list of forms in the database container. If there were 500 forms (and some large systems have this many or more) and the form name started with z, this would take a considerable amount of time. Because there is more than one reference to the form, this process would have to take place multiple times. The `With` command sets up an internal pointer to the form so that all subsequent references to controls, properties, or methods (like `Requery` or `SetFocus`) of the form are much faster.

When you use the `With` keyword and reference the form name, you simply use a dot (.) or an exclamation point (!) to reference a control, property, or method just like the `Forms!FormName` was first. You can see this in Figure 29.12.

For each `With`, you must have an `End With`.

29

Customizing the Ribbon

IN THIS CHAPTER

Working with the default Ribbon

Examining Ribbon architecture

Studying Ribbon controls

Learning the XML necessary to construct Ribbons

Adding VBA callbacks

The Ribbon is the primary way that users interact with Office applications. All Office applications have a Ribbon and support customizing the Ribbon, including Access.

Access is a unique application compared to other Office applications. The main difference is that you use Access to create applications, but you use Word and Excel to create documents. Ribbon customization is different in Access too. While most Office documents are compressed XML documents, Access files don't follow that model. If you've customized the Ribbon in other Office applications, you'll have a head start in Access because you'll already be familiar with the XML. Don't worry if you're new to Ribbon customization. We'll show you everything you need to know.

> **ON THE WEB**
>
> In the `Chapter30.accdb` database, there is a table named Complete_USysRibbons that contains all the data you'd get from following the examples in this chapter. You'll create the USysRibbons table, but because it starts with USys, you won't be able to see it or any other system table until you right-click the Navigation pane, select Navigation Options, and select the Show System Objects check box in the Navigation Options dialog box. Included with the database are several XML files that are used in this chapter.

The Ribbon Hierarchy

The Ribbon is a fairly complex structure and is hierarchical in nature. At the top level are the tabs you see along the top of the Ribbon. Each tab contains one or more groups, each containing one or more controls. The Ribbon is highly adaptable to your current tasks, so the description that follows may not be exactly the same as you see on your screen:

- **Tabs:** The top object in the Ribbon hierarchy. You use tabs to separate the most fundamental operations into logical groups. For instance, the default Ribbon contains five tabs: Home, Create, External Data, Database Tools, and Help. The File tab acts differently from the other tabs. It opens a Backstage area with typical file operations.

- **Groups:** The second highest object in the Ribbon hierarchy. Groups contain any of a number of different types of controls and are used to logically separate operations supported by a Ribbon tab. In Figure 30.1, the Home tab contains seven groups: Views, Clipboard, Sort & Filter, Records, Find, Window, and Text Formatting.

- **Controls:** In Figure 30.1, notice the variety of controls within each group on the Home tab. The Views group contains a single control, while the Text Formatting group contains 18 different controls. Normally, the controls within a group are related to one another, but this is not a hard-and-fast rule.

FIGURE 30.1

The default Ribbon.

> **CAUTION**
>
> The sample files throughout this book use overlapping windows instead of the default tabbed interface. If you're using the tabbed interface, you won't see the Window group on the Home tab of the Ribbon.

As you design your custom Ribbons, you should keep the basic Ribbon hierarchy in mind. Microsoft has spent a great deal of time experimenting with and testing the Ribbon paradigm, and it works well for a wide variety of applications.

You can add a maximum of 100 tabs to a custom Ribbon—a very high limit. The other objects have similarly high limits. Obviously, too many tabs or too many groups can become a real problem for your users. Generally speaking, you should design your Ribbons in a conservative manner, including only the items at each level that your users actually need. Microsoft recommends four or five tabs and never more than seven.

Controls for Access Ribbons

Ribbons can contain buttons, text boxes, labels, separators, check boxes, toggle buttons, edit boxes, and even controls nested within other controls. This chapter explores a few of these controls, but you can find examples showing how to use every type of Ribbon control in Access on the Microsoft Office website (http://office.microsoft.com).

Access features some very interesting controls to use on your custom Ribbons. These controls are used in the default Ribbon and are accessible to the custom Ribbons you add to your applications.

SplitButton

The SplitButton is similar to a traditional button in an Access interface. What makes the SplitButton different is that it is split vertically or horizontally into two different controls. The left (or top side) of the control works as any other button and responds to a single click. The right (or bottom side) of the button includes an arrow that, when clicked, reveals a selection list of single-select options.

An example of a SplitButton (shown in Figure 30.2) is the View button on the Home tab.

FIGURE 30.2

The SplitButton is a powerful Ribbon control.

The top portion of the View button can be clicked to switch to a particular view. In Figure 30.2, the Design view is shown on the top of the button because there's a query open in Datasheet view. What is shown on the top of a SplitButton depends on what you have open and what state it's in. The arrow on the View button can be clicked to reveal a list of other options. Only one option in the SplitButton list can be selected. As soon as an item in the list is selected, the SplitButton list closes, and the action selected by the user is performed.

The button portion of the SplitButton control is independently programmable.

Menu

The Menu control is shown in Figure 30.3. Although the Menu looks very much like a ComboBox or DropDown, they are not the same type of object. Notice that the items in the drop-down list in Figure 30.3 include not only text (Clear All Filters, Filter By Form, and so on) but also an image associated with each item.

30

FIGURE 30.3

The Menu control simplifies a user's selections.

Only one item in the list can be selected at a time, providing an easy-to-understand interface for your users, when a limited number of options exist.

The SplitButton and Menu are similar in many ways. They both expose a list when clicked and present a list of single-select items. The main difference is that a SplitButton is split into two portions (the button portion that executes the default action and the menu portion), whereas the Menu simply drops down the list when clicked.

Gallery

The Gallery presents the user with an abbreviated view of different options for formatting and other tasks. Figure 30.4 shows the Themes Gallery for reports.

Gallery controls are used extensively in Access for displaying options such as those relating to formatting controls and selecting fonts.

Button

A Button can be clicked to perform an action. It does not provide options like a Menu or Gallery, but it can open a dialog box that contains additional options. The Copy button in the Clipboard group of the Home tab is an example of a button. Clicking Copy copies the current selection onto the Clipboard, but it doesn't provide any other options or perform any other actions.

FIGURE 30.4

The Gallery provides the user with a preview of the options.

ToggleButton

A special type of button control, the ToggleButton is used to set a state or condition of the application. ToggleButtons have two states: on and off. When a ToggleButton is in the off state, it appears like a normal button on the Ribbon. When a ToggleButton is clicked to set the on state, its background color changes to indicate its state, and its ScreenTip caption may change. Figure 30.5 shows the Apply Filter ToggleButton in its on state. The change in appearance is an indicator that a filter has been applied. Its ScreenTip changed from Apply Filter to Remove Filter.

FIGURE 30.5

A ToggleButton changes appearance to indicate state.

30

ComboBox

A ComboBox on the Ribbon is very similar to the Combo Box control on a form. It is a combination of a text box and a list box in that you can type directly into a ComboBox or click the down arrow portion of the control to display a list of options. The Font control on the Text Formatting group of the Home tab is an example of a ComboBox control.

CheckBox

A CheckBox control is another control that may seem familiar. It looks and acts just like a check box you put on a form. When a CheckBox has been clicked, a check mark appears in the box; otherwise, the box appears empty. The Required control on the Field Validation group of the Table Tools Fields tab is an example of a CheckBox control.

Special Ribbon features

The Ribbon contains two other special features that are worth noting. Some controls have SuperTips that can expand the amount of information shown in a ScreenTip. Also, the Ribbon can be hidden to increase the screen space available.

SuperTips

The SuperTip is similar to a ScreenTip but larger and it usually displays more information. A SuperTip displays the text that you specify, helping the user understand the purpose of a control. The SuperTip, shown in Figure 30.6, appears as the user hovers the mouse over a control on the Ribbon.

FIGURE 30.6

The SuperTip provides helpful information to the user.

The SuperTip example in Figure 30.6 is displayed when you hover the mouse pointer over the Find button on the Home tab. It's larger than a typical ScreenTip and shows more information, such as the shortcut key and a longer explanation of its function.

Collapsing the Ribbon

By default, the Ribbon is always open on the screen. However, the Ribbon, with all its controls and tabs may be in the way while users work with an application. There are several ways to collapse the Ribbon. The easiest methods are to press Ctrl+F1 or to double-click any tab. Single-clicking any collapsed tab brings the Ribbon back again, but only temporarily; the Ribbon will "auto-collapse" until you double-click a tab (or press Ctrl+F1) to restore the Ribbon to its pinned state. The Ribbon contains a Collapse button in the lower-right corner when it's expanded. When it's hidden, the button disappears and you have to re-pin it with one of the other methods.

Any forms or reports that are open as the Ribbon is collapsed and expanded are moved up or down so that their positions (relative to the Ribbon) remain the same. For example, a form that is open right below the Ribbon moves upward to occupy the same distance between the top of the form and the bottom of the Ribbon area.

Editing the Default Ribbon

Access 2010 added the ability to edit the default Ribbon. Changes made to the Ribbon stay with Access on the machine where the changes were made, but an option to export modifications is available in the Ribbon Designer.

Right-click anywhere on the Ribbon and choose Customize the Ribbon from the shortcut menu to launch the Ribbon Designer. The Customize the Ribbon window (see Figure 30.7) has one list that contains available commands and another that contains selected commands. You select the category of Ribbon you want to modify (File Tab, Main Tabs, Macros, All Commands, Popular Commands, Commands Not in the Ribbon, and so on) from the drop-down above the list on the left side, and then you use the Add and Remove buttons between the lists to add or remove items from the Ribbon.

From the perspective of Access, there is just one Ribbon, but it has a number of Main tabs on it: Print Preview, Home, Create, External Data, Database Tools, Source Control, Add-Ins, and Help. Within a Main tab are a number of groups, such as Views, Clipboard, and Sort & Filter. You cannot add or remove tabs or commands from the default Ribbon, but you can remove individual groups.

You can take away entire built-in groups, but you can't remove individual commands within a group. You can use the buttons below the right list to add new custom tabs or to add new groups within existing Ribbon tabs, and then add commands to the custom group. Using a new custom tab or group is the only way to add commands from the left list to the Ribbon definition on the right side.

You can't add commands directly to tabs. Commands must reside within groups on a tab. It's easy to add a command to a group: select the command from the list on the left, select the custom group to receive the command in the list on the right, and click the Add button between the lists.

30

FIGURE 30.7

The Ribbon Designer allows you to customize the Ribbon.

If you want to remove certain commands from a built-in group, you have to remove the built-in group containing the bad command, add a custom group, move it to the appropriate tab, and then add only the commands you want in the group. Right-click the new group and select Rename from the shortcut menu, or select the new group and click the Rename button under the Customize the Ribbon list. The Rename dialog box appears (see Figure 30.8). Use this dialog box to assign a new name to the group and select the group's icon.

FIGURE 30.8

Renaming a custom group and setting the group's icon.

You can hide built-in Ribbon tabs if you prefer. Notice the check boxes next to the items in the list on the right side of Figure 30.7. Deselecting a box next to a tab hides the tab from the user. If the tab contains commands the user must have, you can add a custom tab (with the New Tab button under the Customize the Ribbon list on the right side of Figure 30.7), and then add custom groups as needed. Finally, add the necessary commands to the custom groups.

In many cases, simply hiding tabs is probably easier than removing them from the Ribbon. If they're hidden, you can easily restore their visibility later on, if you need to.

The Ribbon Designer includes up and down arrows at the far right side for repositioning tabs and groups within tabs. You could, for instance, add a custom group (or use an existing group) and move the most commonly used commands into it with the up- and down-arrow keys.

If the changes you've made don't work out as expected, click the Reset button below the Customize the Ribbon list to return the built-in Ribbon to its original state. The Reset button (notice its drop-down arrow in Figure 30.7) lets you reset the entire Ribbon or just the selected tab.

Click the Import/Export button below the Customize the Ribbon list to export the customizations you've made to the Ribbon as an external file. Alternatively, the list that appears when you click the Import/Export button includes a command to import a customization file and apply it to your Ribbon. Not surprisingly, the customization file is in XML format and is shared by all of the Office 2019 applications.

Using a customization file makes it easy to apply custom Ribbon changes to all users working with an Access 2019 application. It's also a great way to back up the changes you've

30

made if you need to reapply the changes later on. You could, for instance, set up the Ribbon exactly as you want your users to see it, export the customization, and then reset the Ribbon to its original state so that you have access to all Ribbon features during your development cycle.

Working with the Quick Access Toolbar

The Quick Access toolbar is in the upper-left corner of the main Access screen (see Figure 30.9) just above the File tab. The Quick Access toolbar remains visible at all times in Access and provides a handy way to give your users quick access to commonly performed tasks such as opening a database file or sending an object to a printer.

FIGURE 30.9

The Quick Access toolbar remains on the screen at all times.

The Quick Access toolbar is fully customizable. It comes with a list of default controls, some of which are hidden, that you can hide or unhide with the Customize Quick Access Toolbar menu (see Figure 30.9). You can quickly and easily add any of a large number of operations to the Quick Access toolbar. Also, the controls you add are applicable either to the current database or to all Access databases.

The easiest way to add a command to the Quick Access toolbar is to locate the command on the Ribbon, right-click it, and then select Add to Quick Access Toolbar from the shortcut menu that appears. Access adds the selected item to the rightmost position in the Quick Access toolbar.

For more flexibility when modifying the Quick Access toolbar, select More Commands from the shortcut menu to open the Customize the Quick Access Toolbar screen (see Figure 30.10). Like the Ribbon Designer, the Quick Access Toolbar Designer uses a list of available commands and a list of selected commands. The list on the left side of the screen contains items representing every command available in Access, categorized as Popular Commands, Commands Not in the Ribbon, All Commands, and Macros. You select the command category from the drop-down control above the list. The category list also contains entries for all the Ribbon tabs in Access (File, Home, External Data, and so on). Selecting an item from this drop-down list reveals the commands within that category.

FIGURE 30.10

You can easily add new commands to the Quick Access toolbar.

30

The Quick Access toolbar provides a handy way for you to control which commands the users access as they work with your Access applications. The tasks available to the Quick Access toolbar include operations such as backing up the current database, converting the current database to another Access data format, viewing database properties, and linking tables.

Because the Quick Access toolbar is visible to all users, be sure not to include commands (such as Design View) that may be confusing to users or harmful to your applications. Because the Quick Access toolbar is easy to customize, it's not difficult to add the commands you need at the time you need them, instead of leaving them visible to all users all the time.

Use the Add and Remove buttons in the Quick Access Toolbar Designer to move an item from the list on the left to the list on the right. After a command has been added to the Quick Access toolbar, the command is no longer available to be added again, so you can't add the same command more than once.

The Quick Access Toolbar Designer also contains up and down arrows to the right of the selected list that enable you to reorder the left-to-right appearance of the Quick Access toolbar commands.

Be warned that you can add any number of commands to the Quick Access toolbar. When more commands are contained than the Quick Access toolbar can display, a double-right-arrow button appears at the far right side that expands to show the hidden commands. However, because the whole idea of the Quick Access toolbar is to make commands quickly available to users, there is no point in loading up the Quick Access toolbar with dozens of commands that only make it more difficult for the user.

Developing Custom Ribbons

The Ribbon Designer and Quick Access Toolbar Designer provide convenient ways to customize the Access user interface. However, as you've seen, these methods limit the customizations you can make. Using Extensible Markup Language (XML), you have a lot of flexibility in customizing the Ribbon.

Ribbons are not represented by a programmable object model in Access. Ribbon customizations are defined by XML statements contained in a special table named USysRibbons. Access uses the information it finds in the XML to compose and render the Ribbon on the screen.

The Ribbon creation process

Briefly, creating custom Ribbons is a five-step process:

1. **Design the Ribbon and compose the XML that defines the Ribbon.**
2. **Write VBA callback routines (described in the following section) that support the Ribbon's operations.**
3. **Create the USysRibbons table.**
4. **Provide a Ribbon name and add the custom Ribbon's XML to the USysRibbons table.**
5. **Specify the custom Ribbon's name in the Access Options dialog box.**

None of these steps is particularly intuitive, especially when it comes to composing the XML and writing callback routines. Your best bet is to find an example that is reasonably close to what you want and customize its XML to suit your purposes.

Using VBA callbacks

A *callback* is code that is passed to another entity for processing. Each procedure you write to support operations on a Ribbon is passed to the "Ribbon processor" in Access that actually performs the Ribbon's actions. This is very unlike the event-driven code you've been working with in Access. Clicking a button on a form *directly* triggers the code in the button's `Click` event procedure. A Ribbon's callback procedure is linked to the Ribbon but is internally processed by Access and does not directly run in response to the click on the Ribbon.

To fully understand this process, imagine that Access contains a process that constantly monitors activity on the Ribbon. As soon as the user clicks a Ribbon control, the Ribbon processor springs into action, retrieving the callback procedure associated with the control and performing the actions specified in the callback.

This means that there are no `Click`, `DblClick`, or `GotFocus` events associated with the Ribbon in Access. Instead, you bind a callback to a Ribbon control through the XML that defines the Ribbon. Each Ribbon control includes a number of action attributes that can be attached to callbacks, and the Ribbon processor takes over when the user invokes a control's action.

Here is an example. The following XML statements define a button control on a Ribbon:

```
<button id="ViewProducts"
    label="All Products"
    size="large"
    imageMso="FindDialog"
    onAction="OpenProductsForm"
    tag="frmProductsDisplay"/>
```

30

NOTE

These lines are a single XML statement. Line breaks have been added for readability.

Notice the `onAction` attribute in this XML code. Notice also that the `onAction` attribute is set to `OpenProductsForm`. The `onAction` attribute is similar to the events associated with a form's controls. Each interactive Ribbon control (buttons, SplitButtons, and so on) includes the `onAction` attribute. The callback procedure (`OpenProductsForm`, in this example) assigned to the `onAction` attribute is passed to the Ribbon processor when the control's action occurs.

A control's attributes may appear in any order within the control's XML, but they must be spelled correctly. XML is case sensitive, so attributes must be entered exactly as you see in the examples in this chapter and in the `Chapter30.accdb` example database. And, attribute values (like `"FindDialog"`) must be surrounded by double or single quote characters. Both types of quotes are legal in XML, but it's a good practice to choose one and stick with it.

Notice that the button control does not contain a `Click` event. Instead, each interactive control's `onAction` attribute handles whatever action is expected by the control. In the case of a button, the action is a user clicking the button, whereas for a text box, the action is the user typing into the text box. Both of these controls include the `onAction` attribute, but `onAction` means something different for each control.

NOTE

Be aware than `onAction` is not an event. It is just an XML attribute that points to the callback procedure tied to the Ribbon control. The callback procedure runs whenever the user interacts with the control. In this case, the ViewProducts button's callback procedure is invoked when the user clicks the button.

Ribbon controls have several other important attributes, such as `imageMso`, `screentip`, and `supertip`. These attributes are described in the "Adding Ribbon Controls" section, later in this chapter.

TIP

You probably want to see any errors generated by your custom Ribbon during development. By default, Ribbon error reporting is disabled, and you must enable it before you see error messages thrown by the Ribbon. Select the File tab in the upper-left corner of the main Access screen and choose the Options button at the bottom. Next, select the Client Settings tab in the Options dialog box and scroll down to the General section (see Figure 30.11). Make sure the Show Add-In User Interface Errors check box is selected, and then click OK at the bottom of the dialog box. The error messages generated by the Ribbon are invaluable debugging aids. Without these messages, you have no idea what has failed in your custom Ribbons.

FIGURE 30.11

Set the Show Add-in User Interface Errors property to see Ribbon errors.

Creating a Custom Ribbon

Creating Access Ribbons is, at minimum, a five-step process. Each of these steps is described in detail in the following sections. Later you'll see more examples of these steps.

Step 1: Design the Ribbon and build the XML

As with most database objects, the first step to creating a new Access Ribbon is to design it carefully. If you're converting an existing toolbar or menu to an Access Ribbon, you have a pretty good idea of the controls and other items to add to the Ribbon.

The XML document you create for your Ribbon mirrors the design you've laid out. Perhaps the most challenging aspect of composing the Ribbons XML is visualizing how the Ribbon will look, based on the XML behind it. There are no visual cues in a Ribbon XML document that hint at the Ribbon's appearance when rendered in Access. Experience will be your best guide as you work with Ribbon customization, and sometimes trial and error is the only way to achieve a desired objective.

As a final point, Access is extremely fussy about the XML used to compose Ribbons. There is no "parser" in Access that validates the XML as a Ribbon is rendered. If an error exists in the XML document, Access refuses to render the Ribbon, or the Ribbon will be missing elements defined in the XML. This is one reason that using a good XML editor to compose your XML is important. Most often, the only way you know that an error exists in your Ribbon XML code is that Access loads the default Ribbon instead of your custom Ribbon.

Inevitably, Ribbon development in Access requires a number of back-and-forth cycles in which you modify the XML, transfer it to Access, and view the results. You have no way of really knowing how well your XML will work as a Ribbon specification until Access renders the Ribbon on the screen.

"The Basic Ribbon XML" section later in this chapter describes the fundamental XML statements required by Access Ribbons.

For this example, we'll create a new tab on the default Ribbon. The new tab will be named "Messages" and will contain one control that opens a form. First, design a form with one Label control on it containing a message to be displayed. Figure 30.12 shows the form frm-Message, which can be found in the `Chapter30.accdb` database.

FIGURE 30.12

A simple form that displays a message.

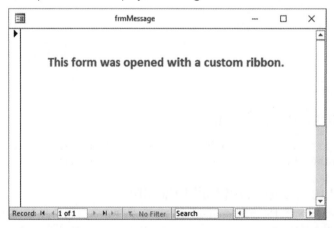

To create the XML that will define the new Ribbon elements, open your favorite XML editor. The examples in this chapter use the XML Notepad application, available for free from Microsoft.com (`www.microsoft.com/en-us/download/details .aspx?id=7973`). Figure 30.13 shows the XML in XML Notepad.

FIGURE 30.13

XML Notepad can be used to write XML.

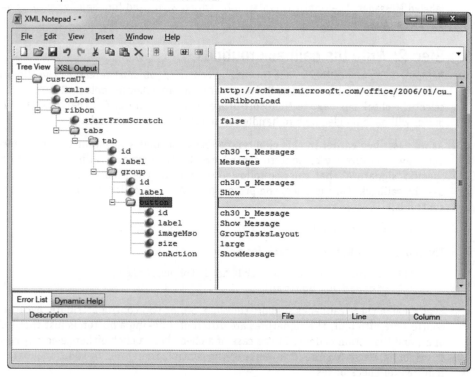

In XML Notepad, you can choose Source from the View menu to see the XML that is generated. Here's the XML for `Message.xml`:

```xml
<?xml version="1.0" encoding="utf-8"?>
<customUI xmlns="http://schemas.microsoft.com/office/2009/07
    /customui" onLoad="onRibbonLoad">
  <ribbon startFromScratch="false">
    <tabs>
      <tab id="ch30_t_Messages" label="Messages">
        <group id="ch30_g_Messages" label="Show">
          <button id="ch30_b_Message" label="Show Message"
           imageMso="GroupTasksLayout" size="large"
            onAction="ShowMessage" />
        </group>
      </tab>
    </tabs>
  </ribbon>
</customUI>
```

30

We'll discuss each of the parts of this XML file later in the chapter. For now, note that this XML creates a button labeled Show Message on a Group labeled Show on a tab labeled Messages. The onAction attribute, which we'll need for the next step, is named ShowMessage.

Step 2: Write the callback routines

Before writing any callback code for Ribbon controls, you must reference the Microsoft Office 16.0 Object Library in the References dialog box (choose Tools ⇨ References, and select the check box next to Microsoft Office 16.0 Object Library). Otherwise, the VBA interpreter will have no idea how to handle references to Ribbon controls.

As we described earlier in this chapter, callback routines are similar to event procedures, but they don't directly respond to control events. Each type of callback routine has a specific "signature" that must be followed in order for the Ribbon processor to locate and use the callback. For instance, the prototype onAction callback signature for a button control is:

```
Public Sub OnAction(control as IRibbonControl)
```

The prototype onAction callback for a check box is:

```
Public Sub OnAction(control As IRibbonControl, _
    pressed As Boolean)
```

Even though these callbacks support the same onAction control attribute, because the controls are different, the signatures are different. Clicking a button is just that—click once, and the action is done. In the case of a check box, a click either selects (pressed = True) or deselects (pressed = False) the control. Therefore, an additional parameter is required for check boxes.

These procedures are just prototypes and do not apply to any particular control on a Ribbon. In practice, the callback procedure for a control is usually named after the control to distinguish it from callback procedures for other controls. For this example, write the following code in a standard module:

```
Public Sub ShowMessage(control As IRibbonControl)

    'Called from Messages > Show > Show Message
    DoCmd.OpenForm "frmMessage"

End Sub
```

Notice that this procedure's declaration matches the prototype for a button control's onAction callback procedure. Although not required, this procedure even contains a comment that identifies the Ribbon control that calls the routine.

Callback routines must be declared with the Public attribute in a standard module, or they can't be seen by the Ribbon process.

The name you apply to callback routines is entirely your choice, as long as the procedure's declaration matches the control's `onAction` signature. Obviously, the procedure's name must match the value you assign to the control's `onAction` attribute, and documenting the procedure's relationship to a Ribbon control is very helpful when it comes time to modify the Ribbon or the callback.

Notice that the preceding callback procedure doesn't reference the control by name. This means that you have to write a uniquely named callback for each control or use a single callback for multiple similar controls.

Step 3: Create the USysRibbons table

Access looks for a table named USysRibbons to see whether any custom Ribbons are in the current database application. This table does not exist by default; if present, it contains the XML that defines the custom Ribbons in the application.

> **NOTE**
>
> USysRibbons is hidden in the Navigation pane by virtue of the USys prefix in its name. (Any database object with USys as the first four characters of its name is automatically hidden in the Navigation pane.) If you want to see USysRibbons in the Navigation pane, you must enable Show System Objects in the Navigation Options: Right-click the Navigation pane title bar, select Navigation Options, and then select Show System Objects in the lower-left corner of the Navigation Options dialog box.

USysRibbons is very simple, containing only three fields (shown in Table 30.1).

TABLE 30.1 The USysRibbons Table Design

Field	Data Type
ID	AutoNumber
RibbonName	Short Text
RibbonXML	Long Text

The ID field just keeps track of the Ribbons in the table. The RibbonName field is used to specify which Ribbon Access should load at startup (described in Step 5, later in this chapter), whereas RibbonXML is a Long Text field containing the XML that defines the Ribbon.

Because USysRibbons is a table, your Access database may actually include the definitions of many different custom Ribbons. However, only one custom Ribbon can be active at a time. Later in this chapter, we cover how to invalidate an existing Ribbon and load a new Ribbon in its place.

You might find good reasons to add additional fields to USysRibbons. For instance, you could add a Notes or Comments field that helps another developer understand how the

30

Ribbon should be used. You could also add a modification date and other fields that help track changes to your custom Ribbons. If you modify USysRibbons, be sure not to remove or rename the three required fields (ID, RibbonName, and RibbonXML). These three fields must exist in USysRibbons and must be named correctly for your custom Ribbons to work.

Step 4: Add XML to USysRibbons

Now you're ready to store your XML in the USysRibbons table. Open the USysRibbons table in Datasheet view. In the RibbonName field, enter **rbnMessages** and move the cursor to the RibbonXml field.

Copy the XML that you created in Step 1 and paste it into the RibbonXml field of USysRibbons. If you're using XML Notepad, open the XML file in XML Notepad and choose View ⇨ Source to output the XML to Windows Notepad. Then copy the XML from there to paste into USysRibbons. Figure 30.14 show USysRibbons with the fields completed.

The XML that was pasted into the RibbonXml field contains a lot of white space. Don't worry about the tabs and line breaks in the XML. However, if you replace existing data in the RibbonXml field, be sure to replace all the existing data. With tabs and line breaks, it can be difficult to know if you've left any remnants from the previous data.

FIGURE 30.14

The USysRibbons table stores the XML for custom Ribbons.

FIGURE 30.15

`frmRibbons` displays the information stored in the `USysRibbons` table.

Step 5: Specify the custom Ribbon property

The last step, before restarting the application, is to open the Current Database properties (choose File ➪ Options ➪ Current Database), scroll to the Ribbons and Toolbar Options section, and select the name of the new Ribbon from the Ribbon Name combo box (see Figure 30.16). The combo box's list contains only the names of custom Ribbons in USysRibbons that were in the table as Access started, so it does not contain the name of the new Ribbon. (Apparently Access reads USysRibbons only one time as Access opens a database.) You have to type the Ribbon's name into the combo box, or restart the application and let Access find the new Ribbon in USysRibbons.

FIGURE 30.16

Specifying the new custom Ribbon in the Current Database options dialog box.

When you close the Access Options dialog box after selecting a new Ribbon Name, Access displays a message that you must close and reopen the database for the changes to take effect. Figure 30.17 shows the message displayed.

FIGURE 30.17

Changes to the Ribbon Name property require a restart of the application.

FIGURE 30.18

The XML produces new Ribbon elements that open a form.

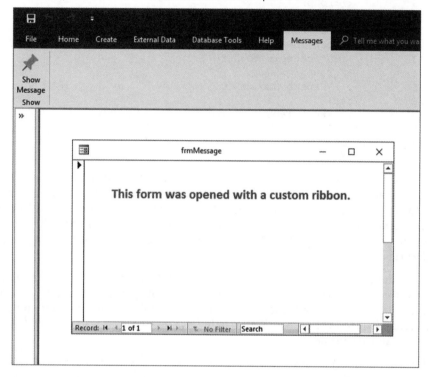

Once Access is restarted, the new tab shows on the default Ribbon. Figure 30.18 shows the new tab, the Show group on that tab, the lone Show Message button, and the form that is opened when the button is clicked.

The Basic Ribbon XML

Take a closer look at the basic XML required by Ribbons. The following XML represents a prototype Ribbon. (Line numbers have been added to make the discussion following this XML easier to understand.)

```
1 <?xml version="1.0" encoding="utf-8"?>
2 <!-- This is a comment in the ribbon's XML -->
3 <customUI xmlns="http://schemas.microsoft.com/office
    /2009/07/customui" onLoad="onRibbonLoad">
4   <ribbon startFromScratch="true">
5     <tabs>
6       <tab id="tab1" ...
```

```
 7              <group id="group1" ... >
 8                  ... Controls go here ...
 9              </group>
10          </tab>
11          <tab id="tab2" ...
12              <group id="group2" ... >
13                  ... Controls go here ...
14              </group>
15              ... Repeat Groups ...
16          </tab>
17          ... Repeat Tabs ...
18      </tabs>
19    </ribbon>
20 </customUI>
```

The first statement (`<?xml version="1.0" encoding="utf-8"?>`) is not required by and does not affect Access Ribbons. It's completely your choice whether to keep this line or not in the USysRibbons table. Well-formed XML includes the version line, and it helps other programs to render the file, so it's a good practice to include it. Line 2 shows how to add a comment to a Ribbon's XML code. The `<!--` and `-->` are standard commenting tags for XML documents.

Line 3 (beginning with `<customUI...`) specifies an XML *namespace* (`xmlns`), an XML document that predefines acceptable tags for the XML statements that follow. The Office namespace defines the Office Ribbon constructs, such as tabs, groups, controls, and so on. Every Ribbon defined in the RibbonXML field in USysRibbons must start with this statement, so be sure it's included.

The statement in line 4 is rather important. The `startFromScratch` directive determines whether you're building an entire Ribbon from scratch or modifying the default Ribbon by adding or taking things away. Depending on your situation, the majority of your custom Ribbons may be built from scratch because the default Ribbon knows nothing about the forms, reports, and other objects and operations in your database. Also, the default Ribbon contains commands that may be dangerous to your application's integrity. For instance, a user could open a form, report, or table in Design view and make changes without your being aware of it. Removing these commands from the user interface is a first line of defense for your applications.

When `startFromScratch` is set to `false`, your custom Ribbon definition is added to the default Ribbon to the right of the built-in tabs. Because Access includes only five tabs by default, you may have enough room for your additional tabs without overcrowding the Ribbon. When `startFromScratch` is set to `true`, none of the default tabs, groups, or controls is shown on the Ribbon. Only what you include in the XML will be displayed.

Most of the tags in an XML file have a corresponding closing tag that defines the end of the section that relates to that tag. All the statements between the opening and closing tags are children of that tag. Lines 19 and 20 are the closing tags for the `Ribbon` and `CustomUI` elements, respectively.

The `<tabs>` (line 5) and `</tabs>` (line 18) tags indicate the beginning and end of the tabs on the Ribbon. Ribbons are hierarchical, with tabs containing groups, which contain controls. The tabs, therefore, are the highest-level objects within a Ribbon and enclose all other Ribbon objects.

Line 6 defines the leftmost tab on the Ribbon. In this example, the tab's name is `tab1`. The other attributes for this tab are not shown but are implied by the ellipsis (...). The ending tag for `tab1` is located on line 10.

Line 7 begins the definition of the first group on `tab1` and line 9 ends this group. Within the group are the controls displayed by the group.

The rest of this prototype Ribbon is simple repetition of the first few items.

> **NOTE**
>
> XML is case sensitive. Be careful to use exactly the same case and spelling for all references in your XML as well as in the callback code driving the Ribbon.

Adding Ribbon Controls

The previous section presented a simple prototype Ribbon. In this example, the controls were indicated by `... Controls go here ...` on lines 8 and 13. In this section, you'll see the XML and the callback procedures for several controls. Many XML attributes are common to more than one control. We won't discuss every attribute for every control; rather, we'll look at the most-used attributes.

Specifying imageMso

Most, but not all, Ribbon controls include an `imageMso` attribute that specifies the picture attached to the control. You can't provide simple references to image files; instead, you must use an `imageMso` identifier for this purpose. Every Ribbon control in the Office 2019 applications has an associated `imageMso` value. You use these values on your custom Access Ribbon controls and provide a label that tells your users the exact purpose of the control.

To find the `imageMso` for a particular Ribbon control, use the Customize the Ribbon window to open a particular Ribbon. Then use the drop-down in the upper left of the designer to select the Ribbon category containing the Ribbon command and hover the mouse over the command's entry in the list (see Figure 30.19).

The `imageMso` for the Layout View command (`ViewsLayoutView`) is shown in parentheses in the ScreenTip that appears near the selected command.

30

The Label control

The Label control is, by far, the simplest and easiest to add to a Ribbon. A Ribbon label is completely analogous to a label you add to an Access form. It contains either hard-coded text or text that is generated by a callback procedure.

Here is a sample label definition:

```
<group id="ch30_g_Settings" label="Settings">
  <labelControl id="lbl1" label="Font Things" />
  <separator id="s1"/>
  <labelControl id="lbl2" label="Choose Font Settings" />
  <checkBox id="chk1" label="Bold" onAction="SetBold"/>
  <checkBox id="chk2" label="Italics" onAction="SetItalics"/>
</group>
```

FIGURE 30.19

Using the Ribbon Designer to obtain a Ribbon command's imageMso attribute.

This XML contains two labels, a separator, and two check boxes. The text in each of these labels is hard-coded, rather than returned by a callback procedure. You can set the label's caption at run time using a callback procedure and the getLabel attribute:

```
<group id="ch30_g_Label" label="Labels">
  <labelControl id="lbl3" getLabel="lbl3_getLabel" />
</group>
```

The preceding XML code uses getLabel to identify the callback procedure that will determine what the label displays. In a standard module, the following procedure will show the current date in the label:

```
Public Sub lbl3_getLabel(control As IRibbonControl, ByRef label)

    label = FormatDateTime(Date, vbLongDate)

End Sub
```

The label argument is passed ByRef, and whichever string is assigned to that argument is displayed in the labelControl. In this example, the FormatDateTime function is used to create a string with the current date.

You can also use one callback procedure to control several labels. In this example, three labels use the same getLabel attribute:

```
<group id="ch30_g_Label" label="Labels">
  <labelControl id="lbl3" getLabel="lbl3_getLabel" />
  <labelControl id="lbl4" getLabel="lbl456_getLabel" />
  <labelControl id="lbl5" getLabel="lbl456_getLabel" />
  <labelControl id="lbl6" getLabel="lbl456_getLabel" />
</group>
```

The lbl456_getLabel callback procedure uses the control's id property to determine which control is calling the procedure:

```
Public Sub lbl456_getLabel(control As IRibbonControl, ByRef label)

    Select Case control.Id
      Case "lbl4"
        label = "This is Label 4"
      Case "lbl5"
        label = "This is Label 5"
      Case "lbl6"
        label = "This is Label 6"
    End Select

End Sub
```

30

> **NOTE**
>
> Most attributes have both a static form and a dynamic form. By prefixing the attribute's name with "get," you transform it from an attribute whose value is set in the XML to an attribute whose value is determined by a callback procedure. For example, the `labelControl` has a `label` attribute and a `getLabel` attribute. Use `label` when you want to set the value in the XML and `getLabel` when you want to set the value dynamically in a VBA callback procedure. An attribute and its `getAttribute` cousin are mutually exclusive. Only specify one or the other in the XML.

The Button control

The Button control is perhaps the most useful and fundamental of all of the Ribbon controls. A button is very simple; it has a label, an `imageMso` attribute for setting the button's image, and an `onAction` attribute that names the callback routine. An example of a button XML is:

```
<button id="btn1" size="large"
  label="Browse"
  imageMso="OutlookGlobe"
  onAction="btn1_onAction" />
```

The `btn1_onAction` callback procedure, shown in the following code, uses the `FollowHyperlink` method of the `Application` object to launch a web browser. The Button Ribbon control does not support double-click actions, so tying a button to a callback procedure is very simple:

```
Public Sub btn1_onAction(control As IRibbonControl)

    Application.FollowHyperlink "http://www.wiley.com"

End Sub
```

Another attribute that you can use with the Button control is the `keytip` attribute. Access assigns key tips to most controls that you add to the Ribbon. Key tips are shown when the Alt key is pressed; they allow you to navigate the Ribbon from the keyboard. You can specify your own key tip with the `keytip` attribute. The XML for the preceding button with a `keytip` attribute looks like this:

```
<button id="btn1" size="large"
label="Browse" keytip="B"
imageMso="OutlookGlobe"
onAction="btn1_onAction" />
```

Figure 30.20 shows the new button with a *B* for the key tip, allowing the user to access the button with an easy-to-remember keyboard shortcut.

FIGURE 30.20

You can specify a custom key tip for controls.

Separators

A *separator* is a graphical element that divides items in a group, as shown in Figure 30.21. Separators contain no text and appear as a vertical line within a group. By themselves, they're not very interesting, but they graphically separate controls that would otherwise be too close within a group.

FIGURE 30.21

Separators provide a way to divide controls within a group.

Here's the XML code for the separators in Figure 30.21:

```
<group id="ch30_g_Separator" label="Separators">
  <labelControl id="lbl7" label="1" />
  <separator id="s2" />
  <labelControl id="lbl8" label="2" />
  <separator id="s3" />
  <labelControl id="lbl9" label="3" />
</group>
```

The only requirement for separators is that each be assigned a unique ID value.

The CheckBox control

The CheckBox control is effective for allowing the user to select any of a number of different options. CheckBox controls are not mutually exclusive, so the user can choose any of the check boxes within a group without affecting other selections.

30

CheckBox controls are established much like any other Ribbon control:

```
<tab id="ch30_t_Outdoor" label="Outdoor">
  <group id="ch30_g_Sports" label="Sports">
    <checkBox id="chkBaseball" label="Baseball" ...
    <checkBox id="chkBasketball" label="Basketball" ...
    <separator id="outdoor_Sep1"/>
    <checkBox id="chkTennis" label="Tennis" ...
    <checkBox id="chkWaterPolo" label="Water Polo" ...
  </group>
  <group id="ch30_g_Camping" label="Camping Supplies">
    <checkBox id="chkTent" label="Tent" ...
    <checkBox id="chkGranola" label="Granola" ...
    <checkBox id="chkLantern" label="Lantern" ...
    <separator id="camping_Sep1"/>
    <button id="btnCamping" imageMso="StartTimer"
      size="large" label="A Big Button" />
  </group>
</tab>
```

> **NOTE**
> We removed some XML and replaced it with ellipsis characters to improve clarity of this example XML.

The tab produced by this XML code is shown in Figure 30.22 (and included in the `ControlExamples.xml` example Ribbon in the `Chapter30.accdb` database).

FIGURE 30.22

CheckBox controls are a good choice when the user needs to be able to select among a number of options.

The Ribbon CheckBox controls shown in Figure 30.22 work exactly as you would expect. The check boxes may be selected individually or in any combination. CheckBox controls are not mutually exclusive, and each control can have its own `onAction` attribute, or multiple controls can share a callback procedure.

The DropDown control

The DropDown control is more complex than the label, button, and check box examples we've covered. It includes a list of items for the user to choose from. Therefore, a DropDown has a number of attributes that define its appearance, as well as callbacks that populate its list:

```
<dropDown
  id="ddLogin"
  label="Login" supertip="Select your employee name...
  screentip="Login Name"
  getItemCount="ddLogin_getItemCount"
  getItemLabel="ddLogin_getItemLabel"
  onAction="ddLogin_onAction" />
```

The id, label, screentip, and supertip attributes define the DropDown control's appearance. The getItemCount and getItemLabel populate the DropDown's list. onAction specifies the callback that handles the control's action. Figure 30.23 shows the DropDown created in this section.

FIGURE 30.23

A DropDown control lists users' names.

The VBA callbacks for a typical DropDown are shown in the following code. Two primary callbacks are required for a DropDown. The first sets the count of items to appear in the list, and the second actually populates the list:

```
Public Sub ddLogin_GetItemCount( _
    control As IRibbonControl, ByRef count)

    count = Nz(DCount("*", "tblSalesPerson"), 0)

End Sub

Public Sub ddLogin_getItemLabel( _
    control As IRibbonControl, index As Integer, ByRef label)

    Dim sName As String

    sName = Nz(DLookup("SalespersonName", _
```

```
                  "tblSalesPerson", "SalesPersonID = " & index + 1), _
                  vbNullString)

         label = sName

    End Sub
```

The first callback (ddLogin_getItemCount) gets the count of items to be placed on the DropDown's list. Notice the ByRef count parameter. This parameter tells the DropDown how many items to accommodate on its list.

The second procedure (ddLogin_getItemLabel) actually retrieves the items for the list. In this case, the procedure pulls the SalesPerson name field from tblSalesPerson using DLookup. ddLogin_getItemLabel is called by the DropDown multiple times; the exact number of calls is determined by the count value established by ddLogin_getItemCount.

An accurate count of values to add to the DropDown is important. The DropDown has no way, other than the count parameter, to know how many items to expect. Setting a count too low means that not all items will be added, whereas setting the count too high means that list contains blank spaces. For instance, if you set the count to ten items but only five are available, then the DropDown's list contains the five items but also five blank spaces.

The ddLogin_getItemLabel routine cheats a little bit to supply this information. Notice the index parameter passed to this routine, which tells the procedure which slot on the drop-down list is being filled when the procedure is called. The DLookup adds 1 to this value and extracts the name of the salesperson whose ID matches this value. This means that the SalesPersonID values have to be sequential, starting with 1, or this procedure will fail.

Extracting data with nonsequential ID values, or where the ID value is non-numeric, requires a bit more work. In the following code, ddLogin_getItemLabel has been rewritten to use a recordset rather than the DLookup function. The ddLogin_onAction procedure uses a recordset in the same way:

```
    Private Const msSQLSALESPERSON As String = _
      "SELECT SalespersonName FROM tblSalesPerson ORDER BY
        SalesPersonName;"

    Public Sub ddLogin_getItemLabel( _
      control As IRibbonControl, index As Integer, ByRef label)

      Dim adRs As ADODB.Recordset

      Set adRs = CurrentProject.Connection.Execute(msSQLSALESPERSON)
      adRs.Move index

      label = adRs.Fields(0).Value

    End Sub
```

```
Public Sub ddLogin_onAction( _
   control As IRibbonControl, id As String, index As Integer)

    Dim rs As DAO.Recordset

    Set rs = CurrentDb.OpenRecordset(msSQLSALESPERSON, _
        dbopendynaset)
    rs.Move index

    MsgBox "You are logged in as " _
        & rs.Fields(0).Value & ".", _
        vbOKOnly, "Logged In"

End Sub
```

Both procedures use the same module-level constant, msSQLSALESPERSON. This ensures that the records are sorted in exactly same order. The Move method moves to the record specified by index, and if the records were in a different order from one procedure to the next, the wrong name would be returned. The name of the salesperson is retrieved using the adRs.Fields(0).Value statement. By controlling the SQL statement in a module-level constant, you can be sure that the first field (.Fields(0)) will contain the proper information.

NOTE

The Ribbon includes three controls that appear similar. The DropDown control discussed in this section shares many visual characteristics with the Menu control (refer to Figure 30.3) and the ComboBox control. (The Font combo box in the Text Formatting group on the Home tab is an example.) The DropDown and ComboBox controls use the getItemCount and getItemLabel callbacks to populate their lists, while the Menu control contains Button elements directly in the XML. You should understand the differences among these controls so that you can choose the best one for your application.

The DropDown control forces the user to select an item on the list and displays the selected item in the control. While the DropDown control looks like a ComboBox control, the user can't edit the value directly.

The ComboBox control works just like a DropDown, except that the user can edit the value directly in the control and is not limited to the items in the list. DropDown controls and CombBox controls are analogous to List Boxes and Combo Boxes that you might use on a form.

The simplest of the three controls, the Menu control, is a list of buttons that perform an action. The value of the selection is not displayed in the control, and the buttons cannot be created dynamically.

The SplitButton Control

The SplitButton control is very useful in situations where the user may select from a number of different options, but one option is used more frequently than the others. An example might be a number of reports, one of which is commonly printed while the others are printed less often. The View SplitButton that's on the Home tab when you're designing a table is a good example (refer to Figure 30.2). The button portion of the View SplitButton changes, depending on the context. If the user is already in Datasheet view, the button changes to Design view and vice versa.

30

The items on a SplitButton's list are contained within <menu> and </menu> tags. Whichever controls (within reason, of course) that appear within these tags show up in the SplitButton's list. The definition of the default button portion of a SplitButton lies outside the <menu> and </menu> tags. In the following code fragment, spbtn1_btn1 is the default button, whereas the other buttons (spbtn1_btn2, spbtn1_btn3, and so on) occupy the SplitButton's list:

```
<group id="ch30_g_Splits" label="Split Button">
  <splitButton id="spbtn1" size="large">
    <button id="spbtn1_btn1"
      imageMso="ModuleInsert"
      label="Button1"
      onAction="spbtn1_onAction" />
    <menu id="spbtn1_menu" itemSize="large">
      <button id="spbtn1_btn2"
        imageMso="OutlookGlobe"
        label="Button2"
        onAction="spbtn1_onAction" />
      <button id="spbtn1_btn3"
        imageMso="OutlookGears"
        label="Button3"
        onAction="spbtn1_onAction" />
      <button id="spbtn1_btn4"
        imageMso="Organizer"
        label="Button4"
        onAction="spbtn1_onAction" />
    </menu>
  </splitButton>
</group>
```

This Ribbon XML example produces the SplitButton shown in Figure 30.24. This example is contained in the rbnControls example in the Chapter30.accdb database.

FIGURE 30.24

A SplitButton is a very useful Ribbon control.

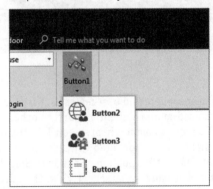

Attaching Ribbons to Forms and Reports

The Ribbon elements we've created so far are always visible. Often, you'll want the Buttons, DropDowns, and Menus that you place on the Ribbon to be available all the time. However, you may have certain Ribbon elements that you want to display only in certain situations. Fortunately, Access provides a simple way to display Ribbons when a form or report is active.

Forms and reports have a RibbonName property that you can set in the Property Sheet or with VBA. The Ribbon Name property in the Property Sheet provides a drop-down for all the Ribbons in the USysRibbons table. Figure 30.25 shows a Ribbon being attached to a form.

FIGURE 30.25

Setting a form's Ribbon Name property.

The rbnAttach XML code is in the FormAttach.xml file included with the sample files for this chapter and is in the USysRibbons table in the Chapter30.accdb example database. Here's the XML:

```xml
<?xml version="1.0" encoding="utf-8"?>
<customUI xmlns="http://schemas.microsoft.com/office/2009/07
    /customui" onLoad="onRibbonLoad">
  <ribbon startFromScratch="false">
    <tabs>
      <tab id="ch30_t_Attach" label="My Form">
        <group id="ch30_g_Attach" label="My Form">
          <button id="ch30_b_Attach" label="My Form"
            imageMso="GroupTasksLayout" size="large" />
        </group>
      </tab>
    </tabs>
  </ribbon>
</customUI>
```

The button doesn't have an `onAction` attribute, so the Ribbon doesn't actually do anything. It's just an example to show how the Ribbon changes when attached to the form. The `startFromScratch` attribute is set to `false` so that the tab is added to the default Ribbon instead of replacing it. Figure 30.26 shows the new tab that is displayed when the form is opened.

FIGURE 30.26

Opening a form opens its Ribbon.

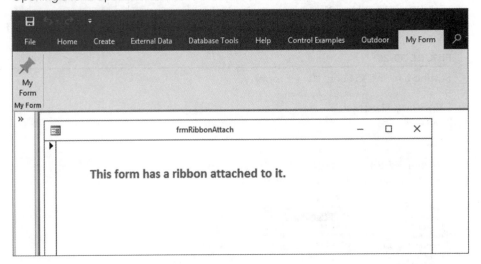

The My Form tab, with its associated controls, is available while the form is open. Closing the form causes the new tab to disappear. The list of Ribbons in the Property Sheet acts like the list in the Access Options dialog box. That is, it doesn't update whenever you add a new Ribbon to USysRibbons. You have to close and reopen your application to update the list.

TIP

Choosing Compact & Repair Database from File ⇨ Info automatically closes and reopens your database. It's a quick option for updating the loaded Ribbons list. It has the added benefit of keeping your database compacted.

Removing the Ribbon Completely

Assume, for a moment, that there are perfectly legitimate reasons why you don't want to use the Ribbon in your applications. Perhaps you've developed a set of effective switch-board forms, or you've mimicked the old-style toolbars and menus with borderless forms. Or, your applications are entirely forms-driven and don't need the flexibility provided by toolbars and Ribbons.

Here's how you can completely remove the Ribbon from the Access interface:

1. **Create a new table called** USysRibbons, **if you haven't already done so.**

2. **If creating the** USysRibbons **table for the first time, add three fields:**
   ID **(AutoNumber),** RibbonName **(Text) and** RibbonXML **(Memo).**

3. **Create a new record with the** RibbonName **set to Blank. It doesn't really matter what you call it.**

4. **Add the following XML to the RibbonXML column:**
   ```
   <CustomUI xmlns="http://schemas.microsoft.com/office/2009
   /07/CustomUI">
    <Ribbon startFromScratch="true"/>
   </CustomUI>
   ```

5. **Restart the database.**

6. **Select the File tab and then the Options button in the Backstage.**

7. **Click the Current Database tab and scroll to the Ribbon and Toolbar Options area.**

8. **In the Ribbon and Toolbar Options area, set the Ribbon Name to Blank (the same name you specified for the** RibbonName **column in Step 3).**

9. **Close and reopen the database.**

This process sets up a dummy Ribbon named Blank that contains no tabs, no groups, and no controls. In effect, you're telling Access to put up an empty Ribbon, which simply removes the Ribbon from the Access user interface. The File tab, however, remains so that you can access Options and change the Ribbon.

30

Preparing Your Access Application for Distribution

IN THIS CHAPTER

Setting options for your current database

Developing your application

Putting the finishing touches on your application

Hardening your application

Securing the Access environment

You're lucky if you have the luxury of developing only single-user, in-house applications and you never have to worry about distributing an application within a company or across the country. Most developers have to prepare an Access application for distribution sooner or later. You don't even have to develop commercial software to deal with distribution; when you develop an application to be run on a dozen workstations in one organization, you need to distribute your application in some form or other.

This chapter covers the issues relevant to distributing Access applications. However, because some of these items—such as error handling and splitting tables—are covered in detail elsewhere in this book, this chapter focuses primarily on setting database options when preparing your application for distribution.

You need to be concerned with many issues when preparing an Access application for distribution. Distributing your application properly not only makes installing and using the application easier for the end user, but also makes updating and maintaining the application easier for you, the application's developer. In addition, the support required for an application is greatly decreased by properly preparing and packaging the database and associated files for distribution.

> **ON THE WEB**
>
> This chapter uses the `Chapter31.accdb` database. If you haven't already copied it onto your machine, you'll need to do so now.
>
> Most of the techniques described in this chapter have been applied to the sample database. In order to open it so that you can see the options, open Access first, and then hold down the Shift key while you click the name of the database to open. Don't release the Shift key until the database has opened. The database has a custom icon as described in this chapter. The icon file won't be in the same place on your computer and you'll have to adjust the settings for it to show properly.

Defining the Current Database Options

Access databases have a number of options that simplify the distribution process. You can access these database options by choosing File ⇨ Options and then selecting the Current Database tab (shown in Figure 31.1). You can use an Autoexec macro to execute initialization code, but the Current Database options enable you to set up certain aspects of your application, thus reducing the amount of startup code that you have to write. It's very important to correctly structure these options before you distribute an Access application.

> **TIP**
>
> Setting the Current Database options saves you many lines of code that you would ordinarily need in order to perform the same functions and enables you to control your application's interface from the moment the user starts it. Always verify the Current Database options before distributing your application.

Application options

The settings in the Application Options section let you define parameters for your database as an application.

Application Title

The text that you provide in the Application Title field displays on the main Access window's title bar. The Application Title is also the text that's displayed in the Windows taskbar when the application is open and running.

> **TIP**
>
> You should always specify an application title for your distributed applications. If you don't, the database name and "Access" appear on the title bar of your application.

FIGURE 31.1

The Current Database options enable you to take control of your application from the moment a user starts it.

Application Icon

The icon that you specify in the Application Icon field displays on the title bar of your application and in the task switcher (Alt+Tab) of Windows. If you check the Use as Form and Report Icon box, this icon is also displayed when a form or report is minimized.

If you don't specify your own icon, Access displays the default Access icon, so you might want to provide an application-specific icon for your application. Using special program icons helps your users distinguish between different Access applications.

> **TIP**
>
> You can create small bitmaps in Microsoft Paint and use a conversion tool to convert a BMP file to the ICO file format. You can also create icons using other graphics programs or search for application icons online.

Display Form

The form you select in the Display Form drop-down list automatically opens when Access starts the application. When the form loads, the Form Load event of the display form fires (if it contains any code), reducing the need to use an Autoexec macro.

> **TIP**
>
> Consider using a splash screen as your startup display form. For more information, see the "A splash screen" section later in this chapter.

Display Status Bar

You can deselect the Display Status Bar check box to remove the status bar from the bottom of the Access screen. (This option is selected by default.)

> **TIP**
>
> The status bar is an informative and easy-to-use tool because it automatically displays key states (such as Caps Lock and Num Lock), as well as the Status Bar Text property for the active control. Instead of hiding the status bar, you should make full use of it and disable it only if you have a very good reason to do so.

Document Window Options

Under Document Window Options, you can choose how the forms and reports look in your distributed application. Your options are:

- **Overlapping Windows:** Overlapping Windows retains the look of previous versions of Access, letting you look at multiple forms at once.
- **Tabbed Documents:** Tabbed Documents (the default) uses a single-document interface (shown in Figure 31.2) similar to recent versions of popular web browsers.

You must close and reopen the current database for the changes to take effect.

The Display Document Tabs check box is only available when you select Tabbed Documents; it turns on or off the tabs that appear at the top of any open database object. This setting turns off only the tabs and does not close tabbed objects themselves.

Use Access Special Keys

If you select this option, users of your application can use accelerator keys that are specific to the Access environment in order to circumvent some security measures, such as unhiding the Navigation pane. If you deselect this option, the following keys are disabled:

- **F11:** Press to show the Navigation pane (if hidden).
- **Ctrl+G:** Press to open the Immediate window in the Visual Basic Editor (VBE).

- **Ctrl+Break:** In Access projects, press to interrupt Access while retrieving records from the server database.
- **Alt+F11:** Press to start the VBE.

FIGURE 31.2

A database with the Tabbed Documents option selected. The tabs let you select which Access object to work with.

TIP

It's a good idea to deselect the Use Access Special Keys check box when distributing the application in order to prevent users from circumventing the options you select; otherwise, users might inadvertently reveal the Navigation pane or VBA code, leading to confusion and other problems.

> **TIP**
>
> When using the Use Access Special Keys property to disable Access's default accelerator keys, you can still use an AutoKeys macro to set your application's shortcut keys.

Compact on Close

Checking the Compact on Close check box tells Access to automatically compact and repair your database when you close it. Some Access developers use Compact on Close as a way to perform this maintenance process each time a user works with a database, while others find it unnecessary. We're in the latter camp, but you can decide for yourself based on the level of activity in your database. You must close and reopen the current database in order for this change to take effect.

> **NOTE**
>
> Access includes a utility named Compact and Repair Database on the Database Tools Ribbon. File-based databases, such as Access, need such a utility to avoid data corruption, optimize performance, and reduce file sizes. As records are added to and deleted from tables, the size of your Access database file can become large.
>
> Compacting an Access database forces Access to rebuild the indexes in all the tables, and physically rearranges tables in primary key order in the ACCDB file. The maintenance operations ensure that your Access databases operate at maximum efficiency.
>
> Keep in mind that compacting a large database might take a considerable amount of time. Plus, Compact on Close only affects the front-end database. Unless your application uses the front end for temporary tables or other operations that cause the front end to bloat, the Compact and Repair Database option may be of minimal benefit to your users.

Remove Personal Information from File Properties on Save

Checking this box automatically removes the personal information from the file properties when you save the file. You must close and reopen the current database for this change to take effect.

Use Windows-Themed Controls on Forms

Checking this box uses your system's Windows theme on the form/report controls. This setting only applies when you use a Windows theme other than the standard theme.

Enable Layout View

The Enable Layout View check box shows or hides the Layout View button on the Access status bar and in the shortcut menus that appear when you right-click an object tab.

> **NOTE**
>
> Remember that you can disable the Layout view for individual objects, so even when you enable this option, Layout view may not be available for certain forms and reports.

Enable Design Changes for Tables in Datasheet View

The Enable Design Changes for Tables in Datasheet View check box allows you to make structural changes to your tables in Datasheet view, as opposed to having to be in Design view. In most well-designed Access applications, the users never see the tables in either Design view or Datasheet view, instead interacting with data via forms. If your application allows viewing tables in Datasheet view, you should uncheck this option to prevent unwanted changes to your tables' designs.

Check for Truncated Number Fields

Checking this option makes numbers appear as ##### when the column is too narrow to display the entire value. (This behavior has been in Excel for a long time.) Unchecking this box truncates values that are too wide to be displayed in the datasheet, which means that users see only a part of the column's value when the column is too narrow and might misinterpret the column's contents.

Picture Property Storage Format

Under Picture Property Storage Format, you can choose how graphic files are stored in the database. Your options are:

- **Preserve Source Image Format (Smaller File Size):** Choose this option if you want to store the image in the original format, which also reduces the database size.

- **Convert All Picture Data to Bitmaps (Compatible with Access 2003 and Earlier):** Choose this option if you want to store all images as bitmaps, which increases the database size but keeps it compatible with previous versions of Access (Access 2003 and earlier).

You have the option to Preserve Source Image Format to conserve disk space by reducing the database file's size. (This option is only available in the ACCDB file format.) When using this option, Access only stores one copy of an image (in its original format) and dynamically generates a bitmap when the image is displayed on a form or report.

Navigation options

The settings in the Navigation section let you define parameters that affect how users navigate your database as an application.

The Display Navigation Pane check box

With most distributed applications, you might never want your users to have direct access to any of your tables, queries, forms, or other database objects. It's far too tempting for a user to try to "improve" a form or report or to make some minor modification to a table or query. Rarely are users really qualified to make such changes to an Access database. Deselecting the Display Navigation Pane option hides the Navigation pane from the user at startup.

> **NOTE**
>
> Unless you also deselect the Use Access Special Keys option (described earlier in this chapter), users can press **F11** to unhide the Navigation pane.

You must close and reopen the current database for this change to take effect.

The Navigation Options button

One nice addition to recent versions of Access is the ability to select which database objects are exposed to users when the Navigation pane is visible at startup. Clicking the Navigation Options button opens the Navigation Options dialog box (shown in Figure 31.3), which you use to change the categories and groups that appear in the Navigation pane.

FIGURE 31.3

The Navigation Options dialog box.

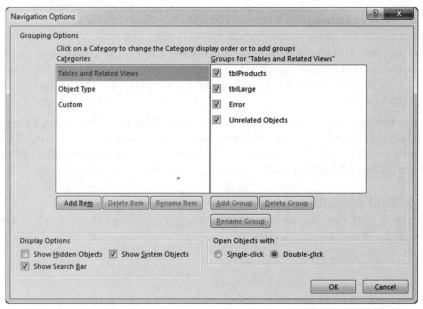

In the Grouping Options section, click a category on the left side of the dialog box to change the category display order or to add groups to the right side of the dialog box. Click the Object Type category to disable viewing of certain Access objects (tables, queries, forms, reports, macros, or modules).

In the Display Options section, you can select the Show Hidden Objects, Show System Objects, and Show Search Bar check boxes.

> **NOTE**
>
> It's usually a good idea to hide the hidden and system objects, which you normally don't want to modify. (They're hidden for a reason!)
>
> The Search Bar (shown in Figure 31.4), on the other hand, is useful in the Navigation pane when you have a lot of objects and want to narrow the list to avoid excessive scrolling, so you should select the Show Search Bar check box. For example, if you wanted to see the objects (tables, forms, etc.) that had the word *Product* in them, you'd type Prod in the Search Bar to limit the tables shown in the Navigation pane.

FIGURE 31.4

The Search Bar appears at the top of the Navigation pane.

In the Open Objects With section of the dialog box, select Single-Click or Double-Click to choose how you open a database object. Double-Click is the default option and is most likely familiar to all your users.

Ribbon and toolbar options

The settings in the Ribbon and Toolbar Options section let you define custom Ribbons and toolbars when using your database as an application. All the options in this section require you to close and reopen the current database for the change to take effect.

 Creating custom Ribbons is explained in Chapter 30.

Ribbon Name

The Ribbon Name option lets you specify a customized (usually trimmed-down) version of the Ribbon. If you don't supply a Ribbon name, Access uses its built-in Ribbon, which might be inappropriate for your application. The default Ribbon contains many controls for modifying database objects, which might lead to problems with your users.

Shortcut Menu Bar

Setting the Shortcut Menu Bar changes the default menu for shortcut menus (right-click menus) to a menu bar that you specify. Using custom shortcut menus that have functionality specific to your application is always preferable.

Allow Full Menus

Checking the Allow Full Menus box determines whether Access displays all the commands in its menus or just the frequently used commands. If you supply custom menus for all your forms and reports and set the Menu Bar property to a custom menu bar, this setting has no effect.

Allow Default Shortcut Menus

The Allow Default Shortcut Menus setting determines whether Access displays its own default shortcut menus when a user right-clicks an object in the Navigation pane or a control on a form or report.

Name AutoCorrect Options

Several chapters in this book mention the problems associated with changing the names of fundamental database objects such as tables and fields within tables. For example, if you change the name of a table, everywhere you refer to that table (a query, a control's `ControlSource` property, VBA code, a macro, and so on) becomes invalid, causing the application to malfunction.

Microsoft added the Name AutoCorrect feature to Access 2000 as a way of helping developers avoid problems that inevitably occur when database objects are renamed. Unfortunately, this feature has never worked quite as well as Microsoft hoped. Primarily, Name AutoCorrect is a major drag on performance. Because Access must constantly monitor activity while Access is used, a database with this option selected runs noticeably slower than it does when the option is turned off. Plus, there are far too many places where an object's name may appear for an AutoCorrect feature to effectively capture every instance when the object is renamed. This is especially true of object names appearing in VBA code; many applications contain hundreds of thousands of lines of VBA code, making it virtually impossible to find and update every object reference.

31

> **TIP**
>
> The Track Name AutoCorrect Info option is turned on by default in Access applications. Unless you find this option useful in your projects, you should consider turning it off, as it has been in the `Chapter31.accdb` example accompanying this chapter.

Developing the Application

Developing an application generally consists of defining the requirements, building the database objects and writing the code, creating the documentation, and testing the application. If you're developing an application for your own use, the requirements are probably in your head. You also may be so familiar with the problem that you're trying to solve that you don't feel a need to formalize the requirements. Consider writing them down anyway as a way to clarify your thoughts and identify any problems early in the development process.

Building to a specification

All databases are meant to solve some problem experienced by users. The problem might be inefficiency in their current methods or the inability to view or retrieve data in a format they need. Or you may simply be converting an obsolete database to a more modern equivalent. The effectiveness of the solution you build will be judged by how well it resolves the problem the users are having. Your best guarantee of success is to carefully plan the application before building any tables, queries, or forms. Only by working to a plan will you know how well the application will solve the user's problem.

Most Access development projects follow this general sequence of events:

1. **Define the problem.** Something is wrong or inadequate with the current methods—a better system is needed and Access appears to be a good candidate to produce the new system.

2. **Determine the requirements.** Interviews with the users yield a description of the basic features the program should provide. The product of these discussions is the *design specification*, a written document that outlines and details the application.

3. **Finalize the specifications.** Review the design specifications with the users to ensure accuracy and completeness.

4. **Design the application.** The developer uses the initial design specification to design the basic structure of the database and its user interface.

5. **Develop the application.** This is where developers spend most of their time. You spend a great deal of time building the tables, queries, forms, and other database objects needed to meet the specification produced in Step 2.

6. **Test.** The developer and client exercise the application to verify that it performs as expected. The application is tested against the requirements defined in the design specification, and discrepancies are noted and corrected for Step 7.

7. **Distribute and roll out.** After the application's performance has been verified, it's distributed to its users. If necessary, users are trained in the application's use and instructed on how to report problems or make suggestions for future versions.

Many Access developers dive right into development without adequately defining the application's objectives or designing the database's structure. Unless the application is incredibly simple, a developer who doesn't work to a specification will surely end up with a buggy, unreliable, and trouble-prone database.

Another major error is allowing the database to stray too far from the initial design specification. Adding lots of bells and whistles to an otherwise simple and straightforward database is all too tempting. If implementation digresses too far from the design specification, the project may fail because too much time is spent on features that don't directly address the users' problems. This is one of the reasons for the third step (finalize the specifications). The developer and the user are essentially entering into a contract at that point, and you might want to include a process to be followed in order for either party to make changes to the specification once it's been agreed upon.

Before any work begins, most professional application developers expect the client to submit a written document describing the intended application and specifying what the program is expected to do. A well-written design specification includes the following information:

- **Expected inputs:** What kind of data (text, numeric, binary) will the database have to handle? Will the data be shared with other applications like Excel or another database system? Does the data exist in a format that is easily imported into an Access database, or will the data have to be re-keyed at run time? Will all the data always be available? Is there a chance that the type might vary? For example, birth dates are obviously dates, but what happens if you know the year of birth but not the month or day?

- **User interface:** Will the users be comfortable with simple forms, or will they need custom menus and Ribbons and other user-interface components? Is context-sensitive online Help required?

- **Expected outputs:** Which kinds of reports are needed by the user? Will simple select queries be adequate to produce the desired results, or are totals, crosstabs, and other advanced queries necessary as well?

The whole point of a design specification is to avoid adding unplanned features that decrease the database's reliability without contributing to its utility. Writing a design specification before beginning the actual implementation will consistently yield the following benefits:

- **A guide to development effort:** Without some kind of design specification, how can you possibly know whether you're building an application that truly meets the client's expectations? As you work through the development phase, you can avoid adding features that don't contribute to the application's objectives and concentrate on those items that the client has identified as having priority.

- **Verification that the application meets expectations:** All aspects of the application must be tested to verify its operation. The best way to conduct testing is to confirm that all design objectives have been met and that no unexpected behavior is observed during the testing phase.

- **Minimization of design changes during implementation:** Many problems can be avoided by sticking to the specification. One of the easiest ways to break an application is to add new features not included in the original design. If the application was properly planned, the specified features will have been designed to work together. Introducing new features after development has begun most likely will result in a less reliable system.

Overall, a well-written design specification provides the basis for creating tight, bulletproof applications that fulfill the user's requirements. At the conclusion of the project, the finished database can be compared to the design specification, and its effectiveness in addressing the original problem can be objectively evaluated. Without a design specification written at the beginning of a project, you have no valid measure of how well the application resolves the problem that inspired the project in the first place.

Creating documentation

Even the best-written Access application will fail if users don't fully understand how to use it. And it's not just the user interface that needs to be understood: the logic of what happens when the user clicks a particular button needs to be understood both by at least some of the users as well as by any technical support staff who might be involved with the application.

While many developers dislike writing documentation, leaving it as a last step that they hopefully won't have time for because they've moved onto another project, documentation really is a "necessary evil."

Documenting the code you write

Over time, changes or additions might be required to the application. Even if you're the one making those changes, the passage of time since you originally wrote the code might mean that even *you* have problems understanding exactly what the code does. Imagine how much harder it'll be if someone else has to figure it out!

Write self-documenting code by using consistent naming conventions for your variables, constants, and procedures. Provide logical names for your procedures that describe simply and clearly what the procedure does. If you can't come up with a reasonable name for a procedure, it may be that you're trying to do too much in one procedure, and you should consider breaking it up. Use comments when necessary, but don't overuse them or they'll never be read and will be quickly out-of-date. Create a comment when you make an important design decision that you want to document or when you use a non-intuitive programming technique that would be otherwise difficult to understand. Comments shouldn't say what is being done (the code should say that on its own) but why it's being done.

Figure 31.5 shows a short procedure that is mostly self-documenting. The procedure, variables, and constants are well named and a comment is included to explain an unusual line of code.

FIGURE 31.5

Produce self-documenting code when possible.

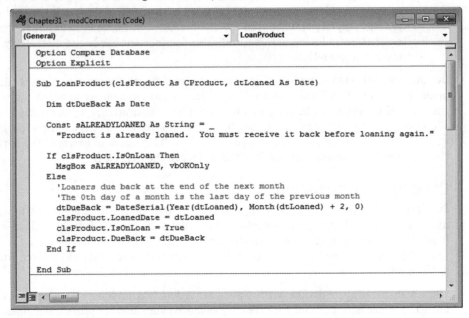

```
Chapter31 - modComments (Code)
(General)                                          LoanProduct

    Option Compare Database
    Option Explicit

    Sub LoanProduct(clsProduct As CProduct, dtLoaned As Date)

      Dim dtDueBack As Date

      Const sALREADYLOANED As String = _
        "Product is already loaned.  You must receive it back before loaning again."

      If clsProduct.IsOnLoan Then
        MsgBox sALREADYLOANED, vbOKOnly
      Else
        'Loaners due back at the end of the next month
        'The 0th day of a month is the last day of the previous month
        dtDueBack = DateSerial(Year(dtLoaned), Month(dtLoaned) + 2, 0)
        clsProduct.LoanedDate = dtLoaned
        clsProduct.IsOnLoan = True
        clsProduct.DueBack = dtDueBack
      End If

    End Sub
```

Name your database objects and controls and don't accept the default names that Access provides for database objects such as forms and controls. The default names are simply a convenience for simple applications and shouldn't be used in professional-quality work.

Documenting the application

The applications you deliver to end users should be accompanied by documentation that explains how the applications are meant to be used. End-user documentation doesn't have to include descriptions of the internal structure or logic behind the user interface. It should, however, explain how the forms and reports work, describe things the users should avoid (for example, changing existing data), and include printouts of sample reports. Use screenshots to illustrate the documentation.

The users of your applications will benefit from the online Help you build into the database. Online Help, of course, means everything from the ScreenTips you attach to the controls on a form to status bar text, to sophisticated context-sensitive and "What's this?" help you see in many Microsoft products.

Testing the application before distribution

As you design your application, consider how you'll test the various aspects of it. Planning your tests during the design phase is the best time because the functions of a form or report will be fresh in your mind. Don't wait until you're completely done developing to start thinking about testing, or you'll have a hard time remembering all the important features that you should test. Write out a test plan during, or shortly after, designing an object in your application (such as a table or form). Don't worry if the test plan isn't perfect, you'll be able to change it before you distribute the application.

Execute your test plans as soon as it's practical to do so. Then execute them again when the whole project is complete and you're ready to distribute it. The first time you execute them assures that you designed the object as you intended. Executing them at the end ensures that future changes didn't introduce bugs. You may find that your tests are no longer valid because of changes you made to the design. Design changes happen all the time during development, and when tests become invalid, you can simply remove them or change them to test the new functionality.

While working through the debugging process of an application, categorize your bugs into one of three categories:

- **Category 1: Catastrophic bugs:** These bugs are absolutely unacceptable—for example, numbers in an accounting application that don't add up the way they should or a routine that consistently causes the application to terminate unexpectedly. If you ship an application with known Category 1 bugs, prepare for your users to revolt!

- **Category 2: Major bugs that have a workaround:** Category 2 bugs are fairly major bugs, but they don't stop users from performing their tasks because some work-around exists in the application. For example, a button that doesn't call a procedure correctly is a bug. If the button is the only way to run the procedure, this bug is a Category 1 bug. But if a corresponding Ribbon command calls the procedure correctly, the bug is a Category 2 bug. Shipping an application with a Category 2 bug is sometimes necessary. Although shipping a bug is never desirable, deadlines sometimes dictate that exceptions need to be made. Category 2 bugs will annoy users but shouldn't render them helpless.

> **TIP**
>
> If you ship an application with known Category 2 bugs, document them! Some developers have a don't-say-anything-and-act-surprised attitude regarding Category 2 bugs. This attitude can frustrate users and waste their time by forcing them to discover not only the problem but also the solution. For example, if you were to ship an application with the Category 2 bug just described, you should include a statement in your application's README file that reads something like this: "The button on the XYZ form does not correctly call feature such-and-such. Please use the corresponding command such-and-such found on the Ribbon. A patch will be made available as soon as possible."

- **Category 3: Small bugs and cosmetic problems:** Category 3 bugs are small issues that don't affect the operation of your application. They may be caption or label misspellings or incorrect text box colors. Category 3 bugs should be fixed soon, but they shouldn't take precedence over Category 1 bugs. They should take precedence over Category 2 bugs only when they're so extreme that the application looks completely unacceptable or when they cause enough trouble for users that a fix is quickly needed.

Categorizing bugs, and approaching them systematically, helps you create a program that looks and behaves the way its users think it should. Sometimes you may feel like you'll never finish your Category 1 list, but you will. You'll be smiling the day you check your bug sheet and realize that you're down to a few Category 2s and a dozen or so Category 3s! Although you might be tempted to skip this beta-testing phase of development, don't. You'll only pay for it in the long run.

> **TIP**
>
> Not all Access features are available when an application is run within the Access runtime environment. You can operate in the runtime environment and use the full version of Access to test for problems with your code and with the runtime environment by using the /Runtime command-line option when starting your Access application.

Polishing Your Application

When your application has been thoroughly tested and appears ready for distribution, spend some time polishing your application.

Giving your application a consistent look and feel

First and foremost, decide on some visual design standards and apply them to your application. This step is incredibly important if you want a professional look and feel to your applications. Figure 31.6 shows a form with samples of different styles of controls.

FIGURE 31.6

Use a consistent style in each object and throughout your application.

Your design decisions may include the following:

- Will text boxes be sunken, flat with a border, flat without a border, chiseled, or raised?
- What back color should text boxes be?
- What color will the forms be?
- Will you use chiseled borders to separate related items or select a sunken or raised border?
- What size will buttons on forms be?
- For forms that have similar buttons, such as Close and Help, in what order will the buttons appear?
- Which accelerator keys will you use on commonly used buttons, such as Close and Help?

- Which control will have focus when the form opens?
- How will the tab order be set?
- What will your Enter key property be for text boxes?
- Will you add some visual indication for when list boxes are multi-select and when they aren't?
- Will you add some visual indication for when combo boxes have their Limit to List property set?

Making your application look and work in a consistent manner is the single most important way to make it appear professional. For ideas on design standards to implement in your applications, spend some time working with some of your favorite programs to see which standards they use.

CAUTION

In the area of look and feel, copying from another developer is generally not considered plagiarism but is instead often looked upon as a compliment. Copying does *not* extend, however, to making use of another application's icons or directly copying the look and feel of a competitor's product; this is a very bad practice.

Adding common professional components

Most professional applications have some similar components. The most common components are the splash screen, an application switchboard, and an About box. These may seem like trivial features, but they can greatly enhance your application's appeal. They don't take much time to implement and should be included in all your distributed applications.

A splash screen

The splash screen (see Figure 31.7 for an example) not only aids in increasing perceived speed of an application but also gives the application a polished, professional appearance from the moment a user runs the program.

ON THE WEB

Figure 31.7 shows the design window for a splash screen template that you can use when building your own applications. This form is included in the `Chapter31.accdb` database. It's named `frmSplashScreen`. Import this form into your application and use it as a template for creating your own splash screen.

Most splash screens contain information such as the following:

- The application's title
- The application's version number
- Your company information
- A copyright notice (© Copyright)

FIGURE 31.7

A splash screen not only increases perceived speed of your application, but it also gives your application a professional appearance.

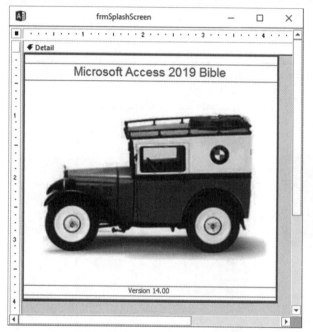

In addition, you might want to include the licensee information and/or a picture on the splash screen. If you use a picture on your splash screen, make it relevant to your application's function. For example, some coins and an image of a check could be used for a check-writing application. If you want, you can also use clip art for your splash screen—just be sure that the picture is clear and concise and doesn't interfere with the text information presented on your splash screen.

To implement the splash screen, have your application load the splash form before it does anything else. (Consider making your splash screen the Display Form in the Application Options, described earlier in this chapter.) When your application finishes all its initialization procedures, close the form. Make the splash form a light form and convert any bitmaps that you place on your splash screen to pictures in order to decrease the splash form's load time.

An application switchboard

An application switchboard is a road map for users to find their way through the functions and forms that are available in the application. Use the switchboard itself as a navigation form, using buttons to display other forms, as shown in the switchboard example in Figure 31.8. This is the switchboard named `frmSwitchboard` created for the Collectible Mini Cars database in this book.

The switchboard provides a familiar place where users can be assured that they won't get lost in the application.

FIGURE 31.8

The switchboard provides a handy way to navigate throughout the application.

TIP

Make sure that the switchboard redisplays whenever the user closes a form.

An About box

The About box (like the one shown in Figure 31.9) contains your company and copyright information, as well as the application name and current version. Including your application's licensee information (if you keep such information) in the About box is also a good idea.

FIGURE 31.9

An About box provides useful information to the user and protects your legal interests.

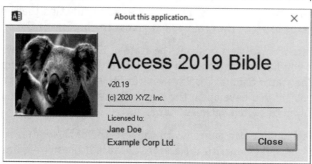

The About box serves as legal notice of ownership and makes your application easier to support by giving your users easy access to the version information. Some advanced About boxes call other forms that display system information. You can make the About box as fancy as you want, but usually a simple one works just fine.

ON THE WEB

Figure 31.9 shows an About box template form that you can use when building your own applications. This form is included in the `Chapter31.accdb` database. It's named `frmAbout`. Import this form into your application and use it as a template for creating your own About box.

The About box should be accessible from a Help menu or from a button on your switchboard form.

Making the Most of Pictures

Most users love pictures, and most developers love to use pictures on buttons. Clear and concise pictures are more intuitive and are more easily recognized than textual captions. Most developers, however, are not graphic artists, and they usually slap together buttons made from any clip art images that are handy. These ugly buttons make an application look clumsy and unprofessional. In addition, pictures that don't clearly show the function of the button make the application harder to use.

Select or create pictures that end users will easily recognize. Avoid abstract pictures or pictures that require specific knowledge to understand them. If your budget permits, consider hiring a professional design firm to create your button pictures. A number of professional image galleries and tools to create and edit buttons are available.

Picture buttons that are well thought out can really make your application look outstanding, as well as make it easier to use.

The status bar

Keeping your users informed about what's happening with your application is an important part of building a good user experience. Access provides a `SysCmd` function that lets you display messages in the status bar (the thin colored bar across the bottom of the screen).

By default, the status bar shows information about the state of the object you're working on. For example, when you have a form open in Design view, the left side of the status bar reads "Design View." The status bar also displays whether the Num Lock key is active. Depending on the type of object you have open, the View buttons on the far right of the status bar provide a quick way to switch between views.

Using `SysCmd`, you can display your own messages on the left side of the status bar. The status bar is a great place to display noncritical messages because it doesn't require any user interaction (other than reading it, of course).

To show a message in the status bar, use the `acSysCmdSetStatus` parameter, as shown in the following code:

```
Private Sub cmdHelpText_Click()

    Const sMSG As String = "Hello, World!"

    SysCmd acSysCmdSetStatus, sMSG

End Sub
```

This code displays `"Hello, World!"` in the status bar, but you can display any string you'd like. However, if the string is longer than Access has space to show, nothing will display. The status bar can also be used to show the user what's happening during a long process. In the following code, the status bar is updated while looping through a large recordset:

```
Private Sub cmdLoop_Click()

    Dim rs As DAO.Recordset
    Dim sSql As String
    Dim lCnt As Long

    sSql = "SELECT * FROM tblLarge;"
    Set rs = CurrentDb.OpenRecordset(sSql, dbOpenSnapshot)
    rs.MoveLast
    rs.MoveFirst

    Do While Not rs.EOF
        lCnt = lCnt + 1
        If lCnt Mod 10 = 0 Then
```

```
      SysCmd acSysCmdSetStatus, "Processing record " & _
         lCnt & " of " & rs.RecordCount
      DoEvents
    End If
    rs.MoveNext
Loop

    SysCmd acSysCmdClearStatus

    rs.Close
    Set rs = Nothing

  End Sub
```

When processing a lot of records, it's useful to display a counter like in the preceding code. This code updates the status bar every tenth record. If it were updated for every record, it would move so fast the user would barely be able to see it. Also, overuse of the status bar can degrade performance, so updating it only as needed helps speed up the process. The Mod function returns the remainder when the first number is divided by the second. When the remainder is zero, the counter is a multiple of 10 and the status bar is updated. Find a multiple that works for your data. The status bar should update frequently enough that the user doesn't think the program has stopped, but not so frequently that the text is a blur or the performance of the process is affected.

A couple of other aspects of the preceding code are worth mentioning. The RecordCount property will not return the total number of records in the recordset until all the records have been accessed. The MoveLast and MoveFirst methods assure that RecordCount will be correct. Inside the loop, the DoEvents keyword is used. While the code is running, it can use all the Windows resources; certain activities, like refreshing the screen, are put on hold until the code stops. That's not very helpful when you're trying to display text in the status bar. DoEvents is a command that briefly gives control to Windows so it can complete any tasks in its events queue.

Figure 31.10 shows the status bar being updated.

FIGURE 31.10

Use the status bar to provide feedback on a long process.

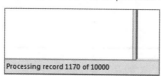

Processing record 1170 of 10000

Near the end of the procedure, the acSysCmdClearStatus parameter is used to return control of the status bar back to Access.

TIP

If you don't want to display a status bar message, but you don't want Access to display one either, you can use `SysCmd` to put a single space in the status bar. The code `SysCmd acSysCmdSetStatus, Space(1)` will keep the status bar blank until you're ready to use it.

A progress meter

Access provides a built-in progress meter in the status bar at the bottom of the main Access window. This progress meter is a rectangle that grows horizontally as a long-running process is executed by Access.

Setting up and using a progress meter requires an initializing step and then setting the meter to its next value. As your code progresses, you don't just increment a counter that is managed by `SysCmd`. You must explicitly set the meter's value to a value between 0 and the maximum you set at initialization.

CAUTION

The following code and demonstration are contained in a form named `frmSysCmdDemo` in the `Chapter31`
`.accdb` database.

Use the `acSysCmdInitMeter` constant to initialize the meter. You must pass some text that is used to label the meter, as well as the meter's maximum value:

```
Private Sub cmdInitMeter_Click()

    Const sSTATUSTEXT As String = "Reading Data"

    mlMeterMax = 100
    mlMeterIncrement = 0
    SysCmd acSysCmdInitMeter, sSTATUSTEXT, mlMeterMax

End Sub
```

This procedure sets the max to 100 and initializes the `mlMeterIncrement` variable to zero. When this procedure is run, the Access status bar appears with an empty progress meter, as shown in Figure 31.11.

FIGURE 31.11

The progress meter after initialization.

Incrementing the meter is a little tricky. In the following subroutine, the module-level variable `mlMeterIncrement` is incremented by 10, and the meter's position is set to the value of `mlMeterIncrement`:

```
Private Sub cmdIncrementMeter_Click()
  mlMeterIncrement = mlMeterIncrement + 10

  If mlMeterIncrement > mlMeterMax Then
    mlMeterIncrement = 0
  End If

  SysCmd acSysCmdUpdateMeter, mlMeterIncrement

End Sub
```

This procedure also checks to see if the value of `mlMeterIncrement` exceeds the maximum set in the initialization routine. If it does, it starts back at zero. That's interesting for a demonstration, but in real-world situations it's best to set the maximum to an appropriate value that won't be exceeded. Figure 31.12 shows the progress meter after the Progress Meter Demo button was clicked and the Increment Meter button was clicked five times. It's easy to see that the meter has moved a distance proportional to the value of `mlMeterIncrement` after being incremented five times.

FIGURE 31.12

The progress meter midway in its movement.

You'll have to choose values for the progress meter's maximum and increment settings in your application. Also, be sure to update the progress meter at appropriate intervals, such as every time one-tenth of a process has run (assuming, of course, that you know ahead of time how many items will be processed or how long an operation may take).

A meter is a valuable way of keeping the user informed of the progress of a lengthy process. Because you control its initial value and the rate at which it increments, you're able to fairly precisely report the application's progress to its users.

The only issue with the default Access progress meter is that it appears at the very bottom of the screen and is easily overlooked by users. Also, if the status bar is hidden through the Display Status Bar option on the Current Database tab of the Access Options dialog box (refer to Figure 31.1), the progress meter can't be seen at all.

If you prefer to keep the status bar hidden and show a progress meter that the users are sure to see, you can create your own progress meter with a form and a couple of label controls. Figure 31.13 shows just such a progress meter. It starts with an unbound form and two label controls. One label is on top of the other and they have the same Top, Left, Height, and Width properties. The label underneath has a lighter BackColor than the label on top.

FIGURE 31.13

A homemade progress meter.

As the program progresses, the top label's Width property is increased, giving the illusion that a darker color is filling a box. The form has certain properties set to give it the look and feel of a progress meter. Table 31.1 shows some of the properties of the form.

TABLE 31.1 Form Properties for a Progress Meter

Property	Value	Description
Pop Up	Yes	Along with Modal, ensures that the form is always on top and other forms can't be selected.
Modal	Yes	Along with Pop Up, ensures that the form is always on top and other forms can't be selected.
Caption	Progress	You can change this property to customize your progress meter.
Allow Datasheet View	No	Progress meters should only be shown in Form view.
Allow Layout View	No	Progress meters should only be shown in Form view.
Auto Center	Yes	Puts the progress meter in the middle of the screen.
Record Selectors	No	Hides the record selectors.
Navigation Buttons	No	Hides the navigation buttons.
Control Box	No	Hides the control box.
Close Button	No	Hides the Close button.
Min Max Buttons	No	Hides the Minimize and Maximize buttons.
Border Style	Dialog	Makes the progress meter appear as a dialog box.

ON THE WEB

In the `Chapter31.accdb` database, the `frmSysCmdDemo` form calls the `frmProgress` form and includes all the code in this section.

To create the progress meter in Figure 31.13, start by adding two custom properties to `frmProgress`. In addition to the form properties built into Access, you can add properties unique to your application. Add a `Max` property to set the maximum length of the progress bar and a `Progress` property to set how far along the process is:

```
Private mlMax As Long
Private mdProgress As Double

Public Property Get Max() As Long
  Max = mlMax
End Property

Public Property Let Max(lMax As Long)
  mlMax = lMax
End Property

Public Property Get Progress() As Double
  Progress = mdProgress
End Property

Public Property Let Progress(dProgress As Double)
  mdProgress = dProgress
End Property
```

The `Property` keyword in VBA is used to define the custom properties. Declare a module-level variable to hold the property's value, like `mlMax`. Then create `Property Get` and `Property Let` procedures to read and write the property, respectively. You can also omit either the `Get` or `Let` property statement if you want to make the property read-only or write-only.

Use the `Form_Load` event to initialize the width of the top label, `lblPmFront`. The underneath label, `lblPmBack`, always stays the same width:

```
Private Sub Form_Load()

  Me.lblPmFront.Width = 0

End Sub
```

The last piece of code behind `frmProgress` is a custom method to update the progress bar. A custom method is simply a sub-procedure declared with the `Public` keyword:

```
Public Sub UpdateProgress(lProgress As Long)

  If lProgress >= Me.Max Then
```

```
      Me.Progress = 1
    Else
      Me.Progress = lProgress / Me.Max
    End If

    Me.lblPmFront.Width = Me.lblPmBack.Width * Me.Progress

  End Sub
```

The first part of the custom method determines if the lProgress argument is greater than the maximum. If it is, Progress is set to 1, or 100%. This way, the progress meter will never go above 100%. If lProgress is less than the max, Progress is set to the ratio of lProgress to the maximum. Finally, the width of lblPmFront is increased by that proportion.

The procedure in the frmSysCmdDemo form that uses this progress meter is shown in the following code. It is very similar to the code used earlier in this chapter to update the status bar when looping through a large recordset:

```
  Private Sub cmdLoopProgress_Click()

    Dim frmProgress As Form
    Dim rs As DAO.Recordset
    Dim sSql As String
    Dim lCnt As Long

    Const sFORMPROGRESS As String = "frmProgress"

    sSql = "SELECT * FROM tblLarge;"
    Set rs = CurrentDb.OpenRecordset(sSql, dbOpenSnapshot)
    rs.MoveLast
    rs.MoveFirst

    DoCmd.OpenForm sFORMPROGRESS
    Set frmProgress = Forms(sFORMPROGRESS)
    frmProgress.Max = rs.RecordCount

    Do While Not rs.EOF
      lCnt = lCnt + 1
      If lCnt Mod 10 = 0 Then
        frmProgress.UpdateProgress lCnt
        DoEvents
      End If
      rs.MoveNext
    Loop

    DoCmd.Close acForm, sFORMPROGRESS
  End Sub
```

In this procedure, the `frmProgress` form is opened and assigned to a variable that allows access to the `Max` property and the `UpdateProgress` method. The `Max` property is set to `rs.RecordCount`, and the `UpdateProgress` method is called within the loop, passing the `lCnt` variable. Finally, the progress form is closed at the end of the procedure.

Making the application easy to start

You shouldn't expect users to locate the Access data file (ACCDB or MDB) or to choose File ⇨ Open in Access to invoke the application. Pinning items to the Windows Start screen isn't difficult. When properly implemented, a program icon creates the impression that the application exists as an entity separate from Access and endows it with a status equivalent to Word, Excel, or other task-oriented programs.

Creating a program icon isn't difficult. Many freeware and shareware versions of icon editors are available online, enabling you to create entirely new icons. The `Chapter31.accdb` example database comes with its own program icon (`Earth.ico`) for you to experiment with. You designate the program icon in the Access startup options (see the "Application options" section earlier in this chapter) or by setting a program icon in File Explorer.

Follow these steps to establish a Windows shortcut for an Access database application:

1. **In the Microsoft Office program folder (usually `C:\Program Files\ Microsoft Office\root\Office16`), locate MSACCESS.EXE.**

2. **Right-click `MSACCESS.EXE` and select Create Shortcut.**

3. **Press F2 while the shortcut is highlighted and enter a new caption for the icon.**

4. **Right-click the icon and select Properties. The icon's Properties dialog box appears.**

5. **Select the Shortcut tab and add a complete path reference to the application's ACCDB or MDB file to the Target text box.**

CAUTION
Be sure not to delete or alter the path to the Access executable file.

In Figure 31.14 the application database's path is `M:\Chapter31.accdb`. Notice that the Target text box contains the path to the Access executable followed by the path to the ACCDB file.

NOTE
If the path to the database includes spaces, you need to put double quotes around the full path.

FIGURE 31.14

It's easy to get Access to automatically open a database from a shortcut icon.

6. **Click the Change Icon button.** The Change Icon dialog box appears.

7. **Click the Browse button and navigate to the icon file (with an ICO extension) you want to use (see Figure 31.14).**

8. **Drag the shortcut to the computer's desktop to provide a convenient way to start the Access application.**

Bulletproofing an Application

Bulletproofing (or hardening) an application is the process of making the application more stable and less prone to problems caused by unskilled users. Bulletproofing involves trapping errors that can be caused by users, such as invalid data entry, attempting to run a function when the application is not ready to run the function, and allowing users to click a Calculate button before all necessary data has been entered. Bulletproofing your application is an additional stage that should be completed in parallel with debugging and should be performed again after the application is working and debugged.

 Chapter 27 discusses error trapping in VBA.

Using error trapping on all Visual Basic procedures

An error-handling routine gives you a chance to display a friendly message to the user, rather than some unintuitive default message box. Figure 31.15 shows a message box with a runtime error "2102," which is probably meaningless to a user; however, it also shows a more-detailed message about a form that's missing or misspelled. The user won't know the name of the form or if it's misspelled or missing. An error-handling routine is needed to provide the user with a more informative and meaningful error message than what's shown in Figure 31.15.

FIGURE 31.15

An error message resulting from a procedure with no error-handling routine.

One of the most important elements of bulletproofing an application is making sure that the application never *crashes* (ceases operation completely and unexpectedly). Although Access provides built-in error processing for most data-entry errors (for example, characters entered into a currency field), automatic processing doesn't exist for VBA code errors. You should include error-handling routines in every VBA procedure, as described in Chapter 27.

When running an application at run time, any untrapped error encountered in your code causes the program to terminate completely. Your users can't recover from such a crash, and serious data loss might occur. Your users have to restart the application after such an application error.

Maintaining usage logs

Usage logs capture information such as the user's name or ID, the date, and the time. They provide valuable information, especially if an error occurs. Although you can easily record too much information, a properly designed usage log will permit you to pinpoint whether a certain type of error always seems to occur when a particular user is working with the system or when a certain query is run.

The logging information you add to a database might include updating a time stamp on records in a table when changes are made. Be aware, however, that the more logging you do, the slower the application becomes. The log information will cause the database to grow as well, unless the log information is stored in another location.

You can even tailor the level of logging to suit individual users or groups of users. Using the information captured on a login form, the application can determine at startup what level of logging to impose during the session. To make reviewing the logs much easier, you can even log to a table located in an external database in a different location on the network.

Usage logs can also provide an excellent way to perform a postmortem on an application that doesn't operate properly. If you have logging in each subroutine and function that might fail at run time, you can see exactly what happened at the time an error occurred, instead of relying on the user's description of the error.

Logging can produce undesirable results when errors occur. For example, an error that causes an endless loop can easily consume all available disk space on the user's computer if each iteration of the loop adds a message to an error log. Use logging wisely. You may want to add logging to *every* procedure in an application during the beta-test process, and reduce the number of calls to the logging procedure just before distributing the application to its users. You may even provide some way that users can turn on logging if they encounter a reproducible problem in a database application.

The function shown in the following listing provides an elementary form of error logging. LogError() writes the following information to a text file in the same location as the database:

- The current date and time
- The procedure name that produced the error
- The error number
- The error description
- The form that was active at the time the error occurred (may be null if no form is open)
- The name of the control that was active at the time the error occurred (may be null if no control is selected)

Using a text file as a log instead of writing to the database keeps the database smaller and improves performance:

```
Public Sub LogError(ProcName As String, _
    ErrNum As Integer, ErrDescription As String)

    Dim sFile As String, lFile As Long
    Dim aLogEntry(1 To 6) As String
```

```
Const sLOGFILE = "Error.log"
Const sLOGDELIM = "|"

On Error Resume Next
sFile = CurrentProject.Path & "\" & sLOGFILE
lFile = FreeFile

aLogEntry(1) = Format(Now, "yyyy-mm-dd hh:mm:ss") 'Date stamp
aLogEntry(2) = ErrNum
aLogEntry(3) = ErrDescription
aLogEntry(4) = ProcName
'The following may be NULL
aLogEntry(5) = Screen.ActiveForm.Name
aLogEntry(6) = Screen.ActiveControl.Name

Open sFile For Append As lFile
Print #lFile, Join(aLogEntry, sLOGDELIM)
Close lFile

End Sub
```

This simple subroutine adds to or creates a text file named `Error.log` in the same directory as the database. Each error encountered is one line in the text file, and each piece of
information is separated by a pipe delimiter.

The most critical items in the error log are the date and time, the error number, and the
error description. The procedure name is useful, but it has to be hard-coded for each procedure (subroutine or function) you log with `LogError()`.

The following procedure intentionally generates an error to test the `LogError` procedure.
A button on the `frmError` form runs this procedure. After the button has been clicked a
few times, the `Error.log` file might look like Figure 31.16:

```
Private Sub cmdError_Click()

  Dim x As Long

  On Error GoTo ErrHandler

  x = 1 / 0

ErrExit:
  Exit Sub

ErrHandler:
  LogError "cmdError_Click", Err.Number, Err.Description
  Resume ErrExit

End Sub
```

FIGURE 31.16

A text file can be used to log errors.

When it's time to review the errors, you can open the text file to see what's happened. You can also import the text file into an Access table to allow you to sort and filter the entries. Figure 31.17 shows `Error.log` imported into a table.

FIGURE 31.17

The error log can be imported into a table.

Once the data has been analyzed, the Error table can be deleted to keep the database small. Importing an error log is a good candidate for saving the import steps so that it can be easily imported the next time you want to review the data.

 See Chapter 6 for more information on importing text files.

Separating tables from the rest of the application

You should separate your code objects (forms, reports, queries, modules, and macros) from your table objects. Many benefits are gained from distributing these objects in separate ACCDB files:

- Network users benefit from speed increases by running the code ACCDB (the database containing the queries, forms, macros, reports, and modules) locally and accessing only the shared data on the network.
- Updates can easily be distributed to users.
- Data can be backed up more efficiently because disk space and time aren't used to continuously back up the code objects.

All professionally distributed applications—especially those intended for network use—should have separate code and data database files.

 Chapter 7 has more information on separating tables from the rest of the database, called *splitting a database.*

Building bulletproof forms

You can take several steps to make each form in an application virtually bulletproof:

- **Consider removing the Control Box, Min, Max, and Close buttons from the form at design time.** Your users will be forced to use the navigation aids you've built into the application to close the form, ensuring that your application is able to test and verify the user's input. When using the tabbed documents interface, the Min and Max buttons don't apply. The Close button is represented by an X at the far right of the tab above the form's body. Removing the Close button from a tabbed form disables the X in the tab but doesn't actually remove it.
- **Always put a Close or Return button on forms to return the user to a previous or next form in the application.** The buttons should appear in the same general location on every form and should be consistently labeled. Don't use Close on one form, Return on another, and Exit on a third.
- **Set the `ViewsAllowed` property of the form to Form at design time.** This setting prevents the user from ever seeing a form as a datasheet.
- **Use modal forms where appropriate.** Keep in mind that modal forms force the user to respond to the controls on the form—the user can't access any other part of the application while a modal form is open.
- **Use your own navigation buttons that check for EOF (end of file) and BOF (beginning of file) conditions on bound forms.** Use the `OnCurrent` event to verify information or set up the form as the user moves from record to record.
- **Use the `StatusBarText` property on every control, to let the user know what's expected in each control.** The `Control TipText` property should also be set on all relevant controls.

> **NOTE**
>
> In order for the `StatusBarText` to be used, the status bar must be displayed (see Figure 31.1).

Validating user input

One of the most important bulletproofing techniques is to simply validate everything the user enters into the database. Capturing erroneous data input during data entry is an important safeguard that you can build into your applications. In many cases, you can use the table-level validation (determined by each field's `ValidationRule` and `ValidationText` properties), but in many other cases you'll want more control over the message the user receives or the actions taken by the database in response to erroneous input.

One of the major problems with the `ValidationRule` property is that it isn't checked until the user actually tabs to the next control, making it impossible to capture bad data entry. You're much better off in many cases validating entries in code. Very often you'll want to validate all controls on a form from the form's `BeforeUpdate` event instead of individually checking each and every control on the form.

Using the /runtime option

If you're not concerned with protecting your application and you just want to prevent users from mistakenly breaking your application by modifying or deleting objects, you can force your application to be run in Access's *runtime mode*. When a database is opened in Access's runtime mode, all the interface elements that allow changes to objects are hidden from the user. In fact, while in runtime mode, it's impossible for a user to access the Navigation pane.

When using the runtime option, you must ensure that your application has a startup form that gives users access to any objects you want them to access. Normally, this is the main menu or main switchboard of your application.

> **TIP**
>
> To assign a form as a startup form, open the database that you want to use, select the File tab, select Options, and select the Current Database tab. Under Application Options, set the Display Form drop-down list to the form you want to be the startup form for the application. Startup forms are covered in more depth in the "Polishing Your Application" section earlier in this chapter.

Earlier in this chapter, in the "Making the application easy to start" section, you read how to create a Windows shortcut that launches an Access application. Forcing run-time behavior in Access is quite easy. Simply add the `/runtime` switch after the reference to the database file in the shortcut properties, as shown in Figure 31.18.

FIGURE 31.18

Adding the /runtime switch to a shortcut.

Encrypting or encoding a database

When security is of utmost importance, one final step that you need to take is to encrypt or encode the database. Access uses strong encryption to secure the data and contents of Access databases.

Follow these steps to encrypt an Access ACCDB database:

1. **Open an existing ACCDB database (Chapter31.accdb) exclusively.** On the File tab, click Open and browse to the file. Click the arrow next to the Open button and choose Open Exclusive.

2. **Click the File button in the upper-left corner of the screen, and select the Encrypt with Password command on the Info tab (see Figure 31.19).**

FIGURE 31.19

Choosing to encrypt an Access database.

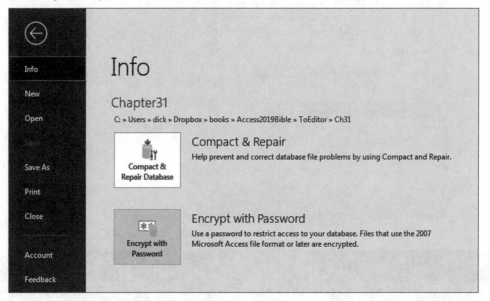

3. **In the Password field, type the password that you want to use to secure the database (see Figure 31.20).** Access does *not* display the password; instead, it shows an asterisk (*) for each letter.

4. **Retype the same password in the Verify field and click OK.**

An encrypted database looks like any other Access application to its users. There is no outward difference in the appearance of the application's forms or reports after encryption. The only difference is that the user is required to provide the password each time the database is opened.

FIGURE 31.20

Providing a password to encrypt an Access database.

When encrypting a database, however, be aware of the following drawbacks:

- **Encrypted databases don't compress from their original size when used with compression programs, such as WinZip or sending it to a compressed (zipped) folder.** Encryption modifies the way that the data is stored on the hard drive so compression utilities have little or no effect.

- **Encrypted databases suffer some performance degradation (up to 15 percent).** Depending on the size of your database and the speed of your computer, this degradation may be imperceptible.

Also, be aware that encrypting a database makes it impossible to access the data or database objects without the proper password. Always maintain an unencrypted backup copy of the database in a secure location in the event that the password is lost or accidentally changed. There is no "universal" password for decrypting an encrypted Access database, and because Access uses strong encryption, there is no way to decrypt the database without the proper password.

Removing a database password

Follow these steps to remove the password from an encrypted database, and restore it to its previous, unencrypted state:

1. **Open the encrypted ACCDB database (for example, Chapter31.accdb) exclusively.**

2. **Click the File button in the upper-left corner of the screen, and select the Decrypt Database command on the Info tab (see Figure 31.21).** The Unset Database Password dialog box appears (see Figure 31.22).

FIGURE 31.21

Choosing to remove a password from an encrypted Access database.

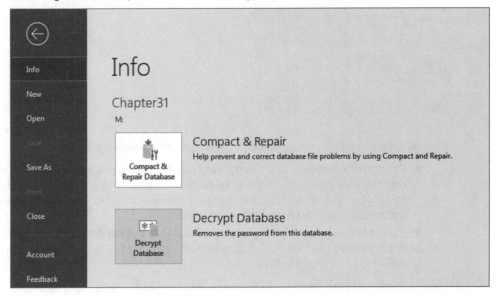

FIGURE 31.22

Providing a password to remove a password from an encrypted Access database.

3. **Enter the database password and click OK.**

Protecting Visual Basic code

You control access to the VBA code in your application by creating a password for the Visual Basic project that you want to protect. When you set a database password for a project, users are prompted to enter the password each time they try to view the Visual Basic code in the database:

> **NOTE**
>
> A Visual Basic project refers to the set of standard and class modules (the code behind forms and reports) that are part of your Access database.

1. **Open the Visual Basic Editor by pressing Alt+F11.**

2. **In the Visual Basic Editor, choose Tools ⇨ Chapter31 Properties. The Project Properties dialog box appears.**

3. **Select the Protection tab (shown in Figure 31.23).**

31

FIGURE 31.23

Creating a project password restricts users from viewing the application's Visual Basic code.

4. **Select the Lock Project for Viewing check box.**

5. **Enter a password in the Password text box.** Access does *not* display the password; instead, it shows a dot for each letter.

6. **Type the password again in the Confirm Password text box and click OK.** This security measure ensures that you don't mistype the password (because you can't see the characters that you type) and mistakenly prevent everyone, including yourself, from accessing the database.

After you save and close the project, users attempting to view the application's code must enter the password. Access prompts for the project password only once per session.

A more secure method of securing your application's code, forms, and reports is to distribute your database as an ACCDE file. When you save your database as an ACCDE file, Access compiles all code modules (including form modules), removes all editable source code, and compacts the database. The new ACCDE file contains no source code but continues to work because it contains a compiled copy of all your code. Not only is this a great way to secure your source code, but it also enables you to distribute databases that are smaller (because they contain no source code) and always keep their modules in a compiled state.

To create an ACCDE file, choose Save As from the File tab, Save Database As, and Make ACCDE, as shown in Figure 31.24.

FIGURE 31.24

Create an ACCDE file to protect your database.

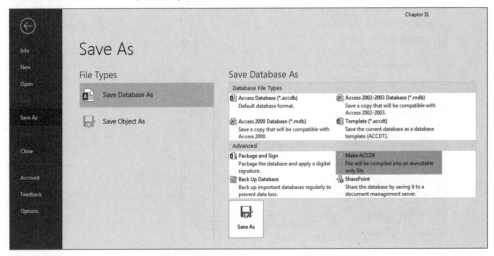

Securing the Environment

A serious Access application must be secured from unauthorized users. The built-in user-level security system (enforced by the ACE database engine, not by Access) provides multiple levels of security. You can, for example, secure a single database object (form, table, report) from individuals, groups, or individuals within groups. A user can even have multiple levels of security (provided the user has been assigned multiple login names). All the Access security objects, their properties, and methods are accessible throughout Access Visual Basic code.

User-level security is available only in the MDB database format. The ACCDB format provides other types of data protection, such as password-protected strong encryption, that is not available in the MDB format. As a developer, you'll have to decide whether user-level security or strong encryption is needed to protect the data in your Access applications.

Setting startup options in code

The options you set on the Current Database tab of the Access Options dialog box (refer to Figure 31.1) apply globally to every user who logs in to the database. There are times when you want to control these options through startup code instead of allowing the global settings to control the application. For example, a database administrator should have access to more of the database controls (menus, the Navigation pane) than a data entry clerk has.

Almost every option you see on the Access Options dialog box can be set through code. As you'll see in the "Setting property values" section, you can use Access VBA to control the setting of the current database properties listed in Table 31.2.

TABLE 31.2 **Startup Option Properties of the Application Object**

Startup Option	Property to Set	Data Type
Application title	AppTitle	dbText
Application icon	AppIcon	dbText
Display form	StartupForm	dbText
Display database window	StartupShowDBWindow	dbBoolean
Display status bar	StartupShowStatusBar	dbBoolean
Menu bar	StartupMenuBar	dbText
Shortcut menu bar	StartupShortcutMenuBar	dbText
Allow full menus	AllowFullMenus	dbBoolean
Allow default shortcut menus	AllowShortcutMenus	dbBoolean
Allow built-in toolbars	AllowBuiltInToolbars	dbBoolean
Allow toolbar changes	AllowToolbarChanges	dbBoolean
Allow viewing code after error	AllowBreakIntoCode	dbBoolean
Use Access special keys	AllowSpecialKeys	dbBoolean

Depending on the username (and password) provided on the login form, you can use VBA code on the splash screen or switchboard form to set or reset any of these properties. Clearly, these properties have a lot to do with controlling the Access environment at startup.

Be aware that many of the database options in Table 31.2, such as AppIcon, require restarting the Access database before they take effect.

Disabling startup bypass

The Access startup properties provide some options for how your users see your application when it starts. Unfortunately, users can bypass your carefully designed startup options by holding down the Shift key as the application starts. Bypassing your startup routines, of course, will reveal the application's design and objects that you've hidden behind the user interface.

Fortunately, the Access designers anticipated the need for bulletproofing an application's startup by providing a database property named AllowBypassKey. This property, which accepts True or False values, disables (or enables) the Shift key bypass at application startup.

> **NOTE**
>
> Because AllowBypassKey is a developer-only property, it isn't built into Access databases. You must create, append, and set this property sometime during the development process. Once appended to the database's Properties collection, you can set and reset it as needed.

Here's the code you need to implement the AllowBypassKey property:

```
Public Sub SetBypass(bFlag As Boolean)

    Dim db As DAO.Database
    Dim pBypass As DAO.Property
    Const sKEYNAME As String = "AllowBypassKey"

    Set db = CurrentDb
    On Error Resume Next
      Set pBypass = db.Properties(sKEYNAME)
    On Error GoTo 0

    If pBypass Is Nothing Then
      Set pBypass = db.CreateProperty(sKEYNAME, dbBoolean, bFlag)
      db.Properties.Append pBypass
    Else
      pBypass.Value = bFlag
    End If

End Sub
```

This procedure first tries to point a variable (pBypass) to the AllowBypassKey property. If the variable is Nothing, then the AllowBypassKey property doesn't exist, and it is created and appended to the database. If it does already exist, its Value property is set to bFlag (the value passed into the procedure).

Setting property values

You use the `CurrentDb` object's `CreateProperty` and `Properties.Append` methods to add each of these properties. In most cases, unless the property has already been set in the Access Options dialog box, the property hasn't been appended to the database's Properties collection. You must make sure the property exists before trying to set its value in code. The following function sets the value of a startup property, creating and appending the property to the Properties collection if the property doesn't exist:

```
Public Function SetStartupProperty(sPropName As String, _
    ePropType As DAO.DataTypeEnum, vPropValue As Variant) As Boolean

    Dim db As DAO.Database
    Dim prp As DAO.Property
    Dim bReturn As Boolean

    Set db = CurrentDb
    On Error Resume Next
      Set prp = db.Properties(sPropName)

      If prp Is Nothing Then
        Set prp = db.CreateProperty(sPropName, ePropType, vPropValue)

        If prp Is Nothing Then
          bReturn = False
        Else
          db.Properties.Append prp
          bReturn = True
        End If
      Else
        prp.Value = vPropValue
        bReturn = True
      End If

      SetStartupProperty = bReturn

End Function
```

Using `SetStartupProperty()` is quite easy. You must know the exact property name and data type of the property before invoking `SetStartupProperty()`. The following subroutine demonstrates how to set a startup property with `SetStartupProperty()`:

```
Sub ChangeAppTitle()

    Dim bSuccess As Boolean

    bSuccess = SetStartupProperty("AppTitle", dbText, "My Application")

    If bSuccess Then
```

```
      MsgBox "Application title has been changed."
   Else
      MsgBox "Application title has not been changed."
   End If

End Sub
```

Notice that the `AppTitle` property is a string data type (`dbText`).

TIP

Use the `RefreshTitleBar` method to see the changes made by setting either the `AppTitle` or `AppIcon` property. The syntax of `RefreshTitleBar` is simple:

`Application.RefreshTitleBar`

Getting property values

Getting the value of a property is much easier than setting a property's value. The `Properties` collection returns the property, and the `Value` property returns the value. The syntax to get the value of the `AppTitle` property is as follows:

```
On Error Resume Next
GetAppTitle = CurrentDb.Properties("AppTitle").Value
```

where `GetAppTitle` is a string variable. The `On Error Resume Next` statement is necessary in case the property has not been set.

Integrating Access with SharePoint

IN THIS CHAPTER

Getting familiar with SharePoint sites

Understanding Access and SharePoint integration

Linking to SharePoint lists

Importing SharePoint lists

Exporting Access tables to SharePoint

Upsizing Access databases to SharePoint

Using SharePoint list templates

Throughout this book you've read about the many features that Microsoft has added to Access over the years. As exciting and interesting as these new capabilities are, they pale in comparison to the ability to upsize Access applications to Windows SharePoint Server. Each recent version of Access has demonstrated greater and greater ability to integrate with SharePoint. The most exciting aspect of this integration is the ability to actually run your Access application as a SharePoint website.

In this chapter, we'll explore the various techniques that allow you to upsize your Access databases to SharePoint. This chapter gives you an understanding of what SharePoint is and how it helps organizations share and collaborate data.

Introducing SharePoint

SharePoint is Microsoft's collaborative server environment, providing tools for sharing documents and data across various organizations within your company network.

SharePoint is typically deployed on a company's network as a series of SharePoint *sites*. A SharePoint site is configured as an intranet site, giving various departments the ability to control their own security, workgroups, documents, and data. These sites can be nested within other sites in a hierarchical fashion.

As with any other website, the pages within a SharePoint site are accessible through a URL that the user can access via a standard web browser.

Although SharePoint is most frequently used for sharing documents, data tables, and other content management tasks, SharePoint is frequently applied to many other applications—for example, to handle the documentation required for product development. A SharePoint site devoted to a development project easily handles the project initiation, tracking, and progress reporting tasks. Because SharePoint easily handles virtually any type of document, project drawings, videos, schematics, photographs, and so on, can be added to the project's SharePoint site for review and comment by project members.

Companies often use SharePoint for distributing human resource and policy documents. Because SharePoint provides user- and group-level security, it's quite easy to grant a particular department access to a SharePoint page while denying other users access to the same page.

SharePoint also logs changes to documents and supports a check-in/check-out paradigm for controlling who is eligible to make changes to existing documents and who is allowed to post new documents and files.

Some of the most common SharePoint deployments are storing of version-controlled documents, such as Word documents and Excel spreadsheets. In many environments, e-mail is used for passing documents back and forth between users. The potential for mixing up different versions of the same document is considerable. Also, storing multiple copies of the same document takes up a lot of disk space. Because SharePoint provides a single source for storing, viewing, and updating documents, many of these issues are eliminated entirely.

Understanding SharePoint Sites

Before going into the detail of describing how Access integrates with SharePoint technology, it's helpful to picture a typical SharePoint site. In this section, you'll get a brief overview of the two most common aspects of a SharePoint site: documents and lists.

> **NOTE**
>
> The topic of SharePoint is vast and worthy of its own book. In that light, we won't be discussing how to create and manage SharePoint lists or document libraries. In this book, we'll assume that your organization has a SharePoint site ready for consumption via Access. If you want to immerse yourself in SharePoint setup and administration, consider picking up the book *Beginning SharePoint 2013: Building Business Solutions with SharePoint,* by Amanda Perran, Shane Perran, Jennifer Mason, and Laura Rogers (Wiley, 2013).

SharePoint documents

Perhaps the most common use of SharePoint is to store shared documents and other files. SharePoint keeps track of files from the moment they're added to a list until they're removed or deleted. Anyone with write-access to a SharePoint site can upload a document for sharing. Figure 32.1 shows a short list of several different types of files uploaded to a SharePoint document library.

FIGURE 32.1

A SharePoint document library.

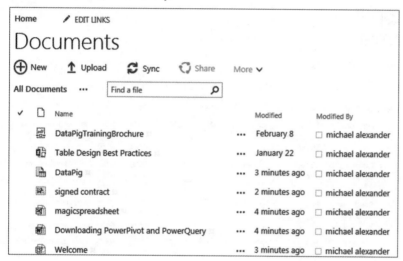

In Figure 32.1, notice that the library contains several different types of documents. Each row in the document list includes an icon indicating the document's type, the document's name, the date it was last modified, and the name of the person who added the document to the list.

SharePoint document libraries support a check-in/check-out paradigm. Only one person at a time is able to check out a document for changes. Although not shown in Figure 32.1, SharePoint records when a document is checked in or out and keeps track of the individuals making changes. SharePoint can even be instructed to roll back document changes to an earlier version, if necessary.

Again, this document-sharing paradigm is most commonly used to share information across organizations, allowing for collaboration between the users of the SharePoint site.

SharePoint lists

In addition to storing and tracking entire documents, SharePoint users can store and share data via SharePoint lists. SharePoint lists are conceptually similar to database tables in that each list consists of rows and columns of data. Each column holds a particular type of data, such as text, a date, or an object (such as a photo). From this simplistic perspective, SharePoint lists are analogous to Access tables.

Figure 32.2 illustrates a typical SharePoint list. As you can see, the relevant information is presented in a single screen. You add a new item, edit an existing item, or delete an item through this same screen.

FIGURE 32.2

A SharePoint list allows for the storage and tracking of data in a table format.

✓	CustomerID	Company	Address	City	State	ZipCode	Phone	Fax	Email
	1	Fun Zone	105 S Dubuque Street	Iowa City	IA	52240	(319) 352-0725	(860) 555-1930	sales@@funzone.com
	2	Exelon Shoppe	123 South Street	Newington	NH	12301	(603) 555-6887	(603) 555-6880	sales@ExelonShoppe.com
	3	Southwest Softies	Rt 9	Pine Plains	NY	12567	(518) 555-6699	(518) 555-6690	schina@SouthwestSofties.com
	4	Pinnacle Playables	560 Broadway	Salem	NH	03079	(603) 555-4422	(603) 555-4420	sampsg@PinnaclePlayables.com
	5	Toys in the	100 Elm	Sunnyville	GA	12305	(478)	(478)	james@ToysInTheBasement.com

SharePoint can manage virtually any type of data you want to share with other people. Although the site shown in Figure 32.2 is designed for a specific purpose, SharePoint is suitable for many other scenarios. For example, an HR department could use a SharePoint list for sharing and tracking required training courses. An IT department could maintain a list of assets, including status and locations. Even smaller organizations like a local bowling club can share and maintain tournament schedules and player rankings as SharePoint lists.

SharePoint easily supports multiple lists, allowing an organization to add as many lists as needed. Unfortunately, unlike Access tables, SharePoint lists are not relational; there is no way to directly relate data in two different SharePoint lists or to query multiple SharePoint lists to find related data. However, SharePoint lists *can* be linked or imported into Access. Linking to SharePoint lists makes data stored on a SharePoint website appear as linked tables in Access.

For the most part, linking to a SharePoint list is no different from linking to a SQL Server database table or other remote data source. However, an important difference is that linked SharePoint lists in Access 2019 are read-only; you can't edit or update the linked SharePoint list.

When linked to an Access application, SharePoint data is available to all the queries, forms, and reports in that application. This means that data entered into SharePoint lists can be viewed in real time and utilized through your Access application, making Access a feature-rich front-end platform for displaying SharePoint content.

> **NOTE**
>
> Many IT organizations today have already implemented a SharePoint environment. It is likely that your organization already has SharePoint running on your network. No one user can simply set up a SharePoint site. If you're interested in using SharePoint, you'll need to contact your IT department to inquire about getting access to a SharePoint site.

Sharing Data between Access and SharePoint

32

Building Access applications with SharePoint data simply means going into an Access application, linking to SharePoint lists, and then writing forms and reports based on those linked tables. A linked SharePoint list appears (to Access) as any other linked data source.

 Turn to Chapter 7 for more on linking to external data.

In addition to linking to SharePoint lists, you may find it helpful to import SharePoint data directly into local Access tables. Imported data is no longer connected to the SharePoint site and is therefore useful in those situations when you need to work with static snapshots of SharePoint lists.

> **NOTE**
>
> Because a SharePoint environment is needed to experiment with the concepts found here, there is no sample database for this chapter. If you're interested in using SharePoint, you'll need to contact your IT department to inquire about getting access to a SharePoint site. You can also find a commercial site, or perhaps even a free demonstration service, to experiment with.

Linking to SharePoint lists

The most fundamental data sharing between Access and SharePoint is for Access to link to a SharePoint list and use the data as with any other linked data source. Follow these steps to link to a SharePoint list:

1. **Click the New Data Source ⇨ From Online Services ⇨ SharePoint List in the Import & Link group on the External Data tab.** The list of more advanced import and linking options (see Figure 32.3) appears.

2. The Get External Data – SharePoint Site dialog box (see Figure 32.4) appears. Here, you can specify your target SharePoint site by entering the site's URL. This dialog box will remember any URL you enter and, when activated again, will show you a

selectable list of the recently used URLs. **Select the "Link to the data source by creating a linked table" option, and click Next.**

FIGURE 32.3

Preparing to link to a SharePoint list.

FIGURE 32.4

The Get External Data – SharePoint Site dialog box.

You must have appropriate permissions to link to a SharePoint list. In fact, without proper permissions, Access can't even display the SharePoint lists on the designated site. SharePoint users are recognized by their membership in Windows Active Directory services and their inclusion in designated SharePoint groups. These topics are beyond the scope of this book, but you should be aware that access to SharePoint sites and SharePoint data is protected by processes similar to any other Windows application.

3. **Enter your username and password.** Once you successfully log in to the SharePoint site, you will be presented with a list of SharePoint lists in the designated SharePoint site. Each item in the list is accompanied by a check box.

4. **Place a check mark next to each list you want linked, and then click OK.** In Figure 32.5, only the Customers SharePoint list is selected for linking, but you can select multiple lists as well.

FIGURE 32.5

Selecting a SharePoint list for linking.

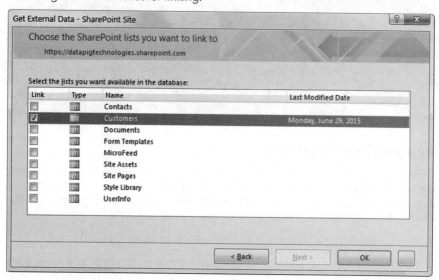

Figure 32.6 shows the linked SharePoint list. The icons indicating linked SharePoint lists look very much like Access table icons. Each linked list is accompanied by an arrow, and the color of the icon has changed to a yellowish-orange color.

The data in the linked table is compatible with Access, and you can build queries, forms, and reports against this data if needed. It's important to remember that the data in the linked list is read-only, meaning you can't update the data in the SharePoint list via Access 2019.

FIGURE 32.6

A linked SharePoint list appears much like any other Access table.

Importing SharePoint lists

Instead of having a live link to SharePoint lists, you may want to import a list. Importing a SharePoint list allows you to simply take a snapshot of the list and bring the data into Access as a stand-alone disconnected table. Unlike a linked SharePoint list, an imported list will not be automatically updated with new SharePoint data.

The steps for importing a SharePoint list are similar to those for linking:

1. **Click the New Data Source drop-down button in the Import & Link group on the External Data tab.** The list of more advanced import and linking options appears.

2. **Select From Online Services ⇨ SharePoint List from the list of online services.** The Get External Data – SharePoint Site dialog box appears.

3. **In the top portion of this dialog box, either select a recently visited SharePoint site or enter a new destination SharePoint URL; then select the Import option, as shown in Figure 32.7.**

FIGURE 32.7

Selecting a SharePoint list for importing.

4. **Enter the appropriate permissions to import a SharePoint list.** You're presented with a list of SharePoint lists in the designated SharePoint site. Each item in the list is accompanied by a check box.

5. **Place a check mark next to each list you want imported, and then click OK.** Access imports your chosen lists into a table (or tables) that can be viewed and utilized like any other standard table through the Navigation pane.

Exporting Access tables to SharePoint

Sometimes you need to transfer data from Access to SharePoint so that SharePoint users have access to the same data as Access users. The following steps export a table from Access to a SharePoint list. Remember, you will need to have proper Write access on the SharePoint site in order to perform this action:

1. **Right-click the table you want to export in the Navigation pane, and then select Export ⇨ SharePoint List (see Figure 32.8).** The Export – SharePoint Site dialog box activates.

2. **Enter or select the target SharePoint site URL (see Figure 32.9).** In addition to pointing to the URL, you have the option of specifying a name for the soon-to-be-created list.

FIGURE 32.8

Exporting a table to SharePoint.

FIGURE 32.9

Select the destination SharePoint site and specify a name for the exported list.

3. **Click the OK button.** If you're prompted for a login, enter a valid SharePoint username and password. When the export is complete, the new SharePoint list will be displayed with the other lists on the SharePoint site.

4. **Click the Close button in Access to dismiss the Export to SharePoint dialog box.**

Note that after exporting data from Access to SharePoint, the two data tables are not connected, so if changes are made in either location, the other application doesn't see the change.

> **NOTE**
>
> You can also export the results of a query to SharePoint. Simply right-click the target query and select Export ⇨ SharePoint List.

Certain fields don't export well to SharePoint. For instance, an OLE Object field is simply left empty on the SharePoint side and contains no data. However, most other field data types are properly translated into compatible SharePoint columns and populated with data from the Access table. Table 32.1 shows how Access data types are translated to compatible column types in SharePoint. Notice that far fewer types of data are available in SharePoint lists than in Access tables. The data types in Table 32.1 are applied any time an Access table is exported to SharePoint.

TABLE 32.1 **SharePoint Data Type Conversion**

Access Data Type	Converted Type in SharePoint
AutoNumber	Number
Text	Single line of text
Memo	Multiple lines of text, limited to 8,192 characters
All Number Types (Byte, Integer, Long Integer, Single, Double, Decimal)	Number
Date/Time	Date and Time
Currency	Currency
Yes/No	YesNo
OLE Object	Single line of text
Calculated	Calculated
Hyperlink	Hyperlink or Picture

Moving Access tables to SharePoint

Instead of simply exporting Access tables to SharePoint, another approach to data sharing is to move all the tables in an Access application to SharePoint as a single export operation and link the new SharePoint lists back to the Access application. All the tables in the Access database are moved to SharePoint and linked back to Access in a single process.

The advantage of moving Access tables to SharePoint is that you can build out your data model in Access, using all convenient tools for table creation, and then upsize the data model to SharePoint. Once the data is in SharePoint, any changes made in SharePoint will be immediately seen in Access.

This level of integration allows SharePoint to be used as the data collaboration and tracking portal, while giving users the benefit of Access's superior user-reporting tools.

Moving Access tables to SharePoint is not one of the import/export features of Access 2019. Instead, the commands necessary to move the entire set of Access tables to SharePoint are on the Database Tools tab of the Ribbon (see Figure 32.10).

FIGURE 32.10

The Move Data group on the Ribbon contains the wizard to upsize to SharePoint.

Clicking the SharePoint command in the Move Data group on the Ribbon opens the Export Tables to SharePoint Wizard dialog box (shown in Figure 32.11). The only information that you need is the URL of the destination SharePoint site; Access handles the rest.

The Next button initiates the export process, which may take more than a few minutes, depending on the number of tables in the Access database, the volume of data in each record, and the efficiency of the SharePoint server hardware and software. You may also be asked for your SharePoint username and password because SharePoint must verify that you have the proper permissions to create objects in the destination SharePoint site.

The newly created SharePoint lists are given the same name. At the conclusion of the process, all the tables in the Access database have been moved to SharePoint and linked back to the Access application. The tables and their data are now stored and managed by SharePoint Services. All that's left in the Access database are logical links to the SharePoint website; the tables and data are no longer stored in the Access database.

Just as with other export processes, you can save the export steps for future use. Access also makes a backup of the Access database file prior to the export process so that you can revert to the prior state, if necessary.

FIGURE 32.11

The Export Tables to SharePoint Wizard dialog box specifies the destination SharePoint site.

32

Things to Note Before Moving Access Tables to SharePoint

Before attempting to upsize your Access tables to SharePoint, keep in mind the following:

- **The export might fail if an Access table name does not conform to SharePoint naming rules.** For example, Access table names may contain spaces and limited punctuation characters, while SharePoint tables are plain text with no spaces. If the export fails, it's likely to be caused by a list-naming violation.

- **All the queries, forms, and reports that are based on the linked tables should function as before, with a few exceptions.** Because of incompatibilities between Access and SharePoint data, not every Access data type migrates to SharePoint. The incompatible fields are created in the SharePoint list, but they're added to the SharePoint list as text columns and are left empty.

- **Export issues are reported in a table named Move to SharePoint Site Issues, with one row for each problem.** A single Access field may generate multiple rows in the issues table. Most export problems are traceable to data incompatibility issues.

- **During the export process, several fields will be added to the SharePoint list that are required for list management on the SharePoint side.** These fields will be available in the linked table in Access but are not included in any of the queries, forms, or reports based on the table before it was exported to SharePoint. These additional fields are listed in the following table. It's possible that you may be able to make use of at least some of these columns, but by and large, they serve no purpose in an Access application.

SharePoint Field Name	Data Type
_OldId	Number (Double)
Content Type	Text
Workflow Instance ID	Text
File Type	Text
Modified	Date/Time
Created	Date/Time
Created By	Text
Modified By	Text
URL Path	Text
Path	Text
Item Type	Text
Encoded Absolute URL	Text

Using SharePoint Templates

In its attempt to solidify the connection between Access and SharePoint, Microsoft has provided yet another approach to integrating Access applications with SharePoint.

Instead of exporting existing Access tables to SharePoint or linking to SharePoint lists, this alternative technique involves building entirely new SharePoint lists within the Access environment. Access 2019 provides SharePoint list *templates*, which contain all the details necessary to build SharePoint lists, including column names and data types and other list properties. This is essentially meant to be a time-saver for anyone who wants to quickly stand up a new list on SharePoint.

The SharePoint templates in Access 2019 cover a number of important business functions: Contacts, Tasks, Issues, and Events, as shown on the Create tab in Figure 32.12. In addition, the Custom list template (near the bottom of the list) allows you to add virtually any combination of SharePoint-compatible columns to an otherwise blank list. The last item in the drop-down list (Existing SharePoint List) provides the same linking capability discussed in the "Linking to SharePoint lists" section, earlier in this chapter.

Selecting an item from the list of SharePoint list templates opens the Create New List dialog box (shown in Figure 32.13). You'll have to provide a SharePoint URL and a name for the new list.

FIGURE 32.12

SharePoint list templates available in Access.

FIGURE 32.13

The Create New List dialog box when creating a new SharePoint list from an Access template.

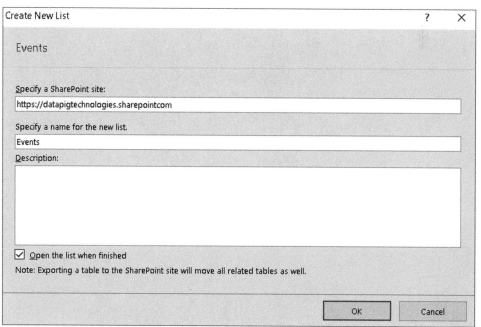

Notice that you don't have an option to modify the template before you create it in SharePoint. This means, of course, that the list will include a predetermined set of columns, each set to a particular data type required for the list's operations.

You may be asked to provide SharePoint credentials as the new list is created. You need administrative rights to add lists to a SharePoint site, so even if you can link to a SharePoint list, you may not be entitled to create an entirely new list.

The newly created list will be automatically added to Access as a linked table that behaves like any other linked SharePoint list.

Index

Symbols and Numerics

& (ampersand), parameter queries, 408
! (exclamation point), parameter queries, 408
. (period), parameter queries, 408
[] (square brackets)
   parameter queries, 406, 408
   wildcard, 430
< > (not equal) comparison operator, 273, 451–452
= (equal) comparison operator, 273, 451–452
> (greater than) comparison operator, 274, 451–452
>= (greater than or equal to) comparison operator, 274, 451–452
< (less than) comparison operator, 273–274, 451–452
<= (less than or equal to) comparison operator, 274, 451–452
+ (addition) mathematical operator, 270, 271
/ (division) mathematical operator, 270, 271
^ (exponentiation) mathematical operator, 270, 272
\ (integer division) mathematical operator, 270, 271–272
* (multiplication) mathematical operator, 270, 271
- (subtraction) mathematical operator, 270, 271
& (concatenation) string operator, 275–276
[!] wildcard, 430
* (asterisk) wildcard, 430
# (pound sign) wildcard, 430
? (question mark) wildcard, 430
1NF (first normal form), 90–93
2NF (second normal form), 94
   decomposition, 97–98
   entities, 96–98
      identifying, 94–96
   exceptions, 98–99
   update anomalies, 95
3NF (third normal form), 99–100

A

Access, as landing pad for data, 173
ACE (Access Connectivity Engine), 20, 901–902
   query optimization, 348–349
Action Catalog, 747
   data actions, 749–751
   data blocks, 748–749
   macro groups, 748
   program flow, 748
action queries, 320
   append queries, 327–332
      SQL statements, 437
      subqueries, 456
   delete queries, 323–326
      SQL statements, 437
      subqueries, 456
   make-table queries, 321–323
      SQL statements, 436
      subqueries, 456
   update queries, 332–336
      SQL statements, 437
      subqueries, 456
Activate event, 849, 853
ActiveX controls, 504
ad hoc joins, 265–266
ADO (ActiveX Data Objects), 763
   Command object, 920–922
   Connection object, 918–920
   library, 917–918
   Recordset object, 922–923
AfterDelConfirm event, 850
AfterDelete event, 744–745
AfterInsert event, 744–745, 850
AfterUpdate event, 744–745, 850, 852
aggregate functions
   Avg, 316
   Count, 317
   domain aggregate functions, 445
   Expression, 318–320
   First, 317
   Group By, 315–316
   Last, 317
   Max, 317
   Min, 317
   StDev, 317
   Sum, 316
   Var, 317
   Where, 318–320

Index

aggregate information in subforms, 572–573
aggregate queries, 311
    descriptive statistics and, 470–471
    versus domain aggregate function, 459
    results to hard tables, 322
aggregation, 165–166
    results, in calculations, 381–382
aggregation functions, Group By, 315–316
aliases
    AS clause (SQL), 433
    column names, 314–315
    correlated subqueries and, 454–455
alignment
    controls, 517–518
    report controls, 687
Allow Additions property, 555
Allow Datasheet View property, 550
Allow Deletions property, 554
Allow Edits property, 554
Allow Filters property, 554
Allow Form View property, 550
Allow Layout View property, 550
Allow Zero Length property, 54
AllowZeroLength property, 65–66
alphanumeric data, 42
ALTER TABLE statement (SQL), 440–442
    ADD clause, 441
    ADD CONSTRAINT clause, 442
    ALTER COLUMN clause, 441
    DROP COLUMN, 441–442
Alternate Row Color drop-down list, 156
ampersand (&), parameter queries, 408
analyses
    calculations, 379–380
        aggregation results in, 381–382
        as argument in function, 382–384
        constants in, 380
        dates, 392–399
        errors, 388–391
        Expression Builder and, 384–388
        fields, 42
        fields in, 381
        null values and, 389–391
        operator precedence and, 388–389
        syntax in expressions, 391
    conditional, 405
        parameter queries, 405–407
And operator, 278–279, 300–302
    select criteria, 286–288

append queries, 327
    conversion failure, 327
    key violations, 327
    lock violations, 327
    subqueries, 456
    validation rule violation, 327
application testing, debugging and, 867–873
applications
    development
        building to specification, 1003–1005
        documentation, 1005–1007
        testing, 1007–1008
    distribution
        Application Options, 994–999
        bulletproofing, 1022–1034
        consistent style, 1009–1022
        development, 1003–1008
        Name AutoCorrect options, 1002
        Navigation options, 999–1001
        Ribbon and Toolbar Options, 1001–1002
        security, 1034–1038
ApplyFilter event, 850
arguments
    calculations as, 381–382
    macros, 706
        Beep, 707
        Message, 707
        Title, 707
        Type, 707
    named arguments, 840–842
    parameters as, 411–414
    procedures, named arguments, 840–842
Array function, 826–827
arrays
    dynamic, 825–826
    fixed, 822–824
    functions
        Array, 826–827
        boundaries, 826
        Join, 828–829
        Split, 827–828
AS clause (SQL), 433
Attachment data type, 42, 48
attachment fields, 84–85
Auto Center property, 550
Auto Resize property, 550
AutoCorrect, 35
AutoNumber data type, 42, 47, 50
    primary keys, 114

AutoSum button, 165–166
Avg aggregate function, 316

B

Back Color property, 557
Background Color drop-down list, 156
background pictures, 580–582
BeforeChange event, 743
BeforeDelConfirm event, 850
BeforeDelete event, 744
BeforeInsert event, 850
BeforeScreenTip event, 849
BeforeUpdate event, 743, 850, 852
Between...And operator, 281, 302, 408–409
binding reports to tables, 629–631
Blank Database option, 18–20
Blank Form command, 491, 492
BMP images, 578, 581
Boolean data type (VBA), 809
Boolean (logical) operators, 270, 278–280
    And, 278–279
    Not, 280
    Or, 279–280
    precedence, 283
    select criteria, 286
Border Style property, 551
bound controls, 506
    user names, 688
bound forms, 547–548
brackets, [ ] (square brackets), 406
breakpoints, debugging and, 881–887
bulleted lists, 674–676
Button Ribbon control, 958–959, 982–983
Byte data type (VBA), 809

C

calculated controls, 506
    unbound, 571
Calculated data type, 42, 48
calculations, 379–380
    aggregation results in, 381–382
    as argument in function, 382–384
    constants in, 380
    dates, 392
        age in years, 394–396
        Date function, 393–396
        DateAdd function, 399–400
        DateSerial function, 401–403

        Day function, 397–399
        days past, 393
        Month function, 397–399
        Weekday function, 397–399
        workdays, 398–399
        Year function, 397–399
    errors, 388–391
    Expression Builder and, 384–388
    fields, 42
    fields in, 381
    null values and, 389–391
    operator precedence and, 388–389
    syntax in expressions, 391
Call Stack window, debugging and, 892–893
Can Grow property, 644–645
Can Shrink property, 644–645
CancelRecordChange action, 749
Caption, 550
Caption property, 54, 63, 546–547
Cascade Delete Related Records, 124
Cascade Related Fields check box, 124
case, changing, 367–368
categories, controls, 504–506
cells, gridlines, 156–158
Change event, 852
character markers, string parsing and, 374–377
Check Box control, 570
check boxes, tallying, 573
CheckBox Ribbon control, 960, 983–984
child table, foreign key, 116
Choose Builder dialog box, 735
ClearMacroError action, 751
Click event, 844, 847, 849, 852
Clipboard, copy and paste in Datasheet window, 148–149
Clipboard group
    Copy option, 535
    Cut option, 535
    Datasheet Ribbon, 134
    Format Painter option, 535
    Paste command
        Paste Append option, 534
        Paste option, 534
        Paste Special option, 534
Close Button property, 551
Close event, 849, 853
Collectible Mini Cars Customers, 38
collections, 903
    Properties collection, 903
color, alternating rows, 156–158

color schemes, reports, 614–616
Column Width dialog box, 153–154
columnar layout, 495
columnar reports, 600, 601–602
columns, 5–6
   adding, 441
   aliases, AS clause, 433
   alignment, 158
   ALTER TABLE statement (SQL), 440–442
      ADD clause, 441
      ALTER COLUMN clause, 441
      DROP COLUMN, 441–442
   altering, 441
   deleting, 441–442
   freezing, 159–160
   hiding/unhiding, 158–159
   names, aliases, 314–315
   ranking columns, 672
   resizing, 153–154
   selecting
      all, 427
      specific, 427
   snaking, 692–696
   vertical lines, 680–682
   width, 153–154
Combo Box control, 568
   Bound Column property, 569
   Column Count property, 569
   Column Heads property, 569
   Column Widths property, 569
   Limit To List property, 569
   List Rows property, 569
   List Width property, 569
   Multi Select property, 570
   Row Source property, 569
   Row Source Type property, 569
   Validation Rule property, 569
   Validation Text property, 569
combo boxes, 542–543
   Organization, 575
   source, 574
   unbound, 937–939
      bookmarks, 941–944
      FindRecord method, 939–941
ComboBox Ribbon control, 960
comma-delimited text files, importing, 185–188
Command Button control
   Hover Color property, 568
   Hover Fore Color property, 568

Picture property, 568
Picture Type property, 568
Pressed Color property, 568
Pressed Fore Color property, 568
Yes/No property, 568
command buttons, query dialog, 587–588
Command object (ADO), 920–922
commands
   Blank Form, 491, 492
   Form, 493–492
   Form Design, 491, 492
   Quick Access toolbar, 26
   Snap to Grid, 518
comma-separated-values text files
   importing, 185–188
   linking to, 223
compacting database, query optimization and, 351
comparison operators, 270, 273
   = (equal), 273, 451–452
   > (greater than), 274, 451–452
   >= (greater than or equal to), 274, 451–452
   < (less than), 273–274, 451–452
   <= (less than or equal to), 274, 451–452
   < > (not equal), 273, 451–452
   precedence, 283
   queries, select queries, 284–285
   subqueries, 451–462
compiling code, application testing and, 871–873
complex criteria, 285–288
   on different lines, 308–309
composite indexes, 76–78
composite primary keys, 72–73, 117–118
concatenation, fields, 364–367
conditional analysis, 405
   functions
      IIf, 414–423
      Switch, 420–423
   parameter queries, 405–407
conditional functions
   IIf
      arguments, 414
      compared to Switch, 421–423
      crosstab analysis, 419–420
      mathematical errors avoidance, 415–416
      nesting, multiple conditions and, 418
      saving steps, 416–418
   Switch
      compared to IIf, 421–423

expressions, 420
    values, 420
conditions, macros, 720–723
Connection object (ADO), 918–920
constants
    in calculations, 380
    declaring, 820
    hard-code values, 821–822
    naming conventions, 821
Control Box property, 551
control events, 851
    AfterUpdate, 852
    BeforeUpdate, 852
    Change, 852
    Click, 852
    DblClick, 852
    Dirty, 852
    Enter, 852
    Exit, 852
    GotFocus, 852
    KeyDown, 852
    KeyPress, 852
    KeyUp, 852
    LostFocus, 852
    MouseDown, 852
    MouseMove, 852
    MouseUp, 852
    NotInList, 852
    Undo, 852
    Updated, 852
    writing, 858–864
Control Source, combo boxes and, 574
controls, 503–504
    ActiveX, 504
    alignment, 517–518, 687
    appearance, 519
    calculated, unbound, 571
    categories, 504–506
    Check Box, 570
    Combo Box, 568
        Bound Column property, 569
        Column Count property, 569
        Column Heads property, 569
        Column Widths property, 569
        Limit To List property, 569
        List Rows property, 569
        List Width property, 569
        Multi Select property, 570
        Row Source property, 569

        Row Source Type property, 569
        Validation Rule property, 569
        Validation Text property, 569
    Command Button
        Hover Color property, 568
        Hover Fore Color property, 568
        Picture property, 568
        Picture Type property, 568
        Pressed Color property, 568
        Pressed Fore Color property, 568
        Yes/No property, 568
    copying, 522
    Date Picker, 541
    deleting, 522
    deselecting, 511–513
    events, 851–852
        writing, 858–864
    Format Painter and, 579
    forms, 16
        adding, 506–511
        attachment, 505
        bound controls, 506
        bound object frame, 505
        button, 505
        calculated controls, 506
        chart, 505
        check box, 505
        combo box, 505
        field list, 508–511
        image, 505
        insert page break, 505
        label, 504
        line, 505
        link, 505
        list box, 505
        navigation control, 505
        option button, 505
        option group, 505
        rectangle, 505
        subform/subreport, 505
        tab control, 505
        text box, 504
        toggle button, 505
        unbound controls, 506
        unbound object frame, 505
        web browser control, 505
    groups, 519–520
    handles, 511–512
    hiding/showing, 677–680

controls *(continued)*
    Image, 577–578
    Label
        cutting, 638–639
        deleting, 638–639
        moving, 640–642
        naming, 527–529
        pasting to section, 640
        properties, 643–644
        reattaching, 522–523
        sizing, 637–638
    List Box, 568
    micro-adjustments, 687
    morphing, 578–579
    moving, 515–516
    naming, 701
    Option Group
        Control Source property, 570
        Default Value property, 570
        Frame Control property, 570
        Option Value property, 570
    placing, 589–590
    properties, 524, 563–564
        appearance, 566–567
        customizing, 565–566
        Design view, 564
        Property Sheet, 565, 566
        settings, 526–527
    Property Sheet, 524–525, 643–644
        Data tab, 525
        Event tab, 525
        Format tab, 525
    reports, placing, 633–634
    resizing, 513–515
    Ribbon, 956
        Button, 958–959, 982–983
        CheckBox, 960, 983–984
        ComboBox, 960
        DropDown, 985–987
        Gallery, 958
        imageMso attribute, 979–980
        Label, 980–982
        Menu, 957–958
        separators, 983
        SplitButton, 957, 987–988
        ToggleButton, 959
    selecting, 511–513
    sizing, automatically, 515
    Tab, 583–584
        Caption property, 585
        Multi Row property, 585
        Picture property, 586
        Style property, 585
        Tab Fixed Height property, 585
        Tab Fixed Width property, 586
    Text Box
        Back Color property, 566–567
        Back Style property, 566–567
        Border Style property, 566–567
        Border Width property, 566–567
        Can Grow property, 644–645
        Can Shrink property, 644–645
        cutting labels, 638–639
        Default Value property, 567
        deleting labels, 638–639
        Font Italic property, 567
        Font Name property, 567
        Font Size property, 567
        Font Underline property, 567
        Font Weight property, 567
        Fore Color property, 567
        Format property, 566
        functions, 637
        Input Mask property, 567
        moving, 640–642
        pasting labels, 640
        properties, 643–644
        sizing, 637–638, 644–645
        Special Effect property, 566–567
        Text Align property, 567
        Text Format property, 567
        Validation Rule property, 567
        Validation Text property, 567
    Toggle Button, 570
    type, changing, 520–522
    Web Browser, Control Source property, 570
Controls group, 504–508
ControlTip Text property, 580
copying
    tables, 82–83
        to another database, 82–83
    values, datasheets, 148–149
correlated subqueries, 453–454
    as expressions, 455
Count aggregate function, 317
Create New Theme Colors dialog box, 614–615
Create New Theme Fonts dialog box, 616

Create tab (Ribbon), 24, 35
    Forms group, 490–491
    Table Design button, 37
    Tables group, 36
CREATE TABLE statement (SQL), 438–440
crosstab queries
    creating manual, 342–345
    Crosstab Query Wizard, 336–342
    customizing
        column heading sort order, 346–348
        defining criteria, 346
    TRANSFORM statement (SQL), 437
Currency data type, 42, 47, 809
Currency format, 55–56
Current event, 850
Cycle property, 555

D

DAO (Data Access Objects), 763, 901–902, 904–905
    Database object, 907–908
    DBEngine, 905
    Field objects, 916–917
    QueryDef object, 909–911
    Recordset object, 911
        counting records, 915–916
        Dynamic type, 911
        Dynaset type, 911
        end/beginning detection, 914–915
        Forward Only type, 911
        navigating recordsets, 912–914
        Snapshot type, 911
        specifying type, 912
        Table type, 911
    TableDef object, 908–909
    Workspace object, 905–906
data, 169–170
    aggregating, 165–166
    alignment, 158
    definition, 5
    events, 850–851
    exporting, 171, 173
    external, 169–170
        External Data tab, 174–175
        linking to, 170, 171–172
        working with, 170
    groups, sorting, 647–650
    importing, 170
        from Access databases, 175–178

        Access objects, 198–200
        from Excel spreadsheets, 178–184
        HTML documents, 197–198
        Outlook folders, 200–202
        SharePoint lists, 185
        from text files, 185–192
        when to use, 172
        XML documents, 192–197
    landing pad, Access as, 173
    linked, limitations, 213–214
    linking to, 170
        when to use, 171–172
    reports
        adding, 688
        assembling, 604–605
        sources, 604–605
    unsupported programs, 173
    working with, 170
data design, 11–13
data entry
    Date/Time data type, 540–541
    Long Text field, 540
    properties and
        Date/Time, 140–141
        Long Text, 141–142
        Number/Currency, 141
        OLE Object, 141
        text, 140
    value lookup, 594–595
Data Entry property, 555
data macros, 742
    collapsing items, 755
    creating, 751–755
    expanding items, 755
    limitations, 757–758
    Macro Builder, 745–747
    moving items, 756
    saving, as XML, 756–757
    table events, 742–743
        AfterDelete, 744–745
        AfterInsert, 744–745
        AfterUpdate, 744–745
        BeforeChange, 743
        BeforeDelete, 744
        BeforeUpdate, 743
data properties
    Allow Additions, 555
    Allow Deletions, 554
    Allow Edits, 554

data properties *(continued)*
  Allow Filters, 554
  Data Entry, 555
  Fetch Defaults, 555
  Filter, 554
  Filter On Load, 554
  Order By, 554
  Order By On Load, 554
  Record Locks, 555
  Record Source, 554
  Recordset Type, 555
data sets
  median, descriptive statistics and, 475–477
  merging, UNION operator, 438–440
  mode, descriptive statistics and, 472–475
  ranking, descriptive statistics and, 471–472
  sampling, random, 477–479
  second quartile, with single query, 457–458
  total row, adding, 330–331
  updatable, 335–336
data sources
  queries, 548
  SQL statements, 548
  tables, 548
Data Type drop-down, 43
data types, 43
  Attachment, 42, 48
  AutoNumber, 42, 47, 50
  Calculated, 42, 48
  converting, 52–53
  Currency, 42, 47
  data validation rules, 49
  Date/Time, 42, 46–47, 140
    entering, 540–541
  Hyperlink, 42, 48
  indexed, 44
  Large Number, 42, 46
  Long Text, 42, 45, 141
    entering, 540
  Lookup Wizard, 42, 49
  Number, 42, 45–46, 141
    bytes, 46
    decimal, 46
    double, 46
    integers, 46
    long integers, 46
    replication ID, 46
    single, 46
  OLE Object, 42, 47–48, 141

reports and, 44
  Short Text, 42, 45
  storage requirements, 43
  validation, automatic, 138–140
  VBA
    Access field types and, 810–811
    Boolean, 809
    Byte, 809
    Currency, 809
    Date, 809
    Decimal, 809
    Double, 810
    Integer, 810
    Long, 810
    Object, 810
    Single, 810
    String, 810
    Variant, 810
  Yes/No, 42, 47
data validation rules, 49
database engine, 20
Database object (DAO), 907–908
Database Splitter, 232–235
Database Tools, Documenter dialog box, 79–80
Database Tools tab (Ribbon), 24
databases, 3
  blank, 18–20
  compacting, query optimization and, 351
  creating, 18–20
  distribution
    Application Options, 994–999
    Name AutoCorrect options, 1002
    Navigation options, 999–1001
    Ribbon and Toolbar Options, 1001–1002
  entity integrity, 71
  exporting to, 202–203
  flat-file, 91, 102–103
  forms, 7, 8
    data-entry forms, 8
    display forms, 8
  importing from, 175–178
  linking to, 214–216
  macros, 7, 9
  manual, 4
  modules, 7
  naming, 19
  objects, 7–9
  queries, 7, 8
  relational databases, 6–7

repairing, query optimization and, 351
reports, 7, 8–9
splitting
    benefits, 229–232
    object location, 232
tables, 7–8
data-entry forms, 8
Datasheet Formatting dialog box,
    157–158
datasheet forms, 501–502
Datasheet Ribbon
    Advanced Filter Options button, 133
    Data sheet Formatting button, 133
    Filter by Selection button, 133
    Home tab, 133
        Clipboard group, 134
        Find group, 134
        Records group, 134
        Sort & Filter group, 134
        Text Formatting group, 135
        Views group, 134
        Window group, 134
    Table Tools group, 136
Datasheet view, 130, 490, 534
    linked data, external, 213
    queries, 131
    switching to, 543–544
    tables, 131
Datasheet window, 131–132
    copy and paste, 148–149
    entering data, 135–137
    fields
        properties, 136
        validation rules, 136
    filtering
        by form, 164–165
        selections, 161–164
    Find and Replace, 143–146
    navigating, 132
        moving between records, 143
        to specific values, 143–146
    Navigation buttons, 133
    new record indicator, 136
    opening datasheets, 135
    records
        adding, 150
        deleting, 150–151
        saving, 138
        sorting, 161

rows, new, 136–137
values, editing, 146–148
datasheets, 5, 130
    alignment, 158
    color, 156–158
    columns, 5–6, 158
        freezing, 159–160
        hiding/unhiding, 158–159
        width, 153–154
    copy and paste, 148–149
    custom, 131
    display, 152–160
    editing, 146
        keystrokes, 147
        values, 146–148
    fields, 5–6, 131
        column width, 153–154
        navigating, 536
        order, 152–153
    filtering
        by form, 164–165
        selections, 161–164
    fonts, 155–156
    gridlines, 156–158
    layouts, saving, 160
    navigating, 132, 142–146
    opening, 135
    records, 5–6
        adding, 150
        deleting, 150–151
        filtering by form, 164–165
        filtering by selection, 161–164
        previewing, 167
        printing, 166–167
        saving, 138, 160
        sorting, 161
    rows
        color, 156–158
        height, 154–155
        new, 136–137
    tables, 131
Date( ) function, 576
date and time
    age in years calculation, 394–396
    data type, 42
    days past, 393
    forms, 576–577
    quarters, 400–401
Date and Time command, 576

Date and Time dialog box, 576–577
date calculations, 392
    age in years, 394–396
    Date function, 393–396
    DateAdd function, 399–400
    DateSerial function, 401–403
    Day function, 397–399
    days past, 393
    Month function, 397–399
    quarters, 400–401
    Weekday function, 397–399
    workdays, 398–399
    Year function, 397–399
date criteria, domain aggregate functions, 463
Date data type (VBA), 809
Date function
    age in years, 394–396
    days past, 393
    in expressions, 394
Date Picker control, 541
DateAdd function, 399–400
DateSerial function, 401–403
Date/Time data type, 42, 46–47
    data entry, 540–541
    properties and, 140
DAvg function, 460
Day function, 397–399
DBEngine object (DAO), 905
DblClick event, 847, 849, 852
DBMS (database management system), 4
DCount function, 460, 465–466
Deactivate event, 849, 853
Debug window, 880–881
debugging, 865
    application testing, 867–868
        code compiling, 871–873
        functions, 868–871
    Auto Data Tips, 886–887
    breakpoints, 881–887
    Call Stack window, 892–893
    compiler directives, 875–878
    Debug window and, 880–881
    Err object, 896–897
    error handling, procedures, 897–898
    error trapping
        On Error GoTo 0, 895
        On Error GoTo Label, 895
        On Error Resume Next, 893–894
        Resume keyword, 896

Immediate window and, 880–881
    Locals window, 887–888
    macros, 733–734
    Stop statements, 883–884
    techniques
        Debug.Print, 878–879
        MsgBox, 874–875
    Watches window, 889–890
        conditional watches, 891–892
Debug.Print, 878–879
Decimal data type (VBA), 809
Decimal Places property, 54
decomposition, 97–98
Default Value property, 54
    Continuous Forms option, 548
    Datasheet option, 548
    Single Form option, 548
    Split Form option, 548
Default View property, 550
Delete event, 850
delete queries, 323–326
    subqueries, 456
DeleteRecord action, 749
deleting
    records, 150–151
    relationships, 126
    tables, 82
deletion anomalies, 100
delimited text files, importing, 185–188
denormalization, 101–102
descriptive statistics, 469
    aggregate queries and, 470–471
    data sets
        median, 475–477
        mode, 472–475
        random sampling, 477–479
    frequency distribution, 483–486
    percentile calculation, 479–481
    quartile calculation, 481–483
    ranking records, 471–472
design
    data design, 11–13
    five-step method, 9–16
    forms, 16, 589
        appearance, 596–597
        behavior, 593–595
        check box tally, 573
        combo boxes, 574–575
        control order, 597

control placement, 596
list boxes, 574–575
properties, 593–594
saving records, 595
Tab Stop property, 573
value lookup, data entry and, 594–595
overall design, 10
report design, 11
banded approach, 622–628
tables, 13–16
Design tab
Controls group, 504–506
Delete Rows, 40, 51
Header/Footer Group, Date and Time command, 576
Indexes, 41
Insert Rows, 40, 51
Primary key, 39
Property Sheet, 40
Themes group, 612–614
colors, 614–616
Design view, 34–35, 490, 534
control properties, 564
form resize, 502–503
null values, 389
reports, 619–620, 631
designing tables, 34–39
designs, forms, subforms, 590–593
Detail section (reports), 624, 626
DFirst function, 461
dialog boxes
Choose Builder, 735
Column Width, 153–154
Create New Theme Colors, 614–615
Create New Theme Fonts, 616
Datasheet Formatting, 157–158
Date and Time, 576–577
Documenter, 79–80
Edit Relationships, 120
Enter Parameter Value, 407
Export - HTML Document, 198
Export XML, 192–193
Field Width, 153–154
Find and Replace, 143–146, 148–149
Grouping Intervals, 607
Indexes, 76–77
information collection and, 586–589
Join Properties, 121–122
Link Specification, 222
modal, 241

Page Setup, 632–633
Paste Table As, 361
Print, 166–167
Print Table Definition, 79–80
queries, 586–587
Cancel button, 589
command buttons, 587–588
control menu, removing, 589
default button, 588
properties, 587
Row Height, 154–155
Show Table, 119–120, 241–242
Summary Options, 608–609
Unhide Columns, 159
Zoom, 540
DIB images, 578
digital certificates, 711–712
digital signatures, 711–712
Dim keyword, 807
Dirty event, 850, 852
display forms, 8
Display When property, 558
DISTINCT predicate (SQL), 432
subqueries, 447
Dividing Lines property, 550
DLast function, 461
DLookup function, 461, 466–468
DMax function, 461
DMin function, 461
DoCmd, 762
Documenter dialog box, 79–80
documents
HTML, importing, 197–198
XML, importing/exporting, 192–197
domain aggregate functions, 445
aggregate queries and, 459
anatomy of, 460
DAvg, 460
DCount, 460, 465–466
DFirst, 461
DLast, 461
DLookup, 461, 466–468
DMax, 461
DMin, 461
DStDev, 461
DStDevP, 461
DSum, 460
DVar, 461
DVarP, 461

domain aggregate functions *(continued)*
    syntax, 461
        date criteria, 463
        number criteria, 462
        text criteria, 462
Double data type (VBA), 810
drop-down lists, Data Type, 43
DropDown Ribbon control, 985–987
DStDev function, 461
DStDevP function, 461
DSum function, 460
duplicate records
    defining, 356
    hiding, 665–668
    locating, 357–359
    removing, 359–361
DVar function, 461
DVarP function, 461
Dynamic recordset type, 911
Dynaset recordset type, 911

E

edge cases, 871
Edit Relationships dialog box, 120
editing, datasheet values
    keystrokes, 147
    uneditable fields, 148
embedded macros, 734–736
empty fields, filling in, 363–364
Enforce Referential Integrity checkbox, 120, 123–124
Enter event, 852
Enter Parameter Value dialog box, 407
entity integrity, 71, 114
Error event, 850, 853
error handling, 728–729
    debugging and, 897–898
    MacroError object, 732–733
    OnError action, 730–732
Euro format, 56
event procedures
    creating, 845–846
    record deletion, 862–864
    running at form closure, 862
    templates, 846
    writing, 858–864
events, 843–844
    Activate, 849, 853
    AfterDelConfirm, 850

AfterInsert, 850
AfterUpdate, 850, 852
ApplyFilter, 850
BeforeDelConfirm, 850
BeforeInsert, 850
BeforeScreenTip, 849
BeforeUpdate, 850, 852
Change, 852
Click, 844, 847, 849, 852
Close, 849, 853
common, 847–856
control events, 851–853
    writing, 858–864
controls, 851–853
Current, 850
data events, 844
DblClick, 847, 849, 852
Deactivate, 849, 853
Delete, 850
Dirty, 850, 852
Enter, 852
Error, 850, 853
error and timing events, 844
Exit, 852
Filter, 850
focus events, 844
form events
    data events, 850–851
    essential events, 848–849
    keyboard events, 849–850
    mouse events, 849–850
    writing, 858–864
Format, 854
forms, 848–849
    data events, 850–851
    keyboard, 848–849
    mouse, 848–849
GotFocus, 849, 852
keyboard events, 844
KeyDown, 847, 849, 852
KeyPress, 847, 849, 852
KeyUp, 847, 849, 852
Load, 849
LostFocus, 849, 852
macros, assigning, 708–709
mouse events, 844
MouseDown, 844, 847, 849, 852
MouseMove, 847, 849, 852
MouseUp, 844, 847, 849, 852

MouseWheel, 847, 849
NoData, 853
NotInList, 852
OnClick, 844
OnMouseDown, 844
OnMouseUp, 844
Open, 849, 853
Page, 853
Print, 854
print events, 844
procedures, creating, 845–846
programming, 844–846
programming events, 844
record deletion, 862–864
report events, 853–854
    section events, 854–856
report section, 854–856
reports, 844–845, 853–854
Resize, 849
Retreat, 854
sequence, 856–858
table events
    AfterDelete, 744–745
    AfterInsert, 744–745
    AfterUpdate, 744–745
    BeforeChange, 743
    BeforeDelete, 744
    BeforeUpdate, 743
Timer, 849
Undo, 850, 852
Unload, 849
Updated, 852
VBA code, 844–845
VBA code triggers, 844–845
windows events, 844
Excel
    linking to, 218–220
    spreadsheets, importing from, 178–184
exclamation point (!), parameter queries, 408
Exit event, 852
ExitForEachRecord action, 749–750
explicit variables, 811–812
Export - HTML Document dialog box, 198
Export XML dialog box, 192–193
exporting, 169–170. *See also* data
    data, 171
        when to, 173
    to databases, 202–203
    External Data tab, 174–175

External Data tab (Ribbon), 174–175
    linking to, 170, 171–172
    ODBC drivers and, 203–205
    publishing to PDF, 206–208
    publishing to XPS, 206–208
    to Word, 205–206
    working with, 170
Expression aggregate function, 318–320
Expression Builder, functions, 385–388
expressions, 269
    aggregation results in, 381–382
    constants and, 380
    correlated subqueries as, 455
    Date function, 394
    fields, 381
    group headers, 653–654
    operators, 269
        Boolean (logical), 270, 278–280
        comparison, 270, 273–274
        mathematical, 270, 271–272
        miscellaneous, 270, 280–282
        string, 270, 275–276
        table properties, 270
    subqueries as, 452–453
    Switch function, 420
    syntax, 291
    update queries, 334–335
external data
    data, 171
        when to, 173
    linking, 210–211
        to Excel, 218–220
        to HTML files, 220–222
        to ODBC sources, 216–217
        to text files, 222–225
External Data tab
    Export group, 174–175
    Import & Link group, New Data Source drop-down, 174
External Data tab (Ribbon), 24
external files, 42

F

Fast Laser Printing property, 556
Fetch Defaults property, 555
field list, controls and, 508–511
field objects, 903
Field Size property, 54

Field Width dialog box, 153–154
fields, 5–6
    adding, 35
    attachment fields, 84–85
    augmenting, 366–367
    blank, filling in, 363–364
    calculations, 42
    in calculations, 381
    Cascade Related Fields check box, 124
    concatenation, 364–365
    data types, 42
    data validation rules, 49
    datasheets, 131
    deleting, 35, 51
    description, entering, 49
    editing, uneditable fields, 148
    empty values, filling in, 363–364
    inserting, 51
    key fields
        foreign, 15
        primary, 15
    moving, 51
    names, parameter queries, 407
    naming, 41
    navigating, 536
    ordering, 152–153
    properties, 53
        Allow Zero Length, 54
        Caption, 54
        Decimal Places, 54
        Default Value, 54
        Field Size, 54
        Format, 54, 55–60
        IME Mode, 55
        IME Sentence Mode, 55
        Indexed, 54
        Input Mask, 54
        New Values, 54
        Required, 54
        Unicode Compression, 54–55
        Validation Rule, 54
        Validation Text, 54
    queries
        deleting, 249
        hiding, 250
        inserting, 249
        multiple, 245–246
        ordering, 248–249
        selecting, QBD grid, 247–248

        single, 244–245
        sort order, 250–252
    renaming, 51–52
    reports, adding, 633–634
    size, 52
    tblCustomers, properties, 68–71
    width, 153–154
Fields tab, 37
File Name box, blank databases, 19
File tab (Ribbon), 24
files
    external, 42
    formats, 20
Filter by Form button, 164–165
Filter By Group option, 21
Filter event, 850
Filter On Load property, 554
Filter property, 554, 582–583
filtering
    Filter By Group option, 21
    forms
        with code, 945–946
        with queries, 947–953
Find and Replace dialog box, 143–145, 370
    Match Case check box, 145
    Match drop-down list, 145
    replacing values, 148–149
    Search Fields as Formatted check box, 145
Find Duplicates Query Wizard, 357–358
Find group, 535
    Datasheet Ribbon, 134
First aggregate function, 317
Fixed format, 56
fixed-width text files
    importing, 188–192
    linking to, 222
flat-file databases, 91, 102–103
FlexFormat( ) function, 686
fonts, formatting, 155–156
footers, 556
Force New Page property, 670–671
foreign keys, 95
    child tables, 116
    referential integrity and, 113
Form command, 491, 493–492
Form Design command, 491, 492, 589
form events
    data events
        AfterDelConfirm, 850

AfterInsert, 850
AfterUpdate, 850
ApplyFilter, 850
BeforeDelConfirm, 850
BeforeInsert, 850
BeforeUpdate, 850
Current, 850
Delete, 850
Dirty, 850
Error, 850
Filter, 850
Undo, 850
essential events, 848–849
    Activate, 849
    BeforeScreenTip, 849
    Close, 849
    Deactivate, 849
    GotFocus, 849
    Load, 849
    LostFocus, 849
    Open, 849
    Resize, 849
    Timer, 849
    Unload, 849
keyboard events
    KeyDown, 849
    KeyPress, 849
    KeyUp, 849
mouse events
    Click, 849
    DblClick, 849
    MouseDown, 849
    MouseMove, 849
    MouseUp, 849
    MouseWheel, 849
writing, 858–864
Form view, 490, 532, 534
Form Wizard, 491, 492–495
Format event, 854
Format Painter, 579
format properties
    Allow Datasheet View, 550
    Allow Form View, 550
    Allow Layout View, 550
    Auto Center, 550
    Auto Resize, 550
    Border Style, 551
    Caption, 550
    Close Button, 551
    Control Box, 551
    Default View, 550
    Dividing Lines, 550
    Grid X, 552
    Grid Y, 552
    Layout for Print, 553
    Min Max Buttons, 551
    Moveable, 553
    Navigation Buttons, 550
    Navigation Caption, 554
    Orientation, 553
    Palette Source, 553
    Picture, 551
    Picture Alignment, 552
    Picture Size Mode, 552
    Picture Tiling, 552
    Picture Type, 551
    Record Selectors, 550
    Save Splitter Bar Position, 554
    Scroll Bars, 550
    Split From Datasheet, 553
    Split From Orientation, 553
    Split From Printing, 554
    Split From Size, 554
    Split From Splitter Bar, 553
    Subdatasheet Expanded, 553
    Subdatasheet Height, 553
    Width, 551
Format property, 54
    Currency, 55–56
    Currency fields, 55–56
    custom numeric, 56–57
    Date/Time, 57–58
    Euro, 56
    Fixed, 56
    Hyperlink, 60
    Long Text, 58–59
    Number, 55
    Number fields, 55–56
    Percent, 56
    Scientific, 56
    Short Text, 58–59
    Standard, 56
    Yes/No, 59–60
formats
    Print Preview, 618–619
    report data
        bulleted lists, 674–676
        numbered lists, 671–675

formats *(continued)*
    reports, 618–619
    text boxes, 686
forms, 7
    blank, 491
    bound forms, 547–548
    closing
        event procedures, 862
        event procedures and, 862
    combo boxes, unbound, 937–944
    controls, 16, 503–504
        adding, 506–511
        attachment, 505
        bound controls, 506
        bound object frame, 505
        button, 505
        calculated controls, 506
        chart, 505
        check box, 505
        combo box, 505
        editing, 538
        field list, 508–511
        image, 505
        insert page break, 505
        label, 504
        line, 505
        link, 505
        list box, 505
        navigation control, 505
        option button, 505
        option group, 505
        order, 597
        placement, 596
        placing, 589–590
        rectangle, 505
        subform/subreport, 505
        Tab, 583–586
        tab control, 505
        text box, 504
        toggle button, 505
        unbound controls, 506
        unbound object frame, 505
        web browser control, 505
    creating, 491–495
        Form Design, 589
    data properties
        Allow Additions, 555
        Allow Deletions, 554
        Allow Edits, 554

        Allow Filters, 554
        Data Entry, 555
        Fetch Defaults, 555
        Filter, 554
        Filter On Load, 554
        Order By, 554
        Order By On Load, 554
        Record Locks, 555
        Record Source, 554
        Recordset Type, 555
    data-entry forms, 8
    datasheet forms, 501–502
    Datasheet item, 491
    Datasheet view, 490
    Date( ) function, 576
    date and time, 576–577
    design, 16, 589
        appearance, 596–597
        behavior, 593–595
        check box tally, 573
        combo boxes, 574–575
        control order, 597
        control placement, 596
        form properties, 593–594
        list boxes, 574–575
        saving records, 595
        Tab Stop property, 573
        value lookup, data entry and, 594–595
    Design view, 490
    dialog forms, 587–589
    display forms, 8
    events, 848–849
        data events, 850–851
        keyboard, 849
        mouse, 849
    Filter property, 582–583
    filtering
        with code, 945–946
        with queries, 947–953
    filtering by, 161–164
    footers, 556
    Form command, 492
    Form Design, 491
    Form view, 490
    Form Wizard, 491, 492–495
    Format Painter and, 579
    format properties
        Allow Datasheet View, 550
        Allow Form View, 550

Allow Layout View, 550
Auto Center, 550
Auto Resize, 550
Border Style, 551
Caption, 550
Close Button, 551
Control Box, 551
Default View, 550
Dividing Lines, 550
Grid X, 552
Grid Y, 552
Layout for Print, 553
Min Max Buttons, 551
Moveable, 553
Navigation Buttons, 550
Navigation Caption, 554
Orientation, 553
Palette Source, 553
Picture, 551
Picture Alignment, 552
Picture Size Mode, 552
Picture Tiling, 552
Picture Type, 551
Record Selectors, 550
Save Splitter Bar Position, 554
Scroll Bars, 550
Split From Datasheet, 553
Split From Orientation, 553
Split From Printing, 554
Split From Size, 554
Split From Splitter Bar, 553
Subdatasheet Expanded, 553
Subdatasheet Height, 553
Width, 551
headers, 556
images, 577–578
background pictures, 580–582
importing, 198–200
layout, 495
columnar, 495
control properties, 558
control text, 560
Field List, 561–562
tab order, 559–560
Layout view, 490
multiple-item forms, 498–500
Navigation form, 491
navigation forms, 496–498
OLE objects, 538–539

opening
with event procedure, 859–861
event procedures, 859–861
page numbers, 576–577
pictures in, 538–539
printing, 544–545
properties
bound forms, 547–548
Caption property, 546–547
Cycle, 555
Default Value, 548
Fast Laser Printing, 556
form other properties, 555–556
format properties, 550–554
Has Module, 556
Modal, 555
Picture, 580–581
Pop Up, 555
Property Sheet, 545
Record Selectors, 549
Ribbon Name, 556
Shortcut Menu, 556
Shortcut Menu Bar, 556
Tag, 556
Use Default Paper Size, 556
viewing form, 548
purpose, 603
records, limiting those shown, 582–583
reports, converting to, 562
versus reports, 603
resizing form area, 502–503
Ribbons, 989–990
ScreenTips, 580
section properties
Back Color, 557
Display When, 558
Height, 557
printing properties, 558
Special Effect, 557
Visible, 557
sizing, 502–503
split forms, 491, 500–501
subforms
adding, 591–593
aggregate information, 572–573
creating, 590–591
LinkChildFields property, 572
LinkMasterFields property, 572
switchboards, 489

forms *(continued)*
   title bar text, 546–547
   values, editing, 537–538
   views, 489–490
      Datasheet, 490
      Design, 490
      Form, 490
      Layout, 490
Forms group, 490–491
   Blank Form command, 491
   Form command, 491
   Form Design command, 491
   Form Wizard, 491
   More Forms command
      Datasheet item, 491
      Modal Dialog item, 491
      Multiple Items item, 491
      Split Form item, 491
   Navigation Form, 491
Forward Only recordset type, 911
freezing columns, 159–160
frequency distribution, descriptive statistics and,
      483–486
`frmIndexTest`, 47
FROM clause (SQL), 427
functions, 637
   aggregate
      `Avg`, 316
      `Count`, 317
      domain aggregate functions, 445
      `Expression`, 318–320
      `First`, 317
      `Group By`, 312, 315–316
      `Last`, 317
      `Max`, 317
      `Min`, 317
      `StDev`, 317
      `Sum`, 316
      `Var`, 317
      `Where`, 318–320
   arguments
      calculations as, 381–382
      parameters as, 411–414
   arrays
      `Array`, 826–827
      boundaries, 826
      `Join`, 828–829
      `Split`, 827–828
   `Count( )`, 701

Date, 393–396
`Date( )`, 576
`DateAdd`, 399–400
`DateSerial`, 401–403
`Day`, 397–399
domain aggregate functions, 460, 461
   date criteria, 463
   `DAvg`, 460
   `DCount`, 460, 465–466
   `DFirst`, 461
   `DLast`, 461
   `DLookup`, 461, 466–468
   `DMax`, 461
   `DMin`, 461
   `DStDev`, 461
   `DStDevP`, 461
   `DSum`, 460, 462–463
   `DVar`, 461
   `DVarP`, 461
   number criteria, 462
   percent of total calculations, 463–464
   running counts, 465–466
   text criteria, 462
   value from previous record, 466–468
`FlexFormat( )`, 686
`IIf`, 414–420
`Month`, 397–399
`Now( )`, 762
`Partition`, 483–486
`Replace`, 370
`Rnd`, 477–479
`String`, 686
`Sum( )`, 699
`Switch`, 420–423
testing, 868–871
VBA, 769–770
   calling, 836–838
   creating, 835–840
   parameters, 836
   sales tax calculation, 838–840
`Weekday`, 397–399
`Year`, 397–399

G

Gallery Ribbon control, 958
GIF images, 578
`GotFocus` event, 849, 852
graph data, 42

Grid X property, 552
Grid Y property, 552
gridlines
    displaying, 156–158
    dragging, 155
Group By aggregate function, 312, 315–316
GROUP BY clause (SQL), 432
Group Footer section (reports), 624
Group Header section (reports), 624
group-by queries, 311. *See also* aggregate queries
Grouping Intervals dialog box, 607
groups
    reports
        alphabetical, 658–662
        by date, 662–665
        defining groups, 607
        headers/footers, 645–647
        levels, 606–607
        page numbers, 670–671
        removing, 648
        sorting, 647–650
    Tables, 36

H

Has Module property, 556
Header/Footer group, Date and Time command,
    576
headers, 556
Height property, 557
help, ScreenTips, 580
Help tab (Ribbon), 24
Hide Duplicates property, 668
hiding
    controls, 677
    page headers, 668–670
    repeating information, 665–668
Home tab (Ribbon), 24, 532–533
    Clipboard group
        Copy option, 535
        Cut option, 535
        Format Painter option, 535
        Paste command, 534
    Datasheet Ribbon
        Clipboard group, 134
        Find group, 134
        Records group, 134
        Sort & Filter group, 134
        Text Formatting group, 135

        Views group, 134
        Window group, 134
    Find group, 535
    Records group, 535
    Sort & Filter group, 535
    Text Formatting group, 536
    Views group, 534
    Window group
        Size to Fit Form, 535
        Switch Windows, 536
HTML documents
    importing, 197–198
    linking to, 220–222
Hyperlink data type, 42, 48

I

ICO images, 578
IIf function
    arguments, 414
    crosstab analysis, 419–420
    mathematical errors avoidance, 415–416
    nesting, multiple conditions and, 418
    saving steps, 416–418
Image control, 577–578
images
    background pictures, 580–582
    BMP, 578, 581
    DIB, 578
    forms, 577–578
    GIF, 578
    ICO, 578
    JPG, 578
    PCX, 578
    PNG, 578
    TIF, 578
    WMF, 578
IME Mode property, 55
IME Sentence Mode property, 55
Immediate window (VBE), 792–793, 880–881
implicit variables, 811–812
Import Spreadsheet Wizard, 181
Import Text Wizard, 186–187
importing
    Access objects, 198–200
    from Access databases, 175–178
    data, 170
        when to use, 172
    from Excel spreadsheets, 178–184

importing *(continued)*
    forms, 198–200
    HTML documents, 197–198
    macros, 198–200
    modules, 198–200
    Outlook folders, 200–202
    queries, 198–200
    reports, 198–200
    SharePoint lists, 185
    tables, 198–200
    from text files, 185–192
    XML documents, 192–197
IN operator, 451
In operator, 281, 299–300
Indexed property, 54, 66–68
Indexes dialog box, 76–77
indexing tables, 73–74
    composite indexes, 76–78
    entry order, 74
    frmIndexTest, 47
    multiple-field indexes, 76–78
    natural order, 74
    physical order, 74
    properties, 77–78
    simple indexes, 74
    when to index, 78–79
inferential statistics, 469
information collection, dialog boxes, 586–589
inner joins, 121, 262–263, 428–429
Input Mask property, 60–63
Input Mask wizard, 62–63
insertion anomalies, 100
Integer data type (VBA), 810
invoice reports, 9
Is operator, 282

J

JET engine (Joint Engine Technology), 20, 901
Join function, 828–829
Join Properties dialog box, 121–122
join tables, 32
    many-to-many relationships, 32
joins
    inner joins, 121, 428–429
    outer joins, 121
        left joins, 429
        right joins, 429
    queries
        ad hoc, 265–266

    deleting, 267
    inner join, 262–263
    left outer join, 263
    right outer join, 264
    types, specifying, 266–267
JPG images, 578

K

key fields
    foreign keys, 15
    primary keys, 15
keyboard events, 848–849
keyboard shortcuts, editing datasheet values, 147
KeyDown event, 847, 849, 852
KeyPress event, 847, 849, 852
keys, 113–114
KeyUp event, 847, 849, 852

L

Label control
    cutting, 638–639
    deleting, 638–639
    moving, 640–642
    pasting to section, 640
    properties, 643–644
    sizing, 637–638
Label Ribbon control, 980–982
labels, controls
    naming, 527–529
    reattaching, 522–523
Large Number data type, 42, 46
Last aggregate function, 317
layout
    forms, 495
        columnar, 495
    reports, 604, 608–609
Layout for Print property, 553
Layout view, 490, 534
layouts, saving, 160
left outer joins, 263
Like operator (SQL)
    selection methods, 430–431
    wildcards, 430
Like string operator, 276–277
    select criteria, 291–294
    wildcards, 277–278, 294
Line method, 681
Link Specification dialog box, 222

Link Spreadsheet Wizard, 220
linked data, limitations, 213–214
Linked Table Manager, 210, 228
linked tables, 211–213
    information, editing, 227–228
    optimization, 226–227
    properties, view, 225–226
    queries, 212
    references, deleting, 227
    refreshing, 228–229
    relationships, 226
linking
    to databases, 214–216
    to Excel, 218–220
    external data, 210–211
    to external data, 170
        when to use, 171–172
    to HTML files, 220–222
    to ODBC sources, 216–217
    to text files, 222–225
List Box control, 568
    Bound Column property, 569
    Column Count property, 569
    Column Heads property, 569
    Column Widths property, 569
    Limit To List property, 569
    List Rows property, 569
    List Width property, 569
    Multi Select property, 570
    Row Source property, 569
    Row Source Type property, 569
    Validation Rule property, 569
    Validation Text property, 569
list boxes, 542–543
lists
    bulleted lists, 674–676
    numbered lists, 671–675
Load event, 849
Locals window, debugging and, 887–888
LogEvent action, 750
logical operators
    And, 278–279
    Not, 280
    Or, 279–280
logical values, 42
Long data type (VBA), 810
Long Text data type, 42, 45, 141
    data entry, 540
Lookup Wizard data type, 42, 49
LostFocus event, 849, 852

M

Macro Builder, 706–707
    Action Catalog, 747
        data actions, 749–751
        data blocks, 748–749
        macro groups, 748
        program flow, 748
    data macros, 745–747
macros, 7, 9, 705–706. *See also* data macros; VBA (Visual
    Basic for Applications)
    arguments, 706
        Beep, 707
        Message, 707
        Title, 707
        Type, 707
    conditions, 720–722
        multiple actions in, 723
    converting to VBA, 737–739
    creating, 706–708
    debugging, 728, 733–734
    embedded, 734–736
    error handling, 728–729
        MacoError object, 732–733
        OnError action, 730–732
    events, assigning to, 708–709
    importing, 198–200
    limitations, 759–760
    mcrBackupContractsAndProducts, 713–716
    mcrMainMenu, 716–720
    mcrReportMenu, 721–722
    multi-action, 713–716
    security, 709–710
        sandbox mode, 710–712
        Trust Center, 712–713
    submacros, 716–720
    variables, temporary, 723–728
    versus VBA, 736–737
Macros & Code group, Macro button, 706–707
mailing label reports, 600, 602–603
make-table queries, 321–323
    removing duplicate records, 362
    subqueries, 456
manual databases, 4
many-to-many relationships, 32, 103–104, 108–110
mathematical operators, 270
    + (addition), 270, 271
    / (division), 270, 271
    ^ (exponentiation), 270
    \ (integer division), 270, 271–272

mathematical operators *(continued)*
    * (multiplication), 270, 271
    - (subtraction), 270, 271
    ^ (exponentiation) operator, 272
    Mod (modulo), 270, 272
    precedence, 282–283
Max aggregate function, 317
mcrBackupContractsAndProducts macro, 713–716
mcrMainMenu macro, 716–720
mcrReportMenu macro, 721–722
median, data sets, descriptive statistics and, 475–477
Menu Ribbon control, 957–958
method, Line, 681
methods
    objects, 903
    OpenDatabase, 907–908
Microsoft Word Mail Merge Wizard, 206
Min aggregate function, 317
Min Max Buttons property, 551
miscellaneous operators, 270
    In, 281
    Between...And, 281, 408
    Is, 282
Mod (modulo) mathematical operator, 270, 272
modal dialogs, 241, 491
Modal property, 555
mode, data sets, descriptive statistics and, 472–475
modules, 7
    importing, 198–200
monetary data, 42
Month function, 397–399
mouse events, 848–849
MouseDown event, 844, 847, 849, 852
MouseMove event, 847, 849, 852
MouseUp event, 844, 847, 849, 852
MouseWheel event, 847, 849
Moveable property, 553
multi-action macros, 713–716
multiple-item forms, 498–500

N

Name AutoCorrect, 33, 35
names
    columns, aliases, 314–315
    control labels, 527–529
    controls, 701
    fields, 41, 51–52
    variables, 803–804
        conventions, 813–815

naming conventions, 33–34
natural primary keys, 118–119
navigation
    datasheets, 132, 536
    Find and Replace, 143–146
    forms, records, 537
    between records, 143
    to specific values, 143–146
Navigation buttons, 133
Navigation Buttons property, 550
Navigation Caption property, 554
Navigation form, 491
navigation forms, 496–498
Navigation pane, 20
    Created Date option, 23
    Custom option, 21–22
    Filter By Group, 21
    Modified Date option, 23
    Navigate To Category, 21
    Object Type option, 22
    Tables and Related Views option, 23
New Values property, 54
NoData event, 853
normalization, 6
    1NF (first normal form), 90–93
    2NF (second normal form), 94
        entities, 94–98
        exceptions, 98–99
    3NF (third normal form), 99–100
    query optimization and, 349
NOT IN operator, 451
Not Like string operator, 276–277
Not operator, 280
NotInList event, 852
Now( ) function, 762
null values, 302–304, 363–364
    calculations and, 389–391
number criteria, domain aggregate functions, 463
Number data type, 42, 45–46, 141
    bytes, 46
    decimal, 46
    double, 46
    integers, 46
    long integers, 46
    replication ID, 46
    single, 46
Number format, 55
numbered lists, 671–675
numbers, increments, 42
numeric data, 42

O

Object Browser (VBE), 794, 903–904
    Options dialog box, Editor tab, 795–797
Object data type (VBA), 810
object tables, 31–32
object types, 691
objects. *See also* DAO (Data Access Objects)
    adding, 35
    collections, 786–788, 903
        Properties collection, 903
    field, 903
    methods, 903
    recordset, 903
ODBC (Open Database Connectivity) standard,
        901
    drivers, exports and, 203–205
    linking to sources, 216–217
Office Backstage view, 25
OLE Object data type, 42, 47–48, 141
OLE Objects, in forms, 538–539
OnClick event, 844
OnError action, 751
one-to-many relationships, 103–104, 107–108
one-to-one relationships, 103–107
OnMouseDown event, 844
OnMouseUp event, 844
Open event, 849, 853
Open Other Files hyperlink, 17
OpenDatabase method, 907–908
operands, 269
operators, 269
    IN, 451
    Boolean (logical), 270, 278–280
    comparison, 270, 273–274
        subqueries, 451–462
    mathematical, 270, 271–272
    miscellaneous, 270, 280–282
    NOT IN, 451
    precedence
        Boolean operators, 283
        comparison operators, 283
        mathematical operators, 282–283
    precedence, calculations and, 388–389
    queries, parameter queries, 408–409
    string, 270, 275–276
    table properties, 270
Option Group control
    Control Source property, 570
    Default Value property, 570
    Frame Control property, 570
    Option Value property, 570
option groups, 542
Options dialog box (VBE), 795
    Auto Data Tips, 797
    Auto Indent, 796
    Auto List Members, 797
    Auto Quick Info, 797
    Auto Syntax Check, 796
    Require Variable Declaration, 796
Or operator, 279–280, 297
    across fields, 305–307
    multiple values, 298
    QBD pane Or cell, 299
    select criteria, 286–288
ORDER BY clause (SQL), 433
Order By On Load property, 554
Order By property, 554
Organization combo boxes, 575
Orientation property, 553
orphans in relational databases, 113
outer joins, 121
    left, 429
    right, 429
outer queries, 447
Outlook, folders, importing, 200–202
output, reports, 599

P

Page event, 853
Page Footer section (reports), 624, 627
Page Header section (reports), 624, 625–626
page headers, hiding, 668–670
page numbers
    forms, 576–577
    report groups, 670–671
Page property, 670–671
Page Setup dialog box, 632–633
Page Setup tab, reports, 632
Palette Source property, 553
parameter queries, 405–407, 947–949
    ampersand (&), 408
    conditional functions
        IIf function, 414–423
        Switch function, 420–423
    exclamation point (!), 408
    field names, 407
    multiple conditions, 408
    operators and, 408–409

parameter queries *(continued)*
  overview, 407
  parameters
    as calculation variables, 411
    as function arguments, 411–414
  partial parameters, 410
  period (.), 408
  prompts, multiple entries, 412–414
  square brackets ([ ]), 406–408
  wildcards, 410
parameters, partial, 410
parent table, primary key, 116
parsing strings, character markers, 374–377
Partition function, 483–486
  Interval argument, 484
  Number argument, 484
  Range Start argument, 484
  Range Stop argument, 484
pass-through queries, 442–444
Paste Table As dialog box, 361
PCX images, 578
PDF files, 618–619
  publishing to, 206–208
Percent format, 56
percentile, descriptive statistics, 479–481
performance, queries, 348–349
period (.) in parameter queries, 408
Picture Alignment property, 552
picture data, 42
Picture property, 551, 580–581
Picture Size Mode property, 552
Picture Tiling property, 552
Picture Type property, 551
pictures, background, 580–582
PNG images, 578
Pop Up property, 555
previewing, records, 167
Primary key button, 72
primary keys, 103–104
  AutoNumber data type, 114
  benefits, 116–117
  composite, 72–73, 117–118
  creating, 72, 119
  deriving, 115
  designating, 117–119
  meaningful, 115
  natural, 118–119
  parent table, 116
  referential integrity and, 113

selecting, 71–72, 114–116
single-field, 117–118
surrogate, 72, 118–119
tables, 442
Print dialog box, 166–167
  Collate, 544
  Copies, 544
  Print Range, 544
Print event, 854
Print Preview, 644
  formats, 618–619
  reports, 611–612
    formats, 618–619
Print Table Definition dialog box, 79–80
printing
  forms, 544–545
  properties, 558
  records, 166–167
  recordsets, 255–256
  reports, 620
    even-odd pages, 684
    queried data, 692
  table designs, 79–81
Private keyword, 808–809
procedures
  event procedures, creating, 845–846
  VBA, 762–764
    calling, 830–831
    compiling, 776
    creating, 830
    declaring, 832
    functions, 762
    statements, 832
    subprocedures, 767–768, 829
    subroutines, 761, 829
    terminators, 832
    variable assignment, 767–769
    variable declaration, 767
programming languages, 761
Project Explorer (VBE), 793
  Toggle Folders, 794
  View Code, 794
  View Object, 794
Project Properties dialog box (VBE), 797
  conditional compilation, 799
  Project Description, 799
  Project Name, 798
  project protection, 800
prompts, parameters, multiple entries, 412–414

properties, 53, 524
  Allow Zero Length, 54
  appearance, 566–567
  Caption, 54
  controls, 563–564
    customizing, 565–566
    Design view, 564
    Property Sheet, 565, 566
    Text Box, 566–567
  data entry and, 567
    Date/Time, 140–141
    Long Text, 141–142
    Number/Currency, 141
    OLE Object, 141
    standard text, 140
  Decimal Places, 54
  Default Value, 54
  dialog forms, 587
  Field Size, 54
  form design, 593–594
  Format, 54, 55–60
  forms
    bound forms, 547–548
    Caption property, 546–547
    Default Value, 548
    form other properties, 555–556
    format properties, 550–554
    Property Sheet, 545
    Record Selectors, 549
    viewing, 548
  IME Mode, 55
  IME Sentence Mode, 55
  Indexed, 54
  indexed tables, 77–78
  Input Mask, 54, 60–63
  labels, 643–644
  New Values, 54
  Required, 54
  RibbonName, 989–990
  section properties
    Back Color, 557
    Display When, 558
    Height, 557
    Special Effect, 557
    Visible, 557
  Special Effect, 565–566
  Split Form Orientation, 501
  Status Bar Text, 532
  tblCustomer, 68–71

text boxes, 643–644
  Unicode Compression, 54–55
  Validation Rule, 54
  Validation Text, 54
Properties collection, 903
Property Sheet, 524–525, 545
  controls, 565, 566
  Data tab, 525
  Event tab, 525
  Format tab, 525
  Label control, 643–644
  Text Box control, 643–644
Public keyword, 807–808

Q

QBE (query by example), 8
qryDialog, query design, 587
quartile, descriptive statistics, 481–483
queries, 4, 7, 8, 240
  action queries, 320
    append queries, 327–332, 437
    delete queries, 323–326, 437
    make-table queries, 321–323
    make-tables queries, 436
    update queries, 332–336, 437
  aggregate, 311–312
    descriptive statistics and, 470–471
  calculations, 240
  capabilities, 240
  columns, resizing, QBD grid, 249
  creating, 241–244
  criteria, 240
  crosstab queries
    creating manual, 342–345
    Crosstab Query Wizard, 336–342
    customizing, 346–348
    TRANSFORM statement (SQL), 437
  data sources, 548
  Datasheet view, 131
  dialog boxes, 586–587
    Cancel button, 589
    command buttons, 587–588
    control menu, removing, 589
    default button, 588
    properties, 587
  fields
    adding, 244–246
    deleting, 249

queries *(continued)*
 field selector, 248
 hiding, 250
 inserting, 249
 multiple, 245–246
 ordering, 248–249
 selecting, 240
 selecting, QBD grid, 247–248
 single, 244–245
 sort order, 250–252
 forms and, 240
 importing, 198–200
 joins
  ad hoc, 265–266
  deleting, 267
  inner join, 262–263
  left outer join, 263
  right outer join, 264
  specifying type, 266–267
 limitations, 260
 linked tables, 212
 parameter queries, 405–407, 947–949
  ampersand (&), 408
  conditional functions, 414–423
  exclamation point (!), 408
  field names, 407
  IIf function, 414–423
  multiple conditions, 408
  operators and, 408–409
  overview, 407
  parameters as calculation variables, 411
  parameters as function arguments, 411–414
  period (.), 408
  square brackets ([ ]), 406–408
  Switch function, 420–423
  wildcards, 410
 pass-through, 442–444
 performance optimization, 348–349
  compacting database, 351
  database normalization, 349
  inboxes in fields, 349–350
  query design optimization, 350–351
  repairing database, 351
 records, sorting, 240
 recordsets, 241
  printing, 255–256
  in reports, 604–605
 reports and, 240
 running, 247

 saving, 256
 select criteria, 252
  comparison operators, 284–285
  criteria, 285–288
  Date fields, 254
  field references, 289
  functions in, 288
  multiple criteria, 297–304
  Numeric fields, 254
  single-field criterion, 289–297
  string criteria, 252–254
  Yes/No fields, 254
 SQL view, 426
 SQL-specific
  ALTER TABLE statement, 440–442
  column manipulation, 440–442
  CREATE TABLE statement, 440
  data set merges, 438–440
  pass-through queries, 442–444
  table creation, 440
  UNION operator, 438–440
 subqueries, 240, 445
  comparison operators, 451–462
  DISTINCT keyword, 447
  as expressions, 452–453
  NOT IN operator, 451
  IN operator, 451
  outer queries, 447
  Query Design view, 446
  restrictions, 447
  SELECT statement, 447
  SELECT TOP PERCENT statement, 447
  SQL statements, 447–450
  table aliases, 447
  uses, 447
 tables
  creating, 240
  editing, 240
  fields, 258
  multiple, 256–260
  names display, 258
  selecting, 240
 updating rules, 259–260
Query Design view, 446
 make-table queries, 321–322
Query Designer, 241
 Query by Design (QBD) grid, 243–244
 table pane
  adding tables, 262

deleting tables, 262
join line, 261
moving tables, 261–262
table/query pane, 242–243
Query Tools Design Ribbon, 244
Query Tools Design tab, Top Values property, 434
QueryDef object (DAO), 909–911
Quick Access toolbar, 25–27, 964
commands, adding, 26, 965
moving items, 966
Undo button, 138, 148

R

RaiseError action, 751
random sampling, data sets, 477–479
ranking columns, 673
RDBMS (relational database management system), 4
Recent (welcome screen), 17
Record Locks property, 555
Record Selectors property, 549, 550
Record Source property, 554, 582–583
bound forms and, 547–548
records, 5–6
adding, 84, 150
blank lines between, 682–684
Datasheet view, 130
new records indicator, 136
deleting, 150–151
duplicate, 355–363
event procedures and, 862–864
duplicate
defining, 356
locating, 357–359
removing, 359–362
filtering
by form, 164–165
by selection, 161–164
forms, limiting those shown, 582–583
navigating, 537
navigating to, 143–146
previewing, 167
printing, 166–167
ranking, descriptive statistics and, 471–472
saving, 138, 160, 544, 595
sorting, 161
Visible property, 677
Records group, 535
Datasheet Ribbon, 134

Recordset object
ADO, 922–923
DAO, 911–916
recordset objects, 903
Recordset Type property, 555
recordsets, 241
counting records, 915–916
Dynamic type, 911
Dynaset type, 911
end/beginning detection, 914–915
Forward Only type, 911
navigating recordsets, 912–914
printing, 255–256
in reports, 604–605
Snapshot type, 911
specifying type, 912
Table type, 911
types, 911
Dynamic type, 911
Dynaset type, 911
Forward Only type, 911
Snapshot type, 911
Table type, 911
Redo command, Quick Access toolbar, 25
references, select criteria, 288
referential integrity, 110–112
application-specific rules, 126–127
cascade delete related records, 124
cascade related fields, 124
enforcing, 119–125
foreign keys, primary keys and, 113
primary keys
foreign keys and, 113
null value, 112
related tables, 6
relational databases, 6–7
joins
inner joins, 121
outer joins, 121
orphans, 113
referential integrity, 110–112
enforcing, 119–125
foreign key values, 113
primary key null value, 112
relationships, 87–90
deleting, 126
joins
inner joins, 121
outer joins, 121

relationships *(continued)*
    many-to-many, 32, 103–104, 108–110
    one-to-many, 103–104, 107–108
    one-to-one, 103–107
    referential integrity, enforcing, 119–125
    relationship creation, 119–125
    viewing all, 125
Relationships window, relationship creation, 119–125
renaming tables, 81–82
repeating information, hiding, 665–668
Replace function, 370
Report Builder, Group, Sort, and Total pane
    alphabetical sort, 658–662
    date sort, 662–665
Report Designer
    layout, 604
    saving reports, 622
Report Footer section (reports), 624, 627–628
Report Header section (reports), 624, 625
Report Wizard, 599, 605–616
    group data, defining, 607
    grouping levels, 606–607
    layout, 609–610
        adjustments, 611–612
    record sort order, 608
    report title, 610–611
    summary options, 608–609
    themes, 612–614
        color schemes, 614–616
reports, 7, 8–9, 599
    banded approach, 622–628
    binding to tables, 629–631
    blank lines between, 683–685
    color schemes, 614–616
    columnar, 600, 601–602
    columns
        layout, 697
        number of, 696
        ranking columns, 672
        size, 697
        snaking, 692–696
        spacing, 696
        vertical lines, 680–682
    combo boxes, displaying all, 690
    controls
        alignment, 687
        micro-adjustments, 687
        modifying appearance, 642
        naming, 701

    placing, 633–634
converting to from forms, 562
data
    adding, 688
    assembling, 604–605
    sources, 604–605
data types and, 44
design, 11
Design View, 619–620
Design view, 619–620, 631
duplicates, hiding, 665–668
events, 844–845, 853–854
    Activate, 853
    Close, 853
    Deactivate, 853
    Error, 853
    NoData, 853
    Open, 853
    Page, 853
    section events, 854
fields, adding, 633–634
Force New Page property and, 650
formats, 618–619
formatting
    bulleted lists, 675–678
    numbered lists, 671–675
versus forms, 603
group headers, 623
    expressions in, 653–654
groups
    alphabetical, 658–662
    by date, 662–665
    defining groups, 607
    headers/footers, 645–647
    levels, 606–607
    page numbers, 670–671
    removing, 648
    sorting, 647–650
headers, creating, 654–656
importing, 198–200
invoice reports, 9
labels
    alignment, 687
    cutting, 638–639
    deleting, 638–639
    moving, 640–642
    pasting to section, 640
    properties, 643–644
    sizing, 637–638

layout, 604, 609–610, 631–633
   adjustments, 611–612
mailing label, 600, 602–603
new, 605–606
page breaks, 650
page headers, 623, 652–653
   hiding, 668–670
page setup, 631–633
Print Preview, 611–612
   formats, 618–619
printing, 620
   even-odd pages, 685–687
   queried data, 693
Product Display, 629
purpose, 603
records, sort order, 608
recordsets, 604–605
repeated information, hiding, 665–668
report section events, 854–856
Report Wizard, 605–616
rows, spacing, 696
saving, 622
sections, 623
   Detail, 624, 626
   Group Footer, 624
   Group Header, 624
   hiding, 648
   lines, 680–682
   moving controls between, 649–650
   page breaks and, 650
   Page Footer, 624, 627
   Page Header, 624, 625–626
   pasting labels, 640
   Report Footer, 624, 627–628
   Report Header, 624, 625
   resizing, 634–636
   sizing, 648–649
summary options, 608–609
tabular, 600–601, 666
text boxes
   adding, 636
   cutting labels, 638–639
   deleting labels, 638–639
   different formats in, 686
   expressions, 636–637
   functions, 637
   moving, 640–642
   pasting labels, 640
   properties, 643–644

   sizing, 637–638
   using, 636
themes, 612–614
   color schemes, 614–616
titles, 610–611
   centering, 687
two-pass processing, 699
viewing, 621–622
Required property, 54, 65
Resize event, 849
resizing, form area, 502–503
Retreat event, 854
Ribbon
   Clipboard group, 956
   collapsing, 961
   contextual tabs, 24
   controls, 956
      Button, 958–959, 982–983
      CheckBox, 960, 983–984
      ComboBox, 960
      DropDown, 985–987
      Gallery, 958
      imageMso attribute, 979–980
      Label, 980–982
      Menu, 957–958
      separators, 983
      SplitButton, 957, 987–988
      ToggleButton, 959
   Create tab, 24, 35, 955
   custom, 966–967
      callbacks, 967–969, 972–973
      properties, 975–977
      USysRibbons, 973–975
      XML and, 969–972
   Database Tools tab, 24, 955
   Datasheet Ribbon, 133
      Advanced Filter Options button, 133
      Clipboard group, 134
      Data sheet Formatting button, 133
      Filter by Selection button, 133
      Find group, 134
      Records group, 134
      Sort & Filter group, 134
      Text Formatting group, 135
      Views group, 134
      Window group, 134
   default, editing, 961–964
   Design tab
      Delete Rows, 40

Ribbon *(continued)*
    Indexes, 41
    Insert Rows, 40
    Primary key, 39
    Property Sheet, 40
  External Data tab, 24, 955
    Export group, 174–175
    Import & Link group, 174
  Fields tab, 37
  File tab, 24, 955
  Find group, 956
  fonts, changing, 156
  forms, 989–990
  Help tab, 24, 955
  hierarchy, 955–961
  Home tab, 24, 532–537, 955
  Page Setup tab, 632
  Query Tools Design Ribbon, 244
  Records group, 956
  removing, 990–991
  reports, 989–990
  Sort & Filter group, 956
  SuperTips, 960–961
  Text Formatting group, 956
  Views group, 956
  Window group, 956
  XML, 977–979
Ribbon Designer, 961–964
Ribbon Name property, 556
right outer joins, 264
Rnd function, 477–479
Row Height dialog box, 154–155
Row Source
  combo boxes and, 574
  properties, 594–595
rows
  color, 156–158
  height, 154–155
  new, 136–137
RunDataMacro action, 750
Running Sum, 671–672

S

sampling, random, data sets, 477–479
sandbox mode, 710–712
Save command, Quick Access toolbar, 25
Save Import Steps, 177
Save Splitter Bar Position property, 554

Saved Imports, 178
saving
  layouts, 160
  queries, 256
  records, 138, 160, 544
  reports, 622
  tables, 81
schema files, XML and, 193
Scientific format, 56
ScreenTips, 580
Scroll Bars property, 550
second quartile, data sets, 457–458
sections, reports
  controls, moving between, 649–650
  hiding, 648
  page breaks and, 650
  properties
    Back Color, 557
    Display When, 558
    Height, 557
    Special Effect, 557
    Visible, 557
  resizing, 634–636
  sizing, 648–649
security
  digital certificates, 711–712
  digital signatures, 711–712
  macros, 709–710
    sandbox mode, 710–712
  Trust Center, 712–713
select criteria
  Boolean operators, 286
  comparison operators, 284–285
  complex, 285–288
    on different lines, 308–309
  field references, 288
  functions in, 288
  multiple
    And operator, 300–302
    Between...And operator, 302, 408
    In operator, 299–300
    Or operator, 297–299
  multiple fields
    And, 304–305
    Or, 304–305
  null data searches, 302–304
  And operators, 286–288
    with Or operator in different fields, 307–308
  Or operators, 286–288

across fields, 305–307
  with And operator in different fields, 307–308
queries, 252
  Date fields, 254
  Numeric fields, 254
  string criteria, 252–254
  Yes/No fields, 254
single-field criterion
  character criteria, 289–291
  Like operator, 291–294
  Memo fields, 289–297
  non-matching values, 294–295
  numeric criteria, 295–296
  OLE objects, 297
  Text fields, 289–297
  true/false criteria, 296–297
  wildcards, 291–294
SELECT statement (SQL)
  FROM clause, 427
  columns
    selecting all, 427
    selecting specific, 427
  subqueries, 447
  syntax, 426
  UNION operator, 438–440
SELECT TOP PERCENT statement, 436
  subqueries, 447
SELECT TOP statement, 433–436
selections, filtering by, 161–164
SendEmail action, 750
separators, Ribbon controls, 983
SetField action, 750
SetLocalVar action, 750
SharePoint, 1039–1041
  Access tables
    exporting to SharePoint, 1051–1049
    moving to SharePoint, 1049–1052
  documents, 1040–1041
  lists, 1041–1043
    importing, 185, 1046–1047
    linking to, 1043–1046
  templates, 1052–1054
Short Text data type, 42, 45
Shortcut Menu Bar property, 556
Shortcut Menu property, 556
Show Table dialog box, 119–120, 241–242
Single data type (VBA), 810
single-field criterion
  Like operator, 291–294

Memo fields, 289–297
non-matching values, 294–295
numeric criteria, 295–296
OLE objects, 297
true/false criteria, 296–297
wildcards, 291–294
single-field primary keys, 117–118
Sizing & Ordering group, 518
snaking columns, 692–696
Snap to Grid command, 518
Snapshot recordset type, 911
Sort & Filter group, 161–162, 535
  Datasheet Ribbon, 134
sound data, 42
Special Effect property, 557, 565–566
Split Form Orientation property, 501
split forms, 500–501
Split From Datasheet property, 553
Split From Orientation property, 553
Split From Printing property, 554
Split From Size property, 554
Split From Splitter Bar property, 553
Split function, 827–828
SplitButton Ribbon control, 957, 987–988
splitting databases
  benefits, 229–232
  Database Splitter, 232–235
  object location, 232
spreadsheets, importing from, 178–184
SQL (Structured Query Language), 8, 425
  clauses
    AS, 433
    AS, 433
    GROUP BY, 432
    ORDER BY, 433
    WHERE, 428–429
  DISTINCT predicate, 432
  Like operator
    selection methods, 430–431
    wildcards, 430
  statements
    action queries, 436–437
    ALTER TABLE, 440–442
    column manipulation, 440–442
    CREATE TABLE, 440
    data set merges, 438–440
    data sources, 548
    pass-through queries, 442–444
    SELECT, 426–427

SQL (Structured Query Language) *(continued)*
    SELECT TOP, 433–436
    SELECT TOP PERCENT, 436
    subqueries, 447
    table creation, 440
    UNION operator, 438–440
SQL view, queries, 426
square brackets ([ ]), parameter queries, 406, 408
Standard format, 56
statistics
    descriptive, 469
        aggregate queries and, 470–471
        data set median, 475–477
        data set mode, 472–475
        frequency distribution, 483–486
        percentile calculation, 479–481
        quartile calculation, 481–483
        ranking records, 471–472
    inferential, 469
Status Bar Text property, 532
StDev aggregate function, 317
Stop statements, 883–884
StopAllMacros action, 750
StopMacro action, 750
String data type (VBA), 810
String function, 686
string operators, 270
    & (concatenation), 275–276
    Like, 276–277
        wildcards, 277–278
    Not Like, 276–277
strings
    parsing, character markers and, 374–377
    spaces, leading, 368–369
Subdatasheet Expanded property, 553
Subdatasheet Height property, 553
Subform control
    LinkChildFields property, 572
    LinkMasterFields property, 572
Subform Wizard, 591–592
subforms
    adding, 591–593
    aggregate information, 572–573
    creating, 590–591
submacros, 716–720
subqueries, 445
    action queries
        append queries, 456
        delete queries, 456
        make-table queries, 456

        update queries, 456
    comparison operators, 451–462
    correlated, 453–454
        as expressions, 453–454
    DISTINCT keyword, 447
    as expressions, 452–453
    NOT IN operator, 451
    IN operator, 451
    outer queries, 447
    parentheses, 446
    Query Design view, 446
    restrictions, 447
    SELECT statement, 447
    SELECT TOP PERCENT statement, 447
    SQL statements, 447–450
    table aliases, 447
    uses, 447
subroutines, VBA, 829
    calling, 829–830
    creating, 831–834
    invoking, 829–830
    running, 829–830
Sum( ) function, 699
Sum aggregate function, 316
Summary Options dialog box, 608–609
SuperTips, 960
surrogate primary keys, 72, 118–119
Switch function
    expressions, 420
    values, 420
switchboards, 489
syntax, expressions, 391

T

Tab control, 583–585
    Caption property, 585
    Multi Row property, 585
    Picture property, 586
    Style property, 585
    Tab Fixed Height property, 585
    Tab Fixed Width property, 586
tabbed windows, 23
tab-delimited text files, importing, 185–188
Table Design button, 37
Table Design window, field names, 41
Table Designer, 37–38
table designs, printing, 79–81
table pane (Query Designer)
    adding tables, 262

deleting tables, 262
join line, 261
moving tables, 261–262
Table recordset type, 911
TableDef object (DAO), 908–909
tables, 4, 5, 7–8
    aliases, AS clause, 433
    Collectible Mini Cars Customers, 38
    columns, ALTER TABLE statement (SQL),
        440–442
    copying, 82–83
    CREATE TABLE statement (SQL), 438–440
    creating, 32–33
        designing, 34–39
    data sources, 548
    Datasheet view, 131
    datasheets, 131
    decomposition, 97–98
    deleting, 82
    design, 13–16
        modifying, 50–68
    events, 742–743
        AfterDelete, 744–745
        AfterInsert, 744–745
        AfterUpdate, 744–745
        BeforeChange, 743
        BeforeDelete, 744
        BeforeUpdate, 743
    fields
        adding, 35
        attachment fields, 84–85
        data types, 42
        deleting, 35, 51
        inserting, 51
        moving, 51
        naming, 41
        properties, 53–68
        renaming, 51–52
        size, 52
    foreign keys, 95
    importing, 198–200
    indexing, 73–74
        composite indexes, 76–78
        entry order, 74
        multiple-field indexes, 76–78
        natural order, 74
        physical order, 74
        properties, 77–78
        simple indexes, 74
        when to index, 78–79

join tables, 32
key fields
    foreign keys, 15
    primary keys, 15
keys, 113–114
linked, 211–213
    editing information, 227–228
    optimization, 226–227
    properties, 225–226
    reference deletion, 227
    relationships, 226
modifying, 35
multiple, 7
object tables, 31–32
primary keys, 103–104, 442
    composite, 72–73
    creating, 72
    selecting, 71–72
Print Table Definition, 79–80
queries
    fields, 258
    multiple, 256–260
    names display, 258
records
    adding, 84
    deleting based on other tables, 335–336
related, 6
relationships, 87–90
    flat-file databases, 102–103
renaming, 81–82
reports, binding, 629–631
Ribbons, 989–990
saving, 81
Tables group, 36
transaction tables, 32
update anomalies, 95
update code, 923–924
    calculated controls, 926–932
    deleting records, 933–936
    fields, 924–926
    new records, 932
Tables group, 36
tabular reports, 600–601, 666
    blank lines, 682–684
Tag property, 556
tblBookOrders table, 91–98
tblCustomers
    AutoNumber fields, 50
    data types, 49–50
    fields, properties, 68–71

templates
  event procedures, 846
  SharePoint, 1052–1054
testing applications, debugging and, 867–873
text
  Find and Replace, 370
  inserting, strings and, 370–374
  Status Bar Text, 532
Text Box control
  Back Color property, 566–567
  Back Style property, 566–567
  Border Style property, 566–567
  Border Width property, 566–567
  Can Grow property, 644–645
  Can Shrink property, 644–645
  cutting labels, 638–639
  Default Value property, 567
  deleting labels, 638–639
  Font Italic property, 567
  Font Name property, 567
  Font Size property, 567
  Font Underline property, 567
  Font Weight property, 567
  Fore Color property, 567
  Format property, 566
  functions, 637
  Input Mask property, 567
  moving, 640–642
  pasting labels, 640
  properties, 643–644
  sizing, 637–638, 644–645
  Special Effect property, 566–567
  Text Align property, 567
  Text Format property, 567
  Validation Rule property, 567
  Validation Text property, 567
text criteria, domain aggregate functions, 463
text files
  delimited, importing, 185–188
  fixed-width, importing, 188–192
  linking to, 222–225
Text Formatting group, 536
  Datasheet Ribbon, 135
themes, reports, 612–616
Themes group, 612–614
  colors, 614–616
TIF images, 578
Timer event, 849
title bar text, Caption property, 546–547

titles, reports, centering, 687
Toggle Button Ribbon control, 570, 959
toolbars, Quick Access, 25–27, 138, 964–966
Tools group, Primary Key, 72
Total row, 165–166
total row, adding, 330–331
Totals, activating, 312–313
Totals button, 165–166
transaction tables, 32
TRANSFORM statement (SQL), crosstabs, 437
transformation
  case, changing, 367–368
  fields
    concatenation, 364–367
    filling in blank, 363–364
  strings
    parsing, character markers and,
      374–377
    spaces, removing, 368–369
  text
    find and replace, 370
    inserting in strings, 370–374
Triple State property, 570
Trust Center, 712–713
two-pass processing of reports, 699

U

unbound combo boxes, 937–939
  bookmarks, 941–944
  FindRecord method, 939–941
unbound controls, 506
  calculated, 571
Undo button, 148
  Quick Access toolbar, 138
Undo command, Quick Access toolbar, 25
Undo event, 850, 852
Unhide Columns dialog box, 159
Unicode Compression property, 54–55
UNION operator, 438–440
Unload event, 849
update anomalies, 95, 100
update queries, 332–336
  expressions, 334–335
  subqueries, 456
Updated event, 852
Use Control Wizards, 506
Use Default Paper Size property, 556
user interface, 563

V

validation, data types, automatic, 138–140
Validation Rule property, 54, 63–65
  referential integrity, 126–127
Validation Text property, 54, 63–65
values, 6
  logical, 42
Var aggregate function, 317
variables, 801
  declarations, 802–806
    Dim keyword, 807
    Private keyword, 808–809
    Public keyword, 807–808
  explicit, 811–812
  implicit, 811–812
  lifetime, 817–818
  naming, 803–804
    conventions, 813–815
  scope, 816–817, 819
  temporary
    macros, 723–727
    VBA and, 727–728
Variant data type (VBA), 810
VBA (Visual Basic for Applications), 4, 9, 759–760.
    See also macros
  ADO (ActiveX Data Objects) and, 763
  arrays
    dynamic, 825–826
    fixed, 822–824
    functions, 826–829
  branching, 777–783
  callbacks, 967–969
  code organization
    comments, 867
    compile frequency, 867
    constants, 866
    modules, 866–867
    naming conventions, 866
    procedure length, 866
    repetition, 867
    variable scope, 866
  code window
    compiling procedures, 776
    IntelliSense, 773–776
    line continuation, 771–772
    multi-statement lines, 772–773
    saving modules, 777
    whitespace, 770–771

constants, 819
  declaring, 820
  hard-code values, 821–822
  naming convention, 821
converting macros, 737–739
DAO (Data Access Objects) and, 763
data types
  Access field types and, 810–811
  Boolean, 809
  Byte, 809
  Currency, 809
  Date, 809
  Decimal, 809
  Double, 810
  Integer, 810
  Long, 810
  Object, 810
  Single, 810
  String, 810
  Variant, 810
debugging, testing applications, 867–873
For Each statement, 790–791
events, triggering, 844–845
extensibility, 763
functions, 762, 769–770, 829
  calling, 829–830, 836–838
  creating, 835–840
  parameters, 836
  sales tax calculation, 838–840
If keyword
  Boolean values, 780–781
  If...Else...End If construct, 779
  If...ElseIf...End If construct, 779
  If...End If construct, 778
  If...Then construct, 778
  nested If statements, 780
keywords, 761
looping
  Do...Loop statement, 783–784
  For...Next statement, 784–786
macro comparison, 736–737
macros, 705–706
methods, 788–789
modules, 762
  class, 764, 766
  saving, 777
  sections, 767
  standard, 764, 765–766
Now( ) function, 762

VBA (Visual Basic for Applications) *(continued)*
 objects, collections, 786–788
 procedures, 762, 763–764
  calling, 830–831
  compiling, 776
  creating, 830
  declaring, 832
  functions, 762
  named arguments, 840–842
  statements, 832
  subprocedures, 767–768, 829
  subroutines, 761, 829
  terminators, 832
  variable assignment, 767–769
  variable declaration, 767
 properties, 788
 Select Case...End Select statement, 781–783
 With statement, 789–790
 statements, 761, 762
 subprocedures, 829
  creating, 831–834
 subroutines, 829
  calling, 829–830
  creating, 831–834
  invoking, 829–830
  running, 829–830
 table updates, 923–924
  calculated controls, 926–932
  deleting records, 933–936
  fields, 924–926
  new records, 932
 variables, 762, 801
  declarations, 802–809
  explicit, 811–812
  implicit, 811–812
  lifetime, 817–818
  naming, 803–804, 813–815
  scope, 816–817, 819
  temporary, 727–728
VBE (Visual Basic Editor)
 Immediate window, 792–793
 Object Browser, 794, 903–904
  Options dialog box, 795–797
 Project Explorer, 793
  Toggle Folders, 794
  View Code, 794
  View Object, 794
 Project Properties dialog box, 797
  conditional compilation, 799
  Project Description, 799

Project Name, 798
 project protection, 800
video data, 42
views
 all relationships, 125
 Datasheet, 130, 490
 Design, 34–35, 490
 Form, 490, 532
 forms, 489–490
  Datasheet, 490
  Design, 490
  Form, 490
  Layout, 490
 Layout, 490
 Office Backstage, 25
Views group
 Datasheet Ribbon, 134
 Datasheet view, 534
 Design view, 534
 Form view, 534
 Layout view, 534
Visible property, 557, 677
Visual Basic Editor, 711

W

Watches window, debugging and, 889–890
 conditional watches, 891–892
Web Browser control, Control Source property, 570
Weekday function, 397–399
welcome screen, 17–18
 Blank Database option, 18–20
 Open Other Files hyperlink, 17
 Recent section, 17
Where aggregate function, 318–320
WHERE clause (SQL), SELECT statement, 428
Width property, 551
wildcard characters
 [!], 430
 * (asterisk), 430
 # (pound sign), 430
 ? (question mark), 430
 [ ] (square brackets), 430
 Find and Replace dialog box, 144
 Like operator, 276–277, 294, 430–431
 parameter queries, 410
 selection criteria, 291–294
Window group
 Datasheet Ribbon
  Size to Fit Form button, 134

Switch Windows button, 134
Size to Fit Form control, 535
Switch Windows control, 536
windows
 Datasheet, 131–135
 tabbed, 23
With keyword, 953
wizards
 Find Duplicates Query Wizard, 357–358
 Form Wizard, 491, 492–495
 Import Spreadsheet, 181
 Import Text, 186–187
 Input Mask, 62–63
 Link Spreadsheet, 220
 Microsoft Word Mail Merge, 206
 Report Wizard, 599, 605–616
 Subform, 591–592
 Use Control Wizards, 506
WMF images, 578
Word
 exporting to, 205–206
 Word Merge, 205–206

workday calculation, 398–399
Workspace object (DAO), 905–906

X

XML (eXtensible Markup Language)
 documents
  exporting, 192–197
  importing, 192–197
  saving macros as, 756–757
 Ribbon, 977–979
XPS files, 618–619
 publishing to, 206–208

Y

Year function, 397–399
Yes/No data type, 42, 47

Z

Zoom dialog box, 540
Zoom window, field data events, 142